Walden and Civil Disobedience

New Riverside Editions

General Editor for the American Volumes
Paul Lauter

STEPHEN CRANE, *The Red Badge of Courage, Maggie: A Girl of the Streets, and Other Selected Writings*
Edited by Phyllis Frus and Stanley Corkin

RALPH WALDO EMERSON, *Selected Writings* and MARGARET FULLER, *Woman in the Nineteenth Century*
Edited by John Carlos Rowe

OLAUDAH EQUIANO, MARY ROWLANDSON, AND OTHERS, *American Captivity Narratives*
Edited by Gordon M. Sayre

HENRY DAVID THOREAU, *Walden and Civil Disobedience*
Edited by Paul Lauter

MARK TWAIN, *Adventures of Huckleberry Finn*
Edited by Susan K. Harris

EDITH WHARTON, *The Age of Innocence*
Edited by Carol J. Singley

Other Riverside Literature Titles

Call and Response: The Riverside Anthology of the African American Literary Tradition
Edited by Patricia Liggins Hill et al.

The Riverside Anthology of Children's Literature, Sixth Edition
Edited by Judith Saltman

The Riverside Anthology of Literature, Third Edition
Edited by Douglas Hunt

The Riverside Anthology of Short Fiction: Convention and Innovation
Edited by Dean Baldwin

The Riverside Chaucer, Third Edition
Edited by Larry D. Benson

The Riverside Milton
Edited by Roy Flannagan

The Riverside Shakespeare, Second Edition
Edited by G. Blakemore Evans et al.

NEW RIVERSIDE EDITIONS

General Editor for the American Volumes
Paul Lauter, Trinity College

Henry David Thoreau

Walden and Civil Disobedience

Complete Texts with Introduction
Historical Contexts • Critical Essays

edited by
Paul Lauter
Trinity College

HOUGHTON MIFFLIN COMPANY
Boston • New York

For Sid and Jules

Senior Sponsoring Editor: Suzanne Phelps Weir
Associate Editor: Jennifer Roderick
Senior Project Editor: Kathryn Dinovo
Senior Cover Design Coordinator: Deborah Azerrad Savona
Manufacturing Manager: Florence Cadran
Senior Marketing Manager: Nancy Lyman
Associate Marketing Manager: Carla Gray

Cover design: Steven Cooley
Cover image: © Corbis/Scott T. Smith

Credits appear on page 440, which constitutes a continuation of the copyright page.

Printed in the U.S.A.

Library of Congress Cataloging-in-Publication Data is available on file.

ISBN: 0-395-98077-1

23456789-QF-04 03 02 01 00

As part of Houghton Mifflin's ongoing
commitment to the environment, this text
has been printed on recycled paper.

Contents

About This Series

Paul Lauter

The Riverside name dates back well over a century. Readers of this book may have seen—indeed, may own—Riverside Editions of works by the best-known nineteenth-century American writers, such as Emerson, Thoreau, Lowell, Longfellow, and Hawthorne. Houghton Mifflin and its predecessor, Ticknor & Fields, were the primary publishers of the New England authors who constituted much of the undisputed canon of American literature until well into the twentieth century. The Riverside Editions of works by these writers, and of some later writers such as Amy Lowell, became benchmarks for distinguished and useful editions of standard American authors for home, library, and classroom.

In the 1950s and 1960s, the Riverside name was used for another series of texts, primarily for the college classroom, of well-known American and British literary works. These paperback volumes, edited by distinguished critics of that generation, were among the most widely used and appreciated of their day. They provided carefully edited texts in a handsome and readable format, with insightful critical introductions. They were books one kept beyond the exam, the class, or even the college experience.

In the last quarter century, however, ideas about the American literary canon have changed. Many scholars want to see a canon that reflects a broader American heritage, including significant literary works by previously marginalized writers, many of them women or men of color. These changes began to be institutionalized in curricula as well as in textbooks such as *The Heath Anthology of American Literature,* which Houghton Mifflin started publishing in 1998. The older Riverside series, excellent in its day, ran the risk of appearing outdated; the editors were long retired or deceased, and the authors were viewed by some as too exclusive.

Yet the name Riverside and the ideas behind it continued to have appeal. The name stood for distinction and worth in the publication of

America's literary heritage. Houghton Mifflin's New Riverside Series, initiated in the year 2000, is designed to uphold the Riverside reputation for excellence while offering a more inclusive range of authors. The Series also provides today's reader with books that contain, in addition to notable literary works, introductions by influential critics, as well as a variety of stimulating materials that bring alive the debates, the conversations, the social and cultural movements within which America's literary classics were formed.

Thus emerged the book you have in hand. Each volume of the New Riverside Editions will contain the basic elements that we think today's readers find interesting and useful: important literary works by significant authors, incisive introductions, and a variety of contextual materials to make the literary text fully engaging. These books will be useful in many kinds of classrooms, but they are also designed to offer the casual reader the enjoyment of a good read in a fresh and accessible format. Among the first group of New Riverside Editions are familiar titles, such as Henry David Thoreau's *Walden* and Mark Twain's *Adventures of Huckleberry Finn.* There are also works in fresh new combinations, such as the collection of early captivity narratives and the volume that pairs texts by Ralph Waldo Emerson and Margaret Fuller. And there are well-known works in distinctively interesting formats, such as the volume containing Edith Wharton's *The Age of Innocence* and the volume of writings by Stephen Crane. Future books will include classics as well as works drawing renewed attention.

The New Riverside Editions will provide discriminating readers with a wide range of important literary works, contextual materials that vividly illuminate those works, and the best of recent critical commentary and analysis. And because we have not confined our editors to a single monotonous format, we think our readers will find that each volume in this new series has a character appropriate to the literary work it presents.

We expect the New Riverside Editions to bring to the twenty-first century the same literary publishing distinction of its nineteenth- and twentieth-century predecessors.

Introduction

Paul Lauter

Henry David Thoreau began to live in the small cottage he had built at Walden Pond on July 4, 1845. He remained there until September 6, 1847, carrying out the activities described in *Walden,* completing much of *A Week on the Concord and Merrimack Rivers,* composing his journal and other works, and visiting friends and acquaintances. On July 24, 1846, while he was living at Walden, Thoreau was arrested and spent a night in the Concord jail for refusing to pay his poll tax, as described in his essay "Civil Disobedience."[1] He delivered one and perhaps two lecture versions of that essay soon after leaving Walden, initially on January 26, 1848. The essay was first published in Elizabeth Peabody's *Aesthetic Papers* in the spring of 1849 as "Resistance to Civil Government." Meanwhile, Thoreau wrote and continued to revise the manuscript of what would become *Walden* until May 1854, when he sent the last of it to the printer. The book was published by Ticknor and Fields, the direct predecessor to Houghton Mifflin, in August 1854. Thoreau made a number of additions and corrections to the book in his personal copy, though it was not published again during his lifetime. "Resistance to Civil Government," retitled more familiarly as "Civil Disobedience," was printed in a posthumous volume, *A Yankee in Canada, with Anti-Slavery and Reform Papers,* probably edited by Sophia Thoreau (the writer's sister) and his friend and first biographer, Ellery Channing, and published by Ticknor and Fields in 1866.

But how did it come about that a man of moderately comfortable origins and many good friendships should wish to take what seemed to some then, and perhaps to others today, as strange or extreme steps, such as choosing to live alone in a woodland shack or going to jail rather than pay-

[1] For the use of this title in this edition, see the last section of the introduction.

ing a modest tax? Such questions are, of course, more easily asked than answered; the answers are the inmost subjects of Thoreau's works included in this volume. At the same time, while Thoreau has become a man of *our* time—as some of the other works in this book suggest—he was also decidedly a man of his own historical moment. We can profitably study his journal and some of his letters, for example, to understand more fully the artistic processes by which he created so rich and complex a work as *Walden.*[2] Yet the genuine toughness, difficulty, contrariness, and especially the struggle of the book can disappear into a paean for Thoreau's artistic genius and for his understanding of natural phenomena.

It is unlikely that Thoreau would have been satisfied with a description of himself constituted dominantly by the labels "artist" and "naturalist." After all, he begins *Walden* with an epigraph insisting that he will "brag as lustily as chanticleer . . . if only to wake my neighbors up." Some critics have argued that his many revisions of the book moved him somewhat away from that initial insistence upon social reform; Robert Sattelmeyer, for example, proposes that "Thoreau became increasingly concerned with his own awakening and less obsessed with waking up his neighbors." In that process, Sattelmeyer suggests, "the book begins to acquire mythic and archetypal dimensions and, in the relative deemphasis of social criticism attendant upon the expansion of these other elements, becomes less topical and more universal in its reference" (64). Such a

---

[2]The most useful studies of the processes by which Thoreau created *Walden* are J. Lyndon Shanley, *The Making of* Walden; Ronald A. Clapper, "The Development of *Walden:* A Generic Text"; Stephen Adams and Donald A. Ross, *Revising Mythologies: The Composition of Thoreau's Major Works,* 162–92; and Robert Sattelmeyer, "The Remaking of *Walden,*" 53–78. Sattelmeyer's summary of the process is useful:

> In 1850, then, Thoreau had a manuscript of *Walden* that only inchoately reflected what he had learned at the pond, that did not embody the new directions his life was taking, and that was in any event probably unsalable. So he ceased thinking of the manuscript as finished, or nearly so. . . . He did not let the book lie fallow, for he drafted into the journal passages of reflection on his life in the woods that were clearly intended for the manuscript and that were eventually added in later revisions. But apparently he did not begin to revise the manuscript as a whole until sometime in 1852. Then he began energetically to work on *Walden* again, adding new material and revising previous drafts in four distinguishable stages, not counting his final fair copy for the printer, between 1852 and 1854. Thus, although there are seven identifiable manuscript drafts (or, more precisely, partial drafts) of *Walden,* ranging from 1846 to 1854, its composition mainly took place in two phases. The first stage includes the first draft written at Walden in 1846–47, along with the second and third drafts that were written nearly together in 1848–49 and that primarily polish material in the first draft. The second stage consists of the four successive partial drafts written between 1852 and the book's publication in 1854 (58).

view of the changes in Thoreau's life have much cogency, and they inform one important way of studying *Walden.* All the same, no one who reads the "Conclusion" of the book can imagine that Thoreau's commitments to social change had diminished at this point. Indeed, at the very time he was bringing *Walden* into its final shape, he was also composing and delivering one of his bitterest and most trenchant political talks, "Slavery in Massachusetts."

Indeed, the problem Thoreau faced in composing his book, and the problem we face in reading it, is how to hold together disparate if not fully contradictory elements. There is a good deal of the mythic and transcendental about *Walden,* just as there is much in it that reflects Thoreau's development as an observer and recorder of nature at work. Still, both *Walden* and "Civil Disobedience" are fundamentally political essays: they have designs on their readers' thoughts and actions. Both argue for certain ways of thinking about and living in the world and against others, particularly in terms of the relationships of individuals to society and to the nation. Nor are they innocent expressions of a set of timeless propositions, but rather arguments grounded in the particular moments of their composition. These arguments remain alive for us not so much because they transcend all times and places but, to the contrary, because of the many ways in which the conditions of life we face at the turn of the twenty-first century echo many of those Thoreau confronted. Were that not the case, Thoreau's prose, wonderful as it is, would be primarily of antiquarian value, like that of, say, Sir Thomas Browne. That a heated argument *against* Thoreau's ideas can still be generated measures how alive they—and he—remain.

It therefore seems faithful (to use one of his key words) to Thoreau's design to think about the ways he emerges in his particular time and place, and how he has been constructed and reconstructed in the century and a half since he wrote these works. Many of the texts that accompany *Walden* and "Civil Disobedience" in this volume have been chosen with such goals in mind. Some were written by Thoreau's contemporaries—like Angelina Grimké, William Lloyd Garrison, and Charles Lane—whose ideas informed his. Others come from the pens of later writers—like Leo Tolstoy, Mohandas K. Gandhi, Martin Luther King Jr.—for whom Thoreau served as inspiration and, in important ways, as mentor. But it would have been easy to choose many other works, especially those from the huge repertoire of mid-nineteenth-century reform and revolutionary literature: Frederick Douglass's 1845 *Narrative,* the Seneca Falls "Declaration of Sentiments" (1848), the "Communist Manifesto" (1848), Margaret Fuller's final dispatches from Italy (1847–49), Harriet Beecher Stowe's *Uncle Tom's Cabin* (1852), Herman Melville's "Benito Cereno"

(1855), Walt Whitman's "Preface" to the 1855 edition of *Leaves of Grass,* just to name a few of the most familiar items from a single ten-year period. It seems helpful—and too little done—to read Thoreau in the light of such works. For both *Walden* and "Civil Disobedience" were products of a historic moment in which many settled social arrangements and cultural norms in America and Europe were brought under intense pressure by fundamental economic and political changes. Many of the writers, thinkers, and reformers of that time struggled for a way to understand those changes and to direct society toward more equitable, moral, and, some hoped, perfectible arrangements than those with which they were forced to contend. A lecture like Emerson's "Man the Reformer" captures something of the outrage at the directions American society had taken, the sense that the corruptions of commercial enterprise, the very system of the division of labor were compromising the fundamental values of the young American democracy. If, on one hand, Thoreau can be seen as a major contributor to that flourishing of creative endeavor that F. O. Matthiessen sixty years ago named the "American Renaissance," he can also be seen as one of those midcentury reformers trying to chart a new direction for living in and changing a world of turmoil and inequality.

Why was Thoreau's historical moment so conflicted and fruitful in the production of reformist, indeed revolutionary, ideas, manifestos, and activities? No single answer can be complete, of course, and different historians provide different emphases. But it is likely that *for Thoreau* the conflicts sprang from two major issues: slavery and industrial capitalism. The two were closely related. The rapid growth of New England industry, particularly in textiles, during the second quarter of the nineteenth century helped fuel the demand for stepped-up production of Southern cotton and other commodities. New technologies like the cotton gin and baling machines helped supply that demand. But plantation owners also tried to increase the slave labor force whenever possible, often to work it harder, and to insist more strongly than ever upon maintaining the South's "peculiar institution."[3] A marriage of economic convenience thus emerged between Northerners involved in key forms of manufacture and trade—shareholders, managers, retailers, workers—and white Southerners invested in

[3] See, for example, Herbert Gutman, *The Black Family in Slavery and Freedom, 1750–1925,* 75–81, 129–32; and Vincent Harding, *There Is a River: The Black Struggle for Freedom in America,* 154–57. In *Roll, Jordan, Roll: The World the Slaves Made,* Eugene Genovese argues that the conditions of slave labor ameliorated in the immediate pre–Civil War period—see "In the Name of Humanity and the Cause of Reform," 49–70—but the evidence, particularly from the point of view of the slaves, and certainly of Northerners sympathetic to them, is ambiguous.

maintaining black servitude. Concurrently, ideological positions had hardened. By the 1840s, abolitionists were being heard—as Garrison had predicted in 1831 they would be. And they had begun to turn toward the political activity that would help shatter the dominant two-party system, generating first the Free Soil and ultimately the Republican parties. Partly in response, partly as a means for rationalizing a whole way of life, Southern ideologues and politicians moved away from the earlier notion of slavery—as a necessary evil that would atrophy in time—toward the view that it was a positive good that ought to be extended to new territories, perhaps by wars like that against Mexico. At the very least, for Southerners, chattel slavery constituted a labor system no worse than what they characterized as the "wage slavery" dominant in northern industry.

Here they tapped into strong feelings of anxiety and guilt, even among those absolutely opposed to slavery in any form. For into the 1830s and 1840s, many Northerners, including industrialists, were opposed to the formation of a "permanent factory population." Form it did, nevertheless. Certainly by the mid- to late-1830s the young Yankee farm women who had constituted the initial workforce of New England factories were being replaced by immigrant workers, men, women and children who had nothing to sell but the labor of their bodies. They owned no property and hardly any tools, had few marketable skills, and lived always on, or over, the edge of economic catastrophe. They could not, like earlier generations of American yeomen, sell their products for a price, only their labor for a wage. Nor could most of the growing urban population supplement wages with the products of farms, woods, or waters. On the other side of the growing economic divide, a "new aristocracy of wealth" had increasingly been emerging, creating a social landscape markedly different from that of the "pleasing uniformity of decent competence" described by J. Hector St. John de Crèvecoeur in *Letters from an American Farmer* (1782).

Thoreau writes in a world marked by an aggressive slavocracy, a complaisant if not collusive northern majority, an increasingly divided system of antagonistic classes, "public and private avarice" that, in Emerson's scandalized words, "make the air we breathe thick and fat." "What deepening twilight"—Whitman would ask—"scum floating atop of the waters, / Who are they as bats and night-dogs askant in the capitol? / What a filthy Presidentiad!" For people like Thoreau, the changed conditions of an industrializing, urbanizing, increasingly divided America cried out for action. But of what kind? In whose name? With what allies? The first set of articles gathered in Part Three of this volume suggests the variety of responses to these questions with which Thoreau would have been familiar.

To begin with, there is Angelina Grimké's "Appeal to the Christian Women of the South." Like Thoreau in "Civil Disobedience," Grimké asserts the right, indeed the duty, of individuals to resist immoral social practices, like slavery, to break unjust laws even if the consequence is jail or ostracism. She writes:

> If for instance, there was a law, which imposed imprisonment or a fine upon me if I manumitted a slave, I would on no account resist that law, I would set the slave free, and then go to prison or pay the fine. If a law commands me to *sin I will break it;* if it calls me to *suffer,* I will let it take its course *unresistingly.* The doctrine of blind obedience and unqualified submission to *any human* power, whether civil or ecclesiastical, is the doctrine of despotism, and ought to have no place among Republicans and Christians.

Grimké herself not only condemned slavery but—violating prohibitions against women speaking in public—carried the abolitionist message into "promiscuous assemblies" of mixed male and female listeners. Unlike Thoreau, whose actions were rooted in a form of radical individualism, Grimké grounds her embrace of civil disobedience in Christian ideology and biblical precedent. Radical evangelical Christianity also forms the basis of William Whipper's 1837 speech at the First African Presbyterian Church in Philadelphia as well as Garrison's manifesto for the Peace Convention held in Boston September 18–20, 1838. Garrisonians took literally the injunction to "resist not one who is evil" but rather to "turn the other cheek," linking nonviolent resistance to slavery to their passionate opposition to war in any form, as well as to other kinds of dissipation or excess, like the consumption of alcohol and, in many cases, fleshly food. Like Thoreau, Garrison insisted upon the necessity of a radical transformation not only of an individual's relationship to government, but of an entire way of life—"where one lived and what one lived for," to adapt Thoreau's language.

This belief in the need to transform life, not just laws or votes or opinions, underlies the articles by Peabody, Bronson Alcott, Lane, Ripley, and Channing. These essays primarily discuss two specific New England efforts at collective reform, Brook Farm and Fruitlands. In both cases, groups of women and men chose to remove themselves, at least somewhat, from the corrupt social and economic priorities of urban life. As was true of Thoreau, a turn toward farming for a living was not the primary goal of these "associationists." As Emerson put it in "Man the Reformer":

> The doctrine of the Farm is merely this, that every man ought to stand in primary relations with the work of the world, ought to do it himself, and not to suffer the accident of his having a purse in his pocket, or his having been bred to some dishonorable and injurious craft, to sever him from

> those duties; and for this reason, that labor is God's education; that he only is a sincere learner, he only can become a master, who learns the secrets of labor, and who by real cunning extorts from nature its sceptre.

For those attracted to collective farms, attaching themselves to the land constituted a necessary as well as a desirable part of their effort to model an entirely new form of social relationship, based not on the cash nexus that characterized capitalism but on forms of cooperation and mutual support.

These articles lay out in some detail the associationists' hopes that moving to intentional rural communities governed by cooperative ideas would enable them to find practical alternatives to the alienation produced by the division of labor and the wage system. They expected to be able to balance intellectual and manual labor and to restore the qualities of play and pleasure that industrial routines had largely excluded from work. And they wished to build concrete alternatives to competitive capitalism that would model a more equitable distribution of the world's goods. They were likewise committed to offering alternatives either to despair or to violent revolution. As the primary associationist newspaper, the *Harbinger,* put it in its June 1846 edition:

> The truth has been revealed to the world: the laws of human progress are discovered. It is for us, for the people of this age and especially this country, to say whether—by obedience to them, we shall have peaceful improvement,—or, by neglect,—misery, discord and violence. (16)

Movement to a rural commune—to use twentieth-century terminology—would, finally, provide the basis for "self-culture," the necessary ingredient, the associationists believed, for a broader reform of the corrupt and oppressive system of chattel and wage slavery, of profit motives and class conflicts they saw as increasingly destroying America's promise.

One of the things that is striking both about these communitarian texts and about many of those included here that postdate Thoreau's work is the strong linkage they display between ideas of personal purification and explicitly radical politics. Gandhi writes at length of the necessary preparations, mental, physical, and moral, for nonviolent action; students active in the American civil rights movement of the early 1960s often participated in training programs designed not only to familiarize them with theories of civil disobedience but with the discipline necessary to its practice. Self-renewal or self-development and social transformation are again and again bound together—as are, we will see, the practices narrated in *Walden* and those recounted in "Civil Disobedience."

But not all reformers shared the associationists' belief in self-culture or in the importance of group action. On the contrary, a reformer like Orestes Brownson inveighed against self-culture, arguing with European socialists like Marx and Engels that the problem lay in the "unequal reparation of the fruits of industry." Self-culture could not, he maintained, be a "remedy for the vices of the social state." Brownson predicted, to the horror of most middle-class New Englanders including the intelligentsia, that a new struggle was at hand "between the operative and his employer, between wealth and labor," that the misery of industrial capitalism would be resolved through a war of "the poor against the rich." If Brownson's analysis sounds, some of the time, like that of a revolutionary communist, his program was quite different. His article ends by calling not for the workers of the world to unite but for societies to rid themselves, in some unspecified way, of priests, banks, and monopolies. However, he shared with the "utopian" associationists a belief in the efficacy of middle-class intellectuals and reformers, like himself, to lead society toward amelioration, whereas "scientific" socialists like Marx and Engels looked to the dynamic of an inevitable class struggle, led by an awakened proletariat, to achieve revolutionary change.

Thoreau obviously did not share Brownson's contempt for self-culture as the key to social betterment. Indeed, the Walden experience can be seen as one version of what the associationists had in mind: an effort to simplify life, to live it fully in relationship to and with a richer understanding of nature and nature's creator. Thoreau also implicitly shared with them a belief in the leadership of people much like himself: that class of educated men and women whose position in the world depended neither on capital, manufacture, and trade nor on the labor of their bodies—a certain elite, in short, who were marked more by education than by labor, more by a cultural network than by connections of money and trade. On the other hand, Thoreau parted company precisely at the word *association*. The Brook Farm Phalanx and the Fruitlands family tried mightily to recruit him. Like Emerson, he was not interested. Or, perhaps, collectivity was simply not his thing. To pull away from the urban world of "getting and spending," to plunge like the loon of Walden Pond deeply into nature, to surface in laughter and joy—these were adventures best conducted by a solitary explorer, not, Thoreau clearly believed, by a "Phalanx." No conversation among reformers, however learned and earnest, could provide the enlightenment generated by Thoreau's lone observation of the flow of sand down the railroad embankment at Walden: "this one hillside illustrated the principle of all the operations of Nature. The Maker of this earth but patented a leaf."

All the same, it is essential to understand that, like the course described and justified in "Civil Disobedience," Thoreau's act of living by himself at Walden Pond was not *only* a work of self-culture, self-purification, or self-assertion. It was not *only* a program to learn more deeply the natural laws that bound up the human, the animate, and the inanimate into a *uni*verse. It was not *only* a writer's endeavor, like a trip down the Concord and Merrimack Rivers, to provide grist for his literary mill. It was all of these things, but like the efforts of those at Brook Farm and at Fruitlands, it was also a means for suggesting and inspiring concrete alternatives to wage slavery and to arrogant commercial culture. It was also, arguably, an attempt to reassert in the affairs of the nation the leadership of a kind of secular New England clerisy, university-educated men—and for the most part, they were men—who might offer not only ideas on paper but the practice of life lived to the beat of a different drummer.

Beyond that, it became an effort to find a course of life in a political landscape increasingly swept, in Matthew Arnold's words, "with confused alarms of struggle and flight." In the 1830s and 1840s, almost all social reformers, and certainly most abolitionists, would have agreed with the nonviolent beliefs so vividly articulated in "Civil Disobedience" and demonstrated again and again in the political practice of Garrison and his followers. But, as Henry Highland Garnet's 1843 speech attests, many—especially African Americans—were becoming restive before the evident failure of moral suasion and reason to end, or even to limit, the slave power. The passage of the Fugitive Slave Law in 1850 seemed to justify those, like John Brown, who had argued all along that only forms of direct pressure on slaveholders, including rebellion and violence, could bring about significant change. By 1860, Frederick Douglass, who had long parted ways with the Garrisonians, would argue in a speech praising Brown that not only had all appeals to Southerners' "sense of justice" been in vain, but that "the very submission of the slave to his chains is held as evidence of his fitness to be a slave. . . . His very non-resistance—what would be here regarded a Christian virtue—is quoted in proof of his cowardice, and his unwillingness to suffer and sacrifice for his liberty" (534, 536). Douglass went on to suggest that slaveholders be subjected to the fear of guerrilla warfare conducted from the Alleghenies and that "the only way to make the Fugitive Slave Law a dead letter is to make a few dead slave-catchers" (537). This is hardly the language of nonviolent civil disobedience.

Nor, it would seem, is Thoreau's in his own speech praising Brown. He has not, to be sure, become an advocate of violent rebellion, but the passage in thought and language from "Civil Disobedience," through

"Slavery in Massachusetts" (1854), to "A Plea for Captain John Brown" (1859–60) is striking. The changes through which Thoreau was moving would not have seemed unfamiliar to those who were active through the 1960s. Then, too, many activists who had begun the decade committed to nonviolence as a way of life as well as a means for achieving racial equality and an end to the war in Vietnam entered the 1970s willing to consider or even to adopt "whatever means were necessary" to bring about change. Neither in the 1850s nor in the 1960s were such shifts in tactics simple or easy. They were often accompanied by contradictory movements: sometimes a retreat from social engagement—"greening out," sometimes a search for personal purification, often a rage against political corruption—and occasionally an outright commitment to armed struggle. It is never easy to retain one's moral compass in a contorted social landscape. In addition to the ways just suggested, Thoreau's difficult relationship to his own book, *Walden,* can be read as a record of his own struggles to find his path through what must have come to seem a moral wilderness, to arrive at a place from which he could, with confidence and hope, at once call his neighbors to account and feel himself in harmony with the "old settler and original proprietor" of Walden Pond. (See chap. 5, "Solitude.")

All of this sounds terribly serious—and it was. But it had a certain comic side to it, as life lived with eyes forever lifted toward changing the world and purifying the self frequently does. Some of that comedy, as well as the pain generated by these utopian exercises, is captured by Louisa May Alcott in "Transcendental Wild Oats." This brief retrospective memoir is included here to amplify what is sometimes too little noted about *Walden,* namely, Thoreau's relentless self-irony. To be sure, many attuned to his ever-playful language will consider his prose quite sufficiently "extra-vagant"; Thoreau can seldom resist a joke, nor does he ever seem to wish to do so. But here we want to attend less to the play of his language as such and more to its effect of disarming the suspicious, not the least of whom is Henry David Thoreau. Modeling life for John or Jonathan (see conclusion, note 32) is, after all, something of a brazen exercise. No less brazen is defying law and one's "civil neighbor," the tax gatherer. No one could casually rationalize such behavior: there is always a difficult balancing act between self-assertion and arrogance, between the asceticism of the committed and the sloppy realities of everyday human life. That tension may be captured in Thoreau's prose by the rapid alterations in tone, in which gestures of play cavort alongside the most serious reflections.

Take, for example, the climactic passage of "Spring," quoted earlier, in which Thoreau announces that "the Maker of this earth but patented a leaf," an assertion of the underlying unity of phenomena both animate (himself included) and inorganic. Immediately after that sentence, Thoreau writes:

> What Champollion will decipher this hieroglyphic for us, that we may turn over a new leaf at last? This phenomenon is more exhilarating to me than the luxuriance and fertility of vineyards. True, it is somewhat excrementitious in its character, and there is no end to the heaps of liver, lights and bowels, as if the globe were turned wrong side outward; but this suggests at least that Nature has some bowels, and there again is mother of humanity.

What are we to make of the tone of this passage? There is the learned reference to the man who first deciphered the hieroglyphics of the Rosetta stone, then the gag about turning over a new leaf, and finally the curious assertion that the presence of bowels demonstrates Nature to be the "mother of humanity." How literally can we take a disquisition on the "excrementitious" character of a railroad embankment? Or the remark in the first paragraph of "Where I Lived" that "the landscape radiated from me accordingly"? We are being kept off balance, lest we become too correct about the speaker or, on the other side, grow hostile to his bumptious ego. The playful language produces a certain ironic distance from—or is it within?—him; he will not hold still long enough for anyone to sit at his feet. Then, too, it may be that Thoreau's own anxiety about the course of life he has chosen here surfaces, wherein the performance of self-irony constitutes a kind of defense against the query: "What are you doing in—or out—there, Henry?"

In any event, the performances are splendid, and part of the fun of *Walden* has to be watching Thoreau taking on and off the cloaks of his various personae. There is the learned scholar, quoting Marcus Porcius Cato and the Zendavestas; there is the scientific naturalist, counting the birds and charting the ponds; there is the aspiring author, flashing his vocabulary. And there is the reformer, very much in Emerson's sense of that word, preparing for the morning star. It is this last Thoreau, who emerges as much from *Walden* as from "Civil Disobedience," on whom this volume's final group of essays, by Tolstoy, John Albert Macy, Gandhi, and King, casts light. All these writers constitute Thoreau not as some guru but as a generative spark in their work for change. They see the force of his ideas in "Civil Disobedience": "Let your life be a counter friction to stop the machine"; "A minority . . . is irresistible when it clogs by its whole weight." It is to these and other such specifically radical injunctions that they refer when they speak of Thoreau's influence on their own political projects. And yet it is clear that *Walden* echoes in their work as well: in Gandhi's understanding of how one prepares oneself and others for

Satyagraha, or nonviolent resistance; in the confidence of Tolstoy and King that people and the institutions of the earth can be transformed because they "are plastic like clay in the hands of the potter."

The challenge of Thoreau may lie precisely in the act of placing together the two works in this book, "Civil Disobedience" and *Walden.* Both his critics and his admirers tend to group themselves about one of these texts, acknowledging the other by distant gestures, nods, and winks. But the full power of Thoreau's writing resides in the dialectic between his supposedly more "political" essays, like "Civil Disobedience," "Slavery in Massachusetts," and "A Plea for Captain John Brown," and his "nature" or "literary" writing, supposedly of different literary species. In fact, readers of this volume may find such categories less useful as they discover, to resurrect a slogan from the feminist movement of the 1960s, the political in the personal—or rather, that political ideas can hardly be imagined, much less put into practice, without a fitting process of inner awakening and self-cultivation. That is the powerful legacy to which the last essays in this book give testimony.

A Note on the Text and Title of "Civil Disobedience" and the Text of *Walden*

An editor has two choices in connection with the text of "Civil Disobedience": base an edition on the version published during Thoreau's lifetime in Elizabeth Peabody's *Aesthetic Papers* (1849) and titled "Resistance to Civil Government," or base it on the posthumous version of the essay published in *A Yankee in Canada, with Anti-Slavery and Reform Papers* (1866) and titled "Civil Disobedience." Title aside, there are some, though not many, meaningful differences between these versions. In recent years the scholarly community has largely chosen to go with the earlier *Aesthetic Papers* text and its title. The later, posthumous text and its title, "Civil Disobedience," have been chosen for this edition for a number of reasons.

To begin with, if one mentions "Civil Disobedience" to informed people almost anywhere in the world, it is instantly recognized—both as an essay and as a political strategy. Indeed, it has become the English-language name for that strategy, wherever it is deployed, as is illustrated by other essays in this volume. Not so "Resistance to Civil Government." Thoreau did not invent the strategy of civil disobedience, but he gave it extraordinarily vivid articulation. It seems a kind of disservice to him, therefore, to detach the name, recognizable worldwide, from the writer who formulated the phrase—that is, unless there is strong and direct scholarly evidence that the title and the later text are corruptions introduced by someone other than Thoreau. No definitive evidence to that effect exists.

On the contrary, the later text corrects a few sentences—not a main concern for Thoreau—and includes two quotations not found in the earlier version. As an editor, I tried to imagine the task of another editor, a sister or close friend of the author, soon after Thoreau's death; it was hard to conceive that he or she simply added quotations (or, for that matter, so strikingly changed the title) without authorial warrant. To be sure, nineteenth-century editors, like many before them, took all sorts of liberties with authors' texts, as the posthumous publication of Emily Dickinson's poems most famously reminds us. But even there, the editors did not add quotations and additional text. No, absent strong evidence to the contrary, we have to assume as much editorial integrity in those who prepared Thoreau's works for publication after his death as we grant to late twentieth-century scholarly editors.

Finally, the biographical record makes clear that the first version of the essay was prepared in some haste, while Thoreau was engaged in bringing *A Week on the Concord and Merrimack Rivers* to press, among other tasks. The extent to which he had time and opportunity to transform what was initially a talk and to certify the text published in *Aesthetic Papers* remains unclear. It is not hard to imagine that he might have wished to improve the text or to add some material—as was his usual practice—though there is little extant holograph evidence that he actually did so. Furthermore, he may well have chosen the earlier title as a sly comment on the work of William Paley, "The Duty of Submission to Civil Government Explained," which he quotes in the essay. But he might also have come to feel that the force of his play was lost as Paley's own work faded from view.

All in all, then, and with great regard for the work of my scholarly colleagues, I came to conclude that both the well-known title and the posthumous text were appropriate, indeed preferable, for this New Riverside Edition.

The notes indicate the few places in which the text printed here differs substantively from that initially published under the title "Resistance to Civil Government."

The text of *Walden* is that of the 1854 edition published in Boston by Ticknor and Fields, incorporating the corrections Thoreau wrote in his own copy, now at the Abernethy Library of Middlebury College. Certain minor mid-nineteenth-century punctuation conventions (e.g., the use of commas or semicolons before dashes or the hyphenation of *to-day*) have been silently changed to conform to current usage. But no changes that might in any way be taken to alter meaning or style have been made in the text.

PART ONE

Civil Disobedience

CIVIL DISOBEDIENCE

by Henry David Thoreau

I heartily accept the motto, "That government is best which governs least;"[1] and I should like to see it acted up to more rapidly and systematically. Carried out, it finally amounts to this, which also I believe—"That government is best which governs not at all;" and when men are prepared for it, that will be the kind of government which they will have. Government is at best but an expedient; but most governments are usually, and all governments are sometimes, inexpedient. The objections which have been brought against a standing army, and they are many and weighty, and deserve to prevail, may also at last be brought against a standing government. The standing army is only an arm of the standing government. The government itself, which is only the mode which the people have chosen to execute their will, is equally liable to be abused and perverted before the people can act through it. Witness the present Mexican war,[2] the work of comparatively a few individuals using the standing government as their tool; for, in the outset, the people would not have consented to this measure.

This American government—what is it but a tradition, though a recent one, endeavoring to transmit itself unimpaired to posterity, but each instant losing some of its integrity? It has not the vitality and force of a single living man; for a single man can bend it to his will. It is a sort of wooden gun to the people themselves.[3] But it is not the less necessary for this; for the people must have some complicated machinery or other, and hear its din, to satisfy that idea of government which they have. Governments show thus how successfully men can be imposed on, even impose on themselves, for their own advantage. It is excellent, we must all allow. Yet this government never of itself furthered any enterprise, but by the alacrity with which it got out of its way. *It* does not keep the country free. *It* does not settle the West. *It* does not educate. The character inherent in the American people has done all that has been accomplished; and it would have done somewhat more, if the government had not sometimes

---

[1] This motto appeared on the title page of the *United States Magazine and Democratic Review,* a literary and political journal. It actually read, "The best government is that which governs least." Some writers have attributed the phrase to Thomas Jefferson, but scholars have been unable to locate it in his writings.

[2] The war between Mexico and the United States, 1846–48, ended with the Treaty of Guadalupe Hidalgo, in which Mexico was forced to cede about a third of its territory, including much of what is now the Southwest of the United States as well as California.

[3] In the original version of the essay, the sentence continued: "and, if ever they should use it in earnest as a real one against each other, it will surely split." Scholars have speculated that the editors of the 1866 edition excised the passage because of the Civil War (ongoing until 1865).

got in its way. For government is an expedient by which men would fain succeed in letting one another alone; and, as has been said, when it is most expedient, the governed are most let alone by it. Trade and commerce, if they were not made of india-rubber,[4] would never manage to bounce over the obstacles which legislators are continually putting in their way; and, if one were to judge these men wholly by the effects of their actions and not partly by their intentions, they would deserve to be classed and punished with those mischievous persons who put obstructions on the railroads.

But, to speak practically and as a citizen, unlike those who call themselves no-government men, I ask for, not at once no government, but *at once* a better government. Let every man make known what kind of government would command his respect, and that will be one step toward obtaining it.

After all, the practical reason why, when the power is once in the hands of the people, a majority are permitted, and for a long period continue, to rule is not because they are most likely to be in the right, nor because this seems fairest to the minority, but because they are physically the strongest. But a government in which the majority rule in all cases cannot be based on justice, even as far as men understand it. Can there not be a government in which majorities do not virtually decide right and wrong, but conscience?—in which majorities decide only those questions to which the rule of expediency is applicable? Must the citizen ever for a moment, or in the least degree, resign his conscience to the legislator? Why has every man a conscience, then? I think that we should be men first, and subjects afterwards. It is not desirable to cultivate a respect for the law, so much as for the right. The only obligation which I have a right to assume is to do at any time what I think right. It is truly enough said that a corporation has no conscience; but a corporation of conscientious men is a corporation *with* a conscience. Law never made men a whit more just; and, by means of their respect for it, even the well-disposed are daily made the agents of injustice. A common and natural result of an undue respect for law is, that you may see a file of soldiers, colonel, captain, corporal, privates, powder-monkeys,[5] and all, marching in admirable order over hill and dale to the wars, against their wills, ay, against their common sense and consciences, which makes it very steep marching indeed, and produces a palpitation of the heart. They have no doubt that it is a damnable business in which they

[4] Crude rubber obtained from latex.
[5] A boy who carried powder from the magazine to the guns aboard a man of war.

are concerned; they are all peaceably inclined. Now, what are they? Men at all? or small movable forts and magazines, at the service of some unscrupulous man in power? Visit the Navy-Yard,[6] and behold a marine, such a man as an American government can make, or such as it can make a man with its black arts—a mere shadow and reminiscence of humanity, a man laid out alive and standing, and already, as one may say, buried under arms with funeral accompaniments, though it may be—

> Not a drum was heard, not a funeral note,
> As his corse to the rampart we hurried;
> Not a soldier discharged his farewell shot
> O'er the grave where our hero was buried.[7]

The mass of men serve the state thus, not as men mainly, but as machines, with their bodies. They are the standing army, and the militia, jailers, constables, *posse comitatus*,[8] etc. In most cases there is no free exercise whatever of the judgment or of the moral sense; but they put themselves on a level with wood and earth and stones; and wooden men can perhaps be manufactured that will serve the purpose as well. Such command no more respect than men of straw or a lump of dirt. They have the same sort of worth only as horses and dogs. Yet such as these even are commonly esteemed good citizens. Others—as most legislators, politicians, lawyers, ministers, and office-holders—serve the state chiefly with their heads; and, as they rarely make any moral distinctions, they are as likely to serve the devil, without *intending* it, as God. A very few—as heroes, patriots, martyrs, reformers in the great sense, and *men*—serve the state with their consciences also, and so necessarily resist it for the most part; and they are commonly treated as enemies by it. A wise man will only be useful as a man, and will not submit to be "clay," and "stop a hole to keep the wind away,"[9] but leave that office to his dust at least—

> I am too high-born to be propertied,
> To be a secondary at control,

[6] Presumably in Boston Harbor.
[7] Charles Wolfe (1791–1823), "Burial of Sir John Moore at Corunna" (1817).
[8] A body of men liable to be called by a sheriff to assist him in keeping the peace.
[9] Shakespeare, *Hamlet* 5.1.236–37.

Or useful serving-man and instrument
To any sovereign state throughout the world.[10]

He who gives himself entirely to his fellow-men appears to them useless and selfish; but he who gives himself partially to them is pronounced a benefactor and philanthropist.

How does it become a man to behave toward this American government today? I answer, that he cannot without disgrace be associated with it. I cannot for an instant recognize that political organization as *my* government which is the *slave's* government also.

All men recognize the right of revolution; that is, the right to refuse allegiance to, and to resist, the government, when its tyranny or its inefficiency are great and unendurable. But almost all say that such is not the case now. But such was the case, they think, in the Revolution of '75.[11] If one were to tell me that this was a bad government because it taxed certain foreign commodities brought to its ports, it is most probable that I should not make an ado about it, for I can do without them. All machines have their friction; and possibly this does enough good to counterbalance the evil. At any rate, it is a great evil to make a stir about it. But when the friction comes to have its machine, and oppression and robbery are organized, I say, let us not have such a machine any longer. In other words, when a sixth of the population of a nation which has undertaken to be the refuge of liberty are slaves, and a whole country is unjustly overrun and conquered by a foreign army, and subjected to military law, I think that it is not too soon for honest men to rebel and revolutionize. What makes this duty the more urgent is the fact that the country so overrun is not our own, but ours is the invading army.

Paley, a common authority with many on moral questions, in his chapter on the "Duty of Submission to Civil Government," resolves all civil obligation into expediency; and he proceeds to say that "so long as the interest of the whole society requires it, that is, so long as the established government cannot be resisted or changed without public inconveniency, it is the will of God . . . that the established government be obeyed—and no longer. This principle being admitted, the justice of every particular case of resistance is reduced to a computation of the quantity of the danger and grievance on the one side, and of the probability and ex-

[10] Shakespeare, *King John* 5.2.79–82.
[11] The American Revolution began with the Battle of Lexington and Concord, April 19, 1775.

pense of redressing it on the other."[12] Of this, he says, every man shall judge for himself. But Paley appears never to have contemplated those cases to which the rule of expediency does not apply, in which a people, as well as an individual, must do justice, cost what it may. If I have unjustly wrested a plank from a drowning man, I must restore it to him though I drown myself.[13] This, according to Paley, would be inconvenient. But he that would save his life, in such a case, shall lose it.[14] This people must cease to hold slaves, and to make war on Mexico, though it cost them their existence as a people.

In their practice, nations agree with Paley; but does any one think that Massachusetts does exactly what is right at the present crisis?

> A drab of state, a cloth-o'-silver slut,
> To have her train borne up, and her soul trail in the dirt.[15]

Practically speaking, the opponents to a reform in Massachusetts are not a hundred thousand politicians at the South, but a hundred thousand merchants and farmers here, who are more interested in commerce and agriculture than they are in humanity, and are not prepared to do justice to the slave and to Mexico, *cost what it may.* I quarrel not with far-off foes, but with those who, near at home, cooperate with, and do the bidding of, those far away, and without whom the latter would be harmless. We are accustomed to say, that the mass of men are unprepared; but improvement is slow, because the few are not materially wiser or better than the many. It is not so important that many should be as good as you, as that there be some absolute goodness somewhere; for that will leaven the whole lump.[16] There are thousands who are *in opinion* opposed to slavery and to the war, who yet in effect do nothing to put an end to them; who, esteeming themselves children of Washington and Franklin, sit down with their hands in their pockets, and say that they know not what to do, and do nothing; who even postpone the question of freedom to the question of free trade, and

[12] William Paley (1743–1805), "The Duty of Submission to Civil Government Explained," chap. 3, book 6 of *The Principles of Moral and Political Philosophy* (1785). Thoreau made a few minor alterations to the passage.

[13] Cf. *De officiis* (*On Duty,* c. 45–44 B.C.E.) by the great Roman orator and statesman Marcus Tullius Cicero (106–43 B.C.E.).

[14] Luke 9.24, Matt. 10.39: "He that findeth his life shall lose it: and he that loseth his life for my sake shall find it." All biblical quotations are from the King James (Authorized) version of 1611.

[15] Cyril Tourneur (1575?–1626), *The Revenger's Tragedy* 4.4.72–73.

[16] I Cor. 5.6–8.

quietly read the prices-current along with the latest advices from Mexico, after dinner, and, it may be, fall asleep over them both. What is the price-current of an honest man and patriot today? They hesitate, and they regret, and sometimes they petition; but they do nothing in earnest and with effect. They will wait, well disposed, for others to remedy the evil, that they may no longer have it to regret. At most, they give only a cheap vote, and a feeble countenance and God-speed, to the right, as it goes by them. There are nine hundred and ninety-nine patrons of virtue to one virtuous man. But it is easier to deal with the real possessor of a thing than with the temporary guardian of it.

All voting is a sort of gaming, like checkers or backgammon, with a slight moral tinge to it, a playing with right and wrong, with moral questions; and betting naturally accompanies it. The character of the voters is not staked. I cast my vote, perchance, as I think right; but I am not vitally concerned that that right should prevail. I am willing to leave it to the majority. Its obligation, therefore, never exceeds that of expediency. Even voting *for the right* is *doing* nothing for it. It is only expressing to men feebly your desire that it should prevail. A wise man will not leave the right to the mercy of chance, nor wish it to prevail through the power of the majority. There is but little virtue in the action of masses of men. When the majority shall at length vote for the abolition of slavery, it will be because they are indifferent to slavery, or because there is but little slavery left to be abolished by their vote. *They* will then be the only slaves. Only *his* vote can hasten the abolition of slavery who asserts his own freedom by his vote.

I hear of a convention to be held at Baltimore, or elsewhere, for the selection of a candidate for the Presidency, made up chiefly of editors, and men who are politicians by profession; but I think, what is it to any independent, intelligent, and respectable man what decision they may come to? Shall we not have the advantage of his wisdom and honesty, nevertheless? Can we not count upon some independent votes? Are there not many individuals in the country who do not attend conventions? But no: I find that the respectable man, so called, has immediately drifted from his position, and despairs of his country, when his country has more reason to despair of him. He forthwith adopts one of the candidates thus selected as the only *available* one, thus proving that he is himself *available* for any purposes of the demagogue. His vote is of no more worth than that of any unprincipled foreigner or hireling native, who may have been bought. O for a man who is a *man,* and, as my neighbor says, has a bone in his back which you cannot pass your hand through! Our statistics are at fault: the population has been returned too large. How many *men* are there to a square thousand miles in this country? Hardly one. Does not America offer any inducement for men to settle here? The American has dwindled into an Odd

Fellow[17]—one who may be known by the development of his organ of gregariousness, and a manifest lack of intellect and cheerful self-reliance; whose first and chief concern, on coming into the world, is to see that the almshouses are in good repair; and, before yet he has lawfully donned the virile garb,[18] to collect a fund for the support of the widows and orphans that may be; who, in short, ventures to live only by the aid of the Mutual Insurance company, which has promised to bury him decently.

It is not a man's duty, as a matter of course, to devote himself to the eradication of any, even the most enormous, wrong; he may still properly have other concerns to engage him; but it is his duty, at least, to wash his hands of it, and, if he gives it no thought longer, not to give it practically his support. If I devote myself to other pursuits and contemplations, I must first see, at least, that I do not pursue them sitting upon another man's shoulders. I must get off him first, that he may pursue his contemplations too. See what gross inconsistency is tolerated. I have heard some of my townsmen say, "I should like to have them order me out to help put down an insurrection of the slaves, or to march to Mexico—see if I would go"; and yet these very men have each, directly by their allegiance, and so indirectly, at least, by their money, furnished a substitute. The soldier is applauded who refuses to serve in an unjust war by those who do not refuse to sustain the unjust government which makes the war; is applauded by those whose own act and authority he disregards and sets at naught; as if the state were penitent to that degree that it hired one to scourge it while it sinned, but not to that degree that it left off sinning for a moment. Thus, under the name of Order and Civil Government, we are all made at last to pay homage to and support our own meanness. After the first blush of sin comes its indifference; and from immoral it becomes, as it were, *un*moral, and not quite unnecessary to that life which we have made.

The broadest and most prevalent error requires the most disinterested virtue to sustain it. The slight reproach to which the virtue of patriotism is commonly liable, the noble are most likely to incur. Those who, while they disapprove of the character and measures of a government, yield to it their allegiance and support are undoubtedly its most conscientious supporters, and so frequently the most serious obstacles to reform. Some are petitioning the State to dissolve the Union, to disregard the requisitions of the President. Why do they not dissolve it themselves—the union between themselves and the State—and refuse to pay their quota into its treasury? Do not they stand in the same relation to the State that the State does to

---

[17] A member of the Independent Order of Odd Fellows, a fraternal organization.

[18] In Rome, adult clothing that a boy was allowed to wear upon reaching age fourteen.

the Union? And have not the same reasons prevented the State from resisting the Union which have prevented them from resisting the State?

How can a man be satisfied to entertain an opinion merely, and enjoy *it?* Is there any enjoyment in it, if his opinion is that he is aggrieved? If you are cheated out of a single dollar by your neighbor, you do not rest satisfied with knowing that you are cheated, or with saying that you are cheated, or even with petitioning him to pay you your due; but you take effectual steps at once to obtain the full amount, and see that you are never cheated again. Action from principle, the perception and the performance of right, changes things and relations; it is essentially revolutionary, and does not consist wholly with anything which was. It not only divides States and churches, it divides families; ay, it divides the *individual,* separating the diabolical in him from the divine.

Unjust laws exist: shall we be content to obey them, or shall we endeavor to amend them, and obey them until we have succeeded, or shall we transgress them at once? Men generally, under such a government as this, think that they ought to wait until they have persuaded the majority to alter them. They think that, if they should resist, the remedy would be worse than the evil. But it is the fault of the government itself that the remedy *is* worse than the evil. *It* makes it worse. Why is it not more apt to anticipate and provide for reform? Why does it not cherish its wise minority? Why does it cry and resist before it is hurt? Why does it not encourage its citizens to be on the alert to point out its faults, and *do* better than it would have them? Why does it always crucify Christ, and excommunicate Copernicus[19] and Luther,[20] and pronounce Washington and Franklin rebels?

One would think, that a deliberate and practical denial of its authority was the only offence never contemplated by government; else, why has it not assigned its definite, its suitable and proportionate, penalty? If a man who has no property refuses but once to earn nine shillings for the State,[21] he is put in prison for a period unlimited by any law that I know, and determined only by the discretion of those who placed him there; but if he should steal ninety times nine shillings from the State, he is soon permitted to go at large again.

If the injustice is part of the necessary friction of the machine of government, let it go, let it go: perchance it will wear smooth—certainly the

[19]Nicolaus Copernicus (1473–1543), Polish astronomer, developed the theory that the planets revolve around the sun. He was not, in fact, excommunicated, though his book on the solar system was banned by Roman Catholic authorities.

[20]Martin Luther (1483–1546) was the initial leader of the Protestant Reformation.

[21]The amount of the poll tax Thoreau had refused to pay.

machine will wear out. If the injustice has a spring, or a pulley, or a rope, or a crank, exclusively for itself, then perhaps you may consider whether the remedy will not be worse than the evil; but if it is of such a nature that it requires you to be the agent of injustice to another, then, I say, break the law. Let your life be a counter friction to stop the machine. What I have to do is to see, at any rate, that I do not lend myself to the wrong which I condemn.

As for adopting the ways which the State has provided for remedying the evil, I know not of such ways. They take too much time, and a man's life will be gone. I have other affairs to attend to. I came into this world, not chiefly to make this a good place to live in, but to live in it, be it good or bad. A man has not everything to do, but something; and because he cannot do *everything*, it is not necessary that he should do *something* wrong. It is not my business to be petitioning the Governor or the Legislature any more than it is theirs to petition me; and if they should not hear my petition, what should I do then? But in this case the State his provided no way: its very Constitution is the evil. This may seem to be harsh and stubborn and unconciliatory; but it is to treat with the utmost kindness and consideration the only spirit that can appreciate or deserves it. So is all change for the better, like birth and death, which convulse the body.

I do not hesitate to say, that those who call themselves Abolitionists should at once effectually withdraw their support, both in person and property, from the government of Massachusetts, and not wait till they constitute a majority of one, before they suffer the right to prevail through them. I think that it is enough if they have God on their side, without waiting for that other one. Moreover, any man more right than his neighbors constitutes a majority of one already.

I meet this American government, or its representative, the State government, directly, and face to face, once a year—no more—in the person of its tax-gatherer; this is the only mode in which a man situated as I am necessarily meets it; and it then says distinctly, Recognize me; and the simplest, the most effectual, and, in the present posture of affairs, the indispensablest mode of treating with it on this head, of expressing your little satisfaction with and love for it, is to deny it then. My civil neighbor, the tax-gatherer, is the very man I have to deal with—for it is, after all, with men and not with parchment that I quarrel—and he has voluntarily chosen to be an agent of the government. How shall he ever know well what he is and does as an officer of the government, or as a man, until he is obliged to consider whether he shall treat me, his neighbor, for whom he has respect, as a neighbor and well-disposed man, or as a maniac and disturber of the peace, and see if he can get over this obstruction to his neighborliness without a ruder and more impetuous thought or speech corresponding with his action. I know this well, that if one thousand, if one hundred, if ten men whom I could name—if ten *honest* men only—ay, if *one* HONEST man, in this State of Massachusetts, *ceasing to hold slaves,* were actually to withdraw from this copartnership, and be locked up in the county jail therefor, it would be the abolition of slavery in America. For it matters not how small the beginning may seem to be: what is once well done is done forever. But we love better to talk about it: that we say is our mission. Reform keeps many scores of newspapers in its service, but not one man. If my esteemed neighbor, the State's ambassador,[22] who will devote his days to the settlement of the question of human rights in the Council Chamber, instead of being threatened with the prisons of Carolina, were to sit down the prisoner of Massachusetts, that State which is so anxious to foist the sin of slavery upon her sister—though at present she can discover only an act of inhospitality to be the ground of a quarrel with her—the Legislature would not wholly waive the subject the following winter.

Under a government which imprisons any unjustly, the true place for a just man is also a prison. The proper place today, the only place which Massachusetts has provided for her freer and less desponding spirits, is in her prisons, to be put out and locked out of the State by her own act, as they have already put themselves out by their principles. It is there that the fugitive slave, and the Mexican prisoner on parole, and the Indian come to plead the wrongs of his race should find them; on that separate, but more free and honorable, ground, where the State places those who are not *with* her, but *against* her—the only house in a slave State in which a free man can abide with honor. If any think that their influence would be lost there, and their voices no longer afflict the ear of the State, that they would not be as an enemy within its walls, they do not know by how much truth is stronger than error, nor how much more eloquently and effectively he can combat injustice who has experienced a little in his own person. Cast your whole vote, not a strip of paper merely, but your whole influence. A minority is powerless while it conforms to the majority; it is not even a minority then; but it is irresistible when it clogs by its whole weight. If the alternative is to keep all just men in prison, or give up war and slavery, the State will not hesitate which to choose. If a thousand men were not to pay their tax-bills this year, that would not be a violent and bloody measure,

[22] In 1844, Samuel Hoar of Concord was sent to Charleston, South Carolina, on behalf of black seamen from Massachusetts who had been threatened with arrest and enslavement if they entered that port. Hoar was expelled from South Carolina by an act of the legislature.

as it would be to pay them, and enable the State to commit violence and shed innocent blood.

This is, in fact, the definition of a peaceable revolution, if any such is possible. If the tax-gatherer, or any other public officer, asks me, as one has done, "But what shall I do?" my answer is, "If you really wish to do anything, resign your office." When the subject has refused allegiance, and the officer has resigned his office, then the revolution is accomplished. But even suppose blood should flow. Is there not a sort of blood shed when the conscience is wounded? Through this wound a man's real manhood and immortality flow out, and he bleeds to an everlasting death. I see this blood flowing now.

I have contemplated the imprisonment of the offender, rather than the seizure of his goods—though both will serve the same purpose—because they who assert the purest right, and consequently are most dangerous to a corrupt State, commonly have not spent much time in accumulating property. To such the State renders comparatively small service, and a slight tax is wont to appear exorbitant, particularly if they are obliged to earn it by special labor with their hands. If there were one who lived wholly without the use of money, the State itself would hesitate to demand it of him. But the rich man—not to make any invidious comparison—is always sold to the institution which makes him rich. Absolutely speaking, the more money, the less virtue; for money comes between a man and his objects, and obtains them for him; and it was certainly no great virtue to obtain it. It puts to rest many questions which he would otherwise be taxed to answer; while the only new question which it puts is the hard but superfluous one, how to spend it. Thus his moral ground is taken from under his feet. The opportunities of living are diminished in proportion as what are called the "means" are increased. The best thing a man can do for his culture when he is rich is to endeavor to carry out those schemes which he entertained when he was poor. Christ answered the Herodians according to their condition. "Show me the tribute-money," said he—and one took a penny out of his pocket—if you use money which has the image of Caesar on it, and which he has made current and valuable, that is, *if you are men of the State,* and gladly enjoy the advantages of Caesar's government, then pay him back some of his own when he demands it. "Render therefore to Caesar that which is Caesar's, and to God those things which are God's"[23]—leaving them no wiser than before as to which was which; for they did not wish to know.

---

[23] Cf. Matt. 22.17–21: "Tell us therefore, What thinkest thou? Is it lawful to give tribute unto Caesar, or not? But Jesus perceived their wickedness, and said, Why tempt ye me,

When I converse with the freest of my neighbors, I perceive that, whatever they may say about the magnitude and seriousness of the question, and their regard for the public tranquillity, the long and the short of the matter is, that they cannot spare the protection of the existing government, and they dread the consequences to their property and families of disobedience to it. For my own part, I should not like to think that I ever rely on the protection of the State. But, if I deny the authority of the State when it presents its tax-bill, it will soon take and waste all my property, and so harass me and my children without end. This is hard. This makes it impossible for a man to live honestly, and at the same time comfortably, in outward respects. It will not be worth the while to accumulate property; that would be sure to go again. You must hire or squat somewhere, and raise but a small crop, and eat that soon. You must live within yourself, and depend upon yourself always tucked up and ready for a start, and not have many affairs. A man may grow rich in Turkey even, if he will be in all respects a good subject of the Turkish government. Confucius said: "If a state is governed by the principles of reason, poverty and misery are subjects of shame; if a state is not governed by the principles of reason, riches and honors are the subjects of shame."[24] No: until I want the protection of Massachusetts to be extended to me in some distant Southern port, where my liberty is endangered, or until I am bent solely on building up an estate at home by peaceful enterprise, I can afford to refuse allegiance to Massachusetts, and her right to my property and life. It costs me less in every sense to incur the penalty of disobedience to the State than it would to obey. I should feel as if I were worth less in that case.

Some years ago, the State met me in behalf of the Church, and commanded me to pay a certain sum toward the support of a clergyman whose preaching my father attended, but never I myself. "Pay," it said, "or be locked up in the jail." I declined to pay.[25] But, unfortunately, another man saw fit to pay it. I did not see why the schoolmaster should be taxed to support the priest, and not the priest the schoolmaster; for I was not the State's schoolmaster, but I supported myself by voluntary subscription. I did not see why the lyceum should not present its tax-bill, and have the State to back its demand, as well as the Church. However, at the request of the se-

---

ye hypocrites? Show me the tribute money. And they brought unto him a penny. And he saith unto them, Whose is this image and superscription? They say unto him, Caesar's. Then saith he unto them, Render therefore unto Caesar the things which are Caesar's; and unto God the things that are God's."

[24] *Analects* 8.13.

[25] After returning from college to Concord, one of Thoreau's first acts was to "sign off" from the local, officially recognized congregation.

lectmen, I condescended to make some such statement as this in writing—"Know all men by these presents, that I, Henry Thoreau, do not wish to be regarded as a member of any incorporated society which I have not joined." This I gave to the town clerk; and he has it. The State, having thus learned that I did not wish to be regarded as a member of that church, has never made a like demand on me since; though it said that it must adhere to its original presumption that time. If I had known how to name them, I should then have signed off in detail from all the societies which I never signed on to; but I did not know where to find a complete list.

I have paid no poll-tax for six years. I was put into a jail once on this account, for one night; and, as I stood considering the walls of solid stone, two or three feet thick, the door of wood and iron, a foot thick, and the iron grating which strained the light, I could not help being struck with the foolishness of that institution which treated me as if I were mere flesh and blood and bones to be locked up. I wondered that it should have concluded at length that this was the best use it could put me to, and had never thought to avail itself of my services in some way. I saw that, if there was a wall of stone between me and my townsmen, there was a still more difficult one to climb or break through before they could get to be as free as I was. I did not for a moment feel confined, and the walls seemed a great waste of stone and mortar. I felt as if I alone of all my townsmen had paid my tax. They plainly did not know how to treat me, but behaved like persons who are underbred. In every threat and in every compliment there was a blunder; for they thought that my chief desire was to stand the other side of that stone wall. I could not but smile to see how industriously they locked the door on my meditations, which followed them out again without let or hindrance, and *they* were really all that was dangerous. As they could not reach me, they had resolved to punish my body; just as boys, if they cannot come at some person against whom they have a spite, will abuse his dog. I saw that the State was half-witted, that it was timid as a lone woman with her silver spoons, and that it did not know its friends from its foes, and I lost all my remaining respect for it, and pitied it.

Thus the State never intentionally confronts a man's sense, intellectual or moral, but only his body, his senses. It is not armed with superior wit or honesty, but with superior physical strength. I was not born to be forced. I will breathe after my own fashion. Let us see who is the strongest. What force has a multitude? They only can force me who obey a higher law than I. They force me to become like themselves. I do not hear of *men* being *forced* to live this way or that by masses of men. What sort of life were that to live? When I meet a government which says to me, "Your money or your life," why should I be in haste to give it my money? It may be in a great strait, and not know what to do: I cannot help that. It must help itself; do as I do. It is not worth the while to snivel about it. I am not responsible for the successful working of the machinery of society. I am not the son of the engineer. I perceive that, when an acorn and a chestnut fall side by side, the one does not remain inert to make way for the other, but both obey their own laws, and spring and grow and flourish as best they can, till one, perchance, overshadows and destroys the other. If a plant cannot live according to its nature, it dies; and so a man.

The night in prison was novel and interesting enough. The prisoners in their shirt-sleeves were enjoying a chat and the evening air in the doorway, when I entered. But the jailer said, "Come, boys, it is time to lock up"; and so they dispersed, and I heard the sound of their steps returning into the hollow apartments. My room-mate was introduced to me by the jailer as "a first-rate fellow and a clever man." When the door was locked, he showed me where to hang my hat, and how he managed matters there. The rooms were whitewashed once a month; and this one, at least, was the whitest, most simply furnished, and probably the neatest apartment in the town. He naturally wanted to know where I came from, and what brought me there; and, when I had told him, I asked him in my turn how he came there, presuming him to be an honest man, of course; and, as the world goes, I believe he was. "Why," said he, "they accuse me of burning a barn; but I never did it." As near as I could discover, he had probably gone to bed in a barn when drunk, and smoked his pipe there; and so a barn was burnt. He had the reputation of being a clever man, had been there some three months waiting for his trial to come on, and would have to wait as much longer; but he was quite domesticated and contented, since he got his board for nothing, and thought that he was well treated.

He occupied one window, and I the other; and I saw that if one stayed there long, his principal business would be to look out the window. I had soon read all the tracts that were left there, and examined where former prisoners had broken out, and where a grate had been sawed off, and heard the history of the various occupants of that room; for I found that even here there was a history and a gossip which never circulated beyond the walls of the jail. Probably this is the only house in the town where verses are composed, which are afterward printed in a circular form, but not published. I was shown quite a long list of verses which were composed by some young men who had been detected in an attempt to escape, who avenged themselves by singing them.

I pumped my fellow-prisoner as dry as I could, for fear I should never see him again; but at length he showed me which was my bed, and left me to blow out the lamp.

It was like travelling into a far country, such as I had never expected to behold, to lie there for one night. It seemed to me that I never had heard the town clock strike before, nor the evening sounds of the village; for we slept with the windows open, which were inside the grating. It was to see my native village in the light of the Middle Ages, and our Concord was turned into a Rhine stream, and visions of knights and castles passed before me. They were the voices of old burghers that I heard in the streets. I was an involuntary spectator and auditor of whatever was done and said in the kitchen of the adjacent village inn—a wholly new and rare experience to me. It was a closer view of my native town. I was fairly inside of it. I never had seen its institutions before. This is one of its peculiar institutions; for it is a shire town.[26] I began to comprehend what its inhabitants were about.

In the morning, our breakfasts were put through the hole in the door, in small oblong-square tin pans, made to fit, and holding a pint of chocolate, with brown bread, and an iron spoon. When they called for the vessels again, I was green enough to return what bread I had left; but my comrade seized it, and said that I should lay that up for lunch or dinner. Soon after he was let out to work at haying in a neighboring field, whither he went every day, and would not be back till noon; so he bade me good-day, saying that he doubted if he should see me again.

When I came out of prison—for some one interfered, and paid that tax—I did not perceive that great changes had taken place on the common, such as he observed who went in a youth and emerged a tottering and gray-headed man; and yet a change had to my eyes come over the scene—the town, and State, and country—greater than any that mere time could effect. I saw yet more distinctly the State in which I lived. I saw to what extent the people among whom I lived could be trusted as good neighbors and friends; that their friendship was for summer weather only; that they did not greatly propose to do right; that they were a distinct race from me by their prejudices and superstitions, as the Chinamen and Malays are; that in their sacrifices to humanity they ran no risks, not even to their property; that after all they were not so noble but they treated the thief as he had treated them, and hoped, by a certain outward observance and a few prayers, and by walking in a particular straight though useless path from time to time, to save their souls. This may be to judge my neighbors harshly; for I believe that many of them are not aware that they have such an institution as the jail in their village.

[26] The seat of county government.

It was formerly the custom in our village, when a poor debtor came out of jail, for his acquaintances to salute him, looking through their fingers, which were crossed to represent the grating of a jail window, "How do ye do?" My neighbors did not thus salute me, but first looked at me, and then at one another, as if I had returned from a long journey. I was put into jail as I was going to the shoemaker's to get a shoe which was mended. When I was let out the next morning, I preceeded to finish my errand, and, having put on my mended shoe, joined a huckleberry party, who were impatient to put themselves under my conduct; and in half an hour—for the horse was soon tackled[27]—was in the midst of a huckleberry field, on one of our highest hills, two miles off, and then the State was nowhere to be seen.

This is the whole history of "My Prisons."[28]

I have never declined paying the highway tax, because I am as desirous of being a good neighbor as I am of being a bad subject; and as for supporting schools, I am doing my part to educate my fellow-countrymen now. It is for no particular item in the tax-bill that I refuse to pay it. I simply wish to refuse allegiance to the State, to withdraw and stand aloof from it effectually. I do not care to trace the course of my dollar, if I could, till it buys a man or a musket to shoot one with—the dollar is innocent—but I am concerned to trace the effects of my allegiance. In fact, I quietly declare war with the State, after my fashion, though I will still make what use and get what advantage of her I can, as is usual in such cases.

If others pay the tax which is demanded of me, from a sympathy with the State, they do but what they have already done in their own case, or rather they abet injustice to a greater extent than the State requires. If they pay the tax from a mistaken interest in the individual taxed, to save his property, or prevent his going to jail, it is because they have not considered wisely how far they let their private feelings interfere with the public good.

This, then, is my position at present. But one cannot be too much on his guard in such a case, lest his action be biased by obstinacy or an undue regard for the opinions of men. Let him see that he does only what belongs to himself and to the hour.

I think sometimes, Why, this people mean well, they are only ignorant; they would do better if they knew how: why give your neighbors this pain to treat you as they are not inclined to? But I think again, This is no rea-

---

[27]Put in harness.

[28]Reference to a play with the title of the autobiography of the Italian revolutionary Silvio Pellico da Saluzzo (1789–1854), *Le mie prigioni: memorie* (1832).

son why I should do as they do, or permit others to suffer much greater pain of a different kind. Again, I sometimes say to myself, When many millions of men, without heat, without ill will, without personal feeling of any kind, demand of you a few shillings only, without the possibility, such is their constitution, of retracting or altering their present demand, and without the possibility, on your side, of appeal to any other millions, why expose yourself to this overwhelming brute force? You do not resist cold and hunger, the winds and the waves, thus obstinately; you quietly submit to a thousand similar necessities. You do not put your head into the fire. But just in proportion as I regard this as not wholly a brute force, but partly a human force, and consider that I have relations to those millions as to so many millions of men, and not of mere brute or inanimate things, I see that appeal is possible, first and instantaneously, from them to the Maker of them, and, secondly, from them to themselves. But if I put my head deliberately into the fire, there is no appeal to fire or to the Maker of fire, and I have only myself to blame. If I could convince myself that I have any right to be satisfied with men as they are, and to treat them accordingly, and not according, in some respects, to my requisitions and expectations of what they and I ought to be, then, like a good Mussulman[29] and fatalist, I should endeavor to be satisfied with things as they are, and say it is the will of God. And, above all, there is this difference between resisting this and a purely brute or natural force, that I can resist this with some effect; but I cannot expect, like Orpheus,[30] to change the nature of the rocks and trees and beasts.

I do not wish to quarrel with any man or nation. I do not wish to split hairs, to make fine distinctions, or set myself up as better than my neighbors. I seek rather, I may say, even an excuse for conforming the laws of the land. I am but too ready to conform to them. Indeed, I have reason to suspect myself on this head; and each year, as the tax-gatherer comes round, I find myself disposed to review the acts and positions of the general and State governments, and the spirit of the people, to discover a pretext for conformity.

> We must affect our country as our parents,
> And if at any time we alienate
> Our love or industry from doing it honor,
> We must respect effects and teach the soul

---

[29] Muslim.

[30] In Greek mythology, Orpheus charmed wild animals and the inhabitants of Hades as well as rocks and trees with his music.

5 Matter of conscience and religion,
And not desire of rule or benefit.[31]

I believe that the State will soon be able to take all my work of this sort out of my hands, and then I shall be no better a patriot than my fellow-countrymen. Seen from a lower point of view, the Constitution, with all its faults, is very good; the law and the courts are very respectable; even this State and this American government are, in many respects, very admirable, and rare things, to be thankful for, such as a great many have described them; but seen from a point of view a little higher, they are what I have described them; seen from a higher still, and the highest, who shall say what they are, or that they are worth looking at or thinking of at all?

However, the government does not concern me much, and I shall bestow the fewest possible thoughts on it. It is not many moments that I live under a government, even in this world. If a man is thought-free, fancy-free, imagination-free, that which *is not* never for a long time appearing *to be* to him, unwise rulers or reformers cannot fatally interrupt him.

I know that most men think differently from myself; but those whose lives are by profession devoted to the study of these or kindred subjects content me as little as any. Statesmen and legislators, standing so completely within the institution, never distinctly and nakedly behold it. They speak of moving society, but have no resting-place without it. They may be men of a certain experience and discrimination, and have no doubt invented ingenious and even useful systems, for which we sincerely thank them; but all their wit and usefulness lie within certain not very wide limits. They are wont to forget that the world is not governed by policy and expediency. Webster[32] never goes behind government, and so cannot speak with authority about it. His words are wisdom to those legislators who contemplate no essential reform in the existing government; but for thinkers, and those who legislate for all time, he never once glances at the subject. I know of those whose serene and wise speculations on this theme would soon reveal the limits of his mind's range and hospitality. Yet, compared with the cheap professions of most reformers, and the still cheaper wisdom and eloquence of politicians in general, his are almost the only sensible and valuable words, and we thank Heaven for him. Comparatively, he is always strong, original, and, above all, practical. Still, his quality is not wisdom, but prudence. The lawyer's truth is not Truth, but

[31] George Peele (1556–1596), *The Battle of Alcazar* (1594) 2.2. This quotation was added in the 1866 edition.
[32] Daniel Webster (1782–1852), U.S. senator from Massachusetts.

consistency or a consistent expediency. Truth is always in harmony with herself, and is not concerned chiefly to reveal the justice that may consist with wrong-doing. He well deserves to be called, as he has been called, the Defender of the Constitution. There are really no blows to be given by him but defensive ones. He is not a leader, but a follower. His leaders are the men of '87.[33] "I have never made an effort," he says, "and never propose to make an effort; I have never countenanced an effort, and never mean to countenance an effort, to disturb the arrangement as originally made, by which the various States came into the Union."[34] Still thinking of the sanction which the Constitution gives to slavery, he says, "Because it was a part of the original compact—let it stand."[35] Notwithstanding his special acuteness and ability, he is unable to take a fact out of its merely political relations, and behold it as it lies absolutely to be disposed of by the intellect—what, for instance, it behooves a man to do here in America today with regard to slavery—but ventures, or is driven, to make some such desperate answer as the following, while professing to speak absolutely, and as a private man—from which what new and similar code of social duties might be inferred? "The manner," says he, "in which the governments of those States where slavery exists are to regulate it is for their own consideration, under their responsibility to their constituents, to the general laws of propriety, humanity, and justice, and to God. Associations formed elsewhere, springing from a feeling of humanity, or any other cause, have nothing whatever to do with it. They have never received any encouragement from me, and they never will."[36]

They who know of no purer sources of truth, who have traced up its stream no higher, stand, and wisely stand, by the Bible and the Constitution, and drink at it there with reverence and humility; but they who behold where it comes trickling into this lake or that pool, gird up their loins once more, and continue their pilgrimage toward its fountainhead.

No man with a genius for legislation has appeared in America. They are rare in the history of the world. There are orators, politicians, and eloquent men, by the thousand; but the speaker has not yet opened his mouth

[33] Members of the Constitutional Convention of 1787.

[34] From Webster's Senate speech of December 22, 1845, on the admission of Texas.

[35] Scholars have not found a source for this Webster quotation. Some have speculated that Thoreau was quoting from memory or perhaps from a corrupted newspaper account.

[36] Thoreau's note here reads: "These extracts have been inserted since the lecture was read." The passage, slightly modified by Thoreau, is from Webster's speech of August 12, 1848, on the exclusion of slavery from the Territories.

to speak who is capable of settling the much-vexed questions of the day. We love eloquence for its own sake, and not for any truth which it may utter, or any heroism it may inspire. Our legislators have not yet learned the comparative value of free trade and of freedom, of union, and of rectitude, to a nation. They have no genius or talent for comparatively humble questions of taxation and finance, commerce and manufactures and agriculture. If we were left solely to the wordy wit of legislators in Congress for our guidance, uncorrected by the seasonable experience and the effectual complaints of the people, America would not long retain her rank among the nations. For eighteen hundred years, though perchance I have no right to say it, the New Testament has been written; yet where is the legislator who has wisdom and practical talent enough to avail himself of the light which it sheds on the science of legislation?

The authority of government, even such as I am willing to submit to—for I will cheerfully obey those who know and can do better than I, and in many things even those who neither know nor can do so well—is still an impure one: to be strictly just, it must have the sanction and consent of the governed. It can have no pure right over my person and property but what I concede to it. The progress from an absolute to a limited monarchy, from a limited monarchy to a democracy, is a progress toward a true respect for the individual. Even the Chinese philosopher[37] was wise enough to regard the individual as the basis of the empire. Is a democracy, such is we know it, the last improvement possible in government? Is it not possible to take a step further towards recognizing and organizing the rights of man? There will never be a really free and enlightened State until the State comes to recognize the individual as a higher and independent power, from which all its own power and authority are derived, and treats him accordingly. I please myself with imagining a State at least which can afford to be just to all men, and to treat the individual with respect as a neighbor; which even would not think it inconsistent with its own repose if a few were to live aloof from it, not meddling with it, nor embraced by it, who fulfilled all the duties of neighbors and fellow-men. A State which bore this kind of fruit, and suffered it to drop off as fast as it ripened, would prepare the way for a still more perfect and glorious State, which also I have imagined, but not yet anywhere seen.

---

[37] Confucius. The sentence "Even the Chinese philosopher . . ." was added in the 1866 edition.

PART TWO

Walden

WALDEN

by Henry David Thoreau

I do not propose to write an ode to dejection, but to brag as lustily as chanticleer in the morning, standing on his roost, if only to wake my neighbors up.

CHAPTER ONE
Economy

When I wrote the following pages, or rather the bulk of them, I lived alone, in the woods, a mile from any neighbor, in a house which I had built myself, on the shore of Walden Pond, in Concord, Massachusetts, and earned my living by the labor of my hands only. I lived there two years and two months. At present I am a sojourner in civilized life again.

I should not obtrude my affairs so much on the notice of my readers if very particular inquiries had not been made by my townsmen concerning my mode of life, which some would call impertinent, though they do not appear to me at all impertinent, but, considering the circumstances, very natural and pertinent. Some have asked what I got to eat; if I did not feel lonesome; if I was not afraid; and the like. Others have been curious to learn what portion of my income I devoted to charitable purposes; and some, who have large families, how many poor children I maintained. I will therefore ask those of my readers who feel no particular interest in me to pardon me if I undertake to answer some of these questions in this book. In most books, the *I*, or first person, is omitted; in this it will be retained; that, in respect to egotism, is the main difference. We commonly do not remember that it is, after all, always the first person that is speaking. I should not talk so much about myself if there were any body else whom I knew as well. Unfortunately, I am confined to this theme by the narrowness of my experience. Moreover, I, on my side, require of every writer, first or last, a simple and sincere account of his own life, and not merely what he has heard of other men's lives; some such account as he would send to his kindred from a distant land; for if he has lived sincerely, it must have been in a distant land to me. Perhaps these pages are more particularly addressed to poor students. As for the rest of my readers, they will accept such portions as apply to them. I trust that none will stretch the seams in putting on the coat, for it may do good service to him whom it fits.

I would fain say something, not so much concerning the Chinese and Sandwich Islanders[1] as you who read these pages, who are said to live in

---

[1] Hawaiian islanders.

New England; something about your condition, especially your outward condition or circumstances in this world, in this town, what it is, whether it is necessary that it be as bad as it is, whether it cannot be improved as well as not. I have travelled a good deal in Concord; and every where, in shops, and offices, and fields, the inhabitants have appeared to me to be doing penance in a thousand remarkable ways. What I have heard of Bramins sitting exposed to four fires and looking in the face of the sun; or hanging suspended, with their heads downward, over flames; or looking at the heavens over their shoulders "until it becomes impossible for them to resume their natural position, while from the twist of the neck nothing but liquids can pass into the stomach;" or dwelling, chained for life, at the foot of a tree; or measuring with their bodies, like caterpillars, the breadth of vast empires; or standing on one leg on the tops of pillars—even these forms of conscious penance are hardly more incredible and astonishing than the scenes which I daily witness. The twelve labors of Hercules[2] were trifling in comparison with those which my neighbors have undertaken; for they were only twelve, and had an end; but I could never see that these men slew or captured any monster or finished any labor. They have no friend Iolas to burn with a hot iron the root of the hydra's head, but as soon as one head is crushed, two spring up.

I see young men, my townsmen, whose misfortune it is to have inherited farms, houses, barns, cattle, and farming tools; for these are more easily acquired than got rid of. Better if they had been born in the open pasture and suckled by a wolf,[3] that they might have seen with clearer eyes what field they were called to labor in. Who made them serfs of the soil? Why should they eat their sixty acres, when man is condemned to eat only his peck of dirt? Why should they begin digging their graves as soon as they are born? They have got to live a man's life, pushing all these things before them, and get on as well as they can. How many a poor immortal soul have I met well nigh crushed and smothered under its load, creeping down the road of life, pushing before it a barn seventy-five feet by forty, its Augean stables never cleansed,[4] and one hundred acres of land, tillage,

---

[2] In Greek mythology, Hercules (Greek Herakles) was the son of Zeus and Alkmene. His "labors" were twelve overwhelmingly difficult tasks, including slaying Hydra, a multi-headed creature who grew two new heads wherever one was cut off. Iolaus, Hercules' nephew, served him as companion and charioteer. He helped defeat Hydra by searing the stumps when Hercules cut off a head, so new ones would not grow in their place.

[3] Romulus and Remus, the founders of the Roman Republic, were supposed to have been suckled by a she-wolf.

[4] One of Hercules' labors was cleaning in one day the stables of Augeias, which had accumulated years of filth left by thousands of cattle.

mowing, pasture, and wood-lot! The portionless, who struggle with no such unnecessary inherited encumbrances, find it labor enough to subdue and cultivate a few cubic feet of flesh.

But men labor under a mistake. The better part of the man is soon ploughed into the soil for compost. By a seeming fate, commonly called necessity, they are employed, as it says in an old book, laying up treasures which moth and rust will corrupt and thieves break through and steal.[5] It is a fool's life, as they will find when they get to the end of it, if not before. It is said that Deucalion and Pyrrha created men by throwing stones over their heads behind them—

> Inde genus durum sumus, experiensque laborum,
> Et documenta damus quâ simus origine nati.

Or, as Raleigh rhymes it in his sonorous way[6]—

> "From thence our kind hard-hearted is, enduring pain and care,
> Approving that our bodies of a stony nature are."

So much for a blind obedience to a blundering oracle, throwing the stones over their heads behind them, and not seeing where they fell.

Most men, even in this comparatively free country, through mere ignorance and mistake, are so occupied with the factitious cares and superfluously coarse labors of life that its finer fruits cannot be plucked by them. Their fingers, from excessive toil, are too clumsy and tremble too much for that. Actually, the laboring man has not leisure for a true integrity day by day; he cannot afford to sustain the manliest relations to men; his labor would be depreciated in the market. He has no time to be any thing but a machine. How can he remember well his ignorance—which his growth requires—who has so often to use his knowledge? We should feed and clothe him gratuitously sometimes, and recruit him with our cordials, before we judge of him. The finest qualities of our nature, like the bloom on fruits, can be preserved only by the most delicate handling. Yet we do not treat ourselves nor one another thus tenderly.

Some of you, we all know, are poor, find it hard to live, are sometimes, as it were, gasping for breath. I have no doubt that some of you who read

---

[5] See Matt. 6.19: "Do not lay up for yourselves treasures upon earth, where moth and rust doth corrupt and where thieves break through and steal."

[6] Thoreau wrote a short essay on Sir Walter Raleigh, whose style he admired. It was incorporated into the "Sunday" section of *A Week on the Concord and Merrimack Rivers* (1849).

this book are unable to pay for all the dinners which you have actually eaten, or for the coats and shoes which are fast wearing or are already worn out, and have come to this page to spend borrowed or stolen time, robbing your creditors of an hour. It is very evident what mean and sneaking lives many of you live, for my sight has been whetted by experience; always on the limits,[7] trying to get into business and trying to get out of debt, a very ancient slough, called by the Latins *aes alienum,* another's brass, for some of their coins were made of brass; still living, and dying, and buried by this other's brass; always promising to pay, promising to pay, tomorrow, and dying today, insolvent; seeking to curry favor, to get custom, by how many modes, only not state-prison offences; lying, flattering, voting, contracting yourselves into a nutshell of civility, or dilating into an atmosphere of thin and vaporous generosity, that you may persuade your neighbor to let you make his shoes, or his hat, or his coat, or his carriage, or import his groceries for him; making yourselves sick, that you may lay up something against a sick day, something to be tucked away in an old chest, or in a stocking behind the plastering, or, more safely, in the brick bank; no matter where, no matter how much or how little.

I sometimes wonder that we can be so frivolous, I may almost say, as to attend to the gross but somewhat foreign form of servitude called Negro Slavery, there are so many keen and subtle masters that enslave both north and south. It is hard to have a southern overseer; it is worse to have northern one; but worst of all when you are the slave-driver of yourself. Talk of a divinity in man! Look at the teamster on the highway, wending to market by day or night; does any divinity stir within him? His highest duty to fodder and water his horses! What is his destiny to him compared with the shipping interests? Does not he drive for Squire Make-a-stir? How godlike, how immortal, is he? See how he cowers and sneaks, how vaguely all the day he fears, not being immortal nor divine, but the slave and prisoner of his own opinion of himself, a fame won by his own deeds. Public opinion is a weak tyrant compared with our own private opinion. What a man thinks of himself, that it is which determines, or rather indicates, his fate. Self-emancipation even in the West Indian provinces of the fancy and imagination—what Wilberforce[8] is there to bring that about? Think, also, of the ladies of the land weaving toilet cushions against the last day, not to betray too green an interest in their fates! As if you could kill time without injuring eternity.

[7] That is, at the limits of one's credit.

[8] William Wilberforce (1759–1833), a leader of the political movement in England to abolish slavery in Britain's West Indian colonies.

The mass of men lead lives of quiet desperation. What is called resignation is confirmed desperation. From the desperate city you go into the desperate country, and have to console yourself with the bravery of minks and muskrats. A stereotyped but unconscious despair is concealed even under what are called the games and amusements of mankind. There is no play in them, for this comes after work. But it is a characteristic of wisdom not to do desperate things.

When we consider what, to use the catechism, is the chief end of man,[9] and what are the true necessaries and means of life, it appears as if men had deliberately chosen the common mode of living because they preferred it to any other. Yet they honestly think there is no choice left. But alert and healthy natures remember that the sun rose clear. It is never too late to give up our prejudices. No way of thinking or doing, however ancient, can be trusted without proof. What every body echoes or in silence passes by as true today may turn out to be falsehood tomorrow, mere smoke of opinion, which some had trusted for a cloud that would sprinkle fertilizing rain on their fields. What old people say you cannot do you try and find that you can. Old deeds for old people, and new deeds for new. Old people did not know enough once, perchance, to fetch fresh fuel to keep the fire a-going; new people put a little dry wood under a pot, and are whirled round the globe with the speed of birds, in a way to kill old people, as the phrase is. Age is no better, hardly so well, qualified for an instructor as youth, for it has not profited so much as it has lost. One may almost doubt if the wisest man has learned any thing of absolute value by living. Practically, the old have no very important advice to give the young, their own experience has been so partial, and their lives have been such miserable failures, for private reasons, as they must believe; and it may be that they have some faith left which belies that experience, and they are only less young than they were. I have lived some thirty years on this planet, and I have yet to hear the first syllable of valuable or even earnest advice from my seniors. They have told me nothing, and probably cannot tell me any thing, to the purpose. Here is life, an experiment to a great extent untried by me; but it does not avail me that they have tried it. If I have any experience which I think valuable, I am sure to reflect that this my Mentors[10] said nothing about.

One farmer says to me, "You cannot live on vegetable food solely, for it furnishes nothing to make bones with"; and so he religiously devotes a

---

[9]The Shorter Catechism of the *New England Primer* says that "the chief end of man" is "to glorify God and to enjoy him forever."

[10]In the *Odyssey*, Mentor was the wise counselor of Telemachus, the son of Odysseus.

part of his day to supplying his system with the raw material of bones; walking all the while he talks behind his oxen, which, with vegetable-made bones, jerk him and his lumbering plough along in spite of every obstacle. Some things are really necessaries of life in some circles, the most helpless and diseased, which in others are luxuries merely, and in others still are entirely unknown.

The whole ground of human life seems to some to have been gone over by their predecessors, both the heights and the valleys, and all things to have been cared for. According to Evelyn,[11] "the wise Solomon prescribed ordinances for the very distances of trees; and the Roman praetors have decided how often you may go into your neighbor's land to gather the acorns which fall on it without trespass, and what share belongs to that neighbor. Hippocrates[12] has even left directions how we should cut our nails; that is, even with the ends of the fingers, neither shorter nor longer. Undoubtedly the very tedium and ennui which presume to have exhausted the variety and the joys of life are as old as Adam. But man's capacities have never been measured; nor are we to judge of what he can do by any precedents, so little has been tried. Whatever have been thy failures hitherto, "be not afflicted, my child, for who shall assign to thee what thou hast left undone?"[13]

We might try our lives by a thousand simple tests; as, for instance, that the same sun which ripens my beans illumines at once a system of earths like ours. If I had remembered this it would have prevented some mistakes. This was not the light in which I hoed them. The stars are the apexes of what wonderful triangles! What distant and different beings in the various mansions of the universe are contemplating the same one at the same moment! Nature and human life are as various as our several constitutions. Who shall say what prospect life offers to another? Could a greater miracle take place than for us to look through each other's eyes for an instant? We should live in all the ages of the world in an hour; ay, in all the worlds of the ages. History, Poetry, Mythology! I know of no reading of another's experience so startling and informing as this would be.

The greater part of what my neighbors call good I believe in my soul to be bad, and if I repent of any thing, it is very likely to be my good be-

[11]John Evelyn (1620–1706), English author and horticulturalist. From his *Sylva; Or, a Discourse of Forest-Trees, and the Propagation of Timber in His Majesties Dominions* (1664).

[12]An ancient Greek physician (c. 300 B.C.E.) whose oath constitutes a common code of medical practice to this day.

[13]From the Hindu Vishnu Purana, poetry addressed to the god Vishnu (the Destroyer) embodying later Hindu religious thought.

havior. What demon possessed me that I behaved so well? You may say the wisest thing you can old man—you who have lived seventy years, not without honor of a kind—I hear an irresistible voice which invites me away from all that. One generation abandons the enterprises of another like stranded vessels.

I think that we may safely trust a good deal more than we do. We may waive just so much care of ourselves as we honestly bestow elsewhere. Nature is as well adapted to our weakness as to our strength. The incessant anxiety and strain of some is a well nigh incurable form of disease. We are made to exaggerate the importance of what work we do; and yet how much is not done by us! or, what if we had been taken sick? How vigilant we are! determined not to live by faith if we can avoid it; all the day long on the alert, at night we unwillingly say our prayers and commit ourselves to uncertainties. So thoroughly and sincerely are we compelled to live, reverencing our life, and denying the possibility of change. This is the only way, we say; but there are as many ways as there can be drawn radii from one centre. All change is a miracle to contemplate; but it is a miracle which is taking place every instant. Confucius said, "To know that we know what we know, and that we do not know what we do not know, that is true knowledge." [14] When one man has reduced a fact of the imagination to be a fact to his understanding, I foresee that all men will at length establish their lives on that basis.

Let us consider for a moment what most of the trouble and anxiety which I have referred to is about, and how much it is necessary that we be troubled, or, at least, careful. It would be some advantage to live a primitive and frontier life, though in the midst of an outward civilization, if only to learn what are the gross necessaries of life and what methods have been taken to obtain them; or even to look over the old day-books of the merchants, to see what it was that men most commonly bought at the stores, what they stored, that is, what are the grossest groceries. For the improvements of ages have had but little influence on the essential laws of man's existence; as our skeletons, probably, are not to be distinguished from those of our ancestors.

By the words, *necessary of life,* I mean whatever, of all that man obtains by his own exertions, has been from the first, or from long use has become, so important to human life that few, if any, whether from savageness, or poverty, or philosophy, ever attempt to do without it. To many creatures there is in this sense but one necessary of life, Food. To the bison

[14] Chinese philosopher (c. 551–478 B.C.E.). From his *Analects* 2.17.

of the prairie it is a few inches of palatable grass, with water to drink; unless he seeks the Shelter of the forest or the mountain's shadow. None of the brute creation requires more than Food and Shelter. The necessaries of life for man in this climate may, accurately enough, be distributed under the several heads of Food, Shelter, Clothing, and Fuel; for not till we have secured these are we prepared to entertain the true problems of life with freedom and a prospect of success. Man has invented, not only houses, but clothes and cooked food; and possibly from the accidental discovery of the warmth of fire, and the consequent use of it, at first a luxury, arose the present necessity to sit by it. We observe cats and dogs acquiring the same second nature. By proper Shelter and Clothing we legitimately retain our own internal heat; but with an excess of these, or of Fuel, that is, with an external heat greater than our own internal, may not cookery properly be said to begin? Darwin, the naturalist, says of the inhabitants of Tierra del Fuego, that while his own party, who were well clothed and sitting close to a fire, were far from too warm, these naked savages, who were farther off, were observed, to his great surprise, "to be streaming with perspiration at undergoing such a roasting."[15] So, we are told, the New Hollander[16] goes naked with impunity, while the European shivers in his clothes. Is it impossible to combine the hardiness of these savages with the intellectualness of the civilized man? According to Liebig, man's body is a stove, and food the fuel which keeps up the internal combustion in the lungs.[17] In cold weather we eat more, in warm less. The animal heat is the result of a slow combustion, and disease and death take place when this is too rapid; or for want of fuel, or from some defect in the draught, the fire goes out. Of course the vital heat is not to be confounded with fire; but so much for analogy. It appears, therefore, from the above list, that the expression, *animal life,* is nearly synonymous with the expression, *animal heat;* for while Food may be regarded as the Fuel which keeps up the fire within us—and Fuel serves only to prepare that Food or to increase the warmth of our bodies by addition from without—Shelter and Clothing also serve only to retain the *heat* thus generated and absorbed.

---

[15] Charles Darwin (1809–1882), English naturalist and developer of the theory of evolution. From his *Journal of Researches into the Geology and Natural History of the Various Countries Visited by H.M.S.* Beagle (1839). Tierra del Fuego, an island, constitutes the southernmost tip of South America.

[16] The aboriginal people of Australia.

[17] Justus Freiherr von Liebig (1803–1873), German chemist. From *Animal Chemistry: Or, Chemistry in Its Applications to Physiology and Pathology by Baron Liebig; Edited from the Author's Manuscript by William Gregory* (1842).

The grand necessity, then, for our bodies, is to keep warm, to keep the vital heat in us. What pains we accordingly take, not only with our Food, and Clothing, and Shelter, but with our beds, which are our night-clothes, robbing the nests and breasts of birds to prepare this shelter within a shelter, as the mole has its bed of grass and leaves at the end of its burrow! The poor man is wont to complain that this is a cold world; and to cold, no less physical than social, we refer directly a great part of our ails. The summer, in some climates, makes possible to man a sort of Elysian life.[18] Fuel, except to cook his Food, is then unnecessary; the sun is his fire, and many of the fruits are sufficiently cooked by its rays; while Food generally is more various, and more easily obtained, and Clothing and Shelter are wholly or half unnecessary. At the present day, and in this country, as I find by my own experience, a few implements, a knife, an axe, a spade, a wheelbarrow, etc., and for the studious, lamplight, stationery, and access to a few books, rank next to necessaries, and can all be obtained at a trifling cost. Yet some, not wise, go to the other side of the globe, to barbarous and unhealthy regions, and devote themselves to trade for ten or twenty years, in order that they may live—that is, keep comfortably warm—and die in New England at last. The luxuriously rich are not simply kept comfortably warm, but unnaturally hot; as I implied before, they are cooked, of course *à la mode*.

Most of the luxuries, and many of the so called comforts of life, are not only not indispensable, but positive hinderances to the elevation of mankind. With respect to luxuries and comforts, the wisest have ever lived a more simple and meagre life than the poor. The ancient philosophers, Chinese, Hindoo, Persian, and Greek, were a class than which none has been poorer in outward riches, none so rich in inward. We know not much about them. It is remarkable that *we* know so much of them as we do. The same is true of the more modern reformers and benefactors of their race. None can be an impartial or wise observer of human life but from the vantage ground of what *we* should call voluntary poverty. Of a life of luxury the fruit is luxury, whether in agriculture, or commerce, or literature, or art. There are nowadays professors of philosophy, but not philosophers. Yet it is admirable to profess because it was once admirable to live. To be a philosopher is not merely to have subtle thoughts, nor even to found a school, but so to love wisdom as to live according to its dictates, a life of simplicity, independence, magnanimity, and trust. It is to solve some of the problems of life, not only theoretically, but practically. The success of great scholars and thinkers is commonly a courtier-like success, not kingly, not

[18]The Elysian fields were, in Greek myth, the home of the blessed dead.

manly. They make shift to live merely by conformity, practically as their fathers did, and are in no sense the progenitors of a nobler race of men. But why do men degenerate ever? What makes families run out? What is the nature of the luxury which enervates and destroys nations? Are we sure that there is none of it in our own lives? The philosopher is in advance of his age even in the outward form of his life. He is not fed, sheltered, clothed, warmed, like his contemporaries. How can a man be a philosopher and not maintain his vital heat by better methods than other men?

When a man is warmed by the several modes which I have described, what does he want next? Surely not more warmth of the same kind, as more and richer food, larger and more splendid houses, finer and more abundant clothing, more numerous incessant and hotter fires, and the like. When he has obtained those things which are necessary to life, there is another alternative than to obtain the superfluities; and that is, to adventure on life now, his vacation from humbler toil having commenced. The soil, it appears, is suited to the seed, for it has sent its radicle downward, and it may now send its shoot upward also with confidence. Why has man rooted himself thus firmly in the earth, but that he may rise in the same proportion into the heavens above? for the nobler plants are valued for the fruit they bear at last in the air and light, far from the ground, and are not treated like the humbler esculents, which, though they may be biennials, are cultivated only till they have perfected their root, and often cut down at top for this purpose, so that most would not know them in their flowering season.

I do not mean to prescribe rules to strong and valiant natures, who will mind their own affairs whether in heaven or hell, and perchance build more magnificently and spend more lavishly than the richest, without ever impoverishing themselves, not knowing how they live—if, indeed, there are any such, as has been dreamed; nor to those who find their encouragement and inspiration in precisely the present condition of things, and cherish it with the fondness and enthusiasm of lovers—and, to some extent, I reckon myself in this number; I do not speak to those who are well employed, in whatever circumstances, and they know whether they are well employed or not—but mainly to the mass of men who are discontented, and idly complaining of the hardness of their lot or of the times, when they might improve them. There are some who complain most energetically and inconsolably of any, because they are, as they say, doing their duty. I also have in my mind that seemingly wealthy, but most terribly impoverished class of all, who have accumulated dross, but know not how to use it, or get rid of it, and thus have forged their own golden or silver fetters.

If I should attempt to tell how I have desired to spend my life in years past, it would probably surprise those of my readers who are somewhat acquainted with its actual history; it would certainly astonish those who know nothing about it. I will only hint at some of the enterprises which I have cherished.

In any weather, at any hour of the day or night, I have been anxious to improve the nick of time, and notch it on my stick too; to stand on the meeting of two eternities, the past and future, which is precisely the present moment; to toe that line. You will pardon some obscurities, for there are more secrets in my trade than in most men's, and yet not voluntarily kept, but inseparable from its very nature. I would gladly tell all that I know about it, and never paint "No Admittance" on my gate.

I long ago lost a hound, a bay horse, and a turtle-dove, and am still on their trail. Many are the travellers I have spoken concerning them, describing their tracks and what calls they answered to. I have met one or two who had heard the hound, and the tramp of the horse, and even seen the dove disappear behind a cloud, and they seemed as anxious to recover them as if they had lost them themselves.[19]

To anticipate, not the sunrise and the dawn merely, but, if possible, Nature herself! How many mornings, summer and winter, before yet any neighbor was stirring about his business, have I been about mine! No doubt, many of my townsmen have met me returning from this enterprise, farmers starting for Boston in the twilight, or woodchoppers going to their work. It is true, I never assisted the sun materially in his rising, but, doubt not, it was of the last importance only to be present at it.

So many autumn, ay, and winter days, spent outside the town, trying to hear what was in the wind, to hear and carry it express! I well-nigh sunk all my capital in it, and lost my own breath into the bargain, running in the face of it. If it had concerned either of the political parties, depend upon it, it would have appeared in the Gazette with the earliest intelligence. At other times watching from the observatory of some cliff or tree, to telegraph any new arrival; or waiting at evening on the hill-tops for the sky to fall, that I might catch something, though I never caught much, and that, manna-wise, would dissolve again in the sun.

[19]Sherman Paul writes about this passage, which has been much discussed by critics, "To one inquisitive correspondent . . . Thoreau explained that these animals *might* represent his 'losses,' but that he had lost 'a far finer and more ethereal treasure, which commonly no loss of . . . will symbolize.'" Paul traces the source to a passage from the Chinese Confucian philosopher Mencius (or Meng-tzu) that Thoreau had selected for the *Dial,* the Transcendentalist magazine for which he had written: "If a man lose his fowls or his dogs, he knows how to seek them. There are those who lose their hearts and know not how to seek them. The duty of the student is no other than to seek his lost heart."

For a long time I was reporter to a journal, of no very wide circulation,[20] whose editor has never yet seen fit to print the bulk of my contributions, and, as is too common with writers, I got only my labor for my pains. However, in this case my pains were their own reward.

For many years I was self-appointed inspector of snow storms and rain storms, and did my duty faithfully; surveyor, if not of highways, then of forest paths and all across-lot routes, keeping them open, and ravines bridged and passable at all seasons, where the public heel had testified to their utility.

I have looked after the wild stock of the town, which give a faithful herdsman a good deal of trouble by leaping fences; and I have had an eye to the unfrequented nooks and corners of the farm; though I did not always know whether Jonas or Solomon worked in a particular field today; that was none of my business. I have watered the red huckleberry, the sand cherry and the nettle tree, the red pine and the black ash, the white grape and the yellow violet, which might have withered else in dry seasons.

In short, I went on thus for a long time, I may say it without boasting, faithfully minding my business, till it became more and more evident that my townsmen would not after all admit me into the list of town officers, nor make my place a sinecure with a moderate allowance. My accounts, which I can swear to have kept faithfully, I have, indeed, never got audited, still less accepted, still less paid and settled. However, I have not set my heart on that.

Not long since, a strolling Indian went to sell baskets at the house of a well-known lawyer in my neighborhood. "Do you wish to buy any baskets?" he asked. "No, we do not want any," was the reply. "What!" exclaimed the Indian as he went out the gate, "do you mean to starve us?" Having seen his industrious white neighbors so well off—that the lawyer had only to weave arguments, and by some magic wealth and standing followed, he had said to himself; I will go into business; I will weave baskets; it is a thing which I can do. Thinking that when he had made the baskets he would have done his part, and then it would be the white man's to buy them. He had not discovered that it was necessary for him to make it worth the other's while to buy them, or at least make him think that it was so, or to make something else which it would be worth his while to buy. I too had woven a kind of basket of a delicate texture, but I had not made

[20] Probably the *Dial,* which flourished from 1840 to 1844. Thoreau also wrote for the *Democratic Review* and other magazines. It is likely that he is also referring to his own journal, which he mined as a source for his books. Thoreau's journal was first published in 1906 in fourteen volumes.

it worth any one's while to buy them.[21] Yet not the less, in my case, did I think it worth my while to weave them, and instead of studying how to make it worth men's while to buy my baskets, I studied rather how to avoid the necessity of selling them. The life which men praise and regard as successful is but one kind. Why should we exaggerate any one kind at the expense of the others?

Finding that my fellow-citizens were not likely to offer me any room in the court house, or any curacy or living any where else, but I must shift for myself, I turned my face more exclusively than ever to the woods, where I was better known. I determined to go into business at once, and not wait to acquire the usual capital, using such slender means as I had already got. My purpose in going to Walden Pond was not to live cheaply nor to live dearly there, but to transact some private business with the fewest obstacles; to be hindered from accomplishing which for want of a little common sense, a little enterprise and business talent, appeared not so sad as foolish.

I have always endeavored to acquire strict business habits; they are indispensable to every man. If your trade is with the Celestial Empire,[22] then some small counting house on the coast, in some Salem harbor, will be fixture enough. You will export such articles as the country affords, purely native products, much ice and pine timber and a little granite, always in native bottoms. These will be good ventures. To oversee all the details yourself in person; to be at once pilot and captain, and owner and underwriter; to buy and sell and keep the accounts; to read every letter received, and write or read every letter sent; to superintend the discharge of imports night and day; to be upon many parts of the coast almost at the same time—often the richest freight will be discharged upon a Jersey shore—to be your own telegraph, unweariedly sweeping the horizon, speaking all passing vessels bound coastwise; to keep up a steady despatch of commodities, for the supply of such a distant and exorbitant market; to keep yourself informed of the state of the markets, prospects of war and peace every where, and anticipate the tendencies of trade and civilization—taking advantage of the results of all exploring expeditions, using new passages and all improvements in navigation—charts to be studied, the position of reefs and new lights and buoys to be ascertained, and ever, and ever, the logarithmic tables to be corrected, for by the error of some

---

[21] Thoreau may be referring to his first book, *A Week on the Concord and Merrimack Rivers* (1849), only a few copies of which had sold.
[22] China.

calculator the vessel often splits upon a rock that should have reached a friendly pier—there is the untold fate of La Perouse[23]—universal science to be kept pace with, studying the lives of all great discoverers and navigators, great adventurers and merchants, from Hanno[24] and the Phoenicians down to our day; in fine, account of stock to be taken from time to time, to know how you stand. It is a labor to task the faculties of a man—such problems of profit and loss, of interest, of tare and tret,[25] and gauging of all kinds in it, as demand a universal knowledge.

I have thought that Walden Pond would be a good place for business, not solely on account of the railroad and the ice trade; it offers advantages which it may not be good policy to divulge; it is a good post and a good foundation. No Neva marshes to be filled; though you must every where build on piles of your own driving. It is said that a flood-tide, with a westerly wind, and ice in the Neva, would sweep St. Petersburg from the face of the earth.[26]

As this business was to be entered into without the usual capital, it may not be easy to conjecture where those means, that will still be indispensable to every such undertaking, were to be obtained. As for Clothing, to come at once to the practical part of the question, perhaps we are led oftener by the love of novelty, and a regard for the opinions of men, in procuring it, than by a true utility. Let him who has work to do recollect that the object of clothing is, first, to retain the vital heat, and secondly, in this state of society to cover nakedness, and he may judge how much of any necessary or important work may be accomplished without adding to his wardrobe. Kings and queens who wear a suit but once, though made by some tailor or dressmaker to their majesties, cannot know the comfort of wearing a suit that fits. They are no better than wooden horses to hang the clean clothes on. Every day our garments become more assimilated to ourselves, receiving the impress of the wearer's character, until we hesitate to lay them aside, without such delay and medical appliances and some

---

[23] Jean-François de Galaup, comte de La Pérouse (1741–1788?), last heard of from Australia in February 1788. His ship subsequently disappeared somewhere in the South Pacific.

[24] Carthaginian navigator (c. 500 B.C.E.). The Greek account attributed to him is known as *Periplus or, Circumnavigation of Africa.*

[25] In the shipping business, *tare* refers to the deduction for the weight of a container and *tret* is an adjustment for damage or waste.

[26] The Russian city of St. Petersburg was built in the delta of the Neva River, much of which was drained for construction.

such solemnity even as our bodies. No man ever stood the lower in my estimation for having a patch in his clothes; yet I am sure that there is greater anxiety, commonly, to have fashionable, or at least clean and unpatched clothes, than to have a sound conscience. But even if the rent is not mended, perhaps the worst vice betrayed is improvidence. I sometimes try my acquaintances by such tests as this—who could wear a patch, or two extra seams only, over the knee? Most behave as if they believed that their prospects for life would be ruined if they should do it. It would be easier for them to hobble to town with a broken leg than with a broken pantaloon. Often if an accident happens to a gentleman's legs, they can be mended; but if a similar accident happens to the legs of his pantaloons, there is no help for it; for he considers, not what is truly respectable, but what is respected. We know but few men, a great many coats and breeches. Dress a scarecrow in your last shift, you standing shiftless by, who would not soonest salute the scarecrow? Passing a cornfield the other day, close by a hat and coat on a stake, I recognized the owner of the farm. He was only a little more weather-beaten than when I saw him last. I have heard of a dog that barked at every stranger who approached his master's premises with clothes on, but was easily quieted by a naked thief. It is an interesting question how far men would retain their relative rank if they were divested of their clothes. Could you, in such a case, tell surely of any company of civilized men, which belonged to the most respected class? When Madam Pfeiffer, in her adventurous travels round the world, from east to west, had got so near home as Asiatic Russia, she says that she felt the necessity of wearing other than a travelling dress, when she went to meet the authorities, for she "was now in a civilized country, where—people are judged of by their clothes."[27] Even in our democratic New England towns the accidental possession of wealth, and its manifestation in dress and equipage alone, obtain for the possessor almost universal respect. But they who yield such respect, numerous as they are, are so far heathen, and need to have a missionary sent to them. Beside, clothes introduced sewing, a kind of work which you may call endless; a woman's dress, at least, is never done.

A man who has at length found something to do will not need to get a new suit to do it in; for him the old will do, that has lain dusty in the garret for an indeterminate period. Old shoes will serve a hero longer than

[27]Ida Pfeiffer (1797–1858), Austrian traveler, from one of her two accounts of round-the-world travel, *A Lady's Voyage Round the World: A Selected Translation from the German of Ida Pfeiffer. By Mrs. Percy Sinnett* (1852).

they have served his valet—if a hero ever has a valet—bare feet are older than shoes, and he can make them do. Only they who go to soirées and legislative halls must have new coats, coats to change as often as the man changes in them. But if my jacket and trousers, my hat and shoes, are fit to worship God in, they will do; will they not? Who ever saw his old clothes—his old coat, actually worn out, resolved into its primitive elements, so that it was not a deed of charity to bestow it on some poor boy, by him perchance to be bestowed on some poorer still, or shall we say richer, who could do with less? I say, beware of all enterprises that require new clothes, and not rather a new wearer of clothes. If there is not a new man, how can the new clothes be made to fit? If you have any enterprise before you, try it in your old clothes. All men want, not something to *do with*, but something to *do*, or rather something to *be*. Perhaps we should never procure a new suit, however ragged or dirty the old, until we have so conducted, so enterprised or sailed in some way, that we feel like new men in the old, and that to retain it would be like keeping new wine in old bottles.[28] Our moulting season, like that of the fowls, must be a crisis in our lives. The loon retires to solitary ponds to spend it. Thus also the snake casts its slough, and the caterpillar its wormy coat, by an internal industry and expansion; for clothes are but outmost cuticle and mortal coil. Otherwise we shall be found sailing under false colors, and be inevitably cashiered at last by our own opinion, as well as that of mankind.

We don garment after garment, as if we grew like exogenous plants by addition without. Our outside and often thin and fanciful clothes are our epidermis or false skin, which partakes not of our life, and may be stripped off here and there without fatal injury; our thicker garments, constantly worn, are our cellular integument, or cortex; but our shirts are our liber or true bark, which cannot be removed without girdling and so destroying the man. I believe that all races at some seasons wear something equivalent to the shirt. It is desirable that a man be clad so simply that he can lay his hands on himself in the dark, and that he live in all respects so compactly and preparedly, that, if an enemy take the town, he can, like the old philosopher, walk out the gate empty-handed without anxiety.[29] While one thick garment is, for most purposes, as good as three thin ones, and cheap clothing can be obtained at prices really to suit customers; while a

---

[28] An echo of Matt. 9.17: "Neither do men put new wine into old bottles: else the bottles break, and the wine runneth out and the bottles perish; but they put new wine into new bottles, and both are preserved."

[29] Bias (c. 570 B.C.E.) was supposed to have fled the sack of his home city, Priene, with only the clothing he wore.

thick coat can be bought for five dollars, which will last as many years, thick pantaloons for two dollars, cowhide boots for a dollar and a half a pair, a summer hat for a quarter of a dollar, and a winter cap for sixty-two and a half cents, or a better be made at home at a nominal cost, where is he so poor that, clad in such a suit, *of his own earning,* there will not be found wise men to do him reverence?

When I ask for a garment of a particular form, my tailoress tells me gravely, "They do not make them so now," not emphasizing the "They" at all, as if she quoted an authority as impersonal as the Fates,[30] and I find it difficult to get made what I want, simply because she cannot believe that I mean what I say, that I am so rash. When I hear this sentence, I am for a moment absorbed in thought, emphasizing to myself each word separately that I may come at the meaning of it, that I may find out by what degree of consanguinity *They* are related to *me,* and what authority they may have in an affair which affects me so nearly; and, finally, I am inclined to answer her with equal mystery, and without any more emphasis of the "they"—"It is true, they did not make them so recently, but they do now." Of what use this measuring of me if she does not measure my character, but only the breadth of my shoulders, as it were a peg to hang the coat on? We worship not the Graces, nor the Parcae,[31] but Fashion. She spins and weaves and cuts with full authority. The head monkey at Paris puts on a traveller's cap, and all the monkeys in America do the same. I sometimes despair of getting any thing quite simple and honest done in this world by the help of men. They would have to be passed through a powerful press first, to squeeze their old notions out of them, so that they would not soon get upon their legs again, and then there would be some one in the company with a maggot in his head, hatched from an egg deposited there nobody knows when, for not even fire kills these things, and you would have lost your labor. Nevertheless, we will not forget that some Egyptian wheat was handed down to us by a mummy.[32]

On the whole, I think that it cannot be maintained that dressing has in this or any country risen to the dignity of an art. At present men make shift to wear what they can get. Like shipwrecked sailors, they put on what they can find on the beach, and at a little distance, whether of space or

---

[30] In Greek mythology, the three goddesses who controlled human fate by spinning, drawing out, and cutting the threads of life.

[31] The Graces, minor Greek and Roman goddesses, personified beauty and symmetry of form; the Parcae were the Roman equivalent of the Fates.

[32] Wheat, among other items of food, household goods, trade, and warfare, was generally buried with mummies.

time, laugh at each other's masquerade. Every generation laughs at the old fashions, but follows religiously the new. We are amused at beholding the costume of Henry VIII, or Queen Elizabeth, as much as if it was that of the King and Queen of the Cannibal Islands. All costume off a man is pitiful or grotesque. It is only the serious eye peering from and the sincere life passed within it, which restrain laughter and consecrate the costume of any people. Let Harlequin[33] be taken with a fit of the colic and his trappings will have to serve that mood too. When the soldier is hit by a cannon ball rags are as becoming as purple.

The childish and savage taste of men and women for new patterns keeps how many shaking and squinting through kaleidoscopes that they may discover the particular figure which this generation requires today. The manufacturers have learned that this taste is merely whimsical. Of two patterns which differ only by a few threads more or less of a particular color, the one will be sold readily, the other lie on the shelf, though it frequently happens that after the lapse of a season the later becomes the most fashionable. Comparatively, tattooing is not the hideous custom which it is called. It is not barbarous merely because the printing is skin-deep and unalterable.

I cannot believe that our factory system is the best mode by which men may get clothing. The condition of the operatives is becoming every day more like that of the English; and it cannot be wondered at, since, as far as I have heard or observed, the principal object is, not that mankind may be well and honestly clad, but, unquestionably, that the corporations may be enriched.[34] In the long run men hit only what they aim at. Therefore, though they should fail immediately, they had better aim at something high.

As for a Shelter, I will not deny that this is now a necessary of life, though there are instances of men having done without it for long periods in colder countries than this. Samuel Laing says that "The Laplander in his skin dress, and in a skin bag which he puts over his head and shoulders, will sleep night after night on the snow—in a degree of cold which would extinguish the life of one exposed to it in any woollen clothing." He had

[33] A comic character from the Italian *commedia dell' arte,* a form of popular improvised comedy that flourished in sixteenth-century Italy, whose costume included multicolored tights.

[34] The factory system was still relatively new in Thoreau's time, and there were those who continued to doubt its economic and moral viability as compared with earlier means for producing commodities like clothing.

seen them asleep thus. Yet he adds, "They are not hardier than other people."[35] But, probably, man did not live long on the earth without discovering the convenience which there is in a house, the domestic comforts, which phrase may have originally signified the satisfactions of the house more than of the family; though these must be extremely partial and occasional in those climates where the house is associated in our thoughts with winter or the rainy season chiefly, and two thirds of the year, except for a parasol, is unnecessary. In our climate, in the summer, it was formerly almost solely a covering at night. In the Indian gazettes a wigwam was the symbol of a day's march, and a row of them cut or painted on the bark of a tree signified that so many times they had camped. Man was not made so large limbed and robust but that he must seek to narrow his world, and wall in a space such as fitted him. He was at first bare and out of doors; but though this was pleasant enough in serene and warm weather, by daylight, the rainy season and the winter, to say nothing of the torrid sun, would perhaps have nipped his race in the bud if he had not made haste to clothe himself with the shelter of a house. Adam and Eve, according to the fable, wore the bower before other clothes. Man wanted a home, a place of warmth, or comfort, first of physical warmth, then the warmth of the affections.

We may imagine a time when, in the infancy of the human race, some enterprising mortal crept into a hollow in a rock for shelter. Every child begins the world again, to some extent, and loves to stay out doors, even in wet and cold. It plays house, as well as horse, having an instinct for it. Who does not remember the interest with which when young he looked at shelving rocks, or any approach to a cave? It was the natural yearning of that portion of our most primitive ancestor which still survived in us. From the cave we have advanced to roofs of palm leaves, of bark and boughs, of linen woven and stretched, of grass and straw, of boards and shingles, of stones and tiles. At last, we know not what it is to live in the open air, and our lives are domestic in more senses than we think. From the hearth to the field is a great distance. It would be well perhaps if we were to spend more of our days and nights without any obstruction between us and the celestial bodies, if the poet did not speak so much from under a roof, or the saint dwell there so long. Birds do not sing in caves, nor do doves cherish their innocence in dovecots.

---

[35] Samuel Laing (1780–1868), English author, visited and wrote about Scandinavia, its people, and the sagas. From his *Journal of a Residence in Norway during the Years 1834, 1835, and 1836; Made with a View to Enquire into the Moral and Political Economy of That Country, and the Condition of Its Inhabitants* (1837).

However, if one designs to construct a dwelling house, it behooves him to exercise a little Yankee shrewdness, lest after all he find himself in a workhouse, a labyrinth without a clew, a museum, an almshouse, a prison, or a splendid mausoleum instead. Consider first how slight a shelter is absolutely necessary. I have seen Penobscot Indians, in this town, living in tents of thin cotton cloth, while the snow was nearly a foot deep around them, and I thought that they would be glad to have it deeper to keep out the wind. Formerly, when how to get my living honestly, with freedom left for my proper pursuits, was a question which vexed me even more than it does now, for unfortunately I am become somewhat callous, I used to see a large box by the railroad, six feet long by three wide, in which the laborers locked up their tools at night, and it suggested to me that every man who was hard pushed might get such a one for a dollar, and, having bored a few auger holes in it, to admit the air at least, get into it when it rained and at night, and hook down the lid, and so have freedom in his love, and in his soul be free. This did not appear the worst, nor by any means a despicable alternative. You could sit up as late as you pleased, and, whenever you got up, go abroad without any landlord or house-lord dogging you for rent. Many a man is harassed to death to pay the rent of a larger and more luxurious box who would not have frozen to death in such a box as this. I am far from jesting. Economy is a subject which admits of being treated with levity, but it cannot so be disposed of. A comfortable house for a rude and hardy race, that lived mostly out of doors, was once made here almost entirely of such materials as Nature furnished ready to their hands. Gookin, who was superintendent of the Indians subject to the Massachusetts Colony, writing in 1674, says, "The best of their houses are covered very neatly, tight and warm, with barks of trees, slipped from their bodies at those seasons when the sap is up, and made into great flakes, with pressure of weighty timber, when they are green. . . . The meaner sort are covered with mats which they make of a kind of bulrush, and are also indifferently tight and warm, but not so good as the former. . . . Some I have seen, sixty or a hundred feet long and thirty feet broad. . . . I have often lodged in their wigwams, and found them as warm as the best English houses." [36] He adds, that they were commonly carpeted and lined within with well-wrought embroidered mats, and were furnished with various utensils. The Indians had advanced so far as to regulate the effect of the wind by a mat suspended over the hole in the roof and moved

[36] Daniel Gookin (1612–1687), whose *Historical Collections of the Indians in New England* . . . was first published in 1792.

by a string. Such a lodge was in the first instance constructed in a day or two at most, and taken down and put up in a few hours; and every family owned one, or its apartment in one.

In the savage state every family owns a shelter as good as the best, and sufficient for its coarser and simpler wants; but I think that I speak within bounds when I say that, though the birds of the air have their nests, and the foxes their holes, and the savages their wigwams, in modern civilized society not more than one half the families own a shelter.[37] In the large towns and cities, where civilization especially prevails, the number of those who own a shelter is a very small fraction of the whole. The rest pay an annual tax for this outside garment of all, become indispensable summer and winter, which would buy a village of Indian wigwams, but now helps to keep them poor as long as they live. I do not mean to insist here on the disadvantage of hiring compared with owning, but it is evident that the savage owns his shelter because it costs so little, while the civilized man hires his commonly because he cannot afford to own it; nor can he, in the long run, any better afford to hire. But, answers one, by merely paying this tax the poor civilized man secures an abode which is a palace compared with the savage's. An annual rent of from twenty-five to a hundred dollars, these are the country rates, entitles him to the benefit of the improvements of centuries, spacious apartments, clean paint and paper, Rumford fire-place,[38] back plastering, Venetian blinds, copper pump, spring lock, a commodious cellar, and many other things. But how happens it that he who is said to enjoy these things is so commonly a *poor* civilized man, while the savage, who has them not, is rich as a savage? If it is asserted that civilization is a real advance in the condition of man—and I think that it is, though only the wise improve their advantages—it must be shown that it has produced better dwellings without making them more costly; and the cost of a thing is the amount of what I will call life which is required to be exchanged for it, immediately or in the long run. An average house in this neighborhood costs perhaps eight hundred dollars, and to lay up this sum will take from ten to fifteen years of the laborer's life, even if he is not encumbered with a family—estimating the pecuniary value of every man's labor at one dollar a day, for if some receive more, others receive

[37] Cf. Matt. 8.22: "And Jesus saith unto him, The foxes have holes, and the birds of the air have nests; but the Son of man hath not where to lay his head."
[38] Benjamin Thompson, Count Rumford (1753–1814), American-born physicist, invented a nonsmoking stove, widely marketed in the United States as the "Rumford Roaster."

less—so that he must have spent more than half his life commonly before *his* wigwam will be earned. If we suppose him to pay a rent instead, this is but a doubtful choice of evils. Would the savage have been wise to exchange his wigwam for a palace on these terms?

It may be guessed that I reduce almost the whole advantage of holding this superfluous property as a fund in store against the future, so far as the individual is concerned, mainly to the defraying of funeral expenses. But perhaps a man is not required to bury himself. Nevertheless this points to an important distinction between the civilized man and the savage; and, no doubt, they have designs on us for our benefit, in making the life of a civilized people an *institution,* in which the life of the individual is to a great extent absorbed, in order to preserve and perfect that of the race. But I wish to show at what a sacrifice this advantage is at present obtained, and to suggest that we may possibly so live as to secure all the advantage without suffering any of the disadvantage. What mean ye by saying that the poor ye have always with you, or that the fathers have eaten sour grapes, and the children's teeth are set on edge?

"As I live, saith the Lord God, ye shall not have occasion any more to use this proverb in Israel."

"Behold all souls are mine; as the soul of the father, so also the soul of the son is mine: the soul that sinneth it shall die."[39]

When I consider my neighbors, the farmers of Concord, who are at least as well off as the other classes, I find that for the most part they have been toiling twenty, thirty, or forty years, that they may become the real owners of their farms, which commonly they have inherited with encumbrances, or else bought with hired money—and we may regard one third of that toil as the cost of their houses—but commonly they have not paid for them yet. It is true, the encumbrances sometimes outweigh the value of the farm, so that the farm itself becomes one great encumbrance, and still a man is found to inherit it, being well acquainted with it, as he says. On applying to the assessors, I am surprised to learn that they cannot at once name a dozen in the town who own their farms free and clear. If you would know the history of these homesteads, inquire at the bank where they are mortgaged. The man who has actually paid for his farm with labor on it is so rare that every neighbor can point to him. I doubt if there are three such men in Concord. What has been said of the merchants, that a very large majority, even ninety-seven in a hundred, are sure to fail, is equally true of the farmers. With regard to the merchants, however, one of

[39] Cf. John 12.8; Matt. 26.11; Ezek. 18.2–4.

them says pertinently that a great part of their failures are not genuine pecuniary failures, but merely failures to fulfil their engagements, because it is inconvenient; that is, it is the moral character that breaks down. But this puts an infinitely worse face on the matter, and suggests, beside, that probably not even the other three succeed in saving their souls, but are perchance bankrupt in a worse sense than they who fail honestly. Bankruptcy and repudiation are the springboards from which much of our civilization vaults and turns its somersets, but the savage stands on the unelastic plank of famine. Yet the Middlesex Cattle Show[40] goes off here with *éclat* annually, as if all the joints of the agricultural machine were suent.[41]

The farmer is endeavoring to solve the problem of a livelihood by a formula more complicated than the problem itself. To get his shoestrings he speculates in herds of cattle. With consummate skill he has set his trap with a hair spring to catch comfort and independence, and then, as he turned away, got his own leg into it. This is the reason he is poor; and for a similar reason we are all poor in respect to a thousand savage comforts, though surrounded by luxuries. As Chapman sings—

> "The false society of men—
> —for earthly greatness
> All heavenly comforts rarefies to air."[42]

And when the farmer has got his house, he may not be the richer but the poorer for it, and it be the house that has got him. As I understand it, that was a valid objection urged by Momus against the house which Minerva made, that she "had not made it movable, by which means a bad neighborhood might be avoided;"[43] and it may still be urged, for our houses are such unwieldy property that we are often imprisoned rather than housed in them; and the bad neighborhood to be avoided is our own scurvy selves. I know one or two families, at least, in this town, who, for nearly a generation, have been wishing to sell their houses in the outskirts and move into the village, but have not been able to accomplish it, and only death will set them free.

---

[40] The annual county agricultural fair.

[41] Dialect for "running smoothly."

[42] George Chapman (c. 1559–1634), *The Tragedy of Caesar and Pompey*, 5.2.

[43] Momus and Minerva were the Roman gods of derision (or disdainful laughter) and wisdom, respectively.

Granted that the *majority* are able at last either to own or hire the modern house with all its improvements. While civilization has been improving our houses, it has not equally improved the men who are to inhabit them. It has created palaces, but it was not so easy to create noblemen and kings. And *if the civilized man's pursuits are no worthier than the savage's, if he is employed the greater part of his life in obtaining gross necessaries and comforts merely, why should he have a better dwelling than the former?*

But how do the poor *minority* fare? Perhaps it will be found, that just in proportion as some have been placed in outward circumstances above the savage, others have been degraded below him. The luxury of one class is counterbalanced by the indigence of another. On the one side is the palace, on the other are the almshouse and "silent poor." The myriads who built the pyramids to be the tombs of the Pharaohs were fed on garlic, and it may be were not decently buried themselves. The mason who finishes the cornice of the palace returns at night perchance to a hut not so good as a wigwam. It is a mistake to suppose that, in a country where the usual evidences of civilization exist, the condition of a very large body of the inhabitants may not be as degraded as that of savages. I refer to the degraded poor, not now to the degraded rich. To know this I should not need to look farther than to the shanties which every where border our railroads, that last improvement in civilization; where I see in my daily walks human beings living in sties, and all winter with an open door, for the sake of light, without any visible, often imaginable, wood pile, and the forms of both old and young are permanently contracted by the long habit of shrinking from cold and misery, and the development of all their limbs and faculties is checked. It certainly is fair to look at that class by whose labor the works which distinguish this generation are accomplished. Such too, to a greater or less extent, is the condition of the operatives of every denomination in England, which is the great workhouse of the world. Or I could refer you to Ireland, which is marked as one of the white or enlightened spots on the map. Contrast the physical condition of the Irish with that of the North American Indian, or the South Sea Islander, or any other savage race before it was degraded by contact with the civilized man. Yet I have no doubt that that people's rulers are as wise as the average of civilized rulers. Their condition only proves what squalidness may consist with civilization. I hardly need refer now to the laborers in our Southern States who produce the staple exports of this country, and are themselves a staple production of the South. But to confine myself to those who are said to be in *moderate* circumstances.

Most men appear never to have considered what a house is, and are actually though needlessly poor all their lives because they think that they must have such a one as their neighbors have. As if one were to wear any sort of coat which the tailor might cut out for him, or gradually leaving off palmleaf hat or cap of woodchuck skin, complain of hard times because he could not afford to buy him a crown! It is possible to invent a house still more convenient and luxurious than we have, which yet all would admit that man could not afford to pay for. Shall we always study to obtain more of these things, and not sometimes to be content with less? Shall the respectable citizen thus gravely teach, by precept and example, the necessity of the young man's providing a certain number of superfluous glowshoes,[44] and umbrellas, and empty guest chambers for empty guests, before he dies? Why should not our furniture be as simple as the Arab's or the Indian's? When I think of the benefactors of the race, whom we have apotheosized as messengers from heaven, bearers of divine gifts to man, I do not see in my mind any retinue at their heels, any car-load of fashionable furniture. Or what if I were to allow—would it not be a singular allowance?—that our furniture should be more complex than the Arab's, in proportion as we are morally and intellectually his superiors! At present our houses are cluttered and defiled with it, and a good house-wife would sweep out the greater part into the dust hole, and not leave her morning's work undone. Morning work! By the blushes of Aurora and the music of Memnon,[45] what should be man's *morning work* in this world? I had three pieces of limestone on my desk, but I was terrified to find that they required to be dusted daily, when the furniture of my mind was all undusted still, and I threw them out the window in disgust. How, then, could I have a furnished house? I would rather sit in the open air, for no dust gathers on the grass, unless where man has broken ground.

It is the luxurious and dissipated who set the fashions which the herd so diligently follow. The traveller who stops at the best houses, so called, soon discovers this, for the publicans presume him to be a Sardanapalus,[46] and if he resigned himself to their tender mercies he would soon be completely emasculated. I think that in the railroad car we are inclined to spend more on luxury than on safety and convenience, and it threatens without attaining these to become no better than a modern drawing room, with its divans, and ottomans, and sunshades, and a hundred other oriental things, which we are taking west with us, invented for

[44] Waterproof overshoes.

[45] The Roman goddess of dawn and her son, whose statue, near Thebes, was supposed to emit music at dawn.

[46] The Greek form of Assurbanipal, a sovereign of Assyria, said to be effeminate and corrupt.

the ladies of the harem and the effeminate natives of the Celestial Empire, which Jonathan[47] should be ashamed to know the names of. I would rather sit on a pumpkin and have it all to myself, than be crowded on a velvet cushion. I would rather ride on earth in an ox cart with a free circulation, than go to heaven in the fancy car of an excursion train and breathe a *malaria* all the way.

The very simplicity and nakedness of man's life in the primitive ages imply this advantage at least, that they left him still but a sojourner in nature. When he was refreshed with food and sleep he contemplated his journey again. He dwelt, as it were, in a tent in this world, and was either threading the valleys, or crossing the plains, or climbing the mountain tops. But lo! men have become the tools of their tools. The man who independently plucked the fruits when he was hungry is become a farmer; and he who stood under a tree for shelter, a housekeeper. We now no longer camp as for a night, but have settled down on earth and forgotten heaven. We have adopted Christianity merely as an improved method of *agri*-culture. We have built for this world a family mansion, and for the next a family tomb. The best works of art are the expression of man's struggle to free himself from this condition, but the effect of our art is merely to make this low state comfortable and that higher state to be forgotten. There is actually no place in this village for a work of *fine* art, if any had come down to us, to stand, for our lives, our houses and streets, furnish no proper pedestal for it. There is not a nail to hang a picture on, nor a shelf to receive the bust of a hero or a saint. When I consider how our houses are built and paid for, or not paid for, and their internal economy managed and sustained, I wonder that the floor does not give way under the visitor while he is admiring the gewgaws upon the mantelpiece, and let him through into the cellar, to some solid and honest though earthy foundation. I cannot but perceive that this so called rich and refined life is a thing jumped at, and I do not get on in the enjoyment of the *fine* arts which adorn it, my attention being wholly occupied with the jump; for I remember that the greatest genuine leap, due to human muscles alone, on record, is that of certain wandering Arabs, who are said to have cleared twenty-five feet on level ground. Without factitious support, man is sure to come to earth again beyond that distance. The first question which I am tempted to put to the proprietor of such impropriety is, Who bolsters you? Are you one of the ninety-seven who fail, or the three who succeed? An-

[47] A popular nineteenth-century name for the ordinary American man. Cf. the last paragraph of *Walden.*

swer me these questions, and then perhaps I may look at your bawbles and find them ornamental. The cart before the horse is neither beautiful nor useful. Before we can adorn our houses with beautiful objects the walls must be stripped, and our lives must be stripped, and beautiful housekeeping and beautiful living be laid for a foundation: now, a taste for the beautiful is most cultivated out of doors, where there is no house and no housekeeper.

Old Johnson, in his "Wonder-Working Providence,"[48] speaking of the first settlers of this town, with whom he was contemporary, tells us that "they burrow themselves in the earth for their first shelter under some hill-side, and, casting the soil aloft upon timber, they make a smoky fire against the earth, at the highest side." They did not "provide them houses," says he, "till the earth, by the Lord's blessing, brought forth bread to feed them," and the first year's crop was so light that "they were forced to cut their bread very thin for a long season." The secretary of the Province of New Netherland, writing in Dutch, in 1650, for the information of those who wished to take up land there, states more particularly, that "those in New Netherland, and especially in New England, who have no means to build farm houses at first according to their wishes, dig a square pit in the ground, cellar fashion, six or seven feet deep, as long and as broad as they think proper, case the earth inside with wood all round the wall, and line the wood with the bark of trees or something else to prevent the caving in of the earth; floor this cellar with plank, and wainscot it overhead for a ceiling, raise a roof of spars clear up, and cover the spars with bark or green sods, so that they can live dry and warm in these houses with their entire families for two, three, and four years, it being understood that partitions are run through those cellars which are adapted to the size of the family. The wealthy and principal men in New England, in the beginning of the colonies, commenced their first dwelling houses in this fashion for two reasons; firstly, in order not to waste time in building, and not to want food the next season; secondly, in order not to discourage poor laboring people whom they brought over in numbers from Fatherland. In the course of three or four years, when the country became adapted to agriculture, they built themselves handsome houses, spending on them several thousands."[49]

---

[48] Edward Johnson (1599?–1672), one of the first settlers of the Massachusetts Bay Colony; *Wonder-Working Providence of Sions Saviour in New England* (1654).

[49] Cornelius Van Tienhoven; his account is found in Edmund Bailey O'Callaghan (1797–1880), *Documents Relative to the Colonial History of the State of New-York* (1849–1851).

In this course which our ancestors took there was a show of prudence at least, as if their principle were to satisfy the more pressing wants first. But are the more pressing wants satisfied now? When I think of acquiring for myself one of our luxurious dwellings, I am deterred, for, so to speak, the country is not yet adapted to *human* culture, and we are still forced to cut our *spiritual* bread far thinner than our forefathers did their wheaten. Not that all architectural ornament is to be neglected even in the rudest periods; but let our houses first be lined with beauty, where they come in contact with our lives, like the tenement of the shellfish, and not overlaid with it. But, alas! I have been inside one or two of them, and know what they are lined with.

Though we are not so degenerate but that we might possibly live in a cave or a wigwam or wear skins today, it certainly is better to accept the advantages, though so dearly bought, which the invention and industry of mankind offer. In such a neighborhood as this, boards and shingles, lime and bricks, are cheaper and more easily obtained than suitable caves, or whole logs, or bark in sufficient quantities, or even well-tempered clay or flat stones. I speak understandingly on this subject, for I have made myself acquainted with it both theoretically and practically. With a little more wit we might use these materials so as to become richer than the richest now are, and make our civilization a blessing. The civilized man is a more experienced and wiser savage. But to make haste to my own experiment.

Near the end of March, 1845, I borrowed an axe and went down to the woods by Walden Pond, nearest to where I intended to build my house, and began to cut down some tall arrowy white pines, still in their youth, for timber. It is difficult to begin without borrowing, but perhaps it is the most generous course thus to permit your fellow-men to have an interest in your enterprise. The owner of the axe,[50] as he released his hold on it, said that it was the apple of his eye; but I returned it sharper than I received it. It was a pleasant hillside where I worked, covered with pine woods, through which I looked out on the pond, and a small open field in the woods where pines and hickories were springing up. The ice in the pond was not yet dissolved, though there were some open spaces, and it was all dark colored and saturated with water. There were some slight flurries of snow during

[50] A. Bronson Alcott (1799–1888), New England transcendentalist and educational reformer, and father of Louisa May Alcott, whose short work "Transcendental Wild Oats," printed in this volume, offers an amusing and often painful look at their family and friends.

the days that I worked there; but for the most part when I came out on to the railroad, on my way home, its yellow sand heap stretched away gleaming in the hazy atmosphere, and the rails shone in the spring sun, and I heard the lark and pewee and other birds already come to commence another year with us. They were pleasant spring days, in which the winter of man's discontent was thawing as well as the earth, and the life that had lain torpid began to stretch itself. One day, when my axe had come off and I had cut a green hickory for a wedge, driving it with a stone, and had placed the whole to soak in a pond hole in order to swell the wood, I saw a striped snake run into the water, and he lay on the bottom, apparently without inconvenience, as long as I staid there, or more than a quarter of an hour; perhaps because he had not yet fairly come out of the torpid state. It appeared to me that for a like reason men remain in their present low and primitive condition; but if they should feel the influence of the spring of springs arousing them, they would of necessity rise to a higher and more ethereal life. I had previously seen the snakes in frosty mornings in my path with portions of their bodies still numb and inflexible, waiting for the sun to thaw them. On the 1st of April it rained and melted the ice, and the early part of the day, which was very foggy, I heard a stray goose groping about over the pond and cackling as if lost, or like the spirit of the fog.

So I went on for some days cutting and hewing timber, and also studs and rafters, all with my narrow axe, not having many communicable or scholar-like thoughts, singing to myself—

Men say they know many things;
But lo! they have taken wings—
The arts and sciences,
And a thousand appliances;
5 The wind that blows
Is all that any body knows.

I hewed the main timbers six inches square, most of the studs on two sides only, and the rafters and floor timbers on one side, leaving the rest of the bark on, so that they were just as straight and much stronger than sawed ones. Each stick was carefully mortised or tenoned by its stump, for I had borrowed other tools by this time. My days in the woods were not very long ones; yet I usually carried my dinner of bread and butter, and read the newspaper in which it was wrapped, at noon, sitting amid the green pine boughs which I had cut off, and to my bread was imparted some of their fragrance, for my hands were covered with a thick coat of pitch. Before I had done I was more the friend than the foe of the pine tree, though I had cut down some of them, having become better acquainted with it. Sometimes a rambler in the wood was attracted by the sound of my axe, and we chatted pleasantly over the chips which I had made.

By the middle of April, for I made no haste in my work, but rather made the most of it, my house was framed and ready for the raising. I had already bought the shanty of James Collins, an Irishman who worked on the Fitchburg Railroad,[51] for boards. James Collins' shanty was considered an uncommonly fine one. When I called to see it he was not at home. I walked about the outside, at first unobserved from within, the window was so deep and high. It was of small dimensions, with a peaked cottage roof, and not much else to be seen, the dirt being raised five feet all around as if it were a compost heap. The roof was the soundest part, though a good deal warped and made brittle by the sun. Doorsill there was none, but a perennial passage for the hens under the door board. Mrs. C. came to the door and asked me to view it from the inside. The hens were driven in by my approach. It was dark, and had a dirt floor for the most part, dank, clammy, and aguish, only here a board and there a board which would not bear removal. She lighted a lamp to show me the inside of the roof and the walls, and also that the board floor extended under the bed, warning me not to step into the cellar, a sort of dust hole two feet deep. In her own words, they were "good boards overhead, good boards all around, and a good window"—of two whole squares originally, only the cat had passed out that way lately. There was a stove, a bed, and a place to sit, an infant in the house where it was born, a silk parasol, gilt-framed looking-glass, and a patent new coffee mill nailed to an oak sapling, all told. The bargain was soon concluded, for James had in the mean while returned. I to pay four dollars and twenty-five cents tonight, he to vacate at five tomorrow morning, selling to nobody else meanwhile: I to take possession at six. It were well, he said, to be there early, and anticipate certain indistinct but wholly unjust claims on the score of ground rent and fuel. This he assured me was the only encumbrance. At six I passed him and his family on the road. One large bundle held their all—bed, coffee-mill, looking-glass, hens—all but the cat, she took to the woods and became a wild cat, and, as I learned afterward, trod in a trap set for woodchucks, and so became a dead cat at last.

I took down this dwelling the same morning, drawing the nails, and removed it to the pond side by small cart-loads, spreading the boards on

[51] The Boston & Fitchburg Railroad, which ran by Walden Pond, plays a prominent role in the book. Fitchburg is west of Concord.

the grass there to bleach and warp back again in the sun. One early thrush gave me a note or two as I drove along the woodland path. I was informed treacherously by a young Patrick that neighbor Seeley, an Irishman, in the intervals of the carting, transferred the still tolerable, straight, and drivable nails, staples, and spikes to his pocket, and then stood when I came back to pass the time of day, and look freshly up, unconcerned, with spring thoughts, at the devastation; there being a dearth of work, as he said. He was there to represent spectatordom, and help make this seemingly insignificant event one with the removal of the gods of Troy.[52]

I dug my cellar in the side of a hill sloping to the south, where a woodchuck had formerly dug his burrow, down through sumach and blackberry roots, and the lowest stain of vegetation, six feet square by seven deep, to a fine sand where potatoes would not freeze in any winter. The sides were left shelving, and not stoned; but the sun having never shone on them, the sand still keeps its place. It was but two hours' work. I took particular pleasure in this breaking of ground, for in almost all latitudes men dig into the earth for an equable temperature. Under the most splendid house in the city is still to be found the cellar where they store their roots as of old, and long after the superstructure has disappeared posterity remark its dent in the earth. The house is still but a sort of porch at the entrance of a burrow.

At length, in the beginning of May, with the help of some of my acquaintances, rather to improve so good an occasion for neighborliness than from any necessity, I set up the frame of my house. No man was ever more honored in the character of his raisers than I.[53] They are destined, I trust, to assist at the raising of loftier structures one day. I began to occupy my house on the 4th of July, as soon as it was boarded and roofed, for the boards were carefully feather-edged and lapped, so that it was perfectly impervious to rain; but before boarding I laid the foundation of a chimney at one end, bringing two cartloads of stones up the hill from the pond in my arms. I built the chimney after my hoeing in the fall, before a fire became necessary for warmth, doing my cooking in the mean while out of doors on the ground, early in the morning: which mode I still think is in some respects more convenient and agreeable than the usual one. When it stormed before my bread was baked, I fixed a few boards over the fire, and sat under them to watch my loaf, and passed some pleasant hours in that

[52] In Virgil's *Aeneid,* book 2, Aeneas removes the images of the gods to Mount Ida.

[53] His "raisers" were Emerson, Alcott, William Ellery Channing the younger, George William, Burrill Curtis, and Edmund Hosmer with his three sons.

way. In those days, when my hands were much employed, I read but little, but the least scraps of paper which lay on the ground, my holder, or tablecloth, afforded me as much entertainment, in fact answered the same purpose as the Iliad.[54]

It would be worth the while to build still more deliberately than I did, considering, for instance, what foundation a door, a window, a cellar, a garret, have in the nature of man, and perchance never raising any superstructure until we found a better reason for it than our temporal necessities even. There is some of the same fitness in a man's building his own house that there is in a bird's building its own nest. Who knows but if men constructed their dwellings with their own hands, and provided food for themselves and families simply and honestly enough, the poetic faculty would be universally developed, as birds universally sing when they are so engaged? But alas! we do like cowbirds and cuckoos, which lay their eggs in nests which other birds have built, and cheer no traveller with their chattering and unmusical notes. Shall we forever resign the pleasure of construction to the carpenter? What does architecture amount to in the experience of the mass of men? I never in all my walks came across a man engaged in so simple and natural an occupation as building his house. We belong to the community. It is not the tailor alone who is the ninth part of a man; it is as much the preacher, and the merchant, and the farmer. Where is this division of labor to end? and what object does it finally serve? No doubt another *may* also think for me; but it is not therefore desirable that he should do so to the exclusion of my thinking for myself.

True, there are architects so called in this country, and I have heard of one[55] at least possessed with the idea of making architectural ornaments have a core of truth, a necessity, and hence a beauty, as if it were a revelation to him. All very well perhaps from his point of view, but only a little better than the common dilettantism. A sentimental reformer in architecture, he began at the cornice, not at the foundation. It was only how to put a core of truth within the ornaments, that every sugar plum in fact might have an almond or caraway seed in it—though I hold that almonds are most wholesome without the sugar—and not how the inhabitant, the indweller, might build truly within and without, and let the ornaments take care of themselves. What reasonable man ever supposed that ornaments

[54]The epic poem by Homer.
[55]Horatio Greenough (1805–1851), the American sculptor, whose ideas about the functionality of architectural decoration Thoreau may not have understood—or approved of.

were something outward and in the skin merely—that the tortoise got his spotted shell, or the shellfish its mother-o'-pearl tints, by such a contract as the inhabitants of Broadway their Trinity Church?[56] But a man has no more to do with the style of architecture of his house than a tortoise with that of its shell: nor need the soldier be so idle as to try to paint the precise *color* of his virtue on his standard. The enemy will find it out. He may turn pale when the trial comes. This man seemed to me to lean over the cornice, and timidly whisper his half truth to the rude occupants who really knew it better than he. What of architectural beauty I now see, I know has gradually grown from within outward, out of the necessities and character of the indweller, who is the only builder—out of some unconscious truthfulness, and nobleness, without ever a thought for the appearance; and whatever additional beauty of this kind is destined to be produced will be preceded by a like unconscious beauty of life. The most interesting dwellings in this country, as the painter knows, are the most unpretending, humble log huts and cottages of the poor commonly; it is the life of the inhabitants whose shells they are, and not any peculiarity in their surfaces merely, which makes them *picturesque;* and equally interesting will be the citizen's suburban box, when his life shall be as simple and as agreeable to the imagination, and there is as little straining after effect in the style of his dwelling. A great proportion of architectural ornaments are literally hollow, and a September gale would strip them off, like borrowed plumes, without injury to the substantials. They can do without *architecture* who have no olives nor wines in the cellar. What if an equal ado were made about the ornaments of style in literature, and the architects of our bibles spent as much time about their cornices as the architects of our churches do? So are made the *belles-lettres* and the *beaux-arts* and their professors. Much it concerns a man, forsooth, how a few sticks are slanted over him or under him and what colors are daubed upon his box. It would signify somewhat, if, in any earnest sense, *he* slanted them and daubed it; but the spirit having departed out of the tenant, it is of a piece with constructing his own coffin—the architecture of the grave, and "carpenter," is but another name for "coffin-maker." One man says, in his despair or indifference to life, take up a handful of the earth at your feet, and paint your house that color. Is he thinking of his last and narrow house? Toss up a copper for it as well. What an abundance of leisure he must have! Why do you take up a handful of dirt? Better paint your house your own complexion; let it turn pale or blush for you. An enterprise to improve the style

[56] The Gothic Revival church in downtown New York, completed in 1846.

of cottage architecture! When you have got my ornaments ready I will wear them.

Before winter I built a chimney, and shingled the sides of my house, which were already impervious to rain, with imperfect and sappy shingles made of the first slice of the log, whose edges I was obliged to straighten with a plane.

I have thus a tight shingled and plastered house, ten feet wide by fifteen long, and eight-feet posts, with a garret and a closet, a large window on each side, two trap doors, one door at the end, and a brick fireplace opposite. The exact cost of my house, paying the usual price for such materials as I used, but not counting the work, all of which was done by myself, was as follows; and I give the details because very few are able to tell exactly what their houses cost, and fewer still, if any, the separate cost of the various materials which compose them:

Item	Cost	Remark
Boards	\$8.03½	mostly shanty boards.
Refuse shingles for roof and sides	4.00	
Laths	1.25	
Two second-hand windows with glass	2.43	
One thousand old brick	4.00	
Two casks of lime	2.40	That was high.
Hair	0.31	More than I needed.
Mantle-tree iron	0.15	
Nails	3.90	
Hinges and screws	0.14	
Latch	0.10	
Chalk	0.01	
Transportation	1.40	I carried a good part on my back.
In all	\$28.12½	

These are all the materials excepting the timber, stones and sand, which I claimed by squatter's right. I have also a small wood-shed adjoining, made chiefly of the stuff which was left after building the house.

I intend to build me a house which will surpass any on the main street in Concord in grandeur and luxury, as soon as it pleases me as much and will cost me no more than my present one.

I thus found that the student who wishes for a shelter can obtain one for a lifetime at an expense not greater than the rent which he now pays annually. If I seem to boast more than is becoming, my excuse is that I brag for humanity rather than for myself; and my shortcomings and inconsistencies do not affect the truth of my statement. Notwithstanding much cant and hypocrisy—chaff which I find it difficult to separate from my wheat, but for which I am as sorry as any man—I will breathe freely and stretch myself in this respect, it is such a relief to both the moral and physical system; and I am resolved that I will not through humility become the devil's attorney. I will endeavor to speak a good word for the truth. At Cambridge College[57] the mere rent of a student's room, which is only a little larger than my own, is thirty dollars each year, though the corporation had the advantage of building thirty-two side by side and under one roof, and the occupant suffers the inconvenience of many and noisy neighbors, and perhaps a residence in the fourth story. I cannot but think that if we had more true wisdom in these respects, not only less education would be needed, because, forsooth, more would already have been acquired, but the pecuniary expense of getting an education would in a great measure vanish. Those conveniences which the student requires at Cambridge or elsewhere cost him or somebody else ten times as great a sacrifice of life as they would with proper management on both sides. Those things for which the most money is demanded are never the things which the student most wants. Tuition, for instance, is an important item in the term bill, while for the far more valuable education which he gets by associating with the most cultivated of his contemporaries no charge is made. The mode of founding a college is, commonly, to get up a subscription of dollars and cents, and then following blindly the principles of a division of labor to its extreme, a principle which should never be followed but with circumspection—to call in a contractor who makes this a subject of speculation, and he employs Irishmen or other operatives actually to lay the foundations, while the students that are to be are said to be fitting themselves for it; and for these oversights successive generations have to pay. I think that it would be *better than this,* for the students, or those who desire to be benefited by it, even to lay the foundation themselves. The student who secures his coveted leisure and retirement by systematically shirking any labor necessary to man obtains but an ignoble and unprofitable leisure, defrauding himself of the experience which alone can make leisure fruitful. "But," says one, "you do not mean that the students should go to work with their hands instead of their heads?" I do not mean that exactly, but I mean something which he might think a good deal like that; I mean that they should not *play* life, or *study* it merely, while the community supports them at this expensive game, but earnestly *live* it from beginning to end. How could youths better learn to live than by at

[57]Harvard College, from which Thoreau graduated in 1837.

once trying the experiment of living? Methinks this would exercise their minds as much as mathematics. If I wished a boy to know something about the arts and sciences, for instance, I would not pursue the common course, which is merely to send him into the neighborhood of some professor, where any thing is professed and practised but the art of life—to survey the world through a telescope or a microscope, and never with his natural eye; to study chemistry, and not learn how his bread is made, or mechanics, and not learn how it is earned; to discover new satellites to Neptune, and not detect the motes in his eyes, or to what vagabond he is a satellite himself; or to be devoured by the monsters that swarm all around him, while contemplating the monsters in a drop of vinegar. Which would have advanced the most at the end of a month—the boy who had made his own jackknife from the ore which he had dug and smelted, reading as much as would be necessary for this—or the boy who had attended the lectures on metallurgy at the Institute in the mean while, and had received a Rogers' penknife[58] from his father? Which would be most likely to cut his fingers? . . . To my astonishment I was informed on leaving college that I had studied navigation!—why, if I had taken one turn down the harbor I should have known more about it. Even the *poor* student studies and is taught only *political* economy, while that economy of living which is synonymous with philosophy is not even sincerely professed in our colleges. The consequence is, that while he is reading Adam Smith, Ricardo, and Say,[59] he runs his father in debt irretrievably.

As with our colleges, so with a hundred "modern improvements"; there is an illusion about them; there is not always a positive advance. The devil goes on exacting compound interest to the last for his early share and numerous succeeding investments in them. Our inventions are wont to be pretty toys, which distract our attention from serious things. They are but improved means to an unimproved end, an end which it was already but too easy to arrive at; as railroads lead to Boston or New York. We are in great haste to construct a magnetic telegraph from Maine to Texas; but Maine and Texas, it may be, have nothing important to communicate. Either is in such a predicament as the man who was earnest to be introduced to a distinguished deaf woman, but when he was presented, and one end of her ear trumpet[60] was put into his hand, had nothing to say. As if the

[58] An imported and thus expensive knife manufactured in Sheffield, England, by Joseph Rodgers and Sons.

[59] Economists all: Adam Smith (1723–1790), David Ricardo (1772–1823), and Jean-Baptiste Say (1767–1832).

[60] Before the development of hearing aids, partially deaf people used a horn-shaped device, the narrow end of which was placed in the ear, with people speaking into the wider end.

main object were to talk fast and not to talk sensibly. We are eager to tunnel under the Atlantic and bring the old world some weeks nearer to the new; but perchance the first news that will leak through into the broad, flapping American ear will be that the Princess Adelaide has the whooping cough.[61] After all, the man whose horse trots a mile in a minute does not carry the most important messages; he is not an evangelist, nor does he come round eating locusts and wild honey. I doubt if Flying Childers[62] ever carried a peck of corn to mill.

One says to me, "I wonder that you do not lay up money; you love to travel; you might take the cars and go to Fitchburg today and see the country." But I am wiser than that. I have learned that the swiftest traveller is he that goes afoot. I say to my friend, Suppose we try who will get there first. The distance is thirty miles; the fare ninety cents. That is almost a day's wages. I remember when wages were sixty cents a day for laborers on this very road. Well, I start now on foot, and get there before night; I have travelled at that rate by the week together. You will in the mean while have earned your fare, and arrive there some time tomorrow, or possibly this evening, if you are lucky enough to get a job in season. Instead of going to Fitchburg, you will be working here the greater part of the day. And so, if the railroad reached round the world, I think that I should keep ahead of you; and as for seeing the country and getting experience of that kind, I should have to cut your acquaintance altogether.

Such is the universal law, which no man can ever outwit, and with regard to the railroad even we may say it is as broad as it is long. To make a railroad round the world available to all mankind is equivalent to grading the whole surface of the planet. Men have an indistinct notion that if they keep up this activity of joint stocks and spades long enough all will at length ride somewhere, in next to no time, and for nothing; but though a crowd rushes to the depot, and the conductor shouts "All aboard!" when the smoke is blown away and the vapor condensed, it will be perceived that a few are riding, but the rest are run over—and it will be called, and will be, "A melancholy accident." No doubt they can ride at last who shall have earned their fare, that is, if they survive so long, but they will probably have lost their elasticity and desire to travel by that time. This spending of the best part of one's life earning money in order to enjoy a questionable liberty during the least valuable part of it, reminds me of the Englishman who went to India to make a fortune first, in order that he

[61] May or may not refer to a specific member of European royalty; probably meant as an imaginary name for any such person.

[62] An eighteenth-century English racehorse, never defeated in a race.

might return to England and live the life of a poet. He should have gone up garret at once. "What!" exclaim a million Irishmen starting up from all the shanties in the land, "is not this railroad which we have built a good thing?" Yes, I answer, *comparatively* good, that is, you might have done worse; but I wish, as you are brothers of mine, that you could have spent your time better than digging in this dirt.

Before I finished my house, wishing to earn ten or twelve dollars by some honest and agreeable method, in order to meet my unusual expenses, I planted about two acres and a half of light and sandy soil near it chiefly with beans, but also a small part with potatoes, corn, peas, and turnips. The whole lot contains eleven acres, mostly growing up to pines and hickories, and was sold the preceding season for eight dollars and eight cents an acre. One farmer said that it was "good for nothing but to raise cheeping squirrels on." I put no manure whatever on this land, not being the owner, but merely a squatter, and not expecting to cultivate so much again, and I did not quite hoe it all once. I got out several cords of stumps in ploughing, which supplied me with fuel for a long time, and left small circles of virgin mould, easily distinguishable through the summer by the greater luxuriance of the beans there. The dead and for the most part unmerchantable wood behind my house, and the driftwood from the pond, have supplied the remainder of my fuel. I was obliged to hire a team and a man for the ploughing, though I held the plough myself. My farm outgoes for the first season were, for implements, seed, work, etc., \$14.72½. The seed corn was given me. This never costs any thing to speak of, unless you plant more than enough. I got twelve bushels of beans, and eighteen bushels of potatoes, beside some peas and sweet corn. The yellow corn and turnips were too late to come to any thing. My whole income from the farm was

	\$23.44.
Deducting the outgoes........	14.72½
There are left................	\$8.71½,

beside produce consumed and on hand at the time this estimate was made of the value of \$4.50—the amount on hand much more than balancing a little grass which I did not raise. All things considered, that is, considering the importance of a man's soul and of today, notwithstanding the short time occupied by my experiment, nay, partly even because of its transient character, I believe that that was doing better than any farmer in Concord did that year.

The next year I did better still, for I spaded up all the land which I required, about a third of an acre, and I learned from the experience of both years, not being in the least awed by many celebrated works on husbandry, Arthur Young[63] among the rest, that if one would live simply and eat only the crop which he raised, and raise no more than he ate, and not exchange it for an insufficient quantity of more luxurious and expensive things, he would need to cultivate only a few rods of ground, and that it would be cheaper to spade up that than to use oxen to plough it, and to select a fresh spot from time to time than to manure the old, and he could do all his necessary farm work as it were with his left hand at odd hours in the summer; and thus he would not be tied to an ox, or horse, or cow, or pig, as at present. I desire to speak impartially on this point, and as one not interested in the success or failure of the present economical and social arrangements. I was more independent than any farmer in Concord, for I was not anchored to a house or farm, but could follow the bent of my genius, which is a very crooked one, every moment. Beside being better off than they already, if my house had been burned or my crops had failed, I should have been nearly as well off as before.

I am wont to think that men are not so much the keepers of herds as herds are the keepers of men, the former are so much the freer. Men and oxen exchange work; but if we consider necessary work only, the oxen will be seen to have greatly the advantage, their farm is so much the larger. Man does some of his part of the exchange work in his six weeks of haying, and it is no boy's play. Certainly no nation that lived simply in all respects, that is, no nation of philosophers, would commit so great a blunder as to use the labor of animals. True, there never was and is not likely soon to be a nation of philosophers, nor am I certain it is desirable that there should be. However, *I* should never have broken a horse or bull and taken him to board for any work he might do for me, for fear I should become a horse-man or a herds-man merely; and if society seems to be the gainer by so doing, are we certain that what is one man's gain is not another's loss, and that the stable-boy has equal cause with his master to be satisfied? Granted that some public works would not have been constructed without this aid, and let man share the glory of such with the ox and horse; does it follow that he could not have accomplished works yet more worthy of himself in that case? When men begin to do, not merely unnecessary

[63] British agriculturalist and author (1741–1820); perhaps his *Rural Oeconomy: Or, Essays on the Practical Parts of Husbandry . . . to Which Is Added, The Rural Socrates: Being Memoirs of a Country Philosopher* (1770), or his *American Husbandry . . .* (1775).

or artistic, but luxurious and idle work, with their assistance, it is inevitable that a few do all the exchange work with the oxen, or, in other words, become the slaves of the strongest. Man thus not only works for the animal within him, but, for a symbol of this, he works for the animal without him. Though we have many substantial houses of brick or stone, the prosperity of the farmer is still measured by the degree to which the barn overshadows the house. This town is said to have the largest houses for oxen, cows, and horses hereabouts, and it is not behindhand in its public buildings; but there are very few halls for free worship or free speech in this county. It should not be by their architecture, but why not even by their power of abstract thought, that nations should seek to commemorate themselves? How much more admirable the Bhagvat-Geeta than all the ruins of the East![64] Towers and temples are the luxury of princes. A simple and independent mind does not toil at the bidding of any prince. Genius is not a retainer to any emperor, nor is its material silver, or gold, or marble, except to a trifling extent. To what end, pray, is so much stone hammered? In Arcadia,[65] when I was there, I did not see any hammering stone. Nations are possessed with an insane ambition to perpetuate the memory of themselves by the amount of hammered stone they leave. What if equal pains were taken to smooth and polish their manners? One piece of good sense would be more memorable than a monument as high as the moon. I love better to see stones in place. The grandeur of Thebes[66] was a vulgar grandeur. More sensible is a rod of stone wall that bounds an honest man's field than a hundred-gated Thebes that has wandered farther from the true end of life. The religion and civilization which are barbaric and heathenish build splendid temples; but what you might call Christianity does not. Most of the stone a nation hammers goes toward its tomb only. It buries itself alive. As for the Pyramids, there is nothing to wonder at in them so much as the fact that so many men could be found degraded enough to spend their lives constructing a tomb for some ambitious booby, whom it would have been wiser and manlier to have drowned in the Nile, and then given his body to the dogs. I might possibly invent some excuse for them and him, but I have no time for it. As for the religion and love of art of the builders, it is much the same all the world over, whether the building be an Egyptian temple or the United States Bank. It costs more than it comes to. The mainspring is vanity, assisted by the love of garlic and bread and butter. Mr. Balcom, a promising young architect, designs it on the back of his

[64] The ancient Hindu text; generally spelled Bhagavad-Gita.
[65] A pastoral area in ancient Greece; by implication, any ideal place.
[66] In the ancient world, the magnificent capital of Upper Egypt.

Vitruvius,[67] with hard pencil and ruler, and the job is let out to Dobson & Sons, stonecutters. When the thirty centuries begin to look down on it, mankind begin to look up at it. As for your high towers and monuments, there was a crazy fellow once in this town who undertook to dig through to China, and he got so far that, as he said, he heard the Chinese pots and kettles rattle; but I think that I shall not go out of my way to admire the hole which he made. Many are concerned about the monuments of the West and the East—to know who built them. For my part, I should like to know who in those days did not build them—who were above such trifling. But to proceed with my statistics.

By surveying, carpentry, and day-labor of various other kinds in the village in the mean while, for I have as many trades as fingers, I had earned \$13.34. The expense of food for eight months, namely, from July 4th to March 1st, the time when these estimates were made, though I lived there more than two years—not counting potatoes, a little green corn, and some peas, which I had raised, nor considering the value of what was on hand at the last date, was

Rice	\$1.73½		
Molasses	1.73	Cheapest form of the saccharine.	
Rye meal	1.04¾		
Indian meal	0.99¾	Cheaper than rye.	
Pork	0.22		
Flour	0.88	Costs more than Indian meal, both money and trouble.	All experiments which failed.
Sugar	0.80		All experiments which failed.
Lard	0.65		All experiments which failed.
Apples	0.25		All experiments which failed.
Dried apple	0.22		All experiments which failed.
Sweet potatoes	0.10		All experiments which failed.
One pumpkin	0.06		All experiments which failed.
One watermelon	0.02		All experiments which failed.
Salt	0.03		All experiments which failed.

Yes, I did eat \$8.74, all told; but I should not thus unblushingly publish my guilt, if I did not know that most of my readers were equally

[67] Vitruvius Pollio (c. 50–26 B.C.E.), Roman architect, author of *De architectura.*

guilty with myself, and that their deeds would look no better in print. The next year I sometimes caught a mess of fish for my dinner, and once I went so far as to slaughter a woodchuck which ravaged my bean-field—effect his transmigration, as a Tartar would say[68]—and devour him, partly for experiment's sake; but though it afforded me a momentary enjoyment, notwithstanding a musky flavor, I saw that the longest use would not make that a good practice, however it might seem to have your woodchucks ready dressed by the village butcher.

Clothing and some incidental expenses within the same dates, though little can be inferred from this item, amounted to

	\$8.40¾
Oil and some household utensils	2.00

So that all the pecuniary outgoes, excepting for washing and mending, which for the most part were done out of the house, and their bills have not yet been received—and these are all and more than all the ways by which money necessarily goes out in this part of the world—were

House	\$28.12½
Farm one year	14.72½
Food eight months...............	8.74
Clothing, etc., eight months........	8.40¾
Oil, etc., eight months	2.00
In all	\$61.99¾

I address myself now to those of my readers who have a living to get. And to meet this I have for farm produce sold

\$23.44	
Earned by day-labor	13.34
In all	\$36.78,

which subtracted from the sum of the outgoes leaves a balance of \$25.21¾ on the one side—this being very nearly the means with which I started,

[68] An inhabitant of the Central Asian area called Tartary or Tatary, where belief in the transmigration of souls was supposedly widespread.

and the measure of expenses to be incurred—and on the other, beside the leisure and independence and health thus secured, a comfortable house for me as long as I choose to occupy it.

These statistics, however accidental and therefore uninstructive they may appear, as they have a certain completeness, have a certain value also. Nothing was given me of which I have not rendered some account. It appears from the above estimate, that my food alone cost me in money about twenty-seven cents a week. It was, for nearly two years after this, rye and Indian meal without yeast, potatoes, rice, a very little salt pork, molasses, and salt, and my drink water. It was fit that I should live on rice, mainly, who loved so well the philosophy of India. To meet the objections of some inveterate cavillers, I may as well state, that if I dined out occasionally, as I always had done, and I trust shall have opportunities to do again, it was frequently to the detriment of my domestic arrangements. But the dining out, being, as I have stated, a constant element, does not in the least affect a comparative statement like this.

I learned from my two years' experience that it would cost incredibly little trouble to obtain one's necessary food, even in this latitude; that a man may use as simple a diet as the animals, and yet retain health and strength. I have made a satisfactory dinner, satisfactory on several accounts, simply off a dish of purslane (*Portulaca oleracea*) which I gathered in my cornfield, boiled and salted. I give the Latin on account of the savoriness of the trivial name. And pray what more can a reasonable man desire, in peaceful times, in ordinary noons, than a sufficient number of ears of green sweet-corn boiled, with the addition of salt? Even the little variety which I used was a yielding to the demands of appetite, and not of health. Yet men have come to such a pass that they frequently starve, not for want of necessaries, but for want of luxuries; and I know a good woman who thinks that her son lost his life because he took to drinking water only.

The reader will perceive that I am treating the subject rather from an economic than a dietetic point of view, and he will not venture to put my abstemiousness to the test unless he has a well-stocked larder.

Bread I at first made of pure Indian meal and salt, genuine hoe-cakes, which I baked before my fire out of doors on a shingle or the end of a stick of timber sawed off in building my house; but it was wont to get smoked and to have a piny flavor. I tried flour also; but have at last found a mixture of rye and Indian meal most convenient and agreeable. In cold weather it was no little amusement to bake several small loaves of this in succession, tending and turning them as carefully as an Egyptian his hatching eggs. They were a real cereal fruit which I ripened, and they had to my senses a fragrance like that of other noble fruits, which I kept in as long as possible by wrapping them in cloths. I made a study of the ancient and indispensable art of bread-making, consulting such authorities as offered, going back to the primitive days and first invention of the unleavened kind, when from the wildness of nuts and meats men first reached the mildness and refinement of this diet, and travelling gradually down in my studies through that accidental souring of the dough which, it is supposed, taught the leavening process, and through the various fermentations thereafter, till I came to "good, sweet, wholesome bread," the staff of life. Leaven, which some deem the soul of bread, the *spiritus* which fills its cellular tissue, which is religiously preserved like the vestal fire—some precious bottle-full, I suppose, first brought over in the Mayflower, did the business for America, and its influence is still rising, swelling, spreading, in cerealian billows over the land—this seed I regularly and faithfully procured from the village, till at length one morning I forgot the rules, and scalded my yeast; by which accident I discovered that even this was not indispensable—for my discoveries were not by the synthetic but analytic process—and I have gladly omitted it since, though most housewives earnestly assured me that safe and wholesome bread without yeast might not be, and elderly people prophesied a speedy decay of the vital forces. Yet I find it not to be an essential ingredient, and after going without it for a year am still in the land of the living; and I am glad to escape the trivialness of carrying a bottle-full in my pocket, which would sometimes pop and discharge its contents to my discomfiture. It is simpler and more respectable to omit it. Man is an animal who more than any other can adapt himself to all climates and circumstances. Neither did I put any sal soda, or other acid or alkali, into my bread. It would seem that I made it according to the recipe which Marcus Porcius Cato[69] gave about two centuries before Christ. "Panem depsticium sic facito. Manus mortariumque bene lavato. Farinam in mortarium indito, aquae paulatim addito, subigitoque pulchre. Ubi bene subegeris, defingito, coquitoque sub testu." Which I take to mean—"Make kneaded bread thus. Wash your hands and trough well. Put the meal into the trough, add water gradually, and knead it thoroughly. When you have kneaded it well, mould it, and bake it under a cover," that is, in a baking-kettle. Not a word about leaven. But I did not always use this staff of life. At one time, owing to the emptiness of my purse, I saw none of it for more than a month.

Every New Englander might easily raise all his own breadstuffs in this land of rye and Indian corn, and not depend on distant and fluctuating

[69] Cato the Censor (234–149 B.C.E.), Roman statesman who also wrote on agricultural subjects, notably in *De agri cultura* and *De re rustica*.

markets for them. Yet so far are we from simplicity and independence that, in Concord, fresh and sweet meal is rarely sold in the shops, and hominy and corn in a still coarser form are hardly used by any. For the most part the farmer gives to his cattle and hogs the grain of his own producing, and buys flour, which is at least no more wholesome, at a greater cost, at the store. I saw that I could easily raise my bushel or two of rye and Indian corn, for the former will grow on the poorest land, and the latter does not require the best, and grind them in a hand-mill, and so do without rice and pork; and if I must have some concentrated sweet, I found by experiment that I could make a very good molasses either of pumpkins or beets, and I knew that I needed only to set out a few maples to obtain it more easily still, and while these were growing I could use various substitutes beside those which I have named. "For," as the Forefathers sang—

> "we can make liquor to sweeten our lips
> Of pumpkins and parsnips and walnut-tree chips."[70]

Finally, as for salt, that grossest of groceries, to obtain this might be a fit occasion for a visit to the seashore, or, if I did without it altogether, I should probably drink the less water. I do not learn that the Indians ever troubled themselves to go after it.

Thus I could avoid all trade and barter, so far as my food was concerned, and having a shelter already, it would only remain to get clothing and fuel. The pantaloons which I now wear were woven in a farmer's family—thank Heaven there is so much virtue still in man; for I think the fall from the farmer to the operative as great and memorable as that from the man to the farmer—and in a new country fuel is an encumbrance. As for a habitat, if I were not permitted still to squat, I might purchase one acre at the same price for which the land I cultivated was sold—namely, eight dollars and eight cents. But as it was, I considered that I enhanced the value of the land by squatting on it.

There is a certain class of unbelievers who sometimes ask me such questions as, if I think that I can live on vegetable food alone; and to strike at the root of the matter at once—for the root is faith—I am accustomed to answer such, that I can live on board nails. If they cannot understand that, they cannot understand much that I have to say. For my part, I am glad to hear of experiments of this kind being tried; as that a young man tried for a fortnight to live on hard, raw corn on the ear, using his teeth for all mortar. The squirrel tribe tried the same and succeeded.

---

[70] From "New England's Annoyances," an anonymous verse from colonial times.

The human race is interested in these experiments, though a few old women who are incapacitated for them, or who own their thirds[71] in mills, may be alarmed.

My furniture, part of which I made myself, and the rest cost me nothing of which I have not rendered an account, consisted of a bed, a table, a desk, three chairs, a looking-glass three inches in diameter, a pair of tongs and andirons, a kettle, a skillet, and a frying-pan, a dipper, a wash-bowl, two knives and forks, three plates, one cup, one spoon, a jug for oil, a jug for molasses, and a japanned lamp. None is so poor that he need sit on a pumpkin. That is shiftlessness. There is a plenty of such chairs as I like best in the village garrets to be had for taking them away. Furniture! Thank God, I can sit and I can stand without the aid of a furniture warehouse. What man but a philosopher would not be ashamed to see his furniture packed in a cart and going up country exposed to the light of heaven and the eyes of men, a beggarly account of empty boxes? That is Spaulding's furniture. I could never tell from inspecting such a load whether it belonged to a so called rich man or a poor one; the owner always seemed poverty-stricken. Indeed, the more you have of such things the poorer you are. Each load looks as if it contained the contents of a dozen shanties; and if one shanty is poor, this is a dozen times as poor. Pray, for what do we *move* ever but to get rid of our furniture, our *exuviae;*[72] at last to go from this world to another newly furnished, and leave this to be burned? It is the same as if all these traps were buckled to a man's belt, and he could not move over the rough country where our lines are cast without dragging them—dragging his trap. He was a lucky fox that left his tail in the trap. The muskrat will gnaw his third leg off to be free. No wonder man has lost his elasticity. How often he is at a dead set! "Sir, if I may be so bold, what do you mean by a dead set?" If you are a seer, whenever you meet a man you will see all that he owns, ay, and much that he pretends to disown, behind him, even to his kitchen furniture and all the trumpery which he saves and will not burn, and he will appear to be harnessed to it and making what headway he can. I think that the man is at a dead set who has got through a knot hole or gateway where his sledge load of furniture cannot follow him. I cannot but feel compassion when I hear some trig, compact-looking man, seemingly free, all girded and ready, speak of his "furniture," as whether it is insured or not. "But what shall I do with my furniture?" My gay butterfly is entangled in a spider's web then. Even those who seem

[71] The "widow's portion" of an inheritance was legally set at a third.
[72] Castoffs.

for a long while not to have any, if you inquire more narrowly you will find have some stored in somebody's barn. I look upon England today as an old gentleman who is travelling with a great deal of baggage, trumpery which has accumulated from long housekeeping, which he has not the courage to burn; great trunk, little trunk, bandbox and bundle. Throw away the first three at least. It would surpass the powers of a well man nowadays to take up his bed and walk, and I should certainly advise a sick one to lay down his bed and run. When I have met an immigrant tottering under a bundle which contained his all—looking like an enormous wen which had grown out of the nape of his neck—I have pitied him, not because that was his all, but because he had all *that* to carry. If I have got to drag my trap, I will take care that it be a light one and do not nip me in a vital part. But perchance it would be wisest never to put one's paw into it.

I would observe, by the way, that it costs me nothing for curtains, for I have no gazers to shut out but the sun and moon, and I am willing that they should look in. The moon will not sour milk nor taint meat of mine, nor will the sun injure my furniture or fade my carpet, and if he is sometimes too warm a friend, I find it still better economy to retreat behind some curtain which nature has provided, than to add a single item to the details of housekeeping. A lady once offered me a mat, but as I had no room to spare within the house, nor time to spare within or without to shake it, I declined it, preferring to wipe my feet on the sod before my door. It is best to avoid the beginnings of evil.

Not long since I was present at the auction of a deacon's effects, for his life had not been ineffectual—

"The evil that men do lives after them."[73]

As usual, a great proportion was trumpery which had begun to accumulate in his father's day. Among the rest was a dried tapeworm. And now, after lying half a century in his garret and other dust holes, these things were not burned; instead of a *bonfire,* or purifying destruction of them, there was an *auction,* or increasing of them. The neighbors eagerly collected to view them, bought them all, and carefully transported them to their garrets and dust holes, to lie there till their estates are settled, when they will start again. When a man dies he kicks the dust.

The customs of same savage nations might, perchance, be profitably imitated by us, for they at least go through the semblance of casting their

---

[73] Shakespeare, *Julius Caesar* 3.3.

slough annually; they have the idea of the thing, whether they have the reality or not. Would it not be well if we were to celebrate such a "busk," or "feast of first fruits," as Bartram describes to have been the custom of the Mucclasse Indians?[74] "When a town celebrates the busk," says he, "having previously provided themselves with new clothes, new pots, pans, and other household utensils and furniture, they collect all their worn out clothes and other despicable things, sweep and cleanse their houses, squares, and the whole town, of their filth, which with all the remaining grain and other old provisions they cast together into one common heap, and consume it with fire. After having taken medicine, and fasted for three days, all the fire in the town is extinguished. During this fast they abstain from the gratification of every appetite and passion whatever. A general amnesty is proclaimed; all malefactors may return to their town."

"On the fourth morning, the high priest, by rubbing dry wood together, produces new fire in the public square, from whence every habitation in the town is supplied with the new and pure flame."

They then feast on the new corn and fruits and dance and sing for three days, "and the four following days they receive visits and rejoice with their friends from neighboring towns who have in like manner purified and prepared themselves."

The Mexicans also practised a similar purification at the end of every fifty-two years, in the belief that it was time for the world to come to an end.

I have scarcely heard of a truer sacrament, that is, as the dictionary defines it, "outward and visible sign of an inward and spiritual grace," than this, and I have no doubt that they were originally inspired directly from Heaven to do thus, though they have no biblical record of the revelation.

For more than five years I maintained myself thus solely by the labor of my hands, and I found, that by working about six weeks in a year, I could meet all the expenses of living. The whole of my winters, as well as most of my summers, I had free and clear for study. I have thoroughly tried school-keeping, and found that my expenses were in proportion, or rather out of proportion, to my income, for I was obliged to dress and train, not to say think and believe, accordingly, and I lost my time into the bargain. As I did not teach for the good of my fellow-man, but simply for a livelihood, this was a failure. I have tried trade; but I found that it would take

---

[74] William Bartram (1739–1823), American naturalist and anthropologist; from his *Travels Through North and South Carolina, Georgia, East and West Florida . . .* (1791).

ten years to get under way in that, and that then I should probably be on my way to the devil. I was actually afraid that I might by that time be doing what is called a good business. When formerly I was looking about to see what I could do for a living, some sad experience in conforming to the wishes of friends being fresh in my mind to tax my ingenuity, I thought often and seriously of picking huckleberries; that surely I could do, and its small profits might suffice—for my greatest skill has been to want but little—so little capital it required, so little distraction from my wonted moods, I foolishly thought. While my acquaintances went unhesitatingly into trade or the professions, I contemplated this occupation as most like theirs; ranging the hills all summer to pick the berries which came in my way, and thereafter carelessly dispose of them; so, to keep the flocks of Admetus.[75] I also dreamed that I might gather the wild herbs, or carry evergreens to such villagers as loved to be reminded of the woods, even to the city, by hay-cart loads. But I have since learned that trade curses every thing it handles; and though you trade in messages from heaven, the whole curse of trade attaches to the business.

As I preferred some things to others, and especially valued my freedom, as I could fare hard and yet succeed well, I did not wish to spend my time in earning rich carpets or other fine furniture, or delicate cookery, or a house in the Grecian or the Gothic style just yet. If there are any to whom it is no interruption to acquire these things, and who know how to use them when acquired, I relinquish to them the pursuit. Some are "industrious," and appear to love labor for its own sake, or perhaps because it keeps them out of worse mischief; to such I have at present nothing to say. Those who would not know what to do with more leisure than they now enjoy, I might advise to work twice as hard as they do—work till they pay for themselves, and get their free papers. For myself I found that the occupation of a day-laborer was the most independent of any, especially as it required only thirty or forty days in a year to support one. The laborer's day ends with the going down of the sun, and he is then free to devote himself to his chosen pursuit, independent of his labor; but his employer, who speculates from month to month, has no respite from one end of the year to the other.

In short, I am convinced, both by faith and experience, that to maintain one's self on this earth is not a hardship but a pastime, if we will live

[75] The Greek god Apollo, banished from Mount Olympus, kept the flocks of King Admetus of Pherae for a year, thus fulfilling an obligation he had incurred by slaying one of the Cyclops, the giants who made thunderbolts for Zeus. (See note 4, chap. 2.)

simply and wisely; as the pursuits of the simpler nations are still the sports of the more artificial. It is not necessary that a man should earn his living by the sweat of his brow, unless he sweats easier than I do.

One young man of my acquaintance, who has inherited some acres, told me that he thought he should live as I did, *if he had the means.* I would not have any one adopt *my* mode of living on any account; for, beside that before he has fairly learned it I may have found out another for myself, I desire that there may be as many different persons in the world as possible; but I would have each one be very careful to find out and pursue *his own* way, and not his father's or his mother's or his neighbor's instead. The youth may build or plant or sail, only let him not be hindered from doing that which he tells me he would like to do. It is by a mathematical point only that we are wise, as the sailor or the fugitive slave keeps the polestar in his eye; but that is sufficient guidance for all our life. We may not arrive at our port within a calculable period, but we would preserve the true course.

Undoubtedly, in this case, what is true for one is truer still for a thousand, as a large house is not proportionally more expensive than a small one, since one roof may cover, one cellar underlie, and one wall separate several apartments. But for my part, I preferred the solitary dwelling. Moreover, it will commonly be cheaper to build the whole yourself than to convince another of the advantage of the common wall; and when you have done this, the common partition, to be much cheaper, must be a thin one, and that other may prove a bad neighbor, and also not keep his side in repair. The only cooperation which is commonly possible is exceedingly partial and superficial; and what little true cooperation there is, is as if it were not, being a harmony inaudible to men. If a man has faith he will cooperate with equal faith every where; if he has not faith, he will continue to live like the rest of the world, whatever company he is joined to. To cooperate, in the highest as well as the lowest sense, means to *get our living together.* I heard it proposed lately that two young men should travel together over the world, the one without money, earning his means as he went, before the mast and behind the plough, the other carrying a bill of exchange in his pocket. It was easy to see that they could not long be companions or cooperate, since one would not *operate* at all. They would part at the first interesting crisis in their adventures. Above all, as I have implied, the man who goes alone can start today; but he who travels with another must wait till that other is ready, and it may be a long time before they get off.

But all this is very selfish, I have heard some of my townsmen say. I confess that I have hitherto indulged very little in philanthropic enterprises.

I have made some sacrifices to a sense of duty, and among others have sacrificed this pleasure also. There are those who have used all their arts to persuade me to undertake the support of some poor family in the town; and if I had nothing to do—for the devil finds employment for the idle—I might try my hand at some such pastime as that. However, when I have thought to indulge myself in this respect, and lay their Heaven under an obligation by maintaining certain poor persons in all respects as comfortably as I maintain myself, and have even ventured so far as to make them the offer, they have one and all unhesitatingly preferred to remain poor. While my townsmen and women are devoted in so many ways to the good of their fellows, I trust that one at least may be spared to other and less humane pursuits. You must have a genius for charity as well as for any thing else. As for Doing-good, that is one of the professions which are full. Moreover, I have tried it fairly, and, strange as it may seem, am satisfied that it does not agree with my constitution. Probably I should not consciously and deliberately forsake my particular calling to do the good which society demands of me, to save the universe from annihilation; and I believe that a like but infinitely greater steadfastness elsewhere is all that now preserves it. But I would not stand between any man and his genius; and to him who does this work, which I decline, with his whole heart and soul and life, I would say, Persevere, even if the world call it doing evil, as it is most likely they will.

I am far from supposing that my case is a peculiar one; no doubt many of my readers would make a similar defence. At doing something—I will not engage that my neighbors shall pronounce it good—I do not hesitate to say that I should be a capital fellow to hire; but what that is, it is for my employer to find out. What *good* I do, in the common sense of that word, must be aside from my main path, and for the most part wholly unintended. Men say, practically, Begin where you are and such as you are, without aiming mainly to become of more worth, and with kindness aforethought go about doing good. If I were to preach at all in this strain, I should say rather, Set about being good. As if the sun should stop when he had kindled his fires up to the splendor of a moon or a star of the sixth magnitude, and go about like a Robin Goodfellow,[76] peeping in at every cottage window, inspiring lunatics, and tainting meats, and making darkness visible, instead of steadily increasing his genial heat and beneficence till he is of such brightness that no mortal can look him in the face, and then, and in the mean while too, going about the world in his own orbit, doing it good, or rather, as a truer philosophy has discovered, the world

[76] Puck, the impish sprite of British folklore.

going about him getting good. When Phaeton, wishing to prove his heavenly birth by his beneficence, had the sun's chariot but one day, and drove out of the beaten track, he burned several blocks of houses in the lower streets of heaven, and scorched the surface of the earth, and dried up every spring, and made the great desert of Sahara, till at length Jupiter hurled him headlong to the earth with a thunderbolt, and the sun, through grief at his death, did not shine for a year.[77]

There is no odor so bad as that which arises from goodness tainted. It is human, it is divine, carrion. If I knew for a certainty that a man was coming to my house with the conscious design of doing me good, I should run for my life, as from that dry and parching wind of the African deserts called the simoom, which fills the mouth and nose and ears and eyes with dust till you are suffocated, for fear that I should get some of his good done to me—some of its virus mingled with my blood. No—in this case I would rather suffer evil the natural way. A man is not a good *man* to me because he will feed me if I should be starving, or warm me if I should be freezing, or pull me out of a ditch if I should ever fall into one. I can find you a Newfoundland dog that will do as much. Philanthropy is not love for one's fellowman in the broadest sense. Howard[78] was no doubt an exceedingly kind and worthy man in his way, and has his reward; but, comparatively speaking, what are a hundred Howards to *us,* if their philanthropy do not help *us* in our best estate, when we are most worthy to be helped? I never heard of a philanthropic meeting in which it was sincerely proposed to do any good to me, or the like of me.

The Jesuits[79] were quite balked by those Indians who, being burned at the stake, suggested new modes of torture to their tormentors. Being superior to physical suffering, it sometimes chanced that they were superior to any consolation which the missionaries could offer; and the law to do as you would be done by fell with less persuasiveness on the ears of those, who, for their part, did not care how they were done by, who loved their enemies after a new fashion, and came very near freely forgiving them all they did.

Be sure that you give the poor the aid they most need, though it be your example which leaves them far behind. If you give money, spend yourself with it, and do not merely abandon it to them. We make curious mistakes sometimes. Often the poor man is not so cold and hungry as he

[77]Thoreau here summarizes the Greek myth of Phaeton, son of Helios, the sun.
[78]John Howard (1726–1790), English philanthropist and pioneer in prison reform who had written a book titled *The State of the Prisons in England and Wales . . .* (1780).
[79]The Society of Jesus, a Roman Catholic religious order.

is dirty and ragged and gross. It is partly his taste, and not merely his misfortune. If you give him money, he will perhaps buy more rags with it. I was wont to pity the clumsy Irish laborers who cut ice on the pond, in such mean and ragged clothes, while I shivered in my more tidy and somewhat more fashionable garments, till, one bitter cold day, one who had slipped into the water came to my house to warm him, and I saw him strip off three pairs of pants and two pairs of stockings ere he got down to the skin, though they were dirty and ragged enough, it is true, and that he could afford to refuse the *extra* garments which I offered him, he had so many *intra* ones. This ducking was the very thing he needed. Then I began to pity myself, and I saw that it would be a greater charity to bestow on me a flannel shirt than a whole slop-shop on him. There are a thousand hacking at the branches of evil to one who is striking at the root, and it may be that he who bestows the largest amount of time and money on the needy is doing the most by his mode of life to produce that misery which he strives in vain to relieve. It is the pious slave-breeder devoting the proceeds of every tenth slave to buy a Sunday's liberty for the rest. Some show their kindness to the poor by employing them in their kitchens. Would they not be kinder if they employed themselves there? You boast of spending a tenth part of your income in charity; may be you should spend the nine tenths so, and done with it. Society recovers only a tenth part of the property then. Is this owing to the generosity of him in whose possession it is found, or to the remissness of the officers of justice?

Philanthropy is almost the only virtue which is sufficiently appreciated by mankind. Nay, it is greatly overrated; and it is our selfishness which overrates it. A robust poor man, one sunny day here in Concord, praised a fellow-townsman to me, because, as he said, he was kind to the poor; meaning himself. The kind uncles and aunts of the race are more esteemed than its true spiritual fathers and mothers. I once heard a reverend lecturer on England, a man of learning and intelligence, after enumerating her scientific, literary, and political worthies, Shakespeare, Bacon, Cromwell, Milton, Newton, and others, speak next of her Christian heroes, whom, as if his profession required it of him, he elevated to a place far above all the rest, as the greatest of the great. They were Penn, Howard, and Mrs. Fry.[80] Every one must feel the falsehood and cant of this. The last were not England's best men and women; only, perhaps, her best philanthropists.

I would not subtract any thing from the praise that is due to philanthropy, but merely demand justice for all who by their lives and works are

[80]William Penn (1644–1718), founder of Pennsylvania; John Howard (see note 78); Elizabeth Gurney Fry (1780–1845), English philanthropist and prison reformer.

a blessing to mankind. I do not value chiefly a man's uprightness and benevolence, which are, as it were, his stem and leaves. Those plants of whose greenness withered we make herb tea for the sick, serve but a humble use, and are most employed by quacks. I want the flower and fruit of a man; that some fragrance be wafted over from him to me, and some ripeness flavor our intercourse. His goodness must not be a partial and transitory act, but a constant superfluity, which costs him nothing and of which he is unconscious. This is a charity that hides a multitude of sins.[81] The philanthropist too often surrounds mankind with the remembrance of his own cast-off griefs as an atmosphere, and calls it sympathy. We should impart our courage, and not our despair, our health and ease, and not our disease, and take care that this does not spread by contagion. From what southern plains comes up the voice of wailing? Under what latitudes reside the heathen to whom we would send light? Who is that intemperate and brutal man whom we would redeem? If any thing ail a man, so that he does not perform his functions, if he have a pain in his bowels even—for that is the seat of sympathy—he forthwith sets about reforming—the world. Being a microcosm himself, he discovers, and it is a true discovery, and he is the man to make it—that the world has been eating green apples; to his eyes, in fact, the globe itself is a great green apple, which there is danger awful to think of that the children of men will nibble before it is ripe; and straightway his drastic philanthropy seeks out the Esquimaux and the Patagonian,[82] and embraces the populous Indian and Chinese villages; and thus, by a few years of philanthropic activity, the powers in the mean while using him for their own ends, no doubt, he cures himself of his dyspepsia, the globe acquires a faint blush on one or both of its cheeks, as if it were beginning to be ripe, and life loses its crudity and is once more sweet and wholesome to live. I never dreamed of any enormity greater than I have committed. I never knew, and never shall know, a worse man than myself.

I believe that what so saddens the reformer is not his sympathy with his fellows in distress, but, though he be the holiest son of God, is his private ail. Let this be righted, let the spring come to him, the morning rise over his couch, and he will forsake his generous companions without apology. My excuse for not lecturing against the use of tobacco is, that I never chewed it; that is a penalty which reformed tobacco-chewers have to pay; though there are things enough I have chewed, which I could lecture against. If you should ever be betrayed into any of these philanthropies, do

[81] Cf. 1 Pet. 4.8: "And above all things have fervent charity among yourselves: for charity shall cover the multitude of sins."
[82] Inhabitants, respectively, of the furthest northern and southern reaches of the Americas.

not let your left hand know what your right hand does,[83] for it is not worth knowing. Rescue the drowning and tie your shoe-strings. Take your time, and set about some free labor.

Our manners have been corrupted by communication with the saints. Our hymn-books resound with a melodious cursing of God and enduring him forever. One would say that even the prophets and redeemers had rather consoled the fears than confirmed the hopes of man. There is nowhere recorded a simple and irrepressible satisfaction with the gift of life, any memorable praise of God. All health and success does me good, however far off and withdrawn it may appear; all disease and failure helps to make me sad and does me evil, however much sympathy it may have with me or I with it. If, then, we would indeed restore mankind by truly Indian, botanic, magnetic, or natural means, let us first be as simple and well as Nature ourselves, dispel the clouds which hang over our own brows, and take up a little life into our pores. Do not stay to be an overseer of the poor, but endeavor to become one of the worthies of the world.

I read in the Gulistan, or Flower Garden, of Sheik Sadi of Shiraz,[84] that "They asked a wise man, saying; Of the many celebrated trees which the Most High God has created lofty and umbrageous, they call none azad, or free, excepting the cypress, which bears no fruit; what mystery is there in this? He replied; Each has its appropriate produce, and appointed season, during the continuance of which it is fresh and blooming, and during their absence dry and withered; to neither of which states is the cypress exposed, being always flourishing; and of this nature are the azads, or religious independents—Fix not thy heart on that which is transitory; for the Dijlah, or Tigris, will continue to flow through Bagdad after the race of caliphs is extinct: if thy hand has plenty, be liberal as the date tree; but if it affords nothing to give away, be an azad, or free man, like the cypress."

Complemental Verses

THE PRETENSIONS OF POVERTY

Thou dost presume too much, poor needy wretch,
To claim a station in the firmament,
Because thy humble cottage, or thy tub,
Nurses some lazy or pedantic virtue

---

[83] Cf. Matt. 6.3: "But when thou doest alms, let not thy left hand know what thy right hand doeth."

[84] Sheikh Muslihu'd-din Saadi (1184?–1291), Persian poet born in Shiraz; from his *The Gulistan, or Rose Garden* (1258); Emerson wrote a preface to a later edition of this popular work.

5 In the cheap sunshine or by shady springs,
With roots and pot-herbs; where thy right hand,
Tearing those humane passions from the mind,
Upon whose stocks fair blooming virtues flourish,
Degradeth nature, and benumbeth sense,
10 And, Gorgon-like, turns active men to stone
We not require the dull society
Of your necessitated temperance,
Or that unnatural stupidity
That knows nor joy nor sorrow; nor your forc'd
15 Falsely exalted passive fortitude
Above the active. This low abject brood,
That fix their seats in mediocrity,
Become your servile minds; but we advance
Such virtues only as admit excess,
20 Brave, bounteous acts, regal magnificence,
All-seeing prudence, magnanimity
That knows no bound, and that heroic virtue
For which antiquity hath left no name,
But patterns only, such as Hercules,
25 Achilles, Theseus. Back to thy loath'd cell;
And when thou seest the new enlightened sphere,
Study to know but what those worthies were.[85]

T. Carew

CHAPTER TWO

Where I Lived, and What I Lived For

At a certain season of our life we are accustomed to consider every spot as the possible site of a house. I have thus surveyed the country on every side within a dozen miles of where I live. In imagination I have bought all the farms in succession, for all were to be bought, and I knew their price. I walked over each farmer's premises, tasted his wild apples, discoursed on husbandry with him, took his farm at his price, at any price, mortgaging it to him in my mind; even put a higher price on it—took every thing but

[85]From the masque *Coelum Britannicum* by Thomas Carew (1595?–1639?), English poet. Thoreau added the title.

a deed of it—took his word for his deed, for I dearly love to talk—cultivated it, and him too to some extent, I trust, and withdrew when I had enjoyed it long enough, leaving him to carry it on. This experience entitled me to be regarded as a sort of real-estate broker by my friends. Wherever I sat, there I might live, and the landscape radiated from me accordingly. What is a house but a *sedes*, a seat?—better if a country seat. I discovered many a site for a house not likely to be soon improved, which some might have thought too far from the village, but to my eyes the village was too far from it. Well, there I might live, I said; and there I did live, for an hour, a summer and a winter life; saw how I could let the years run off, buffet the winter through, and see the spring come in. The future inhabitants of this region, wherever they may place their houses, may be sure that they have been anticipated. An afternoon sufficed to lay out the land into orchard, woodlot, and pasture, and to decide what fine oaks or pines should be left to stand before the door, and whence each blasted tree could be seen to the best advantage; and then I let it lie, fallow perchance, for a man is rich in proportion to the number of things which he can afford to let alone.

My imagination carried me so far that I even had the refusal of several farms—the refusal was all I wanted—but I never got my fingers burned by actual possession. The nearest that I came to actual possession was when I bought the Hollowell place, and had begun to sort my seeds, and collected materials with which to make a wheelbarrow to carry it on or off with; but before the owner gave me a deed of it, his wife—every man has such a wife—changed her mind and wished to keep it, and he offered me ten dollars to release him. Now, to speak the truth, I had but ten cents in the world, and it surpassed my arithmetic to tell, if I was that man who had ten cents, or who had a farm, or ten dollars, or all together. However, I let him keep the ten dollars and the farm too, for I had carried it far enough; or rather, to be generous, I sold him the farm for just what I gave for it, and, as he was not a rich man, made him a present of ten dollars, and still had my ten cents, and seeds, and materials for a wheelbarrow left. I found thus that I had been a rich man without any damage to my poverty. But I retained the landscape, and I have since annually carried off what it yielded without a wheelbarrow. With respect to landscapes—

> "I am monarch of all I *survey*,
> My right there is none to dispute."[1]

---

[1]William Cowper (1731–1800), from "Verses Supposed to Be Written by Alexander Selkirk, during His Solitary Abode in the Island of Juan Fernandez." Thoreau, who worked as a surveyor, italicized the word *survey*.

I have frequently seen a poet withdraw, having enjoyed the most valuable part of a farm, while the crusty farmer supposed that he had got a few wild apples only. Why, the owner does not know it for many years when a poet has put his farm in rhyme, the most admirable kind of invisible fence, has fairly impounded it, milked it, skimmed it, and got all the cream, and left the farmer only the skimmed milk.

The real attractions of the Hollowell farm, to me, were; its complete retirement, being about two miles from the village, half a mile from the nearest neighbor, and separated from the highway by a broad field; its bounding on the river, which the owner said protected it by its fogs from frosts in the spring, though that was nothing to me; the gray color and ruinous state of the house and barn, and the dilapidated fences, which put such an interval between me and the last occupant; the hollow and lichen-covered apple trees, gnawed by rabbits, showing what kind of neighbors I should have; but above all, the recollection I had of it from my earliest voyages up the river, when the house was concealed behind a dense grove of red maples, through which I heard the house-dog bark. I was in haste to buy it, before the proprietor finished getting out some rocks, cutting down the hollow apple trees, and grubbing up some young birches which had sprung up in the pasture, or, in short, had made any more of his improvements. To enjoy these advantages I was ready to carry it on; like Atlas,[2] to take the world on my shoulders—I never heard what compensation he received for that—and do all those things which had no other motive or excuse but that I might pay for it and be unmolested in my possession of it; for I knew all the while that it would yield the most abundant crop of the kind I wanted if I could only afford to let it alone. But it turned out as I have said.

All that I could say, then, with respect to farming on a large scale (I have always cultivated a garden) was that I had had my seeds ready. Many think that seeds improve with age. I have no doubt that time discriminates between the good and the bad; and when at last I shall plant, I shall be less likely to be disappointed. But I would say to my fellows, once for all, As long as possible live free and uncommitted. It makes but little difference whether you are committed to a farm or the county jail.

Old Cato, whose "De Re Rustica" is my "Cultivator,"[3] says, and the only translation I have seen makes sheer nonsense of the passage, "When

---

[2] In Greek mythology, Atlas was punished for taking part in the revolt of the Titans against the gods by being required to support the world on his shoulders.

[3] Roman statesman (239–149 B.C.E.), who also wrote on agricultural subjects, notably in *De agri cultura* and *De re rustica.*

you think of getting a farm, turn it thus in your mind, not to buy greedily; nor spare your pains to look at it, and do not think it enough to go round it once. The oftener you go there the more it will please you, if it is good." I think I shall not buy greedily, but go round and round it as long as I live, and be buried in it first, that it may please me the more at last.

The present was my next experiment of this kind, which I purpose to describe more at length, for convenience, putting the experience of two years into one. As I have said, I do not propose to write an ode to dejection, but to brag as lustily as chanticleer in the morning, standing on his roost, if only to wake my neighbors up.

When first I took up my abode in the woods, that is, began to spend my nights as well as days there, which, by accident, was on Independence day, or the fourth of July, 1845, my house was not finished for winter, but was merely a defence against the rain, without plastering or chimney, the walls being of rough weather-stained boards, with wide chinks, which made it cool at night. The upright white hewn studs and freshly planed door and window casings gave it a clean and airy look, especially in the morning, when its timbers were saturated with dew, so that I fancied that by noon some sweet gum would exude from them. To my imagination it retained throughout the day more or less of this auroral character, reminding me of a certain house on a mountain which I had visited the year before. This was an airy and unplastered cabin, fit to entertain a travelling god, and where a goddess might trail her garments. The winds which passed over my dwelling were such as sweep over the ridges of mountains, bearing the broken strains, or celestial parts only, of terrestrial music. The morning wind forever blows, the poem of creation is uninterrupted; but few are the ears that hear it. Olympus[4] is but the outside of the earth every where.

The only house I had been the owner of before, if I except a boat, was a tent, which I used occasionally when making excursions in the summer, and this is still rolled up in my garret; but the boat, after passing from hand to hand,[5] has gone down the stream of time. With this more substantial shelter about me, I had made some progress toward settling in the world. This frame, so slightly clad, was a sort of crystallization around me, and reacted on the builder. It was suggestive somewhat as a picture in outlines. I did not need to go out doors to take the air, for the atmosphere within had lost none of its freshness. It was not so much within doors as behind a door where I sat, even in the rainiest weather. The Harivansa says, "An

[4]In Greek mythology, Mount Olympus is the home of the gods.
[5]Nathaniel Hawthorne was its next owner.

abode without birds is like a meat without seasoning."[6] Such was not my abode, for I found myself suddenly neighbor to the birds; not by having imprisoned one, but having caged myself near them. I was not only nearer to some of those which commonly frequent the garden and the orchard, but to those wilder and more thrilling songsters of the forest which never, or rarely, serenade a villager—the wood-thrush, the veery, the scarlet tanager, the field-sparrow, the whippoorwill, and many others.

I was seated by the shore of a small pond, about a mile and a half south of the village of Concord and somewhat higher than it, in the midst of an extensive wood between that town and Lincoln, and about two miles south of that our only field known to fame, Concord Battle Ground;[7] but I was so low in the woods that the opposite shore, half a mile off, like the rest, covered with wood, was my most distant horizon. For the first week, whenever I looked out on the pond it impressed me like a tarn high up on the side of a mountain, its bottom far above the surface of other lakes, and, as the sun arose, I saw it throwing off its nightly clothing of mist, and here and there, by degrees, its soft ripples or its smooth reflecting surface was revealed, while the mists, like ghosts, were stealthily withdrawing in every direction into the woods, as at the breaking up of some nocturnal conventicle. The very dew seemed to hang upon the trees later into the day than usual, as on the sides of mountains.

This small lake was of most value as a neighbor in the intervals of a gentle rain storm in August, when, both air and water being perfectly still, but the sky overcast, mid-afternoon had all the serenity of evening, and the wood-thrush sang around, and was heard from shore to shore. A lake like this is never smoother than at such a time; and the clear portion of the air above it being shallow and darkened by clouds, the water, full of light and reflections, becomes a lower heaven itself so much the more important. From a hill-top near by, where the wood had been recently cut off, there was a pleasing vista southward across the pond, through a wide indentation in the hills which form the shore there, where their opposite sides sloping toward each other suggested a stream flowing out in that direction through a wooded valley, but stream there was none. That way I looked between and over the near green hills to some distant and higher ones in the horizon, tinged with blue. Indeed, by standing on tiptoe I could catch a glimpse of some of the peaks of the still bluer and more distant mountain ranges in the northwest, those true-blue coins from heaven's own mint, and also of some portion of the village. But in other directions, even

[6] Hindu epic poem.
[7] Site of the opening battle of the Revolutionary War, April 19, 1775.

from this point, I could not see over or beyond the woods which surrounded me. It is well to have some water in your neighborhood, to give buoyancy to and float the earth. One value even of the smallest well is, that when you look into it you see that earth is not continent but insular. This is as important as that it keeps butter cool. When I looked across the pond from this peak toward the Sudbury meadows, which in time of flood I distinguished elevated perhaps by a mirage in their seething valley, like a coin in a basin, all the earth beyond the pond appeared like a thin crust insulated and floated even by this small sheet of intervening water, and I was reminded that this on which I dwelt was but *dry land*.

Though the view from my door was still more contracted, I did not feel crowded or confined in the least. There was pasture enough for my imagination. The low shrub-oak plateau to which the opposite shore arose, stretched away toward the prairies of the West and the steppes of Tartary,[8] affording ample room for all the roving families of men. "There are none happy in the world but beings who enjoy freely a vast horizon"—said Damodara,[9] when his herds required new and larger pastures.

Both place and time were changed, and I dwelt nearer to those parts of the universe and to those eras in history which had most attracted me. Where I lived was as far off as many a region viewed nightly by astronomers. We are wont to imagine rare and delectable places in some remote and more celestial corner of the system, behind the constellation of Cassiopeia's Chair, far from noise and disturbance. I discovered that my house actually had its site in such a withdrawn, but forever new and unprofaned, part of the universe. If it were worth the while to settle in those parts near to the Pleiades or the Hyades,[10] to Aldebaran or Altair,[11] then I was really there, or at an equal remoteness from the life which I had left behind, dwindled and twinkling with as fine a ray to my nearest neighbor, and to be seen only in moonless nights by him. Such was that part of creation where I had squatted—

"There was a shepherd that did live,
And held his thoughts as high
As were the mounts whereon his flocks
Did hourly feed him by."[12]

[8] An area of Central Asia.
[9] One of the names for the Hindu god Krishna, the central figure of the *Harivansa*.
[10] Like Cassiopeia's Chair, constellations of stars.
[11] Bright stars.
[12] A Jacobean poem published in *Bodenham's 'Belvedére; Or, the Garden of the Muses* (1600).

What should we think of the shepherd's life if his flocks always wandered to higher pastures than his thoughts?

Every morning was a cheerful invitation to make my life of equal simplicity, and I may say innocence, with Nature herself. I have been as sincere a worshipper of Aurora as the Greeks. I got up early and bathed in the pond; that was a religious exercise, and one of the best things which I did. They say that characters were engraven on the bathing tub of king Tching-thang[13] to this effect: "Renew thyself completely each day; do it again, and again, and forever again." I can understand that. Morning brings back the heroic ages. I was as much affected by the faint hum of a mosquito making its invisible and unimaginable tour through my apartment at earliest dawn, when I was sitting with door and windows open, as I could be by any trumpet that ever sang of fame. It was Homer's requiem; itself an Iliad and Odyssey in the air, singing its own wrath and wanderings. There was something cosmical about it; a standing advertisement, till forbidden, of the everlasting vigor and fertility of the world. The morning, which is the most memorable season of the day, is the awakening hour. Then there is least somnolence in us; and for an hour, at least, some part of us awakes which slumbers all the rest of the day and night. Little is to be expected of that day, if it can be called a day, to which we are not awakened by our Genius, but by the mechanical nudgings of some servitor, are not awakened by our own newly-acquired force and aspirations from within, accompanied by the undulations of celestial music, instead of factory bells, and a fragrance filling the air—to a higher life than we fell asleep from; and thus the darkness bear its fruit, and prove itself to be good, no less than the light. That man who does not believe that each day contains an earlier, more sacred, and auroral hour than he has yet profaned, has despaired of life, and is pursuing a descending and darkening way. After a partial cessation of his sensuous life, the soul of man, or its organs rather, are reinvigorated each day, and his Genius tries again what noble life it can make. All memorable events, I should say, transpire in morning time and in a morning atmosphere. The Vedas[14] say, "All intelligences awake with the morning." Poetry and art, and the fairest and most memorable of the actions of men, date from such an hour. All poets and heroes, like Memnon, are the children of Aurora,[15] and emit their music at sunrise. To him whose elastic and vigorous thought keeps pace with the

[13] Ch'en T'ang, founder for the Shang dynasty (1766–1123 B.C.E.).

[14] Hindu scripture.

[15] In Greek mythology, Memnon was the son of Tithonus and Eos (or Aurora, Dawn); his colossal statue, near Egyptian Thebes, was said to emit a musical sound when the first rays of the morning sun struck it.

sun, the day is a perpetual morning. It matters not what the clocks say or the attitudes and labors of men. Morning is when I am awake and there is a dawn in me. Moral reform is the effort to throw off sleep. Why is it that men give so poor an account of their day if they have not been slumbering? They are not such poor calculators. If they had not been overcome with drowsiness they would have performed something. The millions are awake enough for physical labor; but only one in a million is awake enough for effective intellectual exertion, only one in a hundred millions to a poetic or divine life. To be awake is to be alive. I have never yet met a man who was quite awake. How could I have looked him in the face?

We must learn to reawaken and keep ourselves awake, not by mechanical aids, but by an infinite expectation of the dawn, which does not forsake us in our soundest sleep. I know of no more encouraging fact than the unquestionable ability of man to elevate his life by a conscious endeavor. It is something to be able to paint a particular picture, or to carve a statue, and so to make a few objects beautiful; but it is far more glorious to carve and paint the very atmosphere and medium through which we look, which morally we can do. To affect the quality of the day, that is the highest of arts. Every man is tasked to make his life, even in its details, worthy of the contemplation of his most elevated and critical hour. If we refused, or rather used up, such paltry information as we get, the oracles would distinctly inform us how this might be done.

I went to the woods because I wished to live deliberately, to front only the essential facts of life, and see if I could not learn what it had to teach, and not, when I came to die, discover that I had not lived. I did not wish to live what was not life, living is so dear; nor did I wish to practise resignation, unless it was quite necessary. I wanted to live deep and suck out all the marrow of life, to live so sturdily and Spartan-like[16] as to put to rout all that was not life, to cut a broad swath and shave close, to drive life into a corner, and reduce it to its lowest terms, and, if it proved to be mean, why then to get the whole and genuine meanness of it, and publish its meanness to the world; or if it were sublime, to know it by experience, and be able to give a true account of it in my next excursion. For most men, it appears to me, are in a strange uncertainty about it, whether it is of the devil or of God, and have *somewhat hastily* concluded that it is the chief end of man here to "glorify God and enjoy him forever."[17]

---

[16]The Spartans of ancient Greece emphasized a tough and austere life as part of their preparation for military skill.

[17]The Shorter Catechism in the *New England Primer* begins, "Man's chief End is to Glorify God, and to Enjoy Him for ever."

Still we live meanly, like ants; though the fable tells us that we were long ago changed into men;[18] like pygmies we fight with cranes;[19] it is error upon error, and clout upon clout, and our best virtue has for its occasion a superfluous and evitable wretchedness. Our life is frittered away by detail. An honest man has hardly need to count more than his ten fingers, or in extreme cases he may add his ten toes, and lump the rest. Simplicity, simplicity, simplicity! I say, let your affairs be as two or three, and not a hundred or a thousand; instead of a million count half a dozen, and keep your accounts on your thumb nail. In the midst of this chopping sea of civilized life, such are the clouds and storms and quicksands and thousand-and-one items to be allowed for, that a man has to live, if he would not founder and go to the bottom and not make his port at all, by dead reckoning and he must be a great calculator indeed who succeeds. Simplify, simplify. Instead of three meals a day, if it be necessary eat but one; instead of a hundred dishes, five; and reduce other things in proportion. Our life is like a German Confederacy, made up of petty states, with its boundary forever fluctuating, so that even a German cannot tell you how it is bounded at any moment.[20] The nation itself, with all its so called internal improvements, which, by the way, are all external and superficial, is just such an unwieldy and overgrown establishment, cluttered with furniture and tripped up by its own traps, ruined by luxury and heedless expense, by want of calculation and a worthy aim, as the million households in the land; and the only cure for it as for them is in a rigid economy, a stern and more than Spartan simplicity of life and elevation of purpose. It lives too fast. Men think that it is essential that the *Nation* have commerce, and export ice, and talk through a telegraph, and ride thirty miles an hour, without a doubt, whether *they* do or not; but whether we should live like baboons or like men, is a little uncertain. If we do not get out sleepers,[21] and forge rails, and devote days and nights to the work, but go to tinkering upon our *lives* to improve *them,* who will build railroads? And if railroads are not built, how shall we get to heaven in season? But if we stay at home and mind our business, who will want railroads? We do not ride on the railroad; it rides upon us. Did you ever think what those sleepers are that underlie the railroad? Each one is a man, an Irishman, or a Yankee man. The rails are laid on them, and they are covered with sand, and the cars

[18] In Greek mythology, Zeus turned ants into men.

[19] The battle of the pygmies and the cranes is narrated in book 3 of Homer's *Iliad.*

[20] In Thoreau's time, no single German nation existed, but from 1815 to 1866 there was a nebulous confederation of "petty states."

[21] The crossties upon which rails are set.

run smoothly over them. They are sound sleepers, I assure you. And every few years a new lot is laid down and run over; so that, if some have the pleasure of riding on a rail, others have the misfortune to be ridden upon. And when they run over a man that is walking in his sleep, a supernumerary sleeper in the wrong position, and wake him up, they suddenly stop the cars, and make a hue and cry about it, as if this were an exception. I am glad to know that it takes a gang of men for every five miles to keep the sleepers down and level in their beds as it is, for this is a sign that they may sometime get up again.

Why should we live with such hurry and waste of life? We are determined to be starved before we are hungry. Men say that a stitch in time saves nine, and so they take a thousand stitches today to save nine tomorrow. As for *work,* we haven't any of any consequence. We have the Saint Vitus' dance,[22] and cannot possibly keep our heads still. If I should only give a few pulls at the parish bell-rope, as for a fire, that is, without setting the bell, there is hardly a man on his farm in the outskirts of Concord, notwithstanding that press of engagements which was his excuse so many times this morning, nor a boy, nor a woman, I might also say, but would forsake all and follow that sound, not mainly to save property from the flames, but, if we will confess the truth, much more to see it burn, since burn it must, and we, be it known, did not set it on fire—or to see it put out, and have a hand in it, if that is done as handsomely; yes, even if it were the parish church itself. Hardly a man takes a half hour's nap after dinner, but when he wakes he holds up his head and asks, "What's the news?" as if the rest of mankind had stood his sentinels. Some give directions to be waked every half hour, doubtless for no other purpose; and then, to pay for it, they tell what they have dreamed. After a night's sleep the news is as indispensable as the breakfast. "Pray tell me any thing new that has happened to a man any where on this globe,"—and he reads it over his coffee and rolls, that a man has had his eyes gouged out this morning on the Wachito River;[23] never dreaming the while that he lives in the dark unfathomed mammoth cave of this world, and has but the rudiment of an eye himself.

For my part, I could easily do without the post office. I think that there are very few important communications made through it. To speak critically, I never received more than one or two letters in my life—I wrote this some years ago—that were worth the postage. The penny-post is, commonly, an institution through which you seriously offer a man that penny

---

[22] A nervous disease primarily marked by involuntary jerky body movements.

[23] A tributary of the Red River that runs through Arkansas and Louisiana.

for his thoughts which is so often safely offered in jest. And I am sure that I never read any memorable news in a newspaper. If we read of one man robbed, or murdered, or killed by accident, or one house burned, or one vessel wrecked, or one steamboat blown up, or one cow run over on the Western Railroad, or one mad dog killed, or one lot of grasshoppers in the winter—we never need read of another. One is enough. If you are acquainted with the principle, what do you care for a myriad instances and applications? To a philosopher all *news,* as it is called, is gossip, and they who edit and read it are old women over their tea. Yet not a few are greedy after this gossip. There was such a rush, as I hear, the other day at one of the offices to learn the foreign news by the last arrival, that several large squares of plate glass belonging to the establishment were broken by the pressure—news which I seriously think a ready wit might write a twelvemonth or twelve years beforehand with sufficient accuracy. As for Spain, for instance, if you know how to throw in Don Carlos and the Infanta, and Don Pedro and Seville and Granada,[24] from time to time in the right proportions—they may have changed the names a little since I saw the papers—and serve up a bullfight when other entertainments fail, it will be true to the letter, and give us as good an idea of the exact state or ruin of things in Spain as the most succinct and lucid reports under this head in the newspapers: and as for England, almost the last significant scrap of news from that quarter was the revolution of 1649; and if you have learned the history of her crops for an average year, you never need attend to that thing again, unless your speculations are of a merely pecuniary character. If one may judge who rarely looks into the newspapers, nothing new does ever happen in foreign parts, a French revolution not excepted.

What news! how much more important to know what that is which was never old! "Kieou-he-yu (great dignitary of the state of Wei) sent a man to Khoung-tseu to know his news. Khoung-tseu caused the messenger to be seated near him, and questioned him in these teams: What is your master doing? The messenger answered with respect: My master desires to diminish the number of his faults, but he cannot come to the end of them. The messenger being gone, the philosopher remarked: What a worthy messenger! What a worthy messenger!"[25] The preacher, instead of vexing the ears of drowsy farmers on their day of rest at the end of the week—for Sunday is the fit conclusion of an ill-spent week, and not the fresh and brave beginning of a new one—with this one other draggletail of a ser-

[24]People and places involved in the shifting royal politics of Spain, Brazil, and Portugal during the 1830s and 1840s.

[25]Related by Confucius in *Analects* 14.

mon, should shout with thundering voice—"Pause! Avast! Why so seeming fast, but deadly slow?"

Shams and delusions are esteemed for soundest truths, while reality is fabulous. If men would steadily observe realities only, and not allow themselves to be deluded, life, to compare it with such things as we know, would be like a fairy tale and the Arabian Nights' Entertainments.[26] If we respected only what is inevitable and has a right to be, music and poetry would resound along the streets. When we are unhurried and wise, we perceive that only great and worthy things have any permanent and absolute existence—that petty fears and petty pleasures are but the shadow of the reality. This is always exhilarating and sublime. By closing the eyes and slumbering, and consenting to be deceived by shows, men establish and confirm their daily life of routine and habit every where, which still is built on purely illusory foundations. Children, who play life, discern its true law and relations more clearly than men, who fail to live it worthily, but think that they are wiser by experience, that is, by failure. I have read in a Hindoo book, that "there was a king's son, who, being expelled in infancy from his native city, was brought up by a forester, and, growing up to maturity in that state, imagined himself to belong to the barbarous race with which he lived. One of his father's ministers having discovered him, revealed to him what he was, and the misconception of his character was removed, and he knew himself to be a prince. So soul," continues the Hindoo philosopher, "from the circumstances in which it is placed, mistakes its own character, until the truth is revealed to it by some holy teacher, and then it knows itself to be *Brahme*."[27] I perceive that we inhabitants of New England live this mean life that we do because our vision does not penetrate the surface of things. We think that that *is* which *appears* to be. If a man should walk through this town and see only the reality, where, think you, would the "Mill-dam"[28] go to? If he should give us an account of the realities he beheld there, we should not recognize the place in his description. Look at a meeting-house, or a court-house, or a jail, or a shop, or a dwelling-house, and say what that thing really is before a true gaze, and they would all go to pieces in your account of them. Men esteem truth remote, in the outskirts of the system, behind the farthest star, before Adam and after the last man. In eternity there is indeed something true and sublime. But all these times and places and occasions

---

[26] A well-known collection of Arabian, Persian, and Indian tales assembled about the tenth century; also known as *The Thousand and One Nights*.

[27] The spiritual essence or divine function of creation in Hindu thought.

[28] The central gathering spot and place of business in Concord.

are now and here. God himself culminates in the present moment, and will never be more divine in the lapse of all the ages. And we are enabled to apprehend at all what is sublime and noble only by the perpetual instilling and drenching of the reality that surrounds us. The universe constantly and obediently answers to our conceptions; whether we travel fast or slow, the track is laid for us. Let us spend our lives in conceiving then. The poet or the artist never yet had so fair and noble a design but some of his posterity at least could accomplish it.

Let us spend one day as deliberately as Nature, and not be thrown off the track by every nutshell and mosquito's wing that falls on the rails. Let us rise early and fast, or break fast, gently and without perturbation; let company come and let company go, let the bells ring and the children cry—determined to make a day of it. Why should we knock under and go with the stream? Let us not be upset and overwhelmed in that terrible rapid and whirlpool called a dinner, situated in the meridian shallows. Weather this danger and you are safe, for the rest of the way is down hill. With unrelaxed nerves, with morning vigor, sail by it, looking another way, tied to the mast like Ulysses.[29] If the engine whistles, let it whistle till it is hoarse for its pains. If the bell rings, why should we run? We will consider what kind of music they are like. Let us settle ourselves, and work and wedge our feet downward through the mud and slush of opinion, and prejudice, and tradition, and delusion, and appearance, that alluvion which covers the globe, through Paris and London, through New York and Boston and Concord, through church and state, through poetry and philosophy and religion, till we come to a hard bottom and rocks in place, which we can call *reality,* and say, This is, and no mistake; and then begin, having a *point d'appui,* below freshet and frost and fire, a place where you might found a wall or a state, or set a lamp-post safely, or perhaps a gauge, not a Nilometer,[30] but a Realometer, that future ages might know how deep a freshet of shams and appearances had gathered from time to time. If you stand right fronting and face to face to a fact, you will see the sun glimmer on both its surfaces, as if it were a cimeter, and feel its sweet edge dividing you through the heart and marrow, and so you will happily conclude your mortal career. Be it life or death, we crave only reality. If we are

---

[29] To sail past the Sirens, whose song lured men to their deaths, Ulysses (the Roman name for Odysseus) had his men stuff their ears with wax and had himself tied to the mast so that he could hear the Sirens' song but not crash his ship upon the rocks to which the Sirens were leading him.

[30] A supposed instrument of ancient times that measured the rise and fall of the Nile.

really dying, let us hear the rattle in our throats and feel cold in the extremities; if we are alive, let us go about our business.

Time is but the stream I go a-fishing in. I drink at it; but while I drink I see the sandy bottom and detect how shallow it is. Its thin current slides away, but eternity remains. I would drink deeper; fish in the sky, whose bottom is pebbly with stars. I cannot count one. I know not the first letter of the alphabet. I have always been regretting that I was not as wise as the day I was born. The intellect is a cleaver; it discerns and rifts its way into the secret of things. I do not wish to be any more busy with my hands than is necessary. My head is hands and feet. I feel all my best faculties concentrated in it. My instinct tells me that my head is an organ for burrowing, as some creatures use their snout and fore-paws, and with it I would mine and burrow my way through these hills. I think that the richest vein is somewhere hereabouts; so by the divining rod and thin rising vapors I judge; and here I will begin to mine.

CHAPTER THREE
Reading

With a little more deliberation in the choice of their pursuits, all men would perhaps become essentially students and observers, for certainly their nature and destiny are interesting to all alike. In accumulating property for ourselves or our posterity, in founding a family or a state, or acquiring fame even, we are mortal; but in dealing with truth we are immortal, and need fear no change nor accident. The oldest Egyptian or Hindoo philosopher raised a corner of the veil from the statue of the divinity; and still the trembling robe remains raised, and I gaze upon as fresh a glory as he did, since it was I in him that was then so bold, and it is he in me that now reviews the vision. No dust has settled on that robe; no time has elapsed since that divinity was revealed. That time which we really improve, or which is improvable, is neither past, present, nor future.

My residence was more favorable, not only to thought, but to serious reading, than a university; and though I was beyond the range of the ordinary circulating library, I had more than ever come within the influence of those books which circulate round the world, whose sentences were first written on bark, and are now merely copied from time to time on to linen paper. Says the poet Mîr Camar Uddîn Mast,[1] "Being seated to run

[1] Persian and Urdu poet, died 1793.

through the region of the spiritual world; I have had this advantage in books. To be intoxicated by a single glass of wine; I have experienced this pleasure when I have drunk the liquor of the esoteric doctrines." I kept Homer's Iliad on my table through the summer, though I looked at his page only now and then. Incessant labor with my hands, at first, for I had my house to finish and my beans to hoe at the same time, made more study impossible. Yet I sustained myself by the prospect of such reading in future. I read one or two shallow books of travel in the intervals of my work, till that employment made me ashamed of myself, and I asked where it was then that *I* lived.

The student may read Homer or Aeschylus in the Greek without danger of dissipation or luxuriousness, for it implies that he in some measure emulate their heroes, and consecrate morning hours to their pages. The heroic books, even if printed in the character of our mother tongue, will always be in a language dead to degenerate times; and we must laboriously seek the meaning of each word and line, conjecturing a larger sense than common use permits out of what wisdom and valor and generosity we have. The modern cheap and fertile press, with all its translations, has done little to bring us nearer to the heroic writers of antiquity. They seem as solitary, and the letter in which they are printed as rare and curious, as ever. It is worth the expense of youthful days and costly hours, if you learn only some words of an ancient language, which are raised out of the trivialness of the street, to be perpetual suggestions and provocations. It is not in vain that the farmer remembers and repeats the few Latin words which he has heard. Men sometimes speak as if the study of the classics would at length make way for more modern and practical studies; but the adventurous student will always study classics, in whatever language they may be written and however ancient they may be. For what are the classics but the noblest recorded thoughts of man? They are the only oracles which are not decayed, and there are such answers to the most modern inquiry in them as Delphi and Dodona[2] never gave. We might as well omit to study Nature because she is old. To read well, that is, to read true books in a true spirit, is a noble exercise, and one that will task the reader more than any exercise which the customs of the day esteem. It requires a training such as the athletes underwent, the steady intention almost of the whole life to this object. Books must be read as deliberately and reservedly as they were written. It is not enough even to be able to speak the language of that nation by which they are written, for there is a memorable interval between the spoken and the written language, the language heard and the language

[2]The sites of important Greek oracles.

read. The one is commonly transitory, a sound, a tongue, a dialect merely, almost brutish, and we learn it unconsciously, like the brutes, of our mothers. The other is the maturity and experience of that; if that is our mother tongue, this is our father tongue, a reserved and select expression, too significant to be heard by the ear, which we must be born again in order to speak. The crowds of men who merely *spoke* the Greek and Latin tongues in the middle ages were not entitled by the accident of birth to *read* the works of genius written in those languages; for these were not written in that Greek or Latin which they knew, but in the select language of literature. They had not learned the nobler dialects of Greece and Rome, but the very materials on which they were written were waste paper to them, and they prized instead a cheap contemporary literature. But when the several nations of Europe had acquired distinct though rude written languages of their own, sufficient for the purposes of their rising literatures, then first learning revived, and scholars were enabled to discern from that remoteness the treasures of antiquity. What the Roman and Grecian multitude could not *hear,* after the lapse of ages a few scholars *read,* and a few scholars only are still reading it.

However much we may admire the orator's occasional bursts of eloquence, the noblest written words are commonly as far behind or above the fleeting spoken language as the firmament with its stars is behind the clouds. *There* are the stars, and they who can may read them. The astronomers forever comment on and observe them. They are not exhalations like our daily colloquies and vaporous breath. What is called eloquence in the forum is commonly found to be rhetoric in the study. The orator yields to the inspiration of a transient occasion, and speaks to the mob before him, to those who can *hear* him; but the writer, whose more equable life is his occasion, and who would be distracted by the event and the crowd which inspire the orator, speaks to the intellect and heart of mankind, to all in any age who can *understand* him.

No wonder that Alexander[3] carried the Iliad with him on his expeditions in a precious casket. A written word is the choicest of relics. It is something at once more intimate with us and more universal than any other work of art. It is the work of art nearest to life itself. It may be translated into every language, and not only be read but actually breathed from all human lips—not be represented on canvas or in marble only, but be carved out of the breath of life itself. The symbol of an ancient man's

[3] Alexander the Great (356–323 B.C.E.), king of Macedon and conqueror of the Persian Empire and beyond. In his *Lives,* Plutarch records Alexander's practice of carrying the *Iliad.*

thought becomes a modern man's speech. Two thousand summers have imparted to the monuments of Grecian literature, as to her marbles, only a maturer golden and autumnal tint, for they have carried their own serene and celestial atmosphere into all lands to protect them against the corrosion of time. Books are the treasured wealth of the world and the fit inheritance of generations and nations. Books, the oldest and the best, stand naturally and rightfully on the shelves of every cottage. They have no cause of their own to plead, but while they enlighten and sustain the reader his common sense will not refuse them. Their authors are a natural and irresistible aristocracy in every society, and, more than kings or emperors, exert an influence on mankind. When the illiterate and perhaps scornful trader has earned by enterprise and industry his coveted leisure and independence, and is admitted to the circles of wealth and fashion, he turns inevitably at last to those still higher but yet inaccessible circles of intellect and genius, and is sensible only of the imperfection of his culture and the vanity and insufficiency of all his riches, and further proves his good sense by the pains which he takes to secure for his children that intellectual culture whose want he so keenly feels; and thus it is that he becomes the founder of a family.

Those who have not learned to read the ancient classics in the language in which they were written must have a very imperfect knowledge of the history of the human race; for it is remarkable that no transcript of them has ever been made into any modern tongue, unless our civilization itself may be regarded as such a transcript. Homer has never yet been printed in English, nor Aeschylus, nor Virgil even—works as refined, as solidly done, and as beautiful almost as the morning itself; for later writers, say what we will of their genius, have rarely, if ever, equalled the elaborate beauty and finish and the lifelong and heroic literary labors of the ancients. They only talk of forgetting them who never knew them. It will be soon enough to forget them when we have the learning and the genius which will enable us to attend to and appreciate them. That age will be rich indeed when those relics which we call Classics, and the still older and more than classic but even less known Scriptures of the nations, shall have still further accumulated, when the Vaticans shall be filled with Vedas and Zendavestas[4] and Bibles, with Homers and Dantes and Shakespeares, and all the centuries to come shall have successively deposited their trophies in the forum of the world. By such a pile we may hope to scale heaven at last.

---

[4]The Vedas are the oldest Hindu scriptures, written in Vedic, the parent language of Sanskrit. The Zend Avesta is one of the scriptural books of Zoroastrianism.

The works of the great poets have never yet been read by mankind, for only great poets can read them. They have only been read as the multitude read the stars, at most astrologically, not astronomically. Most men have learned to read to serve a paltry convenience, as they have learned to cipher in order to keep accounts and not be cheated in trade; but of reading as a noble intellectual exercise they know little or nothing; yet this only is reading, in a high sense, not that which lulls us as a luxury and suffers the nobler faculties to sleep the while, but what we have to stand on tiptoe to read and devote our most alert and wakeful hours to.

I think that having learned our letters we should read the best that is in literature, and not be forever repeating our *a b ab*s, and words of one syllable, in the fourth or fifth classes, sitting on the lowest and foremost form[5] all our lives. Most men are satisfied if they read or hear read, and perchance have been convicted by the wisdom of one good book, the Bible, and for the rest of their lives vegetate and dissipate their faculties in what is called easy reading. There is a work in several volumes in our Circulating Library entitled Little Reading, which I thought referred to a town of that name which I had not been to. There are those who, like cormorants and ostriches, can digest all sorts of this, even after the fullest dinner of meats and vegetables, for they suffer nothing to be wasted. If others are the machines to provide this provender, they are the machines to read it. They read the nine thousandth tale about Zebulon and Sephronia, and how they loved as none had ever loved before, and neither did the course of their true love run smooth—at any rate, how it did run and stumble, and get up again and go on! how some poor unfortunate got up on to a steeple, who had better never have gone up as far as the belfry; and then, having needlessly got him up there, the happy novelist rings the bell for all the world to come together and hear, O dear! how he did get down again! For my part, I think that they had better metamorphose all such aspiring heroes of universal noveldom into man weathercocks, as they used to put heroes among the constellations, and let them swing round there till they are rusty, and not come down at all to bother honest men with their pranks. The next time the novelist rings the bell I will not stir though the meeting-house burn down. "The Skip of the Tip-Toe-Hop, a Romance of the Middle Ages, by the celebrated author of 'Tittle-Tol-Tan,' to appear in monthly parts; a great rush; don't all come together." All this they read with saucer eyes, and erect and primitive curiosity, and with unwearied gizzard, whose corrugations even yet need no sharpening, just as some little four-year-old

[5] In the front row of the schoolroom with the youngest children.

bencher his two-cent gilt-covered edition of Cinderella—without any improvement, that I can see, in the pronunciation, or accent, or emphasis, or any more skill in extracting or inserting the moral. The result is dulness of sight, a stagnation of the vital circulations, and a general deliquium and sloughing off of all the intellectual faculties. This sort of gingerbread is baked daily and more sedulously than pure wheat or rye-and-Indian in almost every oven, and finds a surer market.

The best books are not read even by those who are called good readers. What does our Concord culture amount to? There is in this town, with a very few exceptions, no taste for the best or for very good books even in English literature, whose words all can read and spell. Even the college-bred and so called liberally educated men here and elsewhere have really little or no acquaintance with the English classics; and as for the recorded wisdom of mankind, the ancient classics and Bibles, which are accessible to all who will know of them, there are the feeblest efforts any where made to become acquainted with them. I know a woodchopper, of middle age, who takes a French paper, not for news as he says, for he is above that, but to "keep himself in practice," he being a Canadian by birth; and when I ask him what he considers the best thing he can do in this world, he says, beside this, to keep up and add to his English. This is about as much as the college bred generally do or aspire to do, and they take an English paper for the purpose. One who has just come from reading perhaps one of the best English books will find how many with whom he can converse about it? Or suppose he comes from reading a Greek or Latin classic in the original, whose praises are familiar even to the so called illiterate; he will find nobody at all to speak to, but must keep silence about it. Indeed, there is hardly the professor in our colleges, who, if he has mastered the difficulties of the language, has proportionally mastered the difficulties of the wit and poetry of a Greek poet, and has any sympathy to impart to the alert and heroic reader; and as for the sacred Scriptures, or Bibles of mankind, who in this town can tell me even their titles? Most men do not know that any nation but the Hebrews have had a scripture. A man, any man, will go considerably out of his way to pick up a silver dollar; but here are golden words, which the wisest men of antiquity have uttered, and whose worth the wise of every succeeding age have assured us of—and yet we learn to read only as far as Easy Reading, the primers and class-books, and when we leave school, the "Little Reading," and story books, which are for boys and beginners; and our reading, our conversation and thinking, are all on a very low level, worthy only of pygmies and manikins.

I aspire to be acquainted with wiser men than this our Concord soil has produced, whose names are hardly known here. Or shall I hear the name of Plato and never read his book? As if Plato were my townsman and

I never saw him—my next neighbor and I never heard him speak or attended to the wisdom of his words. But how actually is it? His Dialogues, which contain what was immortal in him, lie on the next shelf, and yet I never read them. We are under-bred and low-lived and illiterate; and in this respect I confess I do not make any very broad distinction between the illiterateness of my townsman who cannot read at all, and the illiterateness of him who has learned to read only what is for children and feeble intellects. We should be as good as the worthies of antiquity, but partly by first knowing how good they were. We are a race of tit-men,[6] and soar but little higher in our intellectual flights than the columns of the daily paper.

It is not all books that are as dull as their readers. There are probably words addressed to our condition exactly, which, if we could really hear and understand, would be more salutary than the morning or the spring to our lives, and possibly put a new aspect on the face of things for us. How many a man has dated a new era in his life from the reading of a book. The book exists for us perchance which will explain our miracles and reveal new ones. The at present unutterable things we may find somewhere uttered. These same questions that disturb and puzzle and confound us have in their turn occurred to all the wise men; not one has been omitted; and each has answered them, according to his ability, by his words and his life. Moreover, with wisdom we shall learn liberality. The solitary hired man on a farm in the outskirts of Concord, who has had his second birth and peculiar religious experience, and is driven as he believes into silent gravity and exclusiveness by his faith, may think it is not true; but Zoroaster, thousands of years ago, travelled the same road and had the same experience; but he, being wise, knew it to be universal, and treated his neighbors accordingly, and is even said to have invented and established worship among men. Let him humbly commune with Zoroaster then, and through the liberalizing influence of all the worthies, with Jesus Christ himself, and let "our church" go by the board.

We boast that we belong to the nineteenth century and are making the most rapid strides of any nation. But consider how little this village does for its own culture. I do not wish to flatter my townsmen, nor to be flattered by them, for that will not advance either of us. We need to be provoked—goaded like oxen, as we are, into a trot. We have a comparatively decent system of common schools, schools for infants only; but excepting the half-starved Lyceum[7] in the winter, and latterly the puny beginning of

[6] Puny, stunted.

[7] An organization that presented public lectures, one of main forms of entertainment and education for adults in the nineteenth century. Thoreau himself lectured some twenty

a library suggested by the state, no school for ourselves. We spend more on almost any article of bodily aliment or ailment than on our mental aliment. It is time that we had uncommon schools, that we did not leave off our education when we begin to be men and women. It is time that villages were universities, and their elder inhabitants the fellows of universities, with leisure—if they are indeed so well off—to pursue liberal studies the rest of their lives. Shall the world be confined to one Paris or one Oxford forever? Cannot students be boarded here and get a liberal education under the skies of Concord? Can we not hire some Abelard[8] to lecture to us? Alas! what with foddering the cattle and tending the store, we are kept from school too long, and our education is sadly neglected. In this country, the village should in some respects take the place of the nobleman of Europe. It should be the patron of the fine arts. It is rich enough. It wants only the magnanimity and refinement. It can spend money enough on such things as farmers and traders value, but it is thought Utopian to propose spending money for things which more intelligent men know to be of far more worth. This town has spent seventeen thousand dollars on a town-house, thank fortune or politics, but probably it will not spend so much on living wit, the true meat to put into that shell, in a hundred years. The one hundred and twenty-five dollars annually subscribed for a Lyceum in the winter is better spent than any other equal sum raised in the town. If we live in the nineteenth century, why should we not enjoy the advantages which the nineteenth century offers? Why should our life be in any respect provincial? If we will read newspapers, why not skip the gossip of Boston and take the best newspaper in the world at once?—not be sucking the pap of "neutral family" papers, or browsing "Olive-Branches"[9] here in New England. Let the reports of all the learned societies come to us, and we will see if they know any thing. Why should we leave it to Harper & Brothers[10] and Redding & Co.[11] to select our reading? As the nobleman of cultivated taste surrounds himself with whatever conduces to his culture—genius—learning—wit—books—paintings—statuary—music—philosophical instruments, and the like; so let the village do—not stop short at a pedagogue, a parson, a sexton, a parish library, and three selectmen, because our pilgrim forefathers got through a cold winter once on a bleak rock

times for the Concord Lyceum and, as curator, organized its lecture series for a number of years.

[8] Peter Abelard (1079–1142), French philosopher and teacher.

[9] A Methodist weekly.

[10] New York publishing house.

[11] Boston bookselling firm.

with these. To act collectively is according to the spirit of our institutions; and I am confident that, as our circumstances are more flourishing, our means are greater than the nobleman's. New England can hire all the wise men in the world to come and teach her, and board them round the while, and not be provincial at all. That is the *uncommon* school we want. Instead of noblemen, let us have noble villages of men. If it is necessary, omit one bridge over the river, go round a little there, and throw one arch at least over the darker gulf of ignorance which surrounds us.

CHAPTER FOUR
Sounds

But while we are confined to books, though the most select and classic, and read only particular written languages, which are themselves but dialects and provincial, we are in danger of forgetting the language which all things and events speak without metaphor, which alone is copious and standard. Much is published, but little printed. The rays which stream through the shutter will be no longer remembered when the shutter is wholly removed. No method nor discipline can supersede the necessity of being forever on the alert. What is a course of history, or philosophy, or poetry, no matter how well selected, or the best society, or the most admirable routine of life, compared with the discipline of looking always at what is to be seen? Will you be a reader, a student merely, or a seer? Read your fate, see what is before you, and walk on into futurity.

I did not read books the first summer; I hoed beans. Nay, I often did better than this. There were times when I could not afford to sacrifice the bloom of the present moment to any work, whether of the head or hands. I love a broad margin to my life. Sometimes, in a summer morning, having taken my accustomed bath, I sat in my sunny doorway from sunrise till noon, rapt in a revery, amidst the pines and hickories and sumachs, in undisturbed solitude and stillness, while the birds sang around or flitted noiseless through the house, until by the sun falling in at my west window, or the noise of some traveller's wagon on the distant highway, I was reminded of the lapse of time. I grew in those seasons like corn in the night, and they were far better than any work of the hands would have been. They were not time subtracted from my life, but so much over and above my usual allowance. I realized what the Orientals mean by contemplation and the forsaking of works. For the most part, I minded not how the hours went. The day advanced as if to light some work of mine; it was morning, and lo, now it is evening, and nothing memorable is accomplished. Instead of singing like the birds, I silently smiled at my incessant good fortune. As the sparrow had its trill, sitting on the hickory before my door, so had I my chuckle or suppressed warble which he might hear out of my nest. My days were not days of the week, bearing the stamp of any heathen deity,[1] nor were they minced into hours and fretted by the ticking of a clock; for I lived like the Puri Indians, of whom it is said that "for yesterday, today, and tomorrow they have only one word, and they express the variety of meaning by pointing backward for yesterday, forward for tomorrow, and overhead for the passing day."[2] This was sheer idleness to my fellow-townsmen, no doubt; but if the birds and flowers had tried me by their standard, I should not have been found wanting. A man must find his occasions in himself, it is true. The natural day is very calm, and will hardly reprove his indolence.

I had this advantage, at least, in my mode of life, over those who were obliged to look abroad for amusement, to society and the theatre, that my life itself was become my amusement and never ceased to be novel. It was a drama of many scenes and without an end. If we were always indeed getting our living, and regulating our lives according to the last and best mode we had learned, we should never be troubled with ennui. Follow your genius closely enough, and it will not fail to show you a fresh prospect every hour. Housework was a pleasant pastime. When my floor was dirty, I rose early, and, setting all my furniture out of doors on the grass, bed and bedstead making but one budget, dashed water on the floor, and sprinkled white sand from the pond on it, and then with a broom scrubbed it clean and white; and by the time the villagers had broken their fast the morning sun had dried my house sufficiently to allow me to move in again, and my meditations were almost uninterrupted. It was pleasant to see my whole household effects out on the grass, making a little pile like a gypsy's pack, and my three-legged table, from which I did not remove the books and pen and ink, standing amid the pines and hickories. They seemed glad to get out themselves, and as if unwilling to be brought in. I was sometimes tempted to stretch an awning over them and take my seat there. It was worth the while to see the sun shine on these things, and hear the free wind blow on them; so much more interesting most familiar objects look out of doors than in the house. A bird sits on the next bough, life-everlasting

---

[1] Our names for the days of the week are derived from those of Germanic and Roman gods, as in *Wednesday* from Woden and *Saturday* from Saturn.

[2] The Puri were a tribe of eastern Brazil; related by Ida Pfeiffer, *A Lady's Voyage Round the World* (1852).

grows under the table, and blackberry vines run round its legs; pine cones, chestnut burs, and strawberry leaves are strewn about. It looked as if this was the way these forms came to be transferred to our furniture, to tables, chairs, and bedsteads—because they once stood in their midst.

My house was on the side of a hill, immediately on the edge of the larger wood, in the midst of a young forest of pitch pines and hickories, and half a dozen rods from the pond, to which a narrow footpath led down the hill. In my front yard grew the strawberry, blackberry, and life-everlasting, johnswort and goldenrod, shrub-oaks and sand-cherry, blueberry and groundnut. Near the end of May, the sand-cherry (*cerasus pumila*), adorned the sides of the path with its delicate flowers arranged in umbels cylindrically about its short stems, which last, in the fall, weighed down with good sized and handsome cherries, fell over in wreaths like rays on every side. I tasted them out of compliment to Nature, though they were scarcely palatable. The sumach (*rhus glabra*) grew luxuriantly about the house, pushing up through the embankment which I had made, and growing five or six feet the first season. Its broad pinnate tropical leaf was pleasant though strange to look on. The large buds, suddenly pushing out late in the spring from dry sticks which had seemed to be dead, developed themselves as by magic into graceful green and tender boughs, an inch in diameter; and sometimes, as I sat at my window, so heedlessly did they grow and tax their weak joints, I heard a fresh and tender bough suddenly fall like a fan to the ground, when there was not a breath of air stirring, broken off by its own weight. In August, the large masses of berries, which, when in flower, had attracted many wild bees, gradually assumed their bright velvety crimson hue, and by their weight again bent down and broke the tender limbs.

As I sit at my window this summer afternoon, hawks are circling about my clearing; the tantivy of wild pigeons, flying by twos and threes athwart my view, or perching restless on the white-pine boughs behind my house, gives a voice to the air; a fishhawk dimples the glassy surface of the pond and brings up a fish; a mink steals out of the marsh before my door and seizes a frog by the shore; the sedge is bending under the weight of the reed-birds flitting hither and thither; and for the last half hour I have heard the rattle of railroad cars, now dying away and then reviving like the beat of a partridge, conveying travellers from Boston to the country. For I did not live so out of the world as that boy, who, as I hear, was put out to a farmer in the east part of the town, but ere long ran away and came home again, quite down at the heel and homesick. He had never seen such a dull and out-of-the-way place; the folks were all gone off; why, you couldn't even hear the whistle! I doubt if there is such a place in Massachusetts now—

> "In truth, our village has become a butt
> For one of those fleet railroad shafts, and o'er
> Our peaceful plain its soothing sound is—Concord." [3]

The Fitchburg Railroad touches the pond about a hundred rods south of where I dwell. I usually go to the village along its causeway, and am, as it were, related to society by this link. The men on the freight trains, who go over the whole length of the road, bow to me as to an old acquaintance, they pass me so often, and apparently they take me for an employee; and so I am. I too would fain be a track-repairer somewhere in the orbit of the earth.

The whistle of the locomotive penetrates my woods summer and winter, sounding like the scream of a hawk sailing over some farmer's yard, informing me that many restless city merchants are arriving within the circle of the town, or adventurous country traders from the other side. As they come under one horizon, they shout their warning to get off the track to the other, heard sometimes through the circles of two towns. Here come your groceries, country; your rations, countrymen! Nor is there any man so independent on his farm that he can say them nay. And here's your pay for them! screams the countryman's whistle; timber like long battering rams going twenty miles an hour against the city's walls, and chairs enough to seat all the weary and heavy laden that dwell within them. With such huge and lumbering civility the country hands a chair to the city. All the Indian huckleberry hills are stripped, all the cranberry meadows are raked into the city. Up comes the cotton, down goes the woven cloth; up comes the silk, down goes the woollen; up come the books, but down goes the wit that writes them.

When I meet the engine with its train of cars moving off with planetary motion—or, rather, like a comet, for the beholder knows not if with that velocity and with that direction it will ever revisit this system, since its orbit does not look like a returning curve—with its steam cloud like a banner streaming behind in golden and silver wreaths, like many a downy cloud which I have seen, high in the heavens, unfolding its masses to the light—as if this travelling demigod, this cloud-compeller, would ere long take the sunset sky for the livery of his train; when I hear the iron horse

---

[3] Ellery Channing (1818–1901), from "Walden Spring," *The Woodman and Other Poems* (1849). (See chap. 12, note 1.)

make the hills echo with his snort like thunder, shaking the earth with his feet, and breathing fire and smoke from his nostrils (what kind of winged horse or fiery dragon they will put into the new Mythology I don't know), it seems as if the earth had got a race now worthy to inhabit it. If all were as it seems, and men made the elements their servants for noble ends! If the cloud that hangs over the engine were the perspiration of heroic deeds, or as beneficent as that which floats over the farmer's fields, then the elements and Nature herself would cheerfully accompany men on their errands and be their escort.

I watch the passage of the morning cars with the same feeling that I do the rising of the sun, which is hardly more regular. Their train of clouds stretching far behind and rising higher and higher, going to heaven while the cars are going to Boston, conceals the sun for a minute and casts my distant field into the shade, a celestial train beside which the petty train of cars which hugs the earth is but the barb of the spear. The stabler of the iron horse was up early this winter morning by the light of the stars amid the mountains, to fodder and harness his steed. Fire, too, was awakened thus early to put the vital heat in him and get him off. If the enterprise were as innocent as it is early! If the snow lies deep, they strap on his snow-shoes, and with the giant plough plough a furrow from the mountains to the seaboard, in which the cars, like a following drill-barrow, sprinkle all the restless men and floating merchandise in the country for seed. All day the fire-steed flies over the country, stopping only that his master may rest, and I am awakened by his tramp and defiant snarl at midnight, when in some remote glen in the woods he fronts the elements incased in ice and snow; and he will reach his stall only with the morning star, to start once more on his travels without rest or slumber. Or perchance, at evening, I hear him in his stable blowing off the superfluous energy of the day, that he may calm his nerves and cool his liver and brain for a few hours of iron slumber. If the enterprise were as heroic and commanding as it is protracted and unwearied!

Far through unfrequented woods on the confines of towns, where once only the hunter penetrated by day, in the darkest night dart these bright saloons without the knowledge of their inhabitants; this moment stopping at some brilliant station-house in town or city, where a social crowd is gathered, the next in the Dismal Swamp,[4] scaring the owl and fox. The startings and arrivals of the cars are now the epochs in the village day. They go and come with such regularity and precision, and their whistle can be heard so far, that the farmers set their clocks by them, and thus one

[4] An area along the coasts of southern Virginia and northern North Carolina.

well conducted institution regulates a whole country. Have not men improved somewhat in punctuality since the railroad was invented? Do they not talk and think faster in the depot than they did in the stage-office? There is something electrifying in the atmosphere of the former place. I have been astonished at the miracles it has wrought; that some of my neighbors, who, I should have prophesied, once for all, would never get to Boston by so prompt a conveyance, are on hand when the bell rings. To do things "railroad fashion" is now the by-word; and it is worth the while to be warned so often and so sincerely by any power to get off its track. There is no stopping to read the riot act, no firing over the heads of the mob, in this case. We have constructed a fate, an *Atropos,*[5] that never turns aside. (Let that be the name of your engine.) Men are advertised that at a certain hour and minute these bolts will be shot toward particular points of the compass; yet it interferes with no man's business, and the children go to school on the other track. We live the steadier for it. We are all educated thus to be sons of Tell.[6] The air is full of invisible bolts. Every path but your own is the path of fate. Keep on your own track, then.

What recommends commerce to me is its enterprise and bravery. It does not clasp its hands and pray to Jupiter.[7] I see these men every day go about their business with more or less courage and content, doing more even than they suspect, and perchance better employed than they could have consciously devised. I am less affected by their heroism who stood up for half an hour in the front line at Buena Vista,[8] than by the steady and cheerful valor of the men who inhabit the snow-plough for their winter quarters; who have not merely the three-o'clock in the morning courage, which Bonaparte[9] thought was the rarest, but whose courage does not go to rest so early, who go to sleep only when the storm sleeps or the sinews of their iron steed are frozen. On this morning of the Great Snow, perchance, which is still raging and chilling men's blood, I hear the muffled tone of their engine bell from out the fog bank of their chilled breath, which announces that the cars *are coming,* without long delay, notwithstanding the veto of a New England north-east snow storm, and I behold the ploughmen covered with snow and rime, their heads peering above the

[5] One of the three Fates of Greek mythology, who determined when the thread of a person's life would be cut.
[6] Tell was supposed to have shot an arrow through an apple perched on the head of his son.
[7] The chief Roman god.
[8] The site of a major battle (1847) during the war between the United States and Mexico.
[9] Napoleon Bonaparte (1769–1821), French general and emperor.

mould-board which is turning down other than daisies and the nests of field mice, like bowlders of the Sierra Nevada, that occupy an outside place in the universe.

Commerce is unexpectedly confident and serene, alert, adventurous, and unwearied. It is very natural in its methods withal, far more so than many fantastic enterprises and sentimental experiments, and hence its singular success. I am refreshed and expanded when the freight train rattles past me, and I smell the stores which go dispensing their odors all the way from Long Wharf[10] to Lake Champlain, reminding me of foreign parts, of coral reefs, and Indian oceans, and tropical climes, and the extent of the globe. I feel more like a citizen of the world at the sight of the palm-leaf which will cover so many flaxen New England heads the next summer, the Manilla hemp and cocoa-nut husks, the old junk, gunny bags, scrap iron, and rusty nails. This car-load of torn sails is more legible and interesting now than if they should be wrought into paper and printed books. Who can write so graphically the history of the storms they have weathered as these rents have done? They are proof-sheets which need no correction. Here goes lumber from the Maine woods, which did not go out to sea in the last freshet, risen four dollars on the thousand because of what did go out or was split up; pine, spruce, cedar—first, second, third and fourth qualities, so lately all of one quality, to wave over the bear, and moose, and caribou. Next rolls Thomaston lime,[11] a prime lot, which will get far among the hills before it gets slacked. These rags in bales, of all hues and qualities, the lowest condition to which cotton and linen descend, the final result of dress—of patterns which are now no longer cried up, unless it be in Milwaukie, as those splendid articles, English, French, or American prints, ginghams, muslins, etc., gathered from all quarters both of fashion and poverty, going to become paper of one color or a few shades only, on which forsooth will be written tales of real life, high and low, and founded on fact! This closed car smells of salt fish, the strong New England and commercial scent, reminding me of the Grand Banks[12] and the fisheries. Who has not seen a salt fish, thoroughly cured for this world, so that nothing can spoil it, and putting the perseverance of the saints to the blush? with which you may sweep or pave the streets, and split your kindlings, and the teamster shelter himself and his lading against sun wind and rain behind it—and the trader, as a Concord trader once did, hang it up by his

[10] At Boston Harbor.
[11] Thomaston, Maine, a well-known source of lime.
[12] Southeast of Newfoundland, one of the major fishing areas of the North Atlantic.

door for a sign when he commences business, until at last his oldest customer cannot tell surely whether it be animal, vegetable, or mineral, and yet it shall be as pure as a snowflake, and if it be put into a pot and boiled, will come out an excellent dun fish for a Saturday's dinner. Next Spanish hides, with the tails preserving their twist and the angle of elevation they had when the oxen that wore them were careering over the pampas of the Spanish main—a type of all obstinacy, and evincing how almost hopeless and incurable are all constitutional vices. I confess, that practically speaking, when I have learned a man's real disposition, I have no hopes of changing it for the better or worse in this state of existence. As the Orientals say, "A cur's tail may be warmed, and pressed, and bound round with ligatures, and after a twelve years' labor bestowed upon it, still it will retain its natural form." [13] The only effectual cure for such inveteracies as these tails exhibit is to make glue of them, which I believe is what is usually done with them, and then they will stay put and stick. Here is a hogshead of molasses or of brandy directed to John Smith, Cuttingsville, Vermont, some trader among the Green Mountains, who imports for the farmers near his clearing, and now perchance stands over his bulk-head and thinks of the last arrivals on the coast, how they may affect the price for him, telling his customers this moment, as he has told them twenty times before this morning, that he expects some by the next train of prime quality. It is advertised in the Cuttingsville Times.

While these things go up other things come down. Warned by the whizzing sound, I look up from my book and see some tall pine, hewn on far northern hills, which has winged its way over the Green Mountains and the Connecticut, shot like an arrow through the township within ten minutes, and scarce another eye beholds it; going

> "to be the mast
> Of some great ammiral." [14]

And hark! here comes the cattle-train bearing the cattle of a thousand hills,[15] sheepcots, stables, and cow-yards in the air, drovers with their sticks, and shepherd boys in the midst of their flocks, all but the mountain pastures, whirled along like leaves blown from the mountains by the September gales. The air is filled with the bleating of calves and sheep, and the

---

[13] *Hitopadesa: Fables and Proverbs from the Sanskrit,* translated by Sir Charles Wilkins (1750–1836).

[14] John Milton, *Paradise Lost* 1.293–94.

[15] Cf. Psalms 50.10: "For every beast of the forest is mine, and the cattle upon a thousand hills."

hustling of oxen, as if a pastoral valley were going by. When the old bell-weather at the head rattles his bell, the mountains do indeed skip like rams and the little hills like lambs.[16] A car-load of drovers, too, in the midst, on a level with their droves now, their vocation gone, but still clinging to their useless sticks as their badge of office. But their dogs, where are they? It is a stampede to them; they are quite thrown out; they have lost the scent. Methinks I hear them barking behind the Peterboro' Hills,[17] or panting up the western slope of the Green Mountains. They will not be in at the death. Their vocation, too, is gone. Their fidelity and sagacity are below par now. They will slink back to their kennels in disgrace, or perchance run wild and strike a league with the wolf and the fox. So is your pastoral life whirled past and away. But the bell rings, and I must get off the track and let the cars go by—

> What's the railroad to me?
> I never go to see
> Where it ends.
> It fills a few hollows,
> 5 And makes banks for the swallows,
> It sets the sand a-blowing,
> And the blackberries a-growing,

but I cross it like a cart-path in the woods. I will not have my eyes put out and my ears spoiled by its smoke and steam and hissing.

Now that the cars are gone by and all the restless world with them, and the fishes in the pond no longer feel their rumbling, I am more alone than ever. For the rest of the long afternoon, perhaps, my meditations are interrupted only by the faint rattle of a carriage or team along the distant highway.

Sometimes, on Sundays, I heard the bells, the Lincoln, Acton, Bedford,[18] or Concord bell, when the wind was favorable, a faint, sweet, and, as it were, natural melody, worth importing into the wilderness. At a sufficient distance over the woods this sound acquires a certain vibratory hum, as if the pine needles in the horizon were the strings of a harp which it swept. All sound heard at the greatest possible distance produces one and the same effect, a vibration of the universal lyre, just as the intervening atmosphere makes a distant ridge of earth interesting to our eyes by the azure tint it imparts to it. There came to me in this case a melody which

---

[16] Cf. Psalms 114.4: "The mountains skipped like rams, and the little hills like lambs."
[17] An area in southern New Hampshire that can be seen from Concord.
[18] Towns in the vicinity of Concord.

the air had strained, and which had conversed with every leaf and needle of the wood, that portion of the sound which the elements had taken up and modulated and echoed from vale to vale. The echo is, to some extent, an original sound, and therein is the magic and charm of it. It is not merely a repetition of what was worth repeating in the bell, but partly the voice of the wood; the same trivial words and notes sung by a wood-nymph.

At evening, the distant lowing of some cow in the horizon beyond the woods sounded sweet and melodious, and at first I would mistake it for the voices of certain minstrels by whom I was sometimes serenaded, who might be straying over hill and dale; but soon I was not unpleasantly disappointed when it was prolonged into the cheap and natural music of the cow. I do not mean to be satirical, but to express my appreciation of those youths' singing, when I state that I perceived clearly that it was akin to the music of the cow, and they were at length one articulation of Nature.

Regularly at half past seven, in one part of the summer, after the evening train had gone by, the whippoorwills chanted their vespers for half an hour, sitting on a stump by my door, or upon the ridge pole of the house. They would begin to sing almost with as much precision as a clock, within five minutes of a particular time, referred to the setting of the sun, every evening. I had a rare opportunity to become acquainted with their habits. Sometimes I heard four or five at once in different parts of the wood, by accident one a bar behind another, and so near me that I distinguished not only the cluck after each note, but often that singular buzzing sound like a fly in a spider's web, only proportionally louder. Sometimes one would circle round and round me in the woods a few feet distant as if tethered by a string, when probably I was near its eggs. They sang at intervals throughout the night, and were again as musical as ever just before and about dawn.

When other birds are still the screech owls take up the strain, like mourning women their ancient *u-lu-lu*. Their dismal scream is truly Ben Jonsonian.[19] Wise midnight hags! It is no honest and blunt *tu-whit tu-who* of the poets, but, without jesting, a most solemn graveyard ditty, the mutual consolations of suicide lovers remembering the pangs and the delights of supernal love in the infernal groves. Yet I love to hear their wailing, their doleful responses, trilled along the woodside; reminding me sometimes of music and singing birds; as if it were the dark and tearful side of music, the regrets and sighs that would fain be sung. They are the spirits, the low spirits and melancholy forebodings, of fallen souls that once in human shape night-walked the earth and did the deeds of darkness, now ex-

[19] Ben Jonson (1572–1637), English playwright.

piating their sins with their wailing hymns or threnodies in the scenery of their transgressions. They give me a new sense of the variety and capacity of that nature which is our common dwelling. *Oh-o-o-o-o that I never had been bor-r-r-r-n!* sighs one on this side of the pond, and circles with the restlessness of despair to some new perch on the gray oaks. Then—*that I never had been bor-r-r-r-n!* echoes another on the farther side with tremulous sincerity and—*bor-r-r-r-n!* comes faintly from far in the Lincoln woods.

I was also serenaded by a hooting owl. Near at hand you could fancy it the most melancholy sound in Nature, as if she meant by this to stereotype and make permanent in her choir the dying moans of a human being—some poor weak relic of mortality who has left hope behind, and howls like an animal, yet with human sobs, on entering the dark valley, made more awful by a certain gurgling melodiousness—I find myself beginning with the letters gl when I try to imitate it—expressive of a mind which has reached the gelatinous mildewy stage in the mortification of all healthy and courageous thought. It reminded me of ghouls and idiots and insane howlings. But now one answers from far woods in a strain made really melodious by distance—*Hoo hoo hoo, hoorer hoo;* and indeed for the most part it suggested only pleasing associations, whether heard by day or night, summer or winter.

I rejoice that there are owls. Let them do the idiotic and maniacal hooting for men. It is a sound admirably suited to swamps and twilight woods which no day illustrates, suggesting a vast and undeveloped nature which men have not recognized. They represent the stark twilight and unsatisfied thoughts which all have. All day the sun has shone on the surface of some savage swamp, where the single spruce stands hung with usnea lichens, and small hawks circulate above, and the chicadee lisps amid the evergreens, and the partridge and rabbit skulk beneath; but now a more dismal and fitting day dawns, and a different race of creatures awakes to express the meaning of Nature there.

Late in the evening I heard the distant rumbling of wagons over bridges—a sound heard farther than almost any other at night—the baying of dogs, and sometimes again the lowing of some disconsolate cow in a distant barn-yard. In the meanwhile all the shore rang with the trump of bullfrogs, the sturdy spirits of ancient winebibbers and wassailers, still unrepentant, trying to sing a catch in their Stygian lake[20]—if the Walden nymphs will pardon the comparison, for though there are almost no

---

[20] A dismal lake, from the name of the Styx, in Greek myth a river separating the land of the living from that of the dead.

weeds, there are frogs there—who would fain keep up the hilarious rules of their old festal tables, though their voices have waxed hoarse and solemnly grave, mocking at mirth, and the wine has lost its flavor, and become only liquor to distend their paunches, and sweet intoxication never comes to drown the memory of the past, but mere saturation and waterloggedness and distention. The most aldermanic, with his chin upon a heart-leaf, which serves for a napkin to his drooling chaps, under this northern shore quaffs a deep draught of the once scorned water, and passes round the cup with the ejaculation *tr-r-r-oonk, tr-r-r-oonk, tr-r-r-oonk!* and straightway comes over the water from some distant cove the same password repeated, where the next in seniority and girth has gulped down to his mark; and when this observance has made the circuit of the shores, then ejaculates the master of ceremonies, with satisfaction, *tr-r-r-oonk!* and each in his turn repeats the same down to the least distended, leakiest, and flabbiest paunched, that there be no mistake; and then the bowl goes round again and again, until the sun disperses the morning mist, and only the patriarch is not under the pond, but vainly bellowing *troonk* from time to time, and pausing for a reply.

I am not sure that I ever heard the sound of cock-crowing from my clearing, and I thought that it might be worth the while to keep a cockerel for his music merely, as a singing bird. The note of this once wild Indian pheasant is certainly the most remarkable of any bird's, and if they could be naturalized without being domesticated, it would soon become the most famous sound in our woods, surpassing the clangor of the goose and the hooting of the owl; and then imagine the cackling of the hens to fill the pauses when their lords' clarions rested! No wonder that man added this bird to his tame stock—to say nothing of the eggs and drumsticks. To walk in a winter morning in a wood where these birds abounded, their native woods, and hear the wild cockerel crow on the trees, clear and shrill for miles over the resounding earth, drowning the feebler notes of other birds—think of it! It would put nations on the alert. Who would not be early to rise, and rise earlier and earlier every successive day of his life, till he became unspeakably healthy, wealthy, and wise? This foreign bird's note is celebrated by the poets of all countries along with the notes of their native songsters. All climates agree with brave Chanticleer. He is more indigenous even than the natives. His health is ever good, his lungs are sound, his spirits never flag. Even the sailor on the Atlantic and Pacific is awakened by his voice; but its shrill sound never roused me from my slumbers. I kept neither dog, cat, cow, pig, nor hens, so that you would have said there was a deficiency of domestic sounds; neither the churn, nor the spinning wheel, nor even the singing of the kettle, nor the hissing of the urn, nor children crying, to comfort one. An old-fashioned man would have lost his senses or died of ennui before this. Not even rats in the wall, for they were starved out, or rather were never baited in—only squirrels on the roof and under the floor, a whippoorwill on the ridge pole, a blue-jay screaming beneath the window, a hare or woodchuck under the house, a screech-owl or a cat-owl behind it, a flock of wild geese or a laughing loon on the pond, and a fox to bark in the night. Not even a lark or an oriole, those mild plantation birds, ever visited my clearing. No cockerels to crow nor hens to cackle in the yard. No yard! but unfenced Nature reaching up to your very sills. A young forest growing up under your windows, and wild sumachs and blackberry vines breaking through into your cellar; sturdy pitch-pines rubbing and creaking against the shingles for want of room, their roots reaching quite under the house. Instead of a scuttle or a blind blown off in the gale—a pine tree snapped off or torn up by the roots behind your house for fuel. Instead of no path to the front-yard gate in the Great Snow—no gate—no front-yard—and no path to the civilized world!

CHAPTER FIVE
Solitude

This is a delicious evening, when the whole body is one sense, and imbibes delight through every pore. I go and come with a strange liberty in Nature, a part of herself. As I walk along the stony shore of the pond in my shirt sleeves, though it is cool as well as cloudy and windy, and I see nothing special to attract me, all the elements are unusually congenial to me. The bull frogs trump to usher in the night, and the note of the whippoorwill is borne on the rippling wind from over the water. Sympathy with the fluttering alder and poplar leaves almost takes away my breath; yet, like the lake, my serenity is rippled but not ruffled. These small waves raised by the evening wind are as remote from storm as the smooth reflecting surface. Though it is now dark, the wind still blows and roars in the wood, the waves still dash, and some creatures lull the rest with their notes. The repose is never complete. The wildest animals do not repose, but seek their prey now; the fox, and skunk, and rabbit, now roam the fields and woods without fear. They are Nature's watchmen—links which connect the days of animated life.

When I return to my house I find that visitors have been there and left their cards, either a bunch of flowers, or a wreath of evergreen, or a name in pencil on a yellow walnut leaf or a chip. They who come rarely to the woods take some little piece of the forest into their hands to play with by the way, which they leave, either intentionally or accidentally. One has peeled a willow wand, woven it into a ring, and dropped it on my table. I could always tell if visitors had called in my absence, either by the bended twigs or grass, or the print of their shoes, and generally of what sex or age or quality they were by some slight trace left, as a flower dropped, or a bunch of grass plucked and thrown away, even as far off as the railroad, half a mile distant, or by the lingering odor of a cigar or pipe. Nay, I was frequently notified of the passage of a traveller along the highway sixty rods off by the scent of his pipe.

There is commonly sufficient space about us. Our horizon is never quite at our elbows. The thick wood is not just at our door, nor the pond, but somewhat is always clearing, familiar and worn by us, appropriated and fenced in some way, and reclaimed from Nature. For what reason have I this vast range and circuit, some square miles of unfrequented forest, for my privacy, abandoned to me by men? My nearest neighbor is a mile distant, and no house is visible from any place but the hill-tops within half a mile of my own. I have my horizon bounded by woods all to myself; a distant view of the railroad where it touches the pond on the one hand, and of the fence which skirts the woodland road on the other. But for the most part it is as solitary where I live as on the prairies. It is as much Asia or Africa as New England. I have, as it were, my own sun and moon and stars, and a little world all to myself. At night there was never a traveller passed my house, or knocked at my door, more than if I were the first or last man; unless it were in the spring, when at long intervals some came from the village to fish for pouts—they plainly fished much more in the Walden Pond of their own natures, and baited their hooks with darkness—but they soon retreated, usually with light baskets, and left "the world to darkness and to me,"[1] and the black kernel of the night was never profaned by any human neighborhood. I believe that men are generally still a little afraid of the dark, though the witches are all hung, and Christianity and candles have been introduced.

Yet I experienced sometimes that the most sweet and tender, the most innocent and encouraging society may be found in any natural object, even for the poor misanthrope and most melancholy man. There can be no very black melancholy to him who lives in the midst of Nature and has his senses still. There was never yet such a storm but it was Aeolian music[2] to a healthy and innocent ear. Nothing can rightly compel a simple and brave

---

[1] From Thomas Gray (1716–1771), "An Elegy Wrote in a Country Church Yard" (1751).

[2] Aeolus was the ancient Greek god of winds; "Aeolian music" is produced by currents of air playing over a stringed instrument.

man to a vulgar sadness. While I enjoy the friendship of the seasons I trust that nothing can make life a burden to me. The gentle rain which waters my beans and keeps me in the house today is not drear and melancholy, but good for me too. Though it prevents my hoeing them, it is of far more worth than my hoeing. If it should continue so long as to cause the seeds to rot in the ground and destroy the potatoes in the low lands, it would still be good for the grass on the uplands, and, being good for the grass, it would be good for me. Sometimes, when I compare myself with other men, it seems as if I were more favored by the gods than they, beyond any deserts that I am conscious of; as if I had a warrant and surety at their hands which my fellows have not, and were especially guided and guarded. I do not flatter myself, but if it be possible they flatter me. I have never felt lonesome, or in the least oppressed by a sense of solitude, but once, and that was a few weeks after I came to the woods, when, for an hour, I doubted if the near neighborhood of man was not essential to a serene and healthy life. To be alone was something unpleasant. But I was at the same time conscious of a slight insanity in my mood, and seemed to foresee my recovery. In the midst of a gentle rain while these thoughts prevailed, I was suddenly sensible of such sweet and beneficent society in Nature, in the very pattering of the drops, and in every sound and sight around my house, an infinite and unaccountable friendliness all at once like an atmosphere sustaining me, as made the fancied advantages of human neighborhood insignificant, and I have never thought of them since. Every little pine needle expanded and swelled with sympathy and befriended me. I was so distinctly made aware of the presence of something kindred to me, even in scenes which we are accustomed to call wild and dreary, and also that the nearest of blood to me and humanest was not a person nor a villager, that I thought no place could ever be strange to me again.

> "Mourning untimely consumes the sad;
> Few are their days in the land of the living,
> Beautiful daughter of Toscar."[3]

Some of my pleasantest hours were during the long rain storms in the spring or fall, which confined me to the house for the afternoon as well as the forenoon, soothed by their ceaseless roar and pelting; when an early twilight ushered in a long evening in which many thoughts had time to take root and unfold themselves. In those driving north-east rains which

---

[3] From "Croma" in James Macpherson (1736–1796), *Fingal: The Genuine Remains of Ossian* (1761), a work Macpherson attributed to a mythical Celtic hero named Ossian but which he himself had written.

tried the village houses so, when the maids stood ready with mop and pail in front entries to keep the deluge out, I sat behind my door in my little house, which was all entry, and thoroughly enjoyed its protection. In one heavy thunder shower the lightning struck a large pitch-pine across the pond, making a very conspicuous and perfectly regular spiral groove from top to bottom, an inch or more deep, and four or five inches wide, as you would groove a walking-stick. I passed it again the other day, and was struck with awe on looking up and beholding that mark, now more distinct than ever, where a terrific and resistless bolt came down out of the harmless sky eight years ago. Men frequently say to me, "I should think you would feel lonesome down there, and want to be nearer to folks, rainy and snowy days and nights especially." I am tempted to reply to such—This whole earth which we inhabit is but a point in space. How far apart, think you, dwell the two most distant inhabitants of yonder star, the breadth of whose disk cannot be appreciated by our instruments? Why should I feel lonely? is not our planet in the Milky Way? This which you put seems to me not to be the most important question. What sort of space is that which separates a man from his fellows and makes him solitary? I have found that no exertion of the legs can bring two minds much nearer to one another. What do we want most to dwell near to? Not to many men surely, the depot, the post office, the barroom, the meeting-house, the school-house, the grocery, Beacon Hill, or the Five Points,[4] where men most congregate, but to the perennial source of our life, whence in all our experience we have found that to issue, as the willow stands near the water and sends out its roots in that direction. This will vary with different natures, but this is the place where a wise man will dig his cellar. . . . I one evening overtook one of my townsmen, who has accumulated what is called "a handsome property"—though I never got a *fair* view of it—on the Walden road, driving a pair of cattle to market, who inquired of me how I could bring my mind to give up so many of the comforts of life. I answered that I was very sure I liked it passably well; I was not joking. And so I went home to my bed, and left him to pick his way through the darkness and the mud to Brighton—or Bright-town[5]—which place he would reach some time in the morning.

Any prospect of awakening or coming to life to a dead man makes indifferent all times and places. The place where that may occur is always the

[4]Beacon Hill was one of Boston's most fashionable residential districts. Five Points, in New York, was notorious as a center of vice and gang activity.

[5]Brighton is a Boston suburb. "Bright" was a general name used for oxen, just like "Fido" for a dog.

same, and indescribably pleasant to all our senses. For the most part we allow only outlying and transient circumstances to make our occasions. They are, in fact, the cause of our distraction. Nearest to all things is that power which fashions their being. *Next* to us the grandest laws are continually being executed. *Next* to us is not the workman whom we have hired, with whom we love so well to talk, but the workman whose work we are.

"How vast and profound is the influence of the subtile powers of Heaven and of Earth!"

"We seek to perceive them, and we do not see them; we seek to hear them, and we do not hear them; identified with the substance of things, they cannot be separated from them."

"They cause that in all the universe men purify and sanctify their hearts, and clothe themselves in their holiday garments to offer sacrifices and oblations to their ancestors. It is an ocean of subtile intelligences. They are every where, above us, on our left, on our right; they environ us on all sides."[6]

We are the subjects of an experiment which is not a little interesting to me. Can we not do without the society of our gossips a little while under these circumstances—have our own thoughts to cheer us? Confucius says truly, "Virtue does not remain as an abandoned orphan; it must of necessity have neighbors."[7]

With thinking we may be beside ourselves in a sane sense. By a conscious effort of the mind we can stand aloof from actions and their consequences; and all things, good and bad, go by us like a torrent. We are not wholly involved in Nature. I may be either the driftwood in the stream, or Indra[8] in the sky looking down on it. I *may* be affected by a theatrical exhibition; on the other hand, I *may not* be affected by an actual event which appears to concern me much more. I only know myself as a human entity; the scene, so to speak, of thoughts and affections; and am sensible of a certain doubleness by which I can stand as remote from myself as from another. However intense my experience, I am conscious of the presence and criticism of a part of me, which, as it were, is not a part of me, but spectator, sharing no experience, but taking note of it; and that is no more I than it is you. When the play, it may be the tragedy, of life is over, the spectator goes his way. It was a kind of fiction, a work of the imagination only, so

---

[6] Confucius, *The Doctrine of the Mean* 14.
[7] Confucius, *Analects* 4.
[8] In Hindu scripture, the chief god, who wields the thunder and rules over the rain and the air.

far as he was concerned. This doubleness may easily make us poor neighbors and friends sometimes.

I find it wholesome to be alone the greater part of the time. To be in company, even with the best, is soon wearisome and dissipating. I love to be alone. I never found the companion that was so companionable as solitude. We are for the most part more lonely when we go abroad among men than when we stay in our chambers. A man thinking or working is always alone, let him be where he will. Solitude is not measured by the miles of space that intervene between a man and his fellows. The really diligent student in one of the crowded hives of Cambridge College[9] is as solitary as a dervis in the desert. The farmer can work alone in the field or the woods all day, hoeing or chopping, and not feel lonesome, because he is employed; but when he comes home at night he cannot sit down in a room alone, at the mercy of his thoughts, but must be where he can "see the folks," and recreate, and as he thinks remunerate, himself for his day's solitude; and hence he wonders how the student can sit alone in the house all night and most of the day without ennui and "the blues"; but he does not realize that the student, though in the house, is still at work in *his* field, and chopping in *his* woods, as the farmer in his, and in turn seeks the same recreation and society that the latter does, though it may be a more condensed form of it.

Society is commonly too cheap. We meet at very short intervals, not having had time to acquire any new value for each other. We meet at meals three times a day, and give each other a new taste of that old musty cheese that we are. We have had to agree on a certain set of rules, called etiquette and politeness, to make this frequent meeting tolerable and that we need not come to open war. We meet at the post office, and at the sociable, and about the fireside every night; we live thick and are in each other's way, and stumble over one another, and I think that we thus lose some respect for one another. Certainly less frequency would suffice for all important and hearty communications. Consider the girls in a factory—never alone, hardly in their dreams. It would be better if there were but one inhabitant to a square mile, as where I live. The value of a man is not in his skin, that we should touch him.

I have heard of a man lost in the woods and dying of famine and exhaustion at the foot of a tree, whose loneliness was relieved by the grotesque visions with which, owing to bodily weakness, his diseased imagination surrounded him, and which he believed to be real. So also, owing to bodily and mental health and strength, we may be continually cheered

---

[9] Harvard College.

by a like but more normal and natural society, and come to know that we are never alone.

I have a great deal of company in my house; especially in the morning, when nobody calls. Let me suggest a few comparisons, that some one may convey an idea of my situation. I am no more lonely than the loon in the pond that laughs so loud, or than Walden Pond itself. What company has that lonely lake, I pray? And yet it has not the blue devils, but the blue angels in it, in the azure tint of its waters. The sun is alone, except in thick weather, when there sometimes appear to be two, but one is a mock sun. God is alone—but the devil, he is far from being alone; he sees a great deal of company; he is legion. I am no more lonely than a single mullein or dandelion in a pasture, or a bean leaf, or sorrel, or a horse-fly, or a humble-bee. I am no more lonely than the Mill Brook, or a weathercock, or the north star, or the south wind, or an April shower, or a January thaw, or the first spider in a new house.

I have occasional visits in the long winter evenings, when the snow falls fast and the wind howls in the wood, from an old settler and original proprietor, who is reported to have dug Walden Pond, and stoned it, and fringed it with pine woods; who tells me stories of old time and of new eternity; and between us we manage to pass a cheerful evening with social mirth and pleasant views of things, even without apples or cider—a most wise and humorous friend, whom I love much, who keeps himself more secret than ever did Goffe or Whalley;[10] and though he is thought to be dead, none can show where he is buried. An elderly dame, too, dwells in my neighborhood, invisible to most persons, in whose odorous herb garden I love to stroll sometimes, gathering simples and listening to her fables; for she has a genius of unequalled fertility, and her memory runs back farther than mythology, and she can tell me the original of every fable, and on what fact every one is founded, for the incidents occurred when she was young. A ruddy and lusty old dame, who delights in all weathers and seasons, and is likely to outlive all her children yet.

The indescribable innocence and beneficence of Nature—of sun and wind and rain, of summer and winter—such health, such cheer, they afford forever! and such sympathy have they ever with our race, that all Nature would be affected, and the sun's brightness fade, and the winds would sigh humanely, and the clouds rain tears, and the woods shed their leaves

---

[10] William Goffe (1605?–1679?) and Edward Whalley (?–1675?) were two of the judges who signed the death warrant for King Charles I of England; at the Restoration, they fled to Boston, New Haven, Milford, and finally Hadley, Massachusetts, where they remained in hiding from royal agents.

and put on mourning in midsummer, if any man should ever for a just cause grieve. Shall I not have intelligence with the earth? Am I not partly leaves and vegetable mould myself?

What is the pill which will keep us well, serene, contented? Not my or thy great-grandfather's, but our great-grandmother Nature's universal, vegetable, botanic medicines, by which she has kept herself young always, outlived so many old Parrs[11] in her day, and fed her health with their decaying fatness. For my panacea, instead of one of those quack vials of a mixture dipped from Acheron[12] and the Dead Sea,[13] which come out of those long shallow black-schooner looking wagons which we sometimes see made to carry bottles, let me have a draught of undiluted morning air. Morning air! If men will not drink of this at the fountain-head of the day, why, then, we must even bottle up some and sell it in the shops, for the benefit of those who have lost their subscription ticket to morning time in this world. But remember, it will not keep quite till noon-day even in the coolest cellar, but drive out the stopples long ere that and follow westward the steps of Aurora. I am no worshipper of Hygeia, who was the daughter of that old herb-doctor Aesculapius,[14] and who is represented on monuments holding a serpent in one hand, and in the other a cup out of which the serpent sometimes drinks; but rather of Hebe, cupbearer to Jupiter, who was the daughter of Juno and wild lettuce,[15] and who had the power of restoring gods and men to the vigor of youth. She was probably the only thoroughly sound-conditioned, healthy, and robust young lady that ever walked the globe, and wherever she came it was spring.

CHAPTER SIX
Visitors

I think that I love society as much as most, and am ready enough to fasten myself like a bloodsucker for the time to any full-blooded man that comes in my way. I am naturally no hermit, but might possibly sit out the sturdiest frequenter of the barroom, if my business called me thither.

---

[11] Thomas Parr (1483?–1635), an Englishman reputed to have lived 152 years.

[12] One of the five rivers in Greek myth separating the land of the dead from that of the living.

[13] A large salty body of water located on the border of present-day Israel and Jordan.

[14] In Greek mythology, Hygeia was the goddess of health, daughter of Aesclepius, son of Apollo and god of the healing arts.

[15] In Greek mythology, Hebe was the handmaiden of the gods and associated with perpetual youth; she was the daughter of Zeus (Jupiter in Roman myth) and Hera (Juno in Roman myth). In some legends, Hera conceived Hebe after eating wild lettuce.

I had three chairs in my house; one for solitude, two for friendship, three for society. When visitors came in larger and unexpected numbers there was but the third chair for them all, but they generally economized the room by standing up. It is surprising how many great men and women a small house will contain. I have had twenty-five or thirty souls, with their bodies, at once under my roof, and yet we often parted without being aware that we had come very near to one another. Many of our houses, both public and private, with their almost innumerable apartments, their huge halls and their cellars for the storage of wines and other munitions of peace, appear to me extravagantly large for their inhabitants. They are so vast and magnificent that the latter seem to be only vermin which infest them. I am surprised when the herald blows his summons before some Tremont or Astor or Middlesex House,[1] to see come creeping out over the piazza for all inhabitants a ridiculous mouse, which soon again slinks into some hole in the pavement.

One inconvenience I sometimes experienced in so small a house, the difficulty of getting to a sufficient distance from my guest when we began to utter the big thoughts in big words. You want room for your thoughts to get into sailing trim and run a course or two before they make their port. The bullet of your thought must have overcome its lateral and ricochet motion and fallen into its last and steady course before it reaches the ear of the hearer, else it may plough out again through the side of his head. Also, our sentences wanted room to unfold and form their columns in the interval. Individuals, like nations, must have suitable broad and natural boundaries, even a considerable neutral ground, between them. I have found it a singular luxury to talk across the pond to a companion on the opposite side. In my house we were so near that we could not begin to hear—we could not speak low enough to be heard; as when you throw two stones into calm water so near that they break each other's undulations. If we are merely loquacious and loud talkers, then we can afford to stand very near together, cheek by jowl, and feel each other's breath; but if we speak reservedly and thoughtfully, we want to be farther apart, that all animal heat and moisture may have a chance to evaporate. If we would enjoy the most intimate society with that in each of us which is without, or above, being spoken to, we must not only be silent, but commonly so far apart bodily that we cannot possibly hear each other's voice in any case. Referred to this standard, speech is for the convenience of those who are hard of hearing; but there are many fine things which we cannot say if we have to shout. As the conversation began to assume a loftier and grander

[1] Fashionable hotels in Boston, New York, and Concord, respectively.

tone, we gradually shoved our chairs farther apart till they touched the wall in opposite corners, and then commonly there was not room enough.

My "best" room, however, my withdrawing room, always ready for company, on whose carpet the sun rarely fell, was the pine wood behind my house. Thither in summer days, when distinguished guests came, I took them, and a priceless domestic swept the floor and dusted the furniture and kept the things in order.

If one guest came he sometimes partook of my frugal meal, and it was no interruption to conversation to be stirring a hasty-pudding, or watching the rising and maturing of a loaf of bread in the ashes, in the mean while. But if twenty came and sat in my house there was nothing said about dinner, though there might be bread enough for two, more than if eating were a forsaken habit; but we naturally practised abstinence; and this was never felt to be an offence against hospitality, but the most proper and considerate course. The waste and decay of physical life, which so often needs repair, seemed miraculously retarded in such a case, and the vital vigor stood its ground. I could entertain thus a thousand as well as twenty; and if any ever went away disappointed or hungry from my house when they found me at home, they may depend upon it that I sympathized with them at least. So easy is it, though many housekeepers doubt it, to establish new and better customs in the place of the old. You need not rest your reputation on the dinners you give. For my own part, I was never so effectually deterred from frequenting a man's house, by any kind of Cerberus[2] whatever, as by the parade one made about dining me, which I took to be a very polite and roundabout hint never to trouble him so again. I think I shall never revisit those scenes. I should be proud to have for the motto of my cabin those lines of Spenser which one of my visitors inscribed on a yellow walnut leaf for a card:

> "Arrivéd there, the little house they fill,
> Ne looke for entertainment where none was;
> Rest is their feast, and all things at their will:
> The noblest mind the best contentment has."[3]

When Winslow,[4] afterward governor of the Plymouth Colony, went with a companion on a visit of ceremony to Massassoit[5] on foot through

---

[2] In Greek myth, a three-headed dog who guarded the land of the dead, Hades.

[3] *Faerie Queen,* 1.1.35.

[4] Edward Winslow (1595–1655); the account of this event (1621) is given in *The English Plantation at Plymouth* by Nathaniel Morton (1613–1685).

[5] Massassoit (c. 1590–1661) was a Wampanoag chief friendly to the Plymouth settlers.

the woods, and arrived tired and hungry at his lodge, they were well received by the king, but nothing was said about eating that day. When the night arrived, to quote their own words—"He laid us on the bed with himself and his wife, they at the one end and we at the other, it being only plank, laid a foot from the ground, and a thin mat upon them. Two more of his chief men, for want of room, pressed by and upon us; so that we were worse weary of our lodging than of our journey." At one o'clock the next day Massassoit "brought two fishes that he had shot," about thrice as big as a bream; "these being boiled, there were at least forty looked for a share in them. The most ate of them. This meal only we had in two nights and a day; and had not one of us bought a partridge, we had taken our journey fasting." Fearing that they would be lightheaded for want of food and also sleep, owing to "the savages' barbarous singing (for they used to sing themselves asleep)," and that they might get home while they had strength to travel, they departed. As for lodging, it is true they were but poorly entertained, though what they found an inconvenience was no doubt intended for an honor; but as far as eating was concerned, I do not see how the Indians could have done better. They had nothing to eat themselves, and they were wiser than to think that apologies could supply the place of food to their guests; so they drew their belts tighter and said nothing about it. Another time when Winslow visited them, it being a season of plenty with them, there was no deficiency in this respect.

As for men, they will hardly fail one any where. I had more visitors while I lived in the woods than at any other period of my life; I mean that I had some. I met several there under more favorable circumstances than I could any where else. But fewer came to see me upon trivial business. In this respect, my company was winnowed by my mere distance from town. I had withdrawn so far within the great ocean of solitude, into which the rivers of society empty, that for the most part, so far as my needs were concerned, only the finest sediment was deposited around me. Beside, there were wafted to me evidences of unexplored and uncultivated continents on the other side.

Who should come to my lodge this morning but a true Homeric or Paphlagonian[6] man—he had so suitable and poetic a name that I am sorry I cannot print it here—a Canadian, a wood-chopper and post-maker, who can hole fifty posts in a day, who made his last supper on a woodchuck which his dog caught.[7] He, too, has heard of Homer, and, "if it were not

[6]Paphlagonia was an ancient country of Asia Minor whose inhabitants were notorious for being backward and coarse.

[7]The woodchopper was, Thoreau wrote in the manuscript, "Aleck Therien . . . (Terrien,—Alexander the Farmer)."

for books," would "not know what to do rainy days," though perhaps he has not read one wholly through for many rainy seasons. Some priest who could pronounce the Greek itself taught him to read his verse in the testament in his native parish far away; and now I must translate to him, while he holds the book, Achilles' reproof to Patroclus for his sad countenance—"Why are you in tears, Patroclus, like a young girl?"—

> "Or have you alone heard some news from Phthia?
> They say that Menoetius lives yet, son of Actor,
> And Peleus lives, son of Æacus, among the Myrmidons,
> Either of whom having died, we should greatly grieve."[8]

He says, "That's good." He has a great bundle of white-oak bark under his arm for a sick man, gathered this Sunday morning. "I suppose there's no harm in going after such a thing today," says he. To him Homer was a great writer, though what his writing was about he did not know. A more simple and natural man it would be hard to find. Vice and disease, which cast such a sombre moral hue over the world, seemed to have hardly any existence for him. He was about twenty-eight years old, and had left Canada and his father's house a dozen years before to work in the States, and earn money to buy a farm with at last, perhaps in his native country. He was cast in the coarsest mould; a stout but sluggish body, yet gracefully carried, with a thick sunburnt neck, dark bushy hair, and dull sleepy blue eyes, which were occasionally lit up with expression. He wore a flat gray cloth cap, a dingy wool-colored greatcoat, and cowhide boots. He was a great consumer of meat, usually carrying his dinner to his work a couple of miles past my house—for he chopped all summer—in a tin pail; cold meats, often cold woodchucks, and coffee in a stone bottle which dangled by a string from his belt; and sometimes he offered me a drink. He came along early, crossing my bean-field, though without anxiety or haste to get to his work, such as Yankees exhibit. He wasn't a-going to hurt himself. He didn't care if he only earned his board. Frequently he would leave his dinner in the bushes, when his dog had caught a woodchuck by the way, and go back a mile and a half to dress it and leave it in the cellar of the house where he boarded, after deliberating first for half an hour whether he could not sink it in the pond safely till nightfall—loving to dwell long upon these themes. He would say, as he went by in the morning, "How thick the pigeons are! If working every day were not my trade, I could get

[8] *Iliad* 16.13–16.

all the meat I should want by hunting—pigeons, woodchucks, rabbits, partridges—by gosh! I could get all I should want for a week in one day."

He was a skilful chopper, and indulged in some flourishes and ornaments in his art. He cut his trees level and close to the ground, that the sprouts which came up afterward might be more vigorous and a sled might slide over the stumps; and instead of leaving a whole tree to support his corded wood, he would pare it away to a slender stake or splinter which you could break off with your hand at last.

He interested me because he was so quiet and solitary and so happy withal; a well of good humor and contentment which overflowed at his eyes. His mirth was without alloy. Sometimes I saw him at his work in the woods, felling trees, and he would greet me with a laugh of inexpressible satisfaction, and a salutation in Canadian French, though he spoke English as well. When I approached him he would suspend his work, and with half-suppressed mirth lie along the trunk of a pine which he had felled, and, peeling off the inner bark, roll it up into a ball and chew it while he laughed and talked. Such an exuberance of animal spirits had he that he sometimes tumbled down and rolled on the ground with laughter at any thing which made him think and tickled him. Looking round upon the trees he would exclaim—"By George! I can enjoy myself well enough here chopping; I want no better sport." Sometimes, when at leisure, he amused himself all day in the woods with a pocket pistol, firing salutes to himself at regular intervals as he walked. In the winter he had a fire by which at noon he warmed his coffee in a kettle; and as he sat on a log to eat his dinner the chicadees would sometimes come round and alight on his arm and peck at the potato in his fingers; and he said that he "liked to have the little *fellers* about him."

In him the animal man chiefly was developed. In physical endurance and contentment he was cousin to the pine and the rock. I asked him once if he was not sometimes tired at night, after working all day; and he answered, with a sincere and serious look, "Gorrappit, I never was tired in my life." But the intellectual and what is called spiritual man in him were slumbering as in an infant. He had been instructed only in that innocent and ineffectual way in which the Catholic priests teach the aborigines, by which the pupil is never educated to the degree of consciousness, but only to the degree of trust and reverence, and a child is not made a man, but kept a child. When Nature made him, she gave him a strong body and contentment for his portion, and propped him on every side with reverence and reliance, that he might live out his threescore years and ten a child. He was so genuine and unsophisticated that no introduction would serve to introduce him, more than if you introduced a woodchuck to your neighbor. He had got to find him out as you did. He would not play any part.

Men paid him wages for work, and so helped to feed and clothe him; but he never exchanged opinions with them. He was so simply and naturally humble—if he can be called humble who never aspires—that humility was no distinct quality in him, nor could he conceive of it. Wiser men were demigods to him. If you told him that such a one was coming, he did as if he thought that any thing so grand would expect nothing of himself, but take all the responsibility on itself, and let him be forgotten still. He never heard the sound of praise. He particularly reverenced the writer and the preacher. Their performances were miracles. When I told him that I wrote considerably, he thought for a long time that it was merely the handwriting which I meant, for he could write a remarkably good hand himself. I sometimes found the name of his native parish handsomely written in the snow by the highway, with the proper French accent, and knew that he had passed. I asked him if he ever wished to write his thoughts. He said that he had read and written letters for those who could not, but he never tried to write thoughts—no, he could not, he could not tell what to put first, it would kill him, and then there was spelling to be attended to at the same time!

I heard that a distinguished wise man and reformer asked him if he did not want the world to be changed; but he answered with a chuckle of surprise in his Canadian accent, not knowing that the question had ever been entertained before, "No, I like it well enough." It would have suggested many things to a philosopher to have dealings with him. To a stranger he appeared to know nothing of things in general; yet I sometimes saw in him a man whom I had not seen before, and I did not know whether he was as wise as Shakespeare or as simply ignorant as a child, whether to suspect him of a fine poetic consciousness or of stupidity. A townsman told me that when he met him sauntering through the village in his small close-fitting cap, and whistling to himself, he reminded him of a prince in disguise.

His only books were an almanac and an arithmetic, in which last he was considerably expert. The former was a sort of cyclopaedia to him, which he supposed to contain an abstract of human knowledge, as indeed it does to a considerable extent. I loved to sound him on the various reforms of the day, and he never failed to look at them in the most simple and practical light. He had never heard of such things before. Could he do without factories? I asked. He had worn the home-made Vermont gray, he said, and that was good. Could he dispense with tea and coffee? Did this country afford any beverage beside water? He had soaked hemlock leaves in water and drank it, and thought that was better than water in warm weather. When I asked him if he could do without money, he showed the convenience of money in such a way as to suggest and coincide with the most philosophical accounts of the origin of this institution, and the very derivation of the word *pecunia.*[9] If an ox were his property, and he wished to get needles and thread at the store, he thought it would be inconvenient and impossible soon to go on mortgaging some portion of the creature each time to that amount. He could defend many institutions better than any philosopher, because, in describing them as they concerned him, he gave the true reason for their prevalence, and speculation had not suggested to him any other. At another time, hearing Plato's definition of a man—a biped without feathers—and that one exhibited a cock plucked and called it Plato's man, he thought it an important difference that the *knees* bent the wrong way. He would sometimes exclaim, "How I love to talk! By George, I could talk all day!" I asked him once, when I had not seen him for many months, if he had got a new idea this summer. "Good Lord," said he, "a man that has to work as I do, if he does not forget the ideas he has had, he will do well. May be the man you hoe with is inclined to race; then, by gorry, your mind must be there; you think of weeds." He would sometimes ask me first on such occasions, if I had made any improvement. One winter day I asked him if he was always satisfied with himself, wishing to suggest a substitute within him for the priest without, and some higher motive for living. "Satisfied!" said he; "some men are satisfied with one thing, and some with another. One man, perhaps, if he has got enough, will be satisfied to sit all day with his back to the fire and his belly to the table, by George!" Yet I never, by any manoeuvring, could get him to take the spiritual view of things; the highest that he appeared to conceive of was a simple expediency, such as you might expect an animal to appreciate; and this, practically, is true of most men. If I suggested any improvement in his mode of life, he merely answered, without expressing any regret, that it was too late. Yet he thoroughly believed in honesty and the like virtues.

There was a certain positive originality, however slight, to be detected in him, and I occasionally observed that he was thinking for himself and expressing his own opinion, a phenomenon so rare that I would any day walk ten miles to observe it, and it amounted to the re-origination of many of the institutions of society. Though he hesitated, and perhaps failed to express himself distinctly, he always had a presentable thought behind. Yet his thinking was so primitive and immersed in his animal life, that, though more promising than a merely learned man's, it rarely ripened to any thing which can be reported. He suggested that there might be men of genius in the lowest grades of life, however permanently humble and illiterate, who take their own view always, or do not pretend to see at all; who are

[9] Latin for "money," derived from *pecus,* "cattle."

as bottomless even as Walden Pond was thought to be, though they may be dark and muddy.

Many a traveller came out of his way to see me and the inside of my house, and, as an excuse for calling, asked for a glass of water. I told them that I drank at the pond, and pointed thither, offering to lend them a dipper. Far off as I lived, I was not exempted from that annual visitation which occurs, methinks, about the first of April, when every body is on the move; and I had my share of good luck, though there were some curious specimens among my visitors. Half-witted men from the almshouse and elsewhere came to see me; but I endeavored to make them exercise all the wit they had, and make their confessions to me; in such cases making wit the theme of our conversation; and so was compensated. Indeed, I found some of them to be wiser than the so called *overseers* of the poor and selectmen of the town, and thought it was time that the tables were turned. With respect to wit, I learned that there was not much difference between the half and the whole. One day, in particular, an inoffensive, simple-minded pauper, whom with others I had often seen used as fencing stuff, standing or sitting on a bushel in the fields to keep cattle and himself from straying, visited me, and expressed a wish to live as I did. He told me, with the utmost simplicity and truth, quite superior, or rather *inferior*, to any thing that is called humility, that he was "deficient in intellect." These were his words. The Lord had made him so, yet he supposed the Lord cared as much for him as for another. "I have always been so," said he, "from my childhood; I never had much mind; I was not like other children; I am weak in the head. It was the Lord's will, I suppose." And there he was to prove the truth of his words. He was a metaphysical puzzle to me. I have rarely met a fellow-man on such promising ground—it was so simple and sincere and so true all that he said. And, true enough, in proportion as he appeared to humble himself was he exalted. I did not know at first but it was the result of a wise policy. It seemed that from such a basis of truth and frankness as the poor weak-headed pauper had laid, our intercourse might go forward to something better than the intercourse of sages.

I had some guests from those not reckoned commonly among the town's poor, but who should be; who are among the world's poor, at any rate; guests who appeal, not to your hospitality, but to your *hospitalality;* who earnestly wish to be helped, and preface their appeal with the information that they are resolved, for one thing, never to help themselves. I require of a visitor that he be not actually starving, though he may have the very best appetite in the world, however he got it. Objects of charity are not guests. Men who did not know when their visit had terminated, though I went about my business again, answering them from greater and greater remoteness. Men of almost every degree of wit called on me in the migrating season. Some who had more wits than they knew what to do with; runaway slaves with plantation manners, who listened from time to time, like the fox in the fable,[10] as if they heard the hounds a-baying on their track, and looked at me beseechingly, as much as to say,

"O Christian, will you send me back?"

One real runaway slave, among the rest, whom I helped to forward toward the northstar. Men of one idea, like a hen with one chicken, and that a duckling; men of a thousand ideas, and unkempt heads, like those hens which are made to take charge of a hundred chickens, all in pursuit of one bug, a score of them lost in every morning's dew—and become frizzled and mangy in consequence; men of ideas instead of legs, a sort of intellectual centipede that made you crawl all over. One man proposed a book in which visitors should write their names, as at the White Mountains; but, alas! I have too good a memory to make that necessary.

I could not but notice some of the peculiarities of my visitors. Girls and boys and young women generally seemed glad to be in the woods. They looked in the pond and at the flowers, and improved their time. Men of business, even farmers, thought only of solitude and employment, and of the great distance at which I dwelt from something or other; and though they said that they loved a ramble in the woods occasionally, it was obvious that they did not. Restless committed men, whose time was all taken up in getting a living or keeping it; ministers who spoke of God as if they enjoyed a monopoly of the subject, who could not bear all kinds of opinions; doctors, lawyers, uneasy housekeepers who pried into my cupboard and bed when I was out—how came Mrs. ——— to know that my sheets were not as clean as hers?—young men who had ceased to be young, and had concluded that it was safest to follow the beaten track of the professions—all these generally said that it was not possible to do so much good in my position. Ay! there was the rub. The old and infirm and the timid, of whatever age or sex, thought most of sickness, and sudden accident and death; to them life seemed full of danger—what danger is there if you don't think of any?—and they thought that a prudent man would carefully select the safest position, where Dr. B[11] might be on hand at a moment's warning. To them the village was literally a *community*, a league

---

[10]Perhaps from Aesop's fable about the fox and the woodman, in which the fox, pursued by hounds, appeals to the woodman not to betray him.
[11]Josiah Bartlett, one of Concord's physicians.

for mutual defence, and you would suppose that they would not go a-huckleberrying without a medicine chest. The amount of it is, if a man is alive, there is always *danger* that he may die, though the danger must be allowed to be less in proportion as he is dead-and-alive to begin with. A man sits as many risks as he runs. Finally, there were the self-styled reformers, the greatest bores of all, who thought that I was forever singing—

> This is the house that I built;
> This is the man that lives in the house that I built;

but they did not know that the third line was—

> These are the folks that worry the man
> That lives in the house that I built.

I did not fear the hen-harriers, for I kept no chickens; but I feared the men-harriers rather.

I had more cheering visitors than the last. Children come a-berrying, railroad men taking a Sunday morning walk in clean shirts, fishermen and hunters, poets and philosophers, in short, all honest pilgrims, who came out to the woods for freedom's sake, and really left the village behind, I was ready to greet with—"Welcome, Englishmen! welcome, Englishmen!"[12] for I had had communication with that race.

CHAPTER SEVEN
The Bean-Field

Meanwhile my beans, the length of whose rows, added together, was seven miles already planted, were impatient to be hoed, for the earliest had grown considerably before the latest were in the ground; indeed they were not easily to be put off. What was the meaning of this so steady and self-respecting, this small Herculean labor, I knew not. I came to love my rows, my beans, though so many more than I wanted. They attached me to the earth, and so I got strength like Antaeus.[1] But why should I raise them? Only Heaven knows. This was my curious labor all summer—to make this portion of the earth's surface, which had yielded only cinquefoil, blackberries, johnswort, and the like, before, sweet wild fruits and pleasant flowers, produce instead this pulse. What shall I learn of beans or beans of

[12] The words with which the Indian Samoset is supposed to have greeted the Pilgrims.
[1] In Greek mythology, a giant who regained his strength by touching the earth. Hercules killed him by holding him off the ground and then stifling him.

me? I cherish them, I hoe them, early and late I have an eye to them; and this is my day's work. It is a fine broad leaf to look on. My auxiliaries are the dews and rains which water this dry soil, and what fertility is in the soil itself, which for the most part is lean and effete. My enemies are worms, cool days, and most of all woodchucks. The last have nibbled for me a quarter of an acre clean. But what right had I to oust johnswort and the rest, and break up their ancient herb garden? Soon, however, the remaining beans will be too tough for them, and go forward to meet new foes.

When I was four years old, as I well remember, I was brought from Boston to this my native town, through these very woods and this field, to the pond. It is one of the oldest scenes stamped on my memory. And now tonight my flute has waked the echoes over that very water. The pines still stand here older than I; or, if some have fallen, I have cooked my supper with their stumps, and a new growth is rising all around, preparing another aspect for new infant eyes. Almost the same johnswort springs from the same perennial root in this pasture, and even I have at length helped to clothe that fabulous landscape of my infant dreams, and one of the results of my presence and influence is seen in these bean leaves, corn blades, and potato vines.

I planted about two acres and a half of upland; and as it was only about fifteen years since the land was cleared, and I myself had got out two or three cords of stumps, I did not give it any manure; but in the course of the summer it appeared by the arrow-heads which I turned up in hoeing, that an extinct nation had anciently dwelt here and planted corn and beans ere white men came to clear the land, and so, to some extent, had exhausted the soil for this very crop.

Before yet any woodchuck or squirrel had run across the road, or the sun had got above the shrub-oaks, while all the dew was on, though the farmers warned me against it—I would advise you to do all your work if possible while the dew is on—I began to level the ranks of haughty weeds in my bean-field and throw dust upon their heads. Early in the morning I worked barefooted, dabbling like a plastic artist in the dewy and crumbling sand, but later in the day the sun blistered my feet. There the sun lighted me to hoe beans, pacing slowly backward and forward over that yellow gravelly upland, between the long green rows, fifteen rods, the one end terminating in a shrub oak copse where I could rest in the shade, the other in a blackberry field where the green berries deepened their tints by the time I had made another bout. Removing the weeds, putting fresh soil about the bean stems, and encouraging this weed which I had sown, making the yellow soil express its summer thought in bean leaves and blossoms rather than in wormwood and piper and millet grass, making the earth say beans instead of grass—this was my daily work. As I had little aid from horses or cattle, or hired men or boys, or improved implements of husbandry, I was much slower, and became much more intimate with my beans than usual. But labor of the hands, even when pursued to the verge of drudgery, is perhaps never the worst form of idleness. It has a constant and imperishable moral, and to the scholar it yields a classic result. A very *agricola laboriosus*[2] was I to travellers bound westward through Lincoln and Wayland[3] to nobody knows where; they sitting at their ease in gigs, with elbows on knees, and reins loosely hanging in festoons; I the home-staying, laborious native of the soil. But soon my homestead was out of their sight and thought. It was the only open and cultivated field for a great distance on either side of the road, so they made the most of it; and sometimes the man in the field heard more of travellers' gossip and comment than was meant for his ear: "Beans so late! peas so late!"—for I continued to plant when others had begun to hoe—the ministerial husbandman had not suspected it. "Corn, my boy, for fodder; corn for fodder." "Does he *live* there?" asks the black bonnet of the gray coat; and the hard-featured farmer reins up his grateful dobbin to inquire what you are doing where he sees no manure in the furrow, and recommends a little chip dirt, or any little waste stuff, or it may be ashes or plaster. But here were two acres and a half of furrows, and only a hoe for cart and two hands to draw it—there being an aversion to other carts and horses—and chip dirt far away. Fellow-travellers as they rattled by compared it aloud with the fields which they had passed, so that I came to know how I stood in the agricultural world. This was one field not in Mr. Coleman's report.[4] And, by the way, who estimates the value of the crop which Nature yields in the still wilder fields unimproved by man? The crop of *English* hay is carefully weighed, the moisture calculated, the silicates and the potash; but in all dells and pond holes in the woods and pastures and swamps grows a rich and various crop only unreaped by man. Mine was, as it were, the connecting link between wild and cultivated fields; as some states are civilized, and others half-civilized, and others savage or barbarous, so my field was, though not in a bad sense, a half-cultivated field. They were beans cheerfully returning to their wild and primitive state that I cultivated, and my hoe played the *Rans des Vaches*[5] for them.

---

[2] Toiling farmer.

[3] Towns near Concord.

[4] Henry Coleman (1785–1849), Unitarian minister and State Commissioner for the Agricultural Survey of Massachusetts, which was printed in four reports from 1828 to 1841.

[5] A song sung by Swiss cowherds to call their cattle.

Near at hand, upon the topmost spray of a birch, sings the brown-thrasher—or red mavis, as some love to call him—all the morning, glad of your society, that would find out another farmer's field if yours were not here. While you are planting the seed, he cries—"Drop it, drop it—cover it up, cover it up—pull it up, pull it up, pull it up." But this was not corn, and so it was safe from such enemies as he. You may wonder what his rigmarole, his amateur Paganini[6] performances on one string or on twenty, have to do with your planting, and yet prefer it to leached ashes or plaster. It was a cheap sort of top dressing in which I had entire faith.

As I drew a still fresher soil about the rows with my hoe, I disturbed the ashes of unchronicled nations who in primeval years lived under these heavens, and their small implements of war and hunting were brought to the light of this modern day. They lay mingled with other natural stones, some of which bore the marks of having been burned by Indian fires, and some by the sun, and also bits of pottery and glass brought hither by the recent cultivators of the soil. When my hoe tinkled against the stones, that music echoed to the woods and the sky, and was an accompaniment to my labor which yielded an instant and immeasurable crop. It was no longer beans that I hoed, nor I that hoed beans; and I remembered with as much pity as pride, if I remembered at all, my acquaintances who had gone to the city to attend the oratorios. The night-hawk circled overhead in the sunny afternoons—for I sometimes made a day of it—like a mote in the eye, or in heaven's eye, falling from time to time with a swoop and a sound as if the heavens were rent, torn at last to very rags and tatters, and yet a seamless cope remained; small imps that fill the air and lay their eggs on the ground on bare sand or rocks on the tops of hills, where few have found them; graceful and slender like ripples caught up from the pond, as leaves are raised by the wind to float in the heavens; such kindredship is in Nature. The hawk is aerial brother of the wave which he sails over and surveys, those his perfect air-inflated wings answering to the elemental unfledged pinions of the sea. Or sometimes I watched a pair of hen-hawks circling high in the sky, alternately soaring and descending, approaching and leaving one another, as if they were the imbodiment of my own thoughts. Or I was attracted by the passage of wild pigeons from this wood to that, with a slight quivering winnowing sound and carrier haste; or from under a rotten stump my hoe turned up a sluggish portentous and outlandish spotted salamander, a trace of Egypt and the Nile, yet our contemporary. When I paused to lean on my hoe, these sounds and sights I

[6] Nicolo Paganini (1782–1840), Italian virtuoso violinist and composer.

heard and saw any where in the row, a part of the inexhaustible entertainment which the country offers.

On gala days the town fires its great guns,[7] which echo like popguns to these woods, and some waifs of martial music occasionally penetrate thus far. To me, away there in my bean-field at the other end of the town, the big guns sounded as if a puff ball had burst; and when there was a military turnout of which I was ignorant, I have sometimes had a vague sense all the day of some sort of itching and disease in the horizon, as if some eruption would break out there soon, either scarlatina or canker-rash, until at length some more favorable puff of wind, making haste over the fields and up the Wayland road, brought me information of the "trainers."[8] It seemed by the distant hum as if somebody's bees had swarmed, and that the neighbors, according to Virgil's advice, by a faint *tintinnabulum* upon the most sonorous of their domestic utensils, were endeavoring to call them down into the hive again. And when the sound died quite away, and the hum had ceased, and the most favorable breezes told no tale, I knew that they had got the last drone of them all safely into the Middlesex hive, and that now their minds were bent on the honey with which it was smeared.

I felt proud to know that the liberties of Massachusetts and of our fatherland were in such safe keeping; and as I turned to my hoeing again I was filled with an inexpressible confidence, and pursued my labor cheerfully with a calm trust in the future.

When there were several bands of musicians, it sounded as if all the village was a vast bellows, and all the buildings expanded and collapsed alternately with a din. But sometimes it was a really noble and inspiring strain that reached these woods, and the trumpet that sings of fame, and I felt as if I could spit a Mexican with a good relish—for why should we always stand for trifles?—and looked round for a woodchuck or a skunk to exercise my chivalry upon. These martial strains seemed as far away as Palestine, and reminded me of a march of crusaders in the horizon, with a slight tantivy and tremulous motion of the elm-tree tops which overhang the village. This was one of the *great* days; though the sky had from my clearing only the same everlastingly great look that it wears daily, and I saw no difference in it.

It was a singular experience that long acquaintance which I cultivated with beans, what with planting, and hoeing, and harvesting, and thresh-

[7] April 19, the anniversary of the 1775 Battle of Concord, and July 4, Independence Day.
[8] Members of the Concord Artillery, a state militia unit.

ing, and picking over, and selling them—the last was the hardest of all—I might add eating, for I did taste. I was determined to know beans. When they were growing, I used to hoe from five o'clock in the morning till noon, and commonly spent the rest of the day about other affairs. Consider the intimate and curious acquaintance one makes with various kinds of weeds—it will bear some iteration in the account, for there was no little iteration in the labor—disturbing their delicate organizations so ruthlessly, and making such invidious distinctions with his hoe, levelling whole ranks of one species, and sedulously cultivating another. That's Roman wormwood—that's pigweed—that's sorrel—that's piper-grass—have at him, chop him up, turn his roots upward to the sun, don't let him have a fibre in the shade, if you do he'll turn himself t'other side up and be as green as a leek in two days. A long war not with cranes, but with weeds, those Trojans who had sun and rain and dews on their side. Daily the beans saw me come to their rescue armed with a hoe, and thin the ranks of their enemies, filling up the trenches with weedy dead. Many a lusty crest-waving Hector, that towered a whole foot above his crowding comrades, fell before my weapon and rolled in the dust.[9]

Those summer days which some of my contemporaries devoted to the fine arts in Boston or Rome, and others to contemplation in India, and others to trade in London or New York, I thus, with the other farmers of New England, devoted to husbandry. Not that I wanted beans to eat, for I am by nature a Pythagorean,[10] so far as beans are concerned, whether they mean porridge or voting, and exchanged them for rice; but, perchance, as some must work in fields if only for the sake of tropes and expression, to serve a parable-maker one day. It was on the whole a rare amusement, which, continued too long, might have become a dissipation. Though I gave them no manure, and did not hoe them all once, I hoed them unusually well as far as I went, and was paid for it in the end, "there being in truth," as Evelyn says, "no compost or laetation whatsoever comparable to this continual motion, repastination, and turning of the mould with the spade." "The earth," he adds elsewhere, "especially if fresh, has a certain magnetism in it, by which it attracts the salt, power, or virtue (call it either) which gives it life, and is the logic of all the labor and stir we keep about it, to sustain us; all dungings and other sordid temperings being but

---

[9] The references—the battle of pygmies and cranes, Hector—are to the Trojan War, as recounted in Homer's *Iliad*. Hector was the leader of the Trojan forces.

[10] The Greek philosopher and mathematician Pythagoras (582–507? B.C.E.) is supposed to have prohibited his followers from eating beans.

the vicars succedaneous to this improvement."[11] Moreover, this being one of those "worn-out and exhausted lay fields which enjoy their sabbath," had perchance, as Sir Kenelm Digby[12] thinks likely, attracted "vital spirits" from the air. I harvested twelve bushels of beans.

But to be more particular, for it is complained that Mr. Coleman has reported chiefly the expensive experiments of gentlemen farmers, my outgoes were,

For a hoe	$0.54	
Ploughing, harrowing, and furrowing	7.50,	Too much
Beans for seed	3.12½	
Potatoes for seed	1.33	
Peas for seed	0.40	
Turnip seed	0.06	
White line for crow fence	0.02	
Horse cultivator and boy three hours	1.00	
Horse and cart to get crop	0.75	
In all	$14.72½	

My income was (patrem familias vendacem, non emacem esse oportet)[13] from

Nine bushels and twelve quarts of beans sold	$16.94
Five bushels large potatoes	2.50
Nine bushels small	2.25
Grass	1.00
Stalks	0.75
In all	$23.44

Leaving a pecuniary profit, as I have elsewhere said, of $8.71½.

This is the result of my experience in raising beans. Plant the common small white bush bean about the first of June, in rows three feet by eigh-

[11] John Evelyn (1620–1706), who wrote on a number of subjects and probably is best known for his *Diary*. The passages are from his *Terra, A Philosophical Discourse of Earth* (1729).

[12] Sir Kenelm Digby (1603–1665), naval commander and diplomat, who wrote on natural history, among other subjects.

[13] Cato, *De agri cultura:* "The head of a household should be he who sells rather than buys."

teen inches apart, being careful to select fresh round and unmixed seed. First look out for worms, and supply vacancies by planting anew. Then look out for woodchucks, if it is an exposed place, for they will nibble off the earliest tender leaves almost clean as they go; and again, when the young tendrils make their appearance, they have notice of it, and will shear them off with both buds and young pods, sitting erect like a squirrel. But above all harvest as early as possible, if you would escape frosts and have a fair and salable crop; you may save much loss by this means.

This further experience also I gained. I said to myself, I will not plant beans and corn with so much industry another summer, but such seeds, if the seed is not lost, as sincerity, truth, simplicity, faith, innocence, and the like, and see if they will not grow in this soil, even with less toil and manurance, and sustain me, for surely it has not been exhausted for these crops. Alas! I said this to myself; but now another summer is gone, and another, and another, and I am obliged to say to you, Reader, that the seeds which I planted, if indeed they *were* the seeds of those virtues, were wormeaten or had lost their vitality, and so did not come up. Commonly men will only be brave as their fathers were brave, or timid. This generation is very sure to plant corn and beans each new year precisely as the Indians did centuries ago and taught the first settlers to do, as if there were a fate in it. I saw an old man the other day, to my astonishment, making the holes with a hoe for the seventieth time at least, and not for himself to lie down in! But why should not the New Englander try new adventures, and not lay so much stress on his grain, his potato and grass crop, and his orchards—raise other crops than these? Why concern ourselves so much about our beans for seed, and not be concerned at all about a new generation of men? We should really be fed and cheered if when we met a man we were sure to see that some of the qualities which I have named, which we all prize more than those other productions, but which are for the most part broadcast and floating in the air, had taken root and grown in him. Here comes such a subtile and ineffable quality, for instance, as truth or justice, though the slightest amount or new variety of it, along the road. Our ambassadors should be instructed to send home such seeds as these, and Congress help to distribute them over all the land. We should never stand upon ceremony with sincerity. We should never cheat and insult and banish one another by our meanness, if there were present the kernel of worth and friendliness. We should not meet thus in haste. Most men I do not meet at all, for they seem not to have time; they are busy about their beans. We would not deal with a man thus plodding ever, leaning on a hoe or a spade as a staff between his work, not as a mushroom, but partially risen out of the earth, something more than erect, like swallows alighted and walking on the ground:

"And as he spake, his wings would now and then
Spread, as he meant to fly, then close again,"[14]

so that we should suspect that we might be conversing with an angel. Bread may not always nourish us; but it always does us good, it even takes stiffness out of our joints, and makes us supple and buoyant, when we knew not what ailed us, to recognize any generosity in man or Nature, to share any unmixed and heroic joy.

Ancient poetry and mythology suggest, at least, that husbandry was once a sacred art; but it is pursued with irreverent haste and heedlessness by us, our object being to have large farms and large crops merely. We have no festival, nor procession, nor ceremony, not excepting our Cattle-shows and so called Thanksgivings, by which the farmer expresses a sense of the sacredness of his calling, or is reminded of its sacred origin. It is the premium and the feast which tempt him. He sacrifices not to Ceres and the Terrestrial Jove, but to the infernal Plutus rather.[15] By avarice and selfishness, and a grovelling habit, from which none of us is free, of regarding the soil as property, or the means of acquiring property chiefly, the landscape is deformed, husbandry is degraded with us, and the farmer leads the meanest of lives. He knows Nature but as a robber. Cato says that the profits of agriculture are particularly pious or just (*maximeque pius quaestus*), and according to Varro the old Romans "called the same earth Mother and Ceres, and thought that they who cultivated it led a pious and useful life, and that they alone were left of the race of King Saturn."[16]

We are wont to forget that the sun looks on our cultivated fields and on the prairies and forests without distinction. They all reflect and absorb his rays alike, and the former make but a small part of the glorious picture which he beholds in his daily course. In his view the earth is all equally cultivated like a garden. Therefore we should receive the benefit of his light and heat with a corresponding trust and magnanimity. What though I value the seed of these beans, and harvest that in the fall of the year? This broad field which I have looked at so long looks not to me as the principal cultivator, but away from me to influences more genial to it, which water

[14]Francis Quarles (1592–1644), English poet. From "The Shepheards Oracles" (1646), Eglogue 5, ll. 1270–1271.

[15]In Roman mythology, Ceres represented the generative power of nature; "Jove," another name for Jupiter, was the chief god; Plutus, in Greek mythology, was the personification of wealth, originally agricultural.

[16]Marcus Terrentius Varro (116–27 B.C.E.), Roman writer said to have composed almost 600 books; from his *De re rustica*. In Roman mythology, Saturn was of the race of gods preceding that of Jupiter; he was an agricultural god.

and make it green. These beans have results which are not harvested by me. Do they not grow for woodchucks partly? The ear of wheat (in Latin *spica,* obsoletely *speca,* from *spe,* hope) should not be the only hope of the husbandman; its kernel or grain (*granum,* from *gerendo,* bearing) is not all that it bears. How, then, can our harvest fail? Shall I not rejoice also at the abundance of the weeds whose seeds are the granary of the birds? It matters little comparatively whether the fields fill the farmer's barns. The true husbandman will cease from anxiety, as the squirrels manifest no concern whether the woods will bear chestnuts this year or not, and finish his labor with every day, relinquishing all claim to the produce of his fields, and sacrificing in his mind not only his first but his last fruits also.

CHAPTER EIGHT
The Village

After hoeing, or perhaps reading and writing, in the forenoon, I usually bathed again in the pond, swimming across one of its coves for a stint, and washed the dust of labor from my person, or smoothed out the last wrinkle which study had made, and for the afternoon was absolutely free. Every day or two I strolled to the village to hear some of the gossip which is incessantly going on there, circulating either from mouth to mouth, or from newspaper to newspaper, and which, taken in homoeopathic doses, was really as refreshing in its way as the rustle of leaves and the peeping of frogs. As I walked in the woods to see the birds and squirrels, so I walked in the village to see the men and boys; instead of the wind among the pines I heard the carts rattle. In one direction from my house there was a colony of muskrats in the river meadows; under the grove of elms and buttonwoods in the other horizon was a village of busy men, as curious to me as if they had been prairie dogs, each sitting at the mouth of its burrow, or running over to a neighbor's to gossip. I went there frequently to observe their habits. The village appeared to me a great news room; and on one side, to support it, as once at Redding & Company's on State Street, they kept nuts and raisins, or salt and meal and other groceries. Some have such a vast appetite for the former commodity, that is, the news, and such sound digestive organs, that they can sit forever in public avenues without stirring, and let it simmer and whisper through them like the Etesian winds,[1] or as if inhaling ether, it only producing numbness and insensibility to pain—otherwise it would often be painful to hear—without affecting the consciousness. I hardly ever failed, when I rambled through the

[1] Annual Mediterranean winds.

village, to see a row of such worthies, either sitting on a ladder sunning themselves, with their bodies inclined forward and their eyes glancing along the line this way and that, from time to time, with a voluptuous expression, or else leaning against a barn with their hands in their pockets, like caryatides, as if to prop it up. They, being commonly out of doors, heard whatever was in the wind. These are the coarsest mills, in which all gossip is first rudely digested or cracked up before it is emptied into finer and more delicate hoppers within doors. I observed that the vitals of the village were the grocery, the barroom, the post office, and the bank; and, as necessary part of the machinery, they kept a bell, a big gun, and a fire-engine, at convenient places; and the houses were so arranged as to make the most of mankind, in lanes and fronting one another, so that every traveller had to run the gantlet, and every man, woman, and child might get a lick at him. Of course, those who were stationed nearest to the head of the line, where they could most see and be seen, and have the first blow at him, paid the highest prices for their places; and the few straggling inhabitants in the outskirts, where long gaps in the line began to occur, and the traveller could get over walls or turn aside into cow paths, and so escape, paid a very slight ground or window tax. Signs were hung out on all sides to allure him; some to catch him by the appetite, as the tavern and victualling cellar; some by the fancy, as the dry goods store and the jeweller's; and others by the hair or the feet or the skirts, as the barber, the shoemaker, or the tailor. Besides, there was a still more terrible standing invitation to call at every one of these houses, and company expected about these times. For the most part I escaped wonderfully from these dangers, either by proceeding at once boldly and without deliberation to the goal, as is recommended to those who run the gantlet, or by keeping my thoughts on high things, like Orpheus, who, "loudly singing the praises of the gods to his lyre, drowned the voices of the Sirens, and kept out of danger."[2] Sometimes I bolted suddenly, and nobody could tell my whereabouts, for I did not stand much about gracefulness, and never hesitated at a gap in a fence. I was even accustomed to make an irruption into some houses, where I was well entertained, and after learning the kernels and very last sieve-ful of news, what had subsided, the prospects of war and peace, and whether the world was likely to hold together much longer, I was let out through the rear avenues, and so escaped to the woods again.

It was very pleasant, when I staid late in town, to launch myself into the night, especially if it was dark and tempestuous, and set sail from some

[2]In Greek mythology, the music of Orpheus was so beautiful that it not only drowned out the Sirens' song but charmed the guardians and inhabitants of Hades.

bright village parlor or lecture room, with a bag of rye or Indian meal upon my shoulder, for my snug harbor in the woods, having made all tight without and withdrawn under hatches with a merry crew of thoughts, leaving only my outer man at the helm, or even tying up the helm when it was plain sailing. I had many a genial thought by the cabin fire "as I sailed." I was never cast away nor distressed in any weather, though I encountered some severe storms. It is darker in the woods, even in common nights, than most suppose. I frequently had to look up at the opening between the trees above the path in order to learn my route, and, where there was no cart-path, to feel with my feet the faint track which I had worn, or steer by the known relation of particular trees which I felt with my hands, passing between two pines for instance, not more than eighteen inches apart, in the midst of the woods, invariably in the darkest night. Sometimes, after coming home thus late in a dark and muggy night, when my feet felt the path which my eyes could not see, dreaming and absent-minded all the way, until I was aroused by having to raise my hand to lift the latch, I have not been able to recall a single step of my walk, and I have thought that perhaps my body would find its way home if its master should forsake it, as the hand finds its way to the mouth without assistance. Several times, when a visitor chanced to stay into evening, and it proved a dark night, I was obliged to conduct him to the cart-path in the rear of the house, and then point out to him the direction he was to pursue, and in keeping which he was to be guided rather by his feet than his eyes. One very dark night I directed thus on their way two young men who had been fishing in the pond. They lived about a mile off through the woods, and were quite used to the route. A day or two after one of them told me that they wandered about the greater part of the night, close by their own premises, and did not get home till toward morning, by which time, as there had been several heavy showers in the mean while, and the leaves were very wet, they were drenched to their skins. I have heard of many going astray even in the village streets, when the darkness was so thick that you could cut it with a knife, as the saying is. Some who live in the outskirts, having come to town a-shopping in their wagons, have been obliged to put up for the night; and gentlemen and ladies making a call have gone half a mile out of their way, feeling the sidewalk only with their feet, and not knowing when they turned. It is a surprising and memorable, as well as valuable experience, to be lost in the woods any time. Often in a storm, even by day, one will come out upon a well-known road and yet find it impossible to tell which way leads to the village. Though he knows that he has travelled it a thousand times, he cannot recognize a feature in it, but it is as strange to him as if it were a road in Siberia. By night, of course, the perplexity is infinitely greater. In our most trivial walks, we are constantly, though unconsciously, steering like pilots by certain well-known beacons and head-lands, and if we go beyond our usual course we still carry in our minds the bearing of some neighboring cape; and not till we are completely lost, or turned round—for a man needs only to be turned round once with his eyes shut in this world to be lost—do we appreciate the vastness and strangeness of Nature. Every man has to learn the points of compass again as often as he awakes, whether from sleep or any abstraction. Not till we are lost, in other words, not till we have lost the world, do we begin to find ourselves, and realize where we are and the infinite extent of our relations.

One afternoon, near the end of the first summer, when I went to the village to get a shoe from the cobbler's, I was seized and put into jail, because, as I have elsewhere related,[3] I did not pay a tax to, or recognize the authority of, the state which buys and sells men, women, and children, like cattle at the door of its senate-house. I had gone down to the woods for other purposes. But, wherever a man goes, men will pursue and paw him with their dirty institutions, and, if they can, constrain him to belong to their desperate odd-fellow society. It is true, I might have resisted forcibly with more or less effect, might have run "amok" against society; but I preferred that society should run "amok" against me, it being the desperate party. However, I was released the next day, obtained my mended shoe, and returned to the woods in season to get my dinner of huckleberries on Fair-Haven Hill. I was never molested by any person but those who represented the state. I had no lock nor bolt but for the desk which held my papers, not even a nail to put over my latch or windows. I never fastened my door night or day, though I was to be absent several days; not even when the next fall I spent a fortnight in the woods of Maine.[4] And yet my house was more respected than if it had been surrounded by a file of soldiers. The tired rambler could rest and warm himself by my fire, the literary amuse himself with the few books on my table, or the curious, by opening my closet door, see what was left of my dinner, and what prospect I had of a supper. Yet, though many people of every class came this way to the pond, I suffered no serious inconvenience from these sources, and I never missed any thing but one small book, a volume of Homer, which perhaps was improperly gilded, and this I trust a soldier of our camp has found by this time. I am convinced, that if all men were to live as simply as I then did, thieving and robbery would be unknown. These take place only in com-

[3] In "Civil Disobedience."

[4] The journey, one of three Thoreau made to Maine, is recorded in *The Maine Woods,* published in part in 1848 and 1858 and fully in 1864.

munities where some have got more than is sufficient while others have not enough. The Pope's Homers[5] would soon get properly distributed—

> "Nec bella fuerunt,
> Faginus astabat dum scyphus ante dapes."
>
> "Nor wars did men molest,
> When only beechen bowls were in request."[6]

"You who govern public affairs, what need have you to employ punishments? Love virtue, and the people will be virtuous. The virtues of a superior man are like the wind; the virtues of a common man are like the grass; the grass, when the wind passes over it, bends."[7]

CHAPTER NINE
The Ponds

Sometimes, having had a surfeit of human society and gossip, and worn out all my village friends, I rambled still farther westward than I habitually dwell, into yet more unfrequented parts of the town, "to fresh woods and pastures new,"[1] or, while the sun was setting, made my supper of huckleberries and blueberries on Fair Haven Hill, and laid up a store for several days. The fruits do not yield their true flavor to the purchaser of them, nor to him who raises them for the market. There is but one way to obtain it, yet few take that way. If you would know the flavor of huckleberries, ask the cow-boy or the partridge. It is a vulgar error to suppose that you have tasted huckleberries who never plucked them. A huckleberry never reaches Boston; they have not been known there since they grew on her three hills. The ambrosial and essential part of the fruit is lost with the bloom which is rubbed off in the market cart, and they become mere provender. As long as Eternal Justice reigns, not one innocent huckleberry can be transplanted thither from the country's hills.

---

[5] The English poet Alexander Pope (1688–1744) translated both Homer's *Iliad* and *Odyssey*.

[6] Albius Tibullus (c. 60–19 B.C.E.), *Elegies*.

[7] Confucius, *Analects* 12.

[1] John Milton, "Lycidas," l. 193.

Occasionally, after my hoeing was done for the day, I joined some impatient companion who had been fishing on the pond since morning, as silent and motionless as a duck or a floating leaf, and, after practising various kinds of philosophy, had concluded commonly, by the time I arrived, that he belonged to the ancient sect of Cenobites.[2] There was one older man, an excellent fisher and skilled in all kinds of woodcraft, who was pleased to look upon my house as a building erected for the convenience of fishermen; and I was equally pleased when he sat in my doorway to arrange his lines. Once in a while we sat together on the pond, he at one end of the boat, and I at the other; but not many words passed between us, for he had grown deaf in his later years, but he occasionally hummed a psalm, which harmonized well enough with my philosophy. Our intercourse was thus altogether one of unbroken harmony, far more pleasing to remember than if it had been carried on by speech. When, as was commonly the case, I had none to commune with, I used to raise the echoes by striking with a paddle on the side of my boat, filling the surrounding woods with circling and dilating sound, stirring them up as the keeper of a menagerie his wild beasts, until I elicited a growl from every wooded vale and hill-side.

In warm evenings I frequently sat in the boat playing the flute, and saw the perch, which I seemed to have charmed, hovering around me, and the moon travelling over the ribbed bottom, which was strewed with the wrecks of the forest. Formerly I had come to this pond adventurously, from time to time, in dark summer nights, with a companion, and making a fire close to the water's edge, which we thought attracted the fishes, we caught pouts with a bunch of worms strung on a thread; and when we had done, far in the night, threw the burning brands high into the air like skyrockets, which, coming down into the pond, were quenched with a loud hissing, and we were suddenly groping in total darkness. Through this, whistling a tune, we took our way to the haunts of men again. But now I made my home by the shore.

Sometimes, after staying in a village parlor till the family had all retired, I have retired to the woods, and, partly with a view to the next day's dinner, spent the hours of midnight fishing from a boat by moonlight, serenaded by owls and foxes, and hearing, from time to time, the creaking note of some unknown bird close at hand. These experiences were very memorable and valuable to me—anchored in forty feet of water, and twenty or thirty rods from the shore, surrounded sometimes by thousands of small perch and shiners, dimpling the surface with their tails in the moonlight, and communicating by a long flaxen line with mysterious nocturnal

[2] A religious sect; Thoreau is punning on "see no bites."

fishes which had their dwelling forty feet below, or sometimes dragging sixty feet of line about the pond as I drifted in the gentle night breeze, now and then feeling a slight vibration along it, indicative of some life prowling about its extremity, of dull uncertain blundering purpose there, and slow to make up its mind. At length you slowly raise, pulling hand over hand, some horned pout squeaking and squirming to the upper air. It was very queer, especially in dark nights, when your thoughts had wandered to vast and cosmogonal themes in other spheres, to feel this faint jerk, which came to interrupt your dreams and link you to Nature again. It seemed as if I might next cast my line upward into the air, as well as downward into this element which was scarcely more dense. Thus I caught two fishes as it were with one hook.

The scenery of Walden is on a humble scale, and, though very beautiful, does not approach to grandeur, nor can it much concern one who has not long frequented it or lived by its shore; yet this pond is so remarkable for its depth and purity as to merit a particular description. It is a clear and deep green well, half a mile long and a mile and three quarters in circumference, and contains about sixty-one and a half acres; a perennial spring in the midst of pine and oak woods, without any visible inlet or outlet except by the clouds and evaporation. The surrounding hills rise abruptly from the water to the height of forty to eighty feet, though on the southeast and east they attain to about one hundred and one hundred and fifty feet respectively, within a quarter and a third of a mile. They are exclusively woodland. All our Concord waters have two colors at least, one when viewed at a distance, and another, more proper, close at hand. The first depends more on the light, and follows the sky. In clear weather, in summer, they appear blue at a little distance, especially if agitated, and at a great distance all appear alike. In stormy weather they are sometimes of a dark slate color. The sea, however, is said to be blue one day and green another without any perceptible change in the atmosphere. I have seen our river, when, the landscape being covered with snow, both water and ice were almost as green as grass. Some consider blue "to be the color of pure water, whether liquid or solid." But, looking directly down into our waters from a boat, they are seen to be of very different colors. Walden is blue at one time and green at another, even from the same point of view. Lying between the earth and the heavens, it partakes of the color of both. Viewed from a hill-top it reflects the color of the sky, but near at hand it is of a yellowish tint next the shore where you can see the sand, then a light green, which gradually deepens to a uniform dark green in the body of the pond. In some lights, viewed even from a hill-top, it is of a vivid green next the shore. Some have referred this to the reflection of the verdure; but it is equally green there against the railroad sand-bank, and in the spring, before the leaves are expanded, and it may be simply the result of the prevailing blue mixed with the yellow of the sand. Such is the color of its iris. This is that portion, also, where in the spring, the ice being warmed by the heat of the sun reflected from the bottom, and also transmitted through the earth, melts first and forms a narrow canal about the still frozen middle. Like the rest of our waters, when much agitated, in clear weather, so that the surface of the waves may reflect the sky at the right angle, or because there is more light mixed with it, it appears at a little distance of a darker blue than the sky itself; and at such a time, being on its surface, and looking with divided vision, so as to see the reflection, I have discerned a matchless and indescribable light blue, such as watered or changeable silks and sword blades suggest, more cerulean than the sky itself, alternating with the original dark green on the opposite sides of the waves, which last appeared but muddy in comparison. It is a vitreous greenish blue, as I remember it, like those patches of the winter sky seen through cloud vistas in the west before sundown. Yet a single glass of its water held up to the light is as colorless as an equal quantity of air. It is well known that a large plate of glass will have a green tint, owing, as the makers say, to its "body," but a small piece of the same will be colorless. How large a body of Walden water would be required to reflect a green tint I have never proved. The water of our river is black or a very dark brown to one looking directly down on it, and, like that of most ponds, imparts to the body of one bathing in it a yellowish tinge; but this water is of such crystalline purity that the body of the bather appears of an alabaster whiteness, still more unnatural, which, as the limbs are magnified and distorted withal, produces a monstrous effect, making fit studies for a Michael Angelo.[3]

The water is so transparent that the bottom can easily be discerned at the depth of twenty-five or thirty feet. Paddling over it, you may see many feet beneath the surface the schools of perch and shiners, perhaps only an inch long, yet the former easily distinguished by their transverse bars, and you think that they must be ascetic fish that find a subsistence there. Once, in the winter, many years ago, when I had been cutting holes through the ice in order to catch pickerel, as I stepped ashore I tossed my axe back on to the ice, but, as if some evil genius had directed it, it slid four or five rods directly into one of the holes, where the water was twenty-five feet deep.

[3] Renaissance Italian sculptor, architect, and painter (1475–1564), known for his grand, robust figures.

Out of curiosity, I lay down on the ice and looked through the hole, until I saw the axe a little on one side, standing on its head, with its helve erect and gently swaying to and fro with the pulse of the pond; and there it might have stood erect and swaying till in the course of time the handle rotted off, if I had not disturbed it. Making another hole directly over it with an ice chisel which I had, and cutting down the longest birch which I could find in the neighborhood with my knife, I made a slip-noose, which I attached to its end, and, letting it down carefully, passed it over the knob of the handle, and drew it by a line along the birch, and so pulled the axe out again.

The shore is composed of a belt of smooth rounded white stones like paving stones, excepting one or two short sand beaches, and is so steep that in many places a single leap will carry you into water over your head; and were it not for its remarkable transparency, that would be the last to be seen of its bottom till it rose on the opposite side. Some think it is bottomless. It is nowhere muddy, and a casual observer would say that there were no weeds at all in it; and of noticeable plants, except in the little meadows recently overflowed, which do not properly belong to it, a closer scrutiny does not detect a flag nor a bulrush, nor even a lily, yellow or white, but only a few small heart-leaves and potamogetons, and perhaps a water-target or two; all which however a bather might not perceive; and these plants are clean and bright like the element they grow in. The stones extend a rod or two into the water, and then the bottom is pure sand, except in the deepest parts, where there is usually a little sediment, probably from the decay of the leaves which have been wafted on to it so many successive falls, and a bright green weed is brought up on anchors even in midwinter.

We have one other pond just like this, White Pond in Nine Acre Corner, about two and a half miles westerly; but, though I am acquainted with most of the ponds within a dozen miles of this centre, I do not know a third of this pure and well-like character. Successive nations perchance have drank at, admired, and fathomed it, and passed away, and still its water is green and pellucid as ever. Not an intermitting spring! Perhaps on that spring morning when Adam and Eve were driven out of Eden Walden Pond was already in existence, and even then breaking up in a gentle spring rain accompanied with mist and a southerly wind, and covered with myriads of ducks and geese, which had not heard of the fall, when still such pure lakes sufficed them. Even then it had commenced to rise and fall, and had clarified its waters and colored them of the hue they now wear, and obtained a patent of heaven to be the only Walden Pond in the world and distiller of celestial dews. Who knows in how many unremembered nations' literatures this has been the Castalian Fountain?[4] or what nymphs presided over it in the Golden Age? It is a gem of the first water which Concord wears in her coronet.

Yet perchance the first who came to this well have left some trace of their footsteps. I have been surprised to detect encircling the pond, even where a thick wood has just been cut down on the shore, a narrow shelf-like path in the steep hill-side, alternately rising and falling, approaching and receding from the water's edge, as old probably as the race of man here, worn by the feet of aboriginal hunters, and still from time to time unwittingly trodden by the present occupants of the land. This is particularly distinct to one standing on the middle of the pond in winter, just after a light snow has fallen, appearing as a clear undulating white line, unobscured by weeds and twigs, and very obvious a quarter of a mile off in many places where in summer it is hardly distinguishable close at hand. The snow reprints it, as it were, in clear white type alto-relievo.[5] The ornamented grounds of villas which will one day be built here may still preserve some trace of this.

The pond rises and falls, but whether regularly or not, and within what period, nobody knows, though, as usual, many pretend to know. It is commonly higher in the winter and lower in the summer, though not corresponding to the general wet and dryness. I can remember when it was a foot or two lower, and also when it was at least five feet higher, than when I lived by it. There is a narrow sand-bar running into it, with very deep water on one side, on which I helped boil a kettle of chowder, some six rods from the main shore, about the year 1824, which it has not been possible to do for twenty-five years; and on the other hand, my friends used to listen with incredulity when I told them, that a few years later I was accustomed to fish from a boat in a secluded cove in the woods, fifteen rods from the only shore they knew, which place was long since converted into a meadow. But the pond has risen steadily for two years, and now, in the summer of '52, is just five feet higher than when I lived there, or as high as it was thirty years ago, and fishing goes on again in the meadow. This makes a difference of level, at the outside, of six or seven feet; and yet the water shed by the surrounding hills is insignificant in amount, and this overflow must be referred to causes which affect the deep springs. This same summer the pond has begun to fall again. It is remarkable that the

[4] In Greek mythology, a fountain, located on Mount Parnassus, that was the source of poetic inspiration.
[5] High relief; the sculptural technique of projecting a figure from a background in a composition like a frieze.

fluctuation, whether periodical or not, appears thus to require many years for its accomplishment. I have observed one rise and a part of two falls, and I expect that a dozen or fifteen years hence the water will again be as low as I have ever known it. Flints' Pond, a mile eastward, allowing for the disturbance occasioned by its inlets and outlets, and the smaller intermediate ponds also, sympathize with Walden, and recently attained their greatest height at the same time with the latter. The same is true, as far as my observation goes, of White Pond.

This rise and fall of Walden at long intervals serves this use at least; the water standing at this great height for a year or more, though it makes it difficult to walk round it, kills the shrubs and trees which have sprung up about its edge since the last rise, pitch-pines, birches, alders, aspens, and others, and, falling again, leaves an unobstructed shore; for, unlike many ponds and all waters which are subject to a daily tide, its shore is cleanest when the water is lowest. On the side of the pond next my house, a row of pitch pines fifteen feet high has been killed and tipped over as if by a lever, and thus a stop put to their encroachments; and their size indicates how many years have elapsed since the last rise to this height. By this fluctuation the pond asserts its title to a shore, and thus the *shore* is *shorn,* and the trees cannot hold it by right of possession. These are the lips of the lake on which no beard grows. It licks its chaps from time to time. When the water is at its height, the alders, willows, and maples send forth a mass of fibrous red roots several feet long from all sides of their stems in the water, and to the height of three or four feet from the ground, in the effort to maintain themselves; and I have known the high-blueberry bushes about the shore, which commonly produce no fruit, bear an abundant crop under these circumstances.

Some have been puzzled to tell how the shore became so regularly paved. My townsmen have all heard the tradition, the oldest people tell me that they heard it in their youth, that anciently the Indians were holding a pow-wow upon a hill here, which rose as high into the heavens as the pond now sinks deep into the earth, and they used much profanity, as the story goes, though this vice is one of which the Indians were never guilty, and while they were thus engaged the hill shook and suddenly sank, and only one old squaw, named Walden, escaped, and from her the pond was named.[6] It has been conjectured that when the hill shook these stones rolled down its side and became the present shore. It is very certain, at any

[6]Thoreau annotated this passage as follows: "This is told of Alexander's Lake in Killingly Ct. By Barber. v his Con. Hist. Coll."

rate, that once there was no pond here, and now there is one; and this Indian fable does not in any respect conflict with the account of that ancient settler whom I have mentioned, who remembers so well when he first came here with his divining rod, saw a thin vapor rising from the sward, and the hazel pointed steadily downward, and he concluded to dig a well here. As for the stones, many still think that they are hardly to be accounted for by the action of the waves on these hills; but I observe that the surrounding hills are remarkably full of the same kind of stones, so that they have been obliged to pile them up in walls on both sides of the railroad cut nearest the pond; and, moreover, there are most stones where the shore is most abrupt; so that, unfortunately, it is no longer a mystery to me. I detect the paver. If the name was not derived from that of some English locality—Saffron Walden, for instance[7]—one might suppose that it was called, originally, *Walled-in* Pond.

The pond was my well ready dug. For four months in the year its water is as cold as it is pure at all times; and I think that it is then as good as any, if not the best, in the town. In the winter, all water which is exposed to the air is colder than springs and wells which are protected from it. The temperature of the pond water which had stood in the room where I sat from five o'clock in the afternoon till noon the next day, the sixth of March, 1846, the thermometer having been up to 65° to 70° some of the time, owing partly to the sun on the roof, was 42°, or one degree colder than the water of one of the coldest wells in the village just drawn. The temperature of the Boiling Spring[8] the same day was 45°, or the warmest of any water tried, though it is the coldest that I know of in summer, when, beside, shallow and stagnant surface water is not mingled with it. Moreover, in summer, Walden never becomes so warm as most water which is exposed to the sun, on account of its depth. In the warmest weather I usually placed a pailful in my cellar, where it became cool in the night, and remained so during the day; though I also resorted to a spring in the neighborhood. It was as good when a week old as the day it was dipped, and had no taste of the pump. Whoever camps for a week in summer by the shore of a pond, needs only bury a pail of water a few feet deep in the shade of his camp to be independent on the luxury of ice.

There have been caught in Walden, pickerel, one weighing seven pounds, to say nothing of another which carried off a reel with great ve-

---

[7]Thoreau annotated this passage as follows: "Evelyn in his Diary (1654) mentions 'the parish of Saffron Walden, famous for the abundance of Saffron there cultivated, and esteemed the best of any foreign country.'" Saffron Walden is about forty miles from London.

[8]A "bubbling," not hot, spring west of Walden.

locity, which the fisherman safely set down at eight pounds because he did not see him, perch and pouts, some of each weighing over two pounds, shiners, chivins or roach, (*Leuciscus pulchellus,*) a very few breams,[9] and a couple of eels, one weighing four pounds—I am thus particular because the weight of a fish is commonly its only title to fame, and these are the only eels I have heard of here—also, I have a faint recollection of a little fish some five inches long, with silvery sides and a greenish back, somewhat dace-like in its character, which I mention here chiefly to link my facts to fable. Nevertheless, this pond is not very fertile in fish. Its pickerel, though not abundant, are its chief boast. I have seen at one time lying on the ice pickerel of at least three different kinds; a long and shallow one, steel-colored, most like those caught in the river; a bright golden kind, with greenish reflections and remarkably deep, which is the most common here; and another, golden-colored, and shaped like the last, but peppered on the sides with small dark brown or black spots, intermixed with a few faint blood-red ones, very much like a trout. The specific name *reticulatus*[10] would not apply to this, it should be *guttatus* rather.[11] These are all very firm fish, and weigh more than their size promises. The shiners, pouts, and perch also, and indeed all the fishes which inhabit this pond, are much cleaner, handsomer, and firmer fleshed than those in the river and most other ponds, as the water is purer, and they can easily be distinguished from them. Probably many ichthyologists would make new varieties of some of them. There are also a clean race of frogs and tortoises, and a few muscles in it; muskrats and minks leave their traces about it, and occasionally a travelling mud-turtle visits it. Sometimes, when I pushed off my boat in the morning, I disturbed a great mud-turtle which had secreted himself under the boat in the night. Ducks and geese frequent it in the spring and fall, the white-bellied swallows (*Hirundo bicolor*) skim over it, and the peetweets (*Totanus macularius*) "teter" along its stony shores all summer. I have sometimes disturbed a fish-hawk sitting on a white-pine over the water; but I doubt if it is ever profaned by the wing of a gull, like Fair Haven.[12] At most, it tolerates one annual loon. These are all the animals of consequence which frequent it now.

You may see from a boat, in calm weather, near the sandy eastern shore, where the water is eight or ten feet deep, and also in some other

[9] Thoreau annotated this passage as follows: "*Pomotis obesus* [v Nov 26–58] one trout weighing a little over 5 lbs—(Nov. 14–57)."

[10] Netlike.

[11] Speckled.

[12] A bay in the Sudbury River not far from Walden.

parts of the pond, some circular heaps half a dozen feet in diameter by a foot in height, consisting of small stones less than a hen's egg in size, where all around is bare sand. At first you wonder if the Indians could have formed them on the ice for any purpose, and so, when the ice melted, they sank to the bottom; but they are too regular and some of them plainly too fresh for that. They are similar to those found in rivers; but as there are no suckers nor lampreys here, I know not by what fish they could be made. Perhaps they are the nests of the chivin. These lend a pleasing mystery to the bottom.

The shore is irregular enough not to be monotonous. I have in my mind's eye the western indented with deep bays, the bolder northern, and the beautifully scolloped southern shore, where successive capes overlap each other and suggest unexplored coves between. The forest has never so good a setting, nor is so distinctly beautiful, as when seen from the middle of a small lake amid hills which rise from the water's edge; for the water in which it is reflected not only makes the best foreground in such a case, but, with its winding shore, the most natural and agreeable boundary to it. There is no rawness nor imperfection in its edge there, as where the axe has cleared a part, or a cultivated field abuts on it. The trees have ample room to expand on the water side, and each sends forth its most vigorous branch in that direction. There Nature has woven a natural selvage, and the eye rises by just gradations from the low shrubs of the shore to the highest trees. There are few traces of man's hand to be seen. The water laves the shore as it did a thousand years ago.

A lake is the landscape's most beautiful and expressive feature. It is earth's eye; looking into which the beholder measures the depth of his own nature. The fluviatile trees next the shore are the slender eyelashes which fringe it, and the wooded hills and cliffs around are its overhanging brows.

Standing on the smooth sandy beach at the east end of the pond, in a calm September afternoon, when a slight haze makes the opposite shore line indistinct, I have seen whence came the expression, "the glassy surface of a lake." When you invert your head, it looks like a thread of finest gossamer stretched across the valley, and gleaming against the distant pine woods, separating one stratum of the atmosphere from another. You would think that you could walk dry under it to the opposite hills, and that the swallows which skim over might perch on it. Indeed, they sometimes dive below the line, as it were by mistake, and are undeceived. As you look over the pond westward you are obliged to employ both your hands to defend your eyes against the reflected as well as the true sun; for they are equally bright; and if, between the two, you survey its surface critically, it is literally as smooth as glass, except where the skater insects, at equal intervals scattered over its whole extent, by their motions in the sun produce the finest imaginable sparkle on it, or, perchance, a duck plumes itself, or, as I have said, a swallow skims so low as to touch it. It may be that in the distance a fish describes an arc of three or four feet in the air, and there is one bright flash where it emerges, and another where it strikes the water; sometimes the whole silvery arc is revealed; or here and there, perhaps, is a thistle-down floating on its surface, which the fishes dart at and so dimple it again. It is like molten glass cooled but not congealed, and the few motes in it are pure and beautiful like the imperfections in glass. You may often detect a yet smoother and darker water, separated from the rest as if by an invisible cobweb, boom of the water nymphs, resting on it. From a hill-top you can see a fish leap in almost any part; for not a pickerel or shiner picks an insect from this smooth surface but it manifestly disturbs the equilibrium of the whole lake. It is wonderful with what elaborateness this simple fact is advertised—this piscine murder will out—and from my distant perch I distinguish the circling undulations when they are half a dozen rods in diameter. You can even detect a water-bug (*Gyrinus*) ceaselessly progressing over the smooth surface a quarter of a mile off; for they furrow the water slightly, making a conspicuous ripple bounded by two diverging lines, but the skaters glide over it without rippling it perceptibly. When the surface is considerably agitated there are no skaters nor water-bugs on it, but apparently, in calm days, they leave their havens and adventurously glide forth from the shore by short impulses till they completely cover it. It is a soothing employment, on one of those fine days in the fall when all the warmth of the sun is fully appreciated, to sit on a stump on such a height as this, overlooking the pond, and study the dimpling circles which are incessantly inscribed on its otherwise invisible surface amid the reflected skies and trees. Over this great expanse there is no disturbance but it is thus at once gently smoothed away and assuaged, as, when a vase of water is jarred, the trembling circles seek the shore and all is smooth again. Not a fish can leap or an insect fall on the pond but it is thus reported in circling dimples, in lines of beauty, as it were the constant welling up of its fountain, the gentle pulsing of its life, the heaving of its breast. The thrills of joy and thrills of pain are undistinguishable. How peaceful the phenomena of the lake! Again the works of man shine as in the spring. Ay, every leaf and twig and stone and cobweb sparkles now at mid-afternoon as when covered with dew in a spring morning. Every motion of an oar or an insect produces a flash of light; and if an oar falls, how sweet the echo!

In such a day, in September or October, Walden is a perfect forest mirror, set round with stones as precious to my eye as if fewer or rarer. Nothing so fair, so pure, and at the same time so large, as a lake, perchance, lies on the surface of the earth. Sky water. It needs no fence. Nations come and go without defiling it. It is a mirror which no stone can crack, whose quicksilver will never wear off, whose gilding Nature continually repairs; no storms, no dust, can dim its surface ever fresh—a mirror in which all impurity presented to it sinks, swept and dusted by the sun's hazy brush—this the light dust-cloth—which retains no breath that is breathed on it, but sends its own to float as clouds high above its surface, and be reflected in its bosom still.

A field of water betrays the spirit that is in the air. It is continually receiving new life and motion from above. It is intermediate in its nature between land and sky. On land only the grass and trees wave, but the water itself is rippled by the wind. I see where the breeze dashes across it by the streaks or flakes of light. It is remarkable that we can look down on its surface. We shall, perhaps, look down thus on the surface of air at length, and mark where a still subtler spirit sweeps over it.

The skaters and water-bugs finally disappear in the latter part of October, when the severe frosts have come; and then and in November, usually, in a calm day, there is absolutely nothing to ripple the surface. One November afternoon, in the calm at the end of a rain storm of several days' duration, when the sky was still completely overcast and the air was full of mist, I observed that the pond was remarkably smooth, so that it was difficult to distinguish its surface; though it no longer reflected the bright tints of October, but the sombre November colors of the surrounding hills. Though I passed over it as gently as possible, the slight undulations produced by my boat extended almost as far as I could see, and gave a ribbed appearance to the reflections. But, as I was looking over the surface, I saw here and there at a distance a faint glimmer, as if some skater insects which had escaped the frosts might be collected there, or, perchance, the surface, being so smooth, betrayed where a spring welled up from the bottom. Paddling gently to one of these places, I was surprised to find myself surrounded by myriads of small perch, about five inches long, of a rich bronze color in the green water, sporting there and constantly rising to the surface and dimpling it, sometimes leaving bubbles on it. In such transparent and seemingly bottomless water, reflecting the clouds, I seemed to be floating through the air as in a balloon, and their swimming impressed me as a kind of flight or hovering, as if they were a compact flock of birds passing just beneath my level on the right or left, their fins, like sails, set all around them. There were many such schools in the pond, apparently improving the short season before winter would draw an icy shutter over their broad skylight, sometimes giving to the surface an appearance as if a slight breeze struck it, or a few rain-drops fell there. When I approached carelessly and alarmed them, they made a sudden plash and rippling with their tails, as if one had struck the water with a brushy bough, and instantly took refuge in the depths. At length the wind rose, the mist increased, and the waves began to run, and the perch leaped much higher than before, half out of water, a hundred black points, three inches long, at once above the surface. Even as late as the fifth of December, one year, I saw some dimples on the surface, and thinking it was going to rain hard immediately, the air being full of mist, I made haste to take my place at the oars and row homeward; already the rain seemed rapidly increasing, though I felt none on my cheek, and I anticipated a thorough soaking. But suddenly the dimples ceased, for they were produced by the perch, which the noise of my oars had scared into the depths, and I saw their schools dimly disappearing; so I spent a dry afternoon after all.

An old man who used to frequent this pond nearly sixty years ago, when it was dark with surrounding forests, tells me that in those days he sometimes saw it all alive with ducks and other water fowl, and that there were many eagles about it. He came here a-fishing, and used an old log canoe which he found on the shore. It was made of two white-pine logs dug out and pinned together, and was cut off square at the ends. It was very clumsy, but lasted a great many years before it became water-logged and perhaps sank to the bottom. He did not know whose it was; it belonged to the pond. He used to make a cable for his anchor of strips of hickory bark tied together. An old man, a potter, who lived by the pond before the Revolution, told him once that there was an iron chest at the bottom, and that he had seen it. Sometimes it would come floating up to the shore; but when you went toward it, it would go back into deep water and disappear. I was pleased to hear of the old log canoe, which took the place of an Indian one of the same material but more graceful construction, which perchance had first been a tree on the bank, and then, as it were, fell into the water, to float there for a generation, the most proper vessel for the lake. I remember that when I first looked into these depths there were many large trunks to be seen indistinctly lying on the bottom, which had either been blown over formerly, or left on the ice at the last cutting, when wood was cheaper; but now they have mostly disappeared.

When I first paddled a boat on Walden, it was completely surrounded by thick and lofty pine and oak woods, and in some of its coves grape vines had run over the trees next the water and formed bowers under which a boat could pass. The hills which form its shores are so steep, and the woods on them were then so high, that, as you looked down from the west end, it had the appearance of an amphitheatre for some kind of sylvan spectacle. I have spent many an hour, when I was younger, floating over its surface as the zephyr willed, having paddled my boat to the middle, and lying on my back across the seats, in a summer forenoon, dreaming awake, until I was aroused by the boat touching the sand, and I arose to see what shore my fates had impelled me to; days when idleness was the most attractive and productive industry. Many a forenoon have I stolen away, preferring to spend thus the most valued part of the day; for I was rich, if not in money, in sunny hours and summer days, and spent them lavishly; nor do I regret that I did not waste more of them in the workshop or the teacher's desk. But since I left those shores the woodchoppers have still further laid them waste, and now for many a year there will be no more rambling through the aisles of the wood, with occasional vistas through which you see the water. My Muse may be excused if she is silent henceforth. How can you expect the birds to sing when their groves are cut down?

Now the trunks of trees on the bottom, and the old log canoe, and the dark surrounding woods, are gone, and the villagers, who scarcely know where it lies, instead of going to the pond to bathe or drink, are thinking to bring its water, which should be as sacred as the Ganges[13] at least, to the village in a pipe, to wash their dishes with!—to earn their Walden by the turning of a cock or drawing of a plug! That devilish Iron Horse, whose ear-rending neigh is hear throughout the town, has muddied the Boiling Spring with his foot, and he it is that has browsed off all the woods on Walden shore; that Trojan horse, with a thousand men in his belly, introduced by mercenary Greeks! Where is the country's champion, the Moore of Moore Hall,[14] to meet him at the Deep Cut and thrust an avenging lance between the ribs of the bloated pest?

Nevertheless, of all the characters I have known, perhaps Walden wears best, and best preserves its purity. Many men have been likened to it, but few deserve that honor. Though the woodchoppers have laid bare first this shore and then that, and the Irish have built their sties by it, and the railroad has infringed on its border, and the ice-men have skimmed it once, it is itself unchanged, the same water which my youthful eyes fell on; all the change is in me. It has not acquired one permanent wrinkle after all its ripples. It is perennially young, and I may stand and see a swallow dip apparently to pick an insect from its surface as of yore. It struck me again tonight, as if I had not seen it almost daily for more than twenty years—Why, here is Walden, the same woodland lake that I discovered so many years ago; where a forest was cut down last winter another is springing up by its shore as lustily as ever; the same thought is welling up to its surface that was then; it is the same liquid joy and happiness to itself and its Maker, ay, and it *may* be to me. It is the work of a brave man surely, in

[13] A river in India considered sacred by Hindus.
[14] In the old English ballad "The Dragon of Wantley," a hero who kills a dragon.

whom there was no guile![15] He rounded this water with his hand, deepened and clarified it in his thought, and in his will bequeathed it to Concord. I see by its face that it is visited by the same reflection; and I can almost say, Walden, is it you?

It is no dream of mine,
To ornament a line;
I cannot come nearer to God and Heaven
Than I live to Walden even.
5 I am its stony shore,
And the breeze that passes o'er;
In the hollow of my hand
Are its water and its sand,
And its deepest resort
10 Lies high in my thought.

The cars never pause to look at it; yet I fancy that the engineers and firemen and brakemen, and those passengers who have a season ticket and see it often, are better men for the sight. The engineer does not forget at night, or his nature does not, that he has beheld this vision of serenity and purity once at least during the day. Though seen but once, it helps to wash out State-street[16] and the engine's soot. One proposes that it be called "God's Drop."

I have said that Walden has no visible inlet nor outlet, but it is on the one hand distantly and indirectly related to Flints' Pond, which is more elevated, by a chain of small ponds coming from that quarter, and on the other directly and manifestly to Concord River, which is lower, by a similar chain of ponds through which in some other geological period it may have flowed, and by a little digging, which God forbid, it can be made to flow thither again. If by living thus reserved and austere, like a hermit in the woods, so long, it has acquired such wonderful purity, who would not regret that the comparatively impure waters of Flints' Pond should be mingled with it, or itself should ever go to waste its sweetness in the ocean wave?

Flints', or Sandy Pond, in Lincoln, our greatest lake and inland sea, lies about a mile east of Walden. It is much larger, being said to contain

[15] Cf. John 1.47: "Jesus saw Nathanael coming to him, and saith of him, Behold an Israelite indeed, in whom is no guile."
[16] Boston's financial district.

one hundred and ninety-seven acres, and is more fertile in fish; but it is comparatively shallow, and not remarkably pure. A walk through the woods thither was often my recreation. It was worth the while, if only to feel the wind blow on your cheek freely, and see the waves run, and remember the life of mariners. I went a-chestnutting there in the fall, on windy days, when the nuts were dropping into the water and were washed to my feet; and one day, as I crept along its sedgy shore, the fresh spray blowing in my face, I came upon the mouldering wreck of a boat, the sides gone, and hardly more than the impression of its flat bottom left amid the rushes; yet its model was sharply defined, as if it were a large decayed pad, with its veins. It was as impressive a wreck as one could imagine on the sea-shore, and had as good a moral. It is by this time mere vegetable mould and undistinguishable pond shore, through which rushes and flags have pushed up. I used to admire the ripple marks on the sandy bottom, at the north end of this pond, made firm and hard to the feet of the wader by the pressure of the water, and the rushes which grew in Indian file, in waving lines, corresponding to these marks, rank behind rank, as if the waves had planted them. There also I have found, in considerable quantities, curious balls, composed apparently of fine grass or roots, of pipewort perhaps, from half an inch to four inches in diameter, and perfectly spherical. These wash back and forth in shallow water on a sandy bottom, and are sometimes cast on the shore. They are either solid grass, or have a little sand in the middle. At first you would say that they were formed by the action of the waves, like a pebble; yet the smallest are made of equally coarse materials, half an inch long, and they are produced only at one season of the year. Moreover, the waves, I suspect, do not so much construct as wear down a material which has already acquired consistency. They preserve their form when dry for an indefinite period.

Flints' Pond! Such is the poverty of our nomenclature. What right had the unclean and stupid farmer, whose farm abutted on this sky water, whose shores he has ruthlessly laid bare, to give his name to it? Some skin-flint, who loved better the reflecting surface of a dollar, or a bright cent, in which he could see his own brazen face; who regarded even the wild ducks which settled in it as trespassers; his fingers grown into crooked and horny talons from the long habit of grasping harpy-like—so it is not named for me. I go not there to see him nor to hear of him; who never *saw* it, who never bathed in it, who never loved it, who never protected it, who never spoke a good word for it, nor thanked God that he had made it. Rather let it be named from the fishes that swim in it, the wild fowl or quadrupeds which frequent it, the wild flowers which grow by its shores, or some wild man or child the thread of whose history is interwoven with its own; not from him who could show no title to it but the deed which a like-minded neighbor or legislature gave him—him who thought only of its money value; whose presence perchance cursed all the shore; who exhausted the land around it, and would fain have exhausted the waters within it; who regretted only that it was not English hay or cranberry meadow—there was nothing to redeem it, forsooth, in his eyes—and would have drained and sold it for the mud at its bottom. It did not turn his mill, and it was no *privilege* to him to behold it. I respect not his labors, his farm where every thing has its price; who would carry the landscape, who would carry his God, to market, if he could get any thing for him; who goes to market *for* his god as it is; on whose farm nothing grows free, whose fields bear no crops, whose meadows no flowers, whose trees no fruits, but dollars; who loves not the beauty of his fruits, whose fruits are not ripe for him till they are turned to dollars. Give me the poverty that enjoys true wealth. Farmers are respectable and interesting to me in proportion as they are poor—poor farmers. A model farm! where the house stands like a fungus in a muck-heap, chambers for men, horses, oxen, and swine, cleansed and uncleansed, all contiguous to one another! Stocked with men! A great grease-spot, redolent of manures and buttermilk! Under a high state of cultivation, being manured with the hearts and brains of men! As if you were to raise your potatoes in the church-yard! Such is a model farm.

No, no; if the fairest features of the landscape are to be named after men, let them be the noblest and worthiest men alone. Let our lakes receive as true names at least as the Icarian Sea, where "still the shore" a "brave attempt resounds."[17]

Goose Pond, of small extent, is on my way to Flints'; Fair-Haven, an expansion of Concord River, said to contain some seventy acres, is a mile south-west; and White Pond, of about forty acres, is a mile and a half beyond Fair-Haven. This is my lake country.[18] These, with Concord River, are my water privileges; and night and day, year in year out, they grind such grist as I carry to them.

Since the woodcutters, and the railroad, and I myself have profaned Walden, perhaps the most attractive, if not the most beautiful, of all our lakes, the gem of the woods, is White Pond—a poor name from its commonness, whether derived from the remarkable purity of its waters or the

[17] In Greek mythology, Icarus flew too near the sun, which melted the wax of the wings his father, Daedalus, had fashioned; he fell into the sea near Crete, which was consequently named after him.
[18] The Lake Country of England was identified with the English Romantic poets, particularly William Wordsworth.

color of its sands. In these as in other respects, however, it is a lesser twin of Walden. They are so much alike that you would say they must be connected under ground. It has the same stony shore, and its waters are of the same hue. As at Walden, in sultry dog-day weather, looking down through the woods on some of its bays which are not so deep but that the reflection from the bottom tinges them, its waters are of a misty bluish-green or glaucous color. Many years since I used to go there to collect the sand by cart-loads, to make sand-paper with, and I have continued to visit it ever since. One who frequents it proposes to call it Virid Lake. Perhaps it might be called Yellow-Pine Lake, from the following circumstance. About fifteen years ago you could see the top of a pitch-pine, of the kind called yellow-pine hereabouts, though it is not a distinct species, projecting above the surface in deep water, many rods from the shore. It was even supposed by some that the pond had sunk, and this was one of the primitive forest that formerly stood there. I find that even so long ago as 1792, in a "Topographical Description of the Town of Concord," by one of its citizens, in the Collections of the Massachusetts Historical Society, the author,[19] after speaking of Walden and White Ponds, adds: "In the middle of the latter may be seen, when the water is very low, a tree which appears as if it grew in the place where it now stands, although the roots are fifty feet below the surface of the water; the top of this tree is broken off, and at that place measures fourteen inches in diameter." In the spring of '49 I talked with the man who lives nearest the pond in Sudbury, who told me that it was he who got out this tree ten or fifteen years before. As near as he could remember, it stood twelve or fifteen rods from the shore, where the water was thirty or forty feet deep. It was in the winter, and he had been getting out ice in the forenoon, and had resolved that in the afternoon, with the aid of his neighbors, he would take out the old yellow-pine. He sawed a channel in the ice toward the shore, and hauled it over and along and out on to the ice with oxen; but, before he had gone far in his work, he was surprised to find that it was wrong end upward, with the stumps of the branches pointing down, and the small end firmly fastened in the sandy bottom. It was about a foot in diameter at the big end, and he had expected to get a good saw-long, but it was so rotten as to be fit only for fuel, if for that. He had some of it in his shed then. There were marks of an axe and of woodpeckers on the butt. He thought that it might have been a dead tree on the shore, but was finally blown over into the pond, and after the top had become water-logged, while the but-end was still dry and light,

[19] William Jones.

had drifted out and sunk wrong end up. His father, eighty years old, could not remember when it was not there. Several pretty large logs may still be seen lying on the bottom, where, owing to the undulation of the surface, they look like huge water snakes in motion.

This pond has rarely been profaned by a boat, for there is little in it to tempt a fisherman. Instead of the white lily, which requires mud, or the common sweet flag, the blue flag (*Iris versicolor*) grows thinly in the pure water, rising from the stony bottom all around the shore, where it is visited by humming birds in June, and the color both of its bluish blades and its flowers, and especially their reflections, are in singular harmony with the glaucous water.

White Pond and Walden are great crystals on the surface of the earth, Lakes of Light. If they were permanently congealed, and small enough to be clutched, they would, perchance, be carried off by slaves, like precious stones, to adorn the heads of emperors; but being liquid, and ample, and secured to us and our successors forever, we disregard them, and run after the diamond of Kohinoor.[20] They are too pure to have a market value; they contain no muck. How much more beautiful than our lives, how much more transparent than our characters, are they! We never learned meanness of them. How much fairer than the pool before the farmer's door, in which his ducks swim! Hither the clean wild ducks come. Nature has no human inhabitant who appreciates her. The birds with their plumage and their notes are in harmony with the flowers, but what youth or maiden conspires with the wild luxuriant beauty of Nature? She flourishes most alone, far from the towns where they reside. Talk of heaven! ye disgrace earth.

CHAPTER TEN
Baker Farm[1]

Sometimes I rambled to pine groves, standing like temples, or like fleets at sea, full-rigged, with wavy boughs, and rippling with light, so soft and green and shady that the Druids[2] would have forsaken their oaks to worship in them; or to the cedar wood beyond Flints' Pond, where the trees, covered with hoary blue berries, spiring higher and higher, are fit to stand

[20] A famous large diamond, mined in India and now part of the British crown jewels.
[1] The farm lay about a mile southwest of Walden.
[2] An ancient Celtic priesthood; their places of worship were oak groves.

before Valhalla,[3] and the creeping juniper covers the ground with wreaths full of fruit; or to swamps where the usnea lichen hangs in festoons from the white-spruce trees, and toad-stools, round tables of the swamp gods, cover the ground, and more beautiful fungi adorn the stumps, like butterflies or shells, vegetable winkles; where the swamp-pink and dogwood grow, the red alder-berry glows like eyes of imps, the waxwork grooves and crushes the hardest woods in its folds, and the wild-holly berries make the beholder forget his home with their beauty, and he is dazzled and tempted by nameless other wild forbidden fruits, too fair for mortal taste. Instead of calling on some scholar, I paid many a visit to particular trees, of kinds which are rare in this neighborhood, standing far away in the middle of some pasture, or in the depths of a wood or swamp, or on a hilltop; such as the black-birch, of which we have some handsome specimens two feet in diameter; its cousin the yellow-birch, with its loose golden vest, perfumed like the first; the beech, which has so neat a bole and beautifully lichen-painted, perfect in all its details, of which, excepting scattered specimens, I know but one small grove of sizable trees left in the township, supposed by some to have been planted by the pigeons that were once baited with beech nuts near by; it is worth the while to see the silver grain sparkle when you split this wood; the bass; the hornbeam; the *celtis occidentalis,* or false elm, of which we have but one well-grown; some taller mast of a pine, a shingle tree, or a more perfect hemlock than usual, standing like a pagoda in the midst of the woods; and many others I could mention. These were the shrines I visited both summer and winter.

Once it chanced that I stood in the very abutment of a rainbow's arch, which filled the lower stratum of the atmosphere, tinging the grass and leaves around, and dazzling me as if I looked through colored crystal. It was a lake of rainbow light, in which, for a short while, I lived like a dolphin. If it had lasted longer it might have tinged my employments and life. As I walked on the railroad causeway, I used to wonder at the halo of light around my shadow, and would fain fancy myself one of the elect. One who visited me declared that the shadows of some Irishmen before him had no halo about them, that it was only natives that were so distinguished. Benvenuto Cellini tells us in his memoirs,[4] that, after a certain terrible dream or vision which he had during his confinement in the castle of St. Angelo, a resplendent light appeared over the shadow of his head at morning and evening, whether he was in Italy or France, and it was particularly conspicuous when the grass was moist with dew. This was probably the same

[3] In Norse mythology, the noble hall wherein the souls of dead warriors lived.

[4] Italian sculptor, goldsmith, and writer of a famous autobiography (1500–1571).

phenomenon to which I have referred, which is especially observed in the morning, but also at other times, and even by moonlight. Though a constant one, it is not commonly noticed, and, in the case of an excitable imagination like Cellini's, it would be basis enough for superstition. Beside, he tells us that he showed it to very few. But are they not indeed distinguished who are conscious that they are regarded at all?

I set out one afternoon to go a-fishing to Fair-Haven, through the woods, to eke out my scanty fare of vegetables. My way led through Pleasant Meadow, an adjunct of the Baker Farm, that retreat of which a poet has since sung, beginning,

> "Thy entry is a pleasant field,
> Which some mossy fruit trees yield
> Partly to a ruddy brook,
> By gliding musquash undertook,
> 5 And mercurial trout,
> Darting about."[5]

I thought of living there before I went to Walden. I "hooked" the apples, leaped the brook, and scared the musquash and the trout. It was one of those afternoons which seem indefinitely long before one, in which many events may happen, a large portion of our natural life, though it was already half spent when I started. By the way there came up a shower, which compelled me to stand half an hour under a pine, piling boughs over my head, and wearing my handkerchief for a shed; and when at length I had made one cast over the pickerel-weed, standing up to my middle in water, I found myself suddenly in the shadow of a cloud, and the thunder began to rumble with such emphasis that I could do no more than listen to it. The gods must be proud, thought I, with such forked flashes to rout a poor unarmed fisherman. So I made haste for shelter to the nearest hut, which stood half a mile from any road, but so much the nearer to the pond, and had long been uninhabited:

> "And here a poet builded,
> In the completed years,
> For behold a trivial cabin
> That to destruction steers."

---

[5]The poetry in this chapter is that of Thoreau's friend, Ellery Channing, from his "Baker Farm" in *The Woodman and Other Poems* (1849). (See note 1, chap. 12.)

So the Muse fables. But therein, as I found, dwelt now John Field, an Irishman, and his wife, and several children, from the broad-faced boy who assisted his father at his work, and now came running by his side from the bog to escape the rain, to the wrinkled, sibyl-like,[6] cone-headed infant that sat upon its father's knee as in the palaces of nobles, and looked out from its home in the midst of wet and hunger inquisitively upon the stranger, with the privilege of infancy, not knowing but it was the last of a noble line, and the hope and cynosure of the world, instead of John Field's poor starveling brat. There we sat together under that part of the roof which leaked the least, while it showered and thundered without. I had sat there many times of old before the ship was built that floated this family to America. An honest, hard-working, but shiftless man plainly was John Field; and his wife, she too was brave to cook so many successive dinners in the recesses of that lofty stove; with round greasy face and bare breast, still thinking to improve her condition one day; with the never absent mop in one hand, and yet no effects of it visible any where. The chickens, which had also taken shelter here from the rain, stalked about the room like members of the family, too humanized methought to roast well. They stood and looked in my eye or pecked at my shoe significantly. Meanwhile my host told me his story, how hard he worked "bogging" for a neighboring farmer, turning up a meadow with a spade or bog hoe at the rate of ten dollars an acre and the use of the land with manure for one year, and his little broad-faced son worked cheerfully at his father's side the while, not knowing how poor a bargain the latter had made. I tried to help him with my experience, telling him that he was one of my nearest neighbors, and that I too, who came a-fishing here, and looked like a loafer, was getting my living like himself; that I lived in a tight, light, and clean house, which hardly cost more than the annual rent of such a ruin as his commonly amounts to; and how, if he chose, he might in a month or two build himself a palace of his own; that I did not use tea, nor coffee, nor butter, nor milk, nor fresh meat, and so did not have to work to get them; again, as I did not work hard, I did not have to eat hard, and it cost me but a trifle for my food; but as he began with tea, and coffee, and butter, and milk, and beef, he had to work hard to pay for them, and when he had worked hard he had to eat hard again to repair the waste of his system—and so it was as broad as it was long, indeed it was broader than it was long, for he was discontented and wasted his life into the bargain; and yet he had rated it as a gain in coming to America, that here you could get tea, and coffee,

[6]In ancient Greece, sibyls made predictions about the future, often in enigmatic language. They are said to have lived to a great age.

and meat every day. But the only true America is that country where you are at liberty to pursue such a mode of life as many enable you to do without these, and where the state does not endeavor to compel you to sustain the slavery and war and other superfluous expenses which directly or indirectly result from the use of such things. For I purposely talked to him as if he were a philosopher, or desired to be one. I should be glad if all the meadows on the earth were left in a wild state, if that were the consequence of men's beginning to redeem themselves. A man will not need to study history to find out what is best for his own culture. But alas! the culture of an Irishman is an enterprise to be undertaken with a sort of moral bog hoe. I told him, that as he worked so hard at bogging, he required thick boots and stout clothing, which yet were soon soiled and worn out, but I wore light shoes and thin clothing, which cost not half so much, though he might think that I was dressed like a gentleman (which, however, was not the case), and in an hour or two, without labor, but as a recreation, I could, if I wished, catch as many fish as I should want for two days, or earn enough money to support me a week. If he and his family would live simply, they might all go a-huckleberrying in the summer for their amusement. John heaved a sigh at this, and his wife stared with arms a-kimbo, and both appeared to be wondering if they had capital enough to begin such a course with, or arithmetic enough to carry it through. It was sailing by dead reckoning to them, and they saw not clearly how to make their port so; therefore I suppose they still take life bravely, after their fashion, face to face, giving it tooth and nail, not having skill to split its massive columns with any fine entering wedge, and rout it in detail—thinking to deal with it roughly, as one should handle a thistle. But they fight at an overwhelming disadvantage—living, John Field, alas! without arithmetic, and failing so.

"Do you ever fish?" I asked. "O yes, I catch a mess now and then when I am lying by; good perch I catch." "What's your bait?" "I catch shiners with fish-worms, and bait the perch with them." "You'd better go now, John," said his wife with glistening and hopeful face; but John demurred.

The shower was now over, and a rainbow above the eastern woods promised a fair evening; so I took my departure. When I had got without I asked for a dish, hoping to get a sight of the well bottom, to complete my survey of the premises; but there, alas! are shallows and quicksands, and rope broken withal, and bucket irrecoverable. Meanwhile the right culinary vessel was selected, water was seemingly distilled, and after consultation and long delay passed out to the thirsty one—not yet suffered to cool, not yet to settle. Such gruel sustains life here, I thought; so, shutting my eyes, and excluding the notes by a skilfully directed under-current, I drank to genuine hospitality the heartiest draught I could. I am not squeamish in such cases when manners are concerned.

As I was leaving the Irishman's roof after the rain, bending my steps again to the pond, my haste to catch pickerel, wading in retired meadows, in sloughs and bog-holes, in forlorn and savage places, appeared for an instant trivial to me who had been sent to school and college; but as I ran down the hill toward the reddening west, with the rainbow over my shoulder, and some faint tinkling sounds borne to my ear through the cleansed air, from I know not what quarter, my Good Genius seemed to say—Go fish and hunt far and wide day by day—farther and wider—and rest thee by many brooks and hearthsides without misgiving. Remember thy Creator in the days of thy youth.[7] Rise free from care before the dawn, and seek adventures. Let the noon find thee by other lakes, and the night overtake thee every where at home. There are no larger fields than these, no worthier games than may here be played. Grow wild according to thy nature, like these sedges and brakes, which will never become English hay. Let the thunder rumble; what if it threaten ruin to farmers' crops? that is not its errand to thee. Take shelter under the cloud, while they flee to carts and sheds. Let not to get a living be thy trade, but thy sport. Enjoy the land, but own it not. Through want of enterprise and faith men are where they are, buying and selling, and spending their lives like serfs.

O Baker Farm!

"Landscape where the richest element
Is a little sunshine innocent."

. . . .

"No one runs to revel
5 On thy rail-fenced lea."

. . . .

"Debate with no man hast thou,
With questions art never perplexed,
As tame at the first sight as now,
10 In thy plain russet gabardine dressed."

. . . .

"Come ye who love,
And ye who hate,
Children of the Holy Dove,

[7]Cf. Eccles. 12.1: "Remember now thy Creator in the days of thy youth, while the evil days come not, nor the years draw nigh, then thou shalt say, I have no pleasure in them."

15 And Guy Faux[8] of the state,
And hang conspiracies
From the tough rafters of the trees!"

Men come tamely home at night only from the next field or street, where their household echoes haunt, and their life pines because it breathes its own breath over again; their shadows morning and evening reach farther than their daily steps. We should come home from far, from adventures, and perils, and discoveries every day, with new experience and character.

Before I had reached the pond some fresh impulse had brought out John Field, with altered mind, letting go "bogging" ere this sunset. But he, poor man, disturbed only a couple of fins while I was catching a fair string, and he said it was his luck; but when we changed seats in the boat luck changed seats too. Poor John Field! I trust he does not read this, unless he will improve by it—thinking to live by some derivative old country mode in this primitive new country—to catch perch with shiners. It is good bait sometimes, I allow. With his horizon all his own, yet he a poor man, born to be poor, with his inherited Irish poverty or poor life, his Adam's grandmother and boggy ways, not to rise in this world, he nor his posterity, till their wading webbed bog-trotting[9] feet get *talaria*[10] to their heels.

CHAPTER ELEVEN
Higher Laws

As I came home through the woods with my string of fish, trailing my pole, it being now quite dark, I caught a glimpse of a woodchuck stealing across my path, and felt a strange thrill of savage delight, and was strongly tempted to seize and devour him raw; not that I was hungry then, except for that wildness which he represented. Once or twice, however, while I lived at the pond, I found myself ranging the woods, like a half-starved hound, with a strange abandonment, seeking some kind of venison which I might devour, and no morsel could have been too savage for me. The wildest scenes had become unaccountably familiar. I found in myself, and

[8] Guy Fawkes (1570–1606), an English Catholic executed for his role in the Gunpowder Plot, an attempt to blow up the Houses of Parliament and King James I.
[9] *Bog-trotter* was a derisive term for an Irish immigrant.
[10] Winged sandals, or wings growing directly from the ankles, as in ancient Roman images of the god Mercury.

still find, an instinct toward a higher, or, as it is named, spiritual life, as do most men, and another toward a primitive rank and savage one, and I reverence them both. I love the wild not less than the good. The wildness and adventure that are in fishing still recommended it to me. I like sometimes to take rank hold on life and spend my day more as the animals do. Perhaps I have owed to this employment and to hunting, when quite young, my closest acquaintance with Nature. They early introduce us to and detain us in scenery with which otherwise, at that age, we should have little acquaintance. Fishermen, hunters, woodchoppers, and others, spending their lives in the fields and woods, in a peculiar sense a part of Nature themselves, are often in a more favorable mood for observing her, in the intervals of their pursuits, than philosophers or poets even, who approach her with expectation. She is not afraid to exhibit herself to them. The traveller on the prairie is naturally a hunter, on the head waters of the Missouri and Columbia a trapper, and at the Falls of St. Mary[1] a fisherman. He who is only a traveller learns things at second-hand and by the halves, and is poor authority. We are most interested when science reports what those men already know practically or instinctively, for that alone is a true *humanity*, or account of human experience.

They mistake who assert that the Yankee has few amusements, because he has not so many public holidays, and men and boys do not play so many games as they do in England, for here the more primitive but solitary amusements of hunting, fishing and the like have not yet given place to the former. Almost every New England boy among my contemporaries shouldered a fowling piece between the ages of ten and fourteen; and his hunting and fishing grounds were not limited like the preserves of an English nobleman, but were more boundless even than those of a savage. No wonder, then, that he did not oftener stay to play on the common. But already a change is taking place, owing, not to an increased humanity, but to an increased scarcity of game, for perhaps the hunter is the greatest friend of the animals hunted, not excepting the Humane Society.

Moreover, when at the pond, I wished sometimes to add fish to my fare for variety. I have actually fished from the same kind of necessity that the first fishers did. Whatever humanity I might conjure up against it was all factitious, and concerned my philosophy more than my feelings. I speak of fishing only now, for I had long felt differently about fowling, and sold my gun before I went to the woods. Not that I am less humane than others, but I did not perceive that my feelings were much affected. I did not pity

[1]The St. Mary's River flows out of Lake Superior between Michigan and Ontario.

the fishes nor the worms. This was habit. As for fowling, during the last years that I carried a gun my excuse was that I was studying ornithology, and sought only new or rare birds. But I confess that I am now inclined to think that there is a finer way of studying ornithology than this. It requires so much closer attention to the habits of the birds, that, if for that reason only, I have been willing to omit the gun. Yet notwithstanding the objection on the score of humanity, I am compelled to doubt if equally valuable sports are ever substituted for these; and when some of my friends have asked me anxiously about their boys, whether they should let them hunt, I have answered, yes—remembering that it was one of the best parts of my education—*make* them hunters, though sportsmen only at first, if possible, mighty hunters at last, so that they shall not find game large enough for them in this or any vegetable wilderness—hunters as well as fishers of men.[2] Thus far I am of the opinion of Chaucer's nun, who

> "yave not of the text a pulled hen
> That saith that hunters ben not holy men."[3]

There is a period in the history of the individual, as of the race, when the hunters are the "best men," as the Algonquins[4] called them. We cannot but pity the boy who has never fired a gun; he is no more humane, while his education has been sadly neglected. This was my answer with respect to those youths who where bent on this pursuit, trusting that they would soon outgrow it. No humane being, past the thoughtless age of boyhood, will wantonly murder any creature, which holds its life by the same tenure that he does. The hare in its extremity cries like a child. I warn you, mothers, that my sympathies do not always make the usual *philanthropic* distinctions.

Such is oftenest the young man's introduction to the forest, and the most original part of himself. He goes thither at first as a hunter and fisher, until at last, if he has the seeds of a better life in him, he distinguishes his proper objects, as a poet or naturalist it may be, and leaves the gun and fish-pole behind. The mass of men are still and always young in this respect.

---

[2] Cf. Mark 1.17, where Jesus addresses the fishermen Simon and Andrew: "Come ye after me, and I will make you to become fishers of men."

[3] From the General Prologue to Chaucer's *Canterbury Tales;* the lines, however, describe the monk rather than the nun.

[4] An Indian people from the area around the St. Lawrence River.

In some countries a hunting parson is no uncommon sight. Such a one might make a good shepherd's dog, but is far from being the Good Shepherd. I have been surprised to consider that the only obvious employment, except wood-chopping, ice-cutting, or the like business, which ever to my knowledge detained at Walden Pond for a whole half day any of my fellow-citizens, whether fathers or children of the town, with just one exception, was fishing. Commonly they did not think that they were lucky, or well paid for their time, unless they got a long string of fish, though they had the opportunity of seeing the pond all the while. They might go there a thousand times before the sediment of fishing would sink to the bottom and leave their purpose pure; but no doubt such a clarifying process would be going on all the while. The governor and his council faintly remember the pond, for they went a-fishing there when they were boys; but now they are too old and dignified to go a-fishing, and so they know it no more forever. Yet even they expect to go to heaven at last. If the legislature regards it, it is chiefly to regulate the number of hooks to be used there; but they know nothing about the hook of hooks with which to angle for the pond itself, impaling the legislature for a bait. Thus, even in civilized communities, the embryo man passes through the hunter stage of development.

I have found repeatedly, of late years, that I cannot fish without falling a little in self-respect. I have tried it again and again. I have skill at it, and, like many of my fellows, a certain instinct for it, which revives from time to time, but always when I have done I feel that it would have been better if I had not fished. I think that I do not mistake. It is a faint intimation, yet so are the first streaks of morning. There is unquestionably this instinct in me which belongs to the lower orders of creation; yet with every year I am less a fisherman, though without more humanity or even wisdom; at present I am no fisherman at all. But I see that if I were to live in a wilderness I should again be tempted to become a fisher and hunter in earnest. Beside, there is something essentially unclean about this diet and all flesh, and I began to see where housework commences, and whence the endeavor, which costs so much, to wear a tidy and respectable appearance each day, to keep the house sweet and free from all ill odors and sights. Having been my own butcher and scullion and cook, as well as the gentleman for whom the dishes were served up, I can speak from an unusually complete experience. The practical objection to animal food in my case was its uncleanness; and, besides, when I had caught and cleaned and cooked and eaten my fish, they seemed not to have fed me essentially. It was insignificant and unnecessary, and cost more than it came to. A little bread or a few potatoes would have done as well, with less trouble and filth. Like many of my contemporaries, I had rarely for many years used animal food, or tea, or coffee, etc.; not so much because of any ill effects which I had traced to them, as because they were not agreeable to my imagination. The repugnance to animal food is not the effect of experience, but is an instinct. It appeared more beautiful to live low and fare hard in many respects; and though I never did so, I went far enough to please my imagination. I believe that every man who has been earnest to preserve his higher or poetic faculties in the best condition has been particularly inclined to abstain from animal food, and from much food of any kind. It is a significant fact, stated by entomologists, I find it in Kirby and Spence,[5] that "some insects in their perfect state, though furnished with organs of feeding, make no use of them"; and they lay it down as "a general rule, that almost all insects in this state eat much less than in that of larvae. The voracious caterpillar when transformed into a butterfly," . . . "and the gluttonous maggot when become a fly," content themselves with a drop or two of honey or some other sweet liquid. The abdomen under the wings of the butterfly still represents the larva. This is the tid-bit which tempts his insectivorous fate. The gross feeder is a man in the larva state; and there are whole nations in that condition, nations without fancy or imagination, whose vast abdomens betray them.

It is hard to provide and cook so simple and clean a diet as will not offend the imagination; but this, I think, is to be fed when we feed the body; they should both sit down at the same table. Yet perhaps this may be done. The fruits eaten temperately need not make us ashamed of our appetites, nor interrupt the worthiest pursuits. But put an extra condiment into your dish, and it will poison you. It is not worth the while to live by rich cookery. Most men would feel shame if caught preparing with their own hands precisely such a dinner, whether of animal or vegetable food, as is every day prepared for them by others. Yet till this is otherwise we are not civilized, and, if gentlemen and ladies, are not true men and women. This certainly suggests what change is to be made. It may be vain to ask why the imagination will not be reconciled to flesh and fat. I am satisfied that it is not. Is it not a reproach that man is a carniverous animal? True, he can and does live, in a great measure, by preying on other animals; but this is a miserable way—as any one who will go to snaring rabbits, or slaughtering lambs, may learn—and he will be regarded as a benefactor of his race who shall teach man to confine himself to a more innocent and wholesome diet. Whatever my own practice may be, I have no doubt that it is a part of the destiny of the human race, in its gradual improvement, to leave off eating

---

[5] William Kirby (1759–1850) and William Spence (1783–1860) wrote a multivolume *Introduction to Entomology* (1815–1826).

animals, as surely as the savage tribes have left off eating each other when they came in contact with the more civilized.

If one listens to the faintest but constant suggestions of his genius, which are certainly true, he sees not to what extremes, or even insanity, it may lead him; and yet that way, as he grows more resolute and faithful, his road lies. The faintest assured objection which one healthy man feels will at length prevail over the arguments and customs of mankind. No man ever followed his genius till it misled him. Though the result were bodily weakness, yet perhaps no one can say that the consequences were to be regretted, for these were a life in conformity to higher principles. If the day and the night are such that you greet them with joy, and life emits a fragrance like flowers and sweet-scented herbs, is more elastic, more starry, more immortal—that is your success. All nature is your congratulation, and you have cause momentarily to bless yourself. The greatest gains and values are farthest from being appreciated. We easily come to doubt if they exist. We soon forget them. They are the highest reality. Perhaps the facts most astounding and most real are never communicated by man to man. The true harvest of my daily life is somewhat as intangible and indescribable as the tints of morning or evening. It is a little star-dust caught, a segment of the rainbow which I have clutched.

Yet, for my part, I was never unusually squeamish; I could sometimes eat a fried rat with a good relish, if it were necessary. I am glad to have drunk water so long, for the same reason that I prefer the natural sky to an opium-eater's heaven. I would fain keep sober always; and there are infinite degrees of drunkenness. I believe that water is the only drink for a wise man; wine is not so noble a liquor; and think of dashing the hopes of a morning with a cup of warm coffee, or of an evening with a dish of tea! Ah, how low I fall when I am tempted by them! Even music may be intoxicating. Such apparently slight causes destroyed Greece and Rome, and will destroy England and America. Of all ebriosity, who does not prefer to be intoxicated by the air he breathes? I have found it to be the most serious objection to coarse labors long continued, that they compelled me to eat and drink coarsely also. But to tell the truth, I find myself at present somewhat less particular in these respects. I carry less religion to the table, ask no blessing; not because I am wiser than I was, but, I am obliged to confess, because, however much it is to be regretted, with years I have grown more coarse and indifferent. Perhaps these questions are entertained only in youth, as most believe of poetry. My practice is "nowhere," my opinion is here. Nevertheless I am far from regarding myself as one of those privileged ones to whom the Ved refers when it says, that "he who has true faith in the Omnipresent Supreme Being may eat all that exists," that is, is not bound to inquire what is his food, or who prepares it; and even in their case it is to be observed, as a Hindoo commentator has remarked, that the Vedant limits this privilege to "the time of distress."[6]

Who has not sometimes derived an inexpressible satisfaction from his food in which appetite had no share? I have been thrilled to think that I owed a mental perception to the commonly gross sense of taste, that I have been inspired through the palate, that some berries which I had eaten on a hill-side had fed my genius. "The soul not being mistress of herself," says Thseng-tseu, "one looks, and one does not see; one listens, and one does not hear; one eats, and one does not know the savor of food."[7] He who distinguishes the true savor of his food can never be a glutton; he who does not cannot be otherwise. A puritan may go to his brown-bread crust with as gross an appetite as ever an alderman to his turtle. Not that food which entereth into the mouth defileth a man,[8] but the appetite with which it is eaten. It is neither the quality nor the quantity, but the devotion to sensual savors; when that which is eaten is not a viand to sustain our animal, or inspire our spiritual life, but food for the worms that possess us. If the hunter has a taste for mud-turtles, muskrats, and other such savage tid-bits, the fine lady indulges a taste for jelly made of a calf's foot, or for sar-dines from over the sea, and they are even. He goes to the mill-pond, she to her preserve-pot. The wonder is how they, how you and I, can live this slimy beastly life, eating and drinking.

Our whole life is startlingly moral. There is never an instant's truce be-tween virtue and vice. Goodness is the only investment that never fails. In the music of the harp which trembles round the world it is the insisting on this which thrills us. The harp is the travelling patterer for the Universe's Insurance Company, recommending its laws, and our little goodness is all the assessment that we pay. Though the youth at last grows indifferent, the laws of the universe are not indifferent, but are forever on the side of the most sensitive. Listen to every zephyr for some reproof, for it is surely there, and he is unfortunate who does not hear it. We cannot touch a string or move a stop but the charming moral transfixes us. Many an irksome noise, go a long way off, is heard as music, a proud sweet satire on the meanness of our lives.

We are conscious of an animal in us, which awakens in proportion as our higher nature slumbers. It is reptile and sensual, and perhaps cannot

---

[6] Quoted from *Translation of Several Principal Books, Passages, and Texts of the Veds* (1832), trans. Raja Rammohun Roy.

[7] Confucius, *The Great Learning* 7; it was often attributed to Tseng-tzu, a Confucian disciple.

[8] Cf. Matt. 15.11: "Not that which goeth into the mouth defileth a man; but that which cometh out of the mouth, this defileth a man."

be wholly expelled; like the worms which, even in life and health, occupy our bodies. Possibly we may withdraw from it, but never change its nature. I fear that it may enjoy a certain health of its own; that we may be well, yet not pure. The other day I picked up the lower jaw of a hog, with white and sound teeth and tusks, which suggested that there was an animal health and vigor distinct from the spiritual. This creature succeeded by other means than temperance and purity. "That in which men differ from brute beasts," says Mencius, "is a thing very inconsiderable; the common herd lose it very soon; superior men preserve it carefully."[9] Who knows what sort of life would result if we had attained to purity? If I knew so wise a man as could teach me purity I would go to seek him forthwith. "A command over our passions, and over the external senses of the body, and good acts, are declared by the Ved to be indispensable in the mind's approximation to God." Yet the spirit can for the time pervade and control every member and function of the body, and transmute what in form is the grossest sensuality into purity and devotion. The generative energy, which, when we are loose, dissipates and makes us unclean, when we are continent invigorates and inspires us. Chastity is the flowering of man; and what are called Genius, Heroism, Holiness, and the like, are but various fruits which succeed it. Man flows at once to God when the channel of purity is open. By turns our purity inspires and our impurity casts us down. He is blessed who is assured that the animal is dying out in him day by day, and the divine being established. Perhaps there is none but has cause for shame on account of the inferior and brutish nature to which he is allied. I fear that we are such gods or demigods only as fauns and satyrs,[10] the divine allied to beasts, the creatures of appetite, and that, to some extent, our very life is our disgrace.

> "How happy's he who hath due place assigned
> To his beasts and disaforested his mind!
>
> . . . .
>
> Can use his horse, goat, wolf, and ev'ry beast,
> And is not ass himself to all the rest!
> 5 Else man not only is the herd of swine,
> But he's those devils too which did incline
> Them to a headlong rage, and made them worse."[11]

---

[9]The Chinese philosopher Meng-tse, transliterated Mencius (371?–288? B.C.E.); from his *Works*.

[10]In Greek mythology, creatures that were half human, half beast.

[11]From John Donne (1573–1631), "Letter to Sir Edward Herbert, at Julyers," ll. 9–10, 13–17.

All sensuality is one, though it takes many forms; all purity is one. It is the same whether a man eat, or drink, or cohabit, or sleep sensually. They are but one appetite, and we only need to see a person do any one of these things to know how great a sensualist he is. The impure can neither stand nor sit with purity. When the reptile is attacked at one mouth of his burrow, he shows himself at another. If you would be chaste, you must be temperate. What is chastity? How shall a man know if he is chaste? He shall not know it. We have heard of this virtue, but we know not what it is. We speak conformably to the rumor which we have heard. From exertion come wisdom and purity; from sloth ignorance and sensuality. In the student sensuality is a sluggish habit of mind. An unclean person is universally a slothful one, one who sits by a stove, whom the sun shines on prostrate, who reposes without being fatigued. If you would avoid uncleanness, and all the sins, work earnestly, though it be at cleaning a stable. Nature is hard to be overcome, but she must be overcome. What avails it that you are Christian, if you are not purer than the heathen, if you deny yourself no more, if you are not more religious? I know of many systems of religion esteemed heathenish whose precepts fill the reader with shame, and provoke him to new endeavors, though it be to the performance of rites merely.

I hesitate to say these things, but it is not because of the subject—I care not how obscene my *words* are—but because I cannot speak of them without betraying my impurity. We discourse freely without shame of one form of sensuality, and are silent about another. We are so degraded that we cannot speak simply of the necessary functions of human nature. In earlier ages, in some countries, every function was reverently spoken of and regulated by law. Nothing was too trivial for the Hindoo lawgiver, however offensive it may be to modern taste. He teaches how to eat, drink, cohabit, void excrement and urine, and the like, elevating what is mean, and does not falsely excuse himself by calling these things trifles.

Every man is the builder of a temple, called his body, to the god he worships, after a style purely his own, nor can he get off by hammering marble instead. We are all sculptors and painters, and our material is our own flesh and blood and bones. Any nobleness begins at once to refine a man's features, any meanness or sensuality to imbrute them.

John Farmer sat at his door one September evening, after a hard day's work, his mind still running on his labor more or less. Having bathed he sat down to recreate his intellectual man. It was a rather cool evening, and some of his neighbors were apprehending a frost. He had not attended to the train of his thoughts long when he heard some one playing on a flute, and that sound harmonized with his mood. Still he thought of his work; but the burden of his thought was, that though this kept running in his head, and he found himself planning and contriving it against his will, yet it concerned him very little. It was no more than the scurf of his skin, which was constantly shuffled off. But the notes of the flute came home to his ears out of a different sphere from that he worked in, and suggested work for certain faculties which slumbered in him. They gently did away with the street, and the village, and the state in which he lived. A voice said to him—Why do you stay here and live this mean moiling life, when a glorious existence is possible for you? Those same stars twinkle over other fields than these—But how to come out of this condition and actually migrate thither? All that he could think of was to practise some new austerity, to let his mind descend into his body and redeem it, and treat himself with ever increasing respect.

CHAPTER TWELVE
Brute Neighbors

Sometimes I had a companion[1] in my fishing, who came through the village to my house from the other side of the town, and the catching of the dinner was as much a social exercise as the eating of it.

Hermit. I wonder what the world is doing now. I have not heard so much as a locust over the sweet-fern these three hours. The pigeons are all asleep upon their roosts—no flutter from them. Was that a farmer's noon horn which sounded from beyond the woods just now? The hands are coming in to boiled salt beef and cider and Indian bread. Why will men worry themselves so? He that does not eat need not work. I wonder how much they have reaped. Who would live there where a body can never think for the barking of Bose?[2] And O, the housekeeping! to keep bright the devil's door-knobs, and scour his tubs this bright day! Better not keep a house. Say, some hollow tree; and then for morning calls and dinner-parties! Only a wood-pecker tapping. O, they swarm; the sun is too warm there; they are born too far into life for me. I have water from the spring, and a loaf of brown bread on the shelf—Hark! I hear a rustling of the leaves. Is it some ill-fed village hound yielding to the instinct of the chase? or the lost pig which is said to be in these woods, whose tracks I saw after the rain? It comes on apace; my sumachs and sweet-briers tremble—Eh, Mr. Poet, is it you? How do you like the world today?

---

[1] The frequent companion, and model for the "poet" in the dialogue that follows was William Ellery Channing the younger (1818–1901), who wrote the first biography of Thoreau, *Thoreau, The Poet Naturalist* (1873).
[2] A general name for a dog, like "Fido."

Poet. See those clouds; how they hang! That's the greatest thing I have seen today. There's nothing like it in old paintings, nothing like it in foreign lands—unless when we were off the coast of Spain. That's a true Mediterranean sky. I thought, as I have my living to get and have not eaten today, that I might go a-fishing. That's the true industry for poets. It is the only trade I have learned. Come, let's along.

Hermit. I cannot resist. My brown bread will soon be gone. I will go with you gladly soon, but I am just concluding a serious meditation. I think that I am near the end of it. Leave me alone, then, for a while. But that we may not be delayed, you shall be digging the bait meanwhile. Angle-worms are rarely to be met with in these parts, where the soil was never fattened with manure; the race is nearly extinct. The sport of digging the bait is nearly equal to that of catching the fish, when one's appetite is not too keen; and this you may have all to yourself today. I would advise you to set in the spade down yonder among the ground-nuts, where you see the johnswort waving. I think that I may warrant you one worm to every three sods you turn up, if you look well in among the roots of the grass, as if you were weeding. Or, if you choose to go farther, it will not be unwise, for I have found the increase of fair bait to be very nearly as the squares of the distances.

Hermit alone. Let me see; where was I? Methinks I was nearly in this frame of mind; the world lay about at this angle. Shall I go to heaven or a-fishing? If I should soon bring this meditation to an end, would another so sweet occasion be likely to offer? I was as near being resolved into the essence of things as ever I was in my life. I fear my thoughts will not come back to me. If it would do any good, I would whistle for them. When they make us an offer, is it wise to say, We will think of it? My thoughts have left no track, and I cannot find the path again. What was it that I was thinking of? It was a very hazy day. I will just try these three sentences of Con-fut-see;[3] they may fetch that state about again. I know not whether it was the dumps or a budding ecstasy. Mem. There never is but one opportunity of a kind.

Poet. How now, Hermit, is it too soon? I have got just thirteen whole ones, beside several which are imperfect or undersized; but they will do for the smaller fry; they do not cover up the hook so much. Those village worms are quite too large; a shiner may make a meal off one without finding the skewer.

Hermit. Well, then, let's be off. Shall we to the Concord? There's good sport there if the water be not too high.

* * *

[3] Another spelling of Confucius; his name is anglicized as K'ung Fu-tse.

Why do precisely these objects which we behold make a world? Why has man just these species of animals for his neighbors; as if nothing but a mouse could have filled this crevice? I suspect that Pilpay & Co.[4] have put animals to their best use, for they are all beasts of burden, in a sense, made to carry some portion of our thoughts.

The mice which haunted my house were not the common ones, which are said to have been introduced into the country, but a wild native kind not found in the village. I sent one to a distinguished naturalist,[5] and it interested him much. When I was building, one of these had its nest underneath the house, and before I had laid the second floor, and swept out the shavings, would come out regularly at lunch time and pick up the crums at my feet. It probably had never seen a man before; and it soon became quite familiar, and would run over my shoes and up my clothes. It could readily ascend the sides of the room by short impulses, like a squirrel, which it resembled in its motions. At length, as I leaned with my elbow on the bench one day, it ran up my clothes, and along my sleeve, and round and round the paper which held my dinner, while I kept the latter close, and dodged and played at bo-peep with it; and when at last I held still a piece of cheese between my thumb and finger, it came and nibbled it, sitting in my hand, and afterward cleaned its face and paws, like a fly, and walked away.

A phoebe soon built in my shed, and a robin for protection in a pine which grew against the house. In June the partridge (*Tetrao umbellus*), which is so shy a bird, led her brood past my windows, from the woods in the rear to the front of my house, clucking and calling to them like a hen, and in all her behavior proving herself the hen of the woods. The young suddenly disperse on your approach, at a signal from the mother, as if a whirlwind had swept them away, and they so exactly resemble the dried leaves and twigs that many a traveller has placed his foot in the midst of a brood, and heard the whir of the old bird as she flew off, and her anxious calls and mewing, or seen her trail her wings to attract his attention, without suspecting their neighborhood. The parent will sometimes roll and spin round before you in such a dishabille, that you cannot, for a few moments, detect what kind of creature it is. The young squat still and flat, often running their heads under a leaf, and mind only their mother's directions given from a distance, nor will your approach make them run again

---

[4] *Pilpay* or *Bidpai* is a proper name derived from Sanskrit, meaning "master of knowledge" (or of "good counsels"). Bidpai was supposed to be the author of a collection of fables, the *Hitopadesa,* involving animals (see chap. 4, note 13).

[5] Louis Agassiz (1807–1873); Thoreau occasionally collected specimens for him.

and betray themselves. You may even tread on them, or have your eyes on them for a minute, without discovering them. I have held them in my open hand at such a time, and still their only care, obedient to their mother and their instinct, was to squat there without fear or trembling. So perfect is this instinct, that once, when I had laid them on the leaves again, and one accidentally fell on its side, it was found with the rest in exactly the same position ten minutes afterward. They are not callow like the young of most birds, but more perfectly developed and precocious even than chickens. The remarkably adult yet innocent expression of their open and serene eyes is very memorable. All intelligence seems reflected in them. They suggest not merely the purity of infancy, but a wisdom clarified by experience. Such an eye was not born when the bird was, but is coeval with the sky it reflects. The woods do not yield another such a gem. The traveller does not often look into such a limpid well. The ignorant or reckless sportsman often shoots the parent at such a time, and leaves these innocents to fall a prey to some prowling beast or bird, or gradually mingle with the decaying leaves which they so much resemble. It is said that when hatched by a hen they will directly disperse on some alarm, and so are lost, for they never hear the mother's call which gathers them again. These were my hens and chickens.

It is remarkable how many creatures live wild and free though secret in the woods, and still sustain themselves in the neighborhood of towns, suspected by hunters only. How retired the otter manages to live here! He grows to be four feet long, as big as a small boy, perhaps without any human being getting a glimpse of him. I formerly saw the raccoon in the woods behind where my house is built, and probably still heard their whinnering at night. Commonly I rested an hour or two in the shade at noon, after planting, and ate my lunch, and read a little by a spring which was the source of a swamp and of a brook, oozing from under Brister's Hill, half a mile from my field. The approach to this was through a succession of descending grassy hollows, full of young pitch-pines, into a larger wood about the swamp. There, in a very secluded and shaded spot, under a spreading white-pine, there was yet a clean firm sward to sit on. I had dug out the spring and made a well of clear gray water, where I could dip up a pailful without roiling it, and thither I went for this purpose almost every day in midsummer, when the pond was warmest. Thither too the woodcock led her brood, to probe the mud for worms, flying but a foot above them down the bank, while they ran in a troop beneath; but at last, spying me, she would leave her young and circle round and round me, nearer and nearer till within four or five feet, pretending broken wings and legs, to attract my attention, and get off her young, who would already have taken up their march, with faint wiry peep, single file through the swamp, as she directed. Or I heard the peep of the young when I could not see the parent bird. There too the turtle-doves sat over the spring, or fluttered from bough to bough of the soft white-pines over my head; or the red squirrel, coursing down the nearest bough, was particularly familiar and inquisitive. You only need sit still long enough in some attractive spot in the woods that all its inhabitants may exhibit themselves to you by turns.

I was witness to events of a less peaceful character. One day when I went out to my wood-pile, or rather my pile of stumps, I observed two large ants, the one red, the other much larger, nearly half an inch long, and black, fiercely contending with one another. Having once got hold they never let go, but struggled and wrestled and rolled on the chips incessantly. Looking farther, I was surprised to find that the chips were covered with such combatants, that it was not a *duellum,* but a *bellum,* a war between two races of ants, the red always pitted against the black, and frequently two red ones to one black. The legions of these Myrmidons[6] covered all the hills and vales in my wood-yard, and the ground was already strewn with the dead and dying, both red and black. It was the only battle which I have ever witnessed, the only battle-field I ever trod while the battle was raging; internecine war; the red republicans on the one hand, and the black imperialists on the other.[7] On every side they were engaged in deadly combat, yet without any noise that I could hear, and human soldiers never fought so resolutely. I watched a couple that were fast locked in each other's embraces, in a little sunny valley amid the chips, now at noonday prepared to fight till the sun went down, or life went out. The smaller red champion had fastened himself like a vice to his adversary's front, and through all the tumblings on that field never for an instant ceased to gnaw at one of his feelers near the root, having already caused the other to go by the board; while the stronger black one dashed him from side to side, and, as I saw on looking nearer, had already divested him of several of his members. They fought with more pertinacity than bull-dogs. Neither manifested the least disposition to retreat. It was evident that their battle-cry was Conquer or die. In the mean while there came along a single red ant on the hill-side of his valley, evidently full of excitement, who either had despatched his foe, or had not yet taken part in the battle; probably the latter, for he had lost none of his limbs; whose mother had charged him to return with his shield or upon it.[8] Or perchance he was

[6] A warlike people who fought on the side of the Greeks in the Trojan War.
[7] Although critics have speculated that Thoreau was alluding to the Mexican War, he had already described the ant war in "My Books I'd Fain Cast Off, I Cannot Read" (1842).
[8] Supposed to be the injunction of Spartan mothers to their sons.

some Achilles, who had nourished his wrath apart, and had now come to avenge or rescue his Patroclus.[9] He saw this unequal combat from afar—for the blacks were nearly twice the size of the red—he drew near with rapid pace till he stood on his guard within half an inch of the combatants; then watching his opportunity, he sprang upon the black warrior, and commenced his operations near the root of his right fore-leg, leaving the foe to select among his own members; and so there were three united for life, as if a new kind of attraction had been invented which put all other locks and cements to shame. I should not have wondered by this time to find that they had their respective musical bands stationed on some eminent chip, and playing their national airs the while, to excite the slow and cheer the dying combatants. I was myself excited somewhat even as if they had been men. The more you think of it, the less the difference. And certainly there is not the fight recorded in Concord history, at least, if in the history of America, that will bear a moment's comparison with this, whether for the numbers engaged in it, or for the patriotism and heroism displayed. For numbers and for carnage it was an Austerlitz or Dresden.[10] Concord Fight![11] Two killed on the patriots' side, and Luther Blanchard wounded! Why here every ant was a Buttrick—"Fire! for God's sake fire!"—and thousands shared the fate of Davis and Hosmer.[12] There was not one hireling there. I have no doubt that it was a principle they fought for, as much as our ancestors, and not to avoid a three-penny tax on their tea; and the results of this battle will be as important and memorable to those whom it concerns as those of the battle of Bunker Hill, at least.

I took up the chip on which the three I have particularly described were struggling, carried it into my house, and placed it under a tumbler on my window-sill, in order to see the issue. Holding a microscope to the first-mentioned red ant, I saw that, though he was assiduously gnawing at the near fore-leg of his enemy, having severed his remaining feeler, his own breast was all torn away, exposing what vitals he had there to the jaws of the black warrior, whose breast-plate was apparently too thick for him to pierce; and the dark carbuncles of the sufferer's eyes shone with ferocity such as war only could excite. They struggled half an hour longer under the tumbler, and when I looked again the black soldier had severed the heads of his foes from their bodies, and the still living heads were hanging

[9] In the *Iliad,* Achilles, who had sulked in his tent, returned to the battle when his dear friend Patroclus was slain by the Trojans.

[10] Sites of two of the major battles in the Napoleonic Wars.

[11] The first major battle of the American Revolution took place at Concord.

[12] Major John Buttrick (1715–1791) was one of the officers of the Concord militia; Luther Blanchard was wounded, and Isaac Davis and Abner Hosmer were killed.

on either side of him like ghastly trophies at his saddle-bow, still apparently as firmly fastened as ever, and he was endeavoring with feeble struggles, being without feelers and with only the remnant of a leg, and I know not how many other wounds, to divest himself of them; which at length, after half an hour more, he accomplished. I raised the glass, and he went off over the window-sill in that crippled state. Whether he finally survived that combat, and spent the remainder of his days in some Hotel des Invalides,[13] I do not know; but I thought that his industry would not be worth much thereafter. I never learned which party was victorious, nor the cause of the war; but I felt for the rest of that day as if I had had my feelings excited and harrowed by witnessing the struggle, the ferocity and carnage, of a human battle before my door.

Kirby and Spence[14] tell us that the battles of ants have long been celebrated and the date of them recorded, though they say that Huber[15] is the only modern author who appears to have witnessed them. "Aeneas Sylvius,"[16] say they, "after giving a very circumstantial account of one contested with great obstinacy by a great and small species on the trunk of a pear tree," adds that "'This action was fought in the pontificate of Eugenius the Fourth,[17] in the presence of Nicholas Pistoriensis, an eminent lawyer, who related the whole history of the battle with the greatest fidelity.' A similar engagement between great and small ants is recorded by Olaus Magnus,[18] in which the small ones, being victorious, are said to have buried the bodies of their own soldiers, but left those of their giant enemies a prey to the birds. This event happened previous to the expulsion of the tyrant Christiern the Second from Sweden." The battle which I witnessed took place in the Presidency of Polk,[19] five years before the passage of Webster's Fugitive-Slave Bill.[20]

---

[13] A hospital for soldiers and veterans in Paris.

[14] William Kirby (1759–1850) and William Spence (1783–1860) wrote a multivolume *Introduction to Entomology* (1815–1826).

[15] François Huber (1750–1831), Swiss entomologist.

[16] The pseudonym of Pope Pius II (1405–1464), who wrote poetry and historical works.

[17] The reign of Pope Eugenius IV (1431–1437) was marked by conflicts with heretics and by efforts, ultimately unsuccessful, to reconcile the Roman and Greek Churches. Whether Thoreau is playing on these differences is unclear.

[18] Swedish historian and ecclesiastic (1490–1557); in *Historia de Gentibus Septentrionalibus,* (1555).

[19] James K. Polk (1795–1849), eleventh president of the United States, 1845–1849.

[20] Daniel Webster (1782–1852), senator from Massachusetts, did not introduce the Fugitive Slave Bill (1850), but since he was instrumental in its passage, he was excoriated by those holding antislavery views.

Many a village Bose, fit only to course a mud-turtle in a victualling cellar, sported his heavy quarters in the woods, without the knowledge of his master, and ineffectually smelled at old fox burrows and woodchucks' holes; led perchance by some slight cur which nimbly threaded the wood, and might still inspire a natural terror in its denizens—now far behind his guide, barking like a canine bull toward some small squirrel which had treed itself for scrutiny, then, cantering off, bending the bushes with his weight, imagining that he is on the track of some stray member of the jerbilla family. Once I was surprised to see a cat walking along the stony shore of the pond, for they rarely wander so far from home. The surprise was mutual. Nevertheless the most domestic cat, which has lain on a rug all her days, appears quite at home in the woods, and, by her sly and stealthy behavior, proves herself more native there than the regular inhabitants. Once, when berrying, I met with a cat with young kittens in the woods, quite wild, and they all, like their mother, had their backs up and were fiercely spitting at me. A few years before I lived in the woods there was what was called a "winged cat" in one of the farm-houses in Lincoln nearest the pond, Mr. Gilian Baker's. When I called to see her in June, 1842, she was gone a-hunting in the woods, as was her wont (I am not sure whether it was a male or female, and so use the more common pronoun), but her mistress told me that she came into the neighborhood a little more than a year before, in April, and was finally taken into their house, that she was of a dark brownish-gray color, with a white spot on her throat, and white feet, and had a large bushy tail like a fox; that in the winter the fur grew thick and flatted out along her sides, forming strips ten or twelve inches long by two and a half wide, and under her chin like a muff, the upper side loose, the under matted like felt, and in the spring these appendages dropped off. They gave me a pair of her "wings," which I keep still. There is no appearance of a membrane about them. Some thought it was part flying-squirrel or some other wild animal, which is not impossible, for, according to naturalists, prolific hybrids have been produced by the union of the marten and domestic cat. This would have been the right kind of cat for me to keep, if I had kept any; for why should not a poet's cat be winged as well as his horse?[21]

In the fall the loon (*Colymbus glacialis*) came, as usual, to moult and bathe in the pond, making the woods ring with his wild laughter before I had risen. At rumor of his arrival all the Mill-dam sportsmen are on the alert, in gigs and on foot, two by two and three by three, with patent rifles

---

[21] Poets were supposed to ride the winged horse, Pegasus, of Greek mythology.

and conical balls and spy-glasses. They come rustling through the woods like autumn leaves, at least ten men to one loon. Some station themselves on this side of the pond, some on that, for the poor bird cannot be omnipresent; if he dive here he must come up there. But now the kind October wind rises, rustling the leaves and rippling the surface of the water, so that no loon can be heard or seen, though his foes sweep the pond with spy-glasses, and make the woods resound with their discharges. The waves generously rise and dash angrily, taking sides with all waterfowl, and our sportsmen must beat a retreat to town and shop and unfinished jobs. But they were too often successful. When I went to get a pail of water in the morning I frequently saw this stately bird sailing out of my cove within a few rods. If I endeavored to overtake him in a boat, in order to see how he would manoeuvre, he would dive and be completely lost, so that I did not discover him again, sometimes, till the latter part of the day. But I was more than a match for him on the surface. He commonly went off in a rain.

As I was paddling along the north shore one very calm October afternoon, for such days especially they settle on to the lakes, like the milkweed down, having looked in vain over the pond for a loon, suddenly one, sailing out from the shore toward the middle a few rods in front of me, set up his wild laugh and betrayed himself. I pursued with a paddle and he dived, but when he came up I was nearer than before. He dived again, but I miscalculated the direction he would take, and we were fifty rods apart when he came to the surface this time, for I had helped to widen the interval; and again he laughed long and loud, and with more reason than before. He manoeuvred so cunningly that I could not get within half a dozen rods of him. Each time, when he came to the surface, turning his head this way and that, he coolly surveyed the water and the land, and apparently chose his course so that he might come up where there was the widest expanse of water and at the greatest distance from the boat. It was surprising how quickly he made up his mind and put his resolve into execution. He led me at once to the widest part of the pond, and could not be driven from it. While he was thinking one thing in his brain, I was endeavoring to divine his thought in mine. It was a pretty game, played on the smooth surface of the pond, a man against a loon. Suddenly your adversary's checker disappears beneath the board, and the problem is to place yours nearest to where his will appear again. Sometimes he would come up unexpectedly on the opposite side of me, having apparently passed directly under the boat. So long-winded was he and so unweariable, that when he had swum farthest he would immediately plunge again, nevertheless; and then no wit could divine where in the deep pond, beneath the smooth surface, he might be speeding his way like a fish, for he had time and ability to visit the bottom of the pond in its deepest part. It is said that loons have been caught in the New York lakes eighty feet beneath the surface, with hooks set for trout—though Walden is deeper than that. How surprised must the fishes be to see this ungainly visitor from another sphere speeding his way amid their schools! Yet he appeared to know his course as surely under water as on the surface, and swam much faster there. Once or twice I saw a ripple where he approached the surface, just put his head out to reconnoitre, and instantly dived again. I found that it was as well for me to rest on my oars and wait his reappearing as to endeavor to calculate where he would rise; for again and again, when I was straining my eyes over the surface one way, I would suddenly be startled by his unearthly laugh behind me. But why, after displaying so much cunning, did he invariably betray himself the moment he came up by that loud laugh? Did not his white breast enough betray him? He was indeed a silly loon, I thought. I could commonly hear the plash of the water when he came up, and so also detected him. But after an hour he seemed as fresh as ever, dived as willingly and swam yet farther than at first. It was surprising to see how serenely he sailed off with unruffled breast when he came to the surface, doing all the work with his webbed feet beneath. His usual note was this demoniac laughter, yet somewhat like that of a water-fowl; but occasionally, when he had balked me most successfully and come up a long way off, he uttered a long-drawn unearthly howl, probably more like that of a wolf than any bird; as when a beast puts his muzzle to the ground and deliberately howls. This was his looning—perhaps the wildest sound that is ever heard here, making the woods ring far and wide. I concluded that he laughed in derision of my efforts, confident of his own resources. Though the sky was by this time overcast, the pond was so smooth that I could see where he broke the surface when I did not hear him. His white breast, the stillness of the air, and the smoothness of the water were all against him. At length, having come up fifty rods off, he uttered one of those prolonged howls, as if calling on the god of loons to aid him, and immediately there came a wind from the east and rippled the surface, and filled the whole air with misty rain, and I was impressed as if it were the prayer of the loon answered, and his god was angry with me; and so I left him disappearing far away on the tumultuous surface.

For hours, in fall days, I watched the ducks cunningly tack and veer and hold the middle of the pond, far from the sportsman; tricks which they will have less need to practise in Louisiana bayous. When compelled to rise they would sometimes circle round and round and over the pond at a considerable height, from which they could easily see to other ponds and the river, like black motes in the sky; and, when I thought they had gone off thither long since, they would settle down by a slanting flight of a quarter of a mile on to a distant part which was left free; but what beside safety they got by sailing in the middle of Walden I do not know, unless they love its water for the same reason that I do.

CHAPTER THIRTEEN
House-Warming

In October I went a-graping to the river meadows, and loaded myself with clusters more precious for their beauty and fragrance than for food. There too I admired, though I did not gather, the cranberries, small waxen gems, pendants of the meadow grass, pearly and red, which the farmer plucks with an ugly rake, leaving the smooth meadow in a snarl, heedlessly measuring them by the bushel and the dollar only, and sells the spoils of the meads to Boston and New York; destined to be *jammed,* to satisfy the tastes of lovers of Nature there. So butchers rake the tongues of bison out of the prairie grass, regardless of the torn and drooping plant. The barberry's brilliant fruit was likewise food for my eyes merely; but I collected a small store of wild apples for coddling, which the proprietor and travellers had overlooked. When chestnuts were ripe I laid up half a bushel for winter. It was very exciting at that season to roam the then boundless chestnut woods of Lincoln—they now sleep their long sleep under the railroad—with a bag on my shoulder, and a stick to open burrs with in my hand, for I did not always wait for the frost, amid the rustling of leaves and the loud reproofs of the red-squirrels and the jays, whose half-consumed nuts I sometimes stole, for the burrs which they had selected were sure to contain sound ones. Occasionally I climbed and shook the trees. They grew also behind my house, and one large tree which almost overshadowed it, was, when in flower, a bouquet which scented the whole neighborhood, but the squirrels and the jays got most of its fruit; the last coming in flocks early in the morning and picking the nuts out of the burrs before they fell. I relinquished these trees to them and visited the more distant woods composed wholly of chestnut. These nuts, as far as they went, were a good substitute for bread. Many other substitutes might, perhaps, be found. Digging one day for fish-worms I discovered the ground-nut (*Apios tuberosa*) on its string, the potato of the aborigines, a sort of fabulous fruit, which I had begun to doubt if I had ever dug and eaten in childhood, as I had told, and had not dreamed it. I had often since seen its crimpled red velvety blossom supported by the stems of other plants without knowing it to be the same. Cultivation has well nigh exterminated it. It has a sweetish taste, much like that of a frostbitten potato, and I found it better boiled than roasted. This tuber seemed like a faint promise of Nature to rear her own children and feed them simply here at some future period.

In these days of fatted cattle and waving grain-fields, this humble root, which was once the *totem* of an Indian tribe, is quite forgotten, or known only by its flowering vine; but let wild Nature reign here once more, and the tender and luxurious English grains will probably disappear before a myriad of foes, and without the care of man the crow may carry back even the last seed of corn to the great corn-field of the Indian's God in the south-west, whence he is said to have brought it; but the now almost exterminated ground-nut will perhaps revive and flourish in spite of frosts and wildness, prove itself indigenous, and resume its ancient importance and dignity as the diet of the hunter tribe. Some Indian Ceres or Minerva[1] must have been the inventor and bestower of it; and when the reign of poetry commences here, its leaves and string of nuts may be represented on our works of art.

Already, by the first of September, I had seen two or three small maples turned scarlet across the pond, beneath where the white stems of three aspens diverged, at the point of a promontory, next the water. Ah, many a tale their color told! And gradually from week to week the character of each tree came out, and it admired itself reflected in the smooth mirror of the lake. Each morning the manager of this gallery substituted some new picture, distinguished by more brilliant or harmonious coloring, for the old upon the walls.

The wasps came by thousands to my lodge in October, as to winter quarters, and settled on my windows within and on the walls over-head, sometimes deterring visitors from entering. Each morning, when they were numbed with cold, I swept some of them out, but I did not trouble myself much to get rid of them; I even felt complimented by their regarding my house as a desirable shelter. They never molested me seriously, though they bedded with me; and they gradually disappeared, into what crevices I do not know, avoiding winter and unspeakable cold.

Like the wasps, before I finally went into winter quarters in November, I used to resort to the north-east side of Walden, which the sun, reflected from the pitch-pine woods and the stony shore, made the fire-side of the pond; it is so much pleasanter and wholesomer to be warmed by the sun while you can be, than by an artificial fire. I thus warmed myself by the still glowing embers which the summer, like a departed hunter, had left.

When I came to build my chimney I studied masonry. My bricks being second-hand ones required to be cleaned with a trowel, so that I learned more than usual of the qualities of bricks and trowels. The mortar

---

[1] In Roman mythology, the goddesses of harvests and of wisdom, respectively.

on them was fifty years old, and was said to be still growing harder; but this is one of those sayings which men love to repeat whether they are true or not. Such sayings themselves grow harder and adhere more firmly with age, and it would take many blows with a trowel to clean an old wiseacre of them. Many of the villages of Mesopotamia are built of second-hand bricks of a very good quality, obtained from the ruins of Babylon, and the cement on them is older and probably harder still. However that may be, I was struck by the peculiar toughness of the steel which bore so many violent blows without being worn out. As my bricks had been in a chimney before, though I did not read the name of Nebuchadnezzar[2] on them, I picked out as many fireplace bricks as I could find, to save work and waste, and I filled the spaces between the bricks about the fireplace with stones from the pond shore, and also made my mortar with the white sand from the same place. I lingered most about the fireplace, as the most vital part of the house. Indeed, I worked so deliberately, that though I commenced at the ground in the morning, a course of bricks raised a few inches above the floor served for my pillow at night; yet I did not get a stiff neck for it that I remember; my stiff neck is of older date. I took a poet to board for a fortnight[3] about those times, which caused me to be put to it for room. He brought his own knife, though I had two, and we used to scour them by thrusting them into the earth. He shared with me the labors of cooking. I was pleased to see my work rising so square and solid by degrees, and reflected, that, if it proceeded slowly, it was calculated to endure a long time. The chimney is to some extent an independent structure, standing on the ground and rising through the house to the heavens; even after the house is burned it still stands sometimes, and its importance and independence are apparent. This was toward the end of summer. It was now November.

The north wind had already begun to cool the pond, though it took many weeks of steady blowing to accomplish it, it is so deep. When I began to have a fire at evening, before I plastered my house, the chimney carried smoke particularly well, because of the numerous chinks between the boards. Yet I passed some cheerful evenings in that cool and airy apartment, surrounded by the rough brown boards full of knots, and rafters with the bark on high over-head. My house never pleased my eye so much after it was plastered, though I was obliged to confess that it was more comfortable. Should not every apartment in which man dwells be lofty

[2] King of ancient Babylonia (604–561 B.C.E.).
[3] Ellery Channing (see chap. 12, note 1).

enough to create some obscurity over-head, where flickering shadows may play at evening about the rafters? These forms are more agreeable to the fancy and imagination than fresco paintings or other the most expensive furniture. I now first began to inhabit my house, I may say, when I began to use it for warmth as well as shelter. I had got a couple of old fire-dogs to keep the wood from the hearth, and it did me good to see the soot form on the back of the chimney which I had built, and I poked the fire with more right and more satisfaction than usual. My dwelling was small, and I could hardly entertain an echo in it; but it seemed larger for being a single apartment and remote from neighbors. All the attractions of a house were concentrated in one room; it was kitchen, chamber, parlor, and keeping-room;[4] and whatever satisfaction parent or child, master or servant, derive from living in a house, I enjoyed it all. Cato says, the master of a family (*patremfamilias*) must have in his rustic villa "cellam oleariam, vinariam, dolia multa, uti lubeat caritatem expectare, et rei, et virtuti, et gloriae erit," that is, "an oil and wine cellar, many casks, so that it may be pleasant to expect hard times; it will be for his advantage, and virtue, and glory."[5] I had in my cellar a firkin of potatoes, about two quarts of peas with the weevil in them, and on my shelf a little rice, a jug of molasses, and of rye and Indian meal a peck each.

I sometimes dream of a larger and more populous house, standing in a golden age, of enduring materials, and without ginger-bread work, which shall still consist of only one room, a vast, rude, substantial, primitive hall, without ceiling or plastering, with bare rafters and purlins supporting a sort of lower heaven over one's head—useful to keep off rain and snow; where the king and queen posts stand out to receive your homage, when you have done reverence to the prostrate Saturn of an older dynasty[6] on stepping over the sill; a cavernous house, wherein you must reach up a torch upon a pole to see the roof; where some may live in the fire-place, some in the recess of a window, and some on settles, some at one end of the hall, some at another, and some aloft on rafters with the spiders, if they choose; a house which you have got into when you have opened the outside door, and the ceremony is over; where the weary traveller may wash, and eat, and converse, and sleep, without further journey; such a shelter as you would be glad to reach in a tempestuous night, containing all the essentials of a house, and nothing for house-keeping; where you can see all the treasures of the house at one view, and every thing hangs upon its peg

[4] A New England term for the sitting room.

[5] From *De agri cultura.*

[6] In Roman mythology, Saturn was of the race of gods that preceded and was defeated by that of Jupiter.

that a man should use; at once kitchen, pantry, parlor, chamber, storehouse, and garret; where you can see so necessary a thing as a barrel or a ladder, so convenient a thing as a cupboard, and hear the pot boil, and pay your respects to the fire that cooks your dinner and the oven that bakes your bread, and the necessary furniture and utensils are the chief ornaments; where the washing is not put out, nor the fire, nor the mistress, and perhaps you are sometimes requested to move from off the trap-door, when the cook would descend into the cellar, and so learn whether the ground is solid or hollow beneath you without stamping. A house whose inside is as open and manifest as a bird's nest, and you cannot go in at the front door and out at the back without seeing some of its inhabitants; where to be a guest is to be presented with the freedom of the house, and not to be carefully excluded from seven eighths of it, shut up in a particular cell, and told to make yourself at home there—in solitary confinement. Nowadays the host does not admit you to *his* hearth, but has got the mason to build one for yourself somewhere in his alley, and hospitality is the art of *keeping* you at the greatest distance. There is as much secrecy about the cooking as if he had a design to poison you. I am aware that I have been on many a man's premises, and might have been legally ordered off, but I am not aware that I have been in many men's houses. I might visit in my old clothes a king and queen who lived simply in such a house as I have described, if I were going their way; but backing out of a modern palace will be all that I shall desire to learn, if ever I am caught in one.

It would seem as if the very language of our parlors would lose all its nerve and degenerate into *parlaver*[7] wholly, our lives pass at such remoteness from its symbols, and its metaphors and tropes are necessarily so far fetched, through slides and dumb-waiters, as it were; in other words, the parlor is so far from the kitchen and workshop. The dinner even is only the parable of a dinner, commonly. As if only the savage dwelt near enough to Nature and Truth to borrow a trope from them. How can the scholar, who dwells away in the North West Territory[8] or the Isle of Man,[9] tell what is parliamentary in the kitchen?

However, only one or two of my guests were ever bold enough to stay and eat a hasty-pudding with me; but when they saw that crisis approaching they beat a hasty retreat rather, as if it would shake the house to its foundations. Nevertheless, it stood through a great many hasty-puddings.

---

[7] A pun combining *parlor* with *palaver* (chattering, idle talk).

[8] The area in the late eighteenth century that included present-day Ohio, Indiana, Michigan, Wisconsin, and Minnesota.

[9] An island in the Irish Sea.

I did not plaster till it was freezing weather. I brought over some whiter and cleaner sand for this purpose from the opposite shore of the pond in a boat, a sort of conveyance which would have tempted me to go much farther if necessary. My house had in the mean while been shingled down to the ground on every side. In lathing I was pleased to be able to send home each nail with a single blow of the hammer, and it was my ambition to transfer the plaster from the board to the wall neatly and rapidly. I remembered the story of a conceited fellow, who, in fine clothes, was wont to lounge about the village once, giving advice to workmen. Venturing one day to substitute deeds for words, he turned up his cuffs, seized a plasterer's board, and having loaded his trowel without mishap, with a complacent look toward the lathing overhead, made a bold gesture thitherward; and straightway, to his complete discomfiture, received the whole contents in his ruffled bosom. I admired anew the economy and convenience of plastering, which so effectually shuts out the cold and takes a handsome finish, and I learned the various casualties to which the plasterer is liable. I was surprised to see how thirsty the bricks were which drank up all the moisture in my plaster before I had smoothed it, and how many pailfuls of water it takes to christen a new hearth. I had the previous winter made a small quantity of lime by burning the shells of the *Unio fluviatilis,* which our river affords, for the sake of the experiment; so that I knew where my materials came from. I might have got good limestone within a mile or two and burned it myself, if I had cared to do so.

The pond had in the mean while skimmed over in the shadiest and shallowest coves, some days or even weeks before the general freezing. The first ice is especially interesting and perfect, being hard, dark, and transparent, and affords the best opportunity that ever offers for examining the bottom where it is shallow; for you can lie at your length on ice only an inch thick, like a skater insect on the surface of the water, and study the bottom at your leisure, only two or three inches distant, like a picture behind a glass, and the water is necessarily always smooth then. There are many furrows in the sand where some creature has travelled about and doubled on its tracks; and, for wrecks, it is strewn with the cases of cadis worms made of minute grains of white quartz. Perhaps these have creased it, for you find some of their cases in the furrows, though they are deep and broad for them to make. But the ice itself is the object of most interest, though you must improve the earliest opportunity to study it. If you examine it closely the morning after it freezes, you find that the greater part of the bubbles, which at first appeared to be within it, are against its under surface, and that more are continually rising from the bottom; while the ice is as yet comparatively solid and dark, that is, you see the water through it. These bubbles are from an eightieth to an eighth of an inch in diameter, very clear and beautiful, and you see your face reflected in them through the ice. There may be thirty or forty of them to a square inch. There are also already within the ice narrow oblong perpendicular bubbles about half an inch long, sharp cones with the apex upward; or oftener, if the ice is quite fresh, minute spherical bubbles one directly above another, like a string of beads. But these within the ice are not so numerous nor obvious as those beneath. I sometimes used to cast on stones to try the strength of the ice, and those which broke through carried in air with them, which formed very large and conspicuous white bubbles beneath. One day when I came to the same place forty-eight hours afterward, I found that those large bubbles were still perfect, though an inch more of ice had formed, as I could see distinctly by the seam in the edge of a cake. But as the last two days had been very warm, like an Indian summer, the ice was not now transparent, showing the dark green color of the water, and the bottom, but opaque and whitish or gray, and though twice as thick was hardly stronger than before, for the air bubbles had greatly expanded under this heat and run together, and lost their regularity; they were no longer one directly over another, but often like silvery coins poured from a bag, one overlapping another, or in thin flakes, as if occupying slight cleavages. The beauty of the ice was gone, and it was too late to study the bottom. Being curious to know what position my great bubbles occupied with regard to the new ice, I broke out a cake containing a middling sized one, and turned it bottom upward. The new ice had formed around and under the bubble, so that it was included between the two ices. It was wholly in the lower ice, but close against the upper, and was flattish, or perhaps slightly lenticular, with a rounded edge, a quarter of an inch deep by four inches in diameter; and I was surprised to find that directly under the bubble the ice was melted with great regularity in the form of a saucer reversed, to the height of five eighths of an inch in the middle, leaving a thin partition there between the water and the bubble, hardly an eighth of an inch thick; and in many places the small bubbles in this partition had burst out downward, and probably there was no ice at all under the largest bubbles, which were a foot in diameter. I inferred that the infinite number of minute bubbles which I had first seen against the under surface of the ice were now frozen in likewise, and that each, in its degree, had operated like a burning glass on the ice beneath to melt and rot it. These are the little air-guns which contribute to make the ice crack and whoop.

At length the winter set in in good earnest, just as I had finished plastering, and the wind began to howl around the house as if it had not had permission to do so till then. Night after night the geese came lumbering in in the dark with a clangor and a whistling of wings, even after the ground was covered with snow, some to alight in Walden, and some flying low over the woods toward Fair Haven, bound for Mexico. Several times, when returning from the village at ten or eleven o'clock at night, I heard the tread of a flock of geese, or else ducks, on the dry leaves in the woods by a pond-hole behind my dwelling, where they had come up to feed, and the faint honk or quack of their leader as they hurried off. In 1845 Walden froze entirely over for the first time on the night of the 22d of December, Flints' and other shallower ponds and the river having been frozen ten days or more; in '46, the 16th; in '49, about the 31st; and in '50, about the 27th of December; in '52, the 5th of January; in '53, the 31st of December. The snow had already covered the ground since the 25th of November, and surrounded me suddenly with the scenery of winter. I withdrew yet farther into my shell, and endeavored to keep a bright fire both within my house and within my breast. My employment out of doors now was to collect the dead wood in the forest, bringing it in my hands or on my shoulders, or sometimes trailing a dead pine tree under each arm to my shed. An old forest fence which had seen its best days was a great haul for me. I sacrificed it to Vulcan, for it was past serving the god Terminus.[10] How much more interesting an event is that man's supper who has just been forth in the snow to hunt, nay, you might say, steal, the fuel to cook it with! His bread and meat are sweet. There are enough fagots and waste wood of all kinds in the forests of most of our town to support many fires, but which at present warm none, and, some think, hinder the growth of the young wood. There was also the drift-wood of the pond. In the course of the summer I had discovered a raft of pitch-pine logs with the bark on, pinned together by the Irish when the railroad was built. This I hauled up partly on the shore. After soaking two years and then lying high six months it was perfectly sound, though waterlogged past drying. I amused myself one winter day with sliding this piecemeal across the pond, nearly half a mile, skating behind with one end of a log fifteen feet long on my shoulder, and the other on the ice; or I tied several logs together with a birch withe, and then, with a longer birch or alder which had a hook at the end, dragged them across. Though completely waterlogged and almost as heavy as lead, they not only burned long, but made a very hot fire; nay, I thought that they burned better for the soaking, as if the pitch, being confined by the water, burned longer as in a lamp.

---

[10] In Roman mythology, a god of fire and the sacred boundary stone that stood in the great temple of the Capitoline Jupiter, respectively.

Gilpin, in his account of the forest borderers of England, says that "the encroachments of trespassers, and the houses and fences thus raised on the borders of the forest," were "considered as great nuisances by the old forest law, and were severely punished under the name of *purprestures,* as tending *ad terrorem ferarum—ad nocumentum forestae,* etc.,[11] to the frightening of the game and the detriment of the forest. But I was interested in the preservation of the venison and the vert more than the hunters or wood-choppers, and as much as though I had been the Lord Warden himself; and if any part was burned, though I burned it myself by accident, I grieved with a grief that lasted longer and was more inconsolable than that of the proprietors; nay, I grieved when it was cut down by the proprietors themselves. I would that our farmers when they cut down a forest felt some of that awe which the old Romans did when they came to thin, or let in the light to, a consecrated grove (*lucum conlucare*), that is, would believe that it is sacred to some god. The Roman made an expiatory offering, and prayed, Whatever god or goddess thou art to whom this grove is sacred, be propitious to me, my family, and children, etc.

It is remarkable what a value is still put upon wood even in this age and in this new country, a value more permanent and universal than that of gold. After all our discoveries and inventions no man will go by a pile of wood. It is as precious to us as it was to our Saxon and Norman ancestors. If they made their bows of it, we make our gun-stocks of it. Michaux,[12] more than thirty years ago, says that the price of wood for fuel in New York and Philadelphia "nearly equals, and sometimes exceeds, that of the best wood in Paris, though this immense capital annually requires more than three hundred thousand cords, and is surrounded to the distance of three hundred miles by cultivated plains." In this town the price of wood rises almost steadily, and the only question is, how much higher it is to be this year than it was the last. Mechanics and tradesmen who come in person to the forest on no other errand, are sure to attend the wood auction, and even pay a high price for the privilege of gleaning after the wood-chopper. It is now many years that men have resorted to the forest for fuel and the materials of the arts; the New Englander and

---

[11] William Gilpin (1724–1804), English writer and landscape artist; from his *Remarks on Forest Scenery and Other Woodland Views, (Relative Chiefly to Picturesque Beauty). Illustrated by the Scenes of New-Forest in Hampshire* (1791).

[12] François-André Michaux (1770–1855), French botanist; from his *North American Sylva; Or, a Description of the Forest Trees of the United States, Canada, and Nova Scotia, Considered Particularly with Respect to Their Use in the Arts, and Their Introduction into Commerce; to Which Is Added a Description of the Most Useful of the European Trees* (1819).

the New Hollander, the Parisian and the Celt, the farmer and Robinhood, Goody Blake and Harry Gill,[13] in most parts of the world the prince and the peasant, the scholar and the savage, equally require still a few sticks from the forest to warm them and cook their food. Neither could I do without them.

Every man looks at his wood-pile with a kind of affection. I loved to have mine before my window, and the more chips the better to remind me of my pleasing work. I had an old axe which nobody claimed, with which by spells in winter days, on the sunny side of the house, I played about the stumps which I had got out of my bean-field. As my driver prophesied when I was ploughing, they warmed me twice, once while I was splitting them, and again when they were on the fire, so that no fuel could give out more heat. As for the axe, I was advised to get the village blacksmith to "jump" it;[14] but I jumped him, and, putting a hickory helve from the woods into it, made it do. If it was dull, it was at least hung true.

A few pieces of fat pine were a great treasure. It is interesting to remember how much of this food for fire is still concealed in the bowels of the earth. In previous years I had often gone "prospecting" over some bare hill-side, where a pitch-pine wood had formerly stood, and got out the fat pine roots. They are almost indestructible. Stumps thirty or forty years old, at least, will still be sound at the core, though the sap-wood has all become vegetable mould, as appears by the scales of the thick bark forming a ring level with the earth four or five inches distant from the heart. With axe and shovel you explore this mine, and follow the marrowy store, yellow as beef tallow, or as if you had struck on a vein of gold, deep into the earth. But commonly I kindled my fire with the dry leaves of the forest, which I had stored up in my shed before the snow came. Green hickory finely split makes the wood-chopper's kindlings, when he has a camp in the woods. Once in a while I got a little of this. When the villagers were lighting their fires beyond the horizon, I too gave notice to the various wild inhabitants of Walden vale, by a smoky streamer from my chimney, that I was awake.

Light-winged Smoke, Icarian[15] bird,
Melting thy pinions in thy upward flight,
Lark without song, and messenger of dawn,

---

[13] In William Wordsworth's narrative poem "Goody Blake and Harry Gill," Gill denies fuel to the poor woman, who had been trying to steal some; for his harshness, she curses him that he might never be warm.

[14] Flattening or lengthening the end of a piece of metal by hammering it.

[15] In Greek mythology, Icarus flew too near the sun, which melted the wax of the wings his father, Daedalus, had fashioned for him.

Circling above the hamlets as thy nest;
5 Or else, departing dream, and shadowy form
Of midnight vision, gathering up thy skirts;
By night star-veiling, and by day
Darkening the light and blotting out the sun;
Go thou my incense upward from this hearth,
10 And ask the gods to pardon this clear flame.

Hard green wood just cut, though I used but little of that, answered my purpose better than any other. I sometimes left a good fire when I went to take a walk in a winter afternoon; and when I returned, three or four hours afterward, it would be still alive and glowing. My house was not empty though I was gone. It was as if I had left a cheerful housekeeper behind. It was I and Fire that lived there; and commonly my housekeeper proved trustworthy. One day, however, as I was splitting wood, I thought that I would just look in at the window and see if the house was not on fire; it was the only time I remember to have been particularly anxious on this score; so I looked and saw that a spark had caught my bed, and I went in and extinguished it when it had burned a place as big as my hand. But my house occupied so sunny and sheltered a position, and its roof was so low, that I could afford to let the fire go out in the middle of almost any winter day.

The moles nested in my cellar, nibbling every third potato, and making a snug bed even there of some hair left after plastering and of brown paper; for even the wildest animals love comfort and warmth as well as man, and they survive the winter only because they are so careful to secure them. Some of my friends spoke as if I was coming to the woods on purpose to freeze myself. The animal merely makes a bed, which he warms with his body in a sheltered place; but man, having discovered fire, boxes up some air in a spacious apartment, and warms that, instead of robbing himself, makes that his bed, in which he can move about divested of more cumbrous clothing, maintain a kind of summer in the midst of winter, and by means of windows even admit the light, and with a lamp lengthen out the day. Thus he goes a step or two beyond instinct, and saves a little time for the fine arts. Though, when I had been exposed to the rudest blasts a long time, my whole body began to grow torpid, when I reached the genial atmosphere of my house I soon recovered my faculties and prolonged my life. But the most luxuriously housed has little to boast of in this respect, nor need we trouble ourselves to speculate how the human race may be at last destroyed. It would be easy to cut their threads any time with a little sharper blast from the north. We go on dating from Cold Fridays and Great Snows; but a little colder Friday, or greater snow, would put a period to man's existence on the globe.

The next winter I used a small cooking-stove for economy, since I did not own the forest; but it did not keep fire so well as the open fire-place. Cooking was then, for the most part, no longer a poetic, but merely a chemic process. It will soon be forgotten, in these days of stoves, that we used to roast potatoes in the ashes, after the Indian fashion. The stove not only took up room and scented the house, but it concealed the fire, and I felt as if I had lost a companion. You can always see a face in the fire. The laborer, looking into it at evening, purifies his thoughts of the dross and earthiness which they have accumulated during the day. But I could no longer sit and look into the fire, and the pertinent words of a poet recurred to me with new force.

"Never, bright flame, may be denied to me
Thy dear, life imaging, close sympathy.
What but my hopes shot upward e'er so bright?
What but my fortunes sunk so low in night?

5 Why art thou banished from our hearth and hall,
Thou who art welcomed and beloved by all?
Was thy existence then too fanciful
For our life's common light, who are so dull?
Did thy bright gleam mysterious converse hold
10 With our congenial souls? secrets too bold?

Well, we are safe and strong, for now we sit
Beside a hearth where no dim shadows flit,
Where nothing cheers nor saddens, but a fire
Warms feet and hands—nor does to more aspire;
15 By whose compact utilitarian heap
The present may sit down and go to sleep,
Nor fear the ghosts who from the dim past walked,
And with us by the unequal light of the old wood fire talked."[16]

CHAPTER FOURTEEN
Former Inhabitants; and Winter Visitors

I weathered some merry snow storms, and spent some cheerful winter evenings by my fire-side, while the snow whirled wildly without, and even the hooting of the owl was hushed. For many weeks I met no one in my

[16]From "The Wood-Fire" (published in the *Dial* in 1840), by Ellen Sturgis Hooper (1812–1848).

walks but those who came occasionally to cut wood and sled it to the village. The elements, however, abetted me in making a path through the deepest snow in the woods, for when I had once gone through the wind blew the oak leaves into my tracks, where they lodged, and by absorbing the rays of the sun melted the snow, and so not only made a dry bed for my feet, but in the night their dark line was my guide. For human society I was obliged to conjure up the former occupants of these woods. Within the memory of many of my townsmen the road near which my house stands resounded with the laugh and gossip of inhabitants, and the woods which border it were notched and dotted here and there with their little gardens and dwellings, though it was then much more shut in by the forest than now. In some places, within my own remembrance, the pines would scrape both sides of a chaise at once, and women and children who were compelled to go this way to Lincoln alone and on foot did it with fear, and often ran a good part of the distance. Though mainly but a humble route to neighboring villages, or for the woodman's team, it once amused the traveller more than now by its variety, and lingered longer in his memory. Where now firm open fields stretch from the village to the woods, it then ran through a maple swamp on a foundation of logs, the remnants of which, doubtless, still underlie the present dusty highway, from the Stratten, now the Alms House, Farm, to Brister's Hill.

East of my bean-field, across the road, lived Cato Ingraham, slave of Duncan Ingraham, Esquire, gentleman of Concord village; who built his slave a house, and gave him permission to live in Walden Woods—Cato, not Uticensis, but Concordiensis.[1] Some say that he was a Guinea Negro.[2] There are a few who remember his little patch among the walnuts, which he let grow up till he should be old and need them; but a younger and whiter speculator got them at last. He too, however, occupies an equally narrow house at present. Cato's half-obliterated cellar hole still remains, though known to few, being concealed from the traveller by a fringe of pines. It is now filled with the smooth sumach, (*Rhus glabra*), and one of the earliest species of golden-rod (*Solidago stricta*) grows there luxuriantly.

Here, by the very corner of my field, still nearer to town, Zilpha, a colored woman, had her little house, where she spun linen for the townsfolk, making the Walden Woods ring with her shrill singing, for she had a loud

---

[1] Marcus Porcius Cato (95–46 B.C.E.), a chief political antagonist of Julius Caesar, called Uticensis for his death in the North African city of Utica. Thoreau is differentiating him not from his great-grandfather, Cato the Censor, whose *De re rustica* Thoreau is fond of quoting, but from this Cato of Concord.

[2] That is, from Africa.

and notable voice. At length, in the war of 1812, her dwelling was set on fire by English soldiers, prisoners on parole, when she was away, and her cat and dog and hens were all burned up together. She led a hard life, and somewhat inhumane. One old frequenter of these woods remembers, that as he passed her house one noon he heard her muttering to herself over her gurgling pot—"Ye are all bones, bones!" I have seen bricks amid the oak copse there.

Down the road, on the right hand, on Brister's Hill, lived Brister Freeman, "a handy Negro," slave of Squire Cummings once—there where grow still the apple-trees which Brister planted and tended; large old trees now, but their fruit still wild and ciderish to my taste. Not long since I read his epitaph in the old Lincoln burying-ground, a little on one side, near the unmarked graves of some British grenadiers who fell in the retreat from Concord, where he is styled "Sippio Brister"—Scipio Africanus[3] he had some title to be called—"a man of color," as if he were discolored. It also told me, with staring emphasis, when he died; which was but an indirect way of informing me that he ever lived. With him dwelt Fenda, his hospitable wife, who told fortunes, yet pleasantly—large, round, and black, blacker than any of the children of night, such a dusky orb never rose on Concord before or since.

Farther down the hill, on the left, on the old road in the woods, are marks of some homestead of the Stratten family; whose orchard once covered all the slope of Brister's Hill, but was long since killed out by pitch-pines, excepting a few stumps, whose old roots furnish still the wild stocks of many a thrifty village tree.[4]

Nearer yet to town, you come to Breed's location, on the other side of the way, just on the edge of the wood; ground famous for the pranks of a demon not distinctly named in old mythology, who has acted a prominent and astounding part in our New England life, and deserves, as much as any mythological character, to have his biography written one day; who first comes in the guise of a friend or hired man, and then robs and murders the whole family—New England Rum. But history must not yet tell the tragedies enacted here; let time intervene in some measure to assuage and

---

[3]Publius Cornelius Scipio Africanus Major, Roman general (235/6?–183 B.C.E.), awarded his honorary title "Africanus" after defeating the Carthaginians at the battle of Zama.

[4]Thoreau annotated this passage as follows: "Surveying for Cyrus Jarvis Dec. 23d 56—he shows me a deed of this lot containing 6 A. 52 rods all on the W. Wayland Road—& 'consisting of plowland, orcharding & woodland.' sold by Joseph Stratton to Samuel Swan of Concord In holder Aug. 11th 1777."

lend an azure tint to them. Here the most indistinct and dubious tradition says that once a tavern stood; the well the same, which tempered the traveller's beverage and refreshed his steed. Here then men saluted one another, and heard and told the news, and went their ways again.

Breed's hut was standing only a dozen years ago, though it had long been unoccupied. It was about the size of mine. It was set on fire by mischievous boys, one Election night, if I do not mistake. I lived on the edge of the village then, and had just lost myself over Davenant's Gondibert,[5] that winter that I labored with a lethargy—which, by the way, I never knew whether to regard as a family complaint, having an uncle who goes to sleep shaving himself, and is obliged to sprout potatoes in a cellar Sundays, in order to keep awake and keep the Sabbath, or as the consequence of my attempt to read Chalmers' collection of English poetry[6] without skipping. It fairly overcame my Nervii.[7] I had just sunk my head on this when the bells rung fire, and in hot haste the engines rolled that way, led by a straggling troop of men and boys, and I among the foremost, for I had leaped the brook. We thought it was far south over the woods—we who had run to fires before—barn, shop, or dwelling-house, or all together. "It's Baker's barn," cried one. "It is the Codman Place," affirmed another. And then fresh sparks went up above the wood, as if the roof fell in, and we all shouted "Concord to the rescue!" Wagons shot past with furious speed and crushing loads, bearing, perchance, among the rest, the agent of the Insurance Company, who was bound to go however far; and ever and anon the engine bell tingled behind, more slow and sure, and rearmost of all, as it was afterward whispered, came they who set the fire and gave the alarm. Thus we kept on like true idealists, rejecting the evidence of our senses, until at a turn in the road we heard the crackling and actually felt the heat of the fire from over the wall, and realized, alas! that we were there. The very nearness of the fire but cooled our ardor. At first we thought to throw a frog-pond on to it; but concluded to let it burn, it was so far gone and so worthless. So we stood round our engine, jostled one another, expressed our sentiments through speaking trumpets, or in lower tone referred to the great conflagrations which the world has witnessed, including Bascom's shop, and, between ourselves, we thought that, were we there

---

[5]William D'Avenant (1606–1668), English poet and dramatist; *Gondibert* is an unfinished epic of chivalry.

[6]Alexander Chalmers (1759–1834), edited, in twenty-one volumes, *The Works of the English Poets from Chaucer to Cowper* (1810).

[7]A pun on the name of one of the tribes defeated by Julius Caesar during his campaign in Gaul, 57 B.C.E.

in season with our "tub,"[8] and a full frog-pond by, we could turn that threatened last and universal one into another flood. We finally retreated without doing any mischief—returned to sleep and Gondibert. But as for Gondibert, I would except that passage in the preface about wit being the soul's powder—"but most of mankind are strangers to wit, as Indians are to powder."[9]

It chanced that I walked that way across the fields the following night, about the same hour, and hearing a low moaning at this spot, I drew near in the dark, and discovered the only survivor of the family that I know, the heir of both its virtues and its vices, who alone was interested in this burning, lying on his stomach and looking over the cellar wall at the still smouldering cinders beneath, muttering to himself, as is his wont. He had been working far off in the river meadows all day, and had improved the first moments that he could call his own to visit the home of his fathers and his youth. He gazed into the cellar from all sides and points of view by turns, always lying down to it, as if there was some treasure, which he remembered, concealed between the stones, where there was absolutely nothing but a heap of bricks and ashes. The house being gone, he looked at what there was left. He was soothed by the sympathy which my mere presence implied, and showed me, as well as the darkness permitted, where the well was covered up; which, thank Heaven, could never be burned; and he groped long about the wall to find the well-sweep which his father had cut and mounted, feeling for the iron hook or staple by which a burden had been fastened to the heavy end—all that he could now cling to—to convince me that it was no common "rider." I felt it, and still remark it almost daily in my walks, for by it hangs the history of a family.

Once more, on the left, where are seen the well and lilac bushes by the wall, in the now open field, lived Nutting and Le Grosse. But to return toward Lincoln.

Farther in the woods than any of these, where the road approaches nearest to the pond, Wyman the potter squatted, and furnished his townsmen with earthen ware, and left descendants to succeed him. Neither were they rich in worldly goods, holding the land by sufferance while they lived; and there often the sheriff came in vain to collect the taxes, and "attached a chip,"[10] for form's sake, as I have read in his accounts, there being nothing else that he could lay his hands on. One day in midsummer, when I was

---

[8] A hand-drawn fire engine.

[9] From "The Author's Preface." Thoreau appears to have found the poem tedious.

[10] Confiscated some worthless item.

hoeing, a man who was carrying a load of pottery to market stopped his horse against my field and inquired concerning Wyman the younger. He had long ago bought a potter's wheel of him, and wished to know what had become of him. I had read of the potter's clay and wheel in Scripture, but it had never occurred to me that the pots we use were not such as had come down unbroken from those days, or grown on trees like gourds somewhere, and I was pleased to hear that so fictile an art was ever practised in my neighborhood.

The last inhabitant of these woods before me was an Irishman, Hugh Quoil, (if I have spelt his name with coil enough) who occupied Wyman's tenement—Col. Quoil, he was called. Rumor said that he had been a soldier at Waterloo.[11] If he had lived I should have made him fight his battles over again. His trade here was that of a ditcher. Napoleon went to St. Helena;[12] Quoil came to Walden Woods. All I know of him is tragic. He was a man of manners, like one who had seen the world, and was capable of more civil speech than you could well attend to. He wore a great coat in mid-summer, being affected with the trembling delirium, and his face was the color of carmine. He died in the road at the foot of Brister's Hill shortly after I came to the woods, so that I have not remembered him as a neighbor. Before his house was pulled down, when his comrades avoided it as "an unlucky castle," I visited it. There lay his old clothes curled up by use, as if they were himself, upon his raised plank bed. His pipe lay broken on the hearth, instead of a bowl broken at the fountain.[13] The last could never have been the symbol of his death, for he confessed to me that, though he had heard of Brister's Spring, he had never seen it; and soiled cards, kings of diamonds spades and hearts, were scattered over the floor. One black chicken which the administrator could not catch, black as night and as silent, not even croaking, awaiting Reynard,[14] still went to roost in the next apartment. In the rear there was the dim outline of a garden, which had been planted but had never received its first hoeing, owing to those terrible shaking fits, though it was now harvest time. It was overrun with Roman wormwood and beggar-ticks, which last stuck to my clothes for all fruit. The skin of a woodchuck was freshly stretched upon

[11] The battle in Belgium in which England and its allies, under the Duke of Wellington, defeated Napoleon's forces (1815).

[12] The island to which Napoleon was finally exiled and imprisoned.

[13] Cf. Eccles. 12.6: "Or ever the silver cord be loosed, or the golden bowl be broken, or the pitcher be broken at the fountain, or the wheel broken at the cistern."

[14] The proverbial fox.

the back of the house, a trophy of his last Waterloo; but no warm cap or mittens would he want more.

Now only a dent in the earth marks the site of these dwellings, with buried cellar stones, and strawberries, raspberries, thimble-berries, hazel-bushes, and sumachs growing in the sunny sward there; some pitch-pine or gnarled oak occupies what was the chimney nook, and a sweet-scented black-birch, perhaps, waves where the door-stone was. Sometimes the well dent is visible, where once a spring oozed; now dry and tearless grass; or it was covered deep—not to be discovered till some late day—with a flat stone under the sod, when the last of the race departed. What a sorrowful act must that be—the covering up of wells! coincident with the opening of wells of tears. These cellar dents, like deserted fox burrows, old holes, are all that is left where once were the stir and bustle of human life, and "fate, free-will, foreknowledge absolute,"[15] in some form and dialect or other were by turns discussed. But all I can learn of their conclusions amounts to just this, that "Cato and Brister pulled wool;"[16] which is about as edifying as the history of more famous schools of philosophy.

Still grows the vivacious lilac a generation after the door and lintel and the sill are gone, unfolding its sweet-scented flowers each spring, to be plucked by the musing traveller; planted and tended once by children's hands, in front-yard plots—now standing by wall-sides in retired pastures, and giving place to new-rising forests—the last of that stirp, sole survivor of that family. Little did the dusky children think that the puny slip with its two eyes only, which they stuck in the ground in the shadow of the house and daily watered, would root itself so, and outlive them, and house itself in the rear that shaded it, and grown man's garden and orchard, and tell their story faintly to the lone wanderer a half century after they had grown up and died—blossoming as fair, and smelling as sweet, as in that first spring. I mark its still tender, civil, cheerful, lilac colors.

But this small village, germ of something more, why did it fail while Concord keeps its ground? Were there no natural advantages—no water privileges, forsooth? Ay, the deep Walden Pond and cool Brister's Spring—privilege to drink long and healthy draughts at these, all unimproved by these men but to dilute their glass. They were universally a thirsty race. Might not the basket, stable-broom, mat-making, corn-parching, linen-spinning, and pottery business have thrived here, making the wilderness to blossom like the rose, and a numerous posterity have inherited the land of

---

[15] John Milton, *Paradise Lost* 2.560.

[16] Did their everyday tasks.

their fathers? The sterile soil would at least have been proof against a lowland degeneracy. Alas! how little does the memory of these human inhabitants enhance the beauty of the landscape! Again, perhaps, Nature will try, with me for a first settler, and my house raised last spring to be the oldest in the hamlet.

I am not aware that any man has ever built on the spot which I occupy. Deliver me from a city built on the site of a more ancient city, whose materials are ruins, whose gardens cemeteries. The soil is blanched and accursed there, and before that becomes necessary the earth itself will be destroyed. With such reminiscences I repeopled the woods and lulled myself asleep.

At this season I seldom had a visitor. When the snow lay deepest no wanderer ventured near my house for a week or fortnight at a time, but there I lived as snug as a meadow mouse, or as cattle and poultry which are said to have survived for a long time buried in drifts, even without food; or like that early settler's family in the town of Sutton, in this state, whose cottage was completely covered by the great snow of 1717 when he was absent, and an Indian found it only by the hole which the chimney's breath made in the drift, and so relieved the family. But no friendly Indian concerned himself about me; nor needed he, for the master of the house was at home. The Great Snow! How cheerful it is to hear of! When the farmers could not get to the woods and swamps with their teams, and were obliged to cut down the shade trees before their houses, and when the crust was harder cut off the trees in the swamps ten feet from the ground, as it appeared the next spring.

In the deepest snows, the path which I used from the highway to my house, about half a mile long, might have been represented by a meandering dotted line, with wide intervals between the dots. For a week of even weather I took exactly the same number of steps, and of the same length, coming and going, stepping deliberately and with the precision of a pair of dividers in my own deep tracks—to such routine the winter reduces us—yet often they were filled with heaven's own blue. But no weather interfered fatally with my walks, or rather my going abroad, for I frequently tramped eight or ten miles through the deepest snow to keep an appointment with a beech-tree, or a yellow-birch, or an old acquaintance among the pines; when the ice and snow causing their limbs to droop, and so sharpening their tops, had changed the pines into fir-trees; wading to the tops of the highest hills when the snow was nearly two feet deep on a level, and shaking down another snow-storm on my head at every step; or sometimes creeping and floundering thither on my hands and knees, when the hunters had gone into winter quarters. One afternoon I amused myself by watching a barred owl (*Strix nebulosa*) sitting on one of the lower dead limbs of a white-pine, close to the trunk, in broad daylight, I standing within a rod of him. He could hear me when I moved and cronched the snow with my feet, but could not plainly see me. When I made most noise he would stretch out his neck, and erect his neck feathers, and open his eyes wide; but their lids soon fell again, and he began to nod. I too felt a slumberous influence after watching him half an hour, as he sat thus with his eyes half open, like a cat, winged brother of the cat. There was only a narrow slit left between their lids, by which he preserved a peninsular relation to me; thus, with half-shut eyes, looking out from the land of dreams, and endeavoring to realize me, vague object or mote that interrupted his visions. At length, on some louder noise or my nearer approach, he would grow uneasy and sluggishly turn about on his perch, as if impatient at having his dreams disturbed; and when he launched himself off and flapped through the pines, spreading his wings to unexpected breadth, I could not hear the slightest sound from them. Thus, guided amid the pine boughs rather by a delicate sense of their neighborhood than by sight, feeling his twilight way as it were with his sensitive pinions, he found a new perch, where he might in peace await the dawning of his day.

As I walked over the long causeway made for the railroad through the meadows, I encountered many a blustering and nipping wind, for nowhere has it freer play; and when the frost had smitten me on one cheek, heathen as I was, I turned to it the other also.[17] Nor was it much better by the carriage road from Brister's Hill. For I came to town still, like a friendly Indian, when the contents of the broad open fields were all piled up between the walls of the Walden road, and half an hour sufficed to obliterate the tracks of the last traveller. And when I returned new drifts would have formed, through which I floundered, where the busy north-west wind had been depositing the powdery snow round a sharp angle in the road, and not a rabbit's track, nor even the fine print, the small type, of a meadow mouse was to be seen. Yet I rarely failed to find, even in midwinter, some warm and springy swamp where the grass and the skunk-cabbage still put forth with perennial verdure, and some hardier bird occasionally awaited the return of spring.

Sometimes, notwithstanding the snow, when I returned from my walk at evening I crossed the deep tracks of a woodchopper leading from my

---

[17] Cf. Matt. 5.39, Jesus' Sermon on the Mount: "I say unto you, That ye resist not evil, but whosoever shall smite thee on the right cheek, turn to him the other also." This passage constituted the scriptural basis for then-contemporary Christian ideas of nonresistance and pacifism.

door, and found his pile of whittlings on the hearth, and my house filled with the odor of his pipe. Or on a Sunday afternoon, if I chanced to be at home, I heard the cronching of the snow made by the step of a long-headed farmer[18] who from far through the woods sought my house, to have a social "crack;" one of the few of his vocation who are "men on their farms;"[19] who donned a frock instead of a professor's gown, and is as ready to extract the moral out of church or state as to haul a load of manure from his barn-yard. We talked of rude and simple times, when men sat about large fires in cold bracing weather, with clear heads; and when other dessert failed, we tried our teeth on many a nut which wise squirrels have long since abandoned, for those which have the thickest shells are commonly empty.

The one who came from farthest to my lodge, through deepest snows and most dismal tempests, was a poet.[20] A farmer, a hunter, a soldier, a reporter, even a philosopher, may be daunted; but nothing can deter a poet, for he is actuated by pure love. Who can predict his comings and goings? His business calls him out at all hours, even when doctors sleep. We made that small house ring with boisterous mirth and resound with the murmur of much sober talk, making amends then to Walden vale for the long silences. Broadway was still and deserted in comparison. At suitable intervals there were regular salutes of laughter, which might have been referred indifferently to the last uttered or the forthcoming jest. We made many a "bran new" theory of life over a thin dish of gruel, which combined the advantages of conviviality with the clear-headedness which philosophy requires.

I should not forget that during my last winter at the pond there was another welcome visitor,[21] who at one time came through the village, through snow and rain and darkness, till he saw my lamp through the trees, and shared with me some long winter evenings. One of the last of the philosophers—Connecticut gave him to the world—he peddled first her wares, afterwards, as he declares, his brains. These he peddles still, prompting God and disgracing man, bearing for fruit his brain only, like the nut its kernel. I think that he must be the man of the most faith of any alive. His words and attitude always suppose a better state of things than other men are acquainted with, and he will be the last man to be disappointed as the ages revolve. He has no venture in the present. But though compara-

[18] Scholars have speculated that this might be George Minott or Edmund Hosmer.

[19] Emerson had distinguished "man on the farm" from the "farmer," just as he had done with "man thinking" and the "thinker," in "The American Scholar."

[20] Ellery Channing. (See chap. 12, note 1.)

[21] A. Bronson Alcott (1799–1888).

tively disregarded now, when his day comes, laws unsuspected by most will take effect, and masters of families and rulers will come to him for advice.

"How blind that cannot see serenity!"[22]

A true friend of man; almost the only friend of human progress. An Old Mortality,[23] say rather an Immortality, with unwearied patience and faith making plain the image engraven in men's bodies, the God of whom they are but defaced and leaning monuments. With his hospitable intellect he embraces children, beggars, insane, and scholars, and entertains the thought of all, adding to it commonly some breadth and elegance. I think that he should keep a caravansary on the world's highway, where philosophers of all nations might put up, and on his sign should be printed, "Entertainment for man, but not for his beast. Enter ye that have leisure and a quiet mind, who earnestly seek the right road." He is perhaps the sanest man and has the fewest crotchets of any I chance to know; the same yesterday and tomorrow. Of yore we had sauntered and talked, and effectually put the world behind us; for he was pledged to no institution in it, freeborn, *ingenuus*. Whichever way we turned, it seemed that the heavens and the earth had met together, since he enhanced the beauty of the landscape. A blue-robed man, whose fittest roof is the overarching sky which reflects his serenity. I do not see how he can ever die; Nature cannot spare him.

Having each some shingles of thought well dried, we sat and whittled them, trying our knives, and admiring the clear yellowish grain of the pumpkin pine. We waded so gentle and reverently, or we pulled together so smoothly, that the fishes of thought were not scared from the stream, nor feared any angler on the bank, but came and went grandly, like the clouds which float through the western sky, and the mother-o'-pearl flocks which sometimes form and dissolve there. There we worked, revising mythology, rounding a fable here and there, and building castles in the air for which earth offered no worthy foundation. Great Looker! Great Expecter! to converse with whom was a New England Night's Entertainment.[24] Ah! such discourse we had, hermit and philosopher, and the old settler I have spoken of—we three—it expanded and racked my little house; I should not dare to say how many pounds' weight there was above

---

[22]From Thomas Storer (1571–1604), *The Life and Death of Thomas Wolsey Cardinall Diuided into Three Parts: His Aspiring, Triumph, and Death* (1599).

[23]The title of a well-known novel by Sir Walter Scott (1771–1832), in which the main character wanders through Scotland restoring gravestones.

[24] A play on the stories of the *Arabian Nights Entertainment*, also known as *The Thousand and One Nights.*

the atmospheric pressure on every circular inch; it opened its seams so that they had to be calked with much dulness thereafter to stop the consequent leak—but I had enough of that kind of oakum already picked.

There was one other[25] with whom I had "solid seasons," long to be remembered, at his house in the village, and who looked in upon me from time to time; but I had no more for society there.

There too, as every where, I sometimes expected the Visitor who never comes. The Vishnu Purana[26] says, "The house-holder is to remain at eventide in his courtyard as long as it takes to milk a cow, or longer if he pleases, to await the arrival of a guest." I often performed this duty of hospitality, waited long enough to milk a whole herd of cows, but did not see the man approaching from the town.

CHAPTER FIFTEEN
Winter Animals

When the ponds were firmly frozen, they afforded not only new and shorter routes to many points, but new views from their surfaces of the familiar landscape around them. When I crossed Flints' Pond, after it was covered with snow, though I had often paddled about and skated over it, it was so unexpectedly wide and so strange that I could think of nothing but Baffin's Bay.[1] The Lincoln hills rose up around me at the extremity of a snowy plain, in which I did not remember to have stood before; and the fishermen, at an indeterminable distance over the ice, moving slowly about with their wolfish dogs, passed for sealers or Esquimaux, or in misty weather loomed like fabulous creatures, and I did not know whether they were giants or pygmies. I took this course when I went to lecture in Lincoln in the evening,[2] travelling in no road and passing no house between my own hut and the lecture room. In Goose Pond, which lay in my way, a colony of muskrats dwelt, and raised their cabins high above the ice, though none could be seen abroad when I crossed it. Walden, being like the rest usually bare of snow, or with only shallow and interrupted drifts on it, was my yard,

---

[25] Ralph Waldo Emerson (1803–1882), the best known of the Transcendentalists. It was the Emersons with whom Thoreau lived (1841–43), acting as their handyman. And it was through Emerson that Thoreau obtained a position as a tutor (1843), made some of his connections to publishing, and, most important, was enabled to use the land on which he lived at Walden.

[26] A Hindu book of poems addressed to the god Vishnu (the Destroyer).

[1] Part of the Atlantic Ocean, between Greenland and Canada.

[2] Thoreau lectured in lyceums, mainly in the area of Concord. Parts of *Walden,* as well as most of his essays, were first delivered as lectures. "Lyceums" were associations that

where I could walk freely when the snow was nearly two feet deep on a level elsewhere and the villagers were confined to their streets. There, far from the village street, and except at very long intervals, from the jingle of sleigh-bells, I slid and skated, as in a vast moose-yard well trodden, overhung by oak woods and solemn pines bent down with snow or bristling with icicles.

For sounds in winter nights, and often in winter days, I heard the forlorn but melodious note of a hooting owl indefinitely far; such a sound as the frozen earth would yield if struck with a suitable plectrum, the very *lingua vernacula*[3] of Walden Wood, and quite familiar to me at last, though I never saw the bird while it was making it. I seldom opened my door in a winter evening without hearing it; *Hoo hoo hoo, hoorer hoo,* sounded sonorously, and the first three syllables accented somewhat like *how der do;* or sometimes *hoo hoo* only. One night in the beginning of winter, before the pond froze over, about nine o'clock, I was startled by the loud honking of a goose, and, stepping to the door, heard the sound of their wings like a tempest in the woods as they flew low over my house. They passed over the pond toward Fair Haven, seemingly deterred from settling by my light, their commodore honking all the while with a regular beat. Suddenly an unmistakable cat-owl from very near me, with the most harsh and tremendous voice I ever heard from any inhabitant of the woods, responded at regular intervals to the goose, as if determined to expose and disgrace this intruder from Hudson's Bay[4] by exhibiting a greater compass and volume of voice in a native, and *boo-hoo* him out of Concord horizon. What do you mean by alarming the citadel at this time of night consecrated to me? Do you think I am ever caught napping at such an hour, and that I have not got lungs and a larynx as well as yourself? *Boo-hoo, boo-hoo, boo-hoo!* It was one of the most thrilling discords I ever heard. And yet, if you had a discriminating ear, there were in it the elements of a concord such as these plains never saw nor heard.

I also heard the whooping of the ice in the pond, my great bed-fellow in that part of Concord, as if it were restless in its bed and would fain turn over, were troubled with flatulency and bad dreams; or I was waked by the cracking of the ground by the frost, as if some one had driven a team against my door, and in the morning would find a crack in the earth a quarter of a mile long and a third of an inch wide.

---

provided public lectures, as well as concerts and other primary nineteenth-century forms of amusement and education. Many lyceums owned the buildings in which these entertainments took place.

[3]The local language.

[4]A large body of water in north-central Canada.

Sometimes I heard the foxes as they ranged over the snow crust, in moonlight nights, in search of a partridge or other game, barking raggedly and demoniacally like forest dogs, as if laboring with some anxiety, or seeking expression, struggling for light and to be dogs outright and run freely in the streets; for if we take the ages into our account, may there not be a civilization going on among brutes as well as men? They seemed to me to be rudimental, burrowing men, still standing on their defence, awaiting their transformation. Sometimes one came near to my window, attracted by my light, barked a vulpine curse at me, and then retreated.

Usually the red squirrel (*Sciurus Hudsonius*) waked me in the dawn, coursing over the roof and up and down the sides of the house, as if sent out of the woods for this purpose. In the course of the winter I threw out half a bushel of ears of sweet-corn, which had not got ripe, on to the snow crust by my door, and was amused by watching the motions of the various animals which were baited by it. In the twilight and the night the rabbits came regularly and made a hearty meal. All day long the red squirrels came and went, and afforded me much entertainment by their manoeuvres. One would approach at first warily through the shrub-oaks, running over the snow crust by fits and starts like a leaf blown by the wind, now a few paces this way, with wonderful speed and waste of energy, making inconceivable haste with his "trotters," as if it were for a wager, and now as many paces that way, but never getting on more than half a rod at a time; and then suddenly pausing with a ludicrous expression and a gratuitous somerset, as if all the eyes in the universe were fixed on him—for all the motions of a squirrel, even in the most solitary recesses of the forest, imply spectators as much as those of a dancing girl—wasting more time in delay and circumspection than would have sufficed to walk the whole distance—I never saw one walk—and then suddenly, before you could say Jack Robinson,[5] he would be in the top of a young pitch-pine, winding up his clock and chiding all imaginary spectators, soliloquizing and talking to all the universe at the same time—for no reason that I could ever detect, or he himself was aware of, I suspect. At length he would reach the corn, and selecting a suitable ear, brisk about in the same uncertain trigonometrical way to the top-most stick of my wood-pile, before my window, where he looked me in the face, and there sit for hours, supplying himself with a new ear from time to time, nibbling at first voraciously and throwing the half-naked cobs about; till at length he grew more dainty still and played with his food, tasting only the inside of the kernel, and the ear, which was held balanced over the stick by one paw, slipped from his careless grasp and fell

[5] A proverbial expression for sudden quickness.

to the ground, when he would look over at it with a ludicrous expression of uncertainty, as if suspecting that it had life, with a mind not made up whether to get it again, or a new one, or be off; now thinking of corn, then listening to hear what was in the wind. So the little impudent fellow would waste many an ear in a forenoon; till at last, seizing some longer and plumper one, considerably bigger than himself, and skilfully balancing it, he would set out with it to the woods, like a tiger with a buffalo, by the same zig-zag course and frequent pauses, scratching along with it as if it were too heavy for him and falling all the while, making its fall a diagonal between a perpendicular and horizontal, being determined to put it through at any rate—a singularly frivolous and whimsical fellow—and so he would get off with it to where he lived, perhaps carry it to the top of a pine tree forty or fifty rods distant, and I would afterwards find the cobs strewn about the woods in various directions.

At length the jays arrive, whose discordant screams were heard long before, as they were warily making their approach an eighth of a mile off, and in a stealthy and sneaking manner they flit from tree to tree, nearer and nearer, and pick up the kernels which the squirrels have dropped. Then, sitting on a pitch-pine bough, they attempt to swallow in their haste a kernel which is too big for their throats and chokes them; and after great labor they disgorge it, and spend an hour in the endeavor to crack it by repeated blows with their bills. They were manifestly thieves, and I had not much respect for them; but the squirrels, though at first shy, went to work as if they were taking what was their own.

Meanwhile also came the chicadees in flocks, which, picking up the crumbs the squirrels had dropped, flew to the nearest twig, and, placing them under their claws, hammered away at them with their little bills, as if it were an insect in the bark, till they were sufficiently reduced for their slender throats. A little flock of these tit-mice came daily to pick a dinner out of my wood-pile, or the crumbs at my door, with faint flitting lisping notes, like the tinkling of icicles in the grass, or else with sprightly *day day day,* or more rarely, in spring-like days, a wiry summery *phe-be* from the wood-side. They were so familiar that at length one alighted on an armful of wood which I was carrying in, and pecked at the sticks without fear. I once had a sparrow alight upon my shoulder for a moment while I was hoeing in a village garden, and I felt that I was more distinguished by that circumstance than I should have been by any epaulet I could have worn. The squirrels also grew at last to be quite familiar, and occasionally stepped upon my shoe, when that was the nearest way.

When the ground was not yet quite covered, and again near the end of winter, when the snow was melted on my south hill-side and about my wood-pile, the partridges came out of the woods morning and evening to feed there. Whichever side you walk in the woods the partridge bursts away on whirring wings, jarring the snow from the dry leaves and twigs on high, which comes sifting down in the sun-beams like golden dust, for this brave bird is not to be scared by winter. It is frequently covered up by drifts, and, it is said, "sometimes plunges from on wing into the soft snow, where it remains concealed for a day or two." I used to start them in the open land also, where they had come out of the woods at sunset to "bud" the wild apple-trees. They will come regularly every evening to particular trees, where the cunning sportsman lies in wait for them, and the distant orchards next the woods suffer thus not a little. I am glad that the partridge gets fed, at any rate. It is Nature's own bird which lives on buds and diet-drink.

In dark winter mornings, or in short winter afternoons, I sometimes heard a pack of hounds threading all the woods with hounding cry and yelp, unable to resist the instinct of the chase, and the note of the hunting horn at intervals, proving that man was in the rear. The woods ring again, and yet no fox bursts forth on to the open level of the pond, nor following pack pursuing their Actaeon.[6] And perhaps at evening I see the hunters returning with a single brush trailing from their sleigh for a trophy, seeking their inn. They tell me that if the fox would remain in the bosom of the frozen earth he would be safe, or if he would run in a straight line away no fox-hound could overtake him; but, having left his pursuers far behind, he stops to rest and listen till they come up, and when he runs he circles round to his old haunts, where the hunters await him. Sometimes, however, he will run upon a wall many rods, and then leap off far to one side, and he appears to know that water will not retain his scent. A hunter told me that he once saw a fox pursued by hounds burst out on to Walden when the ice was covered with shallow puddles, run part way across, and then return to the same shore. Ere long the hounds arrived, but here they lost the scent. Sometimes a pack hunting by themselves would pass my door, and circle round my house, and yelp and hound without regarding me, as if afflicted by a species of madness, so that nothing could divert them from the pursuit. Thus they circle until they fall upon the recent trail of a fox, for a wise hound will forsake every thing else for this. One day a man came to my hut from Lexington[7] to inquire after his hound that made a large track, and had been hunting for a week by himself. But I fear that he was not the wiser for all I told him, for every time I attempted to answer his questions

---

[6] In Greek mythology, a hunter who, having seen the goddess Artemis at her bath, was turned into a stag, then pursued and torn to pieces by his own hounds.
[7] A town near Concord.

he interrupted me by asking, "What do you do here?" He had lost a dog, but found a man.

One old hunter who has a dry tongue, who used to come to bathe in Walden once every year when the water was warmest, and at such times looked in upon me, told me, that many years ago he took his gun one afternoon and went out for a cruise in Walden Wood; and as he walked the Wayland road he heard the cry of hounds approaching, and ere long a fox leaped the wall into the road, and as quick as thought leaped the other wall out of the road, and his swift bullet had not touched him. Some way behind came an old hound and her three pups in full pursuit, hunting on their own account, and disappeared again in the woods. Late in the afternoon, as he was resting in the thick woods south of Walden, he heard the voice of the hounds far over toward Fair Haven still pursuing the fox; and on they came, their hounding cry which made all the woods ring sounding nearer and nearer, now from Well-Meadow, now from the Baker Farm. For a long time he stood still and listened to their music, so sweet to a hunter's ear, when suddenly the fox appeared, threading the solemn aisles with an easy coursing pace, whose sound was concealed by a sympathetic rustle of the leaves, swift and still, keeping the ground, leaving his pursuers far behind; and, leaping upon a rock amid the woods, he sat erect and listening, with his back to the hunter. For a moment compassion restrained the latter's arm; but that was a short-lived mood, and as quick as thought can follow thought his piece was levelled, and *whang!*—the fox rolling over the rock lay dead on the ground. The hunter still kept his place and listened to the hounds. Still on they came, and now the near woods resounded through all their aisles with their demoniac cry. At length the old hound burst into view with muzzle to the ground, and snapping the air as if possessed, and ran directly to the rock; but spying the dead fox she suddenly ceased her hounding, as if struck dumb with amazement, and walked round and round him in silence; and one by one her pups arrived, and, like their mother, were sobered into silence by the mystery. Then the hunter came forward and stood in their midst, and the mystery was solved. They waited in silence while he skinned the fox, then followed the brush a while, and at length turned off into the woods again. That evening a Weston[8] Squire came to the Concord hunter's cottage to inquire for his hounds, and told how for a week they had been hunting on their own account from Weston woods. The Concord hunter told him what he knew and offered him the skin; but the other declined it and departed. He did

[8] Another town near Concord.

not find his hounds that night, but the next day learned that they had crossed the river and put up at a farm-house for the night, whence, having been well fed, they took their departure early in the morning.

The hunter who told me this could remember one Sam Nutting, who used to hunt bears on Fair Haven Ledges, and exchange their skins for rum in Concord village; who told him, even, that he had seen a moose there. Nutting had a famous fox-hound named Burgoyne—he pronounced it Bugine—which my informant used to borrow. In the "Wast Book"[9] of an old trader of this town, who was also a captain, town-clerk, and representative, I find the following entry. Jan. 18th, 1742–3, "John Melven Cr. by 1 Grey Fox 0—2—3;" they are not now found here; and in his leger, Feb. 7th, 1743, Hezekiah Stratton has credit "by ½ a Catt skin 0—1—4½;"[10] of course, a wild-cat, for Stratton was a sergeant in the old French war, and would not have got credit for hunting less noble game. Credit is given for deer skins also, and they were daily sold. One man still preserves the horns of the last deer that was killed in this vicinity, and another has told me the particulars of the hunt in which his uncle was engaged. The hunters were formerly a numerous and merry crew here. I remember well one gaunt Nimrod[11] who would catch up a leaf by the road-side and play a strain on it wilder and more melodious, if my memory serves me, than any hunting horn.

At midnight, when there was a moon, I sometimes met with hounds in my path prowling about the woods, which would skulk out of my way, as if afraid, and stand silent amid the bushes till I had passed.

Squirrels and wild mice disputed for my store of nuts. There were scores of pitch-pines around my house, from one to four inches in diameter, which had been gnawed by mice the previous winter—a Norwegian winter for them, for the snow lay long and deep, and they were obliged to mix a large proportion of pine bark with their other diet. These trees were alive and apparently flourishing at mid-summer, and many of them had grown a foot, though completely girdled; but after another winter such were without exception dead. It is remarkable that a single mouse should thus be allowed a whole pine tree for its dinner, gnawing round instead of up and down it; but perhaps it is necessary in order to thin these trees, which are wont to grow up densely.

The hares (*Lepus Americanus*) were very familiar. One had her form under my house all winter, separated from me only by the flooring, and she

---

[9] An account or daybook.

[10] Thoreau annotated this passage as follows: "can it be Calf? v. Mott ledger near beginning."

[11] In Gen. 10.9 described as a "mighty hunter."

startled me each morning by her hasty departure when I began to stir—thump, thump, thump, striking her head against the floor timbers in her hurry. They used to come round my door at dusk to nibble the potato parings which I had thrown out, and were so nearly the color of the ground that they could hardly be distinguished when still. Sometimes in the twilight I alternately lost and recovered sight of one sitting motionless under my window. When I opened my door in the evening, off they would go with a squeak and a bounce. Near at hand they only excited my pity. One evening one sat by my door two paces from me, at first trembling with fear, yet unwilling to move; a poor wee thing, lean and bony, with ragged ears and sharp nose, scant tail and slender paws. It looked as if Nature no longer contained the breed of nobler bloods, but stood on her last toes. Its large eyes appeared young and unhealthy, almost dropsical. I took a step, and lo, away it scud with an elastic spring over the snow crust, straightening its body and its limbs into graceful length, and soon put the forest between me and itself—the wild free venison, asserting its vigor and the dignity of Nature. Not without reason was its slenderness. Such then was its nature. (*Lepus, levipes,* light-foot, some think.)

What is a country without rabbits and partridges? They are among the most simple and indigenous animal products; ancient and venerable families known to antiquity as to modern times; of the very hue and substance of Nature, nearest allied to leaves and to the ground—and to one another; it is either winged or it is legged. It is hardly as if you had seen a wild creature when a rabbit or a partridge bursts away, only a natural one, as much to be expected as rustling leaves. The partridge and the rabbit are still sure to thrive, like true natives of the soil, whatever revolutions occur. If the forest is cut off, the sprouts and bushes which spring up afford them concealment, and they become more numerous than ever. That must be a poor country indeed that does not support a hare. Our woods teem with them both, and around every swamp may be seen the partridge or rabbit walk, beset with twiggy fences and horse-hair snares, which some cow-boy tends.

CHAPTER SIXTEEN
The Pond in Winter

After a still winter night I awoke with the impression that some question had been put to me, which I had been endeavoring in vain to answer in my sleep, as what—how—when—where? But there was dawning Nature, in whom all creatures live, looking in at my broad windows with serene and satisfied face, and no question on *her* lips. I awoke to an answered question, to Nature and daylight. The snow lying deep on the earth dotted with young pines, and the very slope of the hill on which my house is placed, seemed to say, Forward! Nature puts no question and answers none which we mortals ask. She has long ago taken her resolution. "O Prince, our eyes contemplate with admiration and transmit to the soul the wonderful and varied spectacle of this universe. The night veils without doubt a part of this glorious creation; but day comes to reveal to us this great work, which extends from earth even into the plains of the ether."[1]

Then to my morning work. First I take an axe and pail and go in search of water, if that be not a dream. After a cold and snowy night it needed a divining rod to find it. Every winter the liquid and trembling surface of the pond, which was so sensitive to every breath, and reflected every light and shadow, becomes solid to the depth of a foot or a foot and a half, so that it will support the heaviest teams, and perchance the snow covers it to an equal depth, and it is not to be distinguished from any level field. Like the marmots in the surrounding hills, it closes its eye-lids and becomes dormant for three months or more. Standing on the snow-covered plain, as if in a pasture amid the hills, I cut my way first through a foot of snow, and then a foot of ice, and open a window under my feet, where, kneeling to drink, I look down into the quiet parlor of the fishes, pervaded by a softened light as through a window of ground glass, with its bright sanded floor the same as in summer; there a perennial waveless serenity reigns as in the amber twilight sky, corresponding to the cool and even temperament of the inhabitants. Heaven is under our feet as well as over our heads.

Early in the morning, while all things are crisp with frost, men come with fishing reels and slender lunch, and let down their fine lines through the snowy field to take pickerel and perch; wild men, who instinctively follow other fashions and trust other authorities than their townsmen, and by their goings and comings stitch towns together in parts where else they would be ripped. They sit and eat their luncheon in stout fear-naughts[2] on the dry oak leaves on the shore, as wise in natural lore as the citizen is in artificial. They never consulted with books, and know and can tell much less than they have done. The things which they practise are said not yet to be known. Here is one fishing for pickerel with grown perch for bait. You look into his pail with wonder as into a summer pond, as if he kept summer locked up at home, or knew where she had retreated. How, pray, did he get these in mid-winter? O, he got worms out of rotten logs since

[1] From the *Mahabarata,* a Sanskrit epic composed in India.
[2] Heavy woolen coats.

the ground froze, and so he caught them. His life itself passes deeper in Nature than the studies of the naturalist penetrate; himself a subject for the naturalist. The latter raises the moss and bark gently with his knife in search of insects; the former lays open logs to their core with his axe, and moss and bark fly far and wide. He gets his living by barking trees. Such a man has some right to fish, and I love to see Nature carried out in him. The perch swallows the grub-worm, the pickerel swallows the perch, and the fisherman swallows the pickerel; and so all the chinks in the scale of being are filled.

When I strolled around the pond in misty weather I was sometimes amused by the primitive mode which some ruder fisherman had adopted. He would perhaps have placed alder branches over the narrow holes in the ice, which were four or five rods apart and an equal distance from the shore, and having fastened the end of the line to a stick to prevent its being pulled through, have passed the slack line over a twig of the alder, a foot or more above the ice, and tied a dry oak leaf to it, which, being pulled down, would show when he had a bite. These alders loomed through the mist at regular intervals as you walked half way round the pond.

Ah, the pickerel of Walden! when I see them lying on the ice, or in the well which the fisherman cuts in the ice, making a little hole to admit the water, I am always surprised by their rare beauty, as if they were fabulous fishes, they are so foreign to the streets, even to the woods, foreign as Arabia to our Concord life. They possess a quite dazzling and transcendent beauty which separates them by a wide interval from the cadaverous cod and haddock whose fame is trumpeted in our streets.[3] They are not green like the pines, nor gray like the stones, nor blue like the sky; but they have, to my eyes, if possible, yet rarer colors, like flowers and precious stones, as if they were the pearls, the animalized *nuclei* or crystals of the Walden water. They, of course, are Walden all over and all through; are themselves small Waldens in the animal kingdom, Waldenses.[4] It is surprising that they are caught here—that in this deep and capacious spring, far beneath the rattling teams and chaises and tinkling sleighs that travel the Walden road, this great gold and emerald fish swims. I never chanced to see its kind in any market; it would be the cynosure of all eyes there. Easily, with a few convulsive quirks, they give up their watery ghosts, like a mortal translated before his time to the thin air of heaven.

---

[3]Fishmongers, who peddled their wares from carts, blew horns to announce their presence.

[4]A pun on the name of a dissenting Christian sect of the twelfth century, founded by Peter Waldo.

As I was desirous to recover the long lost bottom of Walden Pond, I surveyed it carefully, before the ice broke up, early in '46, with compass and chain and sounding line. There have been many stories told about the bottom, or rather no bottom, of this pond, which certainly had no foundation for themselves. It is remarkable how long men will believe in the bottomlessness of a pond without taking the trouble to sound it. I have visited two such Bottomless Ponds in one walk in this neighborhood. Many have believed that Walden reached quite through to the other side of the globe. Some who have lain flat on the ice for a long time, looking down through the illusive medium, perchance with watery eyes into the bargain, and driven to hasty conclusions by the fear of catching cold in their breasts, have seen vast holes "into which a load of hay might be driven," if there were any body to drive it, the undoubted source of the Styx and entrance to the Infernal Regions from these parts. Others have gone down from the village with a "fifty-six"[5] and a wagon load of inch rope, but yet have failed to find any bottom; for while the "fifty-six" was resting by the way, they were paying out the rope in the vain attempt to fathom their truly immeasurable capacity for marvellousness. But I can assure my readers that Walden has a reasonably tight bottom at a not unreasonable, though at an unusual, depth. I fathomed it easily with a cod-line and a stone weighing about a pound and a half, and could tell accurately when the stone left the bottom, by having to pull so much harder before the water got underneath to help me. The greatest depth was exactly one hundred and two feet; to which may be added the five feet which it has risen since, making one hundred and seven. This is a remarkable depth for so small an area; yet not an inch of it can be spared by the imagination. What if all ponds were shallow? Would it not react on the minds of men? I am thankful that this pond was made deep and pure for a symbol. While men believe in the infinite some ponds will be thought to be bottomless.

A factory owner, hearing what depth I had found, thought that it could not be true, for, judging from his acquaintance with dams, sand would not lie at so steep an angle. But the deepest ponds are not so deep in proportion to their area as most suppose, and, if drained, would not leave very remarkable valleys. They are not like cups between the hills; for this one, which is so unusually deep for its area, appears in a vertical section through its centre not deeper than a shallow plate. Most ponds, emptied, would leave a meadow no more hollow than we frequently see. William Gilpin,

[5]Formerly the hundredweight was constituted by one hundred twelve pounds; thus fifty-six is half a hundredweight.

who is so admirable in all that relates to landscapes, and usually so correct, standing at the head of Loch Fyne, in Scotland, which he describes as "a bay of salt water, sixty or seventy fathoms deep, four miles in breadth," and about fifty miles long, surrounded by mountains, observes, "If we could have seen it immediately after the diluvian crash, or whatever convulsion of Nature occasioned it, before the waters gushed in, what a horrid chasm it must have appeared!

> So high as heaved the timid hills, so low
> Down sunk a hollow bottom, broad, and deep,
> Capacious bed of waters—"[6]

But if, using the shortest diameter of Loch Fyne, we apply these proportions to Walden, which, as we have seen, appears already in a vertical section only like a shallow plate, it will appear four times as shallow. So much for the *increased* horrors of the chasm of Loch Fyne when emptied. No doubt many a smiling valley with its stretching cornfields occupies exactly such a "horrid chasm," from which the waters have receded, though it requires the insight and the far sight of the geologist to convince the unsuspecting inhabitants of this fact. Often an inquisitive eye may detect the shores of a primitive lake in the low horizon hills, and no subsequent elevation of the plain have been necessary to conceal their history. But it is easiest, as they who work on the highways know, to find the hollows by the puddles after a shower. The amount of it is, the imagination, give it the least license, dives deeper and soars higher than Nature goes. So, probably, the depth of the ocean will be found to be very inconsiderable compared with its breadth.

As I sounded through the ice I could determine the shape of the bottom with greater accuracy than is possible in surveying harbors which do not freeze over, and I was surprised at its general regularity. In the deepest part there are several acres more level than almost any field which is exposed to the sun, wind and plough. In one instance, on a line arbitrarily chosen, the depth did not vary more than one foot in thirty rods; and generally, near the middle, I could calculate the variation for each one hundred feet in any direction beforehand within three or four inches. Some are accustomed to speak of deep and dangerous holes even in quiet sandy ponds like this, but the effect of water under these circumstances is to level

---

[6]William Gilpin (1724–1804). From *Observations on Several Parts of Great Britain, Particularly the High-Lands of Scotland, Relative Chiefly to Picturesque Beauty, Made in the Year 1776* (1808). Gilpin is quoting from *Paradise Lost,* 7.288–90.

all inequalities. The regularity of the bottom and its conformity to the shores and the range of the neighboring hills were so perfect that a distant promontory betrayed itself in the soundings quite across the pond, and its direction could be determined by observing the opposite shore. Cape becomes bar, and plain shoal, and valley and gorge deep water and channel.

When I had mapped the pond by the scale of ten rods to an inch, and put down the soundings, more than a hundred in all, I observed this remarkable coincidence. Having noticed that the number indicating the greatest depth was apparently in the centre of the map, I laid a rule on the map lengthwise, and then breadthwise, and found, to my surprise, that the line of greatest length intersected the line of greatest breadth *exactly* at the point of greatest depth, notwithstanding that the middle is so nearly level, the outline of the pond far from regular, and the extreme length and breadth were got by measuring into the coves; and I said to myself, Who knows but this hint would conduct to the deepest part of the ocean as well as of a pond or puddle? Is not this the rule also for the height of mountains, regarded as the opposite of valleys? We know that a hill is not highest at its narrowest part.

Of five coves, three, or all which had been sounded, were observed to have a bar quite across their mouths and deeper water within, so that the bay tended to be an expansion of water within the land not only horizontally but vertically, and to form a basin or independent pond, the direction of the two capes showing the course of the bar. Every harbor on the seacoast, also, has its bar at its entrance. In proportion as the mouth of the cove was wider compared with its length, the water over the bar was deeper compared with that in the basin. Given, then, the length and breadth of the cove, and the character of the surrounding shore, and you have almost elements enough to make out a formula for all cases.

In order to see how nearly I could guess, with this experience, at the deepest point in a pond, by observing the outlines of its surface and the character of its shores alone, I made a plan of White Pond, which contains about forty-one acres, and, like this, has no island in it, nor any visible inlet or outlet; and as the line of greatest breadth fell very near the line of least breadth, where two opposite capes approached each other and two opposite bays receded, I ventured to mark a point a short distance from the latter line, but still on the line of greatest length, as the deepest. The deepest part was found to be within one hundred feet of this, still farther in the direction to which I had inclined, and was only one foot deeper, namely, sixty feet. Of course, a stream running through, or an island in the pond, would make the problem much more complicated.

If we knew all the laws of Nature, we should need only one fact, or the description of one actual phenomenon, to infer all the particular results at that point. Now we know only a few laws, and our result is vitiated, not, of course, by any confusion or irregularity in Nature, but by our ignorance of essential elements in the calculation. Our notions of law and harmony are commonly confined to those instances which we detect; but the harmony which results from a far greater number of seemingly conflicting, but really concurring, laws, which we have not detected, is still more wonderful. The particular laws are as our points of view, as, to the traveller, a mountain outline varies with every step, and it has an infinite number of profiles, though absolutely but one form. Even when cleft or bored through it is not comprehended in its entireness.

What I have observed of the pond is no less true in ethics. It is the law of average. Such a rule of the two diameters not only guides us toward the sun in the system and the heart in man, but draw lines through the length and breadth of the aggregate of a man's particular daily behaviors and waves of life into his coves and inlets, and where they intersect will be the height or depth of his character. Perhaps we need only to know how his shores trend and his adjacent country or circumstances, to infer his depth and concealed bottom. If he is surrounded by mountainous circumstances, an Achillean[7] shore, whose peaks overshadow and are reflected in his bosom, they suggest a corresponding depth in him. But a low and smooth shore proves him shallow on that side. In our bodies, a bold projecting brow falls off to and indicates a corresponding depth of thought. Also there is a bar across the entrance of our every cove, or particular inclination; each is our harbor for a season, in which we are detained and partially landlocked. These inclinations are not whimsical usually, but their form, size, and direction are determined by the promontories of the shore, the ancient axes of elevation. When this bar is gradually increased by storms, tides, or currents, or there is a subsidence of the waters, so that it reaches to the surface, that which was at first but an inclination in the shore in which a thought was harbored becomes an individual lake, cut off from the ocean, wherein the thought secures its own conditions, changes, perhaps, from salt to fresh, becomes a sweet sea, dead sea, or a marsh. At the advent of each individual into this life, may we not suppose that such a bar has risen to the surface somewhere? It is true, we are such poor navigators that our thoughts, for the most part, stand off and on upon a harborless coast, are conversant only with the bights of the bays of poesy, or steer for the public ports of entry, and go into the dry docks of science, where they merely refit for this world, and no natural currents concur to individualize them.

[7]The Greek hero Achilles was supposed to have come from the mountainous region of Thessaly.

As for the inlet or outlet of Walden, I have not discovered any but rain and snow and evaporation, though perhaps, with a thermometer and a line, such places may be found, for where the water flows into the pond it will probably be coldest in summer and warmest in winter. When the ice-men were at work here in '46–7, the cakes sent to the shore were one day rejected by those who were stacking them up there, not being thick enough to lie side by side with the rest; and the cutters thus discovered that the ice over a small space was two or three inches thinner than elsewhere, which made them think that there was an inlet there. They also showed me in another place what they thought was a "leach hole," through which the pond leaked out under a hill into a neighboring meadow, pushing me out on a cake of ice to see it. It was a small cavity under ten feet of water; but I think that I can warrant the pond not to need soldering till they find a worse leak than that. One has suggested, that if such a "leach hole" should be found, its connection with the meadow, if any existed, might be proved by conveying some colored powder or sawdust to the mouth of the hole, and then putting a strainer over the spring in the meadow, which would catch some of the particles carried through by the current.

While I was surveying, the ice, which was sixteen inches thick, undulated under a slight wind like water. It is well known that a level cannot be used on ice. At one rod from the shore its greatest fluctuation, when observed by means of a level on land directed toward a graduated staff on the ice, was three quarters of an inch, though the ice appeared firmly attached to the shore. It was probably greater in the middle. Who knows but if our instruments were delicate enough we might detect an undulation in the crust of the earth? When two legs of my level were on the shore and the third on the ice, and the sights were directed over the latter, a rise or fall of the ice of an almost infinitesimal amount made a difference of several feet on a tree across the pond. When I began to cut holes for sounding, there were three or four inches of water on the ice under a deep snow which had sunk it thus far; but the water began immediately to run into these holes, and continued to run for two days in deep streams, which wore away the ice on every side, and contributed essentially, if not mainly, to dry the surface of the pond; for, as the water ran in, it raised and floated the ice. This was somewhat like cutting a hole in the bottom of a ship to let the water out. When such holes freeze, and a rain succeeds, and finally a new freezing forms a fresh smooth ice over all, it is beautifully mottled internally by dark figures, shaped somewhat like a spider's web, what you may call ice rosettes, produced by the channels worn by the water flowing from all sides to a centre. Sometimes, also, when the ice was covered with shallow puddles, I saw a double shadow of myself, one standing on the head of the other, one on the ice, the other on the trees or hill-side.

While yet it is cold January, and snow and ice are thick and solid, the prudent landlord comes from the village to get ice to cool his summer drink; impressively, even pathetically wise, to foresee the heat and thirst of July now in January—wearing a thick coat and mittens! when so many things are not provided for. It may be that he lays up no treasures in this world[8] which will cool his summer drink in the next. He cuts and saws the solid pond, unroofs the house of fishes, and carts off their very element and air, held fast by chains and stakes like corded wood, through the favoring winter air, to wintry cellars, to underlie the summer there. It looks like solidified azure, as, far off, it is drawn through the streets. These ice-cutters are a merry race, full of jest and sport, and when I went among them they were wont to invite me to saw pit-fashion with them, I standing underneath.

In the winter of '46–7 there came a hundred men of Hyperborean[9] extraction swoop down on to our pond one morning, with many carloads of ungainly-looking farming tools, sleds, ploughs, drill-barrows, turf-knives, spades, saws, rakes, and each man was armed with a double-pointed pike-staff, such as is not described in the New-England Farmer or the Cultivator.[10] I did not know whether they had come to sow a crop of winter rye, or some other kind of grain recently introduced from Iceland. As I saw no manure, I judged that they meant to skim the land, as I had done, thinking the soil was deep and had lain fallow long enough. They said that a gentleman farmer, who was behind the scenes, wanted to double his money, which, as I understood, amounted to half a million already; but in order to cover each one of his dollars with another, he took off the only coat, ay, the skin itself, of Walden Pond in the midst of a hard winter. They went to work at once, ploughing, harrowing, rolling, furrowing, in admirable order, as if they were bent on making this a model farm; but when I was looking sharp to see what kind of seed they dropped into the furrow, a gang of fellows by my side suddenly began to hook up the virgin mould itself, with a peculiar jerk, clean down to the sand, or

---

[8] Cf. Matt. 6.19–21: "Lay not up for yourselves treasures upon earth, where moth and rust doth corrupt, and where thieves break through and steal: But lay up for yourselves treasures in heaven, where neither moth nor rust doth corrupt, and where thieves do not break through nor steal: For where your treasure is, there will your heart be also."

[9] In Greek mythology, a tribe from the far north.

[10] Boston weekly newspapers directed to rural readers.

rather the water—for it was a very springy soil—indeed all the *terra firma*[11] there was—and haul it away on sleds, and then I guessed that they must be cutting peat in a bog. So they came and went every day, with a peculiar shriek from the locomotive, from and to some point of the polar regions, as it seemed to me, like a flock of arctic snow-birds. But sometimes Squaw Walden had her revenge, and a hired man, walking behind his team, slipped through a crack in the ground down toward Tartarus,[12] and he who was so brave before suddenly became but the ninth part of a man, almost gave up his animal heat, and was glad to take refuge in my house, and acknowledged that there was some virtue in a stove; or sometimes the frozen soil took a piece of steel out of a ploughshare, or a plough got set in the furrow and had to be cut out.

To speak literally, a hundred Irishmen, with Yankee overseers, came from Cambridge every day to get out the ice. They divided it into cakes by methods too well known to require description, and these, being sledded to the shore, were rapidly hauled off on to an ice platform, and raised by grappling irons and block and tackle, worked by horses, on to a stack, as surely as so many barrels of flour, and there placed evenly side by side, and row upon row, as if they formed the solid base of an obelisk designed to pierce the clouds. They told me that in a good day they could get out a thousand tons, which was the yield of about one acre. Deep ruts and "cradle holes" were worn in the ice, as on *terra firma,* by the passage of the sleds over the same track, and the horses invariably ate their oats out of cakes of ice hollowed out like buckets. They stacked up the cakes thus in the open air in a pile thirty-five feet high on one side and six or seven rods square, putting hay between the outside layers to exclude the air; for when the wind, though never so cold, finds a passage through, it will wear large cavities, leaving slight supports or studs only here and there, and finally topple it down. At first it looked like a vast blue fort or Valhalla; but when they began to tuck the coarse meadow hay into the crevices, and this became covered with rime and icicles, it looked like a venerable moss-grown and hoary ruin, built of azure-tinted marble, the abode of Winter, that old man we see in the almanac—his shanty, as if he had a design to estivate with us. They calculated that not twenty-five per cent. of this would reach its destination, and that two or three per cent. would be wasted in the cars. However, a still greater part of this heap had a different destiny from what was intended; for, either because the ice was found not to keep

[11] Solid earth.

[12] In Greek mythology, a part of the underworld where the wicked received punishment for their misdeeds.

so well as was expected, containing more air than usual, or for some other reason, it never got to market. This heap, made in the winter of '46–7 and estimated to contain ten thousand tons, was finally covered with hay and boards; and though it was unroofed the following July, and a part of it carried off, the rest remaining exposed to the sun, it stood over that summer and the next winter, and was not quite melted till September 1848. Thus the pond recovered the greater part.

Like the water, the Walden ice, seen near at hand, has a green tint, but at a distance is beautifully blue, and you can easily tell it from the white ice of the river or the merely greenish ice of some ponds, a quarter of a mile off. Sometimes one of those great cakes slips from the ice-man's sled into the village street, and lies there for a week like a great emerald, an object of interest to all passers. I have noticed that a portion of Walden which in the state of water was green will often, when frozen, appear from the same point of view blue. So the hollows about this pond will, sometimes, in the winter, be filled with a greenish water somewhat like its own, but the next day will have frozen blue. Perhaps the blue color of water and ice is due to the light and air they contain, and the most transparent is the bluest. Ice is an interesting subject for contemplation. They told me that they had some in the ice-house at Fresh Pond five years old which was as good as ever. Why is it that a bucket of water soon becomes putrid, but frozen remains sweet forever? It is commonly said that this is the difference between the affections and the intellect.

Thus for sixteen days I saw from my window a hundred men at work like busy husbandmen, with teams and horses and apparently all the implements of farming, such a picture as we see on the first page of the almanac; and as often as I looked out I was reminded of the fable of the lark and the reapers,[13] or the parable of the sower,[14] and the like; and now they are all gone, and in thirty days more, probably, I shall look from the same window on the pure sea-green Walden water there, reflecting the clouds and the trees, and sending up its evaporations in solitude, and no traces will appear that a man has ever stood there. Perhaps I shall hear a solitary loon laugh as he dives and plumes himself, or shall see a lonely fisher in his boat, like a floating leaf, beholding his form reflected in the waves, where lately a hundred men securely labored.

Thus it appears that the sweltering inhabitants of Charleston and New Orleans, of Madras and Bombay and Calcutta,[15] drink at my well. In the morning I bathe my intellect in the stupendous and cosmogonal philoso-

[13] Jean de la Fontaine (1621–1695), *Fables*.

[14] Matt. 13.3–9, 18–23.

[15] Major cities in India that bought ice from New England.

phy of the Bhagvat Geeta, since whose composition years of the gods have elapsed, and in comparison with which our modern world and its literature seem puny and trivial; and I doubt if that philosophy is not to be referred to a previous state of existence, so remote is its sublimity from our conceptions. I lay down the book and go to my well for water, and lo! there I meet the servant of the Bramin, priest of Brahma and Vishnu and Indra,[16] who still sits in his temple on the Ganges[17] reading the Vedas, or dwells at the root of a tree with his crust and water jug. I meet his servant come to draw water for his master, and our buckets as it were grate together in the same well. The pure Walden water is mingled with the sacred water of the Ganges. With favoring winds it is wafted past the site of the fabulous islands of Atlantis and the Hesperides,[18] makes the periplus of Hanno,[19] and, floating by Ternate and Tidore[20] and the mouth of the Persian Gulf, melts in the tropic gales of the Indian seas, and is landed in ports of which Alexander only heard the names.[21]

CHAPTER SEVENTEEN
Spring

The opening of large tracts by the ice-cutters commonly causes a pond to break up earlier; for the water, agitated by the wind, even in cold weather wears away the surrounding ice. But such was not the effect on Walden that year, for she had soon got a thick new garment to take the place of the old. This pond never breaks up so soon as the others in this neighborhood, on account both of its greater depth and its having no stream passing through it to melt or wear away the ice. I never knew it to open in the course of a winter, not excepting that of '52–3, which gave the ponds so severe a trial. It commonly opens about the first of April, a week or ten days later than Flints' Pond and Fair-Haven, beginning to melt on the north side and in the shallower parts where it began to freeze. It indicates better than any water hereabouts the absolute progress of the season, being least affected by transient changes of temperature. A severe cold of a few days'

[16] Three of the most important Hindu gods.
[17] A river in India considered sacred by Hindus.
[18] In Greek mythology, islands in the west supposed to be paradisaical.
[19] A Carthaginian explorer who traveled to west Africa.
[20] Islands in the Molucca Sea between the Philippines and Indonesia.
[21] Alexander the Great (356–323 B.C.E.) extended his empire into India but was never able to reach the Ganges, about which he had heard tales, in the eastern part of that country.

duration in March may very much retard the opening of the former ponds, while the temperature of Walden increases almost uninterruptedly. A thermometer thrust into the middle of Walden on the 6th of March, 1847, stood at 32°, or freezing point; near the shore at 33°; in the middle of Flints' Pond, the same day, at 32½°; at a dozen rods from the shore, in shallow water, under ice a foot thick, at 36°. This difference of three and a half degrees between the temperature of the deep water and the shallow in the latter pond, and the fact that a great proportion of it is comparatively shallow, show why it should break up so much sooner than Walden. The ice in the shallowest part was at this time several inches thinner than in the middle. In mid-winter the middle had been the warmest and the ice thinnest there. So, also, every one who has waded about the shores of a pond in summer must have perceived how much warmer the water is close to the shore, where only three or four inches deep, than a little distance out, and on the surface where it is deep, than near the bottom. In spring the sun not only exerts an influence through the increased temperature of the air and earth, but its heat passes through ice a foot or more thick, and is reflected from the bottom in shallow water, and so also warms the water and melts the under side of the ice, at the same time that it is melting it more directly above, making it uneven, and causing the air bubbles which it contains to extend themselves upward and downward until it is completely honey-combed, and at last disappears suddenly in a single spring rain. Ice has its grain as well as wood, and when a cake begins to rot or "comb," that is, assume the appearance of honey-comb, whatever may be its position, the air cells are at right angles with what was the water surface. Where there is a rock or a log rising near to the surface the ice over it is much thinner, and is frequently quite dissolved by this reflected heat; and I have been told that in the experiment at Cambridge to freeze water in a shallow wooden pond, though the cold air circulated underneath, and so had access to both sides, the reflection of the sun from the bottom more than counterbalanced this advantage. When a warm rain in the middle of the winter melts off the snow-ice from Walden, and leaves a hard dark or transparent ice on the middle, there will be a strip of rotten though thicker white ice, a rod or more wide, about the shores, created by this reflected heat. Also, as I have said, the bubbles themselves within the ice operate as burning glasses to melt the ice beneath.

The phenomena of the year take place every day in a pond on a small scale. Every morning, generally speaking, the shallow water is being warmed more rapidly than the deep, though it may not be made so warm after all, and every evening it is being cooled more rapidly until the morning. The day is an epitome of the year. The night is the winter, the morning and evening are the spring and fall, and the noon is the summer. The cracking and booming of the ice indicate a change of temperature. One pleasant morning after a cold night, February 24th, 1850, having gone to Flints' Pond to spend the day, I noticed with surprise, that when I struck the ice with the head of my axe, it resounded like a gong for many rods around, or as if I had struck on a tight drum-head. The pond began to boom about an hour after sunrise, when it felt the influence of the sun's rays slanted upon it from over the hills; it stretched itself and yawned like a waking man with a gradually increasing tumult, which was kept up three or four hours. It took a short siesta at noon, and boomed once more toward night, as the sun was withdrawing his influence. In the right stage of the weather a pond fires its evening gun with great regularity. But in the middle of the day, being full of cracks, and the air also being less elastic, it had completely lost its resonance, and probably fishes and muskrats could not then have been stunned by a blow on it. The fishermen say that the "thundering of the pond" scares the fishes and prevents their biting. The pond does not thunder every evening, and I cannot tell surely when to expect its thundering; but though I may perceive no difference in the weather, it does. Who would have suspected so large and cold and thick-skinned a thing to be so sensitive? Yet it has its law to which it thunders obedience when it should as surely as the buds expand in the spring. The earth is all alive and covered with papillae. The largest pond is as sensitive to atmospheric changes as the globule of mercury in its tube.

One attraction in coming to the woods to live was that I should have leisure and opportunity to see the spring come in. The ice in the pond at length begins to be honey-combed, and I can set my heel in it as I walk. Fogs and rains and warmer suns are gradually melting the snow; the days have grown sensibly longer; and I see how I shall get through the winter without adding to my wood-pile, for large fires are no longer necessary. I am on the alert for the first signs of spring, to hear the chance note of some arriving bird, or the striped squirrel's chirp, for his stores must be now nearly exhausted, or see the woodchuck venture out of his winter quarters. On the 13th of March, after I had heard the bluebird, song-sparrow, and red-wing, the ice was still nearly a foot thick. As the weather grew warmer it was not sensibly worn away by the water, nor broken up and floated off as in rivers, but, though it was completely melted for half a rod in width about the shore, the middle was merely honey-combed and saturated with water, so that you could put your foot through it when six inches thick; but by the next day evening, perhaps, after a warm rain followed by fog, it would have wholly disappeared, all gone off with the fog, spirited away. One year I went across the middle only five days before it disappeared entirely. In 1845 Walden was first completely open on the 1st of April; in '46, the 25th of March; in '47, the 8th of April; in '51, the 28th of March; in '52, the 18th of April; in '53, the 23d of March; in '54, about the 7th of April.

Every incident connected with the breaking up of the rivers and ponds and the settling of the weather is particularly interesting to us who live in a climate of so great extremes. When the warmer days come, they who dwell near the river hear the ice crack at night with a startling whoop as loud as artillery, as if its icy fetters were rent from end to end, and within a few days see it rapidly going out. So the alligator comes out of the mud with quakings of the earth. One old man, who has been a close observer of Nature, and seems as thoroughly wise in regard to all her operations as if she had been put upon the stocks when he was a boy, and he had helped to lay her keel—who has come to his growth, and can hardly acquire more of natural lore if he should live to the age of Methuselah[1]—told me, and I was surprised to hear him express wonder at any of Nature's operations, for I thought that there were no secrets between them, that one spring day he took his gun and boat, and thought that he would have a little sport with the ducks. There was ice still on the meadows, but it was all gone out of the river, and he dropped down without obstruction from Sudbury, where he lived, to Fair-Haven Pond, which he found, unexpectedly, covered for the most part with a firm field of ice. It was a warm day, and he was surprised to see so great a body of ice remaining. Not seeing any ducks, he hid his boat on the north or back side of an island in the pond, and then concealed himself in the bushes on the south side, to await them. The ice was melted for three or four rods from the shore, and there was a smooth and warm sheet of water, with a muddy bottom, such as the ducks love, within, and he thought it likely that some would be along pretty soon. After he had lain still there about an hour he heard a low and seemingly very distant sound, but singularly grand and impressive, unlike any thing he had ever heard, gradually swelling and increasing as if it would have a universal and memorable ending, a sullen rush and roar, which seemed to him all at once like the sound of a vast body of fowl coming in to settle there, and, seizing his gun, he started up in haste and excited; but he found, to his surprise, that the whole body of the ice had started while he lay there, and drifted in to the shore, and the sound he had heard was made by its edge grating on the shore—at first gently nibbled and crumbled off, but at length heaving up and scattering its wrecks along the island to a considerable height before it came to a stand still.

[1]According to Gen. 5.27, Methuselah lived 969 years.

At length the sun's rays have attained the right angle, and warm winds blow up mist and rain and melt the snow banks, and the sun dispersing the mist smiles on a checkered landscape of russet and white smoking with incense, through which the traveller picks his way from islet to islet, cheered by the music of a thousand tinkling rills and rivulets whose veins are filled with the blood of winter which they are bearing off.

Few phenomena gave me more delight than to observe the forms which thawing sand and clay assume in flowing down the side of a deep cut on the railroad through which I passed on my way to the village, a phenomenon not very common on so large a scale, though the number of freshly exposed banks of the right material must have been greatly multiplied since railroads were invented. The material was sand of every degree of fineness and of various rich colors, commonly mixed with a little clay. When the frost comes out in the spring, and even in a thawing day in the winter, the sand begins to flow down the slopes like lava, sometimes bursting out through the snow and overflowing it where no sand was to be seen before. Innumerable little streams overlap and interlace one with another, exhibiting a sort of hybrid product, which obeys half way the law of currents, and half way that of vegetation. As it flows it takes the forms of sappy leaves or vines, making heaps of pulpy sprays a foot or more in depth, and resembling, as you look down on them, the laciniated lobed and imbricated thalluses of some lichens; or you are reminded of coral, of leopards' paws or birds' feet, of brains or lungs or bowels, and excrements of all kinds. It is a truly *grotesque* vegetation, whose forms and color we see imitated in bronze, a sort of architectural foliage more ancient and typical than acanthus, chiccory, ivy, vine, or any vegetable leaves; destined perhaps, under some circumstances, to become a puzzle to future geologists. The whole cut impressed me as if it were a cave with its stalactites laid open to the light. The various shades of the sand are singularly rich and agreeable, embracing the different iron colors, brown, gray, yellowish, and reddish. When the flowing mass reaches the drain at the foot of the bank it spreads out flatter into *strands,* the separate streams losing their semi-cylindrical form and gradually becoming more flat and broad, running together as they are more moist, till they form an almost flat *sand,* still variously and beautifully shaded, but in which you can trace the original forms of vegetation; till at length, in the water itself, they are converted into *banks,* like those formed off the mouths of rivers, and the forms of vegetation are lost in the ripple marks on the bottom.

The whole bank, which is from twenty to forty feet high, is sometimes overlaid with a mass of this kind of foliage, or sandy rupture, for a quarter of a mile on one or both sides, the produce of one spring day. What makes this sand foliage remarkable is its springing into existence thus suddenly. When I see on the one side the inert bank—for the sun acts on one side first—and on the other this luxuriant foliage, the creation of an hour, I am affected as if in a peculiar sense I stood in the laboratory of the Artist who made the world and me—had come to where he was still at work, sporting on this bank, and with excess of energy strewing his fresh designs about. I feel as if I were nearer to the vitals of the globe, for this sandy overflow is something such a foliaceous mass as the vitals of the animal body. You find thus in the very sands an anticipation of the vegetable leaf. No wonder that the earth expresses itself outwardly in leaves, it so labors with the idea inwardly. The atoms have already learned this law, and are pregnant by it. The overhanging leaf sees here its prototype. *Internally,* whether in the globe or animal body, it is a moist thick *lobe,* a word especially applicable to the liver and lungs and the *leaves* of fat, (λείβω, *labor, lapsus,* to flow or slip downward, a lapsing; λοβός, *globus,* lobe, globe; also lap, flap, and many other words,) *externally* a dry thin *leaf,* even as the *f* and *v* are a pressed and dried *b*. The radicals of lobe are *lb,* the soft mass of the *b* (single lobed, or B, double lobed,) with a liquid *l* behind it pressing it forward. In globe, *glb,* the guttural *g* adds to the meaning the capacity of the throat. The feathers and wings of birds are still drier and thinner leaves. Thus, also, you pass from the lumpish grub in the earth to the airy and fluttering butterfly. The very globe continually transcends and translates itself, and becomes winged in its orbit. Even ice begins with delicate crystal leaves, as if it had flowed into moulds which the fronds of water plants have impressed on the watery mirror. The whole tree itself is but one leaf, and rivers are still vaster leaves whose pulp is intervening earth, and towns and cities are the ova of insects in their axils.

When the sun withdraws the sand ceases to flow, but in the morning the streams will start once more and branch and branch again into a myriad of others. You here see perchance how blood vessels are formed. If you look closely you observe that first there pushes forward from the thawing mass a stream of softened sand with a drop-like point, like the ball of the finger, feeling its way slowly and blindly downward, until at last with more heat and moisture, as the sun gets higher, the most fluid portion, in its effort to obey the law to which the most inert also yields, separates from the latter and forms for itself a meandering channel or artery within that, in which is seen a little silvery stream glancing like lightning from one stage of pulpy leaves or branches to another, and ever and anon swallowed up in the sand. It is wonderful how rapidly yet perfectly the sand organizes itself as it flows, using the best material its mass affords to form the sharp edges of its channel. Such are the sources of rivers. In the silicious matter which the water deposits is perhaps the bony system, and in the still finer soil and organic matter the fleshy fibre or cellular tissue. What is man but a mass of thawing clay? The ball of the human finger is but a drop congealed. The fingers and toes flow to their extent from the thawing mass of the body. Who knows what the human body would expand and flow out to under a more genial heaven? Is not the hand a spreading *palm* leaf with its lobes and veins? The ear may be regarded, fancifully, as a lichen, *umbilicaria,* on the side of the head, with its lobe or drop. The lip—*labium,* from *labor*(?)—laps or lapses from the sides of the cavernous mouth. The nose is a manifest congealed drop or stalactite. The chin is a still larger drop, the confluent dripping of the face. The cheeks are a slide from the brows into the valley of the face, opposed and diffused by the cheek bones. Each rounded lobe of the vegetable leaf, too, is a thick and now loitering drop, larger or smaller; the lobes are the fingers of the leaf; and as many lobes as it has, in so many directions it tends to flow, and more heat or other genial influences would have caused it to flow yet farther.

Thus it seemed that this one hillside illustrated the principle of all the operations of Nature. The Maker of this earth but patented a leaf. What Champollion[2] will decipher this hieroglyphic for us, that we may turn over a new leaf at last? This phenomenon is more exhilarating to me than the luxuriance and fertility of vineyards. True, it is somewhat excrementitious in its character, and there is no end to the heaps of liver, lights, and bowels, as if the globe were turned wrong side outward; but this suggests at least that Nature has some bowels, and there again is mother of humanity. This is the frost coming out of the ground; this is Spring. It precedes the green and flowery spring, as mythology precedes regular poetry. I know of nothing more purgative of winter fumes and indigestions. It convinces me that Earth is still in her swaddling clothes, and stretches forth baby fingers on every side. Fresh curls spring from the baldest brow. There is nothing inorganic. These foliaceous heaps lie along the bank like the slag of a furnace, showing that Nature is "in full blast" within. The earth is not a mere fragment of dead history, stratum upon stratum like the leaves of a book, to be studied by geologists and antiquaries chiefly, but living poetry like the leaves of a tree, which precede flowers and fruit—not a fossil earth, but a living earth; compared with whose great central life all animal and vegetable life is merely parasitic. Its throes will heave our exuviae from their graves. You may melt your metals and cast them into the most beautiful

---

[2]Jean-François Champollion (1790–1832) deciphered the hieroglyphs on the Rosetta stone, a basalt stone, found in 1799, on which were inscribed hieroglyphics, demotic characters, and Greek words. Comparing the texts provided the initial clues for deciphering the theretofore unreadable inscriptions of ancient Egyptian civilization.

moulds you can; they will never excite me like the forms which this molten earth flows out into. And not only it, but the institutions upon it, are plastic like clay in the hands of the potter.

Ere long, not only on these banks, but on every hill and plain and in every hollow, the frost comes out of the ground like a dormant quadruped from its burrow, and seeks the sea with music, or migrates to other climes in clouds. Thaw with his gentle persuasion is more powerful than Thor[3] with his hammer. The one melts, the other but breaks in pieces.

When the ground was partially bare of snow, and a few warm days had dried its surface somewhat, it was pleasant to compare the first tender signs of the infant year just peeping forth with the stately beauty of the withered vegetation which had withstood the winter—life-everlasting, golden-rods, pin-weeds, and graceful wild grasses, more obvious and interesting frequently than in summer even, as if their beauty was not ripe till then; even cotton-grass, cat-tails, mulleins, johnswort, hard-hack, meadow-sweet, and other strong stemmed plants, those unexhausted granaries which entertain the earliest birds—decent weeds, at least, which widowed Nature wears. I am particularly attracted by the arching and sheaf-like top of the wool-grass; it brings back the summer to our winter memories, and is among the forms which art loves to copy, and which, in the vegetable kingdom, have the same relation to types already in the mind of man that astronomy has. It is an antique style older than Greek or Egyptian. Many of the phenomena of Winter are suggestive of an inexpressible tenderness and fragile delicacy. We are accustomed to hear this king described as a rude and boisterous tyrant; but with the gentleness of a lover he adorns the tresses of Summer.

At the approach of spring the red-squirrels got under my house, two at a time, directly under my feet as I sat reading or writing, and kept up the queerest chuckling and chirruping and vocal pirouetting and gurgling sounds that ever were heard; and when I stamped they only chirruped the louder, as if past all fear and respect in their mad pranks, defying humanity to stop them. No you don't—*chickaree—chickaree*. They were wholly deaf to my arguments, or failed to perceive their force, and fell into a strain of invective that was irresistible.

The first sparrow of spring! The year beginning with younger hope than ever! The faint silvery warblings heard over the partially bare and moist fields from the blue-bird, the song-sparrow, and the red-wing, as if

---

[3] The god of thunder and war in Norse myth.

the last flakes of winter tinkled as they fell! What at such a time are histories, chronologies, traditions, and all written revelations? The brooks sing carols and glees to the spring. The marsh-hawk sailing low over the meadow is already seeking the first slimy life that awakes. The sinking sound of melting snow is heard in all dells, and the ice dissolves apace in the ponds. The grass flames up on the hillsides like a spring fire—"et primitus oritur herba imbribus primoribus evocata"[4]—as if the earth sent forth an inward heat to greet the returning sun; not yellow but green is the color of its flame—the symbol of perpetual youth, the grass-blade, like a long green ribbon, streams from the sod into the summer, checked indeed by the frost, but anon pushing on again, lifting its spear of last year's hay with the fresh life below. It grows as steadily as the rill oozes out of the ground. It is almost identical with that, for in the growing days of June, when the rills are dry, the grass blades are their channels, and from year to year the herds drink at this perennial green stream, and the mower draws from it betimes their winter supply. So our human life but dies down to its root, and still puts forth its green blade to eternity.

Walden is melting apace. There is a canal two rods wide along the northerly and westerly sides, and wider still at the east end. A great field of ice has cracked off from the main body. I hear a song-sparrow singing from the bushes on the shore—*olit, olit, olit—chip, chip, chip, che char—che wiss, wiss, wiss.* He too is helping to crack it. How handsome the great sweeping curves in the edge of the ice, answering somewhat to those of the shore, but more regular! It is unusually hard, owing to the recent severe but transient cold, and all watered or waved like a palace floor. But the wind slides eastward over its opaque surface in vain, till it reaches the living surface beyond. It is glorious to behold this ribbon of water sparkling in the sun, the bare face of the pond full of glee and youth, as if it spoke the joy of the fishes within it, and of the sands on its shore—a silvery sheen as from the scales of a *leuciscus,*[5] as it were all one active fish. Such is the contrast between winter and spring. Walden was dead and is alive again. But this spring it broke up more steadily, as I have said.

The change from storm and winter to serene and mild weather, from dark and sluggish hours to bright and elastic ones, is a memorable crisis which all things proclaim. It is seemingly instantaneous at last. Suddenly an influx of light filled my house, though the evening was at hand, and the

---

[4] From Varro, *De re rustica:* "Called forth by the early rains, the grass rouses itself for the first time."

[5] A small fish, like a "shiner."

clouds of winter still overhung it, and the eaves were dripping with sleety rain. I looked out the window, and lo! where yesterday was cold gray ice there lay the transparent pond already calm and full of hope as in a summer evening, reflecting a summer evening sky in its bosom, though none was visible overhead, as if it had intelligence with some remote horizon. I heard a robin in the distance, the first I had heard for many a thousand years, methought, whose note I shall not forget for many a thousand more—the same sweet and powerful song as of yore. O the evening robin, at the end of a New England summer day! If I could ever find the twig he sits upon! I mean *he;* I mean *the twig.* This at least is not the *Turdus migratorius.*[6] The pitch-pines and shrub-oaks about my house, which had so long drooped, suddenly resumed their several characters, looked brighter, greener, and more erect and alive, as if effectually cleansed and restored by the rain. I knew that it would not rain any more. You may tell by looking at any twig of the forest, ay, at your very wood-pile, whether its winter is past or not. As it grew darker, I was startled by the *honking* of geese flying low over the woods, like weary travellers getting in late from southern lakes, and indulging at last in unrestrained complaint and mutual consolation. Standing at my door, I could hear the rush of their wings; when, driving toward my house, they suddenly spied my light, and with hushed clamor wheeled and settled in the pond. So I came in, and shut the door, and passed my first spring night in the woods.

In the morning I watched the geese from the door through the mist, sailing in the middle of the pond, fifty rods off, so large and tumultuous that Walden appeared like an artificial pond for their amusement. But when I stood on the shore they at once rose up with a great flapping of wings at the signal of their commander, and when they had got into rank circled about over my head, twenty-nine of them, and then steered straight to Canada, with a regular *honk* from the leader at intervals, trusting to break their fast in muddier pools. A "plump" of ducks rose at the same time and took the route to the north in the wake of their noisier cousins.

For a week I heard the circling groping clangor of some solitary goose in the foggy mornings, seeking its companion, and still peopling the woods with the sound of a larger life than they could sustain. In April the pigeons were seen again flying express in small flocks, and in due time I heard the martins twittering over my clearing, though it had not seemed that the township contained so many that it could afford me any, and I fancied that they were peculiarly of the ancient race that dwelt in hollow trees ere white

---

[6] The common American robin was once categorized by the name Thoreau uses.

men came. In almost all climes the tortoise and the frog are among the precursors and heralds of this season, and birds fly with song and glancing plumage, and plants spring and bloom, and winds blow, to correct this slight oscillation of the poles and preserve the equilibrium of Nature.

As every season seems best to us in its turn, so the coming in of spring is like the creation of Cosmos out of Chaos and the realization of the Golden Age—[7]

> "Eurus ad Auroram, Nabathacaque regna recessit,
> Persidaque, et radiis juga subdita matutinis."

> "The East-Wind withdrew to Aurora and the Nabathaean kingdom,
> And the Persian, and the ridges placed under the morning rays.
> . . . .
> Man was born. Whether that Artificer of things,
> The origin of a better world, made him from the divine seed;
> 5 Or the earth being recent and lately sundered from the high
> Ether, retained some seeds of cognate heaven."[8]

A single gentle rain makes the grass many shades greener. So our prospects brighten on the influx of better thoughts. We should be blessed if we lived in the present always, and took advantage of every accident that befell us, like the grass which confesses the influence of the slightest dew that falls on it; and did not spend our time in atoning for the neglect of past opportunities, which we call doing our duty. We loiter in winter while it is already spring. In a pleasant spring morning all man's sins are forgiven. Such a day is a truce to vice. While such a sun holds out to burn, the vilest sinner may return. Through our own recovered innocence we discern the innocence of our neighbors. You may have known your neighbor yesterday for a thief, a drunkard, or a sensualist, and merely pitied or despised him, and despaired of the world; but the sun shines bright and warm this first spring morning, recreating the world, and you meet him at some serene work, and see how his exhausted and debauched veins expand with still joy and bless the new day, feel the spring influence with the innocence of infancy, and all his faults are forgotten. There is not only an atmosphere of good will about him, but even a savor of holiness groping for expression, blindly and ineffectually perhaps, like a new-born instinct, and for a

---

[7]The Golden Age of harmony and delight occurred, according to Greek mythology, shortly after Cosmos was created out of Chaos.

[8]Ovid, *Metamorphoses* 1.61–62, 78–81.

short hour the south hill-side echoes to no vulgar jest. You see some innocent fair shoots preparing to burst from his gnarled rind and try another year's life, tender and fresh as the youngest plant. Even he has entered into the joy of his Lord.[9] Why the jailer does not leave open his prison doors—why the judge does not dismiss his case—why the preacher does not dismiss his congregation! It is because they do not obey the hint which God gives them, nor accept the pardon which he freely offers to all.

"A return to goodness produced each day in the tranquil and beneficent breath of the morning, causes that in respect to the love of virtue and the hatred of vice, one approaches a little the primitive nature of man, as the sprouts of the forest which has been felled. In like manner the evil which one does in the interval of a day prevents the germs of virtues which began to spring up again from developing themselves and destroys them.

"After the germs of virtue have thus been prevented many times from developing themselves, then the beneficent breath of evening does not suffice to preserve them. As soon as the breath of evening does not suffice longer to preserve them, then the nature of man does not differ much from that of the brute. Men seeing the nature of this man like that of the brute, think that he has never possessed the innate faculty of reason. Are those the true and natural sentiments of man?"[10]

"The Golden Age was first created, which without any avenger
Spontaneously without law cherished fidelity and rectitude.
Punishment and fear were not; nor were threatening words read
On suspended brass; nor did the suppliant crowd fear
5 The words of their judge; but were safe without an avenger.
Not yet the pine felled on its mountains had descended
To the liquid waves that it might see a foreign world,
And mortals knew no shores but their own.
. . . .
There was eternal spring, and placid zephyrs with warm
10 Blasts soothed the flowers born without seed."[11]

On the 29th of April, as I was fishing from the bank of the river near the Nine-Acre-Corner bridge, standing on the quaking grass and willow

---

[9] Cf. Matt. 25.21: "His lord said unto him, Well done, thou good and faithful servant: thou hast been faithful over a few things, I will make thee ruler over many things: enter thou into the joy of thy lord."

[10] From the Chinese philosopher Meng-tse (anglicized Mencius), *Works* 6.1.

[11] Ovid, *Metamorphoses* 1.89–96, 107–08.

roots, where the muskrats lurk, I heard a singular rattling sound, somewhat like that of the sticks which boys play with their fingers, when, looking up, I observed a very slight and graceful hawk, like a night-hawk, alternately soaring like a ripple and tumbling a rod or two over and over, showing the underside of its wings, which gleamed like a satin ribbon in the sun, or like the pearly inside of a shell. This sight reminded me of falconry and what nobleness and poetry are associated with that sport. The Merlin it seemed to me it might be called: but I care not for its name. It was the most ethereal flight I had ever witnessed. It did not simply flutter like a butterfly, nor soar like the larger hawks, but it sported with proud reliance in the fields of air; mounting again and again with its strange chuckle, it repeated its free and beautiful fall, turning over and over like a kite, and then recovering from its lofty tumbling, as if it had never set its foot on *terra firma*. It appeared to have no companion in the universe—sporting there alone—and to need none but the morning and the ether with which it played. It was not lonely, but made all the earth lonely beneath it. Where was the parent which hatched it, its kindred, and its father in the heavens? The tenant of the air, it seemed related to the earth but by an egg hatched some time in the crevice of a crag—or was its native nest made in the angle of a cloud, woven of the rainbow's trimmings and the sunset sky, and lined with some soft midsummer haze caught up from earth? Its eyry now some cliffy cloud.

Beside this I got a rare mess of golden and silver and bright cupreous fishes, which looked like a string of jewels. Ah! I have penetrated to those meadows on the morning of many a first spring day, jumping from hummock to hummock, from willow root to willow root, when the wild river valley and the woods were bathed in so pure and bright a light as would have waked the dead, if they had been slumbering in their graves, as some suppose. There needs no stronger proof of immortality. All things must live in such a light. O Death, where was thy sting? O Grave, where was thy victory, then?[12]

Our village life would stagnate if it were not for the unexplored forests and meadows which surround it. We need the tonic of wildness—to wade sometimes in marshes where the bittern and the meadow-hen lurk, and hear the booming of the snipe; to smell the whispering sedge where only some wilder and more solitary fowl builds her nest, and the mink crawls with its belly close to the ground. At the same time that we are earnest to explore and learn all things, we require that all things be mysterious and

[12] 1 Cor. 15.55: "O death, where is thy sting? O grave, where is thy victory?"

unexplorable, that land and sea be infinitely wild, unsurveyed and unfathomed by us because unfathomable. We can never have enough of Nature. We must be refreshed by the sight of inexhaustible vigor, vast and Titanic features, the sea-coast with its wrecks, the wilderness with its living and its decaying trees, the thunder cloud, and the rain which lasts three weeks and produces freshets. We need to witness our own limits transgressed, and some life pasturing freely where we never wander. We are cheered when we observe the vulture feeding on the carrion which disgusts and disheartens us and deriving health and strength from the repast. There was a dead horse in the hollow by the path to my house, which compelled me sometimes to go out of my way, especially in the night when the air was heavy, but the assurance it gave me of the strong appetite and inviolable health of Nature was my compensation for this. I love to see that Nature is so rife with life that myriads can be afforded to be sacrificed and suffered to prey on one another; that tender organizations can be so serenely squashed out of existence like pulp—tadpoles which herons gobble up, and tortoises and toads run over in the road; and that sometimes it has rained flesh and blood! With the liability to accident, we must see how little account is to be made of it. The impression made on a wise man is that of universal innocence. Poison is not poisonous after all, nor are any wounds fatal. Compassion is a very untenable ground. It must be expeditious. Its pleadings will not bear to be stereotyped.

Early in May, the oaks, hickories, maples, and other trees, just putting out amidst the pine woods around the pond, imparted a brightness like sunshine to the landscape, especially in cloudy days, as if the sun were breaking through mists and shining faintly on the hill-sides here and there. On the third or fourth of May I saw a loon in the pond, and during the first week of the month I heard the whippoorwill, the brown-thrasher, the veery, the wood-pewee, the chewink, and other birds. I had heard the wood-thrush long before. The phoebe had already come once more and looked in at my door and window, to see if my house was cavern-like enough for her, sustaining herself on humming wings with clinched talons, as if she held by the air, while she surveyed the premises. The sulphur-like pollen of the pitch-pine soon covered the pond and the stones and rotten wood along the shore, so that you could have collected a barrel-ful. This is the "sulphur showers" we hear of. Even in Calidas' drama of Sacontala, we read of "rills dyed yellow with the golden dust of the lotus."[13] And so the seasons went rolling on into summer, as one rambles into higher and higher grass.

---

[13] From Sir William Jones (1746–1794), translation (1796) of *Sacontalá; Or, The Fatal Ring: an Indian Drama* by the fifth-century Hindu poet Kalidas.

Thus was my first year's life in the woods completed; and the second year was similar to it. I finally left Walden September 6th, 1847.

Conclusion

To the sick the doctors wisely recommend a change of air and scenery. Thank Heaven, here is not all the world. The buck-eye does not grow in New England, and the mocking-bird is rarely heard here. The wild-goose is more of a cosmopolite than we; he breaks his fast in Canada, takes a luncheon in the Ohio, and plumes himself for the night in a southern bayou. Even the bison, to some extent, keeps pace with the seasons, cropping the pastures of the Colorado only till a greener and sweeter grass awaits him by the Yellow-stone. Yet we think that if rail-fences are pulled down, and stone-walls piled up on our farms, bounds are henceforth set to our lives and our fates decided. If you are chosen town-clerk, forsooth, you cannot go to Tierra del Fuego[1] this summer: but you may go to the land of infernal fire nevertheless. The universe is wider than our views of it.

Yet we should oftener look over the tafferel of our craft, like curious passengers, and not make the voyage like stupid sailors picking oakum.[2] The other side of the globe is but the home of our correspondent. Our voyaging is only great-circle sailing, and the doctors prescribe for diseases of the skin merely. One hastens to Southern Africa to chase the giraffe; but surely that is not the game he would be after. How long, pray, would a man hunt giraffes if he could? Snipes and woodcocks also may afford rare sport; but I trust it would be nobler game to shoot one's self.

"Direct your eye right inward, and you'll find
A thousand regions in your mind
Yet undiscovered. Travel them, and be
Expert in home-cosmography."[3]

What does Africa—what does the West stand for? Is not our own interior white on the chart? black though it may prove, like the coast, when discovered. Is it the source of the Nile, or the Niger, or the Mississippi, or a North-West Passage around this continent, that we would find? Are these

---

[1] The southernmost tip of South America.
[2] Hemp fiber used to caulk seams in a ship; it was obtained by untwisting and picking out the fibers of old rope, a dull and tedious job.
[3] From William Habington (1605–1654), "To My Honoured Friend Sir Ed. P. Knight" from *Castara* (1634). In addition to modernizing the spelling, Thoreau changed "eye-sight" to "eye right."

the problems which most concern mankind? Is Franklin[4] the only man who is lost, that his wife should be so earnest to find him? Does Mr. Grinnell[5] know where he himself is? Be rather the Mungo Park,[6] the Lewis and Clarke[7] and Frobisher,[8] of your own streams and oceans; explore your own higher latitudes—with shiploads of preserved meats to support you, if they be necessary; and pile the empty cans sky-high for a sign. Were preserved meats invented to preserve meat merely? Nay, be a Columbus to whole new continents and worlds within you, opening new channels, not of trade, but of thought. Every man is the lord of a realm beside which the earthly empire of the Czar is but a petty state, a hummock left by the ice. Yet some can be patriotic who have no *self*-respect, and sacrifice the greater to the less. They love the soil which makes their graves, but have no sympathy with the spirit which may still animate their clay. Patriotism is a maggot in their heads. What was the meaning of that South-Sea Exploring Expedition,[9] with all its parade and expense, but an indirect recognition of the fact, that there are continents and seas in the moral world, to which every man is an isthmus or an inlet, yet unexplored by him, but that it is easier to sail many thousand miles through cold and storm and cannibals, in a government ship, with five hundred men and boys to assist one, than it is to explore the private sea, the Atlantic and Pacific Ocean of one's being alone.

> "Erret, et extremos alter scrutetur Iberos.
> Plus habet hic vitae, plus habet ille viae." [10]

---

[4]John Franklin (1786–1847), English explorer who disappeared while attempting to find the Northwest Passage, a way of passing north of the North American continent en route to the East long sought by Europeans. He was still missing when Thoreau wrote, though his remains were later located.

[5]Henry Grinnell (1799–1874), a New York merchant and philanthropist, financed two expeditions to locate Franklin, in 1850 and 1853.

[6]Mungo Park (1771–1806), a Scottish explorer who mapped the course of the Niger River and became an archetypical figure of the European explorer in Africa.

[7]Meriwether Lewis (1774–1809) and William Clark (1770–1838) led an expedition (1804–1806) to map a land route to the Pacific Ocean and thus open the whole continent to trade and American settlement.

[8]Martin Frobisher (1535?–1594), English seaman and explorer, who tried on three occasions to find the Northwest Passage.

[9]An expedition (1838–1842) organized by the U.S. Navy and led by Charles Wilkes (1798–1877) that explored the South Pacific and Antarctic Oceans.

[10]From Claudian (fl. 400 C.E.), "*De sene veronesi*" ["The Old Man of Verona"], an idyll imitating Vergil. Thoreau has modernized the text by substituting "Australians" for the original's "Iberians."

"Let them wander and scrutinize the outlandish Australians.
I have more of God, they more of the road."

It is not worth the while to go round the world to count the cats in Zanzibar.[11] Yet do this even till you can do better, and you may perhaps find some "Symmes' Hole"[12] by which to get at the inside at last. England and France, Spain and Portugal, Gold Coast and Slave Coast, all front on this private sea; but no bark from them has ventured out of sight of land, though it is without doubt the direct way to India. If you would learn to speak all tongues and conform to the customs of all nations, if you would travel farther than all travellers, be naturalized in all climes, and cause the Sphinx[13] to dash her head against a stone, even obey the precept of the old philosopher, and Explore thyself. Herein are demanded the eye and the nerve. Only the defeated and deserters go to the wars, cowards that run away and enlist. Start now on that farthest western way, which does not pause at the Mississippi or the Pacific, nor conduct toward a worn-out China or Japan, but leads on direct a tangent to this sphere, summer and winter, day and night, sun down, moon down, and at last earth down too.

It is said that Mirabeau[14] took to highway robbery "to ascertain what degree of resolution was necessary in order to place one's self in formal opposition to the most sacred laws of society." He declared that "a soldier who fights in the ranks does not require half so much courage as a footpad"—"that honor and religion have never stood in the way of a well-considered and a firm resolve." This was manly, as the world goes; and yet it was idle, if not desperate. A saner man would have found himself often enough "in formal opposition" to what are deemed "the most sacred laws of society," through obedience to yet more sacred laws, and so have tested his resolution without going out of his way. It is not for a man to put himself in such an attitude to society, but to maintain himself in whatever attitude he find himself through obedience to the laws of his being, which will never be one of opposition to a just government, if he should chance to meet with such.

---

[11] An island off the east coast of Africa.

[12] Captain John Cleves Symmes (1780–1829), a retired army officer, believed the earth to be hollow and habitable, and in the early years of the nineteenth century published his theory and attempted to raise funds for an expedition to the pole to prove his case.

[13] In Greek mythology, a winged creature with a woman's head and a lion's body who killed anyone unable to answer her riddle. Oedipus is said to have answered correctly, whereupon the Sphinx, enraged, killed herself.

[14] Honore Riqueti, Count de Mirabeau (1749–1791), French revolutionary leader.

I left the woods for as good a reason as I went there. Perhaps it seemed to me that I had several more lives to live, and could not spare any more time for that one. It is remarkable how easily and insensibly we fall into a particular route, and make a beaten track for ourselves. I had not lived there a week before my feet wore a path from my door to the pond-side; and though it is five or six years since I trod it, it is still quite distinct. It is true, I fear that others may have fallen into it, and so helped to keep it open. The surface of the earth is soft and impressible by the feet of men; and so with the paths which the mind travels. How worn and dusty, then, must be the highways of the world, how deep the ruts of tradition and conformity! I did not wish to take a cabin passage, but rather to go before the mast and on the deck of the world, for there I could best see the moonlight amid the mountains. I do not wish to go below now.

I learned this, at least, by my experiment; that if one advances confidently in the direction of his dreams, and endeavors to live the life he has imagined, he will meet with a success unexpected in common hours. He will put some things behind, will pass an invisible boundary; new, universal, and more liberal laws will begin to establish themselves around and within him; or the old laws be expanded, and interpreted in his favor in a more liberal sense, and he will live with the license of a higher order of beings. In proportion as he simplifies his life, the laws of the universe will appear less complex, and solitude will not be solitude, nor poverty poverty, nor weakness weakness. If you have built castles in the air, your work need not be lost; that is where they should be. Now put the foundations under them.

It is a ridiculous demand which England and America make, that you shall speak so that they can understand you. Neither men nor toad-stools grow so. As if that were important, and there were not enough to understand you without them. As if Nature could support but one order of understandings, could not sustain birds as well as quadrupeds, flying as well as creeping things, and *hush* and *who,* which Bright[15] can understand, were the best English. As if there were safety in stupidity alone. I fear chiefly lest my expression may not be *extra-vagant* enough, may not wander far enough beyond the narrow limits of my daily experience, so as to be adequate to the truth of which I have been convinced. *Extra vagance!* it depends on how you are yarded. The migrating buffalo, which seeks new pastures in another latitude, is not extravagant like the cow which kicks over the pail, leaps the cow-yard fence, and runs after her calf, in milking time. I desire to speak somewhere *without* bounds; like a man in a waking

[15] A proverbial name for an ox.

moment, to men in their waking moments; for I am convinced that I cannot exaggerate enough even to lay the foundation of a true expression. Who that has heard a strain of music feared then lest he should speak extravagantly any more forever? In view of the future or possible, we should live quite laxly and undefined in front, our outlines dim and misty on that side; as our shadows reveal an insensible perspiration toward the sun. The volatile truth of our words should continually betray the inadequacy of the residual statement. Their truth is instantly *translated;* its literal monument alone remains. The words which express our faith and piety are not definite; yet they are significant and fragrant like frankincense to superior natures.

Why level downward to our dullest perception always, and praise that as common sense? The commonest sense is the sense of men asleep, which they express by snoring. Sometimes we are inclined to class those who are once-and-a-half witted with the half-witted, because we appreciate only a third part of their wit. Some would find fault with the morning-red, if they ever got up early enough. "They pretend," as I hear, "that the verses of Kabir have four different senses; illusion, spirit, intellect, and the exoteric doctrine of the Vedas;"[16] but in this part of the world it is considered a ground for complaint if a man's writings admit of more than one interpretation. While England endeavors to cure the potato-rot, will not any endeavor to cure the brain-rot, which prevails so much more widely and fatally?

I do not suppose that I have attained to obscurity, but I should be proud if no more fatal fault were found with my pages on this score than was found with the Walden ice. Southern customers objected to its blue color, which is the evidence of its purity, as if it were muddy, and preferred the Cambridge ice, which is white, but tastes of weeds. The purity men love is like the mists which envelop the earth, and not like the azure ether beyond.

Some are dinning in our ears that we Americans, and moderns generally, are intellectual dwarfs compared with the ancients, or even the Elizabethan men. But what is that to the purpose? A living dog is better than a dead lion.[17] Shall a man go and hang himself because he belongs to the race of pygmies, and not be the biggest pygmy that he can? Let every one mind his own business, and endeavor to be what he was made.

---

[16]From Garcin de Tassy (Joseph-Héliodore-Sagesse-Vertu, 1794–1878), *Histoire de la littérature Hindoui et Hindoustani* (1839); Kabir, a fifteenth-century Indian mystic, tried to harmonize Hindu and Muslim belief systems. The Sikh religion was based in part on his writings.

[17]Eccles. 9.4.

Why should we be in such desperate haste to succeed, and in such desperate enterprises? If a man does not keep pace with his companions, perhaps it is because he hears a different drummer. Let him step to the music which he hears, however measured or far away. It is not important that he should mature as soon as an apple-tree or an oak. Shall he turn his spring into summer? If the condition of things which we were made for is not yet, what were any reality which we can substitute? We will not be shipwrecked on a vain reality. Shall we with pains erect a heaven of blue glass over ourselves, though when it is done we shall be sure to gaze still at the true ethereal heaven far above, as if the former were not?

There was an artist in the city of Kouroo[18] who was disposed to strive after perfection. One day it came into his mind to make a staff. Having considered that in an imperfect work time is an ingredient, but into a perfect work time does not enter, he said to himself, It shall be perfect in all respects, though I should do nothing else in my life. He proceeded instantly to the forest for wood, being resolved that it should not be made of unsuitable material; and as he searched for and rejected stick after stick, his friends gradually deserted him, for they grew old in their works and died, but he grew not older by a moment. His singleness of purpose and resolution, and his elevated piety, endowed him, without his knowledge, with perennial youth. As he made no compromise with Time, Time kept out of his way, and only sighed at a distance because he could not overcome him. Before he had found a stock in all respects suitable the city of Kouroo was a hoary ruin, and he sat on one of its mounds to peel the stick. Before he had given it the proper shape the dynasty of the Candahars[19] was at an end, and with the point of the stick he wrote the name of the last of that race in the sand, and then resumed his work. By the time he had smoothed and polished the staff Kalpa[20] was no longer the pole-star; and ere he had put on the ferule and the head adorned with precious stones, Brahma[21] had awoke and slumbered many times. But why do I stay to mention these things? When the finishing stroke was put to his work, it suddenly expanded before the eyes of the astonished artist into the fairest of all the creations of Brahma. He had made a new system in making a staff, a world with full and fair proportions; in which, though the old cities

[18]The parable is of Thoreau's invention; he uses a number of Hindu names to suggest a certain authenticity. Kouroo was actually a nation rather than a city; in the *Mahabharata,* Kouroo fights the Pandoos.

[19]A made-up dynasty.

[20]A *kalpa* is the period between the creation and the destruction of a world, 4,320,000,000 years, equivalent to one day of Brahma.

[21]Brahma is the supreme Hindu god.

and dynasties had passed away, fairer and more glorious ones had taken their places. And now he saw by the heap of shavings still fresh at his feet, that, for him and his work, the former lapse of time had been an illusion, and that no more time had elapsed than is required for a single scintillation from the brain of Brahma to fall on and inflame the tinder of a mortal brain. The material was pure, and his art was pure; how could the result be other than wonderful?

No face which we can give to a matter will stead us so well at last as the truth. This alone wears well. For the most part, we are not where we are, but in a false position. Through an infirmity of our natures, we suppose a case, and put ourselves into it, and hence are in two cases at the same time, and it is doubly difficult to get out. In sane moments we regard only the facts, the case that is. Say what you have to say, not what you ought. Any truth is better than make-believe. Tom Hyde, the tinker, standing on the gallows, was asked if he had any thing to say. "Tell the tailors," said he, "to remember to make a knot in their thread before they take the first stitch." His companion's prayer is forgotten.

However mean your life is, meet it and live it; do not shun it and call it hard names. It is not so bad as you are. It looks poorest when you are richest. The fault-finder will find faults even in paradise. Love your life, poor as it is. You may perhaps have some pleasant, thrilling, glorious hours, even in a poorhouse. The setting sun is reflected from the windows of the alms-house as brightly as from the rich man's abode; the snow melts before its door as early in the spring. I do not see but a quiet mind may live as contentedly there, and have as cheering thoughts, as in a palace. The town's poor seem to me often to live the most independent lives of any. May be they are simply great enough to receive without misgiving. Most think that they are above being supported by the town; but it oftener happens that they are not above supporting themselves by dishonest means, which should be more disreputable. Cultivate poverty like a garden herb, like sage. Do not trouble yourself much to get new things, whether clothes or friends. Turn the old; return to them. Things do not change; we change. Sell your clothes and keep your thoughts. God will see that you do not want society. If I were confined to a corner of a garret all my days, like a spider, the world would be just as large to me while I had my thoughts about me. The philosopher said: "From an army of three divisions one can take away its general, and put it in disorder; from the man the most abject and vulgar one cannot take away his thought."[22] Do not seek so anxiously to be developed, to subject yourself to many influences to be played on; it

[22] Confucius, *Analects* 9.25.

is all dissipation. Humility like darkness reveals the heavenly lights. The shadows of poverty and meanness gather around us, "and lo! creation widens to our view."[23] We are often reminded that if there were bestowed on us the wealth of Croesus,[24] our aims must still be the same, and our means essentially the same. Moreover, if you are restricted in your range by poverty, if you cannot buy books and newspapers, for instance, you are but confined to the most significant and vital experiences; you are compelled to deal with the material which yields the most sugar and the most starch. It is life near the bone where it is sweetest. You are defended from being a trifler. No man loses ever on a lower level by magnanimity on a higher. Superfluous wealth can buy superfluities only. Money is not required to buy one necessary of the soul.

I live in the angle of a leaden wall, into whose composition was poured a little alloy of bell metal. Often, in the repose of my mid-day, there reaches my ears a confused *tintinnabulum*[25] from without. It is the noise of my contemporaries. My neighbors tell me of their adventures with famous gentlemen and ladies, what notabilities they met at the dinner-table; but I am no more interested in such things than in the contents of the Daily Times. The interest and the conversation are about costume and manners chiefly; but a goose is a goose still, dress it as you will. They tell me of California and Texas, of England and the Indies, of the Hon. Mr. ——— of Georgia or of Massachusetts, all transient and fleeting phenomena, till I am ready to leap from their court-yard like the Mameluke bey.[26] I delight to come to my bearings—not walk in procession with pomp and parade, in a conspicuous place, but to walk even with the Builder of the universe, if I may—not to live in this restless, nervous, bustling, trivial Nineteenth Century, but stand or sit thoughtfully while it goes by. What are men celebrating? They are all on a committee of arrangements, and hourly expect a speech from somebody. God is only the president of the day, and Webster is his orator.[27] I love to weigh, to settle, to gravitate toward that which most strongly and rightfully attracts me—not hang by the beam of the

---

[23] Joseph Blanco White (1775–1841), English poet and mystic. In the poem the line reads, "lo! creation widened in man's view."

[24] King of Lydia, fabled for his wealth.

[25] The ringing of bells (*tintinnabulum*). Cf. *tintinnabulation* in Poe's 1849 poem, "The Bells."

[26] The Mamelukes, a military group, were invited by Mehemet Ali, viceroy of Egypt, to a banquet in 1811. All 460 were slaughtered except, so the story goes, one bey (or officer), who escaped by leaping to his horse from a wall.

[27] Daniel Webster (1782–1852), senator from Massachusetts, a noted orator and a favorite target for Thoreau's scorn.

scale and try to weigh less—not suppose a case, but take the case that is; to travel the only path I can, and that on which no power can resist me. It affords me no satisfaction to commence to spring an arch before I have got a solid foundation. Let us not play at kittlybenders.[28] There is a solid bottom every where. We read that the traveller asked the boy if the swamp before him had a hard bottom. The boy replied that it had. But presently the traveller's horse sank in up to the girths, and he observed to the boy, "I thought you said that this bog had a hard bottom." "So it has," answered the latter, "but you have not got half way to it yet." So it is with the bogs and quicksands of society; but he is an old boy that knows it. Only what is thought, said, or done at a certain rare coincidence is good. I would not be one of those who will foolishly drive a nail into mere lath and plastering; such a deed would keep me awake nights. Give me a hammer, and let me feel for the furrowing. Do not depend on the putty. Drive a nail home and clinch it so faithfully that you can wake up in the night and think of your work with satisfaction—a work at which you would not be ashamed to invoke the Muse.[29] So will help you God, and so only. Every nail driven should be as another rivet in the machine of the universe, you carrying on the work.

Rather than love, than money, than fame, give me truth. I sat at a table where were rich food and wine in abundance, and obsequious attendance, but sincerity and truth were not; and I went away hungry from the inhospitable board. The hospitality was as cold as the ices. I thought that there was no need of ice to freeze them. They talked to me of the age of the wine and the fame of the vintage; but I thought of an older, a newer, and purer wine, of a more glorious vintage, which they had not got, and could not buy. The style, the house and grounds and "entertainment" pass for nothing with me. I called on the king, but he made me wait in his hall, and conducted like a man incapacitated for hospitality. There was a man in my neighborhood who lived in a hollow tree. His manners were truly regal. I should have done better had I called on him.

How long shall we sit in our porticoes practising idle and musty virtues, which any work would make impertinent? As if one were to begin the day with long-suffering, and hire a man to hoe his potatoes; and in the afternoon go forth to practise Christian meekness and charity with goodness aforethought! Consider the China pride[30] and stagnant self-complacency

[28] Running or skating on thin ice without breaking through it.
[29] In Greek mythology, nine daughters of Mnemosyne who performed as goddesses of the various arts. Epic poems traditionally began by invoking the Muse Calliope.
[30] China was considered to be a proud and self-satisfied nation.

of mankind. This generation reclines a little to congratulate itself on being the last of an illustrious line; and in Boston and London and Paris and Rome, thinking of its long descent, it speaks of its progress in art and science and literature with satisfaction. There are the Records of the Philosophical Societies, and the public Eulogies of *Great Men!* It is the good Adam contemplating his own virtue. "Yes, we have done great deeds, and sung divine songs, which shall never die"—that is, as long as *we* can remember them. The learned societies and great men of Assyria[31]—where are they? What youthful philosophers and experimentalists we are! There is not one of my readers who has yet lived a whole human life. These may be but the spring months in the life of the race. If we have had the seven-years' itch, we have not seen the seventeen-year locust yet in Concord. We are acquainted with a mere pellicle of the globe on which we live. Most have not delved six feet beneath the surface, nor leaped as many above it. We know not where we are. Beside, we are sound asleep nearly half our time. Yet we esteem ourselves wise, and have an established order on the surface. Truly, we are deep thinkers, we are ambitious spirits! As I stand over the insect crawling amid the pine needles on the forest floor, and endeavoring to conceal itself from my sight, and ask myself why it will cherish those humble thoughts, and hide its head from me who might, perhaps, be its benefactor, and impart to its race some cheering information, I am reminded of the greater Benefactor and Intelligence that stands over me the human insect.

There is an incessant influx of novelty into the world, and yet we tolerate incredible dulness. I need only suggest what kind of sermons are still listened to in the most enlightened countries. There are such words as joy and sorrow, but they are only the burden of a psalm, sung with a nasal twang, while we believe in the ordinary and mean. We think that we can change our clothes only. It is said that the British Empire is very large and respectable, and that the United States are a first-rate power. We do not believe that a tide rises and falls behind every man which can float the British Empire like a chip, if he should ever harbor it in his mind. Who knows what sort of seventeen-year locust will next come out of the ground? The government of the world I live in was not framed, like that of Britain, in after-dinner conversations over the wine.

The life in us is like the water in the river. It may rise this year higher than man has ever known it, and flood the parched uplands; even this may be the eventful year, which will drown out all our muskrats. It was not always dry land where we dwell. I see far inland the banks which the stream

[31] An ancient empire of western Asia.

anciently washed, before science began to record its freshets. Every one has heard the story which has gone the rounds of New England, of a strong and beautiful bug which came out of the dry leaf of an old table of apple-tree wood, which had stood in a farmer's kitchen for sixty years, first in Connecticut, and afterward in Massachusetts—from an egg deposited in the living tree many years earlier still, as appeared by counting the annual layers beyond it; which was heard gnawing out for several weeks, hatched perchance by the heat of an urn. Who does not feel his faith in a resurrection and immortality strengthened by hearing of this? Who knows what beautiful and winged life, whose egg has been buried for ages under many concentric layers of woodenness in the dead dry life of society, deposited at first in the alburnum of the green and living tree, which has been gradually converted into the semblance of its well-seasoned tomb—heard perchance gnawing out now for years by the astonished family of man, as they sat round the festive board—may unexpectedly come forth from amidst society's most trivial and handselled furniture, to enjoy its perfect summer life at last!

I do not say that John or Jonathan[32] will realize all this; but such is the character of that morrow which mere lapse of time can never make to dawn. The light which puts out our eyes is darkness to us. Only that day dawns to which we are awake. There is more day to dawn. The sun is but a morning star.

---

[32] Proverbial names for British and American men, respectively.

PART THREE

Contexts and Comments

From APPEAL TO THE CHRISTIAN WOMEN OF THE SOUTH

Angelina E. Grimké (1805–1879)

Angelina Grimké was born to a slave-holding family of Charleston, South Carolina. Converted to the Quaker faith by her older sister, Sarah, and inspired by antislavery pamphlets as well as by the courageous actions of antislavery women who had been mobbed in Boston, Angelina issued the "Appeal" in 1836 both as a testimony of conscience and as an effort to win converts to the abolitionist cause among Southerners. She and her sister subsequently lectured on antislavery issues as well as on women's rights; their writings and particularly their appearances on public platforms were considered by many people to be outside the boundaries of "decency" for nineteenth-century women. Such opposition inspired them to write on women's rights as well as on behalf of slaves. Their public careers came to an end in 1838, however, when Angelina married the abolitionist leader Theodore Dwight Weld. Nevertheless, by then the Grimké sisters had in significant ways helped frame the antebellum debates over abolition, women's rights, and the questions of conscience and law to which Thoreau would later address "Civil Disobedience."

"Appeal to the Christian Women of the South" was first published in New York by the American Anti-Slavery Society in 1836. The text that follows is excerpted from that publication. The whole "Appeal" is most conveniently available in *The Public Years of Sarah and Angelina Grimké: Selected Writings, 1835–1839,* edited and annotated by Larry Ceplair (New York: Columbia UP, 1989), pp. 36–79. The annotations are Ceplair's. [Ed.]

Then Mordecai commanded to answer Esther. Think not within thyself that thou shalt escape in the king's house more than all the Jews. For if thou altogether holdest thy peace at this time, then shall there enlargement and deliverance arise to the Jews from another place: but thou and thy father's house shall be destroyed: and who knoweth whether thou art come to the kingdom for such a time as this. And Esther bade them return Mordecai this answer:—and so will I go unto the king, which is not according to law, and if I perish, I perish. *Esth.* 4.*13*–*16*.

Respected Friends,

It is because I feel a deep and tender interest in your present and eternal welfare that I am willing thus publicly to address you. Some of you have loved me as a relative, and some have felt bound to me in Christian sympathy, and Gospel friendship; and even when compelled by a strong sense of duty, to break those outward bonds of union which bound us together as members of the same community, and members of the same religious denomination, you were generous enough to give me credit, for sincerity as a Christian, though you believed I had been most strangely deceived. I thanked you then for your kindness, and I ask you *now,* for the sake of former confidence, and friendship, to read the following pages in the spirit of calm investigation and fervent prayer. It is because you have known me, that I write thus unto you.

But there are other Christian women scattered over the Southern States, a very large number of whom have never seen me, and never heard my name, and who feel *no* interest whatever in *me.* But I feel an interest in *you,* as branches of the same vine from whose root I daily draw the principle of spiritual vitality—Yes! Sisters in Christ I feel an interest in *you,* and often has the secret prayer arisen on your behalf, Lord "open thou their eyes that they may see wondrous things out of thy Law"—It is then, because I *do feel* and *do pray* for you, that I thus address you upon a subject about which of all others, perhaps you would rather not hear any thing; but, "would to God ye could bear with me a little in my folly, and indeed bear with me, for I am jealous over you with godly jealousy." Be not afraid then to read my appeal; it is *not* written in the heat of passion or prejudice, but in that solemn calmness which is the result of conviction and duty. It is true, I am going to tell you unwelcome truths, but I mean to speak those *truths in love,* and remember Solomon says, "faithful are the *wounds* of a friend." I do not believe the time has yet come when *Christian women* "will not endure sound doctrine," even on the subject of slavery, if it is spoken to them in tenderness and love, therefore I now address *you.*

To all of you then, known or unknown, relatives or strangers, (for you are all *one* in Christ,) I would speak. I have felt for you at this time, when unwelcome light is pouring in upon the world on the subject of slavery; light which even Christians would exclude, if they could, from our country, or at any rate from the southern portion of it, saying, as its rays strike the rock bound coasts of New England and scatter their warmth and radiance over her hills and valleys, and from thence travel onward over the Palisades of the Hudson, and down the soft flowing waters of the Delaware and gild the waves of the Potomac, "hitherto shalt thou come and no further"; I know that even professors of His name who has been emphatically called the "Light of the world" would, if they could, build a wall of adamant around the Southern States whose top might reach unto heaven, in order to shut out the light which is bounding from mountain to mountain and from the hills to the plains and valleys beneath, through the vast extent of our Northern States. But believe me, when I tell you, their attempts will be as utterly fruitless as were the efforts of the builders of Babel; and why? Because moral, like natural light, is so extremely subtle in its nature as to overleap all human barriers, and laugh at the puny efforts of man to control it. All the excuses and palliations of this system must inevitably be swept away, just as other "refuges of lies" have been, by the irresistible torrent of a rectified public opinion. "The *supporters* of the slave system," says Jonathan Dymond in his admirable work on the Principles of Morality,[1] "will *hereafter* be regarded with the *same* public feeling, as he who was an advocate for the slave trade *now is.*" It will be, and that very soon, clearly perceived and fully acknowledged by all the virtuous and the candid, that in *principle* it is as sinful to hold a human being in bondage who has been born in Carolina, as one who has been born in Africa. All that sophistry of argument which has been employed to prove, that although it is sinful to send to Africa to procure men and women as slaves, who have never been in slavery, that still, it is not sinful to keep those in bondage who have come down by inheritance, will be utterly overthrown. We must come back to the good old doctrine of our forefathers who declared to the world, "this self evident truth that *all* men are created equal, and that they have certain *inalienable* rights among which are life, *liberty,* and the pursuit of happiness." It is even a greater absurdity to suppose a man can be legally born a slave under *our free Republican* Government, than under the petty despotisms of barbarian Africa. If then, we have no right to enslave an African, surely we can have none to enslave an American; if it is a self evident truth that *all* men, every where and of every

[1]Jonathan Dymond (1796–1828), a British Quaker moralist, published *An Enquiry into the Accordancy of War with the Principles of Christianity* . . . in 1823 and founded a peace society in Exeter in 1825. *Essays on the Principles of Morality, and on the Private and Political Rights of Mankind* was published posthumously in England in 1829. The sisters edited a version of it with notes by Thomas S. Grimké (Philadelphia, Pa.: Ashmead, 1834). [Ceplair's note.]

color are born equal, and have an *inalienable right to liberty,* then it is equally true that *no* man can be born a slave, and no man can ever *rightfully* be reduced to *involuntary* bondage and held as a slave, however fair may be the claim of his master or mistress through will and title-deeds.

But after all, it may be said, our fathers were certainly mistaken, for the Bible sanctions Slavery, and that is the highest authority. Now the Bible is my ultimate appeal in all matters of faith and practice, and it is to *this test* I am anxious to bring the subject at issue between us. Let us then begin with Adam and examine the charter of privileges which was given to him. "Have dominion over the fish of the sea, and over the fowl of the air, and over every living thing that moveth upon the earth." In the eighth Psalm we have a still fuller description of this charter which through Adam was given to all mankind. "Thou madest him to have dominion over the works of thy hands; thou hast put all things under his feet. All sheep and oxen, yea, and the beasts of the field, the fowl of the air, the fish of the sea, and whatsoever passeth through the paths of the seas." And after the flood when this charter of human rights was renewed, we find *no additional* power vested in man. "And the fear of you and the dread of you shall be upon every beast of the earth, and every fowl of the air, and upon all that moveth upon the earth, and upon all the fishes of the sea, into your hand are they delivered." In this charter, although the different kinds of *irrational* beings are so particularly enumerated, and supreme dominion over *all of them* is granted, yet *man is never* vested with this dominion *over his fellow man;* he was never told that any of the human species were put *under his feet;* it was only *all things,* and man, who was created in the image of his Maker, *never* can properly be termed a *thing,* though the laws of Slave States do call him a "chattel personal"; *Man* then, I assert *never* was put *under the feet of man,* by that first charter of human rights which was given by God, to the Fathers of the Antediluvian and Postdiluvian worlds, therefore this doctrine of equality is based on the Bible. . . .

Where, then, I would ask, is the warrant, the justification, or the palliation of American Slavery from Hebrew servitude? How many of the southern slaves would now be in bondage according to the laws of Moses; Not one. You may observe that I have carefully avoided using the term *slavery* when speaking of Jewish servitude; and simply for this reason, that *no such thing* existed among that people; the word translated servant does *not* mean *slave,* it is the same that is applied to Abraham, to Moses, to Elisha and the prophets generally. *Slavery* then *never* existed under the Jewish Dispensation at all, and I cannot but regard it as an aspersion on the character of Him who is "glorious in Holiness" for any one to assert that "*God sanctioned, yea commanded slavery* under the old dispensation." I would fain lift my feeble voice to vindicate Jehovah's character from so foul a slander. If slaveholders are determined to hold slaves as long as they can, let them not dare to say that the God of mercy and of truth *ever* sanctioned such a system of cruelty and wrong. It is blasphemy against Him.

We have seen that the code of laws framed by Moses with regard to servants was designed to *protect them as men and women,* to secure to them their *rights as human beings,* to guard them from oppression and defend them from violence of every kind. . . .

Shall I ask you now my friends, to draw the *parallel* between Jewish *servitude* and American *slavery?* No! For there is *no likeness* in the two systems; I ask you rather to mark the contrast. The laws of Moses *protected servants* in their *rights* as *men and women,* guarded them from oppression and defended them from wrong. The Code Noir[2] of the South *robs the slave of all his rights* as a *man,* reduces him to a chattel personal, and defends the *master* in the exercise of the most unnatural and unwarrantable power over his slave. They each bear the impress of the hand which formed them. The attributers of justice and mercy are shadowed out in the Hebrew code; those of injustice and cruelty, in the Code Noir of America. Truly it was wise in the slaveholders of the South to declare their slaves to be "chattels personal"; for before they could be robbed of wages, wives, children, and friends, it was absolutely necessary to deny they were human beings. It is wise in them, to keep them in abject ignorance, for the strong man armed must be bound before we can spoil his house—the powerful intellect of man must be bound down with the iron chains of nescience before we can rob him of his rights as a man; we must reduce him to a *thing* before we can claim the right to set our feet upon his neck, because it was only *all things* which were originally *put under the feet of man* by the Almighty and Beneficent Father of all, who has declared himself to be *no respecter* of persons, whether red, white or black.

But some have even said that Jesus Christ did not condemn slavery. To this I reply that our Holy Redeemer lived and preached among the Jews only. The laws which Moses had enacted fifteen hundred years previous to his appearance among them, had never been annulled, and these laws protected every servant in Palestine. If then He did not condemn Jewish servitude this does not prove that he would not have condemned such a monstrous system as that of American *slavery,* if that had existed among them. But did not Jesus condemn slavery? Let us examine some of his precepts. "*Whatsoever* ye would that men should do to you, do *ye even so to*

---

[2] The slave code written for the French West Indies in 1685. It was one of the most oppressive of the codes and provided the basis for some of the codes used by southern states, notably Louisiana. [Ceplair's note.]

them[.]" Let every slaveholder apply these queries to his own heart; Am *I* willing to be a slave—Am *I* willing to see *my* wife the slave of another—Am *I* willing to see my mother a slave, or my father, my sister or my brother? If *not,* then in holding others as slaves, I am doing what I would *not* wish to be done to me or any relative I have; and thus have I broken this golden rule which was given *me* to walk by.

But some slaveholders have said, "we were never in bondage to any man," and therefore the yoke of bondage would be insufferable to us, but slaves are accustomed to it, their backs are fitted to the burden. Well, I am willing to admit that you who have lived in freedom would find slavery even more oppressive than the poor slave does, but then you may try this question in another form—Am I willing to reduce *my little child* to slavery? You know that *if it is brought up a slave* it will never know any contrast, between freedom and bondage, its back will become fitted to the burden just as the negro child's does—*not by nature*—but by daily, violent pressure, in the same way that the head of the Indian child becomes flattened by the boards in which it is bound. It has been justly remarked that "*God never made a slave,*" he made man upright; his back was *not* made to carry burdens, nor his neck to wear a yoke, and the *man* must be crushed within him, before *his* back can be *fitted* to the burden of perpetual slavery; and that his back is *not* fitted to it, is manifested by the insurrections that so often disturb the peace and security of slaveholding countries. Who ever heard of a rebellion of the beasts of the field; and why not? simply because *they* were all placed *under the feet of man,* into whose hand they were delivered; it was originally designed that they should serve him, therefore their necks have been formed for the yoke, and their backs for the burden; but *not so with man,* intellectual, immortal man! I appeal to you, my friends, as mothers; Are you willing to enslave *your* children? You start back with horror and indignation at such a question. But why, if slavery is *no wrong* to those upon whom it is imposed? why, if as has often been said, slaves are happier than their masters, free from the cares and perplexities of providing for themselves and their families: why not place *your children* in the way of being supported without your having the trouble to provide for them, or they for themselves? Do you not perceive that as soon as this golden rule of action is applied to *yourselves* that you involuntarily shrink from the test; as soon as *your* actions are weighed in *this* balance of the sanctuary that *you are found wanting?* Try yourselves by another of the Divine precepts, "Thou shalt love thy neighbor as thyself." Can we love a man *as* we love *ourselves*[;] if we do, and continue to do unto him, what we would not wish any one to do to us? Look too, at Christ's example, what does he say of himself, "I came *not* to be ministered unto, but to minister." Can you for a moment imagine the meek, and lowly, and compassionate Saviour, *a Slaveholder?* do you not shudder at this thought as much as at that of his being *a warrior?* But why, if slavery is not sinful? . . .

I have thus, I think, clearly proved to you seven propositions, viz.: First, that slavery is contrary to the declaration of our independence. Second, that it is contrary to the first charter of human rights given to Adam, and renewed to Noah. Third, that the fact of slavery having been the subject of prophecy, furnishes *no* excuse whatever to slavedealers. Fourth, that no such system existed under the patriarchal dispensation. Fifth, that *slavery never* existed under the Jewish dispensation; but so far otherwise, that every servant was placed under the *protection of law,* and care taken not only to prevent all *involuntary* servitude, but all *voluntary perpetual* bondage. Sixth, that slavery in America reduces a *man* to a *thing,* a "chattel personal," *robs him* of *all* his rights as a *human being,* fetters both his mind and body, and protects the *master* in the most unnatural and unreasonable power, whilst it *throws him out* of the protection of law. Seventh, that slavery is contrary to the example and precepts of our holy and merciful Redeemer, and of his apostles.

But perhaps you will be ready to query, why appeal to *women* on this subject? *We* do not make the laws which perpetuate slavery. *No* legislative power is vested in *us; we* can do nothing to overthrow the system, even if we wished to do so. To this I reply, I know you do not make the laws, but I also know that *you are the wives and mothers, the sisters and daughters of those who do;* and if you really suppose *you* can do nothing to overthrow slavery, you are greatly mistaken. You can do much in every way: four things I will name. 1st. You can read on this subject. 2d. You can pray over this subject. 3d. You can speak on this subject. 4th. You can *act* on this subject. I have not placed reading before praying because I regard it more important, but because, in order to pray aright, we must understand what we are praying for; it is only then we can "pray with the understanding and the spirit also."

1. Read then on the subject of slavery. Search the Scriptures daily, whether the things I have told you are true. Other books and papers might be a great help to you in this investigation, but they are not necessary, and it is hardly probable that your Committees of Vigilance[3] will allow you to have any other. The *Bible* then is the book I want you to read in the spirit of inquiry, and the spirit of prayer. Even the enemies of Abolitionists,

---

[3] Self-appointed groups of southern white males organized to confiscate what Southerners termed "incendiary," i.e. abolitionist, literature and generally suppress antislavery speech. [Ceplair's note.]

acknowledge that their doctrines are drawn from it. In the great mob in Boston last autumn,[4] when the books and papers of the Anti-Slavery Society were thrown out of the windows of their office, an individual laid hold of the Bible and was about tossing it out to the ground, when another reminded him that it was the Bible he had in his hand. *"O! 'tis all one,"* he replied, and out went the sacred volume along with the rest. We thank him for the acknowledgment. Yes, *"it is all one,"* for our books and papers are mostly commentaries on the Bible, and the Declaration. Read the *Bible* then, it contains the words of Jesus, and they are spirit and life. Judge for yourselves whether *he sanctioned* such a system of oppression and crime.

2. Pray over this subject. When you have entered into your closets, and shut to the doors, then pray to your father, who seeth in secret, that he would open your eyes to see whether slavery is *sinful,* and if it is, that he would enable you to bear a faithful, open and unshrinking testimony against it, and to do whatsoever your hands find to do, leaving the consequences entirely to him, who still says to us whenever we try to reason away duty from the fear of consequences, *"What is that to thee, follow thou me."* Pray also for that poor slave, that he may be kept patient and submissive under his hard lot, until God is pleased to open the door of freedom to him without violence or bloodshed. Pray too for the master that his heart may be softened, and he made willing to acknowledge, as Joseph's brethren did, "Verily we are guilty concerning our brother," before he will be compelled to add in consequence of Divine judgment, "therefore is all this evil come upon us." Pray also for all your brethren and sisters who are laboring in the righteous cause of Emancipation in the Northern States, England and the world. There is great encouragement for prayer in these words of our Lord. "Whatsoever ye shall ask the Father *in my name,* he *will give* it to you"—Pray then without ceasing, in the closet and the social circle.

---

[4] On October 21, 1835 a Boston Female Anti-Slavery Society meeting was surrounded by a mob, erroneously believing that the British abolitionist, George Thompson, was going to appear. The women reluctantly agreed to adjourn, but the mob, frustrated, tore up the office, seized Garrison, tore his clothes, and put a rope around his chest. He would have been hanged, reports May, if not for the efforts of "several gentlemen, assisted by some of the police and a vigorous hack driver," who then put him in the Leverett Street Jail for safekeeping. Samuel J. May, *Some Recollections of Our Antislavery Conflict* (Boston, Mass.: Fields, Osgood, 1869), p. 156. [Ceplair's note.]

George Thompson (1804–1878), a brilliant orator, was invited by Garrison to make a lecture tour of the United States. He arrived in September 1834, planning to stay three years, but he became the focal point of antiabolitionist mobs, being greeted by twenty in fourteen months. He departed hastily in November 1835. The speeches he gave, however, made a strong impression, especially on New England Methodists. [Ceplair's note.]

3. Speak on this subject. It is through the tongue, the pen, and the press, that truth is principally propagated. Speak then to your relatives, your friends, your acquaintances on the subject of slavery; be not afraid if you are conscientiously convinced it is *sinful,* to say so openly, but calmly, and to let your sentiments be known. If you are served by the slaves of others, try to ameliorate their condition as much as possible; never aggravate their faults, and thus add fuel to the fire of anger already kindled in a master and mistress's bosom; remember their extreme ignorance, and consider them as your Heavenly Father does the *less* culpable on this account, even when they do wrong things. Discountenance *all* cruelty to them, all starvation, all corporal chastisement; these may brutalize and *break* their spirits, but will never bond them to willing, cheerful obedience. If possible, see that they are comfortably and *seasonably* fed, whether in the house or the field; it is unreasonable and cruel to expect slaves to wait for their breakfast until eleven o'clock, when they rise at five or six. Do all you can, to induce their owners to clothe them well, and to allow them many little indulgences which would contribute to their comfort. Above all, try to persuade your husband, father, brothers and sons, that *slavery is a crime against God and man,* and that it is a great sin to keep *human beings* in such abject ignorance; to deny them the privilege of learning to read and write. The Catholics are universally condemned, for denying the Bible to the common people, but, *slaveholders must not* blame them, for *they* are doing the *very same thing,* and for the very same reason, neither of these systems can bear the light which bursts from the pages of that Holy Book. And lastly, endeavour to inculcate submission on the part of the slaves, but whilst doing this be faithful in pleading the cause of the oppressed.

Will *you* behold unheeding,
Life's holiest feelings crushed,
Where *woman's* heart is bleeding,
Shall *woman's* heart be hushed?

4. Act on this subject. Some of you *own* slaves yourselves. If you believe slavery is *Sinful,* set them at liberty, "undo the heavy burdens and let the oppressed go free." If they wish to remain with you, pay them wages, if not let them leave you. Should they remain teach them, and have them taught the common branches of an English education; they have minds and those minds, *ought to be improved.* So precious a talent as intellect, never was given to be wrapt in a napkin and buried in the earth. It is the *duty* of all, as far as they can, to improve their own mental faculties, because we are commanded to love God with *all our minds,* as well as with all our hearts, and we commit a great sin, if we *forbid or prevent* that

cultivation of the mind in others, which would enable them to perform this duty. Teach your servants then to read etc., and encourage them to believe it is their *duty* to learn, if it were only that they might read the Bible.

But some of you will say, we can neither free our slaves nor teach them to read, for the laws of our state forbid it. Be not surprised when I say such wicked laws *ought to be no barrier* in the way of your duty, and I appeal to the Bible to prove this position. What was the conduct of Shiphrah and Puah, when the king of Egypt issued his cruel mandate, with regard to the Hebrew children? "*They* feared *God,* and did *not* as the King of Egypt commanded them, but saved the men children alive." Did these *women* do right in disobeying that monarch? "*Therefore* (says the sacred text,) *God dealt well* with them, and made them houses." Exod. 1. What was the conduct of Shadrach, Meshach, and Abednego, when Nebuchadnezzar set up a golden image in the plain of Dura, and commanded all people, nations, and languages to fall down and worship it? "Be it known, unto thee, (said these faithful *Jews*) O king, that *we will not* serve thy gods, nor worship the image which thou hast set up." Did these men *do right in disobeying the law* of their sovereign: Let their miraculous deliverance from the burning fiery furnace, answer; Dan. 3. What was the conduct of Daniel, when Darius made a firm decree that no one should ask a petition of any man or God for thirty days? Did the prophet cease to pray? No! "When Daniel *knew that the writing was signed,* he went into his house, and his windows being *open* towards Jerusalem, he kneeled upon his knees three times a day, and prayed and gave thanks before his God, as he did aforetime." Did Daniel do right thus to *break* the law of his king? Let his wonderful deliverance out of the mouths of the lions answer; Dan. 7. Look, too, at the Apostles Peter and John. When the rulers of the Jews, "*commanded them not* to speak at all, nor teach in the name of Jesus," what did they say? "Whether it be right in the sight of God, to hearken unto you more than unto God, judge ye." And what did they do? "They spake the word of God with boldness, and with great power gave the Apostles witness of the *resurrection* of the Lord Jesus"; although *this* was the very doctrine, for the preaching of which, they had just been cast into prison, and further threatened. Did these men do right? I leave *you* to answer, who now enjoy the benefits of their labors and sufferings, in that Gospel they dared to preach when positively commanded *not to teach any more* in the name of Jesus; Acts 4.

But some of you may say, if we do free our slaves, they will be taken up and sold, therefore there will be no use in doing it. Peter and John might just as well have said, we will not preach the gospel, for if we do, we shall be taken up and put in prison, therefore there will be no use in our preaching. *Consequences,* my friends, belong no more to *you,* than they did to these apostles. Duty is ours and events are God's. If you think slavery is sinful, all *you* have to do is to set your slaves at liberty, do all you can to protect them, and in humble faith and fervent prayer, commend them to your common Father. He can take care of them; but if for wise purposes he sees fit to allow them to be sold, this will afford you an opportunity of testifying openly, wherever you go, against the crime of *manstealing*. Such an act will be *clear robbery,* and if exposed, might, under the Divine direction, do the cause of Emancipation more good, than any thing that could happen, for "He makes even the wrath of man to praise him, and the remainder of wrath he will restrain."

I know that this doctrine of obeying *God,* rather than man, will be considered as dangerous and heretical by many, but I am not afraid openly to avow it, because it is the doctrine of the Bible; but I would not be understood to advocate resistance to any law however oppressive, if, in obeying it, I was not obliged to commit *sin.* If for instance, there was a law, which imposed imprisonment or a fine upon me if I manumitted a slave, I would on no account resist that law, I would set the slave free, and then go to prison or pay the fine. If a law commands me to *sin I will break it;* if it calls me to *suffer,* I will let it take its course *unresistingly*. The doctrine of blind obedience and unqualified submission to *any human* power, whether civil or ecclesiastical, is the doctrine of despotism, and ought to have no place among Republicans and Christians.

But you will perhaps say, such a course of conduct would inevitably expose us to great suffering. Yes! my Christian friends, I believe it would, but this will *not* excuse you or any one else for the neglect of *duty*. If Prophets and Apostles, Martyrs, and Reformers had not been willing to suffer for the truth's sake, where would the world have been now? If they had said, we cannot speak the truth, we cannot do what we believe is right, because the *laws of our country or public opinion are against us,* where would our holy religion have been now? The Prophets were stoned, imprisoned, and killed by the Jews. And why? Because they exposed and openly rebuked public sins; they opposed public opinion; had they held their peace, they all might have lived in ease and died in favor with a wicked generation. Why were the Apostles persecuted from city to city, stoned, incarcerated, beaten, and crucified? Because they dared to *speak the truth;* to tell the Jews, boldly and fearlessly, that *they* were the *murderers* of the Lord of Glory, and that, however great a stumbling-block the Cross might be to them, there was no other name given under heaven by which men could be saved, but the name of Jesus. Because they declared, even at Athens, the seat of learning and refinement, the self-evident truth, that "they be no gods that are made with men's hands," and exposed to the Grecians the foolishness of worldly wisdom, and the impossibility of salvation but through Christ, whom they despised on account of the ignominious death he died. Because at Rome, the proud mistress of the world, they thundered out the terrors of the law upon that idolatrous, war-making, and slaveholding community. Why were the martyrs stretched upon the rack, gibbeted and burnt, the scorn and diversion of a Nero,[5] whilst their tarred and burning bodies sent up a light which illuminated the Roman capital? Why were the Waldenses[6] hunted like wild beasts upon the mountains of Piedmont, and slain with the sword of the Duke of Savoy and the proud monarch of France [Philip II]? Why were the Presbyterians chased like the partridge over the highlands of Scotland—the Methodists pumped, and stoned, and pelted with rotten eggs—the Quakers incarcerated in filthy prisons, beaten, whipped at the cart's tail, banished and hung? Because they dared to *speak* the *truth,* to *break* the unrighteous *laws* of their country, and chose rather to suffer affliction with the people of God, "not accepting deliverance," even under the gallows. Why were Luther and Calvin persecuted and excommunicated, Cranmer, Ridley, and Latimer burnt?[7] Because they fearlessly proclaimed the truth, though that truth was contrary to public opinion, and the authority of Ecclesiastical councils and conventions. Now all this vast amount of human suffering might have been saved. All these Prophets and Apostles, Martyrs, and Reformers, might have lived and died in peace with all men, but following the example of their great pattern, "they despised the shame, endured the cross, and are now set down on the right hand of the throne of God," having received the glorious welcome of "well *done* good and faithful servants, enter ye into the joy of your Lord."

But you may say we are *women,* how can *our* hearts endure persecution? And why not? Have not *women* stood up in all the dignity and strength of moral courage to be the leaders of the people, and to bear a faithful testimony for the truth whenever the providence of God has called them to do so? Are there no *women* in that noble army of martyrs who are

---

[5] Emperor of Rome, A.D. 54–68. [Ceplair's note.]

[6] Valdens preached a form of primitive Christianity, akin to that of the Apostles, in Lyons (1170–1176). His followers were excommunicated in 1184, and eighty were burned in 1211. [Ceplair's note.]

[7] Martin Luther (1483–1546) and John Calvin (1509–1564) broke with the Roman Catholic church and laid the basis for Protestant Christianity. Thomas Cranmer (1489–1556) was the first Protestant archbishop of Canterbury; Nicholas Ridley (c. 1503–1555) was bishop of Rochester and London; Hugh Latimer (1485–1555) had been bishop of Worcester. The latter three were burned as heretics by order of the Catholic queen of England, Mary I. [Ceplair's note.]

now singing the song of Moses and the Lamb? Who led out the women of Israel from the house of bondage, striking the timbrel, and singing the song of deliverance on the banks of that sea whose waters stood up like walls of crystal to open a passage for their escape? It was a *woman;* Miriam, the prophetess, the sister of Moses and Aaron. Who went up with Barak to Kadesh to fight against Jabin, King of Canaan, into whose hand Israel had been sold because of their iniquities? It was a *woman!* Deborah the wife of Lapidoth, the judge, as well as the prophetess of that backsliding people; Judg. 4.9. Into whose hands was Sisera, the captain of Jabin's host delivered? Into the hand of a *woman.* Jael the wife of Heber! Judg. 6.21. Who dared to *speak the truth* concerning those judgments which were coming upon Judea, when Josiah, alarmed at finding that his people "had not kept the word of the Lord to do after all that was written in the book of the Law," sent to enquire of the Lord concerning these things? It was a *woman.* Huldah the prophetess, the wife of Shallum; 2 Chron. 34.22. Who was chosen to deliver the whole Jewish nation from that murderous decree of Persia's King, which wicked Haman had obtained by calumny and fraud? It was a *woman;* Esther the Queen; yes, weak and trembling *woman* was the instrument appointed by God, to reverse the bloody mandate of the eastern monarch, and save the *whole visible church* from destruction. What human voice first proclaimed to Mary that she should be the mother of our Lord? It was a *woman!* Elizabeth, the wife of Zacharias; Luke 1.42, 43. Who united with the good old Simeon in giving thanks publicly in the temple, when the child, Jesus, was presented there by his parents, "and spake of him to all them that looked for redemption in Jerusalem"? It was a *woman!* Anna the prophetess. Who first proclaimed Christ as the true Messiah in the streets of Samaria, once the capital of the ten tribes? It was a *woman!* Who ministered to the Son of God whilst on earth a despised and persecuted Reformer, in the humble garb of a carpenter? They were *women!* Who followed the rejected King of Israel, as his fainting footsteps trod the road to Calvary? "A great company of people and of *women*": and it is remarkable that to *them alone,* he turned and addressed the pathetic language, "Daughters of Jerusalem, weep not for me, but weep for yourselves and your children." Ah! who sent unto the Roman Governor when he was set down on the judgment seat, saying unto him, "Have thou nothing to do with that just man, for I have suffered many things this day in a dream because of him"? It was a *woman!* the wife of Pilate. Although "*he knew* that for envy the Jews had delivered Christ," yet *he* consented to surrender the Son of God into the hands of a brutal soldiery, after having himself scourged his naked body. Had the *wife* of Pilate sat upon that judgment seat, what would have been the result of the trial of this "just person"?

And who last hung around the cross of Jesus on the mountain of Golgotha? Who first visited the sepulchre early in the morning on the first day of the week, carrying sweet spices to embalm his precious body, not knowing that it was incorruptible and could not be holden by the bands of death? These were *women!* To whom did he *first* appear after his resurrection? It was to a *woman!* Mary Magdalene; Mark 26.9. Who gathered with the apostles to wait at Jerusalem, in prayer and supplication, for "the promise of the Father"; the spiritual blessing of the Great High Priest of his Church, who had entered, *not* into the splendid temple of Solomon, there to offer the blood of bulls, and of goats, and the smoking censer upon the golden altar, but into Heaven itself, there to present his intercessions, after having "given himself for us, an offering and a sacrifice to God for a sweet smelling savor"? *Women* were among that holy company; Acts 1.14. And did *women* wait in vain? Did those who had ministered to his necessities, followed in his train, and wept at his crucifixion, wait in vain? No! No! Did the cloven tongues of fire descend upon the heads of *women* as well as men? Yes, my friends, "it sat upon *each of them*"; Acts 2.3. *Women* as well as men were to be living stones in the temple of grace, and therefore *their* heads were consecrated by the descent of the Holy Ghost as well as those of men. Were *women* recognized as fellow laborers in the gospel field? They were! Paul says in his epistle to the Philippians, "help those *women* who labored with men, in the gospel"; Phil. 4.3. . . .

And what, I would ask in conclusion, have *women* done for the great and glorious cause of Emancipation? Who wrote that pamphlet which moved the heart of Wilberforce[8] to pray over the wrongs, and his tongue to plead the cause of the oppressed African? It was a *woman,* Elizabeth Heyrick. Who labored assiduously to keep the sufferings of the slave continually before the British public? They were *women.* And how did they do it? By their needles, paint brushes and pens, by speaking the truth, and petitioning Parliament for the abolition of slavery. And what was the effect of their labors? Read it in the Emancipation bill[9] of Great Britain. Read it, in the present state of her West India Colonies. Read it, in the impulse which has been given to the cause of freedom in the United States of America. Have English women then done so much for the negro, and shall American women do nothing? Oh no! Already are there sixty female Anti-

[8] William Wilberforce (1759–1833), a British philanthropist and reformer who led the fight to end the slave trade and slavery in the British Empire. [Ceplair's note.]

[9] Parliament, on August 29, 1833, passed a bill, to take effect eleven months hence, freeing slave children under the age of six, and holding the other slaves in an apprenticeship system (six years for field hands, four years for others). Slaveowners were paid twenty million pounds in compensation. Antigua and Bermuda waived the apprenticeship sys-

Slavery Societies in operation. These are doing just what the English women did, telling the story of the colored man's wrongs, praying for his deliverance, and presenting his kneeling image constantly before the public eye on bags and needle-books, card-racks, pen-wipers, pin-cushions, etc. Even the children of the north are inscribing on their handy work, "May the points of our needles prick the slaveholder's conscience." Some of the reports of these Societies exhibit not only considerable talent, but a deep sense of religious duty, and a determination to persevere through evil as well as good report, until every scourge, and every shackle, is buried under the feet of the manumitted slave.

The Ladies' Anti-Slavery Society of Boston was called last fall, to a severe trial of their faith and constancy. They were mobbed by "the gentlemen of property and standing," in that city at their anniversary meeting, and their lives were jeoparded by an infuriated crowd; but their conduct on that occasion did credit to our sex, and affords a full assurance that they will *never* abandon the cause of the slave. The pamphlet, Right and Wrong in Boston,[10] issued by them in which a particular account is given of that "mob of broad cloth in broad day," does equal credit to the head and the heart of her who wrote it. I wish my Southern sisters could read it; they would then understand that the women of the North have engaged in this work from a sense of *religious duty,* and that nothing will ever induce them to take their hands from it until it is fully accomplished. They feel no hostility to you, not bitterness or wrath; they rather sympathize in your trials and difficulties; but they well know that the first thing to be done to help you, is to pour in the light of truth on your minds, to urge you to reflect on, and pray over the subject. This is all *they* can do for you, *you* must work out your own deliverance with fear and trembling, and with the direction and blessing of God, *you can do it.* Northern women may labor to produce a correct public opinion at the North, but if Southern women sit down in listless indifference and criminal idleness, public opinion cannot be rectified and purified at the South. It is manifest to every reflecting mind, that slavery must be abolished; the era in which we live, and the light which is overspreading the whole world on this subject, clearly show that the time cannot be distant when it will be done. Now there are only two ways in which it can be effected, by moral power or physical force, and it is for *you* to choose which of these you prefer. Slavery always has, and

---

tem, and the other colonies so abused it that the act was amended on April 11, 1838, ending the apprenticeship system as of August 1 of that year. [Ceplair's note.]

[10] [Maria Weston Chapman] "Right and Wrong in Boston," *Report of the Boston Female Anti Slavery Society; with a Concise Statement of Events, Previous and Subsequent to the Annual Meeting of 1835* (Boston, Mass.: By the Society, 1836). [Ceplair's note.]

always will produce insurrections wherever it exists, because it is a violation of the natural order of things, and no human power can much longer perpetuate it. The opposers of abolitionists fully believe this; one of them remarked to me not long since, there is no doubt there will be a most terrible overturning at the South in a few years, such cruelty and wrong, must be visited with Divine vengeance soon. Abolitionists believe, too, that this must inevitably be the case if you do not repent, and they are not willing to leave you to perish without entreating you, to save yourselves from destruction; well may they say with the apostle, "am I then your enemy because I tell you the truth," and warn you to flee from impending judgments.

But why, my dear friends, have I thus been endeavoring to lead you through the history of more than three thousand years, and to point you to that great cloud of witnesses who have gone before, "from works to rewards"? Have I been seeking to magnify the sufferings, and exalt the character of woman, that she "might have praise of men"? No! no! my object has been to arouse *you,* as the wives and mothers, the daughters and sisters, of the South, to a sense of your duty as *women,* and as Christian women, on that great subject, which has already shaken our country, from the St. Lawrence and the lakes, to the Gulf of Mexico, and from the Mississippi to the shores of the Atlantic; *and will continue mightily to shake it,* until the polluted temple of slavery fall and crumble into ruin. I would say unto each one of you, "what meanest thou, O sleeper! arise and call upon thy God, if so be that God will think upon us that we perish not." Perceive you not that dark cloud of vengeance which hangs over our boasting Republic? Saw you not the lightnings of Heaven's wrath, in the flame which leaped from the Indian's torch to the roof of yonder dwelling, and lighted with its horrid glare the darkness of midnight? Heard you not the thunders of Divine anger, as the distant roar of the cannon came rolling onward, from the Texian country, where Protestant American Rebels are fighting with Mexican Republicans[11]—for what? For the reestablishment of *slavery;* yes! of American slavery in the bosom of a Catholic Republic, where that system of robbery, violence, and wrong, had been legally abolished for twelve years. Yes! citizens of the United States, after plundering Mexico of her land, are now engaged in deadly conflict for the privilege of fastening chains, and collars, and manacles—upon whom? upon the sub-

[11]The Mexicans won their independence from Spain in 1821, established a republic in 1824, and abolished slavery in 1829. However, the settlers from the United States, who had been invited to settle in the Texas territory, continued to bring in slaves. By 1835, some 20,000 settlers and 4,000 slaves lived in Texas, and relations between the Mexican government and the immigrants had deteriorated. Hostilities between them commenced

jects of some foreign prince? No! upon native born American Republican citizens, although the fathers of these very men declared to the whole world, while struggling to free themselves from the three penny taxes of an English king, that they believed it to be a *self-evident* truth that *all men* were created equal, and had an *unalienable right to liberty.*

Well may the poet exclaim in bitter sarcasm,

The fustian flag that proudly waves
In solemn mockery o'er *a land of slaves.*

Can you not, my friends, understand the signs of the time; do you not see the sword of retributive justice hanging over the South, or are you still slumbering at your posts? Are there no Shiphrahs, no Puahs among you, who will dare in Christian firmness and Christian meekness, to refuse to obey the *wicked laws* which require *woman to enslave, to degrade and to brutalize woman?* Are there no Miriams, who would rejoice to lead out the captive daughters of the Southern States to liberty and light? Are there no Huldahs there who will dare to *speak the truth* concerning the sins of the people and those judgments, which it requires no prophet's eye to see must follow if repentance is not speedily sought? Is there no Esther among you who will plead for the poor devoted slave? Read the history of this Persian queen, it is full of instruction; she at first refused to plead for the Jews; but hear the words of Mordecai, "Think not within thyself, that *thou* shalt escape in the king's house more than all the Jews, for *if thou altogether holdest thy peace at this time,* then shall there enlargement and deliverance arise to the Jews from another place: but *thou and thy father's house shall be destroyed.*" Listen, too, to her magnanimous reply to this powerful appeal; "*I will* go in unto the king, which is *not* according to law, and if I perish, I perish." Yes! if there were but *one* Esther at the South, she *might* save her country from ruin; but let the Christian women there arise, as the Christian women of Great Britain did, in the majesty of moral power, and that salvation is certain. Let them embody themselves in societies, and send petitions up to their different legislatures, entreating their husbands, fathers, brothers, and sons, to abolish the institution of slavery; no longer to subject *woman* to the scourge and the chain, to mental darkness and moral degradation; no longer to tear husbands from their wives, and children

---

in October 1835. The settlers established the Republic of Texas on March 2, 1836, and adopted a constitution that formally recognized the institution of slavery. Independence was won at the battle of San Jacinto, April 21, 1836. Abolitionists fought a fierce, but ultimately losing, propaganda battle against Texas' annexation as a state (1845). [Ceplair's note.]

from their parents; no longer to make men, women, and children, work *without wages;* no longer to make their lives bitter in hard bondage; no longer to reduce *American citizens* to the abject condition of *slaves,* of "chattels personal"; no longer to barter the *image of God* in human shambles for corruptible things such as silver and gold.

The *women of the South can overthrow* this horrible system of oppression and cruelty, licentiousness and wrong. Such appeals to your legislatures would be irresistible, for there is something in the heart of man which *will bend under moral suasion.* There is a swift witness for truth in his bosom, which *will respond to truth* when it is uttered with calmness and dignity. If you could obtain but six signatures to such a petition in only one state, I would say, send up that petition, and be not in the least discouraged by the scoffs and jeers of the heartless, or the resolution of the house to lay it on the table. It will be a great thing if the subject can be introduced into your legislatures in any way, even by *women,* and *they* will be the most likely to introduce it there in the best possible manner, as a matter of *morals* and *religion,* not of expediency or politics. You may petition, too, the different ecclesiastical bodies of the slave states. Slavery must be attacked with the whole power of truth and the sword of the spirit. You must take it up on *Christian* ground, and fight against it with Christian weapons, whilst your feet are shod with the preparation of the gospel of peace. And *you are now* loudly called upon by the cries of the widow and the orphan, to arise and gird yourselves for this great moral conflict, with the whole armour of righteousness upon the right hand and on the left.

There is every encouragement for you to labor and pray, my friends, because the abolition of slavery as well as its existence, has been the theme of prophecy. "Ethiopia (says the Psalmist) shall stretch forth her hands unto God." And is he not doing so? Are not the Christian negroes of the south lifting their hands in prayer for deliverance, just as the Israelites did when their redemption was drawing nigh? Are they not sighing and crying by reason of the hard bondage? And think you, that He, of whom it was said, "and God heard their groaning, and their cry came up unto him by reason of the hard bondage," think you that his ear is heavy that he cannot *now* hear the cries of his suffering children? Or that He who raised up a Moses, an Aaron, and a Miriam, to bring them up out of the land of Egypt from the house of bondage, cannot now, with a high hand and a stretched out arm rid the poor negroes out of the hands of their masters? Surely you believe that his arm is *not* shortened that he cannot save. And would not such a work of mercy redound to his glory? But another string of the harp of prophecy vibrates to the song of deliverance: "But they shall sit every man under his vine, and under his fig-tree, and *none shall make them afraid;* for the mouth of the Lord of Hosts hath spoken it." The *slave* never can do this as long as he is a *slave;* whilst he is a "chattel personal" he can own *no* property; but the time *is to come* when *every* man is to sit under *his own* vine and *his own* fig-tree, and no domineering driver, or irresponsible master, or irascible mistress, shall make him afraid of the chain or the whip. Hear, too, the sweet tones of another string: "Many shall run to and fro, and *knowledge* shall be increased." Slavery is an insurmountable barrier to the increase of knowledge in every community where it exists; *slavery, then, must be abolished before* this prediction can be fulfilled. The last chord I shall touch, will be this, "They shall *not* hurt nor destroy in all my holy mountain."

Slavery, then, must be overthrown before the prophecies can be accomplished, but how are they to be fulfilled? Will the wheels of the millennial car be rolled onward by miraculous power? No! God designs to confer this holy privilege upon *man;* it is through *his* instrumentality that the great and glorious work of reforming the world is to be done. . . .

What can I say more, my friends, to induce *you* to set your hands, and heads, and hearts, to this great work of justice and mercy. Perhaps you have feared the consequences of immediate Emancipation, and been frightened by all those dreadful prophecies of rebellion, bloodshed and murder, which have been uttered. "Let no man deceive you"; they are the predictions of that same "lying spirit" which spoke through the four hundred prophets of old, to Ahab king of Israel, urging him on to destruction. *Slavery* may produce these horrible scenes if it is continued five years longer, but Emancipation *never will.* . . .

There is nothing to fear from immediate Emancipation, but *every thing* from the continuance of slavery.

Sisters in Christ, I have done. As a Southerner, I have felt it was my duty to address you. I have endeavored to set before you the exceeding sinfulness of slavery, and to point you to the example of those noble women who have been raised up in the church to effect great revolutions, and to suffer for the truth's sake. I have appealed to your sympathies as women, to your sense of duty as *Christian women.* I have attempted to vindicate the Abolitionists, to prove the entire safety of immediate Emancipation, and to plead the cause of the poor and oppressed. I have done—I have sowed the seeds of truth, but I well know, that even if an Apollos[12] were to follow in my steps to water them, "*God only* can give the increase." To Him then who is able to prosper the work of his servant's hand, I com-

[12] Apollos, an Alexandrian Jew who became a Christian missionary c. 50 A.D. [Ceplair's note.]

mend this Appeal in fervent prayer, that as he "hath *chosen the weak things of the world,* to confound the things which are mighty," so He may cause His blessing, to descend and carry conviction to the hearts of many Lydias[13] through these speaking pages. Farewell—Count me not your "enemy because I have told you the truth," but believe me in unfeigned affection,

Your sympathizing Friend,
Angelina E. Grimké

From SPEECH DELIVERED AT THE FIRST AFRICAN PRESBYTERIAN CHURCH
Philadelphia, Pennsylvania
16 August 1837

William Whipper (1804?–1876)

Whipper was one of the wealthiest black men in antebellum America, and a mainstay of the American Moral Reform Society, which he helped to found. Born in Lancaster, Pennsylvania, he came to Philadelphia at sixteen, later opening what he called a "free labor and temperance grocery store." He settled in Columbia, Pennsylvania, in 1835, from which he developed a series of successful businesses with another black entrepreneur, Stephen Smith, and from which he also operated one of the major stations of the underground railroad. He helped hundreds of fugitive slaves, aiding many of them to settle in western Canada.

Beginning in the 1830s, Whipper became a mainstay of the black national convention movement, frequently writing resolutions, addresses, and pamphlets. He edited the monthly journal of the American Moral Reform Society, though he came to feel that moral reform, however desirable in itself, would ultimately not

The Black Abolitionist Papers. Vol. 3. Chapel Hill: U of North Carolina P, 1991.

[13]Lydia, the first European convert of St. Paul and his hostess at Philippi. [Ceplair's note.]

lead to the elimination of slavery nor, indeed, racial prejudice. Nevertheless, even after passage of the Fugitive Slave Act (1850), he continued to urge nonviolence, though once the Civil War had begun he helped recruit black soldiers for the Union army. After the war, Whipper continued both his career as a successful businessman and his efforts on behalf of the freed slaves and other black people in the North. [ED.]

Resolved, That the practice of non-resistance to physical aggression, is not only consistent with reason, but the surest method of obtaining a speedy triumph of the principles of universal peace.

Mr. President:

The above resolution presupposes, that if there were no God, to guide, and govern, the destinies of man on this planet, no Bible to light his path through the wilds of sin, darkness and error, and no religion to give him a glorious, and lasting consolation, while traversing the gloomy vale of despondency, and to light up his soul anew, with fresh influence from the fountain of Divine grace—that mankind might enjoy an exalted state of civilization, peace, and quietude, in their social, civil, and international relations, far beyond that which christians now enjoy, who profess to be guided, guarded and protected by the great Author of all good, and the doctrines of the Prince of Peace.

But, sir, while I am assuming the position, that the cause of peace amongst mankind, may be promoted without the scriptures, I would not, for a single moment, sanction the often made assertion, that the doctrines of the holy scriptures justify war—for they are in my humble opinion its greatest enemy. And I further believe, that as soon as they become fully understood, and practically adopted, wars and strifes will cease. I believe that every argument urged in favor of what is termed a "just and necessary war," or physical self-defence, is at enmity with the letter and spirit of the scriptures, and when they emanate from its professed advocates should be repudiated as inimical to the principles they profess, and a reproach to christianity itself. I have said this much in favor of the influence of the scriptures, on the subject of peace. It is neither my intention, nor my province, under the present resolution, to give proofs for my belief by quotations from holy writ. That portion of the discussion, I shall leave to the minister of the *altar* and the learned and biblical theologian. Though I may make a few incidental quotations hereafter, I shall now pass on for a few brief moments to the resolution under consideration.

The resolution asserts, that the practice of non-resistance to physical aggression is consistent with reason. A very distinguished man asserts "that reason is that distinguishing characteristic that separates man from the brute creation," and that this power was bestowed upon him by his Maker, that he might be capable of subduing all subordinate intelligences to his will. It is this power when exerted in its full force, that enables him to conquer the animals of the forest, and which makes him lord of creation. There is a right and a wrong method of reasoning. The latter is governed by our animal impulses and wicked desires, without regard to the end to be attained. The former fixes its premises in great fundamental and unalterable truths—surveys the magnitude of the objects, and the difficulties to be surmounted, and calls to its aid the resources of enlightened wisdom, as a landmark by which to conduct its operations.

It is self evident, that when the greatest difficulties surround us, we should summon our noblest powers. "Man is a being formed for action as well as contemplation." "For this purpose there are interwoven in his constitution, powers, instincts, feelings and affections, which have a reference to his improvement in virtue, and which excite him to promote the happiness of others." When we behold them by their noble sentiments, exhibiting sublime virtues and performing illustrious actions, we ascribe the same to the goodness of their hearts, their great reasoning powers and intellectual abilities. For were it not for these high human endowments, we should never behold men in seasons of calamity, displaying tranquility and fortitude in the midst of difficulties and dangers, enduring poverty and distress with a noble heroism, suffering injuries and affronts with patience and serenity, stifling resentment when they have it in their power to inflict vengeance, displaying kindness and generosity towards enemies and slanderers, submitting to pain and disgrace in order to promote the prosperity of their friends and relatives, or the great interests of the human race.

Such acts may be considered by persons of influence and rank as the offspring of pusillanimity, because they themselves are either incapable of conceiving the purity of the motives from which they emanate, or are too deeply engulfed in the ruder passions of our nature, to allow them to bestow a just tribute to the efforts of enlightened reason. . . .

The great law of love forbids our doing aught against the interests of our fellow men. It is altogether inconsistent with reason and common sense for persons, when they deem themselves insulted by the vulgar aspersions of others, to maltreat their bodies for the acts of their minds. Yet how frequently do we observe those that are blest by nature and education (and if they would but aspire to acts that bear a parallel to their dignified minds, they would shine as illustrious stars in the created throngs), that degrade themselves by practising this barbarous custom, suited only to tyrants—because in this they may be justly ranked with the untutored savages or the animals of the forest, that are impelled only by instinct.

Another fatal error arises from the belief that the only method of maintaining peace is always to be ready for war. The spirit of war can never be destroyed by all the butcheries and persecutions the human mind can invent. The history of all the "bloody tragedies," by which the earth has been drenched by human blood, cannot be justified in the conclusion, for it is the spirit of conquest that feeds it. . . .

[T]he war principle, which is the production of human passions, has never been, nor can ever be, conquered by its own elements. Hence, if we ever expect the word of prophecy to be fulfilled—"when the swords shall be turned into plough-shares, and the spears into pruning-hooks, and that the nations of the earth shall learn war no more,"[1] we must seek the destruction of the principle that animates, quickens, and feeds it, by the elevation of another more powerful, and omnipotent, and preservative; or mankind will continue, age after age, to march on in their mad career, until the mighty current of time will doubtless sweep thousands of millions more into endless perdition, beyond the reach of mercy and the hope of future bliss. Thus the very bones, sinews, muscles, and immortal mind, that God, in his infinite mercy has bestowed on man, that he might work out his own glory and extend the principles of "Righteousness, justice, peace on earth, and good will to their fellow men," are constantly employed in protracting the period when the glorious millennium shall illumine our world, "and righteousness cover the earth as the water of the great deep."

Now let us solemnly ask ourselves, is it reasonable, that for the real or supposed injuries that have been inflicted on mankind from the beginning to the present day, that the attempted redress of the same should have cost so much misery, pain, sweat, blood, tears, and treasure? Most certainly not; since the very means used has measurably entailed the evil a thousand fold on coming generations. If man's superiority over the brute creation consists only in his reasoning powers and rationality of mind, his various methods of practising violence towards his fellow-creatures has in many cases placed him on a level with, and sometimes below, many species of the quadruped race. We search in vain amongst the animal race to find a parallel for their cruelties to each other on their own species, that is faithfully recorded in the history of wars and bloodshed, that have devoured empires, desolated kingdoms, overthrown governments, and well nigh aimed at the total annihilation of the human race. There are many species of animals that are so amiable in their disposition to each other, that they might

[1] Cf. Isa. 2.4. [Ed.]

well be considered an eminent pattern for mankind in their present rude condition. The sheep, the ox, the horse, and many other animals exist in a state of comparative quietude, both among themselves, and the other races of animals when compared with man. And if it were possible for them to know the will of their Author, and enjoy that communion with the Creator of all worlds, all men and all animals, they might justly be entitled to a distinction above all other species of creation, that had made greater departures from the will of the divine government.

It is evidently necessary that man should at all times bear in mind his origin and his end. That it is not because he was born a ruler, and superior to all other orders of creation, that he continually reigns above them—it is because he has made a right use of the powers that God has given him of rising in the scale of existence. The rich bequest of Heaven to man was a natural body, a reasonable soul, and an immortal mind. With these he is rendered capable, through the wisdom of Providence, of ascending to the throne of angels, or descending to the abyss of devils. Hence there seems to be a relation between man and the animal creation that subsists, neither in their origin nor their end, but satisfactorily exhibits that man may exist in a state of purity, as far *superior* to theirs as future happiness is to this world, and as far *inferior* as we are distant from future misery.

There is scarcely a single fact more worthy of indelible record than the utter inefficiency of human punishments to cure human evils. The history of wars exhibits a hopeless, as well as a fatal, lesson to all such enterprises. All the associated powers of human governments have been placed in requisition to quell and subdue the spirit of passion, without improving the condition of the human family. Human bodies have been lacerated with whips and scourges—prisons and penitentiaries have been erected for the immolation of human victims—the gibbet and halter have performed their office—while the increase of crime has kept pace with the genius of punishment, and the whole march of mind seems to have been employed in evading penal enactments and inventing new methods of destroying the blessings of the social state, not recognised by human codes.

If mankind ever expect to enjoy a state of peace and quietude, they must at all times be ready to sacrifice on the altar of principle, the rude passions that animate them. This they can only perform by exerting their reasoning powers. If there be those that desire to overlook the offenses of others, and rise above those inflictions that are the offspring of passion, they must seek for protection in something *higher* than human power. They must place their faith in Him who is able to protect them from danger, or they will soon fall prey to the wicked artifices of their wicked enemies. . . .

I am aware that there are those who consider non-resistance wholly impracticable. But I trust that but few such can be found that have adopted the injunction of the Messiah for their guide and future hope, for he commands us to "love our enemies, bless them that curse you, pray for them that despitefully use you, and persecute you."[2] These words were peculiarly applicable at the period they were uttered, and had a direct reference to the wars and strifes that then convulsed the world, and they are equally applicable at this moment. If the christian church had at her beginning made herself the enemy of war, the evil would doubtless have been abolished throughout christendom. The christians of the present day do not seem to regard the principles of peace as binding, or they are unwilling to become subject to Divine government. Human governments then, as well as now, were too feeble to stay the ravages of passion and crime, and hence there was an evident necessity for the imperious command, "Whomsover shall smite thee on thy right cheek, turn unto him the other also."[3]

And now, Mr. President, I rest my argument on the ground, that whatever is *scriptural* is *right* and, that whatever is right, is reasonable, and from this invulnerable position I mean not to stray, for the sake of any expediency whatever. The doctrine evidently taught by the scriptural quotation, evidently instructs us that resistance to physical aggression is wholly unnecessary as well as unrighteous, and subjects the transgressor to the penalty due from a wilful departure from the moral and Divine law. Therefore every act of disobedience to the commands of Christian duty, in relation to our fellow men, may fairly be deemed unreasonable, as it is at enmity with our true interests and the welfare of human society. We are further instructed to turn away from the *evil one,* rather than waste our strength, influence, and passions in a conflict that must in the end prove very injurious to both.

But someone perhaps is ready to raise an objection against this method of brooking the insults of others, and believes it right to refer to the maxim "that self defence is the first law of nature." I will readily agree that it is the unbounded duty of every individual to defend himself against both the vulgar and false aspersions of a wicked world. But then I contend that his weapons should be his reasoning powers. That since a kind Providence has bestowed on him the power of speech, and the ability to reason, he degrades his Creator by engulfing himself in the turmoils of passion and physical conflict, a mode of warfare practised by barbarous tribes in their native forests, and suited only to those animals that are alone endowed with the powers of instinct. Nor is it possible to suppose that men can pursue such a course, without first parting with their reason. We often see men, while under the

---

[2] Luke 6.27–28. [ED.]

[3] Matt. 5.39—the line of the Bible most cited by advocates of nonresistance. [ED.]

reigning influence of passion, as fit subjects for the lunatic asylum, as any that are confined in the lunatic asylum on account of insanity. In every possible and impartial view we take of the subject, we find that physical conflict militates against the interest of the parties in collision. If I, in conflict with mine enemy, overcome him with my superior physical powers, or my skill in battle, I neither wholly subdue him, or convince him of the justice of my cause. His spirit becomes still more enraged, and he will seek retaliation and conquest on some future occasion that may seem to him more propitious. If I intimidate him I have made him a slave, while I reign a despot; and our relation will continue unnatural, as well as dangerous to each other, until our friendship has become fully restored. And what has been gained by this barbarous method of warfare, when both parties become losers thereby? Yet this single case illustrates the value of all personal conflicts. . . .

[I]f there be a single class of people in these United States on which these duties are more imperative and binding than another, that class is the colored population of this country, both free and enslaved. Situated as we are, among a people that recognize the lawfulness of slavery, and more of whom sympathize with the oppressor than the oppressed, it requires us to pursue our course calmly onward, with much self-denial, patience and perseverance.

We must be prepared at all times to meet the scoffs and scorns of the vulgar and indecent—the contemptible frowns of haughty tyrants and the blighting mildew of a popular and sinful prejudice. If amidst these difficulties we can but possess our souls in patience, we shall finally triumph over our enemies. But among the various duties that devolve on us, not the least is that which relates to ourselves. We must learn on all occasions to rebuke the spirit of violence, both in sentiment and practice. God has said, "vengeance is mine, and I will repay it."[4] The laws of the land guarantee the protection of our persons from personal violence, and whoever for any cause inflicts a single blow on a fellow being, violates the laws of God and of his country, and has no just claim to being regarded as a christian or a good citizen.

As a people we have suffered much from the pestilential influence of mob violence, that has spread its devastating influence over our country.[5] And it is to me no matter of astonishment that they continue to exist. They do but put in practice a common everyday theory that pervades every

[4] Rom. 12.19. [Ed.]

[5] Historians count about thirty-five major riots in the quarter century before the Civil War. Occurring in almost every major American city—Baltimore, Boston, New York,

neighborhood, and almost every family, viz: That it is right, under certain circumstances, to violate all law, both civil and national, and abuse, kick and cuff your fellow man, when they deem that he has offended or insulted the community in which he resides. . . .

The love of power is one of the greatest of human infirmities, and with it comes the usurping influence of despotism, the mother of slavery. Show me any country or people where despotism reigns triumphant, and I will exhibit to your view the spirit of slavery, whether the same be incorporated in their government or not. It is this principle of despotism (which is nothing but an exercise of the corrupt passions) that sends forth its poignant influence over professedly civilized nations, as well as the more barbarous tribes. It is alike in its effects on human interests, whether it emanates from the Czar of Russia, the mild influence of Great Britain, the hotspurs of the South, or the genial clime of Pennsylvania—from the white, the red or the black man—whether he be of European or African descent, or the native Indian that resides in the wilds of the West. The combined action of all these are at war with the principles of peace and the liberty of the world, and retard the period when righteousness shall cover the earth like the waters of the great deep. How different is the exercise of this love of power, when exercised by men or enforced by human governments, to the exercise of Him who holds all power over the heavens, earth and seas, and all that in them is. With God all is order, with man all confusion. The planets perform their annual rotations, the tides ebb and flow, the seas obey his command, the whole government of universal worlds is sustained by his wisdom and power, each unvaryingly performing the course marked out by their great Author, because they are impelled by his love. But with man, governments are impelled by the law of force: hence despotism becomes an ingredient in all human governments.

The power of reason is the noblest gift of heaven to man, because it assimilates man to his Maker, and were he to improve his mind by cultivating his reasoning powers, his acts of life would bear the impress of the Deity indelibly stamped upon them. Governments would be mild in their operation, and the principles of universal peace would govern every heart, and be implanted in every mind. Wars, fighting and strifes would cease; there would be a signal triumph of truth over error; the principles of peace, justice, righteousness and universal love would guide and direct mankind onward in that sublime path marked out by the Great Prince of Peace. . . .

Philadelphia—they were often directed against blacks, Catholics, abolitionists, or others marginalized by the native, and often nativist, population. [Ed.]

DECLARATION OF SENTIMENTS
Adopted by the Peace Convention, held in Boston, September 18, 19, and 20, 1838

William Lloyd Garrison (1805–1879)

In 1831, Garrison established himself in a small Boston office, where, with fellow abolitionist Isaac Knapp, he began printing and issuing the *Liberator,* the first nationally circulated paper in the white community to advocate the immediate abolition of slavery. Within a few years, the paper had helped effect a sea change in antislavery sentiment. Slavery, Garrison argued, was a crime against God and man, the most heinous of crimes. Gradualism and colonization of freed blacks merely perpetuated that crime. Only immediate and unconditional emancipation could halt the erosion of moral integrity that Garrison saw taking place in antebellum America. He was a vociferous and determined advocate of that position for the next thirty years, placing the cause of abolition before all else, including the U.S. Constitution and, if necessary, the Union itself. "No union with slaveholders" was not, with him, an empty slogan.

Garrison also held a set of related beliefs not uncommon among evangelical Christians. These included a commitment to nonresistance, temperance and pacifism as well as to feminism, and he became a leading figure in these and other struggles for reform. Such positions were rooted in millennial beliefs of the early nineteenth century that God's kingdom would be brought in by an active commitment to eradicating not just personal wrongdoing but sinfulness in general from the world. Garrison thus articulated a unified vision of change that placed self-culture in the service of religion, that saw political priorities emerging from deeply held religious values, and that committed its proponents to oppose evil only by nonviolence, persuasion, and prayer.

The text of the "Declaration of Sentiments" Garrison prepared for the Peace Convention held in Boston September 18, 19, and 20, 1838, is derived from *Selections from the Writings and Speeches of William Lloyd Garrison, with an Appendix* (Boston: Walcutt, 1852), pp. 72–77. Negro Universities Press reprinted that edition in 1968. [ED.]

Assembled in Convention, from various sections of the American Union, for the promotion of peace on earth and good will among men, we, the undersigned, regard it as due to ourselves, to the cause which we love, to the country in which we live, and to the world, to publish a Declaration, expressive of the principles we cherish, the purposes we aim to accomplish, and the measures we shall adopt to carry forward the work of peaceful and universal reformation.

We cannot acknowledge allegiance to any human government; neither can we oppose any such government, by a resort to physical force. We recognize but one King and Lawgiver, one Judge and Ruler of mankind. We are bound by the laws of a kingdom which is not of this world; the subjects of which are forbidden to fight; in which Mercy and Truth are met together, and Righteousness and Peace have kissed each other; which has no state lines, no national partitions, no geographical boundaries; in which there is no distinction of rank, or division of caste, or inequality of sex; the officers of which are Peace, its exactors Righteousness, its walls Salvation, and its gates Praise; and which is destined to break in pieces and consume all other kingdoms.

Our country is the world, our countrymen are all mankind. We love the land of our nativity, only as we love all other lands. The interests, rights, and liberties of American citizens are no more dear to us, than are those of the whole human race. Hence, we can allow no appeal to patriotism, to revenge any national insult or injury. The Prince of Peace, under whose stainless banner we rally, came not to destroy, but to save, even the worst of enemies. He has left us an example, that we should follow his steps. "God commendeth his love towards us, in that while we were yet sinners, Christ died for us."

We conceive, that if a nation has no right to defend itself against foreign enemies, or to punish its invaders, no individual possesses that right in his own case. The unit cannot be of greater importance than the aggregate. If one man may take life, to obtain or defend his rights, the same license must necessarily be granted to communities, states, and nations. If he may use a dagger or a pistol, they may employ cannon, bombshells, land and naval forces. The means of self-preservation must be in proportion to the magnitude of interests at stake, and the number of lives exposed to destruction. But if a rapacious and bloodthirsty soldiery, thronging these shores from abroad, with intent to commit rapine and destroy life, may not be resisted by the people or magistracy, then ought no resistance to be offered to domestic troublers of the public peace, or of private security. No obligation can rest upon Americans to regard foreigners as more sacred in their persons than themselves, or to give them a monopoly of wrong-doing with impunity.

The dogma, that all the governments of the world are approvingly ordained of God, and that the powers that be in the United States, in Russia, in Turkey, are in accordance with His will, is not less absurd than impious. It makes the impartial Author of human freedom and equality, unequal and tyrannical. It cannot be affirmed, that the powers that be, in any nation, are actuated by the spirit, or guided by the example of Christ, in the treatment of enemies: therefore, they cannot be agreeable to the will of God: and, therefore, their overthrow, by a spiritual regeneration of their subjects, is inevitable.

We register our testimony, not only against all wars, whether offensive or defensive, but all preparations for war; against every naval ship, every arsenal, every fortification; against the militia system and a standing army; against all military chieftains and soldiers; against all monuments commemorative of victory over a foreign foe, all trophies won in battle, all celebrations in honor of military or naval exploits; against all appropriations for the defence of a nation by force and arms on the part of any legislative body; against every edict of government, requiring of its subjects military service. Hence, we deem it unlawful to bear arms, or to hold a military office.

As every human government is upheld by physical strength, and its laws are enforced virtually at the point of the bayonet, we cannot hold any office which imposes upon its incumbent the obligation to do right, on pain of imprisonment or death. We therefore voluntarily exclude ourselves from every legislative and judicial body, and repudiate all human politics, worldly honors, and stations of authority. If *we* cannot occupy a seat in the legislature, or on the bench, neither can we elect *others* to act as our substitutes in any such capacity.

It follows, that we cannot sue any man at law, to compel him by force to restore any thing which he may have wrongfully taken from us or others; but, if he has seized our coat, we shall surrender up our cloak, rather than subject him to punishment.

We believe that the penal code of the old covenant, An eye for an eye, and a tooth for a tooth, has been abrogated by Jesus Christ; and that, under the new covenant, the forgiveness, instead of the punishment of enemies, has been enjoined upon all his disciples, in all cases whatsoever. To extort money from enemies, or set them upon a pillory, or cast them into prison, or hang them upon a gallows, is obviously not to forgive, but to take retribution. "Vengeance is mine—I will repay, saith the Lord."

The history of mankind is crowded with evidences, proving that physical coercion is not adapted to moral regeneration; that the sinful disposition of man can be subdued only by love; that evil can be exterminated from the earth only by goodness; that it is not safe to rely upon an arm of flesh, upon man, whose breath is in his nostrils, to preserve us from harm; that there is great security in being gentle, harmless, long-suffering, and abundant in mercy; that it is only the meek who shall inherit the earth, for the violent, who resort to the sword, shall perish with the sword. Hence, as a measure of sound policy, of safety to property, life, and liberty, of public quietude and private enjoyment, as well as on the ground of allegiance to Him who is King of kings, and Lord of lords, we cordially adopt the non-resistance principle; being confident that it provides for all possible consequences, will ensure all things needful to us, is armed with omnipotent power, and must ultimately triumph over every assailing force.

We advocate no jacobinical doctrines. The spirit of jacobinism is the spirit of retaliation, violence and murder. It neither fears God, nor regards man. We would be filled with the spirit of Christ. If we abide by our principles, it is impossible for us to be disorderly, or plot treason, or participate in any evil work: we shall submit to every ordinance of man, for the Lord's sake; obey all the requirements of government, except such as we deem contrary to the commands of the gospel; and in no wise resist the operation of law, except by meekly submitting to the penalty of disobedience.

But, while we shall adhere to the doctrines of non-resistance and passive submission to enemies, we purpose, in a moral and spiritual sense, to speak and act boldly in the cause of God; to assail iniquity in high places and in low places; to apply our principles to all existing civil, political, legal, and ecclesiastical institutions; and to hasten the time, when the kingdoms of this world shall become the kingdoms of our Lord and of his Christ, and he shall reign for ever.

It appears to us a self-evident truth, that, whatever the gospel is designed to destroy at any period of the world, being contrary to it, ought now to be abandoned. If, then, the time is predicted, when swords shall be beaten into plough-shares, and spears into pruning-hooks, and men shall not learn the art of war any more, it follows that all who manufacture, sell, or wield those deadly weapons, do thus array themselves against the peaceful dominion of the Son of God on earth.

Having thus briefly, but frankly, stated our principles and purposes, we proceed to specify the measures we propose to adopt, in carrying our object into effect.

We expect to prevail through the foolishness of preaching—striving to commend ourselves unto every man's conscience, in the sight of God. From the press, we shall promulgate our sentiments as widely as practicable. We shall endeavor to secure the co-operation of all persons, of whatever name or sect. The triumphant progress of the cause of Temperance and of Abolition in our land, through the instrumentality of benevolent and voluntary associations, encourages us to combine our own means and efforts for the promotion of a still greater cause. Hence we shall employ lecturers, circulate tracts and publications, form societies, and petition our state and national governments in relation to the subject of Universal Peace. It will be our leading object to devise ways and means for effecting a radical change in the views, feelings and practices of society respecting the sinfulness of war, and the treatment of enemies.

In entering upon the great work before us, we are not unmindful that, in its prosecution, we may be called to test our sincerity, even as in a fiery ordeal. It may subject us to insult, outrage, suffering, yea, even death itself. We anticipate no small amount of misconception, misrepresentation, calumny. Tumults may arise against us. The ungodly and violent, the proud and pharisaical, the ambitious and tyrannical, principalities and powers, and spiritual wickedness in high places, may combine to crush us. So they treated the Messiah, whose example we are humbly striving to imitate. If we suffer with him, we know that we shall reign with him. We shall not be afraid of their terror, neither be troubled. Our confidence is in the Lord Almighty, not in man. Having withdrawn from human protection, what can sustain us but that faith which overcomes the world? We shall not think it strange concerning the fiery trial which is to try us, as though some strange thing had happened unto us; but rejoice, inasmuch as we are partakers of Christ's sufferings. Wherefore, we commit the keeping of our souls to God, in well-doing, as unto a faithful Creator. "For every one that forsakes houses, or brethren, or sisters, or father, or mother, or wife, or children, or lands, for Christ's sake, shall receive an hundred fold, and shall inherit everlasting life."

Firmly relying upon the certain and universal triumph of the sentiments contained in this Declaration, however formidable may be the opposition arrayed against them, in solemn testimony of our faith in their divine origin, we hereby affix our signatures to it; commending it to the reason and conscience of mankind, giving ourselves no anxiety as to what may befall us, and resolving, in the strength of the Lord God, calmly and meekly to abide the issue.

From THE LABORING CLASSES

Orestes A. Brownson (1803–1876)

Brownson was a religious reformer as well as an editor of a series of magazines, including the *Boston Quarterly Review,* which he largely wrote, and *Brownson's Quarterly Review,* which was explicitly his own production. At different times he worked as a minister, founded his own church, supported the short-lived Workingmen's party, got involved with Transcendentalist projects like Brook Farm, and wrote two autobiographical novels, among many other works of opinion and controversy. He converted to Catholicism in 1844 and thereafter devoted much energy to attacking non-Catholic ideas as well as to efforts, not always well received, to reform the church itself.

The text that follows is excerpted from its original publication in the *Boston Quarterly Review,* July 1840: 358–95. [ED.]

Chartism, by Thomas Carlyle

Thomas Carlyle unquestionably ranks among the ablest writers of the day. His acquaintance with literature seems to be almost universal, and there is apparently no art or science with which he is not familiar. He possesses an unrivalled mastery over the resources of the English tongue, a remarkably keen insight into the mysteries of human nature, and a large share of genuine poetic feeling. His works are characterized by freshness and power, as well as by strangeness and singularity, and must be read with interest, even when they cannot be with approbation.

The little work, named at the head of this article, is a fair sample of his peculiar excellences, and also of his peculiar defects. As a work intended to excite attention and lead the mind to an investigation of a great subject, it possesses no ordinary value; but as a work intended to throw light on a difficult question, and to afford some positive directions to the statesman and the philanthropist, it is not worth much. Carlyle, like his imitators in this country, though he declaims against the destructives, possesses in no sense a constructive genius. He is good as a demolisher, but pitiable enough as a builder. No man sees more clearly that the present is defective and unworthy to be retained; he is a brave and successful warrior against it, whether reference be had to its literature, its politics, its philosophy, or its religion; but when the question comes up concerning what ought to be, what should take the place of what is, we regret to say, he affords us no essential aid, scarcely a useful hint. He has fine spiritual instincts, has outgrown materialism, loathes skepticism, sees clearly the absolute necessity of faith in both God and man, and insists upon it with due sincerity and earnestness; but with feelings very nearly akin to despair. He does not appear to have found as yet a faith for himself, and his writings have almost invariably a skeptical tendency. He has doubtless a sort of faith in God, or an overwhelming Necessity, but we cannot perceive that he has any faith in man or in man's efforts. Society is wrong, but he mocks at our sincerest and best directed efforts to right it. It cannot subsist as it is; that is clear: but what shall be done to make it what it ought to be, that he saith not. Of all writers we are acquainted with, he is the least satisfactory. He is dissatisfied with everything himself, and he leaves his readers dissatisfied with everything. Hopeless himself, he makes them also hopeless, especially if they have strong social tendencies, and are hungering and thirsting to work out the regeneration of their race. . . .

Mr. Carlyle, though he gives us few facts, yet shows us that the condition of the workingmen in England is deplorable, and every day growing worse. It has already become intolerable, and hence the outbreak of the Chartists. Chartism is the protest of the working classes against the injustice of the present social organization of the British community, and a loud demand for a new organization which shall respect the rights and well-being of the laborer. . . .

There is no country in Europe, in which the condition of the laboring classes seems to us so hopeless as in that of England. This is not owing to the fact, that the aristocracy is less enlightened, more powerful, or more oppressive in England than elsewhere. The English laborer does not find his worst enemy in the nobility, but in the middling class. The middle class is much more numerous and powerful in England than in any other European country, and is of a higher character. It has always been powerful; for by means of the Norman Conquest it received large accessions from the old Saxon nobility. The Conquest established a new aristocracy, and degraded the old to the condition of Commoners. The superiority of the English Commons is, we suppose, chiefly owing to this fact.

The middle class is always a firm champion of equality, when it concerns humbling a class above it; but it is its inveterate foe, when it concerns elevating a class below it. Manfully have the British Commoners struggled against the old feudal aristocracy, and so successfully that they now constitute the dominant power in the state. To their struggles against the throne and the nobility is the English nation indebted for the liberty it so loudly boasts, and which, during the last half of the last century, so enraptured the friends of Humanity throughout Europe.

But this class has done nothing for the laboring population, the real *proletarii.* It has humbled the aristocracy; it has raised itself to dominion, and it is now conservative—conservative in fact, whether it call itself Whig or Radical. From its near relation to the workingmen, its kindred pursuits with them, it is altogether more hostile to them than the nobility ever were or ever can be. This was seen in the conduct of England towards the French Revolution. So long as that Revolution was in the hands of the middle class, and threatened merely to humble monarchy and nobility, the English nation applauded it; but as soon as it descended to the mass of the people, and promised to elevate the laboring classes, so soon as the starving workingman began to flatter himself, that there was to be a Revolution for him too as well as for his employer, the English nation armed itself and poured out its blood and treasure to suppress it. Everybody knows that Great Britain, boasting of her freedom and of her love of freedom, was the life and soul of the opposition to the French Revolution; and on her head almost alone should fall the curses of Humanity for the sad failure of that glorious uprising of the people in behalf of their imprescriptible, and inalienable rights. Yet it was not the English monarchy, nor the English nobility, that was alone in fault. Monarchy and nobility would have been powerless, had they not had with them the great body of the English Commoners. England fought in the ranks, nay, at the head of the allies, not for monarchy, not for nobility, nor yet for religion; but for trade and manufactures, for her middle class, against the rights and well-being of the workingman; and her strength and efficiency consisted in the strength and efficiency of this class.

Now this middle class, which was strong enough to defeat nearly all the practical benefit of the French Revolution, is the natural enemy of the Chartists. It will unite with the monarchy and nobility against them; and spare neither blood nor treasure to defeat them. Our despair for the poor Chartists arises from the number and power of the middle class. We dread for them neither monarchy nor nobility. Nor should they. Their only real enemy is in the employer. In all countries is it the same. The only enemy of the laborer is your employer, whether appearing in the shape of the master mechanic, or in the owner of a factory. A Duke of Wellington is much more likely to vindicate the rights of labor than an Abbot Lawrence, although the latter may be a very kind-hearted man, and liberal citizen, as we always find *Blackwood's Magazine* more true to the interests of the poor, than we do the *Edinburgh Review,* or even the *London and Westminster.*

Mr. Carlyle, contrary to his wont, in the pamphlet we have named, commends two projects for the relief of the workingmen, which he finds others have suggested—universal education, and general emigration. Universal education we shall not be thought likely to depreciate; but we confess that we are unable to see in it that sovereign remedy for the evils of the social state as it is, which some of our friends do, or say they do. We have little faith in the power of education to elevate a people compelled to labor from twelve to sixteen hours a day, and to experience for no mean portion of the time a paucity of even the necessaries of life, let alone its comforts. Give your starving boy a breakfast before you send him to school, and your tattered beggar a cloak before you attempt his moral and intellectual elevation. A swarm of naked and starving urchins crowded into a schoolroom will make little proficiency in the "Humanities." Indeed, it seems to us most bitter mockery for the well-dressed and well-fed to send the schoolmaster and priest to the wretched hovels of squalid poverty—a mockery at which devils may laugh, but over which angels must weep. Educate the working classes of England; and what then? Will they require less food and less clothing when educated than they do now? Will they be more contented or more happy in their condition? For God's sake beware how you kindle within them the intellectual spark, and make them aware that they too are men, with powers of thought and feeling which ally them by the bonds of brotherhood to their betters. If you will doom them to the external condition of brutes, do in common charity keep their minds and hearts brutish. Render them as insensible as possible, that they may feel the less acutely their degradation, and see the less clearly the monstrous injustice which is done them.

General emigration can at best afford only a temporary relief, for the colony will soon become an empire, and reproduce all the injustice and wretchedness of the mother country. Nor is general emigration necessary. England, if she would be just, could support a larger population than she now numbers. The evil is not from over population, but from the unequal repartition of the fruits of industry. She suffers from over production, and from over production, because her workmen produce not for themselves but for their employers. What then is the remedy? As it concerns England, we shall leave the English statesman to answer. Be it what it may, it will not be obtained without war and bloodshed. It will be found only at the end of one of the longest and severest struggles the human race has ever been engaged in, only by that most dreaded of all wars, the war of the poor against the rich, a war which, however long it may be delayed, will come, and come with all its horrors. The day of vengeance is sure; for the world after all is under the dominion of a Just Providence.

No one can observe the signs of the times with much care, without perceiving that a crisis as to the relation of wealth and labor is approaching.

It is useless to shut our eyes to the fact, and like the ostrich fancy ourselves secure because we have so concealed our heads that we see not the danger. We or our children will have to meet this crisis. The old war between the King and the Barons is well nigh ended, and so is that between the Barons and the Merchants and Manufacturers—landed capital and commercial capital. The business man has become the peer of my Lord. And now commences the new struggle between the operative and his employer, between wealth and labor. Every day does this struggle extend further and wax stronger and fiercer; what or when the end will be God only knows.

In this coming contest there is a deeper question at issue than is commonly imagined; a question which is but remotely touched in your controversies about United States Banks and Sub Treasuries, chartered Banking and free Banking, free trade and corporations, although these controversies may be paving the way for it to come up. We have discovered no presentiment of it in any king's or queen's speech, nor in any president's message. It is embraced in no popular political creed of the day, whether christened Whig or Tory, *Juste-milieu* or Democratic.[1] No popular senator, or deputy, or peer seems to have any glimpse of it; but it is working in the hearts of the million, is struggling to shape itself, and one day it will be uttered, and in thunder tones. Well will it be for him, who, on that day, shall be found ready to answer it.

What we would ask is, throughout the Christian world, the actual condition of the laboring classes, viewed simply and exclusively in their capacity of laborers? They constitute at least a moiety of the human race. We exclude the nobility, we exclude also the middle class, and include only actual laborers, who are laborers and not proprietors, owners of none of the funds of production, neither houses, shops, nor lands, nor implements of

---

[1] The term *Whig* originally referred to the British political group that sought to limit the crown's authority and increase parliamentary power. In the United States, the term referred to the mid-nineteenth-century political grouping, primarily associated with commercial and manufacturing interests, formed to oppose Jacksonian Democrats. Tories were originally supporters of the British monarchy; in Britain the term became a general tag for conservatives. In America the term referred to supporters of the British during the Revolutionary War.

The French philosopher Voltaire is among the most prominent representatives of the ideas of the *juste-milieu,* developed in the nineteenth century into a French political tendency and a journal emphasizing rationality. In the nineteenth century, *Democratic* referred in the United States both to the political party of Jefferson and Jackson and to a political tendency emphasizing broad suffrage, civil rights, and a degree of government activism on behalf of the less fortunate. By mid-century the Democrats had also become committed to leaving the slave system undisturbed. [Ed.]

labor, being therefore solely dependent on their hands. We have no means of ascertaining their precise proportion to the whole number of the race; but we think we may estimate them at one half. In any contest they will be as two to one, because the large class of proprietors who are not employers, but laborers on their own lands or in their own shops will make common cause with them.

Now we will not so belie our acquaintance with political economy as to allege that these alone perform all that is necessary to the production of wealth. We are not ignorant of the fact that the merchant, who is literally the common carrier and exchange dealer, performs a useful service, and is therefore entitled to a portion of the proceeds of labor. But make all necessary deductions on his account, and then ask what portion of the remainder is retained, either in kind or in its equivalent, in the hands of the original producer, the workingman? All over the world this fact stares us in the face, the workingman is poor and depressed, while a large portion of the non-workingmen, in the sense we now use the term, are wealthy. It may be laid down as a general rule, with but few exceptions, that men are rewarded in an inverse ratio to the amount of actual service they perform. Under every government on earth the largest salaries are annexed to those offices, which demand of their incumbents the least amount of actual labor either mental or manual. And this is in perfect harmony with the whole system of repartition of the fruits of industry, which obtains in every department of society. Now here is the system which prevails, and here is its result. The whole class of simple laborers are poor, and in general unable to procure anything beyond the bare necessaries of life.

In regard to labor two systems obtain; one that of slave labor, the other that of free labor. Of the two, the first is, in our judgment, except so far as the feelings are concerned, decidedly the least oppressive. If the slave has never been a free man, we think, as a general rule, his sufferings are less than those of the free laborer at wages. As to actual freedom one has just about as much as the other. The laborer at wages has all the disadvantages of freedom and none of its blessings, while the slave, if denied the blessings, is freed from the disadvantages. We are no advocates of slavery, we are as heartily opposed to it as any modern abolitionist can be; but we say frankly that, if there must always be a laboring population distinct from proprietors and employers, we regard the slave system as decidedly preferable to the system at wages. It is no pleasant thing to go days without food, to lie idle for weeks, seeking work and finding none, to rise in the morning with a wife and children you love, and know not where to procure them a breakfast, and to see constantly before you no brighter prospect than the almshouse. Yet these are no unfrequent incidents in the lives of our laboring population. Even in seasons of general prosperity, when there was only the ordinary cry of "hard times," we have seen hundreds of people in a not very populous village, in a wealthy portion of our common country, suffering for the want of the necessaries of life, willing to work, and yet finding no work to do. Many and many is the application of a poor man for work, merely for his food, we have seen rejected. These things are little thought of, for the applicants are poor; they fill no conspicuous place in society, and they have no biographers. But their wrongs are chronicled in heaven. It is said there is no want in this country. There may be less than in some other countries. But death by actual starvation in this country is, we apprehend, no uncommon occurrence. The sufferings of a quiet, unassuming but useful class of females in our cities, in general sempstresses, too proud to beg or to apply to the alms-house, are not easily told. They are industrious; they do all that they can find to do; but yet the little there is for them to do, and the miserable pittance they receive for it, is hardly sufficient to keep soul and body together. And yet there is a man who employs them to make shirts, trousers, etc., and grows rich on their labors. He is one of our respectable citizens, perhaps is praised in the newspapers for his liberal donations to some charitable institution. He passes among us as a pattern of morality, and is honored as a worthy Christian. And why should he not be, since our *Christian* community is made up of such as he, and since our clergy would not dare question his piety, lest they should incur the reproach of infidelity, and lose their standing, and their salaries? Nay, since our clergy are raised up, educated, fashioned, and sustained by such as he? Not a few of our churches rest on Mammon for their foundation. The basement is a trader's shop.

We pass through our manufacturing villages, most of them appear neat and flourishing. The operatives are well dressed, and we are told, well paid. They are said to be healthy, contented, and happy. This is the fair side of the picture; the side exhibited to distinguished visitors. There is a dark side, moral as well as physical. Of the common operatives, few, if any, by their wages, acquire a competence. A few of what Carlyle terms not inaptly the *body-servants* are well paid, and now and then an agent or an overseer rides in his coach. But the great mass wear out their health, spirits, and morals, without becoming one whit better off than when they commenced labor. The bills of mortality in these factory villages are not striking, we admit, for the poor girls when they can toil no longer go home to die. The average life, working life we mean, of the girls that come to Lowell, for instance, from Maine, New Hampshire, and Vermont, we have been assured, is only about three years. What becomes of them then? Few of them ever marry; fewer still ever return to their native places with reputations unimpaired. "She has worked in a Factory" is almost enough to damn to infamy the most worthy and virtuous girl. We know no sadder sight on earth than one of our factory villages presents, when the bell at break of day, or at the hour of breakfast, or dinner, calls out its hundreds or thousands of operatives. We stand and look at these hardworking men and women hurrying in all directions, and ask ourselves, where go the proceeds of their labors? The man who employs them, and for whom they are toiling as so many slaves, is one of our city nabobs, revelling in luxury; or he is a member of our legislature, enacting laws to put money in his own pocket; or he is a member of Congress, contending for a high Tariff to tax the poor for the benefit of the rich; or in these times he is shedding crocodile tears over the deplorable condition of the poor laborer, while he docks his wages twenty-five per cent; building miniature log cabins, shouting Harrison and "hard cider." And this man too would fain pass for a Christian and a republican. He shouts for liberty, stickles for equality, and is horrified at a Southern planter who keeps slaves.

One thing is certain; that of the amount actually produced by the operative, he retains a less proportion than it costs the master to feed, clothe, and lodge his slave. Wages is a cunning device of the devil, for the benefit of tender consciences, who would retain all the advantages of the slave system, without the expense, trouble, and odium of being slave-holders.

Messrs. Thome and Kimball,[2] in their account of emancipation in the West Indies, establish the fact that the employer may have the same amount of labor done, twenty-five per cent cheaper than the master. What does this fact prove, if not that wages is a more successful method of taxing labor than slavery? We really believe our Northern system of labor is more oppressive, and even more mischievous to morals, than the Southern. We, however, war against both. We have no toleration for either system. We would see the slave a man, but a free man, not a mere operative at wages. This he would not be were he now emancipated. Could the abolitionists effect all they propose, they would do the slave no service. Should emancipation work as well as they say, still it would do the slave no good. He would be a slave still, although with the title and cares of a freeman. If then we had no constitutional objections to abolitionism, we could not, for the reason here implied, be abolitionists.

The slave system, however, in name and form, is gradually disappearing from Christendom. It will not subsist much longer. But its place is taken by the system of labor at wages, and this system, we hold, is no improvement upon the one it supplants. Nevertheless the system of wages will triumph. It is the system which in name sounds honester than slavery,

[2] James A. Thome and J. Horace Kimball, *Emancipation in the West Indies.* [Ed.]

and in substance is more profitable to the master. It yields the wages of iniquity, without its opprobium. It will therefore supplant slavery, and be sustained—for a time.

Now, what is the prospect of those who fall under the operation of this system? We ask, is there a reasonable chance that any considerable portion of the present generation of laborers, shall ever become owners of a sufficient portion of the funds of production, to be able to sustain themselves by laboring on their own capital, that is, as independent laborers? We need not ask this question, for everybody knows there is not. Well, is the condition of a laborer at wages the best that the great mass of the working people ought to be able to aspire to? Is it a condition—nay can it be made a condition—with which a man should be satisfied; in which he should be contented to live and die?

In our own country this condition has existed under its most favorable aspects, and has been made as good as it can be. It has reached all the excellence of which it is susceptible. It is now not improving but growing worse. The actual condition of the workingman today, viewed in all its bearings, is not so good as it was fifty years ago. If we have not been altogether misinformed, fifty years ago, health and industrious habits, constituted no mean stock in trade, and with them almost any man might aspire to competence and independence. But it is so no longer. The wilderness has receded, and already the new lands are beyond the reach of the mere laborer, and the employer has him at his mercy. If the present relation subsist, we see nothing better for him in reserve than what he now possesses, but something altogether worse.

We are not ignorant of the fact that men born poor become wealthy, and that men born to wealth become poor; but this fact does not necessarily diminish the numbers of the poor, nor augment the numbers of the rich. The relative numbers of the two classes remain, or may remain, the same. But be this as it may; one fact is certain, no man born poor has ever, by his wages, as a simple operative, risen to the class of the wealthy. Rich he may have become, but it has not been by his own manual labor. He has in some way contrived to tax for his benefit the labor of others. He may have accumulated a few dollars which he has placed at usury, or invested in trade; or he may, as a master workman, obtain a premium on his journeymen; or he may have from a clerk passed to a partner, or from a workman to an overseer. The simple market wages for ordinary labor, has never been adequate to raise him from poverty to wealth. This fact is decisive of the whole controversy, and proves that the system of wages must be supplanted by some other system, or else one half of the human race must forever be the virtual slaves of the other.

Now the great work for this age and the coming, is to raise up the laborer, and to realize in our own social arrangements and in the actual condition of all men, that equality between man and man, which God has established between the rights of one and those of another. In other words, our business is to emancipate the proletaries, as the past has emancipated the slaves. This is our work. There must be no class of our fellow men doomed to toil through life as mere workmen at wages. If wages are tolerated it must be, in the case of the individual operative, only under such conditions that by the time he is of a proper age to settle in life, he shall have accumulated enough to be an independent laborer on his own capital—on his own farm or in his own shop. Here is our work. How is it to be done?

Reformers in general answer this question, or what they deem its equivalent, in a manner which we cannot but regard as very unsatisfactory. They would have all men wise, good, and happy; but in order to make them so, they tell us that we want not external changes, but internal; and therefore instead of declaiming against society and seeking to disturb existing social arrangements, we should confine ourselves to the individual reason and conscience; seek merely to lead the individual to repentance, and to reformation of life; make the individual a practical, a truly religious man, and all evils will either disappear, or be sanctified to the spiritual growth of the soul.

This is doubtless a capital theory, and has the advantage that kings, hierarchies, nobilities—in a word, all who fatten on the toil and blood of their fellows, will feel no difficulty in supporting it. Nicholas of Russia, the Grand Turk, his Holiness the Pope, will hold us their especial friends for advocating a theory, which secures to them the odor of sanctity even while they are sustaining by their anathemas or their armed legions, a system of things of which the great mass are and must be the victims. If you will only allow me to keep thousands toiling for my pleasure or my profit, I will even aid you in your pious efforts to convert their souls. I am not cruel; I do not wish either to cause, or to see suffering; I am therefore disposed to encourage your labors for the souls of the workingman, providing you will secure to me the products of his bodily toil. So far as the salvation of his soul will not interfere with my income, I hold it worthy of being sought; and if a few thousand dollars will aid you, Mr. Priest, in reconciling him to God, and making fair weather for him hereafter, they are at your service. I shall not want him to work for me in the world to come, and I can indemnify myself for what your salary costs me, by paying him less wages. A capital theory this, which one may advocate without incurring the reproach of a disorganizer, a jacobin, a leveller, and without losing the friendship of the rankest aristocrat in the land.

This theory, however, is exposed to one slight objection, that of being condemned by something like six thousand years' experience. For six thousand years its beauty has been extolled, its praises sung, and its blessings sought, under every advantage which learning, fashion, wealth, and power can secure; and yet under its practical operations, we are assured, that mankind, though totally depraved at first, have been growing worse and worse ever since.

For our part, we yield to none in our reverence for science and religion; but we confess that we look not for the regeneration of the race from priests and pedagogues. They have had a fair trial. They cannot construct the temple of God. They cannot conceive its plan, and they know not how to build. They daub with untempered mortar, and the walls they erect tumble down if so much as a fox attempt to go up thereon. In a word they always league with the people's masters, and seek to reform without disturbing the social arrangements which render reform necessary. They would change the consequents without changing the antecedents, secure to men the rewards of holiness, while they continue their allegiance to the devil. We have no faith in priests and pedagogues. They merely cry peace, peace, and that too when there is no peace, and can be none.

We admit the importance of what Dr. Channing in his lectures on the subject we are treating recommends as "self-culture." Self-culture is a good thing, but it cannot abolish inequality, nor restore men to their rights. As a means of quickening moral and intellectual energy, exalting the sentiments, and preparing the laborer to contend manfully for his rights, we admit its importance, and insist as strenuously as any one on making it as universal as possible; but as constituting in itself a remedy for the vices of the social state, we have no faith in it. As a means it is well, as the end it is nothing.

The truth is, the evil we have pointed out is not merely individual in its character. It is not, in the case of any single individual, of any one man's procuring, nor can the efforts of any one man, directed solely to his own moral and religious perfection, do aught to remove it. What is purely individual in its nature, efforts of individuals to perfect themselves, may remove. But the evil we speak of is inherent in all our social arrangements, and cannot be cured without a radical change of those arrangements. Could we convert all men to Christianity in both theory and practice, as held by the most enlightened sect of Christians among us, the evils of the social state would remain untouched. Continue our present system of trade, and all its present evil consequences will follow, whether it be carried on by your best men or your worst. Put your best men, your wisest, most moral, and most religious men, at the head of your paper money banks, and the evils of the present banking system will remain scarcely diminished. The only way to get rid of its evils is to change the system, not its managers. The evils of slavery do not result from the personal characters of slave masters. They are inseparable from the system, let who will be masters. Make all your rich men good Christians, and you have lessened not the evils of existing inequality in wealth. The mischievous effects of this inequality do not result from the personal characters of either rich or poor, but from itself, and they will continue, just so long as there are rich men and poor men in the same community. You must abolish the system or accept its consequences. No man can serve both God and Mammon. If you will serve the devil, you must look to the devil for your wages; we know no other way.

Let us not be misinterpreted. We deny not the power of Christianity. Should all men become good Christians, we deny not that all social evils would be cured. But we deny in the outset that a man, who seeks merely to save his own soul, merely to perfect his own individual nature, can be a good Christian. The Christian forgets himself, buckles on his armor, and goes forth to war against principalities and powers, and against spiritual wickedness in high places. No man can be a Christian who does not begin his career by making war on the mischievous social arrangements from which his brethren suffer. He who thinks he can be a Christian and save his soul, without seeking their radical change, has no reason to applaud himself for his proficiency in Christian science, nor for his progress towards the kingdom of God. Understand Christianity, and we will admit, that should all men become good Christians, there would be nothing to complain of. But one might as well undertake to dip the ocean dry with a clam-shell, as to undertake to cure the evils of the social state by converting men to the Christianity of the Church.

The evil we have pointed out, we have said, is not of individual creation, and it is not to be removed by individual effort, saving so far as individual effort induces the combined effort of the mass. But whence has this evil originated? How comes it that all over the world the working classes are depressed, are the low and vulgar, and virtually the slaves of the non-working classes? This is an inquiry which has not yet received the attention it deserves. It is not enough to answer, that it has originated entirely in the inferiority by nature of the working classes; that they have less skill and foresight, and are less able than the upper classes, to provide for themselves, or less susceptible of the highest moral and intellectual cultivation. Nor is it sufficient for our purpose to be told, that Providence has decreed that some shall be poor and wretched, ignorant and vulgar; and that others shall be rich and vicious, learned and polite, oppressive and miserable. We do not choose to charge this matter to the will of God. "The foolishness of man perverteth his way, and his heart fretteth against the

Lord." God has made of one blood all the nations of men to dwell on all the face of the earth, and to dwell there as brothers, as members of one and the same family; and although he has made them with a diversity of powers, it would perhaps, after all, be a bold assertion to say that he has made them with an inequality of powers. There is nothing in the actual difference of the powers of individuals, which accounts for the striking inequalities we everywhere discover in their condition. The child of the plebeian, if placed early in the proper circumstances, grows up not less beautiful, active, intelligent, and refined, than the child of the patrician; and the child of the patrician may become as coarse, as brutish as the child of any slave. So far as observation on the original capacities of individuals goes, nothing is discovered to throw much light on social inequalities.

The cause of the inequality, we speak of, must be sought in history, and be regarded as having its root in Providence, or in human nature, only in that sense in which all historical facts have their origin in these. We may perhaps trace it in the first instance to conquest, but not to conquest as the ultimate cause. The Romans in conquering Italy no doubt reduced many to the condition of slaves, but they also found the great mass of the laboring population already slaves. There is everywhere a class distinct from the reigning class, bearing the same relation to it, that the Gibbeonites [sic] did to the Jews.[3] They are principally *Colons,* the cultivators for foreign masters, of a soil of which they seemed to have been dispossessed. Who has dispossessed them? Who has reduced them to their present condition—a condition which under the Roman dominion is perhaps even ameliorated? Who were this race? Whence came they? They appear to be distinct from the reigning race, as were the Helotae from the Doric-Spartan. Were they the aborigines of the territory? Had they once been free? By what concurrence of events have they been reduced to their present condition? By a prior conquest? But mere conquest does not so reduce a population. It may make slaves of the prisoners taken in actual combat, and reduce the whole to tributaries, but it leaves the mass of the population free, except in its political relations. Were they originally savages, subjugated by a civilized tribe? Savages may be exterminated, but they never, so far as we can ascertain, become to any considerable extent "the hewers of wood and drawers of water" to their conquerors. For our part we are disposed to seek the cause of the inequality of conditions of which we speak, in relation, and to charge it to the priesthood. And we are confirmed in this, by what appears to be the instinctive tendency of every,

[3]The inhabitants of Gibeon were condemned by Joshua to be "hewers of wood and drawers of water" (Josh. 9.27), thus menials, workers. [Ed.]

or almost every, social reformer. Men's instincts, in a matter of this kind, are worthier of reliance than their reasonings. Rarely do we find in any age or country, a man feeling himself commissioned to labor for a social reform, who does not feel that he must begin it by making war upon the priesthood. This was the case with the old Hebrew reformers, who are to us the prophets of God; with Jesus, the Apostles, and the early Fathers of the Church; with the French democrats of the last century; and is the case with the Young Germans, and the Socialists, as they call themselves in England, at the present moment. Indeed it is felt at once that no reform can be effected without resisting the priests and emancipating the people from their power.

Historical research, we apprehend, will be found to justify this instinct, and to authorize the eternal hostility of the reformer, the advocate of social progress, to the priesthood. . . .

Having, by breaking down the power of the priesthood and the Christianity of the priests, obtained an open field and freedom for our operations, and by preaching the true Gospel of Jesus, directed all minds to the great social reform needed, and quickened in all souls the moral power to live for it or to die for it; our next resort must be to government, to legislative enactments. Government is instituted to be the agent of society, or more properly the organ through which society may perform its legitimate functions. It is not the master of society; its business is not to control society, but to be the organ through which society effects its will. Society has never to petition government; government is its servant, and subject to its commands.

Now the evils of which we have complained are of a social nature. That is, they have their root in the constitution of society as it is, and they have attained to their present growth by means of social influences, the action of government, of laws, and of systems and institutions upheld by society, and of which individuals are the slaves. This being the case, it is evident that they are to be removed only by the action of society, that is, by government, for the action of society is government.

But what shall government do? Its first doing must be an *un*doing. There has been thus far quite too much government, as well as government of the wrong kind. The first act of government we want, is a still further limitation of itself. It must begin by circumscribing within narrower limits its powers. And then it must proceed to repeal all laws which bear against the laboring classes, and then to enact such laws as are necessary to enable them to maintain their equality. We have no faith in those systems of elevating the working classes, which propose to elevate them without calling in the aid of the government. We must have government, and legislation expressly directed to this end.

But again what legislation do we want so far as this country is concerned? We want first the legislation which shall free the government, whether State or Federal, from the control of the Banks. The Banks represent the interest of the employer, and therefore of necessity interests adverse to those of the employed; that is, they represent the interests of the business community in opposition to the laboring community. So long as the government remains under the control of the Banks, so long it must be in the hands of the natural enemies of the laboring classes, and may be made, nay, will be made, an instrument of depressing them yet lower. It is obvious then that, if our object be the elevation of the laboring classes, we must destroy the power of the Banks over the government, and place the government in the hands of the laboring classes themselves, or in the hands of those, if such there be, who have an identity of interest with them. . . . The present character, standing, and resources of the Bank party, prove to a demonstration that the Banks must be destroyed, or the laborer not elevated. Uncompromising hostility to the whole banking system should therefore be the motto of every working man, and of every friend of Humanity. The system must be destroyed. On this point their must be no misgiving, no subterfuge, no palliation. The system is at war with the rights and interest of labor, and it must go. Every friend of the system must be marked as an enemy to his race, to his country, and especially to the laborer. No matter who he is, in what party he is found, or what name he bears, he is, in our judgment, no true democrat, as he can be no true Christian.

Following the destruction of the Banks, must come that of all monopolies, of all PRIVILEGE. There are many of these. We cannot specify them all; we therefore select only one, the greatest of them all, the privilege which some have of being born rich while others are born poor. It will be seen at once that we allude to the hereditary descent of property, an anomaly in our American system, which must be removed, or the system itself will be destroyed. We cannot now go into a discussion of this subject, but we promise to resume it at our earliest opportunity. We only say now, that as we have abolished hereditary monarchy and hereditary nobility, we must complete the work by abolishing hereditary property. A man shall have all he honestly acquires, so long as he himself belongs to the world in which he acquires it. But his power over his property must cease with his life, and his property must then become the property of the state, to be disposed of by some equitable law for the use of the generation which takes his place. Here is the principle without any of its details, and this is the grand legislative measure to which we look forward. We see no means of elevating the laboring classes which can be effectual without this. And is this a measure to be easily carried? Not at all. It will cost infinitely more than it cost to abolish either hereditary monarchy or hereditary nobility. It is a great measure, and a startling. The rich, the business community, will never voluntarily consent to it, and we think we know too much of human nature to believe that it will ever be effected peaceably. It will be effected only by the strong arm of physical force. It will come, if it ever come at all, only at the conclusion of war, the like of which the world as yet has never witnessed, and from which, however inevitable it may seem to the eye of philosophy, the heart of Humanity recoils with horror.

We are not ready for this measure yet. There is much previous work to be done, and we should be the last to bring it before the legislature. The time, however, has come for its free and full discussion. It must be canvassed in the public mind, and society prepared for acting on it. No doubt they who broach it, and especially they who support it, will experience a due share of contumely and abuse. They will be regarded by the part of the community they oppose, or may be thought to oppose, as "graceless varlets," against whom every man of substance should set his face. But this is not, after all, a thing to disturb a wise man, nor to deter a true man from telling his whole thought. He who is worthy of the name of man, speaks what he honestly believes the interests of his race demand, and seldom disquiets himself about what may be the consequences to himself. Men have, for what they believed the cause of God or man, endured the dungeon, the scaffold, the stake, the cross, and they can do it again, if need be. This subject must be freely, boldly, and fully discussed, whatever may be the fate of those who discuss it.

MAN THE REFORMER

Ralph Waldo Emerson (1803–1882)

It may be that no single piece of Emerson's writing so dramatizes the connections between him and Thoreau as "Man the Reformer." There are sentences that, one could imagine, might have served as epigraphs for some of the chapters of Walden: "A man should have a farm or a mechanical craft for his culture." Or, of a man drawn to writing: "that man ought . . . to ransom himself from the duties of economy, by a certain rigor and privation in his habits. . . . Let him be a cenobite, a pauper, and if need be, celibate also. Let him learn to eat his meals standing, and to relish the taste of fair water and black bread. He may leave to others the costly conveniences of housekeeping. . . . He must live in a chamber, and postpone his self-indulgence. . . ." Or: "Let us learn the meaning of economy. Economy is a high, humane office, a sacrament, when its aim is grand." One could go on in this vein. But it would be no surprise to find such connections, for Emerson provided material and intellectual support as well as inspiration and encouragement for the younger man, as he did for many others, including upcoming writers as dissimilar as Margaret Fuller, Walt Whitman, and Louisa May Alcott. Thoreau lived with the Emersons for long periods of time, acting as gardener, handyman, secretary, childcare provider. Emerson furnished the land at Walden Pond on which Thoreau built his cabin. But Emerson's very support and guidance also confronted Thoreau with a problem central to the latter's development: how to carve out a vocation in the crass, philistine America of the 1840s that would at once be socially responsible and personally independent.

As, in some sense, Emerson was inescapable in Thoreau's life, so is he in much of nineteenth- and now again in twentieth-century American culture. An appealing orator, a brilliant phrasemaker, an original if unsystematic thinker, he was listened to by thousands upon thousands of people all across America; but audiences made of him everything from an heretic to a guru for capitalism. His essays redefined the genre of the secular sermon and jeremiad, but Emerson defied imitators. He was at once widely popular and a sage for advanced intellectuals. At the heart of the remarkable flourishing of culture in and around Concord and Boston during and after midcentury, he sustained the Transcendental Club, coedited the *Dial,* and played a strong role in getting the work of peers published; but many of those closest to him found him remote and deeply inaccessible. While he urged upon American intellectuals a decisive independence of mind, he may be read as underwriting the most rooted and intractable of all American ideological traits: absolute individualism. He was, in short, at once a decisive and yet an ambiguous figure. One wonders, in fact, what the mechanics' apprentices in the audience for "Man the Reformer" made of his remarks about feeling deprived of opportunities for manual labor.

The lecture was read "before the Mechanics' Apprentices' Library Association, Boston, January 25, 1841," according to the table of contents of volume 1 in the Riverside Edition of *Emer-*

son's Complete Works: Nature, *Addresses, and Lectures* (Boston: Houghton, 1883). When it was first published in 1856, the volume was called *Miscellanies: Embracing* Nature, *Addresses, and Lectures.* [Ed.]

Mr. President and Gentlemen:

I wish to offer to your consideration some thoughts on the particular and general relations of man as a reformer. I shall assume that the aim of each young man in this association is the very highest that belongs to a rational mind. Let it be granted that our life, as we lead it, is common and mean; that some of those offices and functions for which we were mainly created are grown so rare in society, that the memory of them is only kept alive in old books and in dim traditions; that prophets and poets, that beautiful and perfect men, we are not now, no, nor have even seen such; that some sources of human instruction are almost unnamed and unknown among us; that the community in which we live will hardly bear to be told that every man should be open to ecstasy or a divine illumination, and his daily walk elevated by intercourse with the spiritual world. Grant all this, as we must, yet I suppose none of my auditors will deny that we ought to seek to establish ourselves in such disciplines and courses as will deserve that guidance and clearer communication with the spiritual nature. And further, I will not dissemble my hope, that each person whom I address has felt his own call to cast aside all evil customs, timidities, and limitations, and to be in his place a free and helpful man, a reformer, a benefactor, not content to slip along through the world like a footman or a spy, escaping by his nimbleness and apologies as many knocks as he can, but a brave and upright man, who must find or cut a straight road to everything excellent on the earth, and not only go honorably himself, but make it easier for all who follow him, to go in honor and with benefit.

In the history of the world the doctrine of Reform had never such scope as at the present hour. Lutherans, Hernhutters, Jesuits, Monks, Quakers, Knox, Wesley, Swedenborg, Bentham, in their accusations of society, all respected something—church or state, literature or history, domestic usages, the market town, the dinner-table, coined money. But now all these and all things else hear the trumpet, and must rush to judgment—Christianity, the laws, commerce, schools, the farm, the laboratory; and not a kingdom, town, statute, rite, calling, man, or woman, but is threatened by the new spirit.

What if some of the objections whereby our institutions are assailed are extreme and speculative, and the reformers tend to idealism; that only shows the extravagance of the abuses which have driven the mind into the opposite extreme. It is when your facts and persons grow unreal and fantastic by too much falsehood, that the scholar flies for refuge to the world of ideas, and aims to recruit and replenish nature from that source. Let ideas establish their legitimate sway again in society, let life be fair and poetic, and the scholars will gladly be lovers, citizens, and philanthropists.

It will afford no security from the new ideas, that the old nations, the laws of centuries, the property and institutions of a hundred cities, are built on other foundations. The demon of reform has a secret door into the heart of every law-maker, of every inhabitant of every city. The fact that a new thought and hope have dawned in your breast should apprise you that in the same hour a new light broke in upon a thousand private hearts. That secret which you would fain keep—as soon as you go abroad, lo! there is one standing on the doorstep, to tell you the same. There is not the most bronzed and sharpened money-catcher who does not, to your consternation, almost quail and shake the moment he hears a question prompted by the new ideas. We thought he had some semblance of ground to stand upon, that such as he at least would die hard; but he trembles and flees. Then the scholar says, "Cities and coaches shall never impose on me again; for, behold every solitary dream of mine is rushing to fulfilment. That fancy I had, and hesitated to utter because you would laugh—lo, the broker, the attorney, the market-man are saying the same thing. Had I waited a day longer to speak, I had been too late. Behold, State Street thinks, and Wall Street doubts, and begins to prophesy!"

It cannot be wondered at, that this general inquest into abuses should arise in the bosom of society, when one considers the practical impediments that stand in the way of virtuous young men. The young man, on entering life, finds the way to lucrative employments blocked with abuses. The ways of trade are grown selfish to the borders of theft, and supple to the borders (if not beyond the borders) of fraud. The employments of commerce are not intrinsically unfit for a man, or less genial to his faculties, but these are now in their general course so vitiated by derelictions and abuses at which all connive, that it requires more vigor and resources than can be expected of every young man, to right himself in them; he is lost in them; he cannot move hand or foot in them. Has he genius and virtue? the less does he find them fit for him to grow in, and if he would thrive in them, he must sacrifice all the brilliant dreams of boyhood and youth as dreams; he must forget the prayers of his childhood; and must take on him the harness of routine and obsequiousness. If not so minded, nothing is left him but to begin the world anew, as he does who puts the spade into the ground for food. We are all implicated, of course, in this charge; it is only necessary to ask a few questions as to the progress of the articles of commerce from the fields where they grew, to our houses, to become aware that we eat and drink and wear perjury and fraud in a hundred commodities. How many articles of daily consumption are furnished us from the West Indies; yet it is said, that, in the Spanish islands, the venality of the officers of the government has passed into usage, and that no article passes into our ships which has not been fraudulently cheapened. In the Spanish islands, every agent or factor of the Americans, unless he be a consul, has taken oath that he is a Catholic, or has caused a priest to make that declaration for him. The abolitionist has shown us our dreadful debt to the Southern negro. In the island of Cuba, in addition to the ordinary abominations of slavery, it appears, only men are bought for the plantations, and one dies in ten every year, of these miserable bachelors, to yield us sugar. I leave for those who have the knowledge the part of sifting the oaths of our custom-houses; I will not inquire into the oppression of the sailors; I will not pry into the usages of our retail trade. I content myself with the fact, that the general system of our trade (apart from the blacker traits, which, I hope, are exceptions denounced and unshared by all reputable men) is a system of selfishness; is not dictated by the high sentiments of human nature; is not measured by the exact law of reciprocity; much less by the sentiments of love and heroism, but is a system of distrust, of concealment, of superior keenness, not of giving but of taking advantage. It is not that which a man delights to unlock to a noble friend; which he meditates on with joy and self-approval in his hour of love and aspiration; but rather what he then puts out of sight, only showing the brilliant result, and atoning for the manner of acquiring, by the manner of expending it. I do not charge the merchant or the manufacturer. The sins of our trade belong to no class, to no individual. One plucks, one distributes, one eats. Everybody partakes, everybody confesses—with cap and knee volunteers his confession, yet none feels himself accountable. He did not create the abuse; he cannot alter it. What is he? an obscure private person who must get his bread. That is the vice—that no one feels himself called to act for man, but only as a fraction of man. It happens therefore that all such ingenuous souls as feel within themselves the irrepressible strivings of a noble aim, who by the law of their nature must act simply, find these ways of trade unfit for them, and they come forth from it. Such cases are becoming more numerous every year.

But by coming out of trade you have not cleared yourself. The trail of the serpent reaches into all the lucrative professions and practices of man. Each has its own wrongs. Each finds a tender and very intelligent conscience a disqualification for success. Each requires of the practitioner a certain shutting of the eyes, a certain dapperness and compliance, an acceptance of customs, a sequestration from the sentiments of generosity and love, a compromise of private opinion and integrity. Nay, the evil custom reaches into the whole institution of property, until our laws which establish and protect it seem not to be the issue of love and reason, but of selfishness. Suppose a man is so unhappy as to be born a saint, with keen perceptions, but with the conscience and love of an angel, and he is to get his living in the world; he finds himself excluded from all lucrative works; he has no farm, and he cannot get one; for, to earn money enough to buy one, requires a sort of concentration toward money, which is the selling himself for a number of years, and to him the present hour is as sacred and inviolable as any future hour. Of course, whilst another man has no land, my title to mine, your title to yours, is at once vitiated. Inextricable seem to be the twinings and tendrils of this evil, and we all involve ourselves in it the deeper by forming connections, by wives and children, by benefits and debts.

Considerations of this kind have turned the attention of many philanthropic and intelligent persons to the claims of manual labor, as a part of the education of every young man. If the accumulated wealth of the past generations is thus tainted—no matter how much of it is offered to us—we must begin to consider if it were not the nobler part to renounce it, and to put ourselves into primary relations with the soil and nature, and, abstaining from whatever is dishonest and unclean, to take each of us bravely his part, with his own hands, in the manual labor of the world.

But it is said, "What! will you give up the immense advantages reaped from the division of labor, and set every man to make his own shoes, bureau, knife, wagon, sails, and needle? This would be to put men back into barbarism by their own act." I see no instant prospect of a virtuous revolution; yet I confess, I should not be pained at a change which threatened a loss of some of the luxuries or conveniences of society, if it proceeded from a preference of the agricultural life out of the belief that our primary duties as men could be better discharged in that calling. Who could regret to see a high conscience and a purer taste exercising a sensible effect on young men in their choice of occupation, and thinning the ranks of competition in the labors of commerce, of law, and of state? It is easy to see that the inconvenience would last but a short time. This would be great action, which always opens the eyes of men. When many persons shall have done this, when the majority shall admit the necessity of reform in all these institutions, their abuses will be redressed, and the way will be open again to the advantages which arise from the division of labor, and a man may select the fittest employment for his peculiar talent again, without compromise.

But quite apart from the emphasis which the times give to the doctrine, that the manual labor of society ought to be shared among all the members, there are reasons proper to every individual, why he should not be deprived of it. The use of manual labor is one which never grows obsolete, and which is inapplicable to no person. A man should have a farm or a mechanical craft for his culture. We must have a basis for our higher accomplishments, our delicate entertainments of poetry and philosophy, in the work of our hands. We must have an antagonism in the tough world for all the variety of our spiritual faculties, or they will not be born. Manual labor is the study of the external world. The advantage of riches remains with him who procured them, not with the heir. When I go into my garden with a spade, and dig a bed, I feel such an exhilaration and health, that I discover that I have been defrauding myself all this time in letting others do for me what I should have done with my own hands. But not only health, but education is in the work. Is it possible that I who get indefinite quantities of sugar, hominy, cotton, buckets, crockery-ware, and letter-paper, by simply signing my name once in three months to a check in favor of John Smith & Co., traders, get the fair share of exercise to my faculties by that act, which nature intended for me in making all these far-fetched matters important to my comfort? It is Smith himself, and his carriers, and dealers, and manufacturers, it is the sailor, the hide-drogher, the butcher, the negro, the hunter, and the planter, who have intercepted the sugar of the sugar, and the cotton of the cotton. They have got the education, I only the commodity. This were all very well if I were necessarily absent, being detained by work of my own, like theirs, work of the same faculties; then should I be sure of my hands and feet, but now I feel some shame before my wood-chopper, my ploughman, and my cook, for they have some sort of self-sufficiency, they can contrive without my aid to bring the day and year round, but I depend on them, and have not earned by use a right to my arms and feet.

Consider further the difference between the first and second owner of property. Every species of property is preyed on by its own enemies, as iron by rust; timber by rot; cloth by moths; provisions by mould, putridity, or vermin; money by thieves; an orchard by insects; a planted field by weeds and the inroad of cattle; a stock of cattle by hunger; a road by rain and frost; a bridge by freshets. And whoever takes any of these things into his possession, takes the charge of defending them from this troop of enemies, or of keeping them in repair. A man who supplies his own want, who builds a raft or a boat to go a-fishing, finds it easy to calk it, or put in a thole-pin, or mend the rudder. What he gets only as fast as he wants for his own ends, does not embarrass him, or take away his sleep with looking after. But when he comes to give all the goods he has year after year collected, in one estate to his son—house, orchard, ploughed land, cattle, bridges, hardware, wooden-ware, carpets, cloths, provisions, books, money—and cannot give him the skill and experience which made or collected these, and the method and place they have in his own life, the son finds his hands full—not to use these things—but to look after them and defend them from their natural enemies. To him they are not means, but masters. Their enemies will not remit; rust, mould, vermin, rain, sun, freshet, fire, all seize their own, fill him with vexation, and he is converted from the owner into a watchman or a watch-dog to this magazine of old and new chattels. What a change! Instead of the masterly good-humor, and sense of power, and fertility of resource in himself; instead of those strong and learned hands, those piercing and learned eyes, that supple body, and that mighty and prevailing heart, which the father had, whom nature loved and feared, whom snow and rain, water and land, beast and fish, seemed all to know and to serve, we have now a puny, protected person, guarded by walls and curtains, stoves and down beds, coaches, and men-servants and women-servants from the earth and the sky, and who, bred to depend on all these, is made anxious by all that endangers those possessions, and is forced to spend so much time in guarding them, that he has quite lost sight of their original use, namely, to help him to his ends—to the prosecution of his love; to the helping of his friend, to the worship of his God, to the enlargement of his knowledge, to the serving of his country, to the indulgence of his sentiment, and he is now what is called a rich man—the menial and runner of his riches.

Hence it happens that the whole interest of history lies in the fortunes of the poor. Knowledge, Virtue, Power, are the victories of man over his necessities, his march to the dominion of the world. Every man ought to have this opportunity to conquer the world for himself. Only such persons interest us, Spartans, Romans, Saracens, English, Americans, who have stood in the jaws of need, and have by their own wit and might extricated themselves, and made man victorious.

I do not wish to overstate this doctrine of labor, or insist that every man should be a farmer, any more than that every man should be a lexicographer. In general, one may say, that the husbandman's is the oldest, and most universal profession, and that where a man does not yet discover in himself any fitness for one work more than another, this may be preferred. But the doctrine of the Farm is merely this, that every man ought to stand in primary relations with the work of the world, ought to do it himself, and not to suffer the accident of his having a purse in his pocket, or his having been bred to some dishonorable and injurious craft, to sever him from those duties; and for this reason, that labor is God's education; that he only is a sincere learner, he only can become a master, who learns the secrets of labor, and who by real cunning extorts from nature its sceptre.

Neither would I shut my ears to the plea of the learned professions, of the poet, the priest, the lawgiver, and men of study generally; namely, that in the experience of all men of that class, the amount of manual labor which is necessary to the maintenance of a family indisposes and disqualifies for intellectual exertion. I know, it often, perhaps usually, happens, that where there is a fine organization apt for poetry and philosophy, that individual finds himself compelled to wait on his thoughts, to waste several days that he may enhance and glorify one; and is better taught by a moderate and dainty exercise, such as rambling in the fields, rowing, skating, hunting, than by the downright drudgery of the farmer and the smith. I would not quite forget the venerable counsel of the Egyptian mysteries, which declared that "there were two pairs of eyes in man, and it is requisite that the pair which are beneath should be closed, when the pair that are above them perceive, and that when the pair above are closed, those which are beneath should be opened." Yet I will suggest that no separation from labor can be without some loss of power and of truth to the seer himself; that, I doubt not, the faults and vices of our literature and philosophy, their too great fineness, effeminacy, and melancholy, are attributable to the enervated and sickly habits of the literary class. Better that the book should not be quite so good, and the bookmaker abler and better, and not himself often a ludicrous contrast to all that he has written.

But granting that for ends so sacred and dear, some relaxation must be had, I think, that if a man find in himself any strong bias to poetry, to art, to the contemplative life, drawing him to these things with a devotion incompatible with good husbandry, that man ought to reckon early with himself, and, respecting the compensations of the Universe, ought to ransom himself from the duties of economy, by a certain rigor and privation in his habits. For privileges so rare and grand, let him not stint to pay a great tax. Let him be a cenobite, a pauper, and if need be, celibate also. Let him learn to eat his meals standing, and to relish the taste of fair water and black bread. He may leave to others the costly conveniences of housekeeping, and large hospitality, and the possession of works of art. Let him feel that genius is a hospitality, and that he who can create works of art needs not collect them. He must live in a chamber, and postpone his self-indulgence, forewarned and forearmed against that frequent misfortune of men of genius—the taste for luxury. This is the tragedy of genius—attempting to drive along the ecliptic with one horse of the heavens and one horse of the earth, there is only discord and ruin and downfall to chariot and charioteer.

The duty that every man should assume his own vows, should call the institutions of society to account, and examine their fitness to him, gains in emphasis, if we look at our modes of living. Is our housekeeping sacred and honorable? Does it raise and inspire us, or does it cripple us instead? I ought to be armed by every part and function of my household, by all my social function, by my economy, by my feasting, by my voting, by my traffic. Yet I am almost no party to any of these things. Custom does it for me, gives me no power therefrom, and runs me in debt to boot. We spend our incomes for paint and paper, for a hundred trifles, I know not what, and not for the things of a man. Our expense is almost all for conformity. It is for cake that we run in debt; 'tis not the intellect, not the heart, not beauty, not worship, that costs so much. Why needs any man be rich? Why must he have horses, fine garments, handsome apartments, access to public houses, and places of amusement? Only for want of thought. Give his mind a new image, and he flees into a solitary garden or garret to enjoy it, and is richer with that dream, than the fee of a county could make him. But we are first thoughtless, and then find that we are moneyless. We are first sensual, and then must be rich. We dare not trust our wit for making our house pleasant to our friend, and so we buy ice-creams. He is accustomed to carpets, and we have not sufficient character to put floor-cloths out of his mind whilst he stays in the house, and so we pile the floor with carpets. Let the house rather be a temple of the Furies of Lacedaemon, formidable and holy to all, which none but a Spartan may enter or so much as behold. As soon as there is faith, as soon as there is society, comfits and cushions will be left to slaves. Expense will be inventive and heroic. We shall eat hard and lie hard, we shall dwell like the ancient Romans in narrow tenements, whilst our public edifices, like theirs, will be worthy, for their proportion, of the landscape in which we set them, for conversation, for art, for music, for worship. We shall be rich to great purposes; poor only for selfish ones.

Now what help for these evils? How can the man who has learned but one art, procure all the conveniences of life honestly? Shall we say all we think?—Perhaps with his own hands. Suppose he collects or makes them ill—yet he has learned their lesson. If he cannot do that—Then perhaps he can go without. Immense wisdom and riches are in that. It is better to go without, than to have them at too great a cost. Let us learn the meaning of economy. Economy is a high, humane office, a sacrament, when its aim is grand; when it is the prudence of simple tastes, when it is practised for freedom, or love, or devotion. Much of the economy which we see in houses is of a base origin, and is best kept out of sight. Parched corn eaten today that I may have roast fowl to my dinner on Sunday, is a baseness; but parched corn and a house with one apartment, that I may be free of all perturbations, that I may be serene and docile to what the mind shall speak, and girt and road-ready for the lowest mission of knowledge or good-will, is frugality for gods and heroes.

Can we not learn the lesson of self-help? Society is full of infirm people, who incessantly summon others to serve them. They contrive everywhere to exhaust for their single comfort the entire means and appliances of that luxury to which our invention has yet attained. Sofas, ottomans, stoves, wine, game-fowl, spices, perfumes, rides, the theatre, entertainments—all these they want, they need, and whatever can be suggested more than these, they crave also, as if it was the bread which should keep them from starving; and if they miss any one, they represent themselves as the most wronged and most wretched persons on earth. One must have been born and bred with them to know how to prepare a meal for their learned stomach. Meantime, they never bestir themselves to serve another person; not they! they have a great deal more to do for themselves than they can possibly perform, nor do they once perceive the cruel joke of their lives, but the more odious they grow, the sharper is the tone of their complaining and craving. Can anything be so elegant as to have few wants and to serve them one's self, so as to have somewhat left to give, instead of being always prompt to grab? It is more elegant to answer one's own needs, than to be richly served; inelegant perhaps it may look today, and to a few, but it is an elegance forever and to all.

I do not wish to be absurd and pedantic in reform. I do not wish to push my criticism on the state of things around me to that extravagant mark, that shall compel me to suicide, or to an absolute isolation from the advantages of civil society. If we suddenly plant our foot, and say—I will neither eat nor drink nor wear nor touch any food or fabric which I do not know to be innocent, or deal with any person whose whole manner of life is not clear and rational, we shall stand still. Whose is so? Not mine; not thine; not his. But I think we must clear ourselves each one by the interrogation, whether we have earned our bread today by the hearty contribution of our energies to the common benefit? and we must not cease to *tend* to the correction of flagrant wrongs, by laying one stone aright every day.

But the idea which now begins to agitate society has a wider scope than our daily employments, our households, and the institutions of property. We are to revise the whole of our social structure, the state, the school, religion, marriage, trade, science, and explore their foundations in our own nature; we are to see that the world not only fitted the former men, but fits us, and to clear ourselves of every usage which has not its roots in our own mind. What is a man born for but to be a Re-former, a Re-maker of what man has made; a renouncer of lies; a restorer of truth and good, imitating that great Nature which embosoms us all, and which sleeps no moment on an old past, but every hour repairs herself, yielding us every morning a new day, and with every pulsation a new life? Let him renounce everything which is not true to him, and put all his practices back on their first thoughts, and do nothing for which he has not the whole world for his reason. If there are inconveniences, and what is called ruin in the way, because we have so enervated and maimed ourselves, yet it would be like dying of perfumes to sink in the effort to re-attach the deeds of every day to the holy and mysterious recesses of life.

The power, which is at once spring and regulator in all efforts of reform, is the conviction that there is an infinite worthiness in man which will appear at the call of worth, and that all particular reforms are the removing of some impediment. Is it not the highest duty that man should be honored in us? I ought not to allow any man, because he has broad lands, to feel that he is rich in my presence. I ought to make him feel that I can do without his riches, that I cannot be bought—neither by comfort, neither by pride—and though I be utterly penniless, and receiving bread from him, that he is the poor man beside me. And if, at the same time, a woman or a child discovers a sentiment of piety, or a juster way of thinking than mine, I ought to confess it by my respect and obedience, though it go to alter my whole way of life.

The Americans have many virtues, but they have not Faith and Hope. I know no two words whose meaning is more lost sight of. We use these words as if they were as obsolete as Selah[1] and Amen. And yet they have the broadest meaning, and the most cogent application to Boston in this year. The Americans have little faith. They rely on the power of a dollar; they are deaf to a sentiment. They think you may talk the north-wind down as easily as raise society; and no class more faithless than the scholars or intellectual men. Now if I talk with a sincere wise man, and my friend, with a poet, with a conscientious youth who is still under the dominion of his own wild thoughts, and not yet harnessed in the team of society to drag with us all in the ruts of custom, I see at once how paltry is all this generation of unbelievers, and what a house of cards their institutions are, and I see what one brave man, what one great thought executed might effect. I see that the reason of the distrust of the practical man in all theory is his inability to perceive the means whereby we work. Look, he says, at the tools with which this world of yours is to be built. As we cannot make a planet, with atmosphere, rivers, and forests, by means of the best carpenters' or engineers' tools, with chemist's laboratory and smith's forge to boot—so neither can we ever construct that heavenly society you prate of, out of foolish, sick, selfish men and women, such as we know them to be. But the believer not only beholds his heaven to be possible, but already to begin to

[1] *Selah* is a biblical term found in a few books of the Hebrew Bible. It is thought to have been either an exclamation or a musical notation. [Ed.]

exist—not by the men or materials the statesman uses, but by men transfigured and raised above themselves by the power of principles. To principles something else is possible that transcends all the power of expedients.

Every great and commanding moment in the annals of the world is the triumph of some enthusiasm. The victories of the Arabs after Mahomet, who, in a few years, from a small and mean beginning, established a larger empire than that of Rome, is an example. They did they knew not what. The naked Derar, horsed on an idea, was found an overmatch for a troop of Roman cavalry. The women fought like men, and conquered the Roman men. They were miserably equipped, miserably fed. They were Temperance troops. There was neither brandy nor flesh needed to feed them. They conquered Asia, and Africa, and Spain, on barley. The Caliph Omar's walking-stick struck more terror into those who saw it, than another man's sword. His diet was barley bread; his sauce was salt; and oftentimes by way of abstinence he ate his bread without salt. His drink was water. His palace was built of mud; and when he left Medina to go to the conquest of Jerusalem, he rode on a red camel, with a wooden platter hanging at his saddle, with a bottle of water and two sacks, one holding barley, and the other dried fruits.

But there will dawn erelong on our politics, on our modes of living, a nobler morning than that Arabian faith, in the sentiment of love. This is the one remedy for all ills, the panacea of nature. We must be lovers, and at once the impossible becomes possible. Our age and history, for these thousand years, has not been the history of kindness, but of selfishness. Our distrust is very expensive. The money we spend for courts and prisons is very ill laid out. We make, by distrust, the thief, and burglar, and incendiary, and by our court and jail we keep him so. An acceptance of the sentiment of love throughout Christendom for a season, would bring the felon and the outcast to our side in tears, with the devotion of his faculties to our service. See this wide society of laboring men and women. We allow ourselves to be served by them, we live apart from them, and meet them without a salute in the streets. We do not greet their talents, nor rejoice in their good fortune, nor foster their hopes, nor in the assembly of the people vote for what is dear to them. Thus we enact the part of the selfish noble and king from the foundation of the world. See, this tree always bears one fruit. In every household, the peace of a pair is poisoned by the malice, slyness, indolence, and alienation of domestics. Let any two matrons meet, and observe how soon their conversation turns on the troubles from their "*help,*" as our phrase is. In every knot of laborers, the rich man does not feel himself among his friends—and at the polls he finds them arrayed in a mass in distinct opposition to him. We complain that the politics of masses of the people are controlled by designing men, and led in opposition to manifest justice and the common weal, and to their own interest. But the people do not wish to be represented or ruled by the ignorant and base. They only vote for these, because they were asked with the voice and semblance of kindness. They will not vote for them long. They inevitably prefer wit and probity. To use an Egyptian metaphor, it is not their will for any long time "to raise the nails of wild beasts, and to depress the heads of the sacred birds." Let our affection flow out to our fellows; it would operate in a day the greatest of all revolutions. It is better to work on institutions by the sun than by the wind. The state must consider the poor man, and all voices must speak for him. Every child that is born must have a just chance for his bread. Let the amelioration in our laws of property proceed from the concession of the rich, not from the grasping of the poor. Let us begin by habitual imparting. Let us understand that the equitable rule is, that no one should take more than his share, let him be ever so rich. Let me feel that I am to be a lover. I am to see to it that the world is the better for me, and to find my reward in the act. Love would put a new face on this weary old world in which we dwell as pagans and enemies too long, and it would warm the heart to see how fast the vain diplomacy of statesmen, the impotence of armies, and navies, and lines of defence, would be superseded by this unarmed child. Love will creep where it cannot go, will accomplish that by imperceptible methods—being its own lever, fulcrum, and power—which force could never achieve. Have you not seen in the woods, in a late autumn morning, a poor fungus or mushroom—a plant without any solidity, nay, that seemed nothing but a soft mush or jelly—by its constant, total, and inconceivably gentle pushing, manage to break its way up through the frosty ground, and actually to lift a hard crust on its head? It is the symbol of the power of kindness. The virtue of this principle in human society in application to great interests is obsolete and forgotten. Once or twice in history it has been tried in illustrious instances, with signal success. This great, overgrown, dead Christendom of ours still keeps alive at least the name of a lover of mankind. But one day all men will be lovers; and every calamity will be dissolved in the universal sunshine.

Will you suffer me to add one trait more to this portrait of man the reformer? The mediator between the spiritual and the actual world should have a great prospective prudence. An Arabian poet describes his hero by saying,

> Sunshine was he
> In the winter day;
> And in the midsummer
> Coolness and shade.

He who would help himself and others, should not be a subject of irregular and interrupted impulses of virtue, but a continent, persisting, immovable person—such as we have seen a few scattered up and down in time for the blessing of the world; men who have in the gravity of their nature a quality which answers to the fly-wheel in a mill, which distributes the motion equably over all the wheels, and hinders it from falling unequally and suddenly in destructive shocks. It is better that joy should be spread over all the day in the form of strength, than that it should be concentrated into ecstasies, full of danger and followed by reactions. There is a sublime prudence, which is the very highest that we know of man, which, believing in a vast future—sure of more to come than is yet seen—postpones always the present hour to the whole life; postpones talent to genius, and special results to character. As the merchant gladly takes money from his income to add to his capital, so is the great man willing to lose particular powers and talents, so that he gain in the elevation of his life. The opening of the spiritual senses disposes men ever to greater sacrifices, to leave their signal talents, their means and skill of procuring a present success, their power and their fame—to cast all things behind, in the insatiable thirst for divine communications. A purer fame, a greater power, rewards the sacrifice. It is the conversion of our harvest into seed. As the farmer casts into the ground the finest ears of his grain, the time will come when we too shall hold nothing back, but shall eagerly convert more than we now possess into means and powers, when we shall be willing to sow the sun and the moon for seeds.

From PLAN OF THE WEST ROXBURY COMMUNITY

Elizabeth Palmer Peabody (1804–1894)

Peabody's was a remarkably active and varied career. She helped start and taught in a number of educational institutions, including Bronson Alcott's widely known Temple School as well as one of the first kindergartens in the United States in 1861. She wrote history textbooks, designed educational charts, and lectured publically on historical subjects. She opened a bookshop in Boston that became a literary center at which Margaret Fuller held her "Conversations," structured discussions of cultural, social, and philosophical issues held primarily for the education of women. From the bookshop she published the Transcendentalists' magazine, the *Dial,* and later her own magazine, *Aesthetic Papers,* which lasted only one issue, but in which appeared Thoreau's "Civil Disobedience." She also issued antislavery pamphlets as well as works by Hawthorne, who was married to her sister, Sophia. Her other sister was married to Horace Mann, probably the most influential educational theorist of the century. Elizabeth Peabody was, in short, at the center of an extraordinary web of intellectual and reform connections throughout the middle years of the nineteenth century.

The article that follows, "Plan of the West Roxbury Community," describes the theory and anticipated practice of the intentional community of Brook Farm. In the section of the article not included, Peabody points to a number of potential pitfalls for the community. It appeared in the *Dial* (January 1842): 361–372. [ED.]

In the last number of the *Dial* were some remarks under the perhaps ambitious title of "A Glimpse of Christ's Idea of Society"; in a note to which, it was intimated, that in this number, would be given an account of an attempt to realize in some degree this great Ideal by a little company in the midst of us as yet without name or visible existence. The attempt is made on a very small scale. A few individuals, who, unknown to each other, under different disciplines of life, reacting from different social evils, but aiming at the same object—of being wholly true to their natures as men and women; have been made acquainted with one another, and have determined to become the Faculty of the Embryo University.

In order to live a religious and moral life worthy the name, they feel it is necessary to come out in some degree from the world, and to form themselves into a community of property, so far as to exclude competition and the ordinary rules of trade—while they reserve sufficient private property, or the means of obtaining it, for all purposes of independence, and isolation at will. They have bought a farm, in order to make agriculture the basis of their life, it being the most direct and simple in relation to nature.

A true life, although it aims beyond the highest star, is redolent of the healthy earth. The perfume of clover lingers about it. The lowing of cattle is the natural bass to the melody of human voices.

On the other hand, what absurdity can be imagined greater than the institution of cities? They originated not in love, but in war. It was war that drove men together in multitudes, and compelled them to stand so close, and build walls around them. This crowded condition produces wants of an unnatural character, which resulted in occupations that regenerated the evil, by creating artificial wants. Even when that thought of grief,

> I know, where'er I go,
> That there hath passed away a glory from the Earth,

came to our first parents, as they saw the angel, with the flaming sword of self-consciousness, standing between them and the recovery of spontaneous Life and Joy, we cannot believe they could have anticipated a time would come, when the sensuous apprehension of Creation—the great symbol of God—would be taken away from their unfortunate children—crowded together in such a manner as to shut out the free breath and the Universal Dome of Heaven, some opening their eyes in the dark cellars of the narrow, crowded streets of walled cities. How could they have believed in such a conspiracy against the soul, as to deprive it of the sun and sky, and glorious apparelled Earth!—The growth of cities, which were the embryo of nations hostile to each other, is a subject worthy the thoughts and pen of the philosophic historian. Perhaps nothing would stimulate courage to seek, and hope to attain social good, so much, as a profound history of the origin, in the mixed nature of man, and the exasperation by society, of the various organized Evils under which humanity groans. Is there anything which exists in social or political life contrary to the soul's Ideal? That thing is not eternal, but finite, saith the Pure Reason. It had a beginning, and so a history. What man has done, man may *undo*. "By man came death: by man also cometh the resurrection from the dead."

The plan of the Community, as an Economy, is in brief this; for all who have property to take stock, and receive a fixed interest thereon; then to keep house or board in commons, as they shall severally desire, at the cost of provisions purchased at wholesale, or raised on the farm; and for all to labor in community, and be paid at a certain rate an hour, choosing their own number of hours, and their own kind of work. With the results of this labor, and their interest, they are to pay their board, and also purchase whatever else they require at cost, at the warehouses of the Community, which are to be filled by the Community as such. To perfect this economy, in the course of time they must have all trades, and all modes of business carried on among themselves, from the lowest mechanical trade, which contributes to the health and comfort of life, to the finest art which adorns it with food or drapery for the mind.

All labor, whether bodily or intellectual, is to be paid at the same rate of wages; on the principle, that as the labor becomes merely bodily, it is a greater sacrifice to the individual laborer, to give his time to it; because time is desirable for the cultivation of the intellect, in exact proportion to ignorance. Besides, intellectual labor involves in itself higher pleasures, and is more its own reward, than bodily labor.

Another reason, for setting the same pecuniary value on every kind of labor, is, to give outward expression to the great truth, that all labor is sacred, when done for a common interest. Saints and philosophers already know this, but the childish world does not; and very decided measures must be taken to equalize labors, in the eyes of the young or the community, who are not beyond the moral influences of the world without them. The community will have nothing done within its precincts, but what is done by its own members, who stand all in social equality—that the children may not "learn to expect one kind of service from Love and Goodwill, and another from the obligation of others to render it"—a grievance of the common society stated, by one of the associated mothers, as destructive of the soul's simplicity. Consequently, as the Universal Education will involve all kinds of operation, necessary to the comforts and elegances of life, every associate, even if he be the digger of a ditch as his highest accomplishment, will be an instructor in that to the young members. Nor will this elevation of bodily labor be liable to lower the tone of manners and refinement in the community. The "children of light" are not altogether unwise in their generation. They have an invisible but all-powerful guard of principles. Minds incapable of refinement, will not be attracted into this association. It is an Ideal community, and only to the ideally inclined will it be attractive; but these are to be found in every rank of life, under every shadow of circumstance. Even among the diggers in the ditch are to be found some, who through religious cultivation, can look down, in meek superiority, upon the outwardly refined, and the book-learned.

Besides, after becoming members of this community, none will be engaged merely in bodily labor. The hours of labor for the Association will be limited by a general law, and can be curtailed at the will of the individual still more; and means will be given to all for intellectual improvement and for social intercourse, calculated to refine and expand. The hours redeemed from labor by community, will not be reapplied to the acquisition of wealth, but to the production of intellectual goods. This community aims to be rich, not in the metallic representative of wealth, but in the wealth itself, which money should represent; namely, LEISURE TO LIVE IN ALL THE FACULTIES OF THE SOUL. As a community, it will traffic with the world at large, in the products of Agricultural labor; and it will sell education to as many young persons as can be domesticated in the families, and enter into the common life with their own children. In the end, it hopes to be enabled to provide—not only all the necessaries, but all the elegances desirable for bodily and for spiritual health; books, apparatus, collections for science, works of art, means of beautiful amusement. These things are to be common to all; and thus that object, which alone gilds and refines the passion for individual accumulation, will no longer exist for desire, and whenever the Sordid passion appears, it will be seen in its naked selfishness. In its ultimate success, the community will realize all the ends which selfishness seeks, but involved in spiritual blessings, which only greatness of soul can aspire after.

And the requisitions on the individuals, it is believed, will make this the order forever. The spiritual good will always be the condition of the temporal. Every one must labor for the community in a reasonable degree, or not taste its benefits. The principles of the organization therefore, and not its probable results in future time, will determine its members. These principles are cooperation in social matters, instead of competition or balance of interests; and individual self-unfolding, in the faith that the whole soul of humanity is in each man and woman. The former is the application of the love of man; the latter of the love of God, to life. Whoever is satisfied with society, as it is; whose sense of justice is not wounded by its common action, institutions, spirit of commerce, has no business with this community; neither has any one who is willing to have other men (needing more time for intellectual cultivation than himself) give their best hours and strength to bodily labor, to secure himself immunity therefrom. And whoever does not measure what society owes to its members of cherishing and instruction, by the needs of the individuals that compose it, has no lot in this new society. Whoever is willing to receive from his fellow men that, for which he gives no equivalent, will stay away from its precincts forever.

But whoever shall surrender himself to its principles, shall find that its yoke is easy and its burden light. Everything can be said of it, in a degree, which Christ said of his kingdom, and therefore it is believed that in some measure it does embody his Idea. For its Gate of entrance is straight and narrow. It is literally a pearl *hidden in a field.* Those only who are willing to lose their life for its sake shall find it. Its voice is that which sent the young man sorrowing away. "Go sell all thy goods and give to the poor, and then come and follow me." "Seek first the kingdom of Heaven, and its righteousness, and all other things shall be added to you."

This principle, with regard to labor, lies at the root of moral and religious life; for it is not more true that "money is the root of all evil," than that *labor is the germ of all good.*

All the work is to be offered for the free choice of the members of the community, at stated seasons, and such as is not chosen, will be hired. But it is not anticipated that any work will be set aside to be hired, for which there is actual ability in the community. It is so desirable that the hired labor should be avoided, that it is believed the work will all be done freely, even though at voluntary sacrifice. If there is some exception at first, it is because the material means are inadequate to the reception of all who desire to go. They cannot go, unless they have shelter; and in this climate, they cannot have shelter unless they can build houses; and they cannot build houses unless they have money. It is not here as in Robinson Crusoe's Island, or in the prairies and rocky mountains of the far west, where the land and the wood are not appropriated. A single farm, in the midst of Massachusetts, does not afford range enough for men to create out of the Earth a living, with no other means; as the wild Indians, or the United States Army in Florida may do.

This plan, of letting all persons choose their own departments of action, will immediately place the Genius of Instruction on its throne. Communication is the life of spiritual life. Knowledge pours itself out upon ignorance by a native impulse. All the arts crave response. "WISDOM CRIES." If every man and woman taught only what they loved, and so many hours as they could naturally communicate, instruction would cease to be a drudgery, and we may add, learning would be no longer a task. The known accomplishments of any of the members of this association have already secured it an interest in the public mind, as a school of literary advantages quite superior. Most of the associates have had long practical experience in the details of teaching, and have groaned under the necessity of taking their method and law from custom or caprice, when they would rather have found it in the nature of the thing taught, and the condition of the pupil to be instructed. Each instructor appoints his hours of study or recitation, and the scholars, or the parents of the children, or the educational committee, choose the studies, for the time, and the pupils submit, as long as they pursue their studies with any teacher, to his regulations.

As agriculture is the basis of their external life, scientific agriculture, connected with practice, will be a prominent part of the instruction from the first. This obviously involves the natural sciences, mathematics, and accounts. But to classical learning justice is also to be done. Boys may be fitted for our colleges there, and even be carried through the college course. The particular studies of the individual pupils, whether old or young, male or female, are to be strictly regulated, according to their inward needs. As the children of the community can remain in the community after they become of age, as associates, if they will; there will not be an entire subserviency to the end of preparing the means of earning a material subsistence, as is frequently the case now. Nevertheless, as they will have had opportunity, in the course of their minority, to earn three or four hundred dollars, they can leave the community at twenty years of age, if they will, with that sufficient capital, which, together with their extensive education, will gain *a subsistence* anywhere, in the best society of the world. It is this feature of the plan, which may preclude from parents any question as to their right to go into this community, and forego forever all hope of great individual accumulation *for their children;* a customary plea for spending life in making money. Their children will be supported at free board, until they are ten years of age; educated gratuitously; taken care of in case of their parents' sickness and death; and they themselves will be supported, after seventy years of age, by the community, unless their accumulated capital supports them.

There are some persons who have entered the community without money. It is believed that these will be able to support themselves and dependents, by less work, more completely, and with more ease than elsewhere; while their labor will be of advantage to the community. It is in no sense an eleemosynary establishment, but it is hoped that in the end it will be able to receive all who have the spiritual qualifications.

It seems impossible that the little organization can be looked on with any unkindness by the world without it. Those, who have not the faith that the principles of Christ's kingdom are applicable to real life in the world, will smile at it, as a visionary attempt. But even they must acknowledge it can do no harm, in any event. If it realizes the hope of its founders, it will immediately become a manifold blessing. Its moral *aura* must be salutary. As long as it lasts, it will be an example of the beauty of brotherly love. If it succeeds in uniting successful labor with improvement in mind and manners, it will teach a noble lesson to the agricultural population, and do something to check that rush from the country to the city, which is now stimulated by ambition, and by something better, even a desire for learning. Many a young man leaves the farmer's life, because only by so doing can he have intellectual companionship and opportunity; and yet, did he but know it, professional life is ordinarily more unfavorable to the perfection of the mind, than the farmer's life; if the latter is lived with wisdom and moderation, and the labor mingled as it might be with study. This community will be a school for young agriculturalists, who may learn within its precincts, not only the skilful practice, but the scientific reasons of their work, and be enabled afterwards to improve their art continuously. It will also prove the best of normal schools, and as such, may claim the interest of those, who mourn over the inefficiency of our common school system, with its present ill-instructed teachers.

It should be understood also, that after all the working and teaching, which individuals of the community may do, they will still have leisure, and in that leisure can employ themselves in connexion with the world around them. Some will not teach at all; and those especially can write books, pursue the Fine Arts, for private emolument if they will, and exercise various functions of men. . . .

From LETTER TO A. BROOKE
Sept. 8, 1843

Charles Lane (1800–1870)
A. Bronson Alcott (1799–1888)

Though he had little formal education, Bronson Alcott read widely, if indiscriminately, while he worked as a young man on a variety of jobs, from peddling to clockmaking. He taught in a number of educational institutions, ultimately opening his own Temple School in 1834. There he formulated and for a while was able to apply his own educational theories, which focused on developing children's emotional, physical, and intellectual abilities rather than simply teaching facts. But like many of his enterprises, the school failed after a brief if luminous period; it was condemned for its advanced, child-centered educational theory, but also for enrolling a mulatto girl in the student body. Moreover, his two-volume work, *Conversations with Children on the Gospels* (1836–37), which utilized real classroom conversations about Jesus, religion, and values, was condemned as blasphemous if not altogether obscene.

Because of his interest in the Transcendentalists, Alcott moved to Concord, where he and his family interacted with Emerson, Thoreau, and others. He contributed to the magazine the *Dial* his characteristically intriguing if haphazard "Orphic Sayings." In 1842, he visited Alcott House in Surrey, England, an experimental school named after him. He returned with Charles Lane, an English disciple, reformer, and writer. The next year, Lane purchased a farm at Harvard, Massachusetts, and with Alcott founded an experimental vegetarian community called Fruitlands. For them, the family constituted the central form of "every human relation consistent with universal good," and the sphere within which learning, joy, and beauty might flourish. Whether from lack of planning or misdirected work, however, they found themselves without food or funds within half a year and were forced to abandon the experiment, a result that considerably depressed

Alcott and nearly divided his own family. Lane would return to England, where he continued to be active in reform circles.

Alcott remained in and around Concord, becoming its superintendent of schools for a time. He was seldom able to support his family financially, and while they suffered from real poverty, he seemed able to sustain a calm and encouraging home life. When his daughter Louisa achieved financial success with her writing, Alcott was enabled to continue to play the role of a peripatetic philosopher in lyceums across the country as well as in Concord.

The letter that follows was originally written to a correspondent, A. Brooke of Oakland, Ohio, and published in the *Herald of Freedom,* September 8, 1843. It appears to have initially been drafted by Lane, though both men signed it. The letter was reprinted, together with other letters and documents relating to Fruitlands, including Louisa May Alcott's "Transcendental Wild Oats," in a volume entitled *Bronson Alcott's Fruitlands* (Boston: Houghton, 1915), compiled by Clara Endicott Sears and later republished with a preface by the director of the Fruitlands Museum (Philadelphia: Porcupine, 1975). [Ed.]

Dear Sir:

Having perused your several letters in the *Herald of Freedom,* and finding, moreover, a general invitation to correspondence from "persons who feel prepared to cooperate in the work of reform upon principles" akin to those you have set forth, I take this public means of communicating with one, who seems to be really desirous of aiding entire human regeneration.

After many years passed in admiration of a better order in human society, with a constant expectation that some beginning would shortly be made, and a continued reliance that some party would make it, the idea has gradually gained possession of my mind, that it is not right thus to linger for the leadings of other men, but that each should at once proceed to live out the proposed life to the utmost possible extent. Assured that the most potent hindrances to goodness abide in the Soul itself; next in the body; thirdly in the house and family; and in the fourth degree only in our neighbors, or in society at large; I have daily found less and less reason to complain of public institutions, or of the dilatoriness of reformers of genetic minds.

Animated by pure reform principles, or rather by pure creative spirit, I have not hesitated to withdraw as far and as fast as hopeful prudence dictated from the practices and principles of the Old World, and acting upon the conviction that whatever others might do, or leave undone, however others might fail in the realization of their ideal good, I, at least, should advance, I have accordingly arrived in that region where I perceive you theoretically, and I hope, actually dwell. I agree with you that it would be well to cross the ocean of Life from the narrow island of selfishness to the broad continent of universal Love at one dash; but the winds are not always propitious, and steam is only a recent invention. I cannot yet boast of a year's emancipation from old England. One free step leads to another; and the third must necessarily precede the fourth, as the second was before the third.

A. Bronson Alcott's visit to England last year opened to me some of the superior conditions for a pure life which this country offers compared to the land of my nativity and that of your ancestors. My love for purity and goodness was sufficiently strong it seems to loosen me from a position as regards pecuniary income, affectionate friends, and mental liberty, which millions there and thousands here might envy. It has happened however that of the many persons with whom Mr. Alcott hoped to act in conjunction and concert, not one is yet fully liberated by Providence to that end. So that instead of forming items in a large enterprise, we are left to be the principal actors in promoting an idea less in extent, but greater in intent, than any yet presented to our observation.

Our removal to this estate in humble confidence has drawn to us several practical coadjustors, and opened many inquiries by letter for a statement of our principles and modes of life. We cannot perhaps turn our replies to better account, than to transcribe some portions of them for your information, and we trust, for your sincere satisfaction. . . .

To us it appears not so much that improved circumstances are to meliorate mankind, as that improved men will originate the superior condition for themselves and others. Upon the Human Will, and not upon circumstances, as some philosophers assert, rests the function, power and duty, of generating a better social state. The human beings in whom the Eternal Spirit has ascended from low animal delights or mere human affections, to a state of spiritual chastity and intuition, are in themselves a divine atmosphere, they *are* superior circumstances and are constant in endeavoring to create, as well as to modify, all other conditions, so that these also shall more and more conduce to the like consciousness in others.

Hence our perseverance in efforts to attain simplicity in diet, plain garments, pure bathing, unsullied dwellings, open conduct, gentle behavior, kindly sympathies, serene minds. These, and several other particulars needful to the true end of man's residence on earth, may be designated the Family Life. Our Happiness, though not the direct object in human energy, may be accepted as the conformation of rectitude, and this is not otherwise attainable than in the Holy Family. The Family in its highest, divinest sense is therefore our true position, our sacred earthly destiny. It comprehends every divine, every human relation consistent with universal good, and all others it rejects, as it disdains all animal sensualities.

The evils of life are not so much social, or political, as personal, and a personal reform only can eradicate them.

Let the Family, furthermore, be viewed as the home of pure social affections, the school of expanding intelligence, the sphere of unbought art, the scene of joyous employment, and we feel in that single sentiment, a fulness of action, of life, of being, which no scientific social contrivance can ensure, nor selfish accident supply.

Family is not dependent upon numbers, nor upon skill, nor riches, but upon union in and with that spirit which alone can bless any enterprise whatever.

On this topic of Family association, it will not involve an entire agreement with the Shakers to say they are at least entitled to deeper consideration than they yet appear to have secured. There are many important acts in their career worthy of observation. It is perhaps most striking that the only really successful extensive Community of interest, spiritual and secular, in modern times was established by A Woman. Again, we witness in this people the bringing together of the two sexes in a new relation, or rather with a new idea of the old relation. This has led to results more harmonic than anyone seriously believes attainable for the human race, either in isolation or association, so long as divided, conflicting family arrangements are permitted. The great secular success of the Shakers; their order, cleanliness, intelligence and serenity are so eminent, that it is worthy of enquiry how far these are attributal to an adherence to their peculiar doctrine.

As to Property, we discover not its just disposal either in individual or social tenures, but in its entire absorption into the New Spirit, which ever gives and never grasps.

While we write, negotiations are entertained for our removal to a place of less inconvenience, by friends who have long waited for some proof of a determination to act up to the idea they have cherished. Many, no doubt, are yet unprepared "to give up all and follow him" (the Spirit) who can importantly aid in the New Advent, and conscientiously accomplish the legal processes needful under the present circumstances. We do not recognize the purchase of land; but its redemption from the debasing state of *proprium,* or property, to divine uses, we clearly understand when those whom the world esteems as owners are found yielding their individual rights to the Supreme Owner. Looking at the subject practically in relation to a climate in which a costly shelter is necessary, and where a family with many children has to be provided for, the possibility of at once stepping boldly out of the toils into which the errors of our predecessors have cast us, is not so evident as it is desirable.

Trade we hope entirely to avoid at an early day. As a nursery for many evil propensities it is almost universally felt to be a most undesirable course. Such needful articles as we cannot yet raise by our own hand labor from the soil, thus redeemed from human ownership, we shall endeavor to obtain by friendly exchanges, and, as nearly as possible, without the intervention of money.

Of all the traffic in which civilized society is involved, that of human labor is perhaps the most detrimental. From the state of serfdom to the receipt of wages may be a step in human progress; but it is certainly full time for taking a new step out of the hiring system.

Our outward exertions are in the first instance directed to the soil, and as our ultimate aim is to furnish an instance of self-sustaining cultivation without the subjugation of either men or cattle, or the use of foul animal manures, we have at the outset to encounter struggles and oppositions somewhat formidable. Until the land is restored to its pristine fertility by the annual return of its own green crops, as sweet and animating manures, the human hand and simple implement cannot wholly supersede the employment of machinery and cattle. So long as cattle are used in agriculture, it is very evident that man will remain a slave, whether he be proprietor or hireling. The driving of cattle beyond their natural and pleasurable exertion; the waiting upon them as cook and chambermaid three parts of the year; the excessive labor of mowing, curing, and housing hay, and of collecting other fodder, and the large extra quantity of land needful to keep up this system, form a continuation of unfavorable circumstances which must depress the human affections so long as it continues, and overlay them by the injurious and extravagant development of the animal and bestial natures in man. It is calculated that if no animal food were consumed, one-fourth of the land now used would suffice for human sustenance. And the extensive tracts of country now appropriated to grazing, mowing, and other modes of animal provision, could be cultivated by and for intelligent and affectionate human neighbors. The sty and the stable too often secure more of the farmer's regard than he bestows on the garden and the children. No hope is there for humanity while Woman is withdrawn from the tender assiduities which adorn her and her household, to the servitudes of the dairy and the flesh pots. If the beasts were wholly absent from man's neighborhood, the human population might be at least four times as dense as it now is without raising the price of land. This would give to the country all the advantages of concentration without the vices which always spring up in the dense city.

Debauchery of both the earthly soil and the human body is the result of this cattle keeping. The land is scourged for crops to feed the animals, whose ordures are used under the erroneous supposition of restoring lost fertility; disease is thus infused into the human body; stimulants and medicines are resorted to for relief, which end in a precipitation of the original evil to a more disastrous depth. These misfortunes which affect not only the body, but by reaction rise to the sphere of the soul, would be avoided, or at least in part, by the disuse of animal food. Our diet is therefore strictly the pure and bloodless kind. No animal substances, neither flesh, butter, cheese, eggs, nor milk, pollute our table or corrupt our bodies, neither tea, coffee, molasses, nor rice, tempts us beyond the bounds of indigenous productions. Our sole beverage is pure fountain water. The native grains, fruits, herbs, and roots, dressed with the utmost cleanliness and regard to their purpose of edifying a healthful body, furnish the pleasantest refections and in the greatest variety requisite to the supply of the various organs. The field, the orchard, the garden, in their bounteous products of wheat, rye, barley, maize, oats, buckwheat, apples, pears, peaches, plums, cherries, currants, berries, potatoes, peas, beans, beets, carrots, melons, and other vines, yield an ample store for human nutrition, without dependence on foreign climes, or the degeneration of shipping and trade. The almost inexhaustible variety of the several stages and sorts of vegetable growth, and the several modes of preparation, are a full answer to the question which is often put by those who have never ventured into the region of a pure and chaste diet: "If you give up flesh meat, upon what then can you live?"

Our other domestic habits are in harmony with those of diet. We rise with early dawn, begin the day with cold bathing, succeeded by a music lesson, and then a chaste repast. Each one finds occupation until the meridian meal, when usually some interesting and deep-searching conversation gives rest to the body and development to the mind. Occupation, according to the season and the weather, engages us out of doors or within, until the evening meal—when we again assemble in social communion, prolonged generally until sunset, when we resort to sweet repose for the next day's activity.

In these steps of reform we do not rely as much on scientific reasoning of physiological skill, as on the Spirit's dictates. The pure soul, by the law of its own nature, adopts a pure diet and cleanly customs; nor needs detailed instruction for daily conduct. On a revision of our proceedings it would seem, that if we were in the right course in our particular instance, the greater part of man's duty consists in leaving alone much that he is in the habit of doing. It is a fasting from the present activity, rather than an increased indulgence in it, which, with patient watchfulness tends to newness of life. "Shall I sip tea or coffee?" the inquiry may be. No; abstain from all ardent, as from alcoholic drinks. "Shall I consume pork, beef, or mutton?" Not if you value health or life. "Shall I stimulate with milk?" No. "Shall I warm my bathing water?" Not if cheerfulness is valuable. "Shall I clothe in many garments?" Not if purity is aimed at. "Shall I prolong my dark hours, consuming animal oil and losing bright daylight in the morning?" Not if a clear mind is an object. "Shall I teach my children the dogmas inflicted on myself, under the pretence that I am transmitting truth?" Nay, if you love them intrude not these between them and the Spirit of all Truth. "Shall I subjugate cattle?" "Shall I trade?" "Shall I claim property in any created thing?" "Shall I interest myself in politics?" To how many of these questions could we ask them deeply enough, could they be heard as having relation to our eternal welfare, would the response be "Abstain"? Be not so active to do, as sincere to be. Being in preference to doing, is the great aim and this comes to us rather by a resigned willingness than a wilful activity—which is indeed a check to all divine growth. Outward abstinence is a sign of inward fulness; and the only source of true progress is inward. We may occupy ourselves actively in human improvements—but these unless inwardly well-impelled, never attain to, but rather hinder, divine progress in man. During the utterance of this narrative it has undergone a change in its personal expression which might offend the hypercritical; but we feel assured that you will kindly accept it as unartful offering of both your friends in ceaseless aspiration.

Charles Lane
A. Bronson Alcott
Harvard, Mass.,
August, 1843

ADDRESS TO THE SLAVES OF THE UNITED STATES OF AMERICA

Henry Highland Garnet (1815–1882)

Forceful resistance to slavery very likely began in the same instant that slavery was itself first imposed by one human being on another. In the United States, however, the mainstream of antislavery thinking in the early nineteenth century held that

From *The Black Abolitionist Papers*. Vol. 3. Chapel Hill: U of North Carolina P, 1991.

nonviolent opposition was simultaneously more moral, more Christian, and more practical as a route to ending the slave system. Still, there were those, like David Walker in his *Appeal to the Colored Citizens of the World* (1829), who argued effectively that it was better to die, or indeed to kill, "in preference to such *servile submission* to the murderous hands of tyrants." Garnet's 1843 "Address to the Slaves of the United States of America," which he delivered before the National Convention of Colored Citizens in Buffalo, fit within this countertradition. It was not that Garnet preached overthrowing slavery by force and violence; indeed, his speech could be taken to support militant nonviolence: "Let every slave throughout this land ['cease to labor for tyrants who will not remunerate you'] . . . and the days of slavery are numbered." Yet his language and tone were not those of nonresistance and reconciliation: "Let your motto be RESISTANCE! RESISTANCE! RESISTANCE!" And certainly the Garrisonian wing of the abolitionist movement, taking the speech as an incitement and a danger, opposed its circulation to slaves and to others.

By the time he delivered it, Garnet was well known as an active abolitionist, a Presbyterian minister, and a supporter of the Liberty party. Born a slave in Maryland, he escaped with his family in 1824, settling finally in New York, where he went to a school for black students. Unable to get a decent job in the city, Garnet shipped out as a cabin boy. In the 1830s, he suffered an injury that brought about the amputation of a leg; that event led to his dedicating himself more fully to study. He graduated from the Oneida Institute in 1840 and thereafter taught school, was ordained, and lectured before leaving the United States in 1850 to live first in Europe and then in Jamaica as a missionary. Returning, he helped to recruit black troops for the Union during the Civil War. Garnet was invited by President Lincoln to deliver a sermon in the House of Representatives, thereby becoming the first black American to enter that august body in any role other than that of a servant. He remained active on behalf of black civil rights throughout the postbellum period, ultimately becoming U.S. minister to Liberia, where he died shortly after taking office.

Brethren and Fellow Citizens:

Your brethren of the north, east, and west have been accustomed to meet together in National Conventions, to sympathize with each other, and to weep over your unhappy condition. In these meetings we have addressed all classes of the free, but we have never until this time, sent a word of consolation and advice to you. We have been contented in sitting still and mourning over your sorrows, earnestly hoping that before this day, your sacred Liberties would have been restored. But, we have hoped in vain. Years have rolled on, and tens of thousands have been borne on streams of blood, and tears, to the shores of eternity. While you have been oppressed, we have also been partakers with you; nor can we be free while you are enslaved. We therefore write to you as being bound with you.

Many of you are bound to us, not only by the ties of common humanity, but we are connected by the more tender relations of parents, wives, husbands, children, brothers, and sisters, and friends. As such we most affectionately address you.

Slavery has fixed a deep gulf between you and us, and while it shuts out from you the relief and consolation which your friends would willingly render, it afflicts and persecutes you with a fierceness which we might not expect to see in the fiends of hell. But still the Almighty Father of Mercies has left to us a glimmering ray of hope, which shines out like a lone star in a cloudy sky. Mankind are becoming wiser, and better—the oppressor's power is fading, and you, every day, are becoming better informed, and more numerous. Your grievances, brethren, are many. We shall not attempt, in this short address, to present to the world all the dark catalogue of this nation's sins, which have been committed upon an innocent people. Nor is it indeed, necessary, for you feel them from day to day, and all the civilized world look upon them with amazement.

Two hundred and twenty-seven years ago, the first of our injured race were brought to the shores of America.[1] They came not with glad spirits to select their homes, in the New World. They came not with their own consent, to find an unmolested enjoyment of the blessings of this fruitful soil. The first dealings which they had with men calling themselves Christians, exhibited to them the worst features of corrupt and sordid hearts; and convinced them that no cruelty is too great, no villainy, and no robbery too abhorrent for even enlightened men to perform, when influenced by avarice, and lust. Neither did they come flying upon the wings of Liberty, to a land of freedom. But, they came with broken hearts, from their beloved native land, and were doomed to unrequited toil, and deep degradation. Nor did the evil of their bondage end at their emancipation by death.

---

[1] Actually the first black Africans were brought to Jamestown, in what is now Virginia, in 1619. [Ed.]

Succeeding generations inherited their chains, and millions have come from eternity into time, and have returned again to the world of spirits, cursed and ruined by American Slavery.

The propagators of the system, or their immediate ancestors, very soon discovered its growing evil, and its tremendous wickedness and secret promises were made to destroy it. The gross inconsistency of a people holding slaves, who had themselves "ferried o'er the wave," for freedom's sake, was too apparent to be entirely overlooked. The voice of Freedom cried, "emancipate your Slaves." Humanity supplicated with tears for the deliverance of the children of Africa. Wisdom urged her solemn plea. The bleeding captive pled his innocence, and pointed to Christianity who stood weeping at the cross. Jehovah frowned upon the nefarious institution, and thunderbolts, red with vengeance, struggled to leap forth to blast the guilty wretches who maintained it. But all was vain. Slavery had stretched its dark wings of death over the land, the Church stood silently by—the priests prophesied falsely, and the people loved to have it so. Its throne is established, and now it reigns triumphantly.

Nearly three millions of your fellow citizens are prohibited by law and public opinion (which in this country is stronger than law) from reading the Book of Life. Your intellect has been destroyed as much as possible, and every ray of light they have attempted to shut out from your minds. The oppressors themselves have become involved in the ruin. They have become weak, sensual, and rapacious. They have cursed you—they have cursed themselves—they have cursed the earth which they have trod. In the language of a Southern statesman, we can truly say "even the wolf, driven back long since by the approach of man, now returns after a lapse of a hundred years, and howls amid the desolation of slavery."

The colonists threw the blame upon England. They said that the mother country entailed the evil upon them, and that they would rid themselves of it if they could. The world thought they were sincere, and the philanthropic pitied them. But time soon tested their sincerity. In a few years, the colonists grew strong and severed themselves from the British Government. Their independence was declared, and they took their station among the sovereign powers of the earth. The declaration was a glorious document. Sages admired it, and the patriotic of every nation reverenced the Godlike sentiments which it contained. When the power of Government returned to their hands, did they emancipate the slaves? No, they rather added new links to our chains. Were they ignorant to the principles of Liberty? Certainly they were not. The sentiments of their revolutionary orators fell in burning eloquence upon their hearts, and with one voice they cried, LIBERTY OR DEATH. O, what a sentence was that! It ran from soul to soul like electric fire, and nerved the arm of thousands to fight in the holy cause of Freedom. Among the diversity of opinions that are entertained in regard to physical resistance, there are but a few found to gainsay that stern declaration. We are among those who do not.

SLAVERY! How much misery is comprehended in that single word. What mind is there that does not shrink from its direful effects? Unless the image of God is obliterated from the soul, all men cherish the love of Liberty. The nice discerning political economist does not regard the sacred right, more than the untutored African who roams in the wilds of Congo. Nor has the one more right to the full enjoyment of his freedom than the other. In every man's mind the good seeds of Liberty are planted, and he who brings his fellow down so low, as to make him contented with a condition of slavery, commits the highest crime against God and man. Brethren, your oppressors aim to do this. They endeavor to make you as much like brutes as possible. When they have blinded the eyes of your mind—when they have embittered the sweet waters of life—when they have shut out the light which shines from the word of God—then, and not till then, has American slavery done its perfect work.

TO SUCH DEGRADATION IT IS SINFUL IN THE EXTREME FOR YOU TO MAKE VOLUNTARY SUBMISSION. The divine commandments, you are in duty bound to reverence, and obey. If you do not obey them you will surely meet with the displeasure of the Almighty. He requires you to love him supremely, and your neighbor as yourself—to keep the Sabbath day holy—to search the Scriptures—and bring up your children with respect for his laws, and to worship no other God but him.[2] But slavery sets all these at naught, and hurls defiance in the face of Jehovah. The forlorn condition in which you are placed does not destroy your moral obligation to God. You are not certain of Heaven, because you suffer yourselves to remain in a state of slavery, where you cannot obey the commandments of the Sovereign of the universe. If the ignorance of slavery is a passport to heaven, then it is a blessing, and not a curse, and you should rather desire its perpetuity than its abolition. God will not receive slavery, nor ignorance, nor any other state of mind, for love, and obedience to him. Your condition does not absolve you from your moral obligation. The diabolical injustice by which your Liberties are cloven down, NEITHER GOD, NOR ANGELS, NOR JUST MEN COMMAND YOU TO SUFFER FOR A SINGLE MOMENT. THEREFORE IT IS YOUR SOLEMN AND IMPERATIVE DUTY TO USE

[2] See Matt. 22.37–40, and Exod. 20.1–17. [ED.]

EVERY MEANS, BOTH MORAL, INTELLECTUAL, AND PHYSICAL, THAT PROMISE SUCCESS. If a band of heathen men should attempt to enslave a race of Christians, and to place their children under the influence of some false religion, surely, heaven would frown upon the men who would not resist such aggression, even to death. If, on the other hand, a band of Christians should attempt to enslave a race of heathen men and to entail slavery upon them, and to keep them in heathenism in the midst of Christianity, the God of heaven would smile upon every effort which the injured might make to disenthrall themselves.

Brethren, it is as wrong for your lordly oppressors to keep you in slavery, as it was for the man thief to steal our ancestors from the coast of Africa. You should therefore now use the same manner of resistance, as would have been just in our ancestors, when the bloody footprints of the first remorseless soul thief was placed upon the shores of our fatherland. The humblest peasant is as free in the sight of God, as the proudest monarch that ever swayed a scepter. Liberty is a spirit sent out from God, and like its great Author, is no respecter of persons.

Brethren, the time has come when you must act for yourselves. It is an old and true saying, that "if hereditary bondsmen would be free, they must themselves strike the blow."[3] You can plead your own cause, and do the work of emancipation better than any other. The nations of the old world are moving in the great cause of universal freedom, and some of them at least, will ere long, do you justice. The combined powers of Europe have placed their broad seal of disapprobation upon the African slave trade. But in the slave holding parts of the United States, the trade is as brisk as ever. They buy and sell you as though you were brute beasts. The North has done much—her opinion of slavery in the abstract is known. But in regard to the South, we adopt the opinion of the *New York Evangelist*—"We have advanced so far, that the cause apparently waits for a more effectual door to be thrown open than has been yet."[4] We are about to point you to that more effectual door. Look around you, and behold the bosoms of your loving wives, heaving with untold agonies! Hear the cries of your poor children! Remember the stripes your fathers bore. Think of the torture and disgrace of your noble mothers. Think of your wretched sisters, loving virtue and purity, as they are driven into

[3] Cf. George Gordon, Lord Byron, *Childe Harold's Pilgrimage*, 2.76:

> Hereditary bondsmen! Know ye not
> Who would be free themselves must strike the blow? [ED.]

[4] Paraphrased from an editorial, "The Anti-Slave Enterprise," from the Presbyterian *New York Evangelist*, 27 July 1843. [ED.]

concubinage, and are exposed to the unbridled lusts of incarnate devils. Think of the undying glory that hangs around the ancient name of Africa—and forget not that you are native-born American citizens, and as such, you are justly entitled to all the rights that are granted to the freest. Think how many tears you have poured out upon the soil which you have cultivated with unrequited toil, and enriched with your blood; and then go to your lordly enslavers, and tell them plainly, that YOU ARE DETERMINED TO BE FREE. Appeal to their sense of justice, and tell them that they have no more right to oppress you, than you have to enslave them. Entreat them to remove the grievous burdens which they have imposed upon you, and to remunerate you for your labor. Promise them renewed diligence in the cultivation of the soil, if they will render to you an equivalent for your services. Point them to the increase of happiness and prosperity in the British West Indies, since the act of Emancipation.[5] Tell them in language which they cannot misunderstand, of the exceeding sinfulness of slavery, and of a future judgment, and of the righteous retributions of an indignant God. Inform them that all you desire, is FREEDOM, and that nothing else will suffice. Do this, and forever after cease to toil for the heartless tyrants, who give you no other reward but stripes and abuse. If they then commence the work of death, they, and not you, will be responsible for the consequences. You had far better all die—*die immediately,* than live slaves, and entail your wretchedness upon your posterity. If you would be free in this generation, here is your only hope. However much you and all of us may desire it, there is not much hope of Redemption without the shedding of blood. If you must bleed, let it all come at once—rather, *die freemen, than live to be slaves.* It is impossible, like the children of Israel, to make a grand Exodus from the land of bondage. THE PHAROES [SIC] ARE ON BOTH SIDES OF THE BLOOD-RED WATERS! You cannot remove en masse, to the dominions of the British Queen—nor can you pass through Florida, and overrun Texas, and at last find peace in Mexico. The propagators of American slavery are spending their blood and treasure, that they may plant the black flag in the heart of Mexico, and riot in the halls of the Montezumas. In the language of the Rev. Robert Hall, when addressing the volunteers of Bristol, who were rushing forth to repel the invasion of Napoleon, who threatened to lay waste the fair homes of England, "Religion is too much interested in your behalf, not to shed over you her most gracious influences."[6]

---

[5] The Emancipation Act of 1833 ended slavery in the British Empire. [ED.]

[6] A Baptist clergyman, Robert Hall, spoke these words in response to Napoleon's threat to invade England in 1804. [ED.]

You will not be compelled to spend much time in order to become inured to hardships. From the first moment that you breathed the air of heaven, you have been accustomed to nothing else but hardships. The heroes of the American Revolution were never put upon harder fare, than a peck of corn, and a few herrings per week. You have not become enervated by the luxuries of life. Your sternest energies have been beaten out upon the anvil of severe trial. Slavery has done this, to make you subservient to its own purposes; but it has done more than this, it has prepared you for any emergency. If you receive good treatment, it is what you could hardly expect; if you meet with pain, sorrow, and even death, these are the common lot of the slaves.

Fellow men! patient sufferers! behold your dearest rights crushed to the earth! See your sons murdered, and your wives, mothers, and sisters, doomed to prostitution! In the name of the merciful God! and by all that life is worth, let it no longer be a debateable question, whether it is better to choose LIBERTY or DEATH!

In 1822, Denmark Vesey, of South Carolina, formed a plan for the liberation of his fellow men. In the whole history of human efforts to overthrow slavery, a more complicated and tremendous plan was never formed. He was betrayed by the treachery of his own people, and died a martyr to freedom. Many a brave hero fell, but History, faithful to her high trust, will transcribe his name on the same monument with Moses, Hampden, Tell, Bruce, and Wallace, Toussaint L'Ouverture, Lafayette and Washington. That tremendous movement shook the whole empire of slavery. The guilty soul thieves were overwhelmed with fear. It is a matter of fact, that at that time, and in consequence of the threatened revolution, the slave states talked strongly of emancipation. But they blew but one blast of the trumpet of freedom, and then laid it aside. As these men became quiet, the slaveholders ceased to talk about emancipation; and now, behold your condition today! Angels sigh over it, and humanity has long since exhausted her tears in weeping on your account!

The patriotic Nathaniel Turner followed Denmark Vesey. He was goaded to desperation by wrong and injustice. By Despotism, his name has been recorded on the list of infamy, but future generations will number him upon the noble and brave.

Next arose the immortal Joseph Cinqué, the hero of the *Amistad*. He was a native African, and by the help of God he emancipated a whole shipload of his fellow men on the high seas. And he now sings of Liberty on the sunny hills of Africa, and beneath his native palm trees, where he hears the lion roar, and feels himself as free as that king of the forest. Next arose Madison Washington, that bright star of freedom, and took his station in the constellation of freedom. He was a slave on board the brig *Creole,* of Richmond, bound to New Orleans, that great slave mart, with a hundred and four others. Nineteen struck for Liberty or death. But one life was taken, and the whole were emancipated, and the vessel was carried into Nassau, New Providence. Noble men! Those who have fallen in freedom's conflict, their memories will be cherished by the true hearted, and the God-fearing, in all future generations; those who are living, their names are surrounded by a halo of glory.

We do not advise you to attempt a revolution with the sword, because it would be INEXPEDIENT. Your numbers are too small, and moreover the rising spirit of the age, and the spirit of the gospel, are opposed to war and bloodshed. But from this moment cease to labor for tyrants who will not remunerate you. Let every slave throughout the land do this, and the days of slavery are numbered. You cannot be more oppressed than you have been—you cannot suffer greater cruelties than you have already. RATHER DIE FREEMEN, THAN LIVE TO BE SLAVES. Remember that you are THREE MILLIONS.

It is in your power so to torment the God-cursed slaveholders, that they will be glad to let you go free. If the scale was turned and black men were the masters, and white men the slaves, every destructive agent and element would be employed to lay the oppressor low. Danger and death would hang over their heads day and night. Yes, the tyrants would meet with plagues more terrible than those of Pharaoh. But you are a patient people. You act as though you were made for the special use of these devils. You act as though your daughters were born to pamper the lusts of your masters and overseers. And worse than all, you tamely submit, while your lords tear your wives from your embraces, and defile them before your eyes. In the name of God we ask, are you men? Where is the blood of your fathers? Has it all run out of your veins? Awake, awake; millions of voices are calling you! Your dead fathers speak to you from their graves. Heaven, as with a voice of thunder, calls on you to arise from the dust.

Let your motto be RESISTANCE! RESISTANCE! RESISTANCE! No oppressed people have ever secured their Liberty without resistance. What kind of resistance you had better make, you must decide by the circumstances that surround you, and according to the suggestion of expediency. Brethren, adieu. Trust in the living God. Labor for the peace of the human race, and remember that you are three millions.

LIFE IN ASSOCIATION

George Ripley (1802–1890)

Ripley graduated from Harvard and for a period of time served as a Unitarian minister. But like Emerson he became dissatisfied with that calling and also embroiled in controversies over interpreting the Bible and allocating religious authority. He left the ministry, became involved with issues of social justice and economic reform, and began to study the work of the French social theorist Charles Fourier. In 1840, he proposed to the Transcendentalist Club a communal living arrangement and the following year, with his wife Sophia Alden Ripley, founded the Brook Farm Institute of Agriculture and Education, to give it its formal name, of which he remained president until 1847. Brook Farm operated both as a farm and a school, offering regular transportation from and to Boston for those interested in its work or desirous of participating in one of its programs. In 1845, the community formally declared itself a Fourierist Phalanx, that is, an intentional community or "association" established on the principles devised by Fourier. Associationists believed that voluntary communities, organized along cooperative or utopian socialist lines and somewhat removed from the hurly-burly of getting and spending, held the key to social amelioration by modeling an alternative to capitalism and by training a new generation in those alternative economic and social relationships. (See the article by William Henry Channing printed in this volume.)

Hawthorne, who lived at the Farm for a period of time, satirized it in his novel *The Blithedale Romance* (1852) as a hothouse of intrigue and deception. In fact, however, it encouraged playfulness, provided opportunities for aesthetic and other pleasures, and tried to find ways of adapting Fourier's prescription for balancing intellectual and physical work in such a way that no individual would have to perform alienated, disagreeable labor. Though Ripley had tried to recruit Emerson and Thoreau, among others, they remained skeptical of participation in any such contrived community. Nevertheless, Brook Farm flourished reasonably well, and its participants had begun to work through practical ways of applying Fourier's theories when a fire in 1846 destroyed a major new building into which most of the community's resources had been sunk. Ripley was forced to sell his own library to pay debts, and the community never recovered from the impact of those events.

Ripley himself had long sustained literary interests that were able to flourish at the Farm. Before going there, he had, with F. H. Hedge, issued fourteen volumes of translations primarily from European literary sources. After leaving Brook Farm, he reasserted those interests, becoming an influential and well-known literary critic for the *New York Tribune*.

The article that follows, "Life in Association," was published in the *Harbinger* (December 1845–June 1846): 32. The paper was published at New York and Boston by the Brook Farm Phalanx and was seen as the major voice of the Associationist movement. [ED.]

The highest life, of which the nature of man is capable, is rarely witnessed, and then forms a signal exception to the general rule.

It is no wonder that theologians have so generally maintained the doctrine of innate, hereditary depravity. This was the only way, by which they could account for the universal prevalence of limited, distorted, noxious forms of character. The idea, on which their dogma was based, sprung from experience, from observation, from a correct knowledge of human action.

For what is every man soon taught by the intercourse of life? Certainly, the subjection of the world to the dominion of evil. He learns to calculate on selfishness, more or less disguised, on falsehood, however glossed over with the appearance of truth, on fraud, which though in fear of public opinion, is always ready to entrap the heedless.

It is an easy inference, that these monstrous evils are the true growth of human nature, that they belong to man as man, that they will never cease while his passions and propensities remain unchanged. A more profound view, however, shows us that the fault is not in the intrinsic elements of human nature, but in the imperfect institutions under which that nature is trained and developed.

The savage is not guilty of the frightful acts of cruelty, which make our eyes start from their sockets, because there is a necessary tendency to brutal ferocity in human nature, but because all the influences that have acted on him, all the excitements that have been applied to his passions, have been adapted to cherish the warlike spirit, to give him a taste for blood, to make revenge a deep joy to his soul, to convert all the sweet emotions of humanity into the spirit of the tiger and wolf. Place the savage in a different situation; let the first words that fall upon his ear be those of Christian gentleness and peace; let him be surrounded by generous and loving hearts; another spirit will be manifested; and you would almost say that he had been endowed with another nature.

The man who is so devoted to gaining wealth, that he appears on 'Change[1] like a walking money-bag, with no ideas beyond his leger and cash-book, with no hope but that of becoming a millionaire, and no fear but that of being surpassed in property by his more lucky neighbor, was not born to be a muck-worm; if he has not the faculties of an archangel, as some one has said, folded up within his bosom, he has the elements of goodness, disinterestedness, a sincere devotion to the common weal, and under more favorable influences, might have been a worthy, useful, and happy man, instead of being a little above the vilest reptile.

We cannot believe that the selfishness, the cold-heartedness, the indifference to truth, the insane devotion to wealth, the fierce antagonisms, the painted hypocrisies, the inward weariness, discontent, apathy, which are every where characteristic of the present order of society, have any permanent basis in the nature of man; they are the poisonous weeds that a false system of culture has produced; change the system and you will see the riches of the soil; a golden fruitage will rejoice your eye; but persist in the mode, which the experience of a thousand years has proved defective, and you can anticipate no better results. Men do not gather grapes of thorns, nor figs of thistles. But if you would rear the vine, and the fig-tree, so that you may enjoy their products in full luxuriance and beauty, you must not plant them in the hot sand, deprive them of the rain and dew of heaven, expose them to destructive insects, or violent animals; but ascertain the cultivation which is adapted to their nature, and surround them with the influences, which God who made the vine and the fig-tree, made also essential to their perfection.

So with the influences of modern society. They do not give fit nutriment to the noblest forms of character. They do not make man what he is intended to be by the constitution of his nature. They help him not to fulfil the destiny which is assigned to him by the Creator. It is because we are convinced that the Associative Order is the Divine Order, that life in Association is the only true life of the soul, just as harmony with outward na-

[1] That is, the Exchange, a place for trading securities or commodities, as in the New York Stock Exchange. [Ed.]

ture is essential to the true life of the body, that we are unwilling to give sleep to our eyes or slumber to our eyelids till we witness the commencement of the great and solemn work, which is to emancipate man from the terrible scourges of a false order of society, and reinstate him in the glorious life for which a benignant Providence has adapted his nature.

From TO THE ASSOCIATIONISTS OF THE UNITED STATES

William Henry Channing (1810–1884)

Like Emerson and Ripley, Channing was a Harvard graduate and a Unitarian minister. The nephew of Thoreau's friend, Ellery Channing, he moved in Transcendentalist circles, often involving himself in efforts at social or religious reform. One of these was Brook Farm, where he served as the corresponding secretary for the American Union of Associationists, formed on May 27, 1846, right in the middle of Thoreau's sojourn at Walden. For a time he edited the *Harbinger,* the newspaper of the Associationist movement published from Brook Farm. He was also a leader of the efforts at the Farm between 1845 and 1846 to apply Fourier's theories systematically to their lived realities. (See the introduction to the article by George Ripley.) After the community dissolved in 1847 following a disastrous fire and the consequent overwhelming debt, Channing moved to England in the 1850s. He spent much of the remainder of his life as a Unitarian minister.

The article that follows appeared in the *Harbinger* (June–December, 1846): 14–16. [Ed.]

Brethren:

Your prompt and earnest cooperation is requested in fulfilling the design of a Society organized May 27, 1846, at Boston, Mass. by a General Convention of the Friends of Association. This design may be learned from . . . its CONSTITUTION. . . .

The plan is a simple one, and its advantages are obvious. We wish to secure unity, concentration and energy in the efforts of Associationists throughout the country. There are thousands of believers in an Order of Society founded upon the Laws of Divine Wisdom, now scattered abroad, whose zeal and influence are dissipated for want of concert of action. Henceforth let us be united. We have a solemn and glorious work before us—

1. To indoctrinate the whole People of the United States, with the Principles of Associative Unity;
2. To prepare for the time when the Nation like one man shall reorganize its townships upon the basis of perfect Justice.

This work is an arduous one, and will demand of us lives of devoted labor for its accomplishment; prejudices are to be removed—changes wrought in the habits of thinking of all classes—a new spirit of Trust in Providence and of Brotherhood awakened—and a band of high-minded, judicious, and efficient persons enlisted to give their talents and means to the practical application of the sublime truths of Universal Unity. We have no time to lose, no strength to waste. Providence, the Age, and the state of the Nation summon us; and with concert of action, patience and firmness, we cannot fail.

A nobler opportunity was certainly never open to men, than that which here and now welcomes Associationists. To us has been given the very Word—which this PEOPLE needs, as a guide in its onward destiny. This is a *Christian Nation;* and Association shows how human societies may be so organized in devout obedience to the Will of God as to become true Brotherhoods, where the command of universal love may be fulfilled indeed. Thus it meets the present wants of Christians, who, sick of sectarian feuds and theological controversies, shocked at the inconsistencies which disgrace the religious world—at the selfishness, ostentation, and caste, which pervade even our worshipping assemblies—at the indifference of man to the claims of his fellow man, throughout our communities in country and city—at the tolerance of monstrous inhumanities by professed ministers and disciples of Him, whose life was love—are longing for churches which may be really Houses of God, glorified with an indwelling spirit of holiness and filled to overflowing with heavenly charity. This is a *Free Nation,* pledged by the laws transmitted from our ancestors—by the declaration of independence—by the fundamental principles of our constitutions and legislation—to secure the Equal Rights of every citizen; and Association shows, how from the first hour of life to the last, every child, every man and woman may have the just claims of a human being practically ensured—to Education, Labor, Property, Protection, Social Position according to Worth, access to the highest opportunities of Refinement and Culture, Collective Friendship, and participation in the privileges of the Common-Wealth. Thus it meets the present wants of Republicans, who, disgusted at the bitterness and barrenness of party conflicts—at the manoeuvres of demagogues and ambitious politicians—at the perpetual recurrence of the same unsettled questions—at the immense waste of time, talents, conscience, character, resources, in this weary circle of debate—seek for some Organization of Industry, which shall banish drones and spendthrifts—secure actual benefits to all genuine producers—unite Capital and Labor in mutually beneficial cooperation—substitute for the aristocracy of wealth, honor and loyal devotedness—and make fellow-citizens truly members together of one body politic. Finally this nation is all astir with *Humane Reforms*—designed to secure greater fidelity to our acknowledged religious and political principles, and to eradicate forever the inhumanities of Slavery, War, Legalized Murder, Cruelty to Criminals, Intemperance, Licentiousness, Poverty, Popular Ignorance, Commercial Fraud, Universal Competition, which practically give the lie to our professions; and Association demonstrates, that all these philanthropic movements are but parts of one Unitary Reform, whose end is *perfect justice to the whole nature and destiny of Man.* Thus it would link together by mutual respect, all who are touched by the various wants and sufferings of our fellow men, and organize them into a mighty cooperative fraternity, devoted not merely to the alleviation of existing distress, but to the removal of the radical causes of human degradation.

Fellow Associationists! Is it not clear from these obvious, familiar, yet impressive considerations, from this brief review of our position, that we have the honor to be the pioneers in the grand work of Construction, which Providence designs as the special mission of our Age? It is undeniable that we have the means entrusted to our keeping—by a faithful use of which this People may surely become—what God designed us to be—what our fathers prayed and labored to make us—what our wonderful system of Confederacies within Confederacies has prepared the way for—what Christendom longs that we shall not fail of—what Humanity is waiting to welcome, in this fulness of time—a NATION OF UNITED FREEMEN.

And not only does the Associative Movement thus embody the very life of our age and nation, and tend to the perfect fulfilment of the commands of God and the aspirations of Man in our land and generation; but, yet more, it presents the only peaceful mode of removing a principle of evil, which even now is rising in deadly struggle against the united forces of Christianity, Liberty, and Humane Reform—and which threatens to render the efforts of philanthropy futile throughout the civilized world.

This principle is the power of *Combined Capital;* and the end which it seeks, and will inevitably attain, unless speedily checked, is an INDUSTRIAL FEUDALISM.

All observant and thoughtful persons, have been long aware—and the fact has now become apparent to popular intelligence—that the dominion of kings and nobles, the ancient influence of birth and hereditary power, have given way in these times to the mighty and fast growing Aristocracy of Wealth. Unquestionably this tribute of respect to the symbol of Productive Good, which Money is, marks an advanced stage of society, and is far more reasonable and just than the previous grants of privilege to military heroes and to politicians. This prevalence of the Aristocracy of Wealth, does indeed show that men are waking up to the dictates of common sense, and are beginning to labor for that end of universal cultivation, which Providence contemplated, in appointing man to be the sovereign of the earth. But the obvious benefits attending this era of prodigious material production must not blind our judgments to the startling phenomena which are forcing themselves upon the attention of statesmen every where. How is it that amidst innumerable and incessant improvements in agriculture, inventions in mechanics, applications of newly discovered forces of nature to the service of man, intensely stimulated powers of production, accumulating national wealth, and such overflowing abundance that markets sufficient to absorb the surplus are in vain sought—poverty, destitution, crime, popular degeneracy are yet increasing in appalling ratio? How is it that with ever new means of binding nation to nation in fraternal union the earth over, by facilities of locomotion, the transfer of intelligence, freer and more rapid exchanges—fellow citizens in each nation are yet becoming more and more widely separated by the impassable gulf of *condition?* How is it, that, when scientific discoveries have put us in possession of all but omnipotent energies for the multiplying and diffusing of every means of outward enjoyment, with only such an outlay of human strength as would promote health, symmetry and pleasure—the working classes are yet every where more and more broken down by unremitted toil, and prematurely wasted away amidst squalor, want and misery; while in horrible mockery of this wide-spread woe, the wealthy classes are more and more prompted to extravagance, ostentation, capricious folly, enfeebling luxury and disgraceful sloth? No individual perverseness can explain a tendency, which thus sweeps into a social hell, whole classes of all nations—and those the very nations most inspired by Christian Piety and most governed by the principles of Social Justice. An evil thus universal must be traced up to a universally operative cause. The radical cause of these monstrous wrongs is *Antagonistic Interests,* showing itself in an endless variety of forms, among which are isolated property-holding, free competition, commercial duplicity, gambling speculations, monopolies, fictitious fluctuations in interest, and finally combinations of capital, in vast joint-stock operations. It is the last of these which peculiarly characterizes our times; and no observer of society can watch this rapidly developing tendency without alarm.

Possessed of the resources which the past has accumulated, commanding the irresistible and irresponsible power of machinery, holding in its hand the threads of the all embracing, all pervading agency of money, tending by natural causes to a compound ratio of increase, Capital, by a necessity as universal as the force of gravity, seeks alliance with Capital, in a world-embracing selfish union, whose claims are superior to loyalty, patriotism, humanity, and religion. Already this power of *Combined Capital* governs courts, guides armies and navies, makes war and peace, determines the policy of nations, dictates legislation, gives the tone to literature, controls custom, sways the pulpit; even now it is rapidly pressing on to universal sovereignty, and the day is not distant when in all civilized lands, and indeed throughout the earth, wherever the influence of civilization extends, its dynasty will be permanently established, unless while there is yet time, the People of all nations rise to reclaim their rights by peaceful revolution.

Peaceful Revolution—let us emphasize each word; because there is imminent danger, that one of these two events will happen; either (1), that the Productive Classes—feeling themselves entangled in an inextricable web of injustice, conscious that their labor is the source of the very riches, in which they are denied participation, and which flow by them in tantalizing streams, maddened by the constant contrast of their own want, care, toil, with their employer's wealth, leisure, ease—will league together in an outbreak of destructive radicalism, such as earth has never seen; or (2) that, heart-broken, dispirited, and weak in body, having no confidence in themselves or one another, distrusting leaders who have always betrayed them, awed by the superior qualifications of those who hold and enjoy the privileges of life, crowded upon by eager hosts of fellow sufferers, and driven each day and hour by the cutting lash of necessity, they will, with dogged apathy, submit to their fate, and in a voluntary servitude more degrading and brutalizing than savage and barbarous societies have ever witnessed, underbid each other, and sell themselves and families for the poor chance of bread, shelter, and rags. From this horrible destiny which awaits the Working-Man, in his hopeless contrast with Machinery moved by Capital, we say there is no escape except by Peaceful Revolution. Destructive radicalism will but ensure a wider wo; and passive submission will but hasten the fast coming era of the reign of Money over Men.

Now Association presents the very means of this Peaceful Revolution. The one encouraging tendency in existing society which seems to rise up providentially in opposition to the growing dominion of Combined Capital, is that of MUTUAL INSURANCE. This movement is certainly full of promise; and it can scarcely stop until it makes the circuit of all the great interests of life, and invents a system of perfect Mutual Guarantees. Still it is but a step in the right direction. In the first place, it is yet to be seen, what this movement will result in, when it is clearly admitted to be a safe and rapid money-making enterprise, as must soon be the case, and when the business is seized upon, as it then surely will be, by Capital in the hands of unscrupulous gamblers. And secondly, no such system can be complete until it ensures the two fundamental Rights—the Right to Labor, and the Right to Property, which can never be done, so long as land is held in individual proprietorship. Yet we gladly welcome Mutual Insurance as a hopeful sign of Social Regeneration, and as a transitional step towards the grand Constructive Reform of Association; we take up and fulfil this popular movement of the age; we present the very system of perfect Mutual Guarantees, which is needed; and in our doctrine of townships based upon the Principles of Joint-Stock Property and Cooperative Industry we hold out to the capitalist and laborer—in contrast with the infernal horrors of Industrial Feudalism—the Eden-like peace and prosperity of Universal Unity.

Brethren! Can men, engaged in so holy and humane a cause as this—which fulfils the Good and destroys the Evil in existing society, throughout our age and nation—which teaches unlimited trust in Divine Love, and commands perfect obedience to the laws of Divine Order among all people—which heralds the near advent of the reign of Heaven on Earth—be timid, indifferent, sluggish? Abiding shame will rest upon us, if we put not forth our highest energies in fulfilment of the present command of Providence. Let us be up and doing with all our might.

The *measures* which you are now requested, at once and energetically to carry out, are the three following:

1. Organize AFFILIATED SOCIETIES, to act in concert with the *American Union of Associationists;* wherever it is possible and as soon as possible, summon the Friends of Association in your vicinity, and adopt a Constitution harmonizing in its main provisions with the Constitution of the Parent Society; call it by the name of a place or a man, prefixed to the words "Union of Associationists"; enrol a large number of high minded, pure, generous, men and women, and keep careful lists of all favorable to the cause; prepare to hold regular meetings, weekly, monthly, quarterly, annual, as may be most expedient, and to discuss privately and publicly the great principles of Associative Unity; correspond with the Parent Society,

and give records of progress; and finally, make arrangements to send a delegation of persons wise in counsel and decided in action, to the next Annual Convention of the American Union.

2. *Circulate* the HARBINGER, and other papers devoted to Association—procure for them *subscribers*—and obtain *insertions of articles and extracts* from them in the most influential presses. The Harbinger is especially commended to your care. The expenses of this paper have been cheerfully borne by the Brook Farm Phalanx—whose best thoughts have been also given gratuitously to its pages—until their late losses. But now it has become impossible for them to prolong its publication, unless by an increase of its subscription list its cost shall be fully covered. *This paper must not be discontinued.* Its loss would be a most disastrous hindrance to the progress of our cause. More fully than ever, will it present, by means of translations and original articles, the most mature views of Associationists in Europe and this country. Let this year witness its subscription list at least doubled. Let each society take several copies—one to be bound as a nucleus for a "Union" Library—others to be placed, also bound, in Public, College, and School Libraries. Obtain from liberal friends contributions. By universal consent the Harbinger merits efficient encouragement, and extensive circulation. See to it, Friends! that its influence be increased and its permanent establishment ensured.

3. *Collect Funds,* for the purpose of defraying the expenses of *Lectures and Tracts.* It is proposed in the autumn and winter to send out lecturers, in bands and singly, as widely as possible. In proportion to the means, can be the extent and duration of this effort. Henceforth let a system of lecturing be steadily pursued; in this way only can the people be aroused to the importance of the Unitary Reform, to which we are devoted. *It is desirable to form a permanent fund, the income of which shall be consecrated for a series of years to this object.* Take measures then straightway for raising an immediate and a permanent fund; and give the Parent Society the earliest information of the sum which you can appropriate to the winter's campaign. It is desirable also to issue at once a series of cheap popular *Tracts on the Principles and Practical details of Association.* How much can you this year and each year contribute for this important end. Be in earnest Friends. Let us work while it is day.

Our White Flag is given to the breeze. Our three-fold motto,

Unity of *Man with Man* in true Society:

Unity of MAN WITH GOD in true Religion:

Unity of Man with Nature in creative Art and Industry:

Is blazoned on its folds. Let hearts, strong in the might of Faith and Hope and Charity, rally to bear it on in triumph. We are sure to conquer.

God will work with us; Humanity will welcome our word of Glad Tidings. The Future is Ours. On! in the Name of the Lord.

William Henry Channing,
Domestic-Corresponding
Secretary of the American
Union of Associationists
Brook Farm, West Roxbury,
June 6th, 1846

TRANSCENDENTAL WILD OATS

A Chapter from an Unwritten Romance

Louisa May Alcott (1832–1888)

Alcott was eleven when her father, Bronson Alcott, took the family off to his experiment in communal living, Fruitlands. The memories of that ill-fated enterprise remained fresh for her, if not always some of the details. It was one among a number of parental experiments that sustained family poverty and pushed Louisa to work as a domestic, seamstress, and teacher to help support her parents and sisters. On the other hand, her father's relationships with people like Emerson, Thoreau, and Elizabeth Peabody enabled young Louisa to relate to them as teachers and mentors. She had begun to write with serious intent by age seventeen, published her first book at twenty-two, and by the end of the decade of the 1860s regularly placed her stories and poems in the prestigious *Atlantic Monthly.* The letters she wrote to her family during the period in which she served as a Civil War nurse were published under the title *Hospital Sketches* (1863), and a novel loosely based on her own employment history, *Work,* came out in 1873. Her most famous book, *Little Women* (1868–69), was enormously popular from the moment of its appearance and, with sequels such as *Little Men,* brought the author both fame and, after years of struggle, a very substantial income. She also wrote a series of short thrillers under pseudonyms, many of them concerned with women trapped into situations they could not, at least in the beginning, control.

"Transcendental Wild Oats" was written in 1873. It was collected in a volume entitled *Bronson Alcott's Fruitlands* (Boston: Houghton, 1915), compiled by Clara Endicott Sears and later republished with a preface by the director of the Fruitlands Museum (Philadelphia: Porcupine, 1975). [ED.]

ORIGINALS OF THE CHARACTERS IN "TRANSCENDENTAL WILD OATS"

TIMON LION .... *Charles Lane*
HIS SON .... *William Lane*
ABEL LAMB .... *A. Bronson Alcott*
SISTER HOPE .... *Mrs. Alcott*
HER DAUGHTERS .... *The Alcott girls*
JOHN PEASE .... *Samuel Bower*
FOREST ABSALOM .... *Abram Everett*
MOSES WHITE .... *Joseph Palmer*
JANE GAGE .... *Anna Page*

On the first day of June, 184–, a large wagon, drawn by a small horse and containing a motley load, went lumbering over certain New England hills, with the pleasing accompaniments of wind, rain, and hail. A serene man with a serene child upon his knee was driving, or rather being driven, for the small horse had it all his own way. A brown boy with a William Penn style of countenance sat beside him, firmly embracing a bust of Socrates. Behind them was an energetic-looking woman, with a benevolent brow, satirical mouth, and eyes brimful of hope and courage. A baby reposed upon her lap, a mirror leaned against her knee, and a basket of provisions danced about at her feet, as she struggled with a large, unruly umbrella. Two blue-eyed little girls, with hands full of childish treasures, sat under one old shawl, chatting happily together.

In front of this lively party stalked a tall, sharp-featured man, in a long blue cloak; and a fourth small girl trudged along beside him through the mud as if she rather enjoyed it.

The wind whistled over the bleak hills; the rain fell in a despondent drizzle, and twilight began to fall. But the calm man gazed as tranquilly into the fog as if he beheld a radiant bow of promise spanning the gray sky. The cheery woman tried to cover every one but herself with the big umbrella. The brown boy pillowed his head on the bald pate of Socrates and slumbered peacefully. The little girls sang lullabies to their dolls in soft, maternal murmurs. The sharp-nosed pedestrian marched steadily on, with the blue cloak streaming out behind him like a banner; and the lively infant splashed through the puddles with a duck-like satisfaction pleasant to behold.

Thus these modern pilgrims journeyed hopefully out of the old world, to found a new one in the wilderness.

The editors of *The Transcendental Tripod* had received from Messrs. Lion & Lamb (two of the aforesaid pilgrims) a communication from which the following statement is an extract—

"We have made arrangements with the proprietor of an estate of about a hundred acres which liberates this tract from human ownership. Here we shall prosecute our effort to initiate a Family in harmony with the primitive instincts of man.

"Ordinary secular farming is not our object. Fruit, grain, pulse, herbs, flax, and other vegetable products, receiving assiduous attention, will afford ample manual occupation, and chaste supplies for the bodily needs. It is intended to adorn the pastures with orchards, and to supersede the labor of cattle by the spade and the pruning-knife.

"Consecrated to human freedom, the land awaits the sober culture of devoted men. Beginning with small pecuniary means, this enterprise must be rooted in a reliance on the succors of an ever-bounteous Providence, whose vital affinities being secured by this union with uncorrupted field and unworldly persons, the cares and injuries of a life of gain are avoided.

"The inner nature of each member of the Family is at no time neglected. Our plan contemplates all such disciplines, cultures, and habits as evidently conduce to the purifying of the inmates.

"Pledged to the spirit alone, the founders anticipate no hasty or numerous addition to their numbers. The kingdom of peace is entered only through the gates of self-denial; and felicity is the test and the reward of loyalty to the unswerving law of Love."

This prospective Eden at present consisted of an old red farm-house, a dilapidated barn, many acres of meadow-land, and a grove. Ten ancient apple-trees were all the "chaste supply" which the place offered as yet; but, in the firm belief that planteous orchards were soon to be evoked from their inner consciousness, these sanguine founders had christened their domain Fruitlands.

Here Timon Lion intended to found a colony of Latter Day Saints, who, under his patriarchal sway, should regenerate the world and glorify his name for ever. Here Abel Lamb, with the devoutest faith in the high ideal which was to him a living truth, desired to plant a Paradise, where Beauty, Virtue, Justice, and Love might live happily together, without the possibility of a serpent entering in. And here his wife, unconverted but faithful to the end, hoped, after many wanderings over the face of the earth, to find rest for herself and a home for her children.

"There is our new abode," announced the enthusiast, smiling with a satisfaction quite undamped by the drops dripping from his hat-brim, as they turned at length into a cart-path that wound along a steep hillside into a barren-looking valley.

"A little difficult of access," observed his practical wife, as she endeavored to keep her various household gods from going overboard with every lurch of the laden ark.

"Like all good things. But those who earnestly desire and patiently seek will soon find us," placidly responded the philosopher from the mud, through which he was now endeavoring to pilot the much-enduring horse.

"Truth lies at the bottom of a well, Sister Hope," said Brother Timon, pausing to detach his small comrade from a gate, whereon she was perched for a clearer gaze into futurity.

"That's the reason we so seldom get at it, I suppose," replied Mrs. Hope, making a vain clutch at the mirror, which a sudden jolt sent flying out of her hands.

"We want no false reflections here," said Timon, with a grim smile, as he crunched the fragments under foot in his onward march.

Sister Hope held her peace, and looked wistfully through the mist at her promised home. The old red house with a hospitable glimmer at its windows cheered her eyes; and, considering the weather, was a fitter refuge than the sylvan bowers some of the more ardent souls might have preferred.

The new-comers were welcomed by one of the elect precious—a regenerate farmer, whose idea of reform consisted chiefly in wearing white cotton raiment and shoes of untanned leather. This costume, with a snowy beard, gave him a venerable, and at the same time a somewhat bridal appearance.

The goods and chattels of the Society not having arrived, the weary family reposed before the fire on blocks of wood, while Brother Moses White regaled them with roasted potatoes, brown bread and water, in two plates, a tin pan, and one mug; his table service being limited. But, having cast the forms and vanities of a depraved world behind them, the elders welcomed hardship with the enthusiasm of new pioneers, and the children heartily enjoyed this foretaste of what they believed was to be a sort of perpetual picnic.

During the progress of this frugal meal, two more brothers appeared. One a dark, melancholy man, clad in homespun, whose peculiar mission was to turn his name hind part before and use as few words as possible. The other was a bland, bearded Englishman, who expected to be saved by eating uncooked food and going without clothes. He had not yet adopted the primitive costume, however; but contented himself with meditatively chewing dry beans out of a basket.

"Every meal should be a sacrament, and the vessels used should be beautiful and symbolical," observed Brother Lamb, mildly, righting the tin pan slipping about on his knees. "I priced a silver service when in town, but it was too costly; so I got some graceful cups and vases of Britannia ware."

"Hardest things in the world to keep bright. Will whiting be allowed in the community?" inquired Sister Hope, with a housewife's interest in labor-saving institutions.

"Such trivial questions will be discussed at a more fitting time," answered Brother Timon, sharply, as he burnt his fingers with a very hot potato. "Neither sugar, molasses, milk, butter, cheese, nor flesh are to be used among us, for nothing is to be admitted which has caused wrong or death to man or beast."

"Our garments are to be linen till we learn to raise our own cotton or some substitute for woollen fabrics," added Brother Abel, blissfully basking in an imaginary future as warm and brilliant as the generous fire before him.

"Haou abaout shoes?" asked Brother Moses, surveying his own with interest.

"We must yield that point till we can manufacture an innocent substitute for leather. Bark, wood, or some durable fabric will be invented in time. Meanwhile, those who desire to carry out our idea to the fullest extent can go barefooted," said Lion, who liked extreme measures.

"I never will, nor let my girls," murmured rebellious Sister Hope, under her breath.

"Haou do you cattle'ate to treat the ten-acre lot? Ef things ain't 'tended to right smart, we shan't hev no crops," observed the practical patriarch in cotton.

"We shall spade it," replied Abel, in such perfect good faith that Moses said no more, though he indulged in a shake of the head as he glanced at hands that had held nothing heavier than a pen for years. He was a paternal old soul and regarded the younger men as promising boys on a new sort of lark.

"What shall we do for lamps, if we cannot use any animal substance? I do hope light of some sort is to be thrown upon the enterprise," said Mrs. Lamb, with anxiety, for in those days kerosene and camphene were not, and gas unknown in the wilderness.

"We shall go without till we have discovered some vegetable oil or wax to serve us," replied Brother Timon, in a decided tone, which caused

Sister Hope to resolve that her private lamp should be always trimmed, if not burning.

"Each member is to perform the work for which experience, strength, and taste best fit him," continued Dictator Lion. "Thus drudgery and disorder will be avoided and harmony prevail. We shall rise at dawn, begin the day by bathing, followed by music, and then a chaste repast of fruit and bread. Each one finds congenial occupation till the meridian meal; when some deep-searching conversation gives rest to the body and development to the mind. Healthful labor again engages us till the last meal, when we assemble in social communion, prolonged till sunset, when we retire to sweet repose, ready for the next day's activity."

"What part of the work do you incline to yourself?" asked Sister Hope, with a humorous glimmer in her keen eyes.

"I shall wait till it is made clear to me. Being in preference to doing is the great aim, and this comes to us rather by a resigned willingness than a wilful activity, which is a check to all divine growth," responded Brother Timon.

"I thought so." And Mrs. Lamb sighed audibly, for during the year he had spent in her family Brother Timon had so faithfully carried out his idea of "being, not doing," that she had found his "divine growth" both an expensive and unsatisfactory process.

Here her husband struck into the conversation, his face shining with the light and joy of the splendid dreams and high ideals hovering before him.

"In these steps of reform, we do not rely so much on scientific reasoning or physiological skill as on the spirit's dictates. The greater part of man's duty consists in leaving alone much that he now does. Shall I stimulate with tea, coffee, or wine? No. Shall I consume flesh? Not if I value health. Shall I subjugate cattle? Shall I claim property in any created thing? Shall I trade? Shall I adopt a form of religion? Shall I interest myself in politics? To how many of these questions—could we ask them deeply enough and could they be heard as having relation to our eternal welfare—would the response be 'Abstain'?"

A mild snore seemed to echo the last word of Abel's rhapsody, for Brother Moses had succumbed to mundane slumber and sat nodding like a massive ghost. Forest Absalom, the silent man, and John Pease, the English member, now departed to the barn; and Mrs. Lamb led her flock to a temporary fold, leaving the founders of the "Consociate Family" to build castles in the air till the fire went out and the symposium ended in smoke.

The furniture arrived next day, and was soon bestowed; for the principle property of the community consisted in books. To this rare library was devoted the best room in the house, and the few busts and pictures that still survived many flittings were added to beautify the sanctuary, for here the family was to meet for amusement, instruction, and worship.

Any housewife can imagine the emotions of Sister Hope, when she took possession of a large, dilapidated kitchen, containing an old stove and the peculiar stores out of which food was to be evolved for her little family of eleven. Cakes of maple sugar, dried peas and beans, barley and hominy, meal of all sorts, potatoes, and dried fruit. No milk, butter, cheese, tea, or meat appeared. Even salt was considered a useless luxury and spice entirely forbidden by these lovers of Spartan simplicity. A ten years' experience of vegetarian vagaries had been good training for this new freak, and her sense of the ludicrous supported her through many trying scenes.

Unleavened bread, porridge, and water for breakfast; bread, vegetables, and water for dinner; bread, fruit, and water for supper was the bill of fare ordained by the elders. No teapot profaned that sacred stove, no gory steak cried aloud for vengeance from her chaste gridiron; and only a brave woman's taste, time, and temper were sacrificed on that domestic altar.

The vexed question of light was settled by buying a quantity of bayberry wax for candles; and, on discovering that no one knew how to make them, pine knots were introduced, to be used when absolutely necessary. Being summer, the evenings were not long, and the weary fraternity found it no great hardship to retire with the birds. The inner light was sufficient for most of them. But Mrs. Lamb rebelled. Evening was the only time she had to herself, and while the tired feet rested the skilful hands mended torn frocks and little stockings, or anxious heart forgot its burden in a book.

So "mother's lamp" burned steadily, while the philosophers built a new heaven and earth by moonlight; and through all the metaphysical mists and philanthropic pyrotechnics of that period Sister Hope played her own little game of "throwing light," and none but the moths were the worse for it.

Such farming probably was never seen before since Adam delved. The band of brothers began by spading garden and field; but a few days of it lessened their ardor amazingly. Blistered hands and aching backs suggested the expediency of permitting the use of cattle till the workers were better fitted for noble toil by a summer of the new life.

Brother Moses brought a yoke of oxen from his farm—at least, the philosophers thought so till it was discovered that one of the animals was a cow; and Moses confessed that he "must be let down easy, for he could n't live on garden sarse entirely."

Great was Dictator Lion's indignation at this lapse from virtue. But time pressed, the work must be done; so the meek cow was permitted to wear the yoke and the recreant brother continued to enjoy forbidden draughts in the barn, which dark proceeding caused the children to regard him as one set apart for destruction.

The sowing was equally peculiar, for, owing to some mistake, the three brethren, who devoted themselves to this graceful task, found when about half through the job that each had been sowing a different sort of grain in the same field; a mistake which caused much perplexity, as it could not be remedied; but, after a long consultation and a good deal of laughter, it was decided to say nothing and see what would come of it.

The garden was planted with a generous supply of useful roots and herbs; but, as manure was not allowed to profane the virgin soil, few of these vegetable treasures ever came up. Purslane reigned supreme, and the disappointed planters ate it philosophically, deciding that Nature knew what was best for them, and would generously supply their needs, if they could only learn to digest her "sallets" and wild roots.

The orchard was laid out, a little grafting done, new trees and vines set, regardless of the unfit season and entire ignorance of the husbandmen, who honestly believed that in the autumn they would reap a bounteous harvest.

Slowly things got into order, and rapidly rumors of the new experiment went abroad, causing many strange spirits to flock thither, for in those days communities were the fashion and transcendentalism raged wildly. Some came to look on and laugh, some to be supported in poetic idleness, a few to believe sincerely and work heartily. Each member was allowed to mount his favorite hobby and ride it to his heart's content. Very queer were some of the riders, and very rampant some of the hobbies.

One youth, believing that language was of little consequence if the spirit was only right, startled new-comers by blandly greeting them with "Good-morning, damn you," and other remarks of an equally mixed order. A second irrepressible being held that all the emotions of the soul should be freely expressed, and illustrated his theory by antics that would have sent him to a lunatic asylum, if, as an unregenerate wag said, he had not already been in one. When his spirit soared, he climbed trees and shouted; when doubt assailed him, he lay upon the floor and groaned lamentably. At joyful periods, he raced, leaped, and sang; when sad, he wept aloud; and when a great thought burst upon him in the watches of the night, he crowed like a jocund cockerel, to the great delight of the children and the great annoyance of the elders. One musical brother fiddled whenever so moved, sang sentimentally to the four little girls, and put a music-box on the wall when he hoed corn.

Brother Pease ground away at his uncooked food, or browsed over the farm on sorrel, mint, green fruit, and new vegetables. Occasionally he took his walks abroad, airily attired in an unbleached cotton *poncho,* which was the nearest approach to the primeval costume he was allowed to indulge in. At midsummer he retired to the wilderness, to try his plan where the woodchucks were without prejudices and huckleberry-bushes were hospitably full. A sunstroke unfortunately spoilt his plan, and he returned to semi-civilization a sadder and wiser man.

Forest Absalom preserved his Pythagorean silence, cultivated his fine dark locks, and worked like a beaver, setting an excellent example of brotherly love, justice, and fidelity by his upright life. He it was who helped overworked Sister Hope with her heavy washes, kneaded the endless succession of batches of bread, watched over the children, and did the many tasks left undone by the brethren, who were so busy discussing and defining great duties that they forgot to perform the small ones.

Moses White placidly plodded about, "chorin' raound," as he called it, looking like an old-time patriarch, with his silver hair and flowing beard, and saving the community from many a mishap by his thrift and Yankee shrewdness.

Brother Lion domineered over the whole concern; for, having put the most money into the speculation, he was resolved to make it pay—as if anything founded on an ideal basis could be expected to do so by any but enthusiasts.

Abel Lamb simply revelled in the Newness, firmly believing that his dream was to be beautifully realized and in time not only little Fruitlands, but the whole earth, be turned into a Happy Valley. He worked with every muscle of his body, for *he* was in deadly earnest. He taught with his whole head and heart; planned and sacrificed, preached and prophesied, with a soul full of the purest aspirations, most unselfish purposes, and desires for a life devoted to God and man, too high and tender to bear the rough usage of this world.

It was a little remarkable that only one woman ever joined this community. Mrs. Lamb merely followed wheresoever her husband led—"as ballast for his balloon," as she said, in her bright way.

Miss Jane Gage was a stout lady of mature years, sentimental, amiable, and lazy. She wrote verses copiously, and had vague yearnings and graspings after the unknown, which led her to believe herself fitted for a higher sphere than any she had yet adorned.

Having been a teacher, she was set to instructing the children in the common branches. Each adult member took a turn at the infants; and, as each taught in his own way, the result was a chronic state of chaos in the minds of these much-afflicted innocents.

Sleep, food, and poetic musings were the desires of dear Jane's life, and she shirked all duties as clogs upon her spirit's wings. Any thought of lend-ing a hand with the domestic drudgery never occurred to her; and when to the question, "Are there any beasts of burden on the place?" Mrs. Lamb answered, with a face that told its own tale, "Only one woman!" the buxom Jane took no shame to herself, but laughed at the joke, and let the stout-hearted sister tug on alone.

Unfortunately, the poor lady hankered after the flesh-pots, and endeavored to stay herself with private sips of milk, crackers, and cheese, and on one dire occasion she partook of fish at a neighbor's table.

One of the children reported this sad lapse from virtue, and poor Jane was publicly reprimanded by Timon.

"I only took a little bit of the tail," sobbed the penitent poetess.

"Yes, but the whole fish had to be tortured and slain that you might tempt your carnal appetite with that one taste of the tail. Know ye not, consumers of flesh meat, that ye are nourishing the wolf and tiger in your bosoms?"

At this awful question and the peal of laughter which arose from some of the younger brethren, tickled by the ludicrous contrast between the stout sinner, the stern judge, and the naughty satisfaction of the young detective, poor Jane fled from the room to pack her trunk and return to a world where fishes' tails were not forbidden fruit.

Transcendental wild oats were sown broadcast that year, and the fame thereof has not yet ceased in the land; for, futile as this crop seemed to outsiders, it bore an invisible harvest, worth much to those who planted in earnest. As none of the members of this particular community have ever recounted their experiences before, a few of them may not be amiss, since the interest in these attempts has never died out and Fruitlands was the most ideal of all these castles in Spain.

A new dress was invented, since cotton, silk, and wool were forbidden as the product of slave-labor, worm-slaughter, and sheep-robbery. Tunics and trowsers of brown linen were the only wear. The women's skirts were longer, and their straw hat-brims wider than the men's, and this was the only difference. Some persecution lent a charm to the costume, and the long-haired, linen-clad reformers quite enjoyed the mild martyrdom they endured when they left home.

Money was abjured, as the root of all evil. The produce of the land was to supply most of their wants, or be exchanged for the few things they could not grow. This idea had its inconveniences; but self-denial was the fashion, and it was surprising how many things one can do without. When they desired to travel, they walked, if possible, begged the loan of a vehicle, or boldly entered car or coach, and, stating their principles to the officials, took the consequences. Usually their dress, their earnest frankness, and gentle resolution won them a passage; but now and then they met with hard usage, and had the satisfaction of suffering for their principles.

On one of these penniless pilgrimages they took passage on a boat, and, when fare was demanded, artlessly offered to talk, instead of pay. As the boat was well under way and they actually had not a cent, there was no help for it. So Brothers Lion and Lamb held forth to the assembled passengers in their most eloquent style. There must have been something effective in this conversation, for the listeners were moved to take up a contribution for these inspired lunatics, who preached peace on earth and good-will to man so earnestly, with empty pockets. A goodly sum was collected; but when the captain presented it the reformers proved that they were consistent even in their madness, for not a penny would they accept, saying, with a look at the group about them, whose indifference or contempt had changed to interest and respect, "You see how well we get on without money"; and so went serenely on their way, with their linen blouses flapping airily in the cold October wind.

They preached vegetarianism everywhere and resisted all temptations of the flesh, contentedly eating apples and bread at well-spread tables, and much afflicting hospitable hostesses by denouncing their food and taking away their appetites, discussing the "horrors of shambles," the "incorporation of the brute in man," and "on elegant abstinence the sign of a pure soul." But, when the perplexed or offended ladies asked what they should eat, they got in reply a bill of fare consisting of "bowls of sunrise for breakfast," "solar seeds of the sphere," "dishes from Plutarch's chaste table," and other viands equally hard to find in any modern market.

Reform conventions of all sorts were haunted by these brethren, who said many wise things and did many foolish ones. Unfortunately, these wanderings interfered with their harvest at home; but the rule was to do what the spirit moved, so they left their crops to Providence and went a-reaping in wider and, let us hope, more fruitful fields than their own.

Luckily, the earthly providence who watched over Abel Lamb was at hand to glean the scanty crop yielded by the "uncorrupted land," which, "consecrated to human freedom," had received "the sober culture of devout men."

About the time the grain was ready to house, some call of the Oversoul wafted all the men away. An easterly storm was coming up and the yellow stacks were sure to be ruined. Then Sister Hope gathered her forces. Three little girls, one boy (Timon's son), and herself, harnessed to clothes-baskets and Russia-linen sheets, were the only teams she could command; but with these poor appliances the indomitable woman got in the grain and saved food for her young, with the instinct and energy of a mother-bird with a brood of hungry nestlings to feed.

This attempt at regeneration had its tragic as well as comic side, though the world only saw the former.

With the first frosts, the butterflies, who had sunned themselves in the new light through the summer, took flight, leaving the few bees to see what honey they had stored for winter use. Precious little appeared beyond the satisfaction of a few months of holy living.

At first it seemed as if a chance to try holy dying also was to be offered them. Timon, much disgusted with the failure of the scheme, decided to retire to the Shakers, who seemed to be the only successful community going.

"What is to become of us?" asked Mrs. Hope, for Abel was heart-broken at the bursting of his lovely bubble.

"You can stay here, if you like, till a tenant is found. No more wood must be cut, however, and no more corn ground. All I have must be sold to pay the debts of the concern, as the responsibility rests with me," was the cheering reply.

"Who is to pay us for what we have lost? I gave all I had—furniture, time—strength, six months of my children's lives—and all are wasted. Abel gave himself body and soul, and is almost wrecked by hard work and disappointment. Are we to have no return for this, but leave to starve and freeze in an old house, with winter at hand, no money, and hardly a friend left; for this wild scheme has alienated nearly all we had. You talk much about justice. Let us have a little, since there is nothing else left."

But the woman's appeal met with no reply but the old one: "It was an experiment. We all risked something, and must bear our losses as we can."

With this cold comfort, Timon departed with his son, and was absorbed into the Shaker brotherhood, where he soon found that the order of things was reversed, and it was all work and no play.

Then the tragedy began for the forsaken little family. Desolation and despair fell upon Abel. As his wife said, his new beliefs had alienated many friends. Some thought him mad, some unprincipled. Even the most kindly thought him a visionary, whom it was useless to help till he took more practical views of life. All stood aloof, saying: "Let him work out his own ideas, and see what they are worth."

He had tried, but it was a failure. The world was not ready for Utopia yet, and those who attempted to found it only got laughed at for their pains. In other days, men could sell all and give to the poor, lead lives devoted to holiness and high thought, and, after the persecution was over, find themselves honored as saints or martyrs. But in modern times these things are out of fashion. To live for one's principles, at all costs, is a dangerous speculation; and the failure of an ideal, no matter how humane and noble, is harder for the world to forgive and forget than bank robbery or the grand swindles of corrupt politicians.

Deep waters now for Abel, and for a time there seemed no passage through. Strength and spirits were exhausted by hard work and too much thought. Courage failed when, looking about for help, he saw no sympathizing face, no hand outstretched to help him, no voice to say cheerily,

"We all make mistakes, and it takes many experiences to shape a life. Try again, and let us help you."

Every door was closed, every eye averted, every heart cold, and no way open whereby he might earn bread for his children. His principles would not permit him to do many things that others did; and in the few fields where conscience would allow him to work, who would employ a man who had flown in the face of society, as he had done?

Then this dreamer, whose dream was the life of his life, resolved to carry out his idea to the bitter end. There seemed no place for him here—no work, no friend. To go begging conditions was as ignoble as to go begging money. Better perish of want than sell one's soul for the sustenance of his body. Silently he lay down upon his bed, turned his face to the wall, and waited with pathetic patience for death to cut the knot which he could not untie. Days and nights went by, and neither food nor water passed his lips. Soul and body were dumbly struggling together, and no word of complaint betrayed what either suffered.

His wife, when tears and prayers were unavailing, sat down to wait the end with a mysterious awe and submission; for in this entire resignation of all things there was an eloquent significance to her who knew him as no other human being did.

"Leave all to God," was his belief; and in this crisis the loving soul clung to this faith, sure that the Allwise Father would not desert this child who tried to live so near to Him. Gathering her children about her, she waited the issue of the tragedy that was being enacted in that solitary room, while the first snow fell outside, untrodden by the footprints of a single friend.

But the strong angels who sustain and teach perplexed and troubled souls came and went, leaving no trace without, but working miracles within. For, when all other sentiments had faded into dimness, all other hopes died utterly; when the bitterness of death was nearly over, when body was past any pang of hunger or thirst, and soul stood ready to depart, the love that outlives all else refused to die. Head had bowed to defeat, hand had grown weary with too heavy tasks, but heart could not grow cold to those who lived in its tender depths, even when death touched it.

"My faithful wife, my little girls—they have not forsaken me, they are mine by ties that none can break. What right have I to leave them alone? What right to escape from the burden and the sorrow I have helped to bring? This duty remains to me, and I must do it manfully. For their sakes, the world will forgive me in time; for their sakes, God will sustain me now."

Too feeble to rise, Abel groped for the food that always lay within his reach, and in the darkness and solitude of that memorable night ate and drank what was to him the bread and wine of a new communion, a new dedication of heart and life to the duties that were left him when the dreams fled.

In the early dawn, when that sad wife crept fearfully to see what change had come to the patient face on the pillow, she found it smiling at her, saw a wasted hand outstretched to her, and heard a feeble voice cry bravely, "Hope!"

What passed in that little room is not to be recorded except in the hearts of those who suffered and endured much for love's sake. Enough for us to know that soon the wan shadow of a man came forth, leaning on the arm that never failed him, to be welcomed and cherished by the children, who never forgot the experiences of that time.

"Hope" was the watchword now; and, while the last logs blazed on the hearth, the last bread and apples covered the table, the new commander, with recovered courage, said to her husband—

"Leave all to God—and me. He has done his part, now I will do mine."

"But we have no money, dear."

"Yes, we have. I sold all we could spare, and have enough to take us away from this snowbank."

"Where can we go?"

"I have engaged four rooms at our good neighbor, Lovejoy's. There we can live cheaply till spring. Then for new plans and a home of our own, please God."

"But, Hope, your little store won't last long, and we have no friends."

"I can sew and you can chop wood. Lovejoy offers you the same pay as he gives his other men; my old friend, Mrs. Truman, will send me all the work I want; and my blessed brother stands by us to the end. Cheer up, dear heart, for while there is work and love in the world we shall not suffer."

"And while I have my good angel Hope, I shall not despair, even if I wait another thirty years before I step beyond the circle of the sacred little world in which I still have a place to fill."

So one bleak December day, with their few possessions piled on an ox-sled, the rosy children perched atop, and the parents trudging arm in arm behind, the exiles left their Eden and faced the world again.

"Ah, me! my happy dream. How much I leave behind that never can be mine again," said Abel, looking back at the lost Paradise, lying white and chill in its shroud of snow.

"Yes, dear; but how much we bring away," answered brave-hearted Hope, glancing from husband to children.

"Poor Fruitlands! The name was as great a failure as the rest!" continued Abel, with a sigh, as a frostbitten apple fell from a leafless bough at his feet.

But the sigh changed to a smile as his wife added, in a half-tender, half-satirical tone—

"Don't you think Apple Slump would be a better name for it, dear?"

A CHURCH MOUSE

Mary Wilkins Freeman (1852–1930)

Many of Freeman's characters in the two hundred and more stories she composed are old and seemingly helpless women of rural New England. Like Freeman herself, they were faced with poverty as well as homelessness or the well-intentioned but misdirected "help" of neighbors. They often turn out, however, to be resourceful and active within the limiting circumstances of country and small-town society. They deploy what few resources they have, like Hetty Fifield in "A Church Mouse," to triumph over ostensibly stronger adversaries. Gandhi would later argue that nonviolence was not the weapon of the weak, but in this story a form of nonviolent direct action along with a sharp tongue provides Hetty with what little power she can muster to retain her place at the thin edge of village life.

Freeman's own early life reflected the threat of poverty and movement from place to place that are Hetty's lot. Freeman was forced by adverse family circumstances to go into domestic service at age twenty-five. Four years later, however, she was able to sell her first piece of writing, and soon thereafter she was regularly placing fiction, juveniles, and essays in major newspapers and magazines in the United States. In all she would publish fifteen volumes of stories, fourteen novels, three plays, three collections of poetry, and eight books for children. Her work, which had seemed old-fashioned to modernists of the 1920s, came back into prominence with the advent of the feminist movement of the 1960s and 1970s.

"A Church Mouse" constituted part of the 1891 volume *A New England Nun and Other Stories* (New York: Harper), from which the text is derived. [ED.]

"I never heard of a woman's bein' saxton."

"I dun' know what difference that makes; I don't see why they shouldn't have women saxtons as well as men saxtons, for my part, nor nobody else neither. They'd keep dusted 'nough sight cleaner. I've seen the dust layin' on my pew thick enough to write my name in a good many times, an' ain't said nothin' about it. An' I ain't goin' to say nothin' now again Joe Sowen, now he's dead an' gone. He did jest as well as most men do. Men git in a good many places where they don't belong, an' where they set as awkward as a cow on a hen-roost, jest because they push in ahead of women. I ain't blamin 'em' I s'pose if I could push in I should, jest the same way. But there ain't no reason that I can see, nor nobody else neither, why a woman shouldn't be saxton."

Hetty Fifield stood in the rowen hay-field before Caleb Gale. He was a deacon, the chairman of the selectmen, and the rich and influential man of the village. One looking at him would not have guessed it. There was nothing imposing about his lumbering figure in his calico shirt and baggy trousers. However, his large face, red and moist with perspiration, scanned the distant horizon with a stiff and reserved air; he did not look at Hetty.

"How'd you go to work to ring the bell?" said he. "It would have to be tolled, too, if anybody died."

"I'd jest as lief ring that little meetin'-house bell as to stan' out here an' jingle a cow-bell," said Hetty; "an' as for tollin', I'd jest as soon toll the bell for Methusaleh,[1] if he was livin' here! I'd laugh if I ain't got strength 'nough for that."

"It takes a kind of a knack."

"If I ain't got as much knack as old Joe Sowen ever had, I'll give up the ship."

"You couldn't tend the fires."

---

[1] Biblical patriarch supposed to have lived 969 years: Gen. 5.27. [ED.]

"Couldn't tend the fires—when I've cut an' carried in all the wood I've burned for forty year! Couldn't keep the fires a-goin' in them two little wood-stoves!"

"It's consider'ble work to sweep the meetin'-house."

"I guess I've done 'bout as much work as to sweep that little meetin'-house, I ruther guess I have."

"There's one thing you ain't thought of."

"What's that?"

"Where'd you live? All old Sowen got for bein' saxton was twenty dollar a year an' we couldn't pay a woman so much as that. You couldn't have enough to pay for your livin' anywheres."

"Where am I goin' to live whether I'm saxton or not?"

Caleb Gale was silent.

There was a wind blowing, the rowen hay drifted round Hetty like a brown-green sea touched with ripples of blue and gold by the asters and golden-rod. She stood in the midst of it like a May-weed that had gathered a slender toughness through the long summer; her brown cotton gown clung about her like a wilting leaf, outlining her harsh little form. She was as sallow as a squaw, and she had pretty black eyes; they were bright, although she was old. She kept them fixed upon Caleb. Suddenly she raised herself upon her toes; the wind caught her dress and made it blow out; her eyes flashed. "I tell you where I'm goin' to live," said she. *"I'm goin' to live in the meetin'-house."*

Caleb looked at her. *"Goin' to live in the meetin'-house!"*

"Yes, I be."

"Live in the meetin'-house!"

"I'd like to know why not."

"Why—you couldn't—live in the meetin'-house. You're crazy."

Caleb flung out the rake which he was holding, and drew it in full of rowen. Hetty moved around in front of him, he raked imperturbably; she moved again right in the path of the rake, then he stopped. "There ain't no sense in such talk."

"All I want is jest the east corner of the back gall'ry, where the chimbly goes up. I'll set up my cookin'-stove there, an' my bed, an' I'll curtain it off with my sunflower quilt, to keep off the wind."

"A cookin'-stove an' a bed in the meetin'-house!"

"Mis' Grout she give me that cookin'-stove, an' that bed I've allers slept on, before she died. She give 'em to me before Mary Anne Thomas, an' I moved 'em out. They air settin' out in the yard now, an' if it rains that stove an' that bed will be spoilt. It looks some like rain now. I guess you'd better give me the meetin'-house key right off."

"You don't think you can move that cookin'-stove an' that bed into the meetin'-house—I ain't goin' to stop to hear such talk."

"My worsted-work, all my mottoes I've done, an' my wool flowers, air out there in the yard."

Caleb raked. Hetty kept standing herself about until he was forced to stop, or gather her in with the rowen hay. He looked straight at her, and scowled; the perspiration trickled down his cheeks. "If I go up to the house can Mis' Gale git me the key to the meetin'-house?" said Hetty.

"No, she can't."

"Be you goin' up before long?"

"No, I ain't." Suddenly Caleb's voice changed: it had been full of stubborn vexation, now it was blandly argumentative. "Don't you see it ain't no use talkin' such nonsense, Hetty? You'd better go right along, an' make up your mind it ain't to be thought of."

"Where be I goin' to-night, then?"

"To-night?"

"Yes; where be I a-goin'?"

"Ain't you got any place to go to?"

"Where do you s'pose I've got any place? Them folks air movin' into Mis' Grout's house, an' they as good as told me to clear out. I ain't got no folks to take me in. I dun' know where I'm goin'; mebbe I can go to your house?"

Caleb gave a start. "We've got company to home," said he, hastily. "I'm 'fraid Mis' Gale wouldn't think it was convenient."

Hetty laughed. "Most everybody in the town has got company," said she.

Caleb dug his rake into the ground as if it were a hoe, then he leaned on it, and stared at the horizon. There was a fringe of yellow birches on the edge of the hayfield; beyond them was a low range of misty blue hills. "You ain't got no place to go to, then?"

"I dun' know of any. There ain't no poor-house here, an' I ain't got no folks."

Caleb stood like a statue. Some crows flew cawing over the field. Hetty waited. "I s'pose that key is where Mis' Gale can find it?" she said, finally.

Caleb turned and threw out his rake with a jerk. "She knows where 'tis; it's hangin' up behind the settin'-room door. I s'pose you can stay there to-night, as long as you ain't got no other place. We shall have to see what can be done."

Hetty scuttled off across the field. "You mustn't take no stove nor bed into the meetin'-house," Caleb called after her, "we can't have that, nohow."

Hetty went on as if she did not hear.

The golden-rod at the sides of the road was turning brown; the asters were in their prime, blue and white ones; here and there were rows of thistles with white tops. The dust was thick; Hetty, when she emerged from Caleb's house, trotted along in a cloud of it. She did not look to the right or left, she kept her small eager face fixed straight ahead, and moved forward like some little animal with the purpose to which it was born strong within it.

Presently she came to a large cottage-house on the right of the road; there she stopped. The front yard was full of furniture, tables and chairs standing among the dahlias and clumps of marigolds. Hetty leaned over the fence at one corner of the yard, and inspected a little knot of household goods set aside from the others. There was a small cooking-stove, a hair trunk, a yellow bedstead stacked up against the fence, and a pile of bedding. Some children in the yard stood in a group and eyed Hetty. A woman appeared in the door—she was small, there was a black smutch on her face, which was haggard with fatigue, and she scowled in the sun as she looked over at Hetty. "Well, got a place to stay in?" said she, in an unexpectedly deep voice.

"Yes, I guess so," replied Hetty.

"I dun' know how in the world I can have you. All the beds will be full—I expect his mother some to-night, an' I'm dreadful stirred up anyhow."

"Everybody's havin' company; I never see anything like it." Hetty's voice was inscrutable. The other woman looked sharply at her.

"You've got a place, ain't you?" she asked, doubtfully.

"Yes, I have."

At the left of this house, quite back from the road, was a little unpainted cottage, hardly more than a hut. There was smoke coming out of the chimney, and a tall youth lounged in the door. Hetty, with the woman and children staring after her, struck out across the field in the little foot-path towards the cottage. "I wonder if she's goin' to stay there?" the woman muttered, meditating.

The youth did not see Hetty until she was quite near him, then he aroused suddenly as if from sleep, and tried to slink off around the cottage. But Hetty called after him. "Sammy," she cried, "Sammy, come back here, I want you!"

"What d'ye want?"

"Come back here!"

The youth lounged back sulkily, and a tall woman came to the door. She bent out of it anxiously to hear Hetty.

"I want you to come an' help me move my stove an' things," said Hetty.

"Where to?"

"Into the meetin'-house."

"The meetin'-house."

"Yes, the meetin'-house."

The woman in the door had sodden hands; behind her arose the steam of a wash-tub. She and the youth stared at Hetty, but surprise was too strong an emotion for them to grasp firmly.

"I want Sammy to come right over an' help me," said Hetty.

"He ain't strong enough to move a stove," said the woman.

"Ain't strong enough!"

"He's apt to git lame."

"Most folks are. Guess I've got lame. Come right along, Sammy!"

"He ain't able to lift much."

"I s'pose he's able to be lifted, ain't he?"

"I dun' know what you mean."

"The stove don't weigh nothin'," said Hetty; "I could carry it myself if I could git hold of it. Come, Sammy!"

Hetty turned down the path, and the youth moved a little way after her, as if perforce. Then he stopped, and cast an appealing glance back at his mother. Her face was distressed. "Oh, Sammy, I'm afraid you'll git sick," said she.

"No, he ain't goin' to get sick," said Hetty. "Come, Sammy." And Sammy followed her down the path.

It was four o'clock then. At dusk Hetty had her gay sunflower quilt curtaining off the chimney-corner of the church gallery; her stove and little bedstead were set up, and she had entered upon a life which endured successfully for three months. All that time a storm brewed; then it broke, but Hetty sailed in her own course for the three months.

It was on a Saturday that she took up her habitation in the meeting-house. The next morning, when the boy who had been supplying the dead sexton's place came and shook the door, Hetty was prompt on the other side. "Deacon Gale said for you to let me in so I could ring the bell," called the boy.

"Go away," responded Hetty. "I'm goin' to ring the bell; I'm saxton."

Hetty rang the bell with vigor, but she made a wild, irregular jangle at first; at the last it was better. The village people said to each other that a new hand was ringing. Only a few knew that Hetty was in the meeting-house. When the congregation had assembled, and saw that gaudy tent pitched in the house of the Lord, and the resolute little pilgrim at the door of it, there was a commotion. The farmers and their wives were stirred out of their Sabbath decorum. After the service was over, Hetty, sitting in a pew corner of the gallery, her little face dark and watchful against the flaming background of her quilt, saw the people below gathering in groups, whispering, and looking at her.

Presently the minister, Caleb Gale, and the other deacon came up the gallery stairs. Hetty sat stiffly erect. Caleb Gale went up to the sunflower quilt, slipped it aside, and looked in. He turned to Hetty with a frown. To-day his dignity was supported by important witnesses. "Did you bring that stove an' bedstead here?"

Hetty nodded.

"What made you do such a thing?"

"What was I goin' to do if I didn't? How's a woman as old as me goin' to sleep in a pew, an' go without a cup of tea?"

The men looked at each other. They withdrew to another corner of the gallery and conferred in low tones; then they went down-stairs and out of the church. Hetty smiled when she heard the door shut. When one is hard pressed, one, however simple, gets wisdom as to vantage-points. Hetty comprehended hers perfectly. She was the propounder of a problem; as long as it was unguessed, she was sure of her foothold as propounder. This little village in which she had lived all her life had removed the shelter from her head; she being penniless, it was beholden to provide her another; she asked it what. When the old woman with whom she had lived died, the town promptly seized the estate for taxes—none had been paid for years. Hetty had not laid up a cent; indeed, for the most of the time she had received no wages. There had been no money in the house; all she had gotten for her labor for a sickly, impecunious old woman was a frugal board. When the old woman died, Hetty gathered in the few household articles for which she had stipulated, and made no complaint. She walked out of the house when the new tenants came in; all she asked was, "What are you going to do with me?" This little settlement of narrow-minded, prosperous farmers, however hard a task charity might be to them, could not turn an old woman out into the fields and highways to seek for food as they would a Jersey cow. They had their Puritan consciences, and her note of distress would sound louder in their ears than the Jersey's bell echoing down the valley in the stillest night. But the question as to Hetty Fifield's disposal was a hard one to answer. There was no almshouse in the village, and no private family was willing to take her in. Hetty was strong and capable; although she was old, she could well have paid for her food and shelter by her labor; but this could not secure her an entrance even among this hard-working and thrifty people, who would ordinarily grasp quickly enough at service without wage in dollars and cents. Hetty had somehow gotten for herself an unfortunate name in the village. She was held in the light of a long-thorned brier among the beanpoles, or a fierce little animal with claws and teeth bared. People were afraid to take her into their families; she had the reputation of always taking her own way, and never heeding the voice of authority. "I'd take her in an' have her give me a lift with the work," said one sickly farmer's wife; "but near's I can find out, I couldn't never be sure that I'd get molasses in the beans, nor saleratus[2] in my sour-milk cakes, if she took a notion not to put it in. I don't dare to risk it."

Stories were about concerning Hetty's authority over the old woman with whom she had lived. "Old Mis' Grout never dared to say her soul was her own," people said. Then Hetty's sharp, sarcastic sayings were repeated; the justice of them made them sting. People did not want a tongue like that in their homes.

Hetty as a church sexton was directly opposed to all their ideas of church decorum and propriety in general; her pitching her tent in the Lord's house was almost sacrilege; but what could they do? Hetty jangled the Sabbath bells for the three months; once she tolled the bell for an old man, and it seemed by the sound of the bell as if his long, calm years had swung by in a weak delirium; but people bore it. She swept and dusted the little meeting-house, and she garnished the walls with her treasures of worsted-work. The neatness and the garniture went far to quiet the dissatisfaction of the people. They had a crude taste. Hetty's skill in fancy-work was quite celebrated. Her wool flowers were much talked of, and young girls tried to copy them. So these wreaths and clusters of red and blue and yellow wool roses and lilies hung as acceptably between the meeting-house windows as pictures of saints in a cathedral.

Hetty hung a worsted motto over the pulpit; on it she set her chiefest treasure of art, a white wax cross with an ivy vine trailing over it, all covered with silver frostwork. Hetty always surveyed this cross with a species of awe; she felt the irresponsibility and amazement of a genius at his own work.

When she set it on the pulpit, no queen casting her rich robes and her jewels upon a shrine could have surpassed her in generous enthusiasm. "I guess when they see that they won't say no more," she said.

But the people, although they shared Hetty's admiration for the cross, were doubtful. They, looking at it, had a double vision of a little wax Virgin upon an altar. They wondered if it savored of popery. But the cross remained, and the minister was mindful not to jostle it in his gestures.

---

[2] Baking soda. [Ed.]

It was three months from the time Hetty took up her abode in the church, and a week before Christmas, when the problem was solved. Hetty herself precipitated the solution. She prepared a boiled dish in the meeting-house, upon a Saturday, and the next day the odors of turnip and cabbage were strong in the senses of the worshippers. They sniffed and looked at one another. This superseding the legitimate savor of the sanctuary, the fragrance of peppermint lozenges and wintergreen, the breath of Sunday clothes, by the homely week-day odors of kitchen vegetables, was too much for the sensibilities of the people. They looked indignantly around at Hetty, sitting before her sunflower hanging, comfortable from her good dinner of the day before, radiant with the consciousness of a great plateful of cold vegetables in her tent for her Sabbath dinner.

Poor Hetty had not many comfortable dinners. The selectmen doled out a small weekly sum to her, which she took with dignity as being her hire; then she had a mild forage in the neighbors' cellars and kitchens, of poor apples and stale bread and pie, paying for it in teaching her art of worsted-work to the daughters. Her Saturday's dinner had been a banquet to her: she had actually bought a piece of pork to boil with the vegetables; somebody had given her a nice little cabbage and some turnips, without a thought of the limitations of her housekeeping. Hetty herself had not a thought. She made the fires as usual that Sunday morning; the meeting-house was very clean, there was not a speck of dust anywhere, the wax cross on the pulpit glistened in a sunbeam slanting through the house. Hetty, sitting in the gallery, thought innocently how nice it looked.

After the meeting, Caleb Gale approached the other deacon. "Somethin's got to be done," said he. And the other deacon nodded. He had not smelt the cabbage until his wife nudged him and mentioned it; neither had Caleb Gale.

In the afternoon of the next Thursday, Caleb and the other two selectmen waited upon Hetty in her tabernacle. They stumped up the gallery stairs, and Hetty emerged from behind the quilt and stood looking at them scared and defiant. The three men nodded stiffly; there was a pause; Caleb Gale motioned meaningly to one of the others, who shook his head; finally he himself had to speak. "I'm 'fraid you find it pretty cold here, don't you, Hetty?" said he.

"No, thank ye; it's very comfortable," replied Hetty, polite and wary.

"It ain't very convenient for you to do your cookin' here, I guess."

"It's jest as convenient as I want. I don't find no fault."

"I guess it's rayther lonesome here nights, ain't it?"

"I'd 'nough sight ruther be alone than have comp'ny, any day."

"It ain't fit for an old woman like you to be livin' alone here this way."

"Well, I dun' know of anything that's any fitter; mebbe you do."

Caleb looked appealingly at his companions; they stood stiff and irresponsive. Hetty's eyes were sharp and watchful upon them all.

"Well, Hetty," said Caleb, "we've found a nice, comfortable place for you, an' I guess you'd better pack up your things, an' I'll carry you right over there." Caleb stepped back a little closer to the other men. Hetty, small and trembling and helpless before them, looked vicious. She was like a little animal driven from its cover, for whom there is nothing left but desperate warfare and death.

"Where to?" asked Hetty. Her voice shrilled up into a squeak.

Caleb hesitated. He looked again at the other selectmen. There was a solemn, far-away expression upon their faces. "Well," said he, "Mis' Radway wants to git somebody, an'—"

"You ain't goin' to take me to that woman's!"

"You'd be real comfortable—"

"I ain't goin'."

"Now, why not, I'd like to know?"

"I don't like Susan Radway, hain't never liked her, an' I ain't goin' to live with her."

"Mis' Radway's a good Christian woman. You hadn't ought to speak that way about her."

"You know what Susan Radway is, jest as well's I do; an' everybody else does too. I ain't goin' a step, an' you might jest as well make up your mind to it."

Then Hetty seated herself in the corner of the pew nearest her tent, and folded her hands in her lap. She looked over at the pulpit as if she were listening to preaching. She panted, and her eyes glittered, but she had an immovable air.

"Now, Hetty, you've got sense enough to know you can't stay here," said Caleb. "You'd better put on your bonnet, an' come right along before dark. You'll have a nice ride."

Hetty made no response.

The three men stood looking at her. "Come, Hetty," said Caleb, feebly; and another selectman spoke. "Yes, you'd better come," he said, in a mild voice.

Hetty continued to stare at the pulpit.

The three men withdrew a little and conferred. They did not know how to act. This was a new emergency in their simple, even lives. They were not constables; these three steady, sober old men did not want to drag an old woman by main force out of the meeting-house, and thrust her into Caleb Gale's buggy as if it were a police wagon.

Finally Caleb brightened. "I'll go over an' git mother," said he. He started with a brisk air, and went down the gallery stairs; the others followed. They took up their stand in the meeting-house yard, and Caleb got into his buggy and gathered up the reins. The wind blew cold over the hill. "Hadn't you better go inside and wait out of the wind?" said Caleb.

"I guess we'll wait out here," replied one; and the other nodded.

"Well, I sha'nt be gone long," said Caleb. "Mother'll know how to manage her." He drove carefully down the hill; his buggy wings rattled in the wind. The other men pulled up their coat collars, and met the blast stubbornly.

"Pretty ticklish piece of business to tackle," said one, in a low grunt.

"That's so," assented the other. Then they were silent, and waited for Caleb. Once in a while they stamped their feet and slapped their mittened hands. They did not hear Hetty slip the bolt and turn the key of the meeting-house door, nor see her peeping at them from a gallery window.

Caleb returned in twenty minutes; he had not far to go. His wife, stout and handsome and full of vigor, sat beside him in the buggy. Her face was red with the cold wind; her thick cashmere shawl was pinned tightly over her broad bosom. "Has she come down yet?" she called out, in an imperious way.

The two selectmen shook their heads. Caleb kept the horse quiet while his wife got heavily and briskly out of the buggy. She went up the meeting-house steps; and reached out confidently to open the door. Then she drew back and looked around. "Why," said she, "the door's locked; she's locked the door. I call this pretty work!"

She turned again quite fiercely, and began beating on the door. "Hetty!" she called, "Hetty, Hetty Fifield! Let me in! What have you locked this door for?"

She stopped and turned to her husband.

"Don't you s'pose the barn key would unlock it?" she asked.

"I don't b'lieve 'twould."

"Well, you'd better go home and fetch it."

Caleb again drove down the hill, and the other men searched their pockets for keys. One had the key of his corn-house, and produced it hopefully, but it would not unlock the meeting-house door.

A crowd seldom gathered in the little village for anything short of a fire; but today in a short time quite a number of people stood on the meeting-house hill, and more kept coming. When Caleb Gale returned with the barn key his daughter, a tall, pretty young girl, sat beside him, her little face alert and smiling in her red hood. The other selectmen's wives toiled eagerly up the hill, with a young daughter of one of them speeding on ahead. Then the two young girls stood close to each other and watched the proceedings. Key after key was tried; men brought all the large keys they could find, running importantly up the hill, but none would unlock the meeting-house door. After Caleb had tried the last available key, stooping and screwing it anxiously, he turned around. "There ain't no use in it, any way," said he; "most likely the door's bolted."

"You don't mean there's a bolt on that door?" cried his wife.

"Yes, there is."

"Then you might jest as well have tore 'round for hen's feathers as keys. Of course she's bolted it if she's got any wit, an' I guess she's got most as much as some of you men that have been bringin' keys. Try the windows."

But the windows were fast. Hetty had made her sacred castle impregnable except to violence. Either the door would have to be forced or a window broken to gain an entrance.

The people conferred with one another. Some were for retreating, and leaving Hetty in peaceful possession until time drove her to capitulate. "She'll open it to-morrow," they said. Others were for extreme measures, and their impetuosity gave them the lead. The project of forcing the door was urged; one man started for a crow-bar.

"They are a parcel of fools to do such a thing," said Caleb Gale's wife to another woman. "Spoil that good door! They'd better leave the poor thing alone till to-morrow. I dun' know what's goin' to be done with her when they git in. I ain't goin' to have father draggin' her over to Mis' Radway's by the hair of her head."

"That's jest what I say," returned the other woman.

Mrs. Gale went up to Caleb and nudged him. "Don't you let them break that door down, father," said she.

"Well, well, we'll see," Caleb replied. He moved away a little; his wife's voice had been drowned out lately by a masculine clamor, and he took advantage of it.

All the people talked at once; the wind was keen, and all their garments fluttered; the two young girls had their arms around each other under their shawls; the man with the crow-bar came stalking up the hill.

"Don't you let them break down that door, father," said Mrs. Gale.

"Well, well," grunted Caleb.

Regardless of remonstrances, the man set the crow-bar against the door; suddenly there was a cry. "There she is!" Everybody looked up. There was Hetty looking out of a gallery window.

Everybody was still. Hetty began to speak. Her dark old face, peering out of the window, looked ghastly; the wind blew her poor gray locks over it. She extended her little wrinkled hands. "Jest let me say one word," said she; "jest one word." Her voice shook. All her coolness was gone. The magnitude of her last act of defiance had caused it to react upon herself like an overloaded gun.

"Say all you want to, Hetty, an' don't be afraid," Mrs. Gale called out.

"I jest want to say a word," repeated Hetty. "Can't I stay here, nohow? It don't seem as if I could go to Mis' Radway's. I ain't nothin' again' her. I s'pose she's a good woman, but she's used to havin' her own way, and I've been livin' all my life with them that was, an' I've had to fight to keep a footin' on the earth, an' now I'm gittin' too old for't. If I can jest stay here in the meetin' house, I won't ask for nothin' any better. I sha'n't need much to keep me, I wa'n't never a hefty eater; an' I'll keep the meetin'-house jest as clean as I know how. An' I'll make some more of them wool flowers. I'll make a wreath to go the whole length of the gallery, if I can git wool 'nough. Won't you let me stay? I ain't complainin', but I've always had a dretful hard time; seems as if now I might take a little comfort the last of it, if I could stay here. I can't go to Mis' Radway's nohow." Hetty covered her face with her hands; her words ended in a weak wail.

Mrs. Gale's voice rang out clear and strong and irrepressible. "Of course you can stay in the meetin'-house," said she; "I should laugh if you couldn't. Don't you worry another mite about it. You sha'n't go one step to Mis' Radway's; you couldn't live a day with her. You can stay jest where you are; you've kept the meetin'-house enough sight cleaner than I've ever seen it. Don't you worry another mite, Hetty."

Mrs. Gale stood majestically, and looked defiantly around; tears were in her eyes. Another woman edged up to her. "Why couldn't she have that little room side of the pulpit, where the minister hangs his hat?" she whispered. "He could hang it somewhere else."

"Course she could," responded Mrs. Gale, with alacrity, "jest as well as not. She can have her stove an' her bed in there, an' be jest as comfortable as can be. I should laugh if she couldn't. Don't you worry, Hetty."

The crowd gradually dispersed, sending out stragglers down the hill until it was all gone. Mrs. Gale waited until the last, sitting in the buggy in state. When her husband gathered up the reins, she called back to Hetty: "Don't you worry one mite more about it, Hetty. I'm comin' up to see you in the mornin'!"

It was almost dusk when Caleb drove down the hill; he was the last of the besiegers, and the feeble garrison was left triumphant.

The next day but one was Christmas, the next night Christmas Eve. On Christmas Eve Hetty had reached what to her was the flood-tide of peace and prosperity. Established in that small, lofty room, with her bed and her stove, with gifts of a rocking-chair and table, and a goodly store of food, with no one to molest or disturb her, she had nothing to wish for on earth. All her small desires were satisfied. No happy girl could have a merrier Christmas than this old woman with her little measure full of gifts. That Christmas Eve Hetty lay down under her sunflower quilt, and all her old hardships looked dim in the distance, like far-away hills, while her new joys came out like stars.

She was a light sleeper; the next morning she was up early. She opened the meeting-house door and stood looking out. The smoke from the village chimneys had not yet begun to rise blue and rosy in the clear frosty air. There was no snow, but over all the hill there was a silver rime of frost; the bare branches of the trees glistened. Hetty stood looking. "Why, it's Christmas mornin'," she said, suddenly. Christmas had never been a gala-day to this old woman. Christmas had not been kept at all in this New England village when she was young. She was led to think of it now only in connection with the dinner Mrs. Gale had promised to bring her to-day.

Mrs. Gale had told her she should have some of her Christmas dinner, some turkey and plum-pudding. She called it to mind now with a thrill of delight. Her face grew momentarily more radiant. There was a certain beauty in it. A finer morning light than that which lit up the wintry earth seemed to shine over the furrows of her old face. "I'm goin' to have turkey an' plum-puddin' to-day," said she; "it's Christmas." Suddenly she started, and went into the meeting-house, straight up the gallery stairs. There in a clear space hung the bell-rope. Hetty grasped it. Never before had a Christmas bell been rung in this village; Hetty had probably never heard of Christmas bells. She was prompted by pure artless enthusiasm and grateful happiness. Her old arms pulled on the rope with a will, the bell sounded peal on peal. Down in the village, curtains rolled up, letting in the morning light; happy faces looked out of the windows. Hetty had awakened the whole village to Christmas Day.

LETTER TO DR. EUGEN HEINRICH SCHMITT

Leo Tolstoy (1828–1910)

Lev Nikolaevich, Count Tolstoy, is among the world's greatest writers. Born into a noble family of considerable wealth, he added to the family's honor and fortune through the enormous success of his novels, stories, and plays. But he was increasingly disturbed by the brutal divide between Russia's elite and the mass of

From *Tolstoy's Writings on Civil Disobedience and Non-Violence*. New York: Bergman, 1967.

peasants who constituted the overwhelming majority of the nation's people. He read widely in the reform literature of the nineteenth century, including in his study works by Garrison, such as the "Declaration of Sentiments" of the Peace Convention, and by Thoreau, including "Civil Disobedience." Gradually Tolstoy developed his own theories of Christian brotherhood, pacifism, and simplicity, and he wrote extensively both to protest the conditions of life for the Russian masses and to propose alternatives to war, hatred, and exploitation. He also attempted, in his old age, to renounce material possessions and to live simply, like the Russian peasants for whom he advocated.

The letter to Dr. Eugen Heinrich Schmitt dates from the mid-1890s. Schmitt was editor of *Ohne Staat* (Without the State), a Budapest journal. "The Beginning of the End" was written January 6, 1897. [ED.]

You write to me that people seem quite unable to understand that to serve the government is incompatible with Christianity.

In just the same way people were long unable to see that indulgences, inquisitions, slavery, and tortures were incompatible with Christianity. But a time came when it was comprehensible; and a time will come when men will understand the incompatibility with Christianity, first of war service (that already is beginning to be felt), and then of service to government in general.

It is now fifty years since a not widely known, but very remarkable, American writer—Thoreau—not only clearly expressed that incompatibility in his admirable essay on "Civil Disobedience" but gave a practical example of such disobedience. Not wishing to be an accomplice or supporter of a government which legalized slavery, he declined to pay a tax demanded of him, and went to prison for it.

Thoreau refused to pay taxes to government, and evidently the same motives as actuated him would prevent men from serving a government. As, in your letter to the minister, you have admirably expressed it: you do not consider it compatible with your moral dignity to work for an institution which represents legalized murder and robbery.

Thoreau was, I think, the first to express this view. People paid scant attention to either his refusal or his article fifty years ago—the thing seemed so strange. It was put down to his eccentricity. Today your refusal attracts some attention, and, as is always the case when new truth is clearly expressed, it evokes a double surprise—first, surprise that a man should say such queer things, and then, surprise that I had not myself discovered what this man is saying; it is so certain and so obvious.

Such a truth as that a Christian must not be a soldier—*i.e.* a murderer—and must not be the servant of an institution maintained by violence and murder, is so certain, so clear and irrefutable, that to enable people to grasp it, discussion, proof, or eloquence are not necessary. For the majority of men to hear and understand this truth, it is only needful that it should be constantly repeated.

The truth that a Christian should not take part in murdering, or serve the chiefs of the murderers for a salary collected from the poor by force, is so plain and indisputable that those who hear it cannot but agree with it. And if a man continues to act contrary to these truths after hearing them, it is only because he is accustomed to act contrary to them, and it is difficult to break the habit. Moreover, as long as most people act as he does, he will not, by acting contrary to the truth, lose the regard of the majority of those who are most respected.

The case is the same as it is with the question of vegetarianism. "A man can live and be healthy without killing animals for food; therefore, if he eats meat, he participates in taking animal life merely for the sake of his appetite. And to act so is immoral." It is so simple and indubitable that it is impossible not to agree with it. But because most people do eat meat, people, on hearing the case stated, admit its justice, and then, laughing, say; "But a good beefsteak is a good thing all the same; and I shall eat one at dinner today with pleasure."

Just in the same way officers in the army, and officials employed in the civil service, treat statements of the incompatibility of Christianity and humanitarianism with military and civil service. "Yes, of course, it's true," says such a man, "but, all the same, it is nice to wear a uniform and epaulets, which serve as an introduction anywhere, and which people respect; and it is still better to know that, whatever happens, your salary will be paid punctually and accurately on the first of each month. So that though your statement of the case is correct, I am nevertheless bent on getting a rise of salary and securing a pension."

The position is admitted to be indubitable; but, in the first place, one need not oneself kill an ox to get beefsteaks. It has already been killed. And one need not oneself collect taxes or murder. The taxes are already collected, and the army already exists. And, secondly, most people have not yet heard this view of things, and do not know that it is wrong to do these things. So that, for the present, one need not refuse a well-cooked beefsteak, or a uniform, and all its advantages, or medals and orders; or, above all, a secure monthly salary; "and as for the future, we shall see when the time comes."

At the root of the matter lies the fact that people have not yet heard the injustice and wickedness of such a way of life stated. And, therefore, it is necessary continually to repeat "Carthago delenda est," and Carthage will certainly fall.

I do not say that government and its power will be destroyed. It will not fall to pieces quickly; there are still too many gross elements among the people to support it. But the Christian support of government will be destroyed—*i.e.* those who do violence will cease to find support for their authority in the sanctity of Christianity. Those who employ violence will be simply violators, and nothing else. And when that is so—when they can no longer cloak themselves with pseudo-Christianity—then the end of all violence will be near.

Let us seek to hasten that end. "Carthago delenda est." Government is violence, Christianity is meekness, non-resistance, love. And, therefore, government cannot be Christian, and a man who wishes to be a Christian must not serve government. Government cannot be Christian. A Christian cannot serve government. Government cannot . . . and so on.

THE BEGINNING OF THE END

During last year, in Holland, a young man named Van der Veer was called on to enter the National Guard. To the summons of the commander, Van der Veer answered in the following letter:

THOU SHALT DO NO MURDER.

> TO M. HERMAN SNEIDERS, *Commandant of the National Guard of the Midelburg district.*
>
> *Dear Sir—*
>
> *Last week I received a document ordering me to appear at the municipal office, to be, according to law, enlisted in the National Guards. As you probably noticed, I did not appear, and this letter is to inform you, plainly and without equivocation, that I do not intend to appear before the commission. I know well that I am taking a heavy responsibility, that you have the*

From *Tolstoy's Writings on Civil Disobedience and Non-Violence.* New York, Bergman, 1967.

right to punish me, and that you will not fail to use this right. But that does not frighten me. The reasons which lead me to this passive resistance seem to me strong enough to outweigh the responsibility I take.

I, who, if you please, am not a Christian, understand better than most Christians the commandment which is put at the head of this letter, the commandment which is rooted in human nature, in the mind of man. When but a boy, I allowed myself to be taught the trade of soldier, the art of killing; but now I renounce it. I would not kill at the command of others, and thus have murder on my conscience without any personal cause or reason whatever.

Can you mention anything more degrading to a human being than carrying out such murder, such massacre? I am unable to kill, even to see an animal killed; therefore I became a vegetarian. And now I am to be ordered to shoot men who have done me no harm; for I take it that it is not to shoot at leaves and branches of trees that soldiers are taught to use guns.

But you will reply, perhaps, that the National Guard is besides, and especially, to keep civic order.

M. Commandant, if order really reigned in our society, if the social organism were really healthy—in other words, if there were in our social relations no crying abuses, if it were not established that one man shall die of hunger while another gratifies his every whim of luxury, then you would see me in the front ranks of the defenders of this orderly state. But I flatly decline to help in preserving the present so-called "social order." Why, M. Commandant, should we throw dust in each other's eyes? We both know quite well what the "preservation of order" means: upholding the rich against the poor toilers, who begin to perceive their rights. Do we not know the role which the National Guard played in the last strike at Rotterdam? For no reason, the Guard had to be on duty hours and hours to watch over the property of the commercial houses which were affected. Can you for a moment suppose that I should shoot down working-people who are acting quite within their rights? You cannot be so blind. Why then complicate the question? Certainly, it is impossible for me to allow myself to be molded into an obedient National Guardsman such as you want and must have.

For all these reasons, but especially because I hate murder by order, I refuse to serve as a National Guardsman, and ask you not to send me either uniform or arms, because I have a fixed resolve not to use them.—I greet you, M. Commandant,

J. K. Van der Veer

This letter, in my opinion, has great importance. Refusals of military service in Christian states began when in Christian states military service appeared. Or rather when the states, the power of which rests upon violence, laid claim to Christianity without giving up violence. In truth, it cannot be otherwise. A Christian, whose doctrine enjoins upon him humility, non-resistance to evil, love to all (even to the most malicious), cannot be a soldier; that is, he cannot join a class of men whose business is to kill their fellow-men. Therefore it is that these Christians have always refused and now refuse military service.

But of true Christians there have always been but few. Most people in Christian countries count as Christians only those who profess the doctrines of some Church, which doctrines have nothing in common, except the name, with true Christianity. That occasionally one in tens of thousands of recruits should refuse to serve did not trouble the hundreds of thousands, the millions, of men who every year accepted military service.

Impossible that the whole enormous majority of Christians who enter upon military service are wrong, and only the exceptions, sometimes uneducated people, are right; while every archbishop and man of learning thinks the service compatible with Christianity. So think the majority, and, untroubled regarding themselves as Christians, they enter the rank of murderers. But now appears a man who, as he himself says, is not a Christian, and who refuses military service, not from religious motives, but from motives of the simplest kind, motives intelligible and common to all men, of whatever religion or nation, whether Catholic, Mohammedan, Buddhist, Confucian, whether Spaniards or Japanese.

Van der Veer refuses military service, not because he follows the commandment, "Thou shalt do no murder," not because he is a Christian, but because he holds murder to be opposed to human nature. He writes that he simply abhors all killing, and abhors it to such a degree that he becomes a vegetarian just to avoid participation in the killing of animals; and, above all, he says, he refuses military service because he thinks "murder by order," that is, the obligation to kill those whom one is ordered to kill (which is the real nature of military service), is incompatible with man's uprightness.

Alluding to the usual objection that if he refuses others will follow his example, and the present social order will be destroyed, he answers that he does not wish to preserve the present social order, because it is bad, because in it the rich dominate the poor, which ought not to be. So that, even if he had any other doubts as to the propriety of serving or not serving, the one consideration that in serving as a soldier he must, by carrying arms and threatening to kill, support the oppressing rich against the oppressed poor, would compel him to refuse military service.

If Van der Veer were to give as the reason for his refusal his adherence to the Christian religion, those who now join the military service could say, "We are no sectarians, and do not acknowledge Christianity; therefore we do not see the need to act as you do."

But the reasons given by Van der Veer are so simple, clear, and universal that it is impossible not to apply them each to his own case. As things are, to deny the force of these reasons in one's own case, one must say:

"I like killing, and am ready to kill, not only evil-disposed people, but my own oppressed and unfortunate fellow-countrymen, and I perceive nothing wrong in the promise to kill, at the order of the first officer who comes across me, whomever he bids me kill."

Here is a young man. In whatever surroundings, family, creed, he has been brought up, he has been taught that he must be good, that it is bad to strike and kill, not only men, but even animals; he has been taught that a man must value his uprightness, which uprightness consists in acting according to conscience. This is equally taught to the Confucian in China, the Shintoist in Japan, the Buddhist, and the Mohammedan. Suddenly, after being taught all this, he enters the military service, where he is required to do the precise opposite of what he has been taught. He is told to fit himself for wounding and killing, not animals, but men; he is told to renounce his independence as a man, and obey, in the business of murder, men whom he does not know, utter strangers to him.

To such a command, what right answer can a man of our day make? Surely, only this, "I do not wish to, and I will not."

Exactly this answer Van der Veer gives. And it is hard to invent any reply to him and to those who, in a similar position, do as he does.

One may not see this point, through attention not having been called to it; one may not understand the import of an action, as long as it remains unexplained. But once pointed out and explained, one can no longer fail to see, or feign blindness to what is quite obvious.

There may still be found men who do not reflect upon their action in entering military service, and men who want war with foreign people, and men who would continue the oppression of the laboring class, and even men who like murder for murder's sake. Such men can continue as soldiers; but even they cannot now fail to know that there are others, the best men in the world—not only among Christians, but among Mohammedans, Brahmanists, Buddhists, Confucians—who look upon war and soldiers with aversion and contempt, and whose number grows hourly. No arguments can talk away this plain fact, that a man with any sense of his own dignity cannot enslave himself to an unknown, or even a known, master whose business is killing. Now just in this consists military service, with all its compulsion of discipline.

"But consider the consequences to him who refuses," I am told. "It is all very well for you, an old man exempted from this exaction, and safe by your position to preach martyrdom; but what about those to whom you preach, and who, believing in you, refuse to serve, and ruin their young lives?"

"But what can I do?"—I answer those who speak thus. "Because I am old, must I therefore not point out the evil which I clearly, unquestionably see, seeing it precisely because I am old and have lived and thought for long? Must a man who stands on the far side of the river, beyond the reach of that ruffian whom he sees compelling one man to murder another, not cry out to the slayer, bidding him to refrain, for the reason that such interference will still more enrage the ruffian? Moreover, I by no means see why the government, persecuting those who refuse military service, does not turn its punishment upon me, recognizing in me an instigator. I am not too old for persecution, for any and all sorts of punishments, and my position is a defenseless one. At all events, whether blamed and persecuted or not, whether those who refuse military service are persecuted or not, I, whilst I live, will not cease from saying what I now say; for I cannot refrain from acting according to my conscience." Just in this very thing is Christian truth powerful, irresistible; namely, that, being the teaching of truth, in affecting men it is not to be governed by outside considerations. Whether young or old, whether persecuted or not, he who adopts the Christian, the true, conception of life, cannot shrink from the claims of his conscience. In this is the essence and peculiarity of Christianity, distinguishing it from all other religious teachings; and in this is its unconquerable power.

Van der Veer says he is not a Christian. But the motives of his refusal and action are Christian. He refuses because he does not wish to kill a brother man; he does not obey, because the commands of his conscience are more binding upon him than the commands of men. Precisely on this account is Van der Veer's refusal so important. Thereby he shows that Christianity is not a sect or creed which some may profess and others reject; but that it is naught else than a life's following of that light of reason which illumines all men. The merit of Christianity is not that it prescribes to men such and such acts, but that it foresees and points out the way by which all mankind must go and does go.

Those men who now behave rightly and reasonably do so, not because they follow prescriptions of Christ, but because that line of action which was pointed out eighteen hundred years ago has now become identified with human conscience.

This is why I think the action and letter of Van der Veer are of great import.

As a fire lit on a prairie or in a forest will not die out until it has burned all that is dry and dead, and therefore combustible, so the truth, once articulated in human utterance, will not cease its work until all falsehood, appointed for destruction, surrounding and hiding the truth on all sides as it does, is destroyed. The fire smolders long; but as soon as it flashes into flame, all that can burn burns quickly.

So with the truth, which takes long to reach a right expression, but once that clear expression in word is given, falsehood and wrong are soon to be destroyed. One of the partial manifestations of Christianity—the idea that men can live without the institution of slavery—although it had been included in the Christian concept, was clearly expressed, so it seems to me, only by writers at the end of the eighteenth century. Up to that time, not only the ancient pagans, as Plato and Aristotle, but even men near to us in time, and Christians, could not imagine a human society without slavery. Thomas More could not imagine even a Utopia without slavery. So also men of the beginning of this century could not imagine the life of man without war. Only after the Napoleonic wars was the idea clearly expressed that man can live without war. And now a hundred years have gone since the first clear expression of the idea that mankind can live without slavery; and there is no longer slavery in Christian nations. And there shall not pass away another hundred years after the clear utterance of the idea that mankind can live without war, before war shall cease to be. Very likely some form of armed violence will remain, just as wage-labor remains after the abolition of slavery; but, at least, wars and armies will be abolished in the outrageous form, so repugnant to reason and moral sense, in which they now exist.

Signs that this time is near are many. These signs are such as the helpless position of governments, which more and more increase their armaments; the multiplication of taxation and the discontent of the nations; the extreme degree of efficiency with which deadly weapons are constructed; the activity of congresses and societies of peace; but above all, the refusals of individuals to take military service. In these refusals is the key to the solution of the question. You say that military service is necessary; that, without soldiers, disasters will happen to us. That may be; but, holding the idea of right and wrong which is universal among men today, yourselves included, I cannot kill men to order. So that if, as you say, military service is essential—then arrange it in some way not so contradictory to my, and your, conscience. But, until you have so arranged it, do not claim from me what is against my conscience, which I can by no means disobey.

Thus, inevitably, and very soon, must answer all honest and reasonable men; not only the men of Christendom, but even Mohammedans and the so-called heathen, the Brahmanists, Buddhists, and Confucians. Maybe, by the power of inertia, the soldiering trade will go on for some time to come; but even now the question stands solved in the human conscience, and with every day, every hour, more and more men come to the same solution; and to stay the movement is, at this juncture, not possible. Every recognition of a truth by man, or rather, every deliverance from an error, as in the case of slavery before our eyes, is always attained through a conflict between the awakening conscience and the inertia of the old condition.

At first the inertia is so powerful, the conscience so weak, that the first attempt to escape from error is met only with astonishment. The new truth seems madness. Is it proposed to live without slavery? Then who will work? Is it proposed to live without fighting? Then everybody will come and conquer us.

But the power of conscience grows, inertia weakens, and astonishment is changing to sneers and contempt. "The Holy Scriptures acknowledge masters and slaves. These relations have always been, and now come these wiseacres who want to change the whole world;" so men spoke concerning slavery. "All the scientists and philosophers recognize the lawfulness, and even sacredness, of war; and are we immediately to believe that there is no need of war?"

So men speak concerning war. But conscience continues to grow and to become clear; the number increases of those who recognize the new truth, and sneer and contempt give place to subterfuge and trickery. Those who support the error make slow to understand and admit the incongruity and cruelty of the practice they defend, but think its abolition impossible just now, so delaying its abolition indefinitely. "Who does not know that slavery is an evil? But men are not yet ripe for freedom, and liberation will produce horrible disasters"—men used to say concerning slavery, forty years ago. "Who does not know that war is an evil? But while mankind is still so bestial, abolition of armies will do more harm than good," men say concerning war today.

Nevertheless, the idea is doing its work; it grows, it burns the falsehood; and the time has come when the madness, the uselessness, the harmfulness, and wickedness of the error are so clear (as it happened in the sixties with slavery in Russia and America) that even now it is impossible to justify it. Such is the present position as to war. Just as, in the sixties, no attempts were made to justify slavery, but only to maintain it; so today no man attempts any longer to justify war and armies, but only tries, in silence, to use the inertia which still supports them, knowing very well that this cruel and immoral organization for murder, which seems so powerful, may at any moment crumble down, never more to be raised.

Once a drop of water oozes through the dam, once a brick falls out from a great building, once a mesh comes loose in the strongest net—the dam bursts, the building falls, the net unweaves. Such a drop, such a brick, such a loosed mesh, it seems to me, is the refusal of Van der Veer, explained by reasons universal to all mankind.

Upon this refusal of Van der Veer like refusals must follow more and more often. As soon as these become numerous, the very men (their name is legion) who the day before said, "It is impossible to live without war," will say at once that they have this long time declared the madness and immorality of war, and they will advise everybody to follow Van der Veer's example. Then, of wars and armies, as these are now, there will remain only the recollection.

And this time is coming.

THOREAU

John Albert Macy (1877–1932)

Macy was among the earliest scholars of American literature, publishing his best-known book on the subject, *The Spirit of American Literature,* in 1908. He was also a political activist, joining the Socialist party in 1911, publishing a volume on *Socialism in America* (Garden City: Doubleday, 1916), and editing the *Nation* magazine from 1922 to 1923. He also taught at the progressive Rand School of Social Science in New York. He had earlier married the companion and teacher of Helen Keller, Anne Sullivan; with her help he had edited Keller's *The Story of My Life* (New York: Grosset, 1905), a book that widely influenced ideas about education and especially the possibility of teaching the disabled.

Macy brings to his discussion of Thoreau, and particularly his similarities to and differences from Tolstoy, both his literary training and his political activism. His essay therefore presents a way of reading Thoreau both as a great figure in American literature and as a political commentator whose words were as appropriate for Macy's time (and ours) as for Thoreau's own.

The essay "Thoreau" constitutes Chapter 10 of *The Spirit of American Literature* (New York: Doubleday, 171–88). [Ed.]

When Thoreau died, Emerson wrote: "The country knows not yet, or in the least part how great a son it has lost." In fifty years the country, the world, has learned more of this great son. Friends and editors have assembled one by one the eleven volumes of the standard edition; and the recent publication of his complete journal indicates that there are readers who regard the least of his notes as worthy of preservation. The growing cult of the open air, the increasing host of amateur prodigals returning to nature, have given fresh vogue to his sketches of woods and waters. But, for all that, the man is not yet fully understood. Lowell's unsympathetic essay, product of a mind from which poetry and youth had evaporated, and of a social outlook grown conventionally decorous, has carried inevitable authority. Like Macaulay's essay on Bacon and Jeffrey's blundering miscomprehension of Wordsworth, it is an example of how one great reputation may for a period smother and distort another. Stevenson's popular essay, written in his half dramatic attitude of athletic good-cheer and arm-in-arm sympathy with a hooray-boy world, is based on a misconception of Thoreau's character and his message as a whole. It overemphasizes the gentle reservation with which Emerson tempers his praise. Emerson in a few words sets forth the rounded integrity of Thoreau's work and personality; in one place he makes a comment upon his fellow-philosopher's proneness to negation and opposition. The comment, in its place, is just to Thoreau and expresses Emerson's more inclusive amiability. Stevenson singles out from Emerson's total estimate the negative characteristic, and stiffens it into an anti-social asceticism which is not foreign to Thoreau's nature but is by no means its dominant quality.

That original minds stand above the comprehension of mediocre minds of their own period and of later times is a fact observable everywhere in the history of the human intellect. More than that, some minds are not merely above the common herd; they are in advance of the best culture of their day and must await the intelligence of later generations to give them full recognition. Emerson and Holmes were as comprehensible to their generation as to ours. Whitman and Thoreau were trail-blazers; they went before to survey regions where later comers find a broad highway. Thoreau's vision shot beyond the horizon which bounded and still bounds the sight even of that part of the world which fancies itself liberal and emancipated.

"I am," says Thoreau, "a poet, a mystic and a transcendentalist." He was all that, and, moreover, he was an anarchist. He was the one anarchist of great literary power in a nation of slavish conformity to legalism, where obedience to statute and maintenance of "order" are assiduously inculcated as patriotic virtues by the social powers which profit from other peoples' docility. "Walden" and "A Week on the Concord and Merrimac Rivers" have been accepted as classics. The essays on "Forest Trees" and "Wild Apples" were to be found in a school reader twenty-five years ago. But the ringing revolt of the essay on "Civil Disobedience" is still silenced under the thick respectability of our times. The ideas in it could not today be printed in the magazine which was for years owned by the publishers of Thoreau's complete works. Boston Back Bay would shiver! It would not do, really, to utter aloud Thoreau's ideas in a society whose leading university, Thoreau's alma mater, has recently ruled, "that the halls of the university shall not be open for persistent or systematic propaganda on contentious questions of contemporaneous social, economic, political or religious interests." That is, let the university offer fifty courses in philosophy, history and literature which is dead enough not to be dangerous to vested authority, but let it not take any part in philosophy, history, or literature which is in the making! The application of Thoreau's principles to the injustices of our present political and industrial life would be condemned as disloyally "un-American" in the community where he lived and which is now owned, body and soul, factory and college, by State Street. Thoreau's intellectual kinsmen are not there. For an adequate recognition of the value of Thoreau's challenge to authority one turns to no living New Englander, but to that other solitary and indignant moralist, Tolstoy.

On the right of the individual to withhold his sanction of word and deed from a government by any minority or majority which is engaged in dishonest practices and enforces brutal laws, the American and the Russian philosopher are mainly in accord. Each says to government: "You may take me and break me because you are physically strong, but willing party to your legalized system of plunder and murder I will not be." The government against which Tolstoy rebelled is melodramatically barbarous, so that liberal minds all over the world find themselves in sympathy with him. It is easy to protest against tyranny on the other side of the planet. Thoreau's government (which is so like the present government of the United States that the change of a word or two, the insertion of modern instances, makes his essay as pertinent as if written yesterday)—Thoreau's government skulks behind the pacific mask of democracy; it deforms children, kills men and ruins women by common consent and not by the cossack forces of a picturesquely tyrannous Czar. The prosperous and so-called cultivated classes who manage for us our industrial, educational, literary and religious affairs, hold up horrified hands at Russia, but naturally have no quarrel with the system of government at home which leaves them in peace and offers them a career of ease. Therefore in the gallery of ideas through which admiring American youth is conducted, Thoreau's portrait of government is discreetly turned to the wall. His nature books, his poetic notes on the seasons, are recommended to an ever-growing number of readers. The flaming eloquence of his social philosophy, the significance, the conclusion of his experiment in individualism, is ignored. We praise Tolstoy, even in cultivated Boston, but we remain unacquainted with our own spiritual liberator.

One difference between Tolstoy and Thoreau is vital, a difference in personal circumstances. Tolstoy was born a landed aristocrat. He struggled in vain to bring the conduct of his life into accord with his beliefs. He desired to be a workman, but could only dabble in manual toil. In spite of his attempt to renounce copyright, his world-famous fictions brought money to his family. Circumstances enmeshed him, and his titanic struggle to extricate himself entangled him more and more, and made him a tragic figure. His life came to an impotent conclusion; only death, as in some Greek tragedy, could restore dignity and moral consistency. Thoreau, on the other hand, was born poor; he remained a bachelor; he earned his living by productive labour; and thus he had the good fortune to be able to practise his philosophy. He was not directly, nor by any economic indirection, dependent for his bread on another man. Tolstoy, an agonized prisoner in a wealth which he thought polluted him, may well have envied the Yankee pencil-whittler and land surveyor, a jack-of-all-trades and master of several, who did his honest day's work beside the common labourers of the world. The leisure which he spent in the company of sages, poets, and prophets, whose peer he was, he earned with his hands. He was spared the humiliation of writing sermons on freedom in time won at the expense of some other man's freedom.

"If I devote myself to other pursuits and contemplations," he says, "I must first see, at least, that I do not pursue them sitting upon another man's shoulders. I must get off him first, that he may pursue his contemplations, too."

One other difference between Tolstoy and Thoreau is essential; it springs from that primary difference in their social stations. Tolstoy groaned beneath the agony of a suffering world; he took upon himself the sins of his class. His long cry of pain, which the work of his last twenty years hurls at the dull ears of humanity, is unrelieved except by a sad, half-rationalized Christianity, confessedly unconsoling. He tortured himself with an almost morbid sense of responsibility for evils remote from his private duties, evils which he could not help. Thoreau, on the contrary, enjoyed life. "I came into this world," he says, "not chiefly to make this a good place to live in, but to live in it, be it good or bad." When they put him in jail for refusing on principle to pay his poll tax (he had nothing on which to impose a property tax), he did not make a martyr of himself, but with his mouth slightly awry wrote five dryly humorous pages about "My Prisons," in which legal contrivances are made to look not merely oppressive but ridiculous. He laughs at the jailer and official, his neighbours in their attitudes as policeman and soldier. A man of humour, one might think, would be ashamed to appear on a street in Thoreau's town in blue uniform with a star on his breast, lest Thoreau emerge suddenly from the woods and contemplate the insignia of authority with a faintly acid smile.

Thoreau is not a theorist who argues himself into anarchism by the routes of bookish reasoning. The philosophy of anarchism was not in his lifetime so highly developed, codified and rationalized as it is now; and it is doubtful if Thoreau would have had much patience with its elaborately systematic arguments in support of an unsystematic conduct of life. "To speak practically and as a citizen," he says, "unlike those who call themselves no-government men, I ask for, not at once no government, but at once a better government." He was no selfish opponent of the inconveniences of society. The state might have his money if it used it for useful, or at worst, harmless enterprises, such as building roads. He was willing to conform with any peaceful nonsense or extravagance. "One cannot be too much on his guard . . . lest his action be biased by obstinacy or an undue regard for the opinions of men." He simply asked not to be made accessory to legalized crime. He had no disposition to reform the world, though he joined the abolitionists, like all decent New Englanders of all creeds and political principles. "The government does not concern me much, and I shall bestow the fewest possible thoughts on it."

That was a fair and a practical attitude for a freeman in an agricultural nation like America sixty years ago, where he who had skill to work could get a living somehow. A complexly organized industrial system has since grown up in America, all the good land is occupied, or at least fenced with titles, and today even so capable a man as Thoreau would find it difficult to support himself in decency with a half day's work. Thoreau's views fitted his time and his community. Tolstoy, holding the same views, fifty years later, was trying to hark back to conditions that the world of production had outlived even in Russia. What Thoreau, the maker of pencils, would say to a modern pencil-factory where he, like other workmen, would have to apply for a job, or make no pencils, we can only guess, Yankee-wise. We guess that he would have understood it shrewdly and inspected its machinery with the eye of a born mechanic, and not have protested against it as his epigone, Tolstoy, protested against the advance of modern industry.

With the great changes that have come in the relations between a workman and his tools, some of Thoreau's single-handed individualism has grown obsolete. So far forth as it concerns those practices of government and habits of society which have not appreciably altered or improved, it remains a much-needed word of rebellion. "How does it become a man to behave toward this American government today? I cannot for an instant recognize that political organization as my government which is the slave's government also." For "black slave," which he means, substitute "white slave" or "child labourer" and the sentence stands vividly pertinent to the blessed year 1912. "This people," he said, "must cease to make war on Mexico, though it cost them their existence as a people." Substitute "Philippines" for "Mexico," and the sentence is part of many an honest man's belief this morning. "The standing army," says Thoreau, "is only an arm of the standing government. The government itself, which is only the mode which the people have chosen to execute their will, is equally liable to be abused and perverted before the people can act through it. Witness the present Mexican War, the work of comparatively few individuals using the standing army as their tool." Was that written yesterday when, under pretence of preserving law and order on the Mexican frontier, the financial powers in control of these United States, investors in Mexican "securities," sent an army of freeborn American soldiers to the Rio Grande?

The entire essay on "Civil Disobedience" should be read by us timorous moderns to renerve us in time of abuse. We have, it seems, lost the art of speaking so eloquently and courageously, but we can make the most of a man who spoke for us sixty years ago and whose work it is respectable to quote, for he is an established New England classic.

Thoreau was not concerned primarily with government, because he was so situated that he could turn his back on it and not suffer. In his time an independent man could enjoy liberty of utterance and occupation. Thoreau asked to be let alone, and he was let alone. Non-interference between him and the government was mutual and friendly, except when the tax-collector reached his official hand into the Concord woods and seized that distinguished poll, enumerated as H. D. Thoreau, occupation, surveyor.

Thoreau's work is a long notebook of "surveyor's" jottings, a continuous journal, all autobiographic, some sections of which are assembled into essays.

His first book, "A Week on the Concord and Merrimac Rivers," consists of seven discursive essays on a multitude of subjects. There is rather more reflection upon literature and life in general than narrative of the week's experiences. This insurgent and original man, who lives near the heart of nature, who, like Whitman, regards a woodchuck's hole as a cosmic fact, is a critic of literature, a reader of Elizabethan poets. In a later book, "Cape Cod," he recites the sonorities of Homer on the Yankee sands. In his first book he recites the beauties of nature reclining on the bosom of oriental religion and British poetry.

On Saturday he paddles out on the river. The purling of the water, the echoes of civilization on the banks are vividly realized. But by Sunday morning the little stream has flowed into the vasty deeps of Hindoo and Greek philosophy, and when the Sabbath evening comes we have added nothing to our knowledge of local geography but have listened to one of the very best essays on books. The paragraphs on style form one of the most melodious of all discourses on the art of expression; Thoreau exemplifies the art he is explaining. Whoever enjoys the inconsistency of man may note that for ten pages, in the skilful cadences of a practised "scholar," Thoreau dwells on the merit of the brief word, the eloquence of unlettered men, the farmer's call to his team and other primitive, manly modes of speech. He pays his warmest tribute, however, not to the style of the Concord farmer, but to—Sir Walter Raleigh.

"Sir Walter Raleigh might well be studied, if only for the excellence of his style, for he is remarkable in the midst of so many masters. There is a natural emphasis in his style, like a man's tread, and a breathing space between the sentences, which the best of modern writing does not furnish. His chapters are like English parks, or say rather like a Western forest, where the larger growth keeps down the underwood, and one may ride on horseback through the openings. All the distinguished writers of that period possess a greater vigor and naturalness than the more modern—for it is allowed to slander our own time—and when we read a quotation from one of them in the midst of a modern author, we seem to have come suddenly upon a greener ground, a greater depth and strength of soil. It is as if a green bough were laid across the page, and we are refreshed as by the sight of fresh grass in midwinter or early spring. You have constantly the warrant of life and experience in what you read. The little that is said is eked out by the implication of the much that was done. . . . The word which is best said came nearest to not being spoken at all, for it is cousin to a deed which the speaker could have better done. Nay, almost it must have taken the place of a deed by some urgent necessity, even by some misfortune, so that the truest writer will be some captive knight, after all. And perhaps the Fates had some such design, when, having stored Raleigh so richly with the substance of life and experience, they made him a fast prisoner, and compelled him to make his words his deeds and transfer to his expression the emphasis and sincerity of his action."

Beautiful, fluent, and suggestive! But meanwhile what has become of our village anarchist, whom even the tax collector cannot make a captive knight, but who is paddling idly on a New England river—for a week?

On Tuesday a fine description of daybreak from a mountain, an experience not of this week but of another year; on Wednesday a fine sermon on friendship; on Thursday the story of Hannah Dustan and her justifiably murderous exploit among the Indians, accompanied by a discourse on epic stories and history. On Friday "the wind blew steadily downstream, so that we kept our sails set, and lost not a moment of the forenoon by delays, but from early morning until noon were continually dropping downward. With our hands on the steering paddle, which was thrust deep into the river, or bending to the oar, which indeed we rarely relinquished, we felt each palpitation in the veins of our steed, and each impulse of the wings which drew us above. The current of our thoughts made as sudden bends as the river"—and so he steers into a fine discussion of Ossian. He returns into the current to glide past Tyngsboro and Chelmsford, "holding in one hand half a tart country apple pie"—thence back into a beautiful eddy of thought about poetry, and the week is ended—a leisurely week covering ages of human thought.[1]

Of this interesting book, full of exquisite reflections and of as deep wisdom as ever came out of the universe by way of Concord, the author sold two hundred copies; the rest he took back from the printer and stored in a garret, a transaction which he records with unresentful dry humour.

His next book, the only other which he lived to see in print, is "Walden," his masterpiece, a greater book than the "Week," of the same tone and texture, but informed by a more explicit unifying philosophy of life. It records his actual experiment in individualism. It is alive with the reality of daily doings and is rounded to a higher reality, to one man's complete view of the life worth living and the destiny of the race. Emerson, paying his frugal way by lecturing and writing, makes many observations about society and solitude, the place of the individual in nature, but he lives among men and does not know from experience the effect of abiding sole and self-dependent in the midst of an unpopulated wood. Thoreau, investigator and surveyor, tries solitude for two years, makes nature a laboratory, and brings back the record of his experiment. "Walden" is one of those whole, profound books in which the best of an author is distilled. In

[1] [A. Bronson] Alcott said that this book was "Virgil, White of Selbourne and Izaak Walton and Yankee settler all in one." This is intended as high praise and does express the varied wealth of the book. But Alcott could not turn a lofty intention into words without getting something wrong. There is about as much of Virgil in Thoreau as there is of Seneca! [Macy's note]

his two years by the pond Thoreau observed sharply what he could do with nature and what nature did to him; he pondered at leisure over what it all meant and made, not a collection of random jottings, but a summarized report.

Thoreau does not, as some people imagine, argue the case for the wilderness as against the town; on the contrary he loves best the cultivated land with people on it. He merely uses the wilderness to try himself in; he goes where the nature ingredients are unmixed with other things, as an experimenter in dietetics isolates his "food-squad" to increase human knowledge, not to please their palates. Thoreau tells what he lived for, how he lived, and thereby throws light on what humanity lives for. His attitude is neither modest nor magisterial; it is sometimes rather disdainful, his reflections on the life that his neighbours led are often coolly contemptuous. But for the most part he is setting forth *his* life and makes *his* conclusions clear, without urging them upon the reader's acceptance. He probes into the economies of an unthinking prosperity like other radical philosophers; but whereas the satiric dissections of a Carlyle leave the world a ruin and the pieces not worth picking up, Thoreau builds a courageous and cheerfully remodelled life, practical for him at least, and though not to be foisted on the world like a reformer's nostrum, valuable to any neighbour who will read intelligently. "So I lived," he seems to say; "so I believed; so I found out and realized *my* sense of life. Take it or leave it. My experience taught me that to build a fine house to live in is less important than to build a good man to live in it. If that is not a practical ideal, please examine my bean account and see if by your own dull bread-winning, cake-stealing standards of life, I did not prove myself a competent husbandman."

Thoreau does not turn his back on responsibilities nor flaunt his idleness in the sweaty face of humanity; he is a conscientiously busy man, busy about his life and needs, and not unmindful of the needs of others; he holds his head up honestly, the equal of the thoughtless driven toiler, and is much his superior in the satisfaction of man's need for high meditation. The philosophy of "Walden" is near to the selfish self-culture of the unsocial Greek. States cannot be built on it any more than they can be built on Epictetus or on Plato's "Republic," but like them Thoreau stimulates the individual to examine himself and see where he stands in the midst of the solar system, to inquire what his activities amount to and what is the motive of them.

There is more in "Walden" than philosophy and unsocial experiment in the business of making a living. It is full of the poetry of the open world, an "hypaethral" book, unroofed to the skies. The birds fly and sing and the trees bud. Sometimes they have their technical names, for Thoreau is too clever to know less about a thing he sees than does some commonplace naturalist of the schools; but a naturalist he avowedly is not. He says in his Journal that the Secretary of the Association for the Advancement of Science asked him to fill in the blanks of a circular letter by way of answering certain questions, "among which the most important one was, what branch of science I was especially interested in. . . . I felt that it would be to make myself a laughing stock of the scientific community to describe to them that branch of science which especially interests me, inasmuch as they do not believe in a science which deals with the higher law. . . . How absurd that though I probably stand as near to Nature as any of them, and am by constitution as good an observer as most, yet a true account of my relation to Nature should excite their ridicule only." Again he writes in the Journal: "Man cannot afford to be a naturalist, to look at Nature directly, but with only the side of his eye. He must look through and beyond her. To look at her is as fatal as to look at the head of Medusa. It turns the man of science to stone." Thoreau is, as he prayed to be, a "hunter of the beautiful." He is in league with the stones of the field, and the beasts of the field are at peace with him. He is a better naturalist than most men of literary imagination, and he has more imagination than most naturalists.

There are two kinds of mystics. One shrouds himself in his cloudy dreams, mistaking his murky vision for fact. The other, open-eyed and cheerful amid the sunlit world, feels himself near the heart of living things. The one is a theologian; the other is a poet. For all his interest in the hazier transcendentalists and his admiration for the stupendous absurdities of Swedenborg, Thoreau is less near to the religious mystic than to the nature poet of all times, and especially to Wordsworth. Thoreau's spirit is to that of a poet, though his verses are not good, for he was wanting in "the decisive gift of lyrical expression," as Emerson says of Plato and might have said of himself. Like his contemporaries, Thoreau misreads Nature as a collection of moral lessons, but he is not blind to her naked loveliness, and he finds her lessons not austere, but consoling. "Not by constraint or severity shall you have access to true wisdom, but by abandonment and childlike mirthfulness. If you would know aught, be gay before it."

Mystic and transcendentalist, he is not a foggy-minded dreamer with his head lost in vacant unrealities. He lived not ascetically, but heartily, and could have said on his deathbed like Hazlitt that he had had a happy life. He did not shrink from facts like some other poets who have fled stricken to the shadowy woods. He looked upon things courageously. But he had his private criteria of what was worth looking at. His quarrel with politicians is characteristic. He is contemptuous of them, not because they are engaged in sordid matters, not because they are "practical" (the sentimentalist's charge against them), but because they are not earnestly busy at the tasks they pretend to engage in. They are poor politicians. "They who have been bred in the school of politics fail now and always to face the facts," he says.

In his wonderful essay, "Life Without Principle," he says: "I have often been surprised when one has with confidence proposed to me, a grown man, to embark in some enterprise of his, as if I had absolutely nothing to do, my life having been a complete failure hitherto. . . . No, no! I am not without employment at this stage of the voyage. To tell the truth, I saw an advertisement for able-bodied seamen, when I was a boy, sauntering in my native port, and as soon as I came of age, I embarked." So he sailed, a clear-eyed steersman, content and confident as in the canoe which he paddled on Concord River, to that morrow—the concluding words of "Walden"—"which mere lapse of time can never make to dawn. The light which puts out our eyes is darkness to us. Only that day dawns to which we are awake. There is more day to dawn. The sun is but a morning-star."

A SELECTION FROM HIS WRITINGS, 1919–1940

Mohandas K. Gandhi (1869–1948)

Called "Mahatma," or great-souled, Gandhi was the leader of the Indian struggle for liberation from British rule. His primary strategy for changing the political and social landscape of India was what he called *Satyagraha,* which he defined as "soul force," and which entailed the application of nonviolent resistance or civil disobedience to achieve particular changes in policy or practice. After studying law in London and practicing it in India, Gandhi went to South Africa in 1893. There he first developed his theory of what he then called "passive resistance" and put it into practice in order to defend the rights of Asian immigrants against the racist practices of the government.

Gandhi returned to India in 1914 and shortly thereafter organized the movement of *Satyagraha* (literally, "clinging to truth; civil disobedience"), primarily to win independence for his country. Frequently arrested by British authorities, he became president of the Indian National Congress from 1925 to 1934. He led campaigns against British goods, especially textiles, learning to spin and weave native cloth and refusing to dress in anything but homespun. He also used the fast as a method of protest, threatening to "fast unto death" in 1932 in order to change official policy toward the lowest caste of Hindus, the "untouchables." Gandhi's emaciated frame, clad in white homespun, became a familiar icon of anticolonial resistance and of movements for social justice throughout the world. He remained active until January 30, 1948, when he was assassinated by a Hindu nationalist opposed to Gandhi's efforts to reconcile Hindus and Muslims in the Indian subcontinent.

The selections that follow were edited and arranged by Bharatan Kumarappa, who published them in a volume entitled *Non-Violent Resistance* (New York: Schocken, 1951). The selections are derived from *Young India,* a weekly English language journal edited by Gandhi from 1919 to 1930; *Harijan; a Journal of Applied Gandhiism,* a weekly journal published between 1933 and 1955 and conducted during his life by Gandhi; and from Gandhi's book *Hind Swaraj, Or Indian Home Rule* (Madras: Ganesh, 1919). [Ed.]

Satyagraha, Civil Disobedience, Passive Resistance, Non-Co-operation

Satyagraha is literally holding on to Truth and it means, therefore, Truth-force. Truth is soul or spirit. It is, therefore, known as soul-force. It excludes the use of violence because man is not capable of knowing the absolute truth and, therefore, not competent to punish. The word was coined in South Africa to distinguish the non-violent resistance of the Indians of South Africa from the contemporary 'passive resistance' of the suffragettes and others. It is not conceived as a weapon of the weak.

Passive resistance is used in the orthodox English sense and covers the suffragette movement as well as the resistance of the Non-conformists. Passive resistance has been conceived and is regarded as a weapon of the weak. Whilst it avoids violence, being not open to the weak, it does not exclude its use if, in the opinion of a passive resister, the occasion demands it. However, it has always been distinguished from armed resistance and its application was at one time confined to Christian martyrs.

Civil Disobedience is civil breach of unmoral statutory enactments. The expression was, so far as I am aware, coined by Thoreau to signify his own resistance to the laws of a slave State. He has left a masterly treatise on the duty of Civil Disobedience. But Thoreau was not perhaps an out

Young India, 23 Mar. 1921.

and out champion of non-violence. Probably, also, Thoreau limited his breach of statutory laws to the revenue law, i.e. payment of taxes. Whereas the term Civil Disobedience as practised in 1919 covered a breach of any statutory and unmoral law. It signified the resister's outlawry in a civil, i.e., non-violent manner. He invoked the sanctions of the law and cheerfully suffered imprisonment. It is a branch of Satyagraha.

Non-co-operation predominantly implies withdrawing of co-operation from the State that in the non-co-operator's view has become corrupt and excludes Civil Disobedience of the fierce type described above. By its very nature, non-co-operation is even open to children of understanding and can be safely practised by the masses. Civil Disobedience presupposes the habit of willing obedience to laws without fear of their sanctions. It can, therefore, be practised only as a last resort and by a select few in the first instance at any rate. Non-co-operation, too, like Civil Disobedience is a branch of Satyagraha which includes all non-violent resistance for the vindication of Truth.

Satyagraha[1]

For the past thirty years I have been preaching and practising Satyagraha. The principles of Satyagraha, as I know it today, constitute a gradual evolution.

Satyagraha differs from Passive Resistance as the North Pole from the South. The latter has been conceived as a weapon of the weak and does not exclude the use of physical force or violence for the purpose of gaining one's end, whereas the former has been conceived as a weapon of the strongest and excludes the use of violence in any shape or form.

The term *Satyagraha* was coined by me in South Africa to express the force that the Indians there used for full eight years and it was coined in order to distinguish it from the movement then going on in the United Kingdom and South Africa under the name of Passive Resistance.

Its root meaning is holding on to truth, hence truth-force. I have also called it Love-force or Soul-force. In the application of Satyagraha I discovered in the earliest stages that pursuit of truth did not admit of violence being inflicted on one's opponent but that he must be weaned from error by patience and sympathy. For what appears to be truth to the one may appear to be error to the other. And patience means self-suffering. So the doc-

---

Young India, 14 Jan. 1920.

[1] Extract from a statement by Gandhi to the Hunter Committee. [Bharatan Kumarappa's note.]

trine came to mean vindication of truth not by infliction of suffering on the opponent but on one's self.

But on the political field the struggle on behalf of the people mostly consists in opposing error in the shape of unjust laws. When you have failed to bring the error home to the lawgiver by way of petitions and the like, the only remedy open to you, if you do not wish to submit to error, is to compel him by physical force to yield to you or by suffering in your own person by inviting the penalty for the breach of the law. Hence Satyagraha largely appears to the public as Civil Disobedience or Civil Resistance. It is civil in the sense that it is not criminal.

The lawbreaker breaks the law surreptitiously and tries to avoid the penalty, not so the civil resister. He ever obeys the laws of the State to which he belongs, not out of fear of the sanctions but because he considers them to be good for the welfare of society. But there come occasions, generally rare, when he considers certain laws to be so unjust as to render obedience to them a dishonour. He then openly and civilly breaks them and quietly suffers the penalty for their breach. And in order to register his protest against the action of the law givers, it is open to him to withdraw his co-operation from the State by disobeying such other laws whose breach does not involve moral turpitude.

In my opinion, the beauty and efficacy of Satyagraha are so great and the doctrine so simple that it can be preached even to children. It was preached by me to thousands of men, women and children commonly called indentured Indians with excellent results. . . .

Means and Ends

Reader: Why should we not obtain our goal, which is good, by any means whatsoever, even by using violence? Shall I think of the means when I have to deal with a thief in the house? My duty is to drive him out anyhow. You seem to admit that we have received nothing, and that we shall receive nothing by petitioning. Why, then, may we not do so by using brute force? And, to retain what we may receive we shall keep up the fear by using the same force to the extent that it may be necessary. You will not find fault with a continuance of force to prevent a child from thrusting its foot into fire? Somehow or other we have to gain our end.

Editor: Your reasoning is plausible. It has deluded many. I have used similar arguments before now. But I think I know better now, and I shall endeavour to undeceive you. Let us first take the argument that we are

Hind Swaraj. Madras: Ganesh, 1919, chap. 16.

justified in gaining our end by using brute force because the English gained theirs by using similar means. It is perfectly true that they used brute force and that it is possible for us to do likewise, but by using similar means we can get only the same thing that they got. You will admit that we do not want that. Your belief that there is no connection between the means and the end is a great mistake. Through that mistake even men who have been considered religious have committed grievous crimes. Your reasoning is the same as saying that we can get a rose through planting a noxious weed. If I want to cross the ocean, I can do so only by means of a vessel; if I were to use a cart for that purpose, both the cart and I would soon find the bottom. "As is the God, so is the votary," is a maxim worth considering. Its meaning has been distorted and men have gone astray. The means may be likened to a seed, the end to a tree; and there is just the same inviolable connection between the means and the end as there is between the seed and the tree. I am not likely to obtain the result flowing from the worship of God by laying myself prostrate before Satan. If, therefore, any one were to say: "I want to worship God; it does not matter that I do so by means of Satan," it would be set down as ignorant folly. We reap exactly as we sow. The English in 1833 obtained greater voting power by violence. Did they by using brute force better appreciate their duty? They wanted the right of voting, which they obtained by using physical force. But real rights are a result of performance of duty; these rights they have not obtained. We, therefore, have before us in England the force of everybody wanting and insisting on his rights, nobody thinking of his duty. And, where everybody wants rights, who shall give them to whom? I do not wish to imply that they do no duties. They don't perform the duties corresponding to those rights; and as they do not perform that particular duty, namely, acquire fitness, their rights have proved a burden to them. In other words, what they have obtained is an exact result of the means they adopted. They used the means corresponding to the end. If I want to deprive you of your watch, I shall certainly have to fight for it; if I want to buy your watch, I shall have to pay for it; and if I want a gift, I shall have to plead for it; and, according to the means I employ, the watch is stolen property, my own property, or a donation. Thus we see three different results from three different means. Will you still say that means do not matter?

Now we shall take the example given by you of the thief to be driven out. I do not agree with you that the thief may be driven out by any means. If it is my father who has come to steal I shall use one kind of means. If it is an acquaintance I shall use another; and in the case of a perfect stranger I shall use a third. If it is a white man, you will perhaps say you will use means different from those you will adopt with an Indian thief. If it is a weakling, the means will be different from those to be adopted for dealing with an equal in physical strength; and if the thief is armed from top to toe, I shall simply remain quiet. Thus we have a variety of means between the father and the armed man. Again, I fancy that I should pretend to be sleeping whether the thief was my father or that strong armed man. The reason for this is that my father would also be armed and I should succumb to the strength possessed by either and allow my things to be stolen. The strength of my father would make me weep with pity; the strength of the armed man would rouse in me anger and we should become enemies. Such is the curious situation. From these examples we may not be able to agree as to the means to be adopted in each case. I myself seem clearly to see what should be done in all these cases, but the remedy may frighten you. I therefore hesitate to place it before you. For the time being I will leave you to guess it, and if you cannot, it is clear you will have to adopt different means in each case. You will also have seen that any means will not avail to drive away the thief. You will have to adopt means to fit each case. Hence it follows that your duty is not to drive away the thief by any means you like.

Let us proceed a little further. That well-armed man has stolen your property; you have harboured the thought of his act; you are filled with anger; you argue that you want to punish that rogue, not for your own sake, but for the good of your neighbours; you have collected a number of armed men, you want to take his house by assault; he is duly informed of it, he runs away; he too is incensed. He collects his brother robbers, and sends you a defiant message that he will commit robbery in broad daylight. You are strong, you do not fear him, you are prepared to receive him. Meanwhile, the robber pesters your neighbours. They complain before you. You reply that you are doing all for their sake, you do not mind that your own goods have been stolen. Your neighbours reply that the robber never pestered them before, and that he commenced his depredations only after you declared hostilities against him. You are between Scylla and Charybdis. You are full of pity for the poor men. What they say is true. What are you to do? You will be disgraced if you now leave the robber alone. You, therefore, tell the poor men: "Never mind. Come, my wealth is yours, I will give you arms, I will teach you how to use them; you should belabour the rogue; don't you leave him alone." And so the battle grows; the robbers increase in numbers; your neighbours have deliberately put themselves to inconvenience. Thus the result of wanting to take revenge upon the robber is that you have disturbed your own peace; you are in perpetual fear of being robbed and assaulted; your courage has given place to cowardice. If you will patiently examine the argument, you will see that I have not overdrawn the picture. This is one of the means. Now let us examine the other. You set this armed robber down as an ignorant brother; you intend to reason with him at a suitable opportunity; you argue that he is, after all, a fellow man; you do not know what prompted him to steal. You, therefore, decide that, when you can, you will destroy the man's motive for stealing. Whilst you are thus reasoning with yourself, the man comes again to steal. Instead of being angry with him you take pity on him. You think that this stealing habit must be a disease with him. Henceforth, you, therefore, keep your doors and windows open, you change your sleeping-place, and you keep your things in a manner most accessible to him. The robber comes again and is confused as all this is new to him; nevertheless, he takes away your things. But his mind is agitated. He inquires about you in the village, he comes to learn about your broad and loving heart, he repents, he begs your pardon, returns you your things, and leaves off the stealing habit. He becomes your servant, and you will find for him honourable employment. This is the second method. Thus, you see, different means have brought about totally different results. I do not wish to deduce from this that robbers will act in the above manner or that all will have the same pity and love like you, but I only wish to show that fair means alone can produce fair results, and that, at least in the majority of cases, if not indeed in all, the force of love and pity is infinitely greater than the force of arms. There is harm in the exercise of brute force, never in that of pity. . . .

Pre-Requisites for Satyagraha[2]

Public opposition is effective only where there is strength behind it. What does a son do when he objects to some action of his father? He requests the father to desist from the objectionable course, i.e. presents respectful petitions. If the father does not agree in spite of repeated prayers, he non-co-operates with him to the extent even of leaving the paternal roof. This is pure justice. Where father and son are uncivilized, they quarrel, abuse each other and often even come to blows. An obedient son is ever modest, ever peaceful and ever loving. It is only his love which on due occasion compels him to non-co-operate. The father himself understands this loving non-co-operation. He cannot endure abandonment by or separation from the son, is distressed at heart and repents. Not that it always happens thus. But the son's duty of non-co-operation is clear.

Such non-co-operation is possible between a prince and his people. In particular circumstances it may be the people's duty. Such circumstances can exist only where the latter are by nature fearless and are lovers of lib-

Young India, 8 Jan. 1925.

[2] From Gandhi's Presidential Speech at the third Kathiawad Political Conference, Bhavnagar. [Bharatan Kumarappa's note.]

erty. They generally appreciate the laws of the State and obey them voluntarily without the fear of punishment. Reasoned and willing obedience to the laws of the State is the first lesson in non-co-operation.

The second is that of tolerance. We must tolerate many laws of the State, even when they are inconvenient. A son may not approve of some orders of the father and yet he obeys them. It is only when they are unworthy of tolerance and immoral that he disobeys them. The father will at once understand such respectful disobedience. In the same way it is only when a people have proved their active loyalty by obeying the many laws of the State that they acquire the right of Civil Disobedience.

The third lesson is that of suffering. He who has not the capacity of suffering cannot non-co-operate. He who has not learnt to sacrifice his property and even his family when necessary can never non-co-operate. It is possible that a prince enraged by non-co-operation will inflict all manner of punishments. There lies the test of love, patience, and strength. He who is not ready to undergo the fiery ordeal cannot non-co-operate. A whole people cannot be considered fit or ready for non-co-operation when only an individual or two have mastered these three lessons. A large number of the people must be thus prepared before they can non-co-operate. The result of hasty non-co-operation can only lead to harm. Some patriotic young men who do not understand the limitations noted by me grow impatient. Previous preparation is needed for non-co-operation as it is for all important things. A man cannot become a non-co-operator by merely wishing to be one. Discipline is obligatory. I do not know that many have undergone the needful discipline in any part of Kathiawad. And when the requisite discipline has been gone through probably non-co-operation will be found to be unnecessary.

As it is, I observe the necessity for individuals to prepare themselves in Kathiawad as well as in other parts of India. Individuals must cultivate the spirit of service, renunciation, truth, non-violence, self-restraint, patience, etc. They must engage in constructive work in order to develop these qualities. Many reforms would be effected automatically if we put in a good deal of silent work among the people.

Qualifications for Satyagraha

Satyagraha presupposes self-discipline, self-control, self-purification, and a recognized social status in the person offering it. A Satyagrahi must never forget the distinction between evil and the evil-doer. He must not

---

Young India, 8 Aug. 1929.

harbour ill-will or bitterness against the latter. He may not even employ needlessly offensive language against the evil person, however unrelieved his evil might be. For it should be an article of faith with every Satyagrahi that there is none so fallen in this world but can be converted by love. A Satyagrahi will always try to overcome evil by good, anger by love, untruth by truth, *himsa* [violence] by *ahimsa* [nonviolence]. There is no other way of purging the world of evil. Therefore a person who claims to be a Satyagrahi always tries by close and prayerful self-introspection and self-analysis to find out whether he is himself completely free from the taint of anger, ill-will and such other human infirmities, whether he is not himself capable of those very evils against which he is out to lead a crusade. In self-purification and penance lies half the victory of a Satyagrahi. A Satyagrahi has faith that the silent and undemonstrative action of truth and love produces far more permanent and abiding results than speeches or such other showy performances.

But although Satyagraha can operate silently, it requires a certain amount of action on the part of a Satyagrahi. A Satyagrahi, for instance, must first mobilize public opinion against the evil which he is out to eradicate, by means of a wide and intensive agitation. When public opinion is sufficiently roused against a social abuse even the tallest will not dare to practise or openly to lend support to it. An awakened and intelligent public opinion is the most potent weapon of a Satyagrahi. When a person supports a social evil in total disregard of unanimous public opinion, it indicates a clear justification for his social ostracism. But the object of social ostracism should never be to do injury to the person against whom it is directed. Social ostracism means complete non-co-operation on the part of society with the offending individual; nothing more, nothing less, the idea being that a person who deliberately sets himself to flout society has no right to be served by society. For all practical purposes this should be enough. Of course, special action may be indicated in special cases and the practice may have to be varied to suit the peculiar features of each individual case.

Requisite Qualifications

The four days' fast set me thinking of the qualifications required in a Satyagrahi. Though they were carefully considered and reduced to writing in 1921 they seem to have been forgotten.

In Satyagraha, it is never the numbers that count; it is always the quality, more so when the forces of violence are uppermost.

Harijan, 25 Mar. 1939.

Then it is often forgotten that it is never the intention of a Satyagrahi to embarrass the wrong-doer. The appeal is never to his fear; it is, must be, always to his heart. The Satyagrahi's object is to convert, not to coerce, the wrong-doer. He should avoid artificiality in all his doings. He acts naturally and from inward conviction.

Keeping these observations before his mind's eye, the reader will perhaps appreciate the following qualifications which, I hold, are essential for every Satyagrahi in India:

1. He must have a living faith in God, for He is his only Rock.
2. He must believe in truth and non-violence as his creed and therefore have faith in the inherent goodness of human nature which he expects to evoke by his truth and love expressed through his suffering.
3. He must be leading a chaste life and be ready and willing for the sake of his cause to give up his life and his possessions.
4. He must be a habitual *khadi*[3]-wearer and spinner. This is essential for India.
5. He must be a teetotaller and be free from the use of other intoxicants in order that his reason may be always unclouded and his mind constant.
6. He must carry out with a willing heart all the rules of discipline as may be laid down from time to time.
7. He should carry out the jail rules unless they are specially devised to hurt his self-respect.

The qualifications are not to be regarded as exhaustive. They are illustrative only.

Physical Training for the Satyagrahi

Ahimsa [non-violence] requires certain duties which can be done only by those with a trained physique. It is, therefore, most necessary to consider what kind of physical training a non-violent person should receive.

Very few of the rules applying to a violent army will apply to a non-violent body. A violent army will not have its arms for show but for definitely destructive purposes. A non-violent body will have no use for such weapons and will, therefore, beat its swords into plough-shares and spears into pruning hooks, and will shrink from the thought of using them as lethal weapons. The violent soldier will be trained in the use of violence

[3]Handspun and handwoven cloth. [ED.]

Harijan, 13 Oct. 1940.

by being taught to shoot. The non-violent soldier will have no time for this pastime. He will get all his training through nursing the sick, saving those in danger at the risk of his own life, patrolling places which may be in fear of thieves and dacoits, and in laying down his life, if necessary, in dissuading them from their purpose. Even the uniforms of the two will differ. The violent man will wear a coat of mail for his protection, and his uniform will be such as can dazzle people. The uniform of the non-violent man will be simple, in conformity with the dress of the poor, and betokening humility. Its purpose will be just to keep him from heat and cold and rain. A violent soldier's protection will be his arms, no matter how much he takes God's name. He will not shrink from spending millions on armaments. The first and last shield and buckler of the non-violent person will be his unwavering faith in God. And the minds of the two will be as poles asunder. The violent man will always be casting about for plans to work the destruction of his enemy and will pray to God to fulfil his purpose. The national anthem of the British people is worth considering in this connection. It prays to God to save the King, to frustrate the enemy's knavish tricks, and to destroy him. Millions of Englishmen sing this anthem aloud with one voice standing respectfully. If God is the Incarnation of Mercy, He is not likely to listen to such prayer, but it cannot but affect the minds of those who sing it, and in times of war it simply kindles their hatred and anger to white heat. The one condition of winning a violent war is to keep the indignation against the enemy burning fiercely.

In the dictionary of the non-violent there is no such word as an external enemy. But even for the supposed enemy he will have nothing but compassion in his heart. He will believe that no man is intentionally wicked, that there is no man but is gifted with the faculty to discriminate between right and wrong, and that if that faculty were to be fully developed, it would surely mature into non-violence. He will therefore pray to God that He may give the supposed enemy a sense of right and bless him. His prayer for himself will always be that the spring of compassion in him may ever be flowing, and that he may ever grow in moral strength so that he may face death fearlessly.

Thus since the minds of both will differ as the poles, their physical training will also differ in the same degree.

We all know more or less what military training is like. But we have hardly ever thought that non-violent training must be of a different kind. Nor have we ever cared to discover whether in the past such training was given anywhere in the world. I am of opinion that it used to be given in the past and is even now being given in a haphazard way. The various exercises of *Hatha Yoga* are in this direction. The physical training given by means of these imparts among other things physical health, strength, agility, and the capacity to bear heat and cold. Shri Kuvalayanandji is making scientific researches in the technique and benefits of these exercises. I have no knowledge of the progress he has made, nor do I know whether he is making his experiments with *ahimsa* as his goal. My reference to *Hatha Yoga* is meant only with a view to showing that this ancient type of non-violent training still exists, though I know that there is room in it for improvement. I do not know either that the author of this science had any idea of mass non-violence. The exercises had at their back the desire for individual salvation. The object of the various exercises was to strengthen and purify the body in order to secure control of the mind. The mass non-violence we are now thinking of applies to people of all religions and therefore the rules that may be framed must be such as can be accepted by all believers in *ahimsa*. And then as we are thinking of a non-violent army, that is to say, of bringing into being a Satyagraha *sangha* [commune], we can but build anew accepting the old as our foundation. Let us then think of the physical training required by a Satyagrahi. If the Satyagrahi is not healthy in mind and body, he may perhaps fail in mustering complete fearlessness. He should have the capacity to stand guard at a single spot day and night; he must not fall ill even if he has to bear cold and heat and rain; he must have the strength to go to places of peril, to rush to scenes of fire, and the courage to wander about alone in desolate jungles and haunts of death; he will bear, without a grumble, severe beatings, starvation and worse, and will keep to his post of duty without flinching; he will have the resourcefulness and capacity to plunge into a seemingly impenetrable scene of rioting; he will have the longing and capacity to run with the name of God on his lips to the rescue of men living on the top storeys of buildings enveloped in flames; he will have the fearlessness to plunge into a flood in order to rescue people being carried off by it or to jump down a well to save a drowning person.

This list can be extended *ad libitum*. The substance of it all is that we should cultivate the capacity to run to the rescue of people in danger and distress and to suffer cheerfully any amount of hardship that may be inflicted upon us. He who accepts this fundamental principle will easily be able to frame rules of physical training for Satyagrahis. I have a firm conviction that the very foundation of this training is faith in God. If that is absent, all the training one may have received is likely to fail at the critical moment.

Let no one poohpooh my statement by saying that the Congress has many people who are ashamed to take the name of God. I am simply trying to state the view in terms of the science of Satyagraha as I have known and developed it. The only weapon of the Satyagrahi is God, by whatsoever name one knows Him. Without Him the Satyagrahi is devoid of strength before an opponent armed with monstrous weapons. Most people lie prostrate before physical might. But he who accepts God as his only Protector will remain unbent before the mightiest earthly power.

As faith in God is essential in a Satyagrahi, even so is *brahmacharya* [celibacy]. Without *brahmacharya* the Satyagrahi will have no lustre, no inner strength to stand unarmed against the whole world. *Brahmacharya* may have here the restricted meaning of conservation of the vital energy brought about by sexual restraint, and not the comprehensive definition I have given of it. He who intends to live on spare diet and without any external remedies, and still wants to have physical strength, has need to conserve his vital energy. It is the richest capital man can ever possess. He who can preserve it ever gains renewed strength out of it. He who uses it up, consciously or unconsciously, will ultimately be impotent. His strength will fail him at the right moment. I have often written about the ways and means of conserving this energy. Let the reader turn to my writings and carry out the instructions. He who lusts with the eye or the touch can never conserve his vital energy, nor the man who lusts after flesh-pots. Those who hope to conserve this energy without strict observance of the rules will no more succeed than those who hope to swim against the current without being exhausted. He who restrains himself physically and sins with his thoughts will fare worse than he who, without professing to observe *brahmacharya,* lives the life of a restrained householder. For he who lusts with the thought will ever remain unsated and will end his life a moral wreck and burden on the earth. Such a one can never be a full Satyagrahi. Nor can one who hankers after wealth and fame.

This is the foundation of the physical training for a Satyagrahi. The detailed structure of the course can easily be built in consonance with this foundation.

It should now be clear that in the physical training of a Satyagrahi there is no room for lethal weapons like the sword or the spear. For far more terrible weapons than we have seen are in existence today, and newer ones are being invented every day. Of what fear will a sword rid him who has to cultivate the capacity to overcome all fear—real or imaginary? I have not yet heard of a man having shed all fear by learning sword-play. Mahavir and others who imbibed *ahimsa* did not do so because they knew the use of weapons, but because, in spite of the knowledge of their use, they shed all fear.

A slight introspection will show that he who has always depended on the sword will find it difficult to throw it away. But having deliberately discarded it he is likely to find his *ahimsa* more lasting than that of him who, not knowing its use, fancies he will not fear it. But that does not mean that in order to be truly non-violent one must beforehand possess and know the use of arms. By parity of reasoning, one might say that only a thief can be honest, only a diseased person can be healthy, and only a dissolute person can be a *brachmachari*. The fact is that we have formed the habit of thinking along traditional grooves and will not get out of them. And as we cannot take a detached view, we cannot draw the right conclusions and get caught in delusive snares.

If I have the time, I hope to present the reader with a model course of training.

Civil Disobedience

Civil disobedience was on the lips of every one of the members of the All India Congress Committee. Not having really ever tried it, every one appeared to be enamoured of it from a mistaken belief in it as a sovereign remedy for our present-day ills. I feel sure that it can be made such if we can produce the necessary atmosphere for it. For individuals there always is that atmosphere except when their civil disobedience is certain to lead to bloodshed. I discovered this exception during the Satyagraha days. But even so a call may come which one dare not neglect, cost it what it may. I can clearly see the time coming to me when I *must* refuse obedience to every single State-made law, even though there may be a certainty of bloodshed. When neglect of the call means a denial of God, civil disobedience becomes a peremptory duty.

Mass civil disobedience stands on a different footing. It can only be tried in a calm atmosphere. It must be the calmness of strength not weakness, of knowledge not ignorance. Individual civil disobedience may be and often is vicarious. Mass civil disobedience may be and often is selfish in the sense that individuals expect personal gain from their disobedience. Thus in South Africa, Kallenbach and Polak offered vicarious civil disobedience. They had nothing to gain. Thousands offered it because they expected personal gain also in the shape, say, of the removal of the annual poll-tax levied upon ex-indentured men and their wives and grown-up children. It is sufficient in mass civil disobedience if the resisters understand the working of the doctrine.

It was in a practically uninhabited tract of country that I was arrested in South Africa when I was marching into a prohibited area with over two to three thousand men and some women. The company included several Pathans and others who were able-bodied men. It was the greatest testimony of merit the Government of South Africa gave to the movement.

Young India, 4 Aug. 1921.

They knew that we were as harmless as we were determined. It was easy enough for that body of men to cut to pieces those who arrested me. It would have not only been a most cowardly thing to do, but it would have been a treacherous breach of their own pledge, and it would have meant ruin to the struggle for freedom and the forcible deportation of every Indian from South Africa. But the men were no rabble. They were disciplined soldiers and all the better for being unarmed. Though I was torn from them, they did not disperse, nor did they turn back. They marched on to their destination till they were, every one of them, arrested and imprisoned. So far as I am aware, this was an instance of discipline and non-violence for which there is no parallel in history. Without such restraint I see no hope of successful mass civil disobedience here.

We must dismiss the idea of overawing the Government by huge demonstrations every time some one is arrested. On the contrary, we must treat arrest as the normal condition of the life of a non-co-operator. For we must seek arrest and imprisonment, as a soldier who goes to battle seeks death. We expect to bear down the opposition of the Government by courting and not by avoiding imprisonment, even though it be by showing our supposed readiness to be arrested and imprisoned *en masse*. Civil disobedience then emphatically means our desire to surrender to a single unarmed policeman. Our triumph consists in thousands being led to the prisons like lambs to the slaughter house. If the lambs of the world had been willingly led, they would have long ago saved themselves from the butcher's knife. Our triumph consists again in being imprisoned for no wrong whatsoever. The greater our innocence, the greater our strength and the swifter our victory.

As it is, this Government is cowardly, we are afraid of imprisonment. The Government takes advantage of our fear of gaols. If only our men and women welcome gaols as health-resorts, we will cease to worry about the dear ones put in gaols which our countrymen in South Africa used to nickname His Majesty's Hotels.

We have too long been mentally disobedient to the laws of the State and have too often surreptitiously evaded them, to be fit all of a sudden for civil disobedience. Disobedience to be civil has to be open and non-violent.

Complete civil disobedience is a state of peaceful rebellion—a refusal to obey every single State-made law. It is certainly more dangerous than an armed rebellion. For it can never be put down if the civil resisters are prepared to face extreme hardships. It is based upon an implicit belief in the absolute efficiency of innocent suffering. By noiselessly going to prison a civil resister ensures a calm atmosphere. The wrong-doer wearies of wrong-doing in the absence of resistance. All pleasure is lost when the victim betrays no resistance. A full grasp of the conditions of successful civil resistance is necessary at least on the part of the representatives of the people before we can launch out on an enterprise of such magnitude. The quickest remedies are always fraught with the greatest danger and require the utmost skill in handling them. It is my firm conviction that if we bring about a successful boycott of foreign cloth, we shall have produced an atmosphere that would enable us to inaugurate civil disobedience on a scale that no Government can resist. I would, therefore, urge patience and determined concentration on Swadeshi upon those who are impatient to embark on mass civil disobedience.

From *STRIDE TOWARD FREEDOM*

Martin Luther King Jr. (1929–1968)

King came from a family deeply involved with the African-American Baptist church and with civil rights activism. His grandfather, the Rev. A. D. Williams, was pastor of Ebenezer Baptist church in Atlanta and a founder of the Atlanta chapter of the National Association for the Advancement of Colored People (NAACP). His father, Martin Luther King Sr., also served as the pastor of the Ebenezer church and was active in the civil rights struggle. King himself attended Morehouse College in Atlanta, then pursued theological studies at Crozer Theological Seminary in Chester, Pennsylvania, and at Boston University, from which he received a doctorate in 1955. King decided to return to the South after graduation and took up the post of minister of the Dexter Avenue Baptist Church in Montgomery, Alabama. A few months later, Rosa Parks refused to go to the back of a city bus and was arrested; black citizens decided to boycott the bus system until they received equal treatment; and King was elected president of the Montgomery Improvement Association, which directed the continuing boycott. King's house was bombed, he and other boycott leaders were convicted of conspiring to damage the bus company's operations, and the city and state tried in every way they could to intimidate the black community. Nevertheless, the buses were desegregated after the U.S. Supreme Court ruled Alabama's segregation laws unconstitutional.

After 1956, King increasingly devoted himself to the growing civil rights movement, especially to the Southern Christian Leadership Conference (SCLC), which he had helped to found.

He published his first book, *Stride toward Freedom: The Montgomery Story,* in 1958. The following year he visited India in order to learn more about Mohandas Gandhi's nonviolent campaigns. King led or participated in a series of efforts to win equal public accommodations, voting rights, and desegregated schools for black Americans. In many ways, he became an unofficial spokesperson for the mainstream of black America, most notably at the 1963 March on Washington, at which he gave his most famous speech, "I Have a Dream," to over a quarter of a million intent listeners. Participating directly in the campaigns he led, King was often the target of hostile whites, North as well as South; he was also the object of scrutiny and disruption directed by the head of the Federal Bureau of Investigation, J. Edgar Hoover, who considered King's determination to end segregation and his growing opposition to the Vietnam war as somehow "un-American." Nevertheless, King persisted in using nonviolent direct actions to pursue the goals of the movement, and in December 1964, he received the Nobel Peace Prize. Increasingly, King came to see that more fundamental changes in the economic structure and political priorities of the United States were necessary to achieve real social justice, and he began a somewhat unsuccessful Poor People's Campaign. He was assassinated on April 4, 1968, during an effort to support a garbage workers' strike in Memphis.

The text that follows is part of his 1958 book, *Stride toward Freedom: The Montgomery Story* (New York: Harper). The brief statement, "A Legacy of Creative Protest," was published in 1962 in a special issue of the *Massachusetts Review* devoted to Thoreau. [ED.]

. . . Finally, the Negro himself has a decisive role to play if integration is to become a reality. Indeed, if first-class citizenship is to become a reality for the Negro he must assume the primary responsibility for making it so. Integration is not some lavish dish that the federal government or the white liberal will pass out on a silver platter while the Negro merely furnishes the appetite. One of the most damaging effects of past segregation on the personality of the Negro may well be that he has been victimized with the delusion that others should be more concerned than himself about his citizenship rights.

In this period of social change, the Negro must come to see that there is so much he himself can do about his plight. He may be uneducated or poverty-stricken, but these handicaps must not prevent him from seeing that he has within his being the power to alter his fate. The Negro can take direct action against injustice without waiting for the government to act or a majority to agree with him or a court to rule in his favor.

Oppressed people deal with their oppression in three characteristic ways. One way is acquiescence: the oppressed resign themselves to their doom. They tacitly adjust themselves to oppression, and thereby become conditioned to it. In every movement toward freedom some of the oppressed prefer to remain oppressed. Almost twenty-eight hundred years ago Moses set out to lead the children of Israel from the slavery of Egypt to the freedom of the promised land. He soon discovered that slaves do not always welcome their deliverers. They become accustomed to being slaves. They would rather bear those ills they have, as Shakespeare pointed out, than flee to others that they know not of. They prefer the "fleshpots of Egypt" to the ordeals of emancipation.

There is such a thing as the freedom from exhaustion. Some people are so worn down by the yoke of oppression that they give up. A few years ago in the slum areas of Atlanta, a Negro guitarist used to sing almost daily: "Ben down so long that down don't bother me." This is the type of negative freedom and resignation that often engulfs the life of the oppressed.

But this is not the way out. To accept passively an unjust system is to cooperate with that system; thereby the oppressed become as evil as the oppressor. Noncooperation with evil is as much a moral obligation as is cooperation with good. The oppressed must never allow the conscience of the oppressor to slumber. Religion reminds every man that he is his brother's keeper. To accept injustice or segregation passively is to say to the oppressor that his actions are morally right. It is a way of allowing his conscience to fall asleep. At this moment the oppressed fails to be his brother's keeper. So acquiescence—while often the easier way—is not the moral way. It is the way of the coward. The Negro cannot win the respect of his oppressor by acquiescing; he merely increases the oppressor's arrogance and contempt. Acquiescence is interpreted as proof of the Negro's inferiority. The Negro cannot win the respect of the white people of the South or the peoples of the world if he is willing to sell the future of his children for his personal and immediate comfort and safety.

A second way that oppressed people sometimes deal with oppression is to resort to physical violence and corroding hatred. Violence often brings about momentary results. Nations have frequently won their independence in battle. But in spite of temporary victories, violence never brings permanent peace. It solves no social problem; it merely creates new and more complicated ones.

Violence as a way of achieving racial justice is both impractical and immoral. It is impractical because it is a descending spiral ending in destruction for all. The old law of an eye for an eye leaves everybody blind. It is immoral because it seeks to humiliate the opponent rather than win his understanding; it seeks to annihilate rather than to convert. Violence is immoral because it thrives on hatred rather than love. It destroys community and makes brotherhood impossible. It leaves society in monologue rather than dialogue. Violence ends by defeating itself. It creates bitterness in the survivors and brutality in the destroyers. A voice echoes through time saying to every potential Peter, "Put up your sword." History is cluttered with the wreckage of nations that failed to follow this command.

If the American Negro and other victims of oppression succumb to the temptation of using violence in the struggle for freedom, future generations will be the recipients of a desolate night of bitterness, and our chief legacy to them will be an endless reign of meaningless chaos. Violence is not the way.

The third way open to oppressed people in their quest for freedom is the way of nonviolent resistance. Like the synthesis in Hegelian philosophy, the principle of nonviolent resistance seeks to reconcile the truths of two opposites—acquiescence and violence—while avoiding the extremes and immoralities of both. The nonviolent resister agrees with the person who acquiesces that one should not be physically aggressive toward his opponent but he balances the equation by agreeing with the person of violence that evil must be resisted. He avoids the nonresistance of the former and the violent resistance of the latter. With nonviolent resistance, no individual or group need submit to any wrong, nor need anyone resort to violence in order to right a wrong.

It seems to me that this is the method that must guide the actions of the Negro in the present crisis in race relations. Through nonviolent resistance the Negro will be able to rise to the noble height of opposing the unjust system while loving the perpetrators of the system. The Negro must work passionately and unrelentingly for full stature as a citizen, but he must not use inferior methods to gain it. He must never come to terms with falsehood, malice, hate, or destruction.

Nonviolent resistance makes it possible for the Negro to remain in the South and struggle for his rights. The Negro's problem will not be solved by running away. He cannot listen to the glib suggestion of those who would urge him to migrate en masse to other sections of the country. By grasping his great opportunity in the South he can make a lasting contribution to the moral strength of the nation and set a sublime example of courage for generations yet unborn.

By nonviolent resistance, the Negro can also enlist all men of good will in his struggle for equality. The problem is not a purely racial one, with Negroes set against whites. In the end, it is not a struggle between people at all, but a tension between justice and injustice. Nonviolent resistance is not aimed against oppressors but against oppression. Under its banner consciences, not racial groups, are enlisted.

If the Negro is to achieve the goal of integration, he must organize himself into a militant and nonviolent mass movement. All three elements are indispensable. The movement for equality and justice can only be a success if it has both a mass and militant character; the barriers to be overcome require both. Nonviolence is an imperative in order to bring about ultimate community.

A mass movement of a militant quality that is not at the same time committed to nonviolence tends to generate conflict, which in turn breeds anarchy. The support of the participants and the sympathy of the uncommitted are both inhabited by the threat that bloodshed will engulf the community. This reaction in turn encourages the opposition to threaten and resort to force. When, however, the mass movement repudiates violence while moving resolutely toward its goal, its opponents are revealed as the instigators and practitioners of violence if it occurs. Then public support is magnetically attracted to the advocates of nonviolence, while those who employ violence are literally disarmed by overwhelming sentiment against their stand.

Only through a nonviolent approach can the fears of the white community be mitigated. A guilt-ridden white minority lives in fear that if the Negro should ever attain power, he would act without restraint or pity to revenge the injustices and brutality of the years. It is something like a parent who continually mistreats a son. One day that parent raises his hand to strike the son, only to discover that the son is now as tall as he is. The parent is suddenly afraid—fearful that the son will use his new physical power to repay his parent for all the blows of the past.

The Negro, once a helpless child, has now grown up politically, culturally, and economically. Many white men fear retaliation. The job of the Negro is to show them that they have nothing to fear, that the Negro understands and forgives and is ready to forget the past. He must convince the white man that all he seeks is justice, *for both himself and the white man.* A mass movement exercising nonviolence is an object lesson in power under discipline, a demonstration to the white community that if such a movement attained a degree of strength, its would use its power creatively and not vengefully.

Nonviolence can touch men where the law cannot reach them. When the law regulates behavior it plays an indirect part in molding public sentiment. The enforcement of the law is itself a form of peaceful persuasion. But the law needs help. The courts can order desegregation of the public schools. But what can be done to mitigate the fears, to disperse the hatred, violence, and irrationality gathered around school integration, to take the initiative out of the hands of racial demagogues, to release respect for the law? In the end, for laws to be obeyed, men must believe they are right.

Here nonviolence comes in as the ultimate form of persuasion. It is the method which seeks to implement the just law by appealing to the conscience of the great decent majority who through blindness, fear, pride, or irrationality have allowed their consciences to sleep.

The nonviolent resisters can summarize their message in the following simple terms: We will take direct action against injustice without waiting for other agencies to act. We will not obey unjust laws or submit to unjust practices. We will do this peacefully, openly, cheerfully because our aim is to persuade. We adopt the means of nonviolence because our end is a community at peace with itself. We will try to persuade with our words, but if our words fail, we will try to persuade with our acts. We will always be willing to talk and seek fair compromise, but we are ready to suffer when necessary and even risk our lives to become witnesses to the truth as we see it.

The way of nonviolence means a willingness to suffer and sacrifice. It may mean going to jail. If such is the case the resister must be willing to fill the jail houses of the South. It may even mean physical death. But if physical death is the price that a man must pay to free his children and his white brethren from a permanent death of the spirit, then nothing could be more redemptive.

What is the Negro's best defense against acts of violence inflicted upon him? As Dr. Kenneth Clark has said so eloquently, "His only defense is to meet every act of barbarity, illegality, cruelty and injustice toward an individual Negro with the fact that one hundred more Negroes will present themselves in his place as potential victims." Every time one Negro school teacher is fired for believing in integration, a thousand others should be ready to take the same stand. If the oppressors bomb the home of one Negro for his protest, they must be made to realize that to press back the rising tide of the Negro's courage they will have to bomb hundreds more, and even then they will fail.

Faced with this dynamic unity, this amazing self-respect, this willingness to suffer, and this refusal to hit back, the oppressor will find, as oppressors have always found, that he is glutted with his own barbarity. Forced to stand before the world and his God splattered with the blood of his brother, he will call an end to his self-defeating massacre.

American Negroes must come to the point where they can say to their white brothers, paraphrasing the words of Gandhi: "We will match your capacity to inflict suffering with our capacity to endure suffering. We will meet your physical force with soul force. We will not hate you, but we cannot in all good conscience obey your unjust laws. Do to us what you will and we will still love you. Bomb our homes and threaten our children; send your hooded perpetrators of violence into our communities and drag us out on some wayside road, beating us and leaving us half dead, and we will still love you. But we will soon wear you down by our capacity to suffer. And in winning our freedom we will so appeal to your heart and conscience that we will win you in the process."

Realism impels me to admit that many Negroes will find it difficult to follow the path of nonviolence. Some will consider it senseless; some will argue that they have neither the strength nor the courage to join in such a mass demonstration of nonviolent action. As E. Franklin Frazier points out in *Black Bourgeoisie,* many Negroes are occupied in a middle-class struggle for status and prestige. They are more concerned about "conspicuous consumption" than about the cause of justice, and are probably not prepared for the ordeals and sacrifices involved in nonviolent action. Fortunately, however, the success of this method is not dependent on its unanimous acceptance. A few Negroes in every community, unswervingly committed to the nonviolent way, can persuade hundreds of others at least to use nonviolence as a technique and serve as the moral force to awaken the slumbering national conscience. Thoreau was thinking of such a creative minority when he said: "I know this well, that if one thousand, if one hundred, if ten men whom I could name—if ten honest men only—aye, if one honest man, in the state of Massachusetts, ceasing to hold slaves, were actually to withdraw from the copartnership, and be locked up in the county jail therefore, it would be the abolition of slavery in America. For it matters not how small the beginning may seem to be, what is once well done is done forever."

Mahatma Gandhi never had more than one hundred persons absolutely committed to his philosophy. But with this small group of devoted followers, he galvanized the whole of India, and through a magnificent feat of nonviolence challenged the might of the British Empire and won freedom for his people.

This method of nonviolence will not work miracles overnight. Men are not easily moved from their mental ruts, their prejudiced and irrational feelings. When the underprivileged demand freedom, the privileged first react with bitterness and resistance. Even when the demands are couched in nonviolent terms, the initial response is the same. Nehru once remarked that the British were never so angry as when the Indians resisted them with nonviolence, that he never saw eyes so full of hate as those of the British troops to whom he turned the other cheek when they beat him with lathis.

But nonviolent resistance at least changed the minds and hearts of the Indians, however impervious the British may have appeared. "We cast away our fear," says Nehru. And in the end the British not only granted freedom to India but came to have a new respect for the Indians. Today a mutual friendship based on complete equality exists between these two peoples within the Commonwealth.

In the South too, the initial white reaction to Negro resistance has been bitter. I do not predict that a similar happy ending will come to Montgomery in a few months, because integration is more complicated than independence. But I know that the Negroes of Montgomery are already walking straighter because of the protest. And I expect that this generation of Negro children throughout the United States will grow up stronger and better because of the courage, the dignity, and the suffering of the nine children of Little Rock, and their counterparts in Nashville, Clinton, and Sturges. And I believe that the white people of this country are being affected too, that beneath the surface this nation's conscience is being stirred.

The nonviolent approach does not immediately change the heart of the oppressor. It first does something to the hearts and souls of those committed to it. It gives them new self-respect; it calls up resources of strength and courage that they did not know they had. Finally it reaches the opponent and so stirs his conscience that reconciliation becomes a reality.

I suggest this approach because I think it is the only way to reestablish the broken community. Court orders and federal enforcement agencies will be of inestimable value in achieving desegregation. But desegregation is only a partial, though necessary, step toward the ultimate goal which we seek to realize. Desegregation will break down the legal barriers, and bring men together physically. But something must happen so to touch the hearts and souls of men that they will come together, not because the law says it, but because it is natural and right. In other words, our ultimate goal is integration which is genuine intergroup and interpersonal living. Only through nonviolence can this goal be attained, for the aftermath of nonviolence is reconciliation and the creation of the beloved community.

It is becoming clear that the Negro is in for a season of suffering. As victories for civil rights mount in the federal courts, angry passions and deep prejudices are further aroused. The mountain of state and local segregation laws still stands. Negro leaders continue to be arrested and harassed under city ordinances, and their homes continue to be bombed. State laws continue to be enacted to circumvent integration. I pray that, recognizing the necessity of suffering, the Negro will make of it a virtue. To suffer in a righteous cause is to grow to our humanity's full stature. If only to save himself from bitterness, the Negro needs the vision to see the ordeals of this generation as the opportunity to transfigure himself and

American society. If he has to go to jail for the cause of freedom, let him enter it in the fashion Gandhi urged his countrymen, "as the bridegroom enters the bride's chamber"—that is, with a little trepidation but with a great expectation.

Nonviolence is a way of humility and self-restraint. We Negroes talk a great deal about our rights, and rightly so. We proudly proclaim that three-fourths of the people of the world are colored. We have the privilege of watching in our generation the great drama of freedom and independence as it unfolds in Asia and Africa. All of these things are in line with the work of providence. We must be sure, however, that we accept them in the right spirit. In an effort to achieve freedom in America, Asia, and Africa we must not try to leap from a position of disadvantage to one of advantage, thus subverting justice. We must seek democracy and not the substitution of one tyranny for another. Our aim must never be to defeat or humiliate the white man. We must not become victimized with a philosophy of black supremacy. God is not interested merely in the freedom of black men, and brown men, and yellow men; God is interested in the freedom of the whole human race.

The nonviolent approach provides an answer to the long debated question of gradualism versus immediacy. On the one hand it prevents one from falling into the sort of patience which is an excuse for do-nothingism and escapism, ending up in standstillism. On the other hand it saves one from the irresponsible words which estrange without reconciling and the hasty judgment which is blind to the necessities of social process. It recognizes the need for moving toward the goal of justice with wise restraint and calm reasonableness. But it also recognizes the immorality of slowing up in the move toward justice and capitulating to the guardians of an unjust status quo. It recognizes that social change cannot come overnight. But it causes one to work as if it were a possibility the next morning.

Through nonviolence we avoid the temptation of taking on the psychology of victors. Thanks largely to the noble and invaluable work of the NAACP, we have won great victories in the federal courts. But we must not be self-satisfied. We must respond to every decision with an understanding of those who have opposed us, and with acceptance of the new adjustments that the court orders pose for them. We must act in such a way that our victories will be triumphs for good will in all men, white and Negro.

Nonviolence is essentially a positive concept. Its corollary must always be growth. On the one hand nonviolence requires noncooperation with evil; on the other hand it requires cooperation with the constructive forces of good. Without this constructive aspect noncooperation ends where it begins. Therefore, the Negro must get to work on a program with a broad range of positive goals.

One point in the Negro's program should be a plan to improve his own economic lot. Through the establishment of credit unions, savings and loan associations, and cooperative enterprises the Negro can greatly improve his economic status. He must develop habits of thrift and techniques of wise investment. He must not wait for the end of the segregation that lies at the basis of his economic deprivation; he must act now to lift himself up by his own bootstraps.

The constructive program ahead must include a campaign to get Negroes to register and vote. Certainly they face many external barriers. All types of underhand methods are still being used in the South to prevent the Negroes from voting, and the success of these efforts is not only unjust, it is a real embarrassment to the nation we love and must protect. The advocacy of free elections in Europe by American officials is hypocrisy when free elections are not held in great sections of America.

But external resistance is not the only present barrier to Negro voting. Apathy among the Negroes themselves is also a factor. Even where the polls are open to all, Negroes have shown themselves too slow to exercise their voting privileges. There must be a concerted effort on the part of Negro leaders to arouse their people from their apathetic indifference to this obligation of citizenship. In the past, apathy was a moral failure. Today, it is a form of moral and political suicide.

The constructive program ahead must include a vigorous attempt to improve the Negro's personal standards. It must be reiterated that the standards of the Negro as a group lag behind not because of an inherent inferiority, but because of the fact that segregation does exist. The "behavior deviants" within the Negro community stem from the economic deprivation, emotional frustration, and social isolation which are the inevitable concomitants of segregation. When the white man argues that segregation should continue because of the Negro's lagging standards, he fails to see that the standards lag because of segregation.

Yet Negroes must be honest enough to admit that our standards do often fall short. One of the sure signs of maturity is the ability to rise to the point of self-criticism. Whenever we are objects of criticism from white men, even though the criticisms are maliciously directed and mixed with half-truths, we must pick out the elements of truth and make them the basis of creative reconstruction. We must not let the fact that we are the victims of injustice lull us into abrogating responsibility for our own lives.

Our crime rate is far too high. Our level of cleanliness is frequently far too low. Too often those of us who are in the middle class live above our means, spend money on nonessentials and frivolities, and fail to give to serious causes, organizations, and educational institutions that so desperately need funds. We are too often loud and boisterous, and spend far too much on drink. Even the most poverty-stricken among us can purchase a ten-cent bar of soap; even the most uneducated among us can have high morals. Through community agencies and religious institutions Negro leaders must develop a positive program through which Negro youth can become adjusted to urban living and improve their general level of behavior. Since crime often grows out of a sense of futility and despair, Negro parents must be urged to give their children the love, attention, and sense of belonging that a segregated society deprives them of. By improving our standards here and now we will go a long way toward breaking down the arguments of the segregationist.

This then must be our present program: Nonviolent resistance to all forms of racial injustice, including state and local laws and practices, even when this means going to jail; and imaginative, bold, constructive action to end the demoralization caused by the legacy of slavery and segregation, inferior schools, slums, and second-class citizenship. The nonviolent struggle, if conducted with the dignity and courage already shown by the people of Montgomery and the children of Little Rock, will in itself help end the demoralization; but a new frontal assault on the poverty, disease, and ignorance of a people too long ignored by America's conscience will make victory more certain.

In short, we must work on two fronts. On the one hand, we must continue to resist the system of segregation which is the basic cause of our lagging standards; on the other hand we must work constructively to improve the standards themselves. There must be a rhythmic alternation between attacking the causes and healing the effects.

This is a great hour for the Negro. The challenge is here. To become the instruments of a great idea is a privilege that history gives only occasionally. Arnold Toynbee says in *A Study of History* that it may be the Negro who will give the new spiritual dynamic to Western civilization that it so desperately needs to survive. I hope this is possible. The spiritual power that the Negro can radiate to the world comes from love, understanding, good will, and nonviolence. It may even be possible for the Negro, through adherence to nonviolence, so to challenge the nations of the world that they will seriously seek an alternative to war and destruction. In a day when Sputniks and Explorers dash through outer space and guided ballistic missiles are carving highways of death through the stratosphere, nobody can win a war. Today the choice is no longer between violence and nonviolence. It is either nonviolence or nonexistence. The Negro may be God's appeal to this age—an age drifting rapidly to its doom. The eternal appeal takes the form of a warning: "All who take the sword will perish by the sword."

A LEGACY OF CREATIVE PROTEST

During my early college days I read Thoreau's essay on civil disobedience for the first time. Fascinated by the idea of refusing to cooperate with an evil system, I was so deeply moved that I re-read the work several times. I became convinced then that non-cooperation with evil is as much a moral obligation as is cooperation with good. No other person has been more eloquent and passionate in getting this idea across than Henry David Thoreau. As a result of his writings and personal witness we are the heirs of a legacy of creative protest. It goes without saying that the teachings of Thoreau are alive today, indeed, they are more alive today than ever before. Whether expressed in a sit-in at lunch counters, a freedom ride into Mississippi, a peaceful protest in Albany, Georgia, a bus boycott in Montgomery, Alabama, it is an outgrowth of Thoreau's insistence that evil must be resisted and no moral man can patiently adjust to injustice.

From John H. Hicks, ed. *Thoreau in Our Season*. Amherst: U of Massachusetts P., 1966.

Works Cited

Adams, Stephen, and Donald A. Ross. *Revising Mythologies: The Composition of Thoreau's Major Works*. Charlottesville: UP of Virginia, 1988.

Clapper, Ronald A. "The Development of *Walden:* A Generic Text." Diss. U of California, 1967.

Douglass, Frederick. Speech on John Brown. Tremont Temple, Boston. Dec. 1860. *The Life and Writing of Frederick Douglass*. Ed. Philip S. Foner. Vol. 2. New York: International, 1950.

Emerson, Ralph Waldo. *Emerson's Complete Works*. Riverside ed. 12 vols. Boston: Houghton, 1883–93.

Genovese, Eugene. *Roll, Jordan, Roll: The World the Slaves Made*. New York: Pantheon, 1972.

Gutman, Herbert. *The Black Family in Slavery and Freedom, 1750–1925*. New York: Vintage, 1977.

Harding, Vincent. *There Is a River: The Black Struggle for Freedom in America*. New York: Harcourt, 1981.

Paul, Sherman. *The Shores of America: Thoreau's Inward Exploration*. Urbana: U of Illinois P, 1958.

Sattelmeyer, Robert. "The Remaking of *Walden*." *Writing the American Classics*. Ed. James Barbour and Tom Quirk. Chapel Hill: U of North Carolina P, 1990. 53–78.

Shanley, J. Lyndon. *The Making of* Walden. Chicago: U of Chicago P, 1957.

Thome, James A., and J. Horace Kimball. *Emancipation in the West Indies: A Six Months' Tour in Antigua, Barbados, and Jamaica, in the Year 1837*. New York: Anti-Slavery Soc., 1839.

Thoreau, Henry David. *Early Essays and Miscellanies.* Ed. Joseph J. Moldenhauer and Edwin Moser. Writings of Henry D. Thoreau. Princeton: Princeton UP, 1975.

———. *Reform Papers.* Ed. Wendell Glick. Writings of Henry D. Thoreau. Princeton: Princeton UP, 1975.

———. *Walden.* Ed. J. Lyndon Shanley. Introd. Joyce Carol Oates. Princeton: Princeton UP, 1989.

———. *A Week on the Concord and Merrimack Rivers.* Ed. Carl Hovde, et al. Writings of Henry D. Thoreau. Princeton: Princeton UP, 1980.

Walker, David. "Appeal to the Colored Citizens of the World." *Walker's Appeal, in Four Articles [by] David Walker. An Address to the Slaves of the United States of America [by] Henry Highland Garnet.* American Negro, His History and Literature. New York: Arno, 1969.

For Further Reading

Adams, Stephen, and Donald Ross, Jr. *Revising Mythologies: The Composition of Thoreau's Major Works.* Charlottesville: UP of Virginia, 1988.

Bickman, Martin. *Walden: Volatile Truths.* New York: Twayne, 1992.

Borst, Raymond R., comp. and ed. *The Thoreau Log: A Documentary Life of Henry David Thoreau, 1817–1862.* New York: Hall, 1992.

Bridgman, Richard. *Dark Thoreau.* Lincoln: U of Nebraska P, 1982.

Buell, Lawrence. *The Environmental Imagination: Thoreau, Nature Writing, and the Formation of American Culture.* Cambridge: Harvard UP, 1995.

Cavell, Stanley. *The Senses of Walden.* New York: Viking, 1972.

Clapper, Ronald A. "The Development of *Walden*: A Generic Text." Diss. U of California, 1967.

Douglass, Frederick. *The Life and Writings of Frederick Douglass.* Ed. Philip S. Foner. Vols. 1 and 2. New York: International Publishers, 1950.

Fink, Steven. *Prophet in the Marketplace: Thoreau's Development as a Professional Writer.* Princeton: Princeton UP, 1992.

Foster, David R. *Thoreau's Country: Journey through a Transformed Landscape.* Cambridge: Harvard UP, 1999.

Gandhi, Mohandas K. *Non-Violent Resistance (Satyagraha).* Ed. Bharatan Kumarappa. New York: Schocken, 1961.

Garrison, William Lloyd. *Selections from the Writings and Speeches of William Lloyd Garrison.* Rpt. of 1852 ed. New York: Negro Universities P, 1968.

Glick, Wendell. *The Recognition of Henry David Thoreau: Selected Criticism since 1848.* Ann Arbor: U of Michigan P, 1969.

Golemba, Henry. *Thoreau's Wild Rhetoric.* New York: New York UP, 1990.

Grimké, Angelina, and Sarah Grimké. *The Public Years of Sarah and Angelina Grimké: Selected Writings, 1835–1839.* Ed. Larry Ceplair. New York: Columbia UP, 1989.

Harding, Walter. *The Days of Henry Thoreau.* New York: Knopf, 1965.

Harding, Walter, George Brenner, and Paul A. Doyle, eds. *Henry David Thoreau: Studies and Commentaries.* Madison: Fairleigh Dickinson UP, 1972.

Hicks, John, ed. *Thoreau in Our Season.* Amherst: U of Massachusetts P, 1966.

Howarth, William. *The Book of Concord: Thoreau's Life as a Writer.* New York: Viking, 1982.

King, Martin Luther, Jr. *A Testament of Hope: The Essential Writings and Speeches of Martin Luther King, Jr.* Ed. James M. Washington. San Francisco: HarperCollins, 1986.

Lebeaux, Richard. *Thoreau's Seasons.* Amherst: U of Massachusetts P, 1984.

Mabee, Carleton. *Black Freedom: The Nonviolent Abolitionists from 1830 through the Civil War.* New York: Macmillan, 1970.

Meyer, Michael. *Several More Lives to Live: Thoreau's Political Reputation in America.* Westport: Greenwood, 1977.

Myerson, Joel, ed. *The Cambridge Companion to Henry David Thoreau.* Cambridge: Cambridge UP, 1995.

———. *Critical Essays on Henry David Thoreau's* Walden. Boston: Hall, 1988.

Neufeldt, Leonard N. *The Economist: Henry Thoreau and Enterprise.* New York: Oxford UP, 1989.

Oehlschlaeger, Fritz, and George Hendrick. *Toward the Making of Thoreau's Modern Reputation: Selected Correspondence of S. A. Jones, A. W. Hosmer, H. S. Salt, H. G. O. Blake, and D. Ricketson.* Urbana: U of Illinois P, 1979.

Paul, Sherman. *The Shores of America: Thoreau's Inward Exploration.* Urbana: U of Illinois P, 1958.

Peck, Daniel H. *Thoreau's Morning Work: Memory and Perception in "A Week on the Concord and Merrimack Rivers," the Journal, and* Walden. New Haven: Yale UP, 1990.

Porte, Joel. *Emerson and Thoreau: Transcendentalists in Conflict.* Middletown: Wesleyan UP, 1966.

Ripley, C. Peter, et al., eds. *The Black Abolitionist Papers.* Vols. 3 and 4. Chapel Hill: U of North Carolina P, 1991.

Salt, Henry Stephens. *Life of Henry David Thoreau.* Ed. George Hendrick, Willene Hendrick, and Fritz Oehlschlaeger. Unpublished 1908 rev. of 1890 work. Urbana: U of Illinois P, 1993.

Sattelmeyer, Robert. "The Remaking of *Walden.*" *Writing the American Classics.* Ed. James Barbour and Tom Quirk. Chapel Hill: U of North Carolina P, 1990. 53–78.

Sayre, Robert F., ed. *New Essays on* Walden. Cambridge: Cambridge UP, 1992.

Scharnhorst, Gary. *Henry David Thoreau: A Case Study in Canonization.* Columbia: Camden, 1993.

———. *Henry David Thoreau: An Annotated Bibliography of Comment and Criticism before 1900.* New York: Garland, 1992.

Schneider, Richard J. *Approaches to Teaching Thoreau's* Walden *and Other Works.* New York: MLA, 1996.

Sears, Clara Endicott, comp. and ed. *Bronson Alcott's* Fruitlands. Rpt. of 1915 ed. Philadelphia: Porcupine, 1975.

Shanley, J. Lyndon. *The Making of* Walden, *With the Text of the First Version.* Chicago: U of Chicago P, 1957.

Sibley, Mulford Q., ed. *The Quiet Battle: Writings on the Theory and Practice of Non-Violent Resistance.* Garden City: Anchor, 1963.

Smith, Craig R. *Defender of the Union: The Oratory of Daniel Webster.* New York: Greenwood, 1989.

Taylor, Bob Pepperman. *America's Bachelor Uncle: Thoreau and American Polity.* Lawrence: UP of Kansas, 1996.

Teichgraeber, Richard F. *Sublime Thoughts/Penny Wisdom: Situating Emerson and Thoreau in the American Market.* Baltimore: Johns Hopkins UP, 1995.

Thoreau, Henry David. *Reform Papers.* Ed. Wendell Glick. Princeton: Princeton UP, 1973.

———. *The Variorum* Walden. Ed. Walter Harding. New York: Twayne, 1962.

———. *Walden.* Ed. J. Lyndon Shanley. Princeton: Princeton UP, 1971.

Tolstoy, Leo. *Tolstoy's Writings on Civil Disobedience and Non-Violence.* 1899. Trans. Aylmer Mande. New York: Bergman, 1967.

Whitman, Walt. *Leaves of Grass. A Textual Variorum of the Printed Poems.* Ed. Sculley Bradley, et al. [New York]: New York UP, 1980.

Credits